Clinical Psychology in Britain
Historical Perspectives

Edited by
John Hall
David Pilgrim
and
Graham Turpin

Division of Clinical Psychology

History of Psychology Centre
Monograph No 2

British Library Cataloguing-in-Publication Data

A catalogue record for this book is available from the British Library.

ISBN: 978-1-85433-731-3

Printed and published by
The British Psychological Society
St Andrews House
48 Princess Road East
Leicester LE1 7DR
www.bps.org.uk

Contents

Preface and acknowledgements

This book has been written to offer an informed history of clinical psychology in Britain up to 2010. The chapters describe, and at times critique, the development of clinical psychology research, practice and training in Britain from a number of perspectives. These include the development of theories and underpinning philosophical rationales, an understanding of the contribution of people, places and organisations, and the processes of professionalisation.

The book identifies key transitions and changes in the work and thinking of clinical psychologists, and analyses the factors and constraints that have contributed to them. It situates British clinical psychology in relation to wider fields of research and practice in applied psychology in health care, such as health psychology, clinical neuropsychology and forensic psychology. It explores the relationship between disciplinary and professional issues, and places developments within their policy, political and economic context. But there is no justification for any healthcare profession if it does not address the needs and concerns of those it seeks to help, so an important opening chapter addresses users' perspectives.

We have edited this volume for four reasons:

- There is no published history of clinical psychology in Britain, which we have taken here to include the four UK home nations of England, Northern Ireland, Scotland and Wales, with a note on the Republic of Ireland. Leslie Hearnshaw, the most significant British historian of psychology of his generation, published a history of British psychology covering the years 1840 to 1940 (Hearnshaw, 1964). A history of psychology in Britain (Bunn et al., 2001) was published to mark the centenary of the British Psychological Society (BPS), and the most recent published chapters are the entries by Alan Collins on England and by Nicholas Wade on Scotland in the *Oxford Handbook of the History of Psychology* (2012). Histories have been written for both occupational psychology (Shimmin & Wallis, 1994) and for educational psychology (Arnold & Hardy, 2013). The ways in which each field of applied psychology has developed in different countries is distinctive, and so clinical psychology has developed in Britain – and in different home nations within the UK, and in Ireland – in ways reflecting political, social and conceptual factors specific to each country.
- 2016 marks the 50th anniversary of the formation of the Division of Clinical Psychology of the BPS in 1966. The publication of this book in December 2015 helps to set the scene for that Golden Anniversary year.
- We are still just in reach of living memories of the earliest years of the National Health Service, through the recollections of those who worked directly with the leading figures of the early profession. A number of the chapters are written by psychologists who were working in the 1960s, and include interview material from psychologists working in the early 1950s, such as Peter Mittler. Sadly, during the writing of this book, other leading figures have died, including among others Alan Clarke, John Graham-White, Michael Humphrey, David Smail and Ed Miller.
- An understanding of where any profession or discipline has come from, and the

context in which it has grown, helps us to understand where it may go, in ideas, practice and policy. We reflect as editors in the final chapter on the cross-cutting themes that have emerged within these narratives and what, if anything, history tells us about the profession's future goals and direction.

As editors we faced the issue of how to write this history, or rather these histories. There are at least three forms of authorship for writing professional histories. One is for it to be written by a single senior figure from that profession, such as with the history of the Royal College of Psychiatrists (Bewley, 2008). Another is to commission a professional historian to write it, such as with the history of physiotherapy (Barclay, 1994).

A third way is to invite contributions from those who know most about their own fields of practice. We have taken this last route, offering multiple histories and narratives. This was the form adopted by Geoff Bunn and his colleagues for their centenary BPS history volume, and partly for that reason the title of this book mirrors theirs. We are mindful of the advantages and disadvantages of this primarily internalist emphasis. It emerges from lived experience and detailed knowledge accumulated over many years, but it may tend towards the descriptive and celebratory in its form of historical narrative. However, contributions also include critiques of the profession, and its undergirding body of knowledge within the discipline of psychology.

There is a tension in any book of this type between exploring issues in depth, and covering every area of practice. We have been guided by viewing as our primary readership final-year trainee and recently qualified clinical psychologists, who we have seen as proxy for a wider readership of applied psychologists working in health care. But this is not a textbook, nor an 'official' history. We hope not only psychologists but also historians and other interested professionals will find the book of interest.

We want to thank most of all two groups of people. The preparation of the book and the publication has been supported by both the Committee of the Division of Clinical Psychology (DCP) of the BPS, and the History of Psychology Centre of the BPS, following a proposal from David Pilgrim and John Hall, which had its origins in a conversation between them at the annual meeting of the BPS History and Philosophy of Psychology Section in 2012. We acknowledge the unfailing support of both of the chairs of the Division since then, Peter Kinderman and Richard Pemberton, with Cath Burley as the liaison link with the Division, and the manager of the BPS History of Psychology Centre, Peter Dillon-Hooper, for their initial and ongoing personal support, for giving us editorial freedom, and for arranging funding for the project.

In particular the funding for a part-time historian researcher, Sarah Marks, has enabled us both to support chapter authors in accessing primary sources, and given all of us some understanding of how to write this unusual historical genre. Sarah was appointed to this post in March 2014, and she has worked closely with us as editors, and tirelessly to support chapter authors in a number of ways. Sarah guided us and our authors on writing historically and researching the various relevant archives. Without her help many of the chapters within the book would be incomplete, or partial stories would have been told. But her most important contribution has been to alert us to critical reflection on some of our internalist narratives.

Secondly, we want to thank our chapter authors, for their contributions, which have involved them in the task (unfamiliar to most of them) of accessing primary archival sources, and the more familiar (and enjoyable) task of interviewing other witnesses. Most of them are clinical psychologists, and many of them are not only witnesses to the events they report, but have also been principal agents in contributing to those events. Their chapters include personal memories of their own experiences. Other authors are historians or academic psychologists who already had a knowledge of their field, and we welcome their complementary viewpoint, with no partisan motives in their accounts.

The writing of this book has been a collaborative and collegial exercise. One of our first steps was to create a scoping group, which included a number of the present chapter authors, and also Clare Crellin, Peter Kinderman, Philip Loring and Ed Miller (who died in May 2015). Together we brainstormed both the content and the style of the book, and the present volume has been largely shaped by their ideas. We have benefited from the ongoing advice of Rhodri Hayward, of Queen Mary University of London, who has been in effect our senior historian adviser during the project. Chapter authors have sought advice and comment from other colleagues. Some authors have acknowledged these by name, but we thank all of those who have helped us in this way – they know who they are. We have contributed to a number of other events, including 'pub quizzes' for final-year clinical psychology trainees, and met with a number of other colleagues, including the national Group of Trainers in Clinical Psychology, who have given us further guidance.

Histories of professions are inherently a difficult literary genre, with the risk of being celebratory and internalist. So this book should be seen in the context of the histories of other healthcare professions and disciplines. Unsurprisingly most attention has been paid to histories of doctors and general nurses, but there are histories of mental health nursing (Nolan, 1993), occupational therapy (Wilcock, 2002) and social work (Payne, 2005). So the book is also intended as a contribution to wider debates on the professionalisation of health care and on the psychologisation of society, as well as the applications of psychology to health care in the cultural and political context of Britain since the inception of the NHS.

Chapter authors have made use of BPS archival material, including BPS Council and DCP minutes and papers, for example, and other audio and written material: we thank Mike Maskill, the BPS archivist in London, for his help. The main BPS archives are held at the Wellcome Library, and the BPS book and journal collection is held at the University of London library at Senate House, and we thank the library staff of both. Three sites on the main BPS website are of particular interest to the general reader: there are websites for the History of Psychology Centre (hopc.bps.org.uk) and for the archives (archives.bps.org.uk) and a timeline for the origins of psychology (origins.bps.org.uk).

John Hall, David Pilgrim & Graham Turpin

References

Arnold, C. & Hardy, J. (2013). *British educational psychology: The first hundred years.* HoPC Monograph No. 1. Leicester: British Psychological Society.

Barclay, J. (1994). *In good hands: The history of the Chartered Society of Physiotherapy, 1894–1994.* Oxford: Butterworth-Heinemann.

Bewley, T. (2008). *Madness to mental illness: A history of the Royal College of Psychiatrists.* London: RCPsych Publications.

Bunn, G.C., Lovie, A.D. & Richards, G.D. (Eds.) (2001). *Psychology in Britain: Historical essays and personal reflections.* Leicester: BPS Books.

Collins, A. (2012). England. In D.B. Baker (Ed.), *Oxford handbook of the history of psychology* (pp.182–210). Oxford: Oxford University Press.

Hearnshaw, L.S. (1964). *A short history of British psychology: 1840–1940.* London: Methuen.

Nolan, P. (1993). *A history of mental health nursing.* London: Chapman & Hall.

Payne, M. (2005). *The origins of social work.* Basingstoke: Palgrave.

Shimmin, S. & Wallis, D. (1994). *Fifty years of occupational psychology in Britain.* Leicester: British Psychological Society.

Wade, N.J. (2012). Scotland. In D.B. Baker (Ed.), *Oxford handbook of the history of psychology* (pp.462–495). Oxford: Oxford University Press.

Wilcock, A. (2002). *Occupation for health: Vol. 2. A journey from prescription to self health.* London: British Association and College of Occupational Therapists.

About the contributors

Carole Allan trained as a clinical psychologist at the University of Glasgow where she became Clinical Director of the DClinPsy programme, and then Professional Lead for Psychology for NHS Greater Glasgow and Clyde. She is currently undertaking clinical practice and consultancy on an independent basis. Roles within the BPS include being President of the Society, and Chair of the Professional Practice Board.

Paul Bennett qualified as a clinical psychologist from the Plymouth course. After working in Cardiff, he moved to South Birmingham Psychology Services where he was the psychologist in a coronary heart disease programme and took his PhD at Birmingham University. Since then he has held clinical psychology posts in Bristol, Gwent and, finally, Swansea, and academic posts at the Universities of Bristol, Cardiff and Swansea, He was Research Director on the Bristol clinical psychology training programme. He is now full-time Professor of Clinical Health Psychology at the University of Swansea, with research interests including emotional and behavioural responses to illness or the threat of illness.

Michael Berger trained as a clinical psychologist at the Institute of Psychiatry, followed by a London University PhD. He was a lecturer at the Institute and staff psychologist for the child and adolescent services at the Maudsley and Bethlem Royal Hospitals and then moved to the Institute of Education as Senior Lecturer in Child Development. He was head of child psychology services at St George's Hospital, London and then District Psychologist for Wandsworth. He left to establish and run the Clinical Psychology Doctorate at Royal Holloway University of London, where he is now Emeritus Professor of Clinical Psychology.

Gillian Bowden trained as a clinical psychologist with South East Thames Regional Health Authority. She worked clinically in adult mental health and primary care NHS settings in South East London for several years before moving to Norfolk, where she is a consultant clinical psychologist with an NHS Trust and an honorary senior lecturer with the University of East Anglia. She was awarded an MBE in 2009 for services to mental health in Norfolk.

Cath Burley trained at Leicester University before working with older people in Leicestershire, Peterborough and Cambridgeshire, latterly as Head of Older People's Psychology Services. Actively involved with the training courses at Leicester and UEA, where she has an honorary senior lecturer position, she enjoyed seeing psychologists' enthusiasm for working in this specialty grow. A member of the Psychologists' Special Interest Group on the Elderly (PSIGE) since its inception, she served on the first committee and later rejoined the committee for 10 years, recently finishing her term as outgoing chair. She is now DCP Membership Services Unit Director.

Alan Carr obtained his first degrees in psychology at University College Dublin (UCD), and a PhD in clinical psychology from Queen's University Kingston, Ontario. He then worked as a clinical psychologist in the NHS in Norfolk before joining the UCD School of Psychology in 1992, where he now has a personal chair. He founded the UCD doctoral programme in clinical psychology, and has served as Head of the UCD School of Psychology. He has a clinical practice at Clanwilliam Family Therapy Institute, Dublin, and has produced over 20 volumes on clinical psychology, family therapy and positive psychology.

Jennifer Clegg qualified as a clinical psychologist via the BPS Diploma route with Forth Valley Health Board, largely at the Royal Scottish National Hospital where 2000 children and adults with intellectual disability (ID) were resident. A PhD from University of Nottingham on relationships in adults with ID framed subsequent qualification as a family therapist at the University of Leeds. Clinical posts in Lanarkshire, Exeter and Bury preceded her current joint appointment as Associate Professor, University of Nottingham and Consultant Clinical Psychologist, Nottinghamshire Health care NHS Trust. She is on the executive committee of two International Association for the Scientific Study of Intellectual and Developmental Disabilities (IASSIDD) groups.

Alan Collins is a Senior Lecturer in Psychology at Lancaster University. Trained as a cognitive psychologist, he developed his main research interest in the history of psychology during the late 1990s. He has published in various areas of history, including publications on notable British figures such as Kenneth Craik and Oliver Zangwill, and on particular areas such as the concept of information and popular works in memory improvement. He has been Chair of the BPS History and Philosophy of Psychology Section, and is currently Chair of the BPS History of Psychology Centre Committee.

Fabian Davis trained as a clinical psychologist in the SE Thames region. Since 1990 he has been lead consultant in community and social inclusion in Bromley. He developed English social inclusion policy and practice at the Sainsbury Centre, National Institute of Mental Health (NIMH) and Care Services Improvement Partnership (CSIP), representing the BPS as inclusion lead. He was the founding chair of the DCP Psychosis and Complex Mental Health Faculty. He has taught and published on social capital, inclusion, early intervention and recovery. He is an associate of the Centre for Citizenship and Community.

Juliet Foster is currently a Lecturer in Social Psychology at the Department of Psychology and Fellow and Senior Tutor of Murray Edwards College, University of Cambridge. She completed an MSc in social psychology at the London School of Economics, and a PhD at the University of Cambridge before taking up a Research Fellowship in Social Psychology at Corpus Christi College, Cambridge. She has long-standing research interests in understandings of mental health problems, and specialises in qualitative analysis. Recently she has begun working on the relationship between social psychology and history.

David Griffiths trained as a clinical psychologist at the Institute of Psychiatry, and worked there as a lecturer in the rehabilitation unit until 1971. From 1971 to 1975, he was Senior Lecturer in Clinical Psychology at the Welsh National School of Medicine in Cardiff. From 1975 to 1985 he was the Regional Clinical Tutor for Wales, and in 1985 he became the Director of the South Wales Training Course. He held this post until his retirement in 2003, and from 1994 he was Joint Director in close partnership with Dr Roger Young.

Gisli Gudjonsson is Emeritus Professor of Forensic Psychology at King's College London and Professor of Psychology at Reykjavik University. He trained as a clinical psychologist at the University of Surrey and completed his PhD with Lionel Haward. Prior to his retirement from King's College in 2012 he was the Head of Forensic Psychology Services for the Lambeth Forensic Services and Medium Secure Unit at the South London and Maudsley NHS Trust (SLaM). He currently holds an honorary clinical contract at Broadmoor Hospital. He was awarded a BPS Lifetime Achievement Award in 2009 and was appointed CBE in 2011 for services to clinical psychology.

John Hall trained as a clinical psychologist and obtained his PhD, supervised by H. Gwynne Jones, at Leeds University. He worked in Norfolk, Leeds and Cardiff before moving to Oxfordshire in 1980 where he was Head Clinical Psychologist and Senior Clinical Lecturer in Clinical Psychology at Oxford University, and was for five years Consultant Adviser in Clinical Psychology to the Department of Health. He is now Visiting Professor of Mental Health, and Research Associate at the Centre for the History of Medicine, at Oxford Brookes University. He was awarded the BPS Professional Affairs Board Lifetime Achievement Award in 2010.

Gillian Hardy trained as a clinical psychologist and obtained her PhD at the University of Leeds. She is Professor of Clinical Psychology at the University of Sheffield, where she is Director of the Clinical Psychology Unit. She has been joint Editor of the *British Journal of Clinical Psychology* and Chair of the BPS Committee of Training in Clinical Psychology.

Dougal Hare started out as a social psychologist but has been a clinical psychologist for over 20 years, working with people with intellectual and developmental disabilities. He espouses a left-wing and empiricist approach to history, and yields to none in his admiration for George Orwell.

Katherine Hubbard is currently studying for her PhD at the University of Surrey. She trained as a social psychologist but is currently working on the history of psychology for her doctoral research. Her work focuses on the British projective test movement and she adopts a queer feminist perspective in her critical approach to history.

Bernard Kat trained as a clinical psychologist through in-service training in Manchester leading to the BPS Diploma. He is also a health psychologist. He initiated services with GP practices in Northumberland and then managed psychology services in North Durham for 18 years. He chaired the Division of Clinical Psychology from 1980 to 1983. He is Director of Psynapse (Psychological Services) Ltd and a founding Director of the Centre for Applied Psychology Ltd and the Psychology Partnerships Community Interest Company.

Gary Latchford studied for a PhD in Edinburgh with Colwyn Trevarthen in 1989, after which he completed clinical psychology training in Leeds in 1991. Since that time he has worked with adults with physical illness, particularly cystic fibrosis. His clinical practice is at St James's University Hospital in Leeds. Since 1996 he has also worked on the clinical psychology training programme at Leeds University, where he became Joint Programme Director in 2014.

Tony Lavender trained at the Institute of Psychiatry, and his doctorate, on service evaluation in mental health, was from Kings College London. He has taken a leading role nationally in workforce development. He was previously joint chair of the BPS/NIMHE group looking at 'New Ways of Working for Applied Psychologists' and is currently the BPS representative on the NHS/Centre for Workforce Intelligence's Psychologists and Psychological Therapists Workforce Group. He is Pro-Vice Chancellor (Research & Knowledge Exchange) at Canterbury Christ Church University in addition to his professorial appointment there.

Susan Llewelyn trained as a clinical psychologist in Leeds and Nottingham, and worked clinically in the NHS for 10 years before becoming a lecturer in psychology at Nottingham University, also obtaining her PhD at the University of Sheffield. She then became a trainer in clinical psychology, becoming Course Director first in Edinburgh University and subsequently in Oxford. Since 2006 she has been Professor of Clinical Psychology at Harris Manchester College, Oxford University.

Sarah Marks trained as a historian at University College London. Her research and teaching interests cover the history of science and medicine in modern Europe, with particular emphasis on mental health, psychology and psychiatry. She is currently a Junior Research Fellow at Murray Edwards College, University of Cambridge, and a Research Associate at UCL's Centre for the History of Psychological Disciplines and Department of Science and Technology Studies.

Chris McCusker completed his PhD at Queen's University Belfast (QUB) and his clinical psychology training at the Institute of Psychiatry. He has combined academic and research activity with clinical practice in joint university and NHS appointments throughout his career. He is currently Director of Clinical Psychology Training at QUB. He is a past chair of the DCP in Northern Ireland, and current Chair of the BPS Committee for Training in Clinical Psychology.

Tom McMillan has been the Professor of Clinical Neuropsychology at the University of Glasgow since 1999. He was previously Professor of Clinical Psychology at the University of Surrey and Director of Clinical Neuropsychology for South East

Thames Regional Neurosciences Centre. He worked at the Institute of Psychiatry in London as lecturer and research worker for 10 years. He has published original research on brain injury, with a particular interest in head injury. He was the President of the International Brain Injury Association from 2010 to 2012 and was awarded the BPS Division of Neuropsychology Lifetime Achievement Award in 2014.

Steve Melluish worked for many years as a clinical psychologist within adult mental health and primary care services in Nottingham. He is interested in community psychology and issues of culture and psychology. He currently works as Head of Clinical Practice on the University of Leicester DClin Programme.

Kathy Nairne trained as a clinical psychologist at the Institute of Psychiatry, and worked in the NHS in mental health for 33 years. She was head of the Primary Care Psychology and Counselling Service in Lewisham from 1992 to 2013, becoming Clinical Director of the Lewisham Improving Access to Psychological Therapies (IAPT) service, as well as Head of Psychology for Lewisham. She is now working independently, providing consultancy, mentoring and clinical supervision.

Glenys Parry trained as a clinical psychologist through the South East Thames Regional Training Course and BPS Diploma, and has continued to practise as a psychologist and psychotherapist while undertaking research, management and health policy roles. After working with the Medical Research Council (MRC) Social and Applied Psychology Unit at the University of Sheffield, where she obtained her PhD, she was Academic Director of Clinical Psychology Training in Wessex. Later posts include Director of Psychology Services in Sheffield, and Senior Officer for Psychology and Psychotherapy Policy at the Department of Health, and she is now Professor of Applied Psychological Therapies at the University of Sheffield.

Nimisha Patel trained as a clinical psychologist at the University of Hull and went on to complete a Master's in international human rights. She has worked in the NHS and in civil society organisations, in the UK and internationally, specialising in the areas of antidiscrimination, torture and gender-based gross human rights violations. She is currently Professor of Clinical Psychology at the University of East London and Director of the International Centre for Health and Human Rights.

David Pilgrim trained as a clinical psychologist at the University of Liverpool and went on to complete a PhD on NHS psychotherapy and then a Master's in sociology. Since then his career has been split between clinical work and academic life. He is currently Professor of Health and Social Policy at the University of Liverpool and Visiting Professor of Clinical Psychology at the University of Southampton.

Peter Rankin trained in clinical psychology in Liverpool and in clinical neuropsychology and neuroscience in London. He is a Consultant Paediatric Neuropsychologist at Great Ormond Street Hospital for Children and Director of Clinical Neuropsychology Training at UCL Institute of Child Health. He is current Chair of the BPS Division of Neuropsychology.

Anne Richardson trained as a clinical psychologist at the Institute of Psychiatry. She worked in the NHS as regional tutor for the MSc/DClinPsy programme at the University of East London and as joint course director at University College London. Subsequently, she worked as Mental Health Policy Adviser at the Department of Health, and then as Head of Mental Health. She currently works in the independent sector providing policy consultancy and independent inquiries into serious incidents in the NHS.

Geoff Shepherd trained initially at the Institute of Psychiatry, qualifying in 1972. He has worked primarily in the NHS as a clinical practitioner, applied researcher and manager, mainly in Cambridge. He has also worked outside the NHS, as Head of Research at the Sainsbury Centre for Mental Health (1994–1997) and joint Chief Executive of the Health Advisory Service (1997–2002). He currently holds a visiting chair in the Department of Health Services Research at the Institute of Psychiatry. Since 2007 he has led a group delivering a national programme to help local services better support recovery, Implementing Recovery through Organisational Change (ImROC).

John Stewart trained as a historian at Oxford Polytechnic and at the University of London. His research and publication interests include health and social welfare in modern Britain and the history of child psychiatry. He is Emeritus Professor of Health History at Glasgow Caledonian University, and a Research Associate at the Wellcome Unit for the History of Medicine, Oxford University.

Graham Turpin trained as a clinical psychologist at the Institute of Psychiatry and was a senior lecturer at Plymouth Polytechnic on the MSc/DClinPsy programme. He went on to establish clinical training at the University of Sheffield, where he is now Emeritus Professor. He has been chair of the Division of Clinical Psychology and acted as a National Advisor to the Department of Health's IAPT programme.

Katie Aafjes-van Doorn completed her graduate degree in clinical psychology in Amsterdam, the Netherlands. Following this, she obtained a Master's in psychological research and a doctorate in clinical psychology at the University of Oxford. Since moving to California, her career has been split between clinical and research work. She currently works clinically as a postdoctoral researcher at the Access Institute, a psychoanalytic psychotherapy clinic in San Francisco, and collaborates on a variety of therapy process–outcome research projects.

Michael Wang trained at Manchester University and worked in clinical practice before moving to Hull University, where he became Professor of Clinical Psychology, leading the unique combined bachelors-doctoral programme in clinical psychology. He moved to Leicester in 2005 as Professor of Clinical Psychology and Course Director. His research interests are in the areas of anaesthesia and adult mental health, and he is also a practising clinical neuropsychologist. He was chair of the Division of Clinical Psychology in 2002/2003, when he was closely involved in the New Ways of Working Initiative.

Bob Woods trained as a clinical psychologist at Newcastle University and worked initially in Newcastle. Subsequently he combined extensive clinical work with older people with academic appointments at the Institute of Psychiatry, London and University College London. Since 1996, he has been Professor of Clinical Psychology of Older People at Bangor University, Wales. He established and leads the Dementia Services Development Centre Wales and NEURODEM Cymru, the dementia research network for Wales.

Roger Young trained as a clinical psychologist in South Wales. He worked in child and adolescent services before joining the South Wales Clinical Psychology Training Programme. He was initially appointed as the Assistant/Clinical Director and thereafter he was employed as the Programme Director until 2007. He is now an independent clinical psychologist working primarily within the area of public law/child care proceedings.

Susan Young trained as a clinical psychologist at University College London after having completed a PhD at the Institute of Psychiatry, Psychology and Neuroscience. She currently works as a senior lecturer clinical academic based at the Centre for Mental Health, Department of Medicine, Imperial College London. She holds an honorary clinical contract at Broadmoor Hospital for her work as Director of Forensic R&D in the West London Mental Health Trust.

William Yule trained as a clinical psychologist at the Institute of Psychiatry after a first degree in psychology at the University of Aberdeen, and received his doctoral degree for his studies of specific reading retardation. He worked for nearly all his career at the Institute, and is now Emeritus Professor of Applied Child Psychology. His main research interests have included autism, training teachers to use behavioural techniques, and the effects of trauma on children and adolescents. The Bill Yule Adolescent Unit at the Bethlem Royal Hospital was named in his honour in July 2005, and he was awarded the Aristotle Prize of the European Federation of Psychology Associations in 2007.

Guide to structure of the book

Part 1: Background

The introduction gives an outline of the development of psychology as a discipline from the mid-19th century, and the early development of clinical psychology in the United States. It also describes the development of the National Health Service in Britain, both as a unique form of healthcare administration and as the cradle within which clinical psychology has grown in Britain. Clinical psychology services should be meeting the needs of those who use them, so chapter 2 outlines both the broader history of the engagement of healthcare professionals with service users, and the specific history of the profession's engagement with the views and needs of users of their services. Both of these chapters set the scene for the following parts and chapters.

Part 2: Contexts

The ideas and practice of clinical psychology have arisen in a multidimensional social and political context, and Part 2 explores a number of those dimensions. There was a 'pre-history' before the Second World War, and the complex social changes in Britain following the war contributed further to the ways in which applied psychology began to develop. As the numbers of clinical psychologists grew slowly from the 1960s, they organised themselves, primarily but not solely, through subsystems of the British Psychological Society. Three interlocking issues have been both drivers and constraints upon the development of clinical psychology: government policy and spending on 'psychological' aspects of health care; the training systems required to produce clinical psychologists, when for most of the period there have been major shortages of clinical psychologists; and relationships with other professions, including the relatively new range of other providers of psychological services. The Institute of Psychiatry, based at the Maudsley Hospital, London, has been a leading centre for a significant training and research community of clinical psychologists, which has continued to be a major resource for the profession.

Part 3: Psychological Roles

Clinical psychologists carry out a range of functions. The initial expectation of clinical psychologists was that they would be both assessors and researchers, contributing to an agenda for a more scientific approach to mental illness and handicap. Both of these skills continue to be significant aspects of clinical practice and ongoing research, alongside the increasing involvement of psychologists in how best to organise health care. The most significant role change for psychologists followed the beginning of distinctively psychological forms of intervention from the late 1950s, which from the later 1960s meant that the main expectation of psychologists would be as therapists. This expectation has led to both a number of policy initiatives promoting psychological therapies, and also a proliferation of therapeutic modalities.

Part 4: Work with Client Groups

Clinical psychologists work with a range of different presented clinical problems, usually seen as different client groups, although the psychological aspects of their care often cross over client group boundaries. Work with children and young people was the focus of the first clinical psychologists, and continues to be a major field of work. Work with adults with mental health needs followed from the late 1940s, and has since grown to be the largest single area of work, which has itself developed a range of specialist subfields. Work with people with intellectual disabilities was the third early field of work. Work with older people has grown considerably, reflecting the ageing population of Britain. The fourth early field of work, with people with neuropsychological problems, has developed in a number of ways, so much that there is now a separate Division of Neuropsychology within the BPS. Similarly, work with people with other medical problems, and work in the field of forensic clinical psychology, represent major developments beyond the mental health field, and to levels of specialisation of practice justifying separate Divisions of Health and Forensic Psychology.

Part 5: National and International Perspectives

Clinical psychology has developed differently in different countries of the world. Psychologists from abroad have come to work in Britain, and British psychologists have worked abroad, both contributing to a reappraisal of what forms of psychology are appropriate to different cultures, not least the increasingly multicultural nature of Britain. The UK itself is made up of four home nations, whose own differences (with the Republic of Ireland) have contributed to different clinical psychology narratives.

Part 6: Reflections

The single chapter in this final part gathers together and critically examines the main themes that have emerged in the book, and their implications and challenges both for the future of applied psychology in health care in Britain, and for the place of historical understanding for psychologists

Part 1
Background

Chapter 1 Introduction

John Hall, David Pilgrim & Graham Turpin

This introductory chapter gives an outline of the development of psychology as a discipline from the mid-19th century, and the later interrelated concepts of clinical, medical and abnormal psychology. The professional practice of clinical psychology began in the United States, but under circumstances very different from the status of psychology in Britain at the same period. The chapter also describes the interacting roles of the British Psychological Society and the universities in contributing to the shape and size of psychology as a discipline. As the NHS is the dominant employer of clinical psychologists, its structures and conditions of employment have been a major influence in how the profession has developed.

What is psychology? ...

Introductory text books on psychology usually refer to the long history of philosophical and medical thought that led to the modern concept of 'psychology', and then see the establishment of a psychological laboratory by Wilhelm Wundt (1832–1920) at the University of Leipzig in 1879 as a defining point in that history. While there is a long history of thinking about what are now seen as psychological topics, examining the second of these historical 'tropes', or conventional narratives, helps to understand how modern academic and scientific psychology achieved its current position.

Graham Richards (2010), in his critical account of the history of psychology, identifies the middle of the 19th century as the point when a discipline calling itself psychology can be considered to exist. He sees two developments as supplying both an integrative framework for the emerging discipline, and scientific procedures for pursuing them. These are evolutionary thought, associated with the work of Charles Darwin and Herbert Spencer, and the appearance in Germany of the methodologies identified with Gustav Fechner and Wilhelm Wundt. He also sees the statistical tradition of Galton and Pearson as influential, a tradition underpinning the whole field of psychometrics and psychological assessment (see chapter 10).

Leslie Hearnshaw's introduction to the history of psychology in Britain (Hearnshaw, 1964) similarly suggests that the work of Alexander Bain (1818–1903) marks a turning point in British psychology in four ways: he defines psychology more clearly than before; he lays an accurate physiological foundation for psychology; the requirements of scientific method are better understood; and his *The Senses and the Intellect* (1855) is considered 'the first text book of psychology written in the modern manner'.

For English-speaking psychologists, Wundt has 'unduly dominated our picture of late 19th-century psychological thought' (Richards, 2010, p.39) and is a controversial figure. Hearnshaw sees *three* figures – G.T. Fechner (1801–1887), Hermann von Helmholtz (1821–1894) and Wundt – as laying the foundations of modern psychology from their shared background in experimental physiology (Hearnshaw, 1987, chapter 9). The attention paid to Wundt is only partly because of the laboratory he founded, but also because he attracted numerous American postgraduate students from the 1880s. It is then possible to see Wundt as an early psychologist conferring status on the discipline through his good experimental credentials. The debate about Wundt is a salutary example of the tangle between the actual contribution of a psychologist as actor, and the contribution of audiences in revering teachers and leaders (Rieber, 2003).

Scientific psychology developed in German universities, and the modern research university developed from the model of the University of Berlin, founded by Wilhelm von Humboldt in 1810 (Rüegg, 2004, pp.3–31). The emphasis on research also led in turn to the creation of a new form of research degree, the Doctorate in Philosophy (PhD). The German model of universities was influential in the United States, and as the American psychologists who had studied in Germany returned to academic posts in the United States with their new knowledge and doctoral degrees, the United States proved highly receptive to the new discipline.

The era after the American Civil War saw the foundation of numerous secular universities, such as the postgraduate Johns Hopkins University, with a growing demand for postgraduate education. William James (1842–1910) became professor of psychology at Harvard in 1889, and in 1890 published *The Principles of Psychology*, a landmark in the history of psychology in the United States. He was a central figure in the developments from 1880, alongside G.S. Hall, who had completed a doctorate under Wundt, and was a driving force in the institutionalisation of psychology in America, founding not only the American Psychological Association (APA) in 1892 – the first national psychological society in the world – but also the *American Journal of Psychology* in 1887.

Alongside this academic and laboratory tradition, derived from a physiological background, are other clinical traditions, derived from both an organic and psychodynamic background. The long history of lunacy, based mostly in asylums, had generated a medical approach to diagnosis exemplified by the work of Emil Kraepelin (1856–1926). He had studied at Leipzig, and later worked at Heidelberg and Munich, and through successive editions of his Textbook (see Kraepelin, 1899) laid the foundation for a system of psychiatric diagnosis that underpins present-day practice (but see the historical account and critique of Kraepelin's work by Bentall, 2004). Sigmund Freud (1856–1939) was based in Vienna for most of his life. Following a fellowship in Paris in 1885 with the French neurologist Jean-Martin Charcot, he became interested in hypnosis, and from 1895 was publishing papers and books (such as his *Psychopathology of Everyday Life*, 1904/2003) on his ideas and therapeutic methods, which led to the development of psychoanalysis. Unlike Kraepelin, he formed a school of followers, early members of which included Carl Jung and Alfred Adler.

The 'psychological' foundations for clinical psychology are thus primarily German and American, and include the academic and laboratory traditions of Wundt, Fechner and von Helmholtz, the clinical traditions of Kraepelin and Freud, the American influence of James and Hall, and the British statistical traditions of Galton and Pearson. The First International Congress of Psychology was held at Paris 1889, and the following Congresses, all growing in size, confirmed an international consensus around the nature of the new discipline of psychology.

...and what is clinical, medical or abnormal psychology?

In 1945 the Council of the British Psychological Society (BPS) said that the term 'clinical psychologist' was 'not necessarily meaningless, but...liable to too much ambiguity and misunderstanding to be used by the Society' (BPS, 1945, p.50). How could this be?

The first use of the adjective 'clinical' in connection with psychology has conventionally been seen as referring to the practice of the psychological clinic set up in 1896 by Lightner Witmer of the University of Pennsylvania. This clinic was mainly for 'retarded children' and for children with physical defects associated with delayed development, and would probably now be called a child development clinic. William Healey also set up a clinic in a court setting in Chicago in 1909 to study antisocial behaviour. Misiak and Sexton (1966) explicitly contrast the two models, describing Witmer's model as essentially psychoeducational, following the Wundt and Kraepelin tradition, and as being 'static and segmented', and Healey's clinic as following the tradition of Freud and the French School, and as a 'dynamic total approach'.

There is at least one other earlier use of the term clinical psychology, in a pamphlet published in Edinburgh in 1861 entitled *The Clinical Teaching of Psychology* by James Crichton-Browne, a leading Scottish doctor. He wrote that the medical authorities 'will be compelled at length to incorporate clinical psychology with the other departments of professional education, and to require a study of it in every aspirant to medical education'. He was writing at a period before the emergence of scientific psychology and Freudian psychology, and it is apparent in the text that what he means by psychology is what would now be termed psychopathology or psychiatry, but he uses the terms 'clinical', 'medical', and 'practical' psychology with equal meaning.

A number of other terms have been used to describe the range of activities now undertaken by present-day clinical psychologists. The term 'medical psychology' has been widely used. Confusingly, the professional organisation for British psychiatrists, formed in 1841 as the Association of Medical Officers of Asylums and Hospitals for the Insane, was later known as the Medico-Psychological Association, and from 1926 until 1970 as the Royal Medico-Psychological Association (RMPA). The Medical Section of the British Psychological Society (BPS) published the *British Journal of Medical Psychology*, which was in practice an outlet for mainly psychodynamic papers. During the First World War the medically qualified doctors W.H.R. Rivers, C.S. Myers and W. McDougall were termed psychologists in the British Army (see Shephard, 2014). Abnormal psychology has been taken to refer to the psychology of 'abnormal' mental states and behaviour, most frequently those associated with psychological distress, and some early books with this title are in fact descriptions of psychopathology written by psychiatrists. H.J. Eysenck's monumental *Handbook of Abnormal Psychology* (1960) is an important example of a British text in this field, and was followed by a number of textbooks directed at the medical student market, such as that by Miller and Morley (1986).

Early American and British usage of the terms 'clinical', 'medical', and 'abnormal' psychology thus became confounded. Any of these terms and definitions not only claimed intellectual and scientific territory, but positioned that knowledge professionally. Another approach to understanding the term is to see how it has been used by British clinical psychologists. The academic Oliver Zangwill thought in 1965 that 'clinical psychology involves people as well as problems, flair as well as training, art as well as science...above all the clinical psychologist has to learn to be useful, to doctors, their patients and to his own discipline' (Zangwill, 1965, p.18). The practitioner Mahesh Desai (1967), in his chair's address to the first scientific meeting of the newly established Division of Clinical Psychology, talked of the main functions of clinical psychologists as clinical assessment of patients in relation to their problems (which he also saw as formulation of opinions on the nature of the patient's condition), participation in treatment, guidance and rehabilitation, research, and teaching. The Division of Clinical Psychology of the BPS (Toogood, 2010) defines it as follows: 'Clinical psychology aims to reduce psychological distress and to enhance and promote psychological well-being by the systematic application of knowledge derived from psychological theory and data'.

In Britain the term 'clinical psychology' is now used widely, sometimes when strictly speaking an individual psychologist should be described as a health or forensic psychologist, or clinical neuropsychologist (see chapters 19, 21 and 22). In this book we have not sought to define the boundaries between these closely related branches of applied psychology. The term medical psychology continues to be used to describe the applications of psychology in general medical settings, but it would be archaic for psychiatrists now to describe themselves in that way. Abnormal psychology continues to be used to describe the psychological theories and processes used to explain both the problems presented by patients and some of the psychological variation within the 'normal' population.

An American legacy?

A number of accounts of the early history of clinical psychology as a profession in Britain have been published, claiming for example that 'clinical psychologists in Great Britain were from the start greatly influenced by their American counterparts' (Liddell, 1983). Was this true?

A detailed history of the development of clinical psychology in the United States has been written by Reisman (1991). There were at least three influences on early American 'clinical psychology'. One was psychometrics: Alfred Binet (1857–1911) had founded the first laboratory of physiological psychology at the Sorbonne in Paris in 1889, and collaborated with Theodore Simon, a psychiatrist, to produce the ground-breaking 30-item Binet–Simon scale, which Henry Goddard, a former student of G.S. Hall, revised to make the scale more suitable for general use in America. Second, the mental hygiene movement was initiated by Clifford Beers: from his own experiences at a psychiatric hospital he wrote an autobiography, *A Mind That Found Itself* (1908/1950), and with the support of William James and the leading psychiatrist Adolf Meyer, the National Committee for Mental Hygiene was formed in 1909. Third, Freud's early work was becoming known in America and G.S. Hall, impressed by his work, invited Freud, along with Jung and others, to Clark University in 1909 and as part of this visit a number of lectures were given promoting psychoanalysis.

During the First World War American psychologists were developing their clinical work. At the 1917 APA convention a group of concerned clinicians met and formed the American Association of Clinical Psychologists (AACP). An under-acknowledged figure in this initiative was Leta Hollingworth, who was the first secretary of the AACP, and the first woman to have a leading role in American clinical psychology (Routh, 1994). The AACP was absorbed into the APA, so is the direct ancestor of the APA Division of Clinical Psychology. A number of American clinical journals were well established by the 1930s, including the *Journal of Clinical Psychology* and the *Journal of Abnormal and Social Psychology*; a wide range of formal psychometric tests had been developed; and by 1937 the eminent R.S. Woodworth could write an article drawing on the history of clinical psychology (Woodworth, 1937). The massive support for clinical psychology training by the US Veterans Administration from the 1940s was primarily to assist in the rehabilitation of US servicemen engaged in the Second World War, driven by ideas of social utility, reflecting the prewar existence of an identifiable group of clinical psychologists.

What then was the legacy of this as far as the UK was concerned? Two other new professions contributing significantly to mental health care had been developed in Britain before the Second World War, both of which were directly influenced by American practice. Psychiatric social work had been introduced in a carefully planned way, with the first training course in London in 1930 and the establishment of a professional organisation paid for by the anglophile American Commonwealth Fund (Stewart, 2013). Occupational therapy had developed at the same time, with the first trained occupational therapist appointed in Britain, at a hospital at Aberdeen, having trained in the United States. The first training course in Britain was set up at Dorset House in Bristol in 1930, with the first principal of the training course also having trained in the United States (Wilcock, 2002).

It is difficult to establish any similar direct funding or training links with America for clinical psychologists. The psychological clinic set up by Witmer was not the primary inspiration for the child guidance clinics set up in Britain and Scotland in the 1920s (Stewart, 2013). While H.J. Eysenck from the Maudsley Hospital was funded by the Rockefeller Foundation in 1947 to visit training courses in America, his mind was made up before he went and there is little evidence he learned from his trip (Buchanan, 2010), while the person responsible for training at the Maudsley, M.B. Shapiro, did not visit the United States early in his career. Considerable attention was paid in the United States to effective training, as shown by the APA's Shakow Report of September 1947, and by the Boulder conference of 1949 that put forward the scientist-practitioner model of training, but references to American training precedents are not prominent in early post-war British psychological publications (see chapter 24). There are no known early examples of an American-trained clinical psychologist occupying a senior post in Britain, although from the 1970s there were a few senior psychologists, such as Roger Squier in Kent.

Although the professionalisation of clinical psychology in Britain was conducted some decades after American developments, the extent to which it was directly informed by American practice is unclear, although American journals, other publications and test materials were used widely in Britain from the Second World War. In America there was massive federal funding and established university departments. In Britain there were no home-grown clinical psychology journals, no public budget for training and few home-produced psychological tests. There could hardly have been a worse period to start a new healthcare profession in Britain than in the 1940s.

Psychology in Britain

Psychology was far slower to become established as an academic discipline in Britain compared to both Germany and the United States. The period of most relevance to this book is around the Second World War: there were only five professors of psychology in Britain in 1939, the first being at Kings College London, with C.S. Myers as the first professor (but only part-time) in 1906. Three other noteworthy appointments were at University College London, where Cyril Burt followed C.E. Spearman in 1931; at Cambridge, where Frederic Bartlett was appointed in 1931; and at Edinburgh, where James Drever (primus) was also appointed in 1931 (Hearnshaw, 1964).

Before the Second World War there were at least three ways in which the term 'psychology' would have been understood by the general public in Britain. First, there was the tradition of scientific psychology already outlined, taught in universities and teacher training colleges and still emerging from the disciplines of philosophy, physiology and education. Second, there was the 'New Psychology', deriving from the tradition of psychoanalysis. Third, there was a strong tradition of popular or folk psychology, supported by a number of magazines and by organisations such as the British Federation of Psychologists (Thomson, 2006). It would not have been self-evident to even a reasonably educated person what the term 'psychology' meant on its own, or what knowledge or skills to expect of someone who called themselves simply 'a psychologist', let alone a clinical psychologist.

The role of the British Psychological Society

By the end of the 19th century, more universities had been founded in Britain, and 'science' had become institutionalised. In 1876 the Physiological Society was established, building on the expansion of both physiological research and the teaching of physiology to medical students, with meetings centred on the presentation of scientific papers for discussion. What would seem more natural when psychologists in Britain, many with research interests in physiological psychology, wanted to establish a psychological society, than that they should look to the Physiological Society for a model?

The present British Psychological Society (BPS) was formed at a meeting at University College, London, in 1901 – an earlier attempt to set up a 'Psychological Society of Great Britain' had failed after just four years, probably through an emphasis on spiritualism, and a failure to engage with the metropolitan intellectual elite (Richards, 2001). The 10 people who met in 1901 were an assorted group of academics and educationalists, including the physiologist Frederic Mott, already an FRS; W.H.R. Rivers, later famous for his anthropological work and therapeutic work in the First World War; and one woman, Sophie Bryant, headmistress of the North London Collegiate School. Their aim was 'to advance scientific psychological research, and to further the cooperation of investigators in the different branches of psychology'. The membership criteria were limited to those who were 'recognised teachers in some branch of psychology, or who have published work of recognisable value', so the BPS was formed in the mould of a select learned society.

In 1910 the Society had a membership of less than one hundred, and this had risen to 717 in 1927 (Hearnshaw, 1964). The major reason for this increase was the decision taken in 1919, led by C.S. Myers, to open the doors to those who were 'interested' in psychology, mostly people who were interested in the applications of psychology in the educational, industrial and 'medical' fields. The possibility that these three groups might form organisations of their own was one stimulus to change the membership criteria, but the accompanying substantial increase in membership subscriptions placed the Society for the first time in a reasonably stable financial position (Edgell, 1947).

Three 'Sections' were formed within the Society, one for each of these three fields of interest. The field of education was the first in which an applied psychologist was employed, by the half-time appointment of Cyril (later Sir Cyril) Burt to London County Council in 1913. The industrial field was boosted by the creation in 1921, again by Myers, of the National Institute of Industrial Psychology (NIIP), the largest employer of psychologists before the Second World War. Most of the members of the Medical Section were engaged in some form of psychotherapy in private practice; many of them were doctors who did not see the Medico Psychological Association (MPA), dominated by the asylum superintendents, as their natural institutional home.

At the beginning of the Second World War the BPS was both a learned society and an open-membership association, which was legally incorporated as a limited company in 1941, giving it a number of new powers. The governing body was the Council, made up of the elected officers, directly elected members, and representatives of the different subsections of the Society, crucially the three Sections (Education, Industrial, and Medical), and the editors of the associated journals. The Council reserved to itself all major decisions regarding communication with outside bodies, but there were no structures for professional psychologists. There were a number of ramifications of this structure. A number of the officers of the Society were also medically qualified, so as professional issues began to arise the position of the BPS on an issue could be put forward by representatives who were medically qualified, creating a potential conflict of interest. Quite apart from professional psychologists, a group of young experimental psychologists felt that the BPS did not meet their needs, and in 1946 the Experimental Psychology Group was formed, following an initiative by Oliver Zangwill, in intent and method remarkably similar to the initial meeting of the BPS in 1901 (Mollon, 2006).

The next major step for the BPS was the closure of membership in 1958, restricting full membership to those who possessed a formal qualification in psychology, normally an honours degree with psychology as the main content of the degree. The BPS laid down criteria for the acceptability of such degrees for membership, and by requiring entrants to a range of postgraduate courses, including clinical psychology, to meet those criteria it effectively controlled – and continues to control – entry to all fields of applied psychology in Britain: in 2014 the BPS approved 800 different psychology courses.

A Royal Charter was granted in 1965, conferring the right to be consulted on a range of government issues, and also to set up a chartering procedure, protecting the title of members. Following the grant of the Royal Charter, British educational psychologists formed a separate organisation as both a trade union and a professional body, the Association of Educational Psychologists (AEP), whose objectives were to 'raise the profile of educational psychologists', the implication being that they considered this was not achievable within the BPS (Martin, 2013, p.53). It was not therefore axiomatic that the BPS would remain the umbrella organisation for all British psychologists. In the United States a split has occurred, with the American Psychological Society being formed in 1988 (now renamed as the Association for Psychological Science) to represent experimental psychologists, who were concerned that the APA (continuing as the larger organisation) was more concerned with practitioner issues.

The role of the universities

The supply of candidates for clinical psychology postgraduate training is crucially dependent on the capacity of university psychology departments. Indeed, the health and vitality of a discipline is often assessed by the number of its university departments, the numbers of its faculty and the overall numbers of students enrolled on its courses, as reviewed by the International Benchmarking Review of UK Psychology (ESRC, 2011, pp.1–37). Psychology within the UK was a late developer compared to its counterparts in Germany and the United States. During the first half of the 20th century, psychology as a discipline was expanding quickly in these countries and this was due to the accompanying expansion in numbers of universities and colleges. The UK, by contrast, had a much more conservative higher education establishment (Hearnshaw, 1969) and university expansion did not come about until the 1960s, both by the establishment of completely new campus-based universities and by former 'colleges of advanced technology' (CATS) being awarded university status, both preceding and after the Robbins Report on higher education (Committee on Higher Education, 1963). University education became more available to both older students and those without the conventional school background, to an increasing proportion of whom psychology was an attractive subject (see Anderson, 2006).

From 1960 to 1969 the number of chairs established in psychology had increased from 13 to 21, together with a doubling of the BPS membership from 1595 to 3356 (Hearnshaw, 1969). Up to the late 1980s the numbers of single honours psychology programmes accredited by the BPS were approximately doubling every 10 years, until there were 109 programmes accredited during 1985–1989, resulting in just over 2000 new graduates per year in 1989 for UK universities. From the 1990s onwards there was a massive step change in the expansion of both courses and student numbers, and in the next five years 310 programmes were accredited, rising to just under 500 programmes in 2014 (L. Horder, BPS Partnership and Accreditation Manager, personal communication, January, 2015). The increase in programmes was associated with a large increase in students, so there were 5645 psychology graduates in 1996.

There may be several factors behind this growth. A-level psychology was becoming increasingly popular, reflected in an annual growth rate of 14 per cent between 1985 and 1997, the third fastest growth rate for any GCE A-level subject. By 1997 there were over 27,000 A-level candidates within psychology (Holdstock & Radford, 1998). As psychology as a discipline was adopted by polytechnics and 'new universities' (post-1992) they typically had larger intakes of students than their more conventional counterparts, with a shift in their teaching philosophy from the traditional university laboratory approach, reliant on small practical classes, to larger lecture-based modes of delivery. More recent figures for the number of applicants demonstrate continuing growth. For example, in 2009 there were 17,761 UCAS applicants and 15,385 accepted onto courses. As a subject area psychology is now one of the top three most popular subjects for study at UK universities, only outmatched in absolute terms by the numbers of medical students, or in growth rates by student numbers within economics (ESRC, 2011). Current estimates are 91,000 students, including 18,000 postgraduates (Hulme, 2014).

What is the impact of the discipline's popularity on the profession of clinical psychology? As discussed in chapter 7, even in the 1970s the Trethowan Report (DHSS, 1977) commented on the ready availability of psychology graduates. Clearly supply far outstrips demand for clinical psychology training, but there are both challenges and opportunities in this situation. If the profession is to serve minorities within the population, then one requirement is that the psychology workforce matches that diversity. The sheer numbers of psychology graduates ought to ensure that minority groups (e.g. members of ethnic minorities, and gay and lesbian people) have better opportunities for recruitment into the profession (Turpin & Coleman, 2010; Turpin & Fensom, 2004). The profession needs to actively encourage and welcome these graduates into its fold, and ensure that its values and practices are relevant to minority groups and cultures (Williams et al., 2006). The second opportunity is to encourage more psychology graduates into careers in other health professions, including support roles for applied psychologists.

How many clinical psychologists were there?

It is difficult to answer the question 'What is the size of the profession?' with precision, for a number of reasons. Statistics for England and Wales were the ones usually quoted in official reports, but these figures of course omitted Scotland and Northern Ireland. Figures could be quoted as either numbers of psychologists, or as full-time equivalents (FTE). Figures could be based on NHS employees, or on BPS membership lists. So the following data are only as good as contemporary methods of collection and aggregation: it is impossible to present whole-time equivalents for the whole of Britain on a consistent basis across the period. One of the most careful recent calculations (Turner et al., in press) gives numbers for clinical psychologists employed by the NHS in England and Wales only (see Table 1.1). Figures for the BPS and BPS subsystems are derived from annual reports of the Committee of Professional Psychologists (Mental Health) (CPP(MH)) and the BPS membership lists (see Table 1.2).

Figures for the subgroups within the CPP(MH) show those who were members of the child and adult subsections separately. In 1951 there were 211 and 17 members of the two sections respectively. The figures for 1966 show that at that point there were fewer clinical psychologists than educational psychologists, while in 2010 there were over three times more clinical psychologists than educational psychologists in the respective Divisions of the BPS.

Precisely because of doubts about the reliability of official figures, the DCP periodically organised workforce surveys. One of the most careful surveys (Scrivens & Charlton, 1985), commissioned by the Steering Group on Health Services Information, gave 1486 clinical psychologists in post in England in 1985, with 1734 established posts. This report also showed that 70 per cent of NHS districts had fewer than nine psychologists in post, and that 30 per cent of districts had fewer than four

Table 1.1 NHS clinical psychologists in England and Wales 1950–2010/11 (Turner et al., in press)

Year	*psychologists*
1950	<121
1960	179
1970	399
1980	1078
1990/91	2200
2000/01	5316
2010/11	8837

Table 1.2 Members of the BPS, and members of relevant BPS subsystems 1945–2010

Year	*BPS members*	*CPP(MH) members up to 1965 DCP members from 1966*
1945	1164	77
1950	1897	208
1955	2345	350
1960	2655	425
1965	3587	479
1966	3300	163*
1970	3811	362
1980	7655	966
1990	14,105	1574
2000	26,809	4210
2010	48,195	9554

*The CPP(MH) became the DCP in 1966; the fall in membership is due to educational psychologists moving to their own Division.

posts. Sample figures for Northern Ireland are 10 individuals in 1967, 68 in 1998, and 257 (230 FTE) in 2013. Sample figures for Scotland are 10 FTE in 1948, 94 FTE by 1976; in 2000 there were 428 individuals (360 FTE) and in 2014 795 individuals (668 FTE) (see chapter 23). What all of these figures show is that during the first decade of the NHS only a minority of mental illness or mental handicap hospitals employed even one psychologist.

The statistics from the current statutory registration body, the Health and Care Professions Council, are more reliable. Disentangling the numbers for August 2014 for all categories of practitioner psychologists shows that 8854 psychologists were registered as only clinical psychologists (7242 women and 1603 men, so 82 per cent female). Another 470 psychologists are registered with various combinations of clinical with forensic, health, counselling and educational psychology (one person is registered as clinical, counselling, forensic and health), giving 9324 individuals currently registered as a clinical psychologist (HCPC, 2015).

The British National Health Service

The creation of the NHS

The origins of the profession of clinical psychology are interlinked with the creation and subsequent development of the British National Health Service (NHS). The two-volume official history of the NHS by Charles Webster (1988, 1996) gives detailed information on many of the points made in this section. Developments within the profession have been in response to demands placed on it by the NHS as its major employer, and the great majority of funding for training has been from the NHS. This symbiotic relationship between the development of a state healthcare system and the profession of clinical psychology is unique to the UK (see chapter 24).

Before the Second World War economic depression, and a failure to reform health, education and social services, meant that there was no overall coordination in Britain of the patchwork of state-funded, locally funded, voluntary and privately funded services. Hospitals for people with mental disorders and mental handicap were provided and managed by county and borough councils, and poor law institutions were locally managed. Provision by the most prestigious teaching hospitals, managed by Boards of Governors, was however uncoordinated, and the charitable 'registered' English mental hospitals – including the Bethlem Hospital and the Retreat at York – were administered on the same pattern and similarly were located because of historical patterns of local philanthropy. The consequences of the lack of any planning of hospitals were most apparent in London, and over a period of 50 years the twin principles slowly emerged of regionalised hospital planning, and of hospital planning centred around major teaching (then voluntary) hospitals, with a clearer functional relationship between these hospitals and other general hospitals. As the possibility of war loomed from 1938, the government created the Emergency Medical Service (EMS), which created groups of hospitals on the basis of a number of 'regions' throughout the country.

During the Second World War national priority was given to every activity directed at survival of the state through military action, yet during the war major social welfare and educational policies were being prepared. In 1941 Sir William Beveridge, a 61-year-old civil servant, was asked by Britain's wartime coalition government to chair a committee on the coordination of social insurance as part of the process of post-war reconstruction. The Beveridge Report was finally published in December 1942, and laid the foundations of a comprehensive health and welfare system. The Report provided 'the vital kick to the "five giants" programme that formed the core of the post-war welfare state: social security, health, education, housing and a policy of full employment' (Timmins, 1995). In Beveridge's terms these meant tackling poverty, disease, ignorance, squalor and unemployment.

The landslide victory of the Labour Party at the 1945 General Election followed six years of great loss of life, social upheaval and economic and financial hardship. The new government nationalised a number of industries (such as the rail system), and there was an expectation of political and organisational reform of welfare services. Aneurin 'Nye' Bevan was appointed Minister of Health with a seat in the Cabinet, and in 1946 the National Health Service Act was passed. It promoted 'the establishment in England and Wales of a comprehensive health service designed to secure improvement in the physical and mental health of people of England and Wales and the prevention, diagnosis and treatment of illness'. On the 'appointed day' of 5 July 1948, the National Health Service had arrived.

> [The NHS] was the first health system in any Western society to offer free medical care to the entire population. It was, furthermore, the first comprehensive system to be based not on the insurance principle, with entitlement following contributions, but on the national provision of services available to everyone. It thus offered free and universal entitlement to State-provided medical care. At the time of its creation, it was a unique example of the collectivist provision of health care in a market society. (Klein, 1983, p.1)

NHS structures

The 1946 NHS Act divided England into 14 Regional Hospital Boards (RHBs), related to the Regions established for the EMS, and there were five RHBs in Scotland. The Act created three types of healthcare management (the tripartite system). General medical and other practitioner services were managed by 'Executive Councils' and local health authority clinics, all of which were the responsibility of the new RHBs. Public health services, and usually child guidance clinics, continued to be managed by local education authorities. All hospitals (other than teaching hospitals), were organised into 'groups', managed by 700 separate Hospital Management Committees (HMCs). For general hospitals these typically centred around one or more larger non-teaching hospitals, while mental illness and mental handicap hospitals were typically managed by their own dedicated HMCs. Teaching hospitals were directly responsible to the Ministry of Health, and were managed by Boards of Governors. This hierarchical RHB and HMC structure was to remain fundamentally unchanged until 1974.

This apparently neat structure concealed a number of significant differences between regions and within regions. While some were highly urbanised and compact, such as the Birmingham RHB, others were both more rural and extended, such as the South Western RHB, going all the way west from Gloucester. There were significant differences in funding, so that while the London Metropolitan Regions were relatively overfunded for their population, the Northern and East Anglia Regions were underfunded. For example, in 1955/56 the South West Metropolitan RHB, with 10.5 per cent of the population, had 13.1 per cent of the revenue allocation (Webster, 1988, section vii, chapter VIII).

What this meant in practice for the psychologists beginning to work in the NHS was that they were employed to work in specific hospitals, which had no tradition of cooperating with similar types of hospital within the same region. However, the coordination of funding for training for the various professional groups was carried out at regional level. Regional funding was central to the establishment of new clinical psychology training courses developed in the 1960s, so as the demand for psychologists grew, the key targets in lobbying for training funds were both the regional psychiatric advisory committee and the regional medical officer.

This original structure had a number of disadvantages, most obviously that the full range of health services for any one locality were provided by a number of individual HMCs, whose catchment areas did not match local government boundaries, so that social care was difficult to coordinate with health care. The Local Government Act of 1972 reorganised the structure of local authorities to match the expected areas of the proposed health authorities, and the linked NHS Reorganisation Act was passed in July 1973, the exact 25th anniversary of the introduction of the NHS. In the implementation of the new scheme from 1974, a regional structure was retained, but with the 14 RHBs now renamed as Regional Health Authorities (RHAs). The Boards of Governors and HMCs were replaced by 90 Area Health Authorities (AHAs) run by an area team of officers, and 200 District Management Teams, each with a community health council and an elaborate parallel professional advisory machinery. The new AHAs essentially matched the new local authority areas, subdivided into Districts in large counties and cities; in Scotland the regional tier was abolished, with Health Boards being comparable to the English AHAs. The new Health Authorities and Boards brought together all hospital, community and practitioner services (organised through Family Practitioner Committees), and included the previously separate teaching hospitals. This enabled for the first time comprehensive planning of both clinical services and medical training, as well as social care, for the total population. This ethos of coordination of all area services also led to the creation of lead area posts for all clinical professions, including Area Psychologists.

In 1979 the Royal Commission on the NHS published a report which was critical of the 1974 NHS reorganisation on the basis of too many managerial tiers and administrators, leading to wasted money and a failure to make quick decisions, so in 1982 Area Health Authorities were abolished, leaving Districts and Regions to run the hospital units and GPs. Also in 1982 Roy Griffiths published his influential 1983 letter that recommended the introduction of General Managers (rather than administrators operating through consensus management) to Regions, Districts and Hospital Community Units, and establishing an NHS Executive at the centre.

From the later 1980s the increasing cost of the NHS became a political battlefield, with the escalating cost of acute hospital care being the driver. The consultative White Paper *Working for Patients* (Griffiths, 1989) led to 10 working papers. These introduced the concept of the 'purchaser–provider split' to create an 'internal market' within the NHS, in which Health Authorities would be purchasers, and hospitals would become self-governing Trusts, and along with other private hospitals would become providers. GPs were a second set of purchasers, with practices with over 1000 patients becoming fundholders. The new NHS Trusts were introduced in 'waves', the first wave of Trusts dominated by larger acute hospitals. These changes were also associated with the abolition of the former RHAs, their place taken by a tier of eight regional offices of the Department of Health and the new NHS Executive.

Further reforms to the NHS were introduced by the Labour Government in 1997, when 'The New NHS: Modern, Dependable' was published, laying out their vision, with key organisational structures being Strategic Health Authorities, Trusts and Primary Care Groups. In July 1998 'A First Class Service' was published, which set out how the vision was to be operationalised through the introduction of quality assurance systems. This led to the establishment of the National Institute for Clinical Excellence (NICE) to evaluate the evidence of the effectiveness of treatments, and National Service Frameworks for each health field to guide how the services should be delivered. In 2002 the Primary Care Groups became Primary Care NHS Trusts, with a major role in commissioning non-specialist health services, accompanied by the creation of 28 Strategic Health Authorities, which replaced the previous more numerous DHAs.

The period between 1948 and 1974 can now be seen as one of atypical organisational stability in the NHS, and the period between 1977 and around 1990 as providing a structure which enabled clinical psychology services to develop within a framework where psychologists had a significant degree of control over their working practices. An enduring feature of the changes of the past 20 years has been a stronger voice for GPs, and a shift towards more provision of services at the primary care level. The bewildering rate of organisational change constitutes a real challenge to clinical staff, where services to patients and communities are disrupted by the continuing reorganisation of local teams and changes in managers and budgets, and the flood of complex documents and practice guidance requires constant vigilance by national leaders and senior local psychologists.

Conditions of employment for psychologists in the NHS – the Whitley system

Before and during the Second World War, there were no national agreements about salaries or other conditions of employment for psychologists. With the creation of the new NHS, it became clear that a common framework needed to be created to formalise the roles and employment of educational and clinical psychologists within the health and education services. Before the war a national collective bargaining mechanism had been created for both the civil service and local government, involving separate management sides and staff sides, known as the Whitley system. It offered a relevant precedent for the new NHS, and in the early parliamentary debates on pay arrangements in the new health scheme the Minister gave assurances that a Whitley scheme would be an essential feature of the new service (Ross, 1952). In the spirit of this assurance, the Minister of Health, Aneurin Bevan, met with organisations in their perceived order of importance 'ending for the sake of prudence or completeness with minor groups such as medical auxiliaries, and with cognoscenti from alternative medicine, such as herbalists and homeopaths' (Webster, 1988, p.89). The Whitley framework was thus simply taken over for the NHS, although it did not include doctors.

The full Whitley Council system comprised a general council for matters of common interest, and nine functional councils, each dealing with a specific profession or group of workers. 'Professional and Technical Group A' (PTA) dealt with all graduate non-medical staff (who originally were almost entirely biochemists and physicists), and early negotiations were successful in placing clinical psychologists, as a graduate group, in PTA (see chapter 6). Each council had a 'management side', made up of representative senior managers from RHBs and the Ministry of Health, and a 'staff side' made up of representatives of staff organisations (and indirectly the professional bodies) acting as trade unions. The trade union for psychologists was originally the Association of Scientific Workers (AScW), which became through successive mergers ASTMS in 1969, MSF in 1988, Amicus in 2002, and since 2007 Unite (now the largest trade union in the UK).

The first Whitley circular relating to clinical psychologists (PTA Circular No.10) was issued on 7 February 1952, nearly four years after the NHS had come into being (only significant PTA circulars are reviewed here: others simply gave revised rates of pay). It laid down the qualifications for appointment as a clinical psychologist, requiring the possession of an honours degree in psychology of a British or Irish University (or equivalent). Appointment could be to one of four grades. Assistants (starting salary £380) had to have at least one year's training before they could become Psychologists (who had to be at least 25 years old) – earning £530 a year at the bottom of the scale. They in turn could become Seniors if they held a 'post of greater responsibility'. Top Grade psychologists in 1952 had to occupy a post of 'exceptional responsibility', when they were paid a minimum salary of £1300 and a maximum of £1600. There was no requirement for any specified form of postgraduate training before entry to the psychologist grade. Subsequent circulars, apart from announcing new pay scales, successively refined the grading structure and criteria for different grades (Hall & Lavender, 2012).

The 1957 set of Whitley circulars (HM (57) 81 and Part II of PTA circular 52) for the first time formally recognised 'approved training courses'. Three courses in clinical psychology were approved: at the University of London Institute of Psychiatry; at the Crichton Royal, Dumfries (a leading Scottish mental hospital); and at the Adult Department of the Tavistock Clinic in London. Significantly four courses in educational psychology – all in London – were approved, only for work with children, although in practice once in an NHS post psychologists could and did move to other fields of work. Entry to the profession was also possible through what was called the 'probationer' system – essentially a supervised apprenticeship, with at first no requirement for any form of formal examination – which ended in 1983.

AL (PTA) 2/82, published in 1982, introduced a completely new approach to grading Principal and Top Grade posts, setting out explicit criteria for posts, including a stipulation of the number of psychologists accountable to a post to meet the grading criteria. The next major revision of the grading system was announced in AL (SP) 3/90, which introduced a new four-grade system, and the introduction of a common pay spine, in a radical restructuring requiring the assessment of every post against a number of factors, in practice difficult to interpret. This guidance was issued against the background of the linked reviews of psychology staffing and function by the independent Management Advisory Service (MAS, 1989), and the NHS Manpower Planning Advisory Group (MPAG, 1990). Agenda for Change (Department of Health, 2004) signalled a totally new approach to the grading of posts, by introducing a system of grading for individual posts that was common to all health professions other than doctors, marking the end of the preferential salary scales available to psychologists by virtue of their postgraduate training.

For over 50 years Whitley Regulations controlled the conditions of employment of most NHS employees, including psychologists. The Whitley circulars in the early years offered guidance to NHS employers who would have had no previous experience in recruiting and appointing clinical psychologists, and they created a degree of national consistency in how psychologists were employed. Mechanistic they may have been, but they controlled conditions of employment, influenced how psychologists made career choices and of course told psychologists how much they would be paid.

References

Anderson, R. (2006). *British universities past and present.* London: Continuum.

Bain, A. (1855). *The senses and the intellect.* London: Longmans Green.

Beers, C. (1950). *A mind that found itself.* New York: Doubleday. (Original work published 1908)

Bentall, R. (2004). *Madness explained.* London: Penguin.

Beveridge, W. (1942). *Social insurance and allied services.* Cmd 6404. London: HMSO.

British Psychological Society (1945). The usage of certain terms in applied psychology. *British Journal of Psychology, 35*(2), 50.

Buchanan, R.D. (2010). *Playing with fire: The controversial career of Hans J Eysenck.* Oxford: Oxford University Press.

Committee on Higher Education (1963). *Higher education: Report of the Committee 1961–63.* (Chairman Lord Robbins). Cmnd 2154. London: HMSO.

Crichton Browne, J. (1861). *The clinical teaching of psychology: A valedictory address.* Edinburgh: James Nichol.

Department of Health (1997). *The new NHS: Modern, dependable.* Cm 3807. London: Author.

Department of Health (2004). *Agenda for change.* London: Author.

Department of Health and Social Security (1977). *The role of psychologists in the health service (Trethowan Report).* London: HMSO.

Desai, M. (1967). The concept of clinical psychology. *Bulletin of the British Psychological Society, 20*(69), 29–39.

Edgell, B. (1947). The British Psychological Society. *British Journal of Psychology, 37,* 113–132.

ESRC (2011). *International benchmarking review of UK Psychology. RCUK/BPS/AHPD/EPS.* Swindon: RCUK.

Eysenck, H.J. (Ed.) (1960). *Handbook of abnormal psychology: An experimental approach.* London: Pitman.

Freud, S. (2003). *Psychopathology of everyday life.* Harmondsworth: Penguin Classics. (Original work published 1904)

Griffiths, R. (1989). *Working for patients.* London: Department of Health.

Hall, J. & Lavender, T. (2012). Another diamond jubilee: The world of Whitley Circulars. *Clinical Psychology Forum, 240,* 13–15.

Health and Care Professions Council (2014). *Annual report 2014.* London: Author.

Hearnshaw, L.S. (1964). *A short history of British psychology: 1840–1940.* London: Methuen.

Hearnshaw, L.S. (1969). Psychology in Great Britain: An introductory historical essay. In B.M. Foss (Ed.), *Supplement to the Bulletin of the British Psychological Society* (pp.3–9). London: British Psychological Society.

Hearnshaw, L.S. (1987). *The shaping of modern psychology: An historical introduction.* London: Routledge.

Holdstock, L. & Radford, J. (1998). Psychology passes its 1997 exams (well... er... almost). *The Psychologist, 11*(8), 367–368.

Hulme, J. (2014). Psychological literacy – from classroom to real world. *The Psychologist, 27,* 932–935.

James, W. (1890). *Principles of psychology* (2 vols.). London: Macmillan.

Klein, R. (1983). *The politics of the NHS.* London: Longman.

Kraepelin, E. (1899). *Psychiatrie. Ein Lehrbuch für Studierende und Aertze.* Leipzig: Barth.

Liddell, A. (1983). Professional development. In A. Liddell (Ed.), *The practice of clinical psychology in Great Britain* (pp.3–12). Chichester: Wiley.

Management Advisory Service. (1989). *Review of clinical psychology services.* Cheltenham: Author.

Manpower Planning Advisory Group (1990). *Manpower Planning Advisory Group report on clinical psychology.* London: Department of Health.

Martin, H. (2013). From ascertainment to re-construction: 1944–1978. In C. Arnold & J. Hardy (Eds.), *British educational psychology: The first hundred years* (pp.49–56). Leicester: British Psychological Society.

Miller, E. & Morley, S. (1986). *Investigating abnormal behaviour.* London: Weidenfeld & Nicolson.

Misiak, H. & Sexton, V.S. (1966). *History of psychology.* New York: Grune & Stratton.

Mollon, J.D. (2006). *History of the Experimental Psychology Society.* www.eps.ac.uk/index.php/history

Reisman, J.M. (1991). *A history of clinical psychology* (2nd edn). New York: Brunner-Routledge.

Richards, G.D. (2001). Edward Cox, the Psychological Society of Great Britain (1875–1879) and the meaning of an institutional failure. In G.C. Bunn, A.D. Lovie & G.D. Richards (Eds.), *Psychology in Britain: Historical essays and personal reflections* (pp.33–53). Leicester: BPS Books.

Richards, G.D. (2010). *Putting psychology in its place: Critical historical perspectives* (3rd edn). London: Routledge.

Rieber, R. (Ed.) (2003). *Wilhelm Wundt in history: The making of a scientific psychology.* New York: Plenum Press.

Ross, J.S. (1952). *The National Health Service in Great Britain: An historical and descriptive study.* Oxford: Oxford University Press.

Routh, D.K. (1994). *Clinical psychology since 1917: Science, practice and organisation.* New York: Plenum Press.

Royal Commission on NHS (1979). *Report of the Royal Commission on the NHS* (Chairman Sir Alec Merrison). London: HMSO.

Rüegg, W. (Ed.) (2004). *A history of the university in Europe: Vol. III. Universities in the 19th and early 20th centuries.* New York: Cambridge University Press.

Scrivens, E. & Charlton, D. (1985). *The nature and size of clinical psychology services within health districts in England.* Bath Social Policy Papers No 6. Bath: University of Bath.

Shephard, B. (2014). *Headhunters: The search for a science of the mind.* London: Bodley Head.

Stewart, J. (2013). *Child guidance in Britain, 1918–1955.* London: Pickering & Chatto.

Thomson, M. (2006). *Psychological subjects: Identity, culture and health in 20th century Britain.* Oxford: Oxford University Press.

Timmins, N. (1995). *The five giants: A biography of the Welfare State.* London: Harper Collins.

Toogood, R. (Ed.) (2010). *The core purpose and philosophy of the profession.* Leicester: British Psychological Society.

Turner, J., Hayward, R., Angel, K. et al. (in press). The history of mental health services in modern England. *Medical History.*

Turpin, G. & Coleman, G. (2010). Clinical psychology and diversity: Progress and continuing challenges. *Psychology, Learning and Teaching, 9,* 17–27.

Turpin, G. & Fensom, P. (2004). *Widening access within undergraduate psychology education and its implications for professional psychology: Gender, disability and ethnic diversity.* Leicester: British Psychological Society.

Webster, C. (1988). *The health services since the War: Vol. I. Problems of health care: The National Health Service before 1957.* London: HMSO.

Webster, C. (1996). *The health services since the War: Vol. II. Government and health care: The National Health Service 1958–79.* London: HMSO.

Whitley Professional and Technical Council (1952, 1957, 1982, 1990). Whitley Council Circulars: PTA circular 5. RHB (52) 11, HMC (52), BG (52); PTA Circular 52, Part II, HM (58) Advance Letters: AL (PTA) 2/82; AL (SP) 3/90. London: Ministry of Health and Department of Health.

Wilcock, A. (2002). *Occupation for health, volume 2: A journey from prescription to self health.* London: British Association and College of Occupational Therapists.

Williams, P.E., Turpin, G. & Hardy, G. (2006). Clinical psychology service provision and ethnic diversity within the UK: A review of the literature. *Clinical Psychology and Psychotherapy, 13,* 324–338.

Woodworth, R.S. (1937). The future of clinical psychology. *Journal of Consulting Psychology, 1,* 4–5.

Zangwill, O.L. (1965). In defence of clinical psychology. *Bulletin of the British Psychological Society, 20*(69), 29–39.

Chapter 2 Engaging with the views and needs of users of psychological services

Juliet Foster

Introduction

Defining the terms used in the title of this chapter is a daunting task. 'Views' may seem initially obvious, and we can take this to mean opinions, ideas and preferences, but 'needs' may complicate the issue further: who defines what constitutes the need of a user? Are only needs expressed by users relevant, and what of situations in which other interested parties (whether professionals or those personally connected to a user) feel that the user may have other needs? In particular, what if these needs do not correlate with the needs that users may feel that they have? So far, so complicated. Similarly, defining users of psychological services is also not without its problems, and indeed is related to the first complication. Are users purely those individuals who are referred to a psychologist? What about carers, families, partners, parents and so on? There is a long history of work that highlights the possibilities of tension between carers' and users' perspectives on a variety of issues (see, for example, work on expressed emotion by Vaughan & Leff, 1976); similarly, mental health organisations that have attempted to incorporate the views of multiple stakeholders have often struggled (Wallcraft et al., 2003). The use of the term 'users' itself is also contentious: a shift away from use of the term 'patients' towards terms such as 'users' and 'clients' has occurred for numerous reasons, some of which will be discussed below, and yet there is often dissatisfaction among those labelled by these terms. The term 'user' is largely disliked (Simmons et al., 2010), and is often seen as implying that someone is a 'drain' on resources (J.L.H. Foster, 2007); 'clients', as an alternative, can be seen as too consumerist (McGuire-Snieckus et al., 2003). Some clinical psychologists take particular issue with the term 'users': D. Law (personal communication, 21 November, 2014) points out that it can be viewed as defining individuals in relation to only one part of their experience, while Newnes (2005, p.18) maintains that 'the term service users can be seen as, necessarily, placing people in a one-down position, thus justifying the expert status and salaries of professionals and simultaneously creating an illusion that people have power in the service they are using'. Use of these terms in this chapter should not imply uncritical acceptance, and it is notable, as Newnes (2005) argues, that activists in the area tend to reject the term 'user' and prefer 'survivor', although this may be associated with more extreme distress. G. Turpin (personal communication, 1 December 2014) also makes the point that preferences for different terms can vary in different contexts, and that within primary care the term 'patient' is still common.

This chapter will attempt to elaborate on some of these points in more detail as it considers the way that psychology – and in particular clinical psychology –

has engaged with the wide variety of users of psychological services. The role of clinical psychology in engaging with users' views and needs will be placed in the context of wider health service engagement with users; in particular, psychiatry's engagement is of particular interest, and indeed has received considerable attention in recent years. Another theme that will be addressed throughout is the different levels of engagement that are possible with users' views and needs: these can range from the individual through local and finally national levels. Different concerns might well be more or less relevant at different levels, and the story of engagement at different levels may well also differ.

A definition of 'users'

Putting to one side for a moment the problems of employing the term 'user' described above, it is important to clarify the classification of a 'user' within clinical psychology. As already highlighted, it can be problematic to differentiate between someone who might be using psychological services and those around that individual. Many approaches within clinical psychology rely on a sense of considering people within their social environment (Cromby et al., 2013), and so merely considering the 'user' in isolation is unlikely to be productive in many cases. An excellent example of this comes from Gold's (2000) consideration of clinical psychologists and pain management: having identified the relationship between the behaviour of significant others (in particular) and various issues related to the experience of pain (including intensity, mood, coping styles, etc.), it is problematic to focus purely on the individual without also working with family members. Tombs and Griggs (2000) discuss similar programmes that aim to work with the parents of 'troubled' adolescents, with a view not only to supporting them and reducing their own stress but also enabling them to adopt strategies to complement psychological interventions. Karen Dodd (personal communication, 9 January 2015) also points out that within services for people with learning disabilities, the phrase 'people who use services' is often preferred as it is seen as fitting in better with a person-centred agenda.

However, problems arise if there is a mismatch between the views and needs of users and their families and friends. Clarke provides a thoughtful consideration of this, reflecting on experience as a former service user and current carer:

> The service user and carer agenda can often be different and conflicting, and I understand that some services see the carer as the service user. I don't believe that where one party is involved the other ought to be automatically included, but I fear that if we fall into the habit of using 'service user' as a shorthand we will eventually forget that in most cases there is an important distinction to be made and that the role of the carer ought never to be forgotten. (Clarke, 2014, p.10)

S. Foster (2010) makes a similar point in arguing that psychological services frequently fail to engage with carers in basic interaction, let alone in more formal programmes, despite the benefits of these being evident. While these are impassioned pleas on behalf of carers, there are others who feel that it is more often the actual service user whose views and needs may be overlooked in comparison with those of the carer: this is often the case with people who use mental health services (see, for example, the tension in organisations that try to represent the views of both carers and users, mentioned above, Wallcraft et al., 2003), but might also be an issue in other services that focus on those who are perceived as vulnerable, such as children (Dexter et al., 2012) or people with learning difficulties (Jingree & Finlay, 2012).

A short history of user involvement – work outside the services

When we consider the way that users have attempted and succeeded to engage with professionals themselves, it is clear that very significant work has gone on outside the health services.

Although clinical psychology's focus is much broader than mental health, the mental health service user movement provides a useful case study here, in that it has developed in interesting ways in relation to providers of psychological and psychiatric services. While some mental health organisations have developed to represent the variety of people with an interest in mental health (users, carers, families, academics, etc.), others have not, and have explicitly excluded those who are not users (or former users) themselves (O'Hagan, 1993). The mental health service user and survivor movement developed against a background of the limited opportunities of those labelled 'mad', 'mentally ill' and so on to be heard within society throughout history. Although it is possible to trace some stories through art and literature (Gilman, 1988), this lack of first-person accounts could be regarded as paralleling a similar absence of patient narratives in other areas: many theorists have argued that an emphasis on a biomedical understanding of illness leaves little room for the perspective of the patient (Hyden, 1997). However, users labelled 'mentally ill' might have experienced particular problems in presenting their perspective, for both practical and ideological reasons. Practically, people diagnosed with a mental illness (or labelled 'mad') were routinely segregated away from society for the two hundred years in which asylums and psychiatric hospitals dominated the landscape (both metaphorically and literally) (J.L.H. Foster, 2014). More ideologically, many diagnoses of a mental health problem involve patients being deemed by professionals to lack insight into their own condition and state of mind (Beresford, 2005). Thus it becomes all too easy to dismiss whatever an individual has to say as being the result of their psychopathology, and not what they would say if they were not experiencing those mental health problems (J.L.H. Foster, 2007); users' views may be seen historically as a form of subjugated knowledge (Foucault, 1976).

However, the mental health service user/survivor movement offers an opportunity for collective representation, action and activism. Some theorists (e.g. Campbell, 2005, 2013) argue that the first example of such a group in Britain was the Alleged Lunatics' Friend Society,[1] founded in 1845 (Hunter & MacAlpine, 1962): this association fought for the rights of those who felt that they were wrongly incarcerated, and also for reasonable treatment of all those confined to asylums. It also campaigned for reform of laws relating to madness (Wise, 2012). Despite its often

[1] The Society was originally called the Lunatics' Friend Society, changing its name after a couple of months.

negative reception from the public and from those involved in legislation, it is rightly seen as a forerunner to the advocacy movement: as Hervey states: 'All its proposals bespeak the desire that whenever possible lunatics should be treated as adults capable of making decisions for themselves' (1986, p.254).

After the deaths of several of its key members in the 1860s, the Society drew to a close, and there was little similar activity in Britain for some time. Indeed, Peter Campbell (2005), in his excellent summary of the mental health service user movement in the UK, recognises the 1985 meeting between activists from the UK and other countries at the Mind/World Federation of Mental Health Congress in Brighton as being the most significant first step in the development of a full service user contribution, although he does place this in the context of the significant work that had gone on in the 1970s involving the Mental Patients' Union, which broke up into a number of other smaller groups. Although the amount of activity in Britain at this time was more questionable, it is clear that mental health service user/survivor and advocacy organisations developed more quickly at this time in other countries, such as the United States and the Netherlands (Barnes & Bowl, 2001). During the past 30 years there has been a proliferation of different kinds of mental health service user organisation group: what is clear from the review by Wallcraft et al. (2003) is that while there are many points in common, there is also diversity between the aims and objectives of many of these. As Campbell observes: 'Speaking in broad terms, in 1985 service users were nowhere; in 2005 they are everywhere' (2005, p.74).

The most relevant point for this chapter is how far groups might see their role as one of supporting the wider mental health services (and perhaps supplementing support in some ways) with those that see their role as challenging the mental health services more explicitly. The point I wish to emphasise is that it is wrong to assume that the health services (of any kind) necessarily initiate engagement with user views: users have views and ways of expressing these that exist outside the health services, and may not always want to engage with mainstream services and professionals (an example is Mad Pride). While this point is perhaps best illustrated by the mental health service user movement, it is also important to bear this in mind when considering users of other services.

User involvement and changes within the health services

However, engagement has also clearly occurred within the health services, and I will now consider this in more depth. First, I wish to stress the importance of the wider context of change within the health services. The drive to engage users within health services has come from political sources as well as from users and health professionals themselves.

The significant changes that have occurred in the health services in general over the past 60 years, and clinical psychology's role within them, are detailed extensively elsewhere in this volume (chapter 1) and need careful consideration. Ideological, political and practical changes in the way that services are organised go hand in hand with views on what is and is not appropriate when it comes to engagement with users. A very large body of literature details these changes. Some of this comes from academia, and especially from the social sciences: for example, Hogg (2009) focuses on the health services in general in the UK. Parliamentary documents also include summaries of the developments in patient involvement in the health services (e.g. House of Commons Health Committee, 2007). Other work has looked at particular sections of the health services, with mental health services receiving particular attention: Rogers and Pilgrim (2001) detail the impact that models of democratisation and consumerism within the health services had on the way that patient and service user perspectives became more central to service planning, provision and delivery within the mental health services. In the context of this chapter, the most important point to note is that public, patient and/or user involvement of different kinds in the health services has been first encouraged and then enshrined for some time: Barnes (1999) highlights the significant developments up until the end of the 20th century, starting with the Community Health Councils that were initiated in 1974. She notes not only significant legislation and policies such as the 1992 'Patients' Charter', but also the many reasons behind these changes and developments. Other guidelines on obtaining and using users' views in the health services have been available from a number of bodies for more than 20 years (see, for example, McIver, 1991). More recently, the Children and Young People's IAPT programme has also had a significant impact: D. Law (personal communication, 21 November 2014) sees user engagement as fundamental to this.

It is important to recognise that the models of democratisation and of consumerism differ fundamentally in their interests in user involvement and engagement, and that this has important consequences. Barnes (1999) points out the different motivations behind the promotion and pursuit of user involvement by the Conservative government which was in power in the UK from 1979 to1997 and the Labour government which took power in 1997. She argues that Conservative policies were motivated by a desire to minimise the power of professionals and bureaucrats and allow more active consumers to flourish; Labour, in contrast, preferred to draw on ideas of partnership. However, it would be a mistake to assume that ideologies always alter in line with government policies at ground level, and it is clear that many people working and using health services will draw on different ideas of the value (or otherwise) of user involvement. A consumerist approach may well still be taken by some. Beresford (2013) argues that this consumerist approach limits the role of the service user, in that user engagement becomes more of an exercise in market research and customer satisfaction. It is certainly the case that some studies that have aimed to consider users' views and needs right across the health services clearly aim to increase adherence to treatment or to bring users' views more in line with those of professionals. These programmes undoubtedly place 'expert' professional understanding as central and see users' views that might differ from these as detrimental, and as an obstacle to be overcome. This differs very significantly from programmes and studies that take a more democratic model and see knowledge as something which varies within different groups, and needs to be understood in that context (Felton & Stickely, 2004). The arguments surrounding 'expertise by experience' come into play here, and will be discussed in more depth later in this chapter.

Mental health presents a particular case when we consider engagement with users' views and needs from a more philosophical perspective. Diagnosis of mental health problems involves characterisation 'by definition, by some degree of temporary or permanent irrationality' (Rogers & Pilgrim, 2001, p.111), a point already mentioned above. This seems to have led to problems in accepting users' views on a variety of issues. Institutionally, this has also meant that developments in user involvement in the mental health services have been slower than elsewhere in the health services. Rogers and Pilgrim (2001) argue that mental health professionals' problematic responses to user engagement can be divided into four categories: (a) users' views that do not fit in with professional perspectives are rejected; (b) users' irrationality is emphasised; (c) the assumption is made that all users and carers' views will be the same; and (d) users' views are altered so that they can be brought in line with those of professionals.

However, much of this consideration tends to focus on psychiatry, although there is also relevant work within nursing (Reed, 2011) and social work (Beresford, 2013). Historically, as discussed above, psychiatry has been less interested in the views of users; the content of what was said by users was often dismissed as a symptom of their psychopathology. The antipsychiatrists, of course, took an early stand against this perspective, exemplified in the way in which Laing (1959) took issue with Kraepelin's (1905) assumption that the catatonic patient who had just delivered a monologue clearly both mocking and criticising his doctors had '"*not given us a single piece of useful information.* His talk was… *only a series of disconnected sentences having no relation whatever to the general situation*"'(Kraepelin, 1905, cited in Laing, 1959, p.30; Laing's italics).

While it is not advisable to assume that all psychiatrists have historically adopted this position, it is possible to discern a broader shift, in some ways, in psychiatry's position with regard to users' views and needs in the latter part of the 20th century. At first, the interest in users' views was very much centred on patient satisfaction (perhaps bringing to mind Beresford's, 2013, warning above): Moncrieff and Crawford (2001) note the rise in such articles on the topic in the *British Journal of Psychiatry* from 1995. There is little sense, at least at first, that users' views of their own mental health may be of equal interest to that of professionals, but assessments of services become more common; many of these draw on quality of life measurements, comparing for example, groups of users who attend different models of service (Warner et al., 1999) or use different medication (Awad & Vorugarti, 1999).

Clinical psychology's engagement

This leads to the interesting question as to how far clinical psychology – specifically – has engaged with the user movement and with users' views and whether this has differed from other professions within the health services.

A uniform position from clinical psychology on users' views and needs is hard to find: indeed, it could even be argued that any position was hard to find at the end of the 20th century. In a special issue of the *Clinical Psychology Forum* on involving service users, published in April 2001, Newnes (2001) states:

> Our profession is not conspicuously interested in advocacy and user involvement, at least if the pages of Clinical Psychology Forum are much to go by. In the last 10 years, Forum has published around 1200 papers. Forty of these have been on user views of services. Two have been by users and 14 have been on advocacy and patients' councils. Of the latter, half have been from one psychology service. (Newnes, 2001, p.18)

A more recent discussion (Hayward et al., 2010) suggests that user involvement is 'like Marmite' for clinical psychologists, in that they either love it or hate it. This may, in part, be due to the profession's own philosophical and practical position: Pilgrim (2007) argues that clinical psychology has, in many ways, maintained a similar position to psychiatry: he claims that there have been both financial incentives (e.g. in the form of research funding) for this, but also 'epistemological trends' (p.544), noting that cognitive behavioural therapy arose through clinical work, not specifically from within psychology (Beck, 1979). Diamond (2010) is also critical of the way that clinical psychology has all too often mimicked psychiatry.

Other practical reasons are also relevant here: Rogers and Pilgrim (2001) highlight the relative youth of the profession (compared in particular with psychiatry), its diversity in perspectives and its relative lack of power. Until the 2007 amendments to the Mental Health Act, psychiatrists had a much greater legal role in the treatment of people with mental health problems, and, of course, in prescribing medication. It is also worth mentioning that, as highlighted in Lavender and Turpin's chapter in this volume, the number of clinical psychologists at the start of the 1990s was still limited, since expansion in training had not yet occurred. In many services (and even in entire hospitals) there would only be one clinical psychologist (if indeed there was one at all) and so there was clearly little opportunity for collective practical engagement with users' views and needs. Repper and Perkins (2003) also point out that (at least at the point at which they were writing) clinical psychologists tended to work more within outpatient clinics and so were focused on individuals who were not experiencing such extreme distress or disability, although this is disputed by G. Turpin (personal communication, 1 December 2014) who points out that many psychologists played a significant role in resettlement and rehabilitation services during the closure of large psychiatric hospitals. Since clinical psychologists often work in multidisciplinary teams, it can be hard to separate any particular approach from that of other professionals (K. Dodd, personal communication, 9 January 2015).

However, whether or not the status of the profession of clinical psychology was fundamental or not, and whether the practicalities and problems that the profession faced were also a contributory factor, it would seem that clinical psychology's engagement with users' views and needs lagged behind that of some other health professions by up to 10 years.

Nevertheless, the publication of the special issue of *Clinical Psychology Forum* in 2001 is testament to the fact that work with users' views and needs had been going on in many areas within clinical psychology even if it had not perhaps received the mainstream attention it had within psychiatry. The special issue contains a number of theoretical articles considering user involvement, including one by Campbell (2001), himself a survivor, and another by May (2001), a clinical psychologist and former service user. Additionally, it contains articles on engaging with users with learning disabilities (Cheseldine et al., 2001), mental health problems (Teggart et al., 2001), children (Wolpert et al., 2001) and people with HIV/AIDS (HIV/AIDS Special Interest Group, 2001). In 2003, the BPS's Division of Clinical Psychology also initiated a working group to develop a service user and carer group, as discussed later in this chapter. There are also other examples of long-standing engagement and collaboration, such as Young Minds (D. Law, personal communication, 21 November 2014) and People First (K. Dodd, personal communication, 9 January 2015). In some ways, this reflects another interesting issue as we consider service users' views and needs: the diversity of users with whom clinical psychologists work, and their experiences, may be a further reason why a comprehensive approach within clinical psychology to working with users' views and needs was slower to come about than in other areas of the mental health services and health services.

Levels of engagement with users' views and needs

Much of the discussion in this chapter so far implicitly or explicitly draws on the fact that there are multiple ways and multiple levels at which it is possible for clinical psychologists to engage with users' views and needs. These levels mirror explicit discussion in different areas of the literature. In their introduction to the 2010 special issue of *Clinical Psychology Forum* on service user and carer involvement, Haywood et al. (2010) suggest that we think of user involvement both within and outside the therapeutic context. The Department of Health's In the Public Interest document (NHS Confederation, 1998) maintains that engagement with patients and the public is seen here as beneficial for the NHS, for individuals themselves, for public health and for communities and societies more broadly.

In this next section, I intend to consider these levels of engagement in more depth. I will focus on theory and practice in engagement on three levels: individual, local and national. It is essential to remember, of course, that these levels are interrelated and affect one another.

The individual level

As discussed in the introduction to this chapter, listening and engaging with the views and needs of users is (or at least should be) at the very heart of the patient–professional interaction, and current practice reflects how this has developed. In their review of the development of psychological therapies, Cromby et al. (2013) detail the position of the individual in treatment in behaviour therapy, client-centred therapy, family therapy and cognitive behavioural therapy. Without considering the views of users on their experience, the professional is unlikely to be able to make any judgement; without considering the needs of users, the professional is unlikely to be able to formulate a plan of action. However, consideration of whether users' needs and views are fundamentally at the heart of user–professional interaction (both in theory and in practice) has long been a theme within the literature. Many of these criticisms stem from a concern that a biomedical approach within the health services privileges the professional (scientific) point of view which leaves little room for patient perspectives (Kleinman, 1980). Has clinical psychology, specifically, taken a different perspective on these interactions? To some extent, the answer to this question may lie in how far clinical psychologists have aligned themselves to the biomedical perspective, and, subsequently, how far the biomedical model has moved in regarding patient views as more central. Cromby et al. argue that the situation varies:

> Clinical psychology also has its own culture, which at times is able to work alongside a psychiatric one, as it must operate in the context of a mental health team, while at

> other times may oppose psychiatry and create a new set of rituals and practices that can work independently (though of course clinical psychologists are still by and large employed by medical institutions). (Cromby et al., 2013, p.58)

For some critics, the association with psychiatry may always be too problematic: recent debates in the pages of *Clinical Psychology Forum* about the value, or otherwise, of psychiatric diagnoses within clinical psychology (Ganley, 2014; Pilgrim, 2014) are evidence of this. Indeed, the fact that the line between psychiatrists and clinical psychologists is so blurred in the public mind may also be instructive here: both the NHS and the Royal College of Psychiatrists have pages on their websites which list the differences. Any significant differences between the approaches taken by psychiatry and clinical psychology may not be obvious to the wider world: indeed, a special issue of *Clinical Psychology Forum* in September 2014 on the relationship between psychology and psychiatry suggested that this confusion is also current among some other professionals, students and service users.

The local and national level

In some ways, it is hard to fully separate out the local and the national, since they inevitably influence one another in numerous ways. On a local level, and in line with national policies, hospitals and health services now routinely involve users in planning, evaluation and so on. Users might be involved in different ways: as individuals they may be invited to sit on relevant committees or other bodies; as groups they may be consulted about services more broadly. Engagement at this level starts from within the health services. However, there is of course engagement that will begin from outside the health services at a local level: local advocacy groups press for change (Campbell, 2005); health consumer groups (both local and national) lobby on particular issues (Baggott et al., 2005). Many clinical psychologists have been involved with such groups, the Hearing Voices movement being one good example,

Local organisations may differ in their approaches and aims from national ones: Wallcraft et al.'s (2003) study of mental health organisations in the UK found that local groups often saw their role as more specific to the concerns of users in their areas and were less concerned with influencing policy at a wider level. However, this may not always be the case. Some organisations, such as MIND, work both through a national organisation and local groups. Clinical psychology's engagement with users' views and needs at the national level may come in different forms. The British Psychological Society's Division of Clinical Psychology initiated consultation on a group for users and carers in 2003. A Constitution and Terms of Reference document for this group, initially referred to as the Service Users Liaison Committee, was established at this time and stated that the purpose of the group 'will be to provide user representatives with access to, and influence on, the structures and policies of the DCP and to ensure that the style and content of discussion in the DCP adequately reflects the user perspective'. References to 'users' were later changed to 'service users' to avoid confusion with substance abuse. Mike Wang, who was chair of the DCP at the time, saw it as essential that any users and carers who became involved in the group should not only have direct experience of using clinical psychology services, but that they should also have experience of committees that would allow them to 'hold their own' against clinical psychologists and other professionals in meetings (M. Wang, personal communication, 10 January 2015). Advertisements were placed in the national press, and more than one hundred applications were received. This led to the creation of the Service User and Carer Liaison Committee. An induction programme from this time also shows that new members of this group were given detailed information on the structure and function of the BPS and DCP as well as on issues relating to clinical psychology more broadly. More recently, at the very start of 2014, *Clinical Psychology Forum* introduced an 'Experts by Experience' column, and in the first of these stated that from March 2014 the Service User and Carer Group would become the DCP Experts by Experience.[2] A users and carers column had also been included in the volume under a different name for a few years prior to this.

There are two other areas that are of particular interest here. One is the engagement of users in issues pertaining to the recruitment (both interviewing and training) of professionals and the other is in research. As Campbell (2013) points out, while all mental health professions are required to draw on service users and carers in training, the way that this is developed and put into practice varies significantly, and can be fairly cursory, although as discussion below shows, this is by no means always the case.

Many professions within the health services have included users in selection panels for some time for both training courses and in job interviews. The Nottingham Advocacy Group made a call for more routine involvement of service users in this way in 1997, and Long et al. (2000) published an in-depth analysis of the involvement of a service user in an interview for a mental health post, with Cheseldine et al. (2001) doing likewise a year later for a post related to learning disabilities. Both provided recommendations for effective involvement in future interview panels.

Another development in recruitment is the way that service users and survivors have been sought to fill specific posts because of their history of service use; again, this has been a particular theme within the mental health services. While it has always been the case that some professionals have experienced (and in some cases continue to experience) mental health problem (Rippere & Williams, 1985), these were, until relatively recently, often hidden and certainly not seen as being part of the job specification. There are now a number of 'user professionals' of various kinds who reflect on their own experiences of mental distress and the way that it informs their own clinical practice (e.g. Harding, 2010; May, 2000), lecturing (Holttum, 2010) or research (e.g. Rose, 2003).

Involving service users and carers within training and education programmes in a variety of ways, without a doubt, gives them greater power and also enables their perspectives and voices to be heard more clearly by those who will be working in the health profession in the future. The DCP published a comprehensive 'Good Practice Guide' on this topic in 2007, developed by the DCP Service User and Carer Liaison Committee and the University of Surrey (and Mark Hayward and

---

2 Although editions of *Clinical Psychology Forum* in 2014 continued to use the 'Experts by Experience' column, there was also continued use of the Service User and Carer Group name.

Barbara Riddell in particular). It addresses a wide variety of issues surrounding user engagement in training, and includes a large number of examples and direct quotations from those involved. However, there are both theoretical and practical issues which still need attention. Theoretically, the reasons behind user involvement and the way in which it is actualised need careful analysis: Riddell (2010) points out that too often user involvement has been a 'bolt-on' to training courses and not fundamental or integral to the programme as a whole. There are clearly now examples that move beyond this, and papers that detail the courses at several institutions make this very clear (Atkins et al., 2010; Cooke & Hayward, 2010; Pembroke & Hadfield, 2010; Riddell, 2010). However, barriers may well still remain: Felton and Stickely (2004) detail the concerns which mental health nursing lecturers have over employing users within their training sessions: while many cite advantages such as increasing awareness and empathy, they also highlight a number of barriers, many of which seem to revolve around representations of service users as unreliable and often vulnerable.

Engaging with users within research has a slightly longer history than some of the initiatives discussed in this chapter. Much of this went on outside the health services, and involved mental health organisations in the first instance: the People First study is an excellent example of this (Rogers et al., 1993). However, as Beresford (2013) points out, there are multiple ways in which service users can be included in research: they can be added to research teams in a more superficial way; they can be full collaborators involved at all stages of the research; finally, they can lead the research fully (and independently of other professional researchers). Rose (Rose et al., 1998, Rose, 2001) has been pivotal in developing guidelines for user-focused monitoring, first at the Centre for Mental Health and more recently at the Service User Research Enterprise at the Institute of Psychiatry. However, the point of user-led research is precisely that there is less of a role (if indeed there is any) for professionals, and this is a significant development that has much less to do with professional engagement with users' views, apart from professionals being able to respond appropriately to the findings of the projects.

At the national level, engagement with users and carers may continue to involve working with larger charities and organisations. Many organisations, such as MIND and BILD, involve a combination of professionals, users, carers and others with common objectives, although it is notable that many of these organisations do have their own 'user branch' and others (especially those which involve more grassroots activism) do not admit 'allies' (O'Hagan, 1993). Harper (2010) reflects on his own experience of engaging with service user and survivor organisations outside his professional working life, and especially on the benefits of collective action. Smaller groups can also have an impact at national level: Keith Oliver (personal communication, 25 November 2014) discusses the role that the Kent-based organisation The Forget Me Nots has had, not only in interviewing and training clinical psychologists, but also in reviewing documentation on dementia for the British Psychological Society.

However, an important point is also raised by Harper (2010) in relation to the common interests, or otherwise, of clinical psychologists and users. The discussions that led up to the changes to the Mental Health Act in 2007 are an interesting example of this. Many organisations opposed the proposed changes and a collaboration between professionals, users, carers and others developed in the form of the Mental Health Alliance: the arguments put forward by the Mental Health Alliance were well received in many quarters and gained significant sympathy in the media (see J.L.H. Foster, 2006, for more discussion of this). The Mental Health Alliance included a number of professional organisations among its members, including the Royal College of Psychiatrists, the Royal College of General Practitioners and the British Association of Social Workers. Harper (2010) suggests that the interests of the profession of clinical psychology were, perhaps, at odds with the interests of service users during some of these discussions: the proposed changes to the Act allowed for an extension of the influence of the profession of clinical psychology and so Harper (2010) suggests that other aspects of the proposed changes which were more problematic for service users (such as the impaired judgement clause) were somewhat overlooked by clinical psychologists who were keen to ensure the passage of the parts of the Act that were more beneficial to them professionally.

The influence of psychology is also visible in other ways at this time. Pickersgill (2012) points out that treatment that was provided in the dangerous and severe personality disorder (DSPD) units which were also established was also very much focused on psychological therapy and not on medication or forms of treatment that had their roots in psychiatry.

Problems, challenges and the future

This chapter has attempted to provide a review of the many and varied ways in which clinical psychology has, and has not, engaged with the views and needs of users over the years. Inevitably, given the breadth and depth of the topic, it is incomplete.

While significant developments have taken place, and clinical psychology has without a doubt engaged with those views and needs in more serious and varied ways over the past 15 years, challenges remain: many of these have been alluded to in this chapter. Accusations of tokenism are still relevant (Campbell, 2013). Some users may still be seen as less suited to inclusion in relevant processes: the arguments regarding mental health service users have been well-rehearsed above, but the same is also true of young people and children who might be seen as too vulnerable and powerless to be able to contribute fully (Dexter et al., 2012). When mental health service user groups and organisations at the national and local level engage with services, their views may not be representative of wider service users: Wallcraft et al. (2003) found that very few services users felt part of the mental health service user movement, a point also discussed at length by Campbell (2013). The same may also be true of other health interest groups. D. Law (personal communication, 21 November, 2014) points out that in services for children and adolescents, white female users' views have often been overrepresented; he highlights the importance of seeking to engage with a variety of different groups and cites the MAC (Music and Change) programme started by Charlie Allcock as an example of outreach and engagement that fully engaged with the needs of a community that was hard to reach.

The practicalities of user involvement also need careful thought: Keith Oliver (personal communication, 25 November 2014) discusses the barriers to participation that can be set up to user participation if enough consideration is not given to issues such as timing of meetings and events, or transport for users. Karen Dodd (personal communication, 9 January 2015) also points out that some users of psychological services might be particularly prone to acquiesce in discussion with clinical psychologists if they do not understand the terms being used to discuss an issue: language is crucial. Funding is also a perennial problem. Diamond (2010) sounds a cautionary note when he draws attention to the fact that across Nottingham eight years before his paper was published, 78 per cent of rehabilitation teams had users involved in their recruitment procedures; on reviewing this at the time of preparing his paper, he suggested that this figure had dropped to 20 per cent. Salaried user posts had also decreased; user positions that did exist were often 'by invitation', making, Diamond (2010) argues, a truly critical voice less likely.

Another problem is that putting in place appropriate structures for engaging with the views and needs of users does not automatically lead to change associated with those views and needs. Crawford et al. (2002) reviewed literature on user involvement in the health services in general and found that while there was a large number of papers detailing the methods with which to involve users, there were very few on the effects of user involvement on services, and very little review of the successes or otherwise of such efforts. This concern was echoed by the House of Commons Health Committee when they argued:

> Throughout the inquiry we heard that what matters is not patient and public involvement structures but effective involvement of patients and the public. Structures and procedures… will have little effect if the health service is not prepared to listen and make changes as a result. (House of Commons Health Committee, 2007, p.5)

There may be multiple reasons why this is the case. An excellent example of the wider factors that may prevent full engagement with users' and carers' views and needs comes from a study by Tickle et al. (2014) of clinical psychologists' views of the recovery movement. They suggested that their participants 'are aware of the emergence of recovery-oriented approaches but feel unable to incorporate them in practice because of perceptions of being bound by both their own limitations and those of their circumstances including issues of risk, thus giving rise to dilemmas in professional practice' (p.105). This is a good example of the need to remember that engagement with users' views and needs does not happen in isolation. It takes place against a background of changes and developments within the health services, and within broader society, that involves political, economic, social and cultural factors. The views of politicians and the public continue to have an impact in multiple ways.

However, these final notes of caution should not detract from two issues – the importance of engaging with users' and carers' views and needs, and the developments that have occurred within clinical psychology, the health services and society more broadly as a result of this engagement. Challenges to definitions of expertise and consideration of the potential contributions to knowledge and understanding from different groups are not only essential to the development of all professions within the health services, but also to the ways in which we understand health-related issues of all kinds within wider society.

References

Atkins, E., Hart, L., O'Brien, C. & Davidson, T. (2010). Service users and carers as placement advisers: Part 2 – personal reflections on novel relationships. *Clinical Psychology Forum, 209*, 23–27.

Awad, A.G. & Vorugarti, L.N.P. (1999). Quality of life and new anti-psychotics in schizophrenia: Are patients better off? *International Journal of Social Psychiatry, 45*(4), 268–275.

Baggott, R., Allsop, J. & Jones, K. (2005). *Speaking for patients and carers.* Basingstoke: Palgrave.

Barnes, M. (1999). *Public Expectations – from paternalism to partnership: Changing relationships in health and health services.* Policy futures for UK health, No. 10. London: The Nuffield Trust.

Barnes, M. & Bowl, R. (2001). *Taking over the asylum: Empowerment and mental health.* Basingstoke: Palgrave.

Beck, A. (1979). *Cognitive therapy of depression.* New York: Guilford Press.

Beresford P. (2005). Theory and practice of user involvement: Making the connection with public policy and practice. In L. Lowes & I. Hulatt (Eds.), *Involving service users in health and social care research* (pp.6–17). Routledge, London.

Beresford, P. (2013). From 'other' to involved: User involvement in research: An emerging paradigm. *Nordic Social Work Research, 3*(2),139–148.

Campbell, P. (2001). Surviving social inclusion. *Clinical Psychology Forum, 150*, 6–15.

Campbell, P. (2005). From little acorns: The mental health survivor movement. In A. Bell & P. Lindley (Eds.), *Beyond the water towers: The unfinished revolution in mental health services 1985–2005* (pp.73–82). London: Sainsbury Centre for Mental Health.

Campbell, P. (2013). Service users and survivors. In J. Cromby, D. Harper & P. Reavey (Eds.), *Psychology, mental health and distress* (pp.139–154). Basingstoke: Palgrave.

Cheseldine, S., Anderson, G. & Mappin, R. (2001). Learning disability services: Involving service users in interviews. *Clinical Psychology Forum, 150*, 27–29.

Clarke, J. (2014). Behind the label. *Clinical Psychology Forum, 259*, 10–11.

Cooke, A. & Hayward, M. (2010). Service-users and carers as placement advisors: Part I – getting started. *Clinical Psychology Forum, 209*, 21–22.

Crawford, M.J., Rutter, D., Manley, C. et al. (2002). Systematic review of involving patients in the planning and development of health care. *British Medical Journal, 325*(7375),1263.

Cromby, J., Harper, D. & Reavey, P. (2013). *Psychology, mental health and distress.* Basingstoke: Palgrave.

Dexter, G., Larkin, M. & Newnes, C. (2012). A qualitative exploration of child clinical psychologists' understanding of user involvement. *Clinical Child Psychology and Psychiatry, 17*(2), 246–265.

Diamond, B. (2010). User involvement: Corporate and captive. *Clinical Psychology Forum, 209*, 16–20.

Felton, A. & Stickely, T. (2004). Pedagogy, power and service user involvement. *Journal of Psychiatric Mental Health Nursing, 11*(1), 89–98.

Foster, J.L.H. (2006). Media presentation of the Mental Health Bill and representations of mental health problems. *Journal of Community and Applied Social Psychology, 16*, 285–300.

Foster, J.L.H. (2007). *Journeys through mental illness: Clients' experiences and understandings of mental distress.* Basingstoke: Palgrave.

Foster, J.L.H. (2014). What can social psychologists learn from architecture? The asylum as example. *Journal for the Theory of Social Behaviour, 44*(2), 131–147.

Foster, S. (2010). Don't just involve carers: Engage them and reap the benefits! *Clinical Psychology Forum, 209*, 13–15.

Foucault, M. (1976). Two lectures. In C. Gordon (Ed.), *Michel Foucault: Power/knowledge: Selected interviews and other writings, 1972–1977* (pp.78–109). New York: Pantheon Books.

Ganley, A. (2014). An alternative voice. *Clinical Psychology Forum, 259*, 2.

Gilman, S. (1988). *Disease and representation: Images of illness from madness to AIDS.* Ithaca: Cornell University Press.

Gold, A. (2000). Involving significant others in pain management group programmes: A survey of current practice in the UK. *Clinical Psychology Forum, 138*, 26–30.

Harding, E. (2010). User involvement: Why bother? Trainee clinical psychologist and/or service user? *Clinical Psychology Forum, 209*, 42–45.

Harper, D. (2010). Tensions and dilemmas in clinical psychology's relationship with the service user movement. *Clinical Psychology Forum, 209*, 35–38.

Haywood, M., Cooke, A., Goodbody, L. & Good, R. (2010). Editorial: Service user and carer involvement – why bother? *Clinical Psychology Forum, 209,* 7–8.

Hervey, N. (1986). Advocacy or folly: The Alleged Lunatics' Friend Society 1845–1863. *Medical History, 30,* 245–275.

HIV/AIDS Special Interest Group (2001). User involvement and clinical psychology services in HIV/AIDS. *Clinical Psychology Forum, 150,* 49–50.

Hogg, C. (2009). *Citizens, consumers and the NHS: Capturing voices.* Basingstoke: Palgrave.

Holttum, S. (2010). From student to service user to research lecturer on a clinical psychology programme: A personal view on why clinical psychology training needs service user involvement. *Clinical Psychology Forum, 209,* 39–41.

House of Commons Health Committee (2007). *Patient and public involvement in the NHS: Third report of Session 2006–07.* London: Author.

Hunter, R. & MacAlpine, I. (1962). John Thomas Perceval (1803–1876): Patient and reformer. *Medical History, 6*(2), 391–395.

Hyden, L.-C. (1997). Illness and narrative. *Sociology of Health and Illness, 19*(1), 48–69.

Jingree, T. & Finlay, W.M.L. (2012). 'It's all got so politically correct now': Parents' talk about empowering individuals with learning disabilities. *Sociology of Health and Illness, 34*(3), 412–428.

Kleinman, A. (1980). *Patients and healers in the context of culture.* Berkley: University of California Press.

Kraepelin, E. (1905). *Lectures on clinical psychiatry.* London: Ballière, Tindall & Cox.

Laing, R.D. (1959). *The divided self.* Harmondsworth: Penguin.

Long, N., Newnes, C. & Maclachlan, A. (2000). Involving service users in employing clinical psychologists. *Clinical Psychology Forum, 138,* 39–42.

May, R. (2000). Routes to recovery from psychosis: The roots of a clinical psychologist. *Clinical Psychology Forum, 146,* 6–10.

May, R. (2001). Crossing the 'them and us' barriers: An inside perspective on user involvement in clinical psychology. *Clinical Psychology Forum, 150,* 14–17.

McGuire-Snieckus, R., McCabe, R. & Priebe, S. (2003). Patient, client or service user? A survey of patient preferences of dress and address of six mental health professions. *Psychiatric Bulletin, 27,* 305–308.

McIver, S. (1991). *Obtaining the views of users of mental health services.* London: King's Fund Centre for Health Services Development.

Moncrieff, J. & Crawford, M.J. (2001). British psychiatry in the 20th century – observations from a psychiatric journal. *Social Science and Medicine, 53,* 349–356.

National Health Service Confederation (1998). *In the public interest: Developing a strategy for public participation.* Leeds: NHSE.

Newnes, C. (2001). Clinical psychology, user involvement and advocacy. *Clinical Psychology Forum, 150,* 18–22.

Newnes, C. (2005). *Constructing the service-user.* www.davidsmail.info/newnes.htm.

O'Hagan, M. (1993). *Stopovers on my way home from Mars.* London: Survivors Speak Out.

Pembroke, L. & Hadfield, J. (2010). Psychological research mentored by a survivor activist: Having your cake and eating it! *Clinical Psychology Forum, 209,* 9–12.

Pickersgill M. (2012). Standardising antisocial personality disorder: The social shaping of a psychiatric technology. *Sociology of Health & Illness, 24*(4), 544–559.

Pilgrim, D. (2007). The survival of psychiatric diagnosis. *Social Science and Medicine, 65,* 536–547.

Pilgrim, D. (2014). Correspondence. *Clinical Psychology Forum, 258,* 2.

Reed, A. (2011). *Nursing in partnership with patients and carers.* Exeter: Learning Matters Ltd.

Repper, J. & Perkins, R. (2003). *Social inclusion and recovery: A model for mental health practice.* London: Ballière Tindall.

Riddell, B. (2010). Getting our foot in the door: Service users and carers making progress in clinical psychology training – a personal view. *Clinical Psychology Forum, 209,* 32–34.

Rippere, V. & Williams, R. (1985). *Wounded healers: Mental health workers' experiences of depression.* New York: Wiley, .

Rogers, A. & Pilgrim, D. (2001). *Mental health policy in Britain.* Basingstoke: Palgrave.

Rogers, A., Pilgrim, D. & Lacey, R. (1993). *Experiencing psychiatry: Users' views of services.* Basingstoke: MIND/Macmillan.

Rose, D. (2001). *Users' voices: The perspectives of mental health service users on community and hospital care.* London: Sainsbury Centre for Mental Health.

Rose, D. (2003). 'Having a diagnosis is a qualification for the job'. *British Medical Journal, 236,* 1331.

Rose, D., Ford, R., Lindley, P. & Gawith, L. (1998). *In our experience: User-focused monitoring of mental health services.* London: Sainsbury Centre for Mental Health.

Simmons, P., Hawley, C.J., Gale, T.M. & Sivakuvaran, T. (2010) Service user, patient, client, user or survivor: Describing recipients of mental health services. *The Psychiatrist Online, 34,* 2–23.

Teggart, T., Duffin, B. & Gharbaoui, S. (2001). Mapping our future together. *Clinical Psychology Forum, 150,* 30–33.

Tickle, A., Brown, D. & Hayward, M. (2014). Can we risk recovery? A grounded theory of clinical psychologists' perceptions of risk and recovery-oriented mental health services. *Psychological Psychotherapy, 87*(1), 96–110.

Tombs, D. & Griggs, H. (2000). Surviving adolescents: A group for parents. *Clinical Psychology Forum, 138,* 31–35.

Vaughn, C.E. & Leff, J. (1976). The measurement of expressed emotion in the families of psychiatric patients. *British Journal of Social and Clinical Psychology, 15,* 157–165.

Wallcraft J., Read, J. & Sweeney, A. (2003). *On our own terms: A report on the mental health service user movement.* London: Sainsbury Centre for Mental Health

Warner, R., Huxley, P. & Berg, T. (1999). An evaluation of the impact of clubhouse membership on quality of life and treatment utilisation. *International Journal of Social Psychiatry, 45*(4), 310–320.

Wise, S. (2012) *Inconvenient people: Lunacy, liberty and the mad-doctors in Victorian England.* London: The Bodley Head.

Wolpert, M., Maguire P. & Rowland, A. (2001). Should children be seen and not heard? *Clinical Psychology Forum, 150,* 43–46.

Part 2
Contexts

Chapter 3 Psychology in context: From the First World War to the National Health Service

John Stewart

In 1945 the British Psychological Society (BPS) put forward suggestions for 'The Usage of Certain Terms in Applied Psychology'. So while the terms 'child psychologist' and 'vocational psychologist' were clearly definable, the expression 'clinical psychologist', although not necessarily meaningless, was among those 'liable to too much ambiguity and misunderstanding' (British Psychological Society, 1945; also Hall, 2007). Such insecurities notwithstanding, that the phrase 'clinical psychologist' was being used at all suggests that there were those who saw a definite clinical role for psychologists, and that in certain fields it was already being practised. This chapter explores psychology's early history from the interwar period down to the foundation of the National Health Service (NHS) in the late 1940s. We start with the historical context of the 1920s and 1930s, and psychology's place therein. Next comes a discussion of two areas identifiable as early stages in clinical psychology's development, educational psychology and industrial and vocational psychology. As we shall see, these had made headway before 1939 and this leads into a discussion of the Second World War and the impetus it provided for what was now more clearly emerging as clinical psychology. A concluding passage then assesses the place of clinical psychology in the immediate aftermath of the Second World War in the light of the preceding sections. The chapter's case study is William McDougall, an enigmatic figure but important nonetheless in clinical psychology's early history and, before the First World War, one of Britain's leading psychologists.

The pre-1939 historical context and psychology's place in it

The period under discussion in this chapter as a whole forms part of what the historian Eric Hobsbawm (1994) has called 'The Age of Extremes'. It was characterised by the economic and social upheavals of the interwar era, the rise in the same period of overtly irrationalist political movements such as fascism, and thereafter the coming and aftermath of the most destructive war in human history (only 20 years after another traumatic conflict). In science, the tenets of Newtonian physics were being challenged by accounts of the physical world which posited, for example, the uncertainty principle – an unstable world in an unstable universe. But while science could be unsettling it was also accorded a high intellectual and cultural status (Hobsbawm, 1994). Science's power was to be most strikingly manifested in the atomic weapons which ended the Second World War and ushered in the era of the Cold War. In an associated development, the 20th century saw what the historian Harold Perkin has described as the 'triumph of the professional ideal' and the consequent 'plateau of professional society' (Perkin, 1989, pp.359ff.). The century thus saw the rise of the 'expert', although the nature and value of such expertise, including psychological expertise, has been critically examined from various social science perspectives (e.g. Rose, 1985, 1989, 1992).

In the years preceding the Second World War psychology was presented with both opportunities and challenges. During the Great War 'shell shock' had been treated by some medically trained psychologists, including McDougall, C.S. Myers and W.H.R. Rivers. These three had previously participated in the famous Torres Straits expedition, a landmark in the history of British anthropology and which of itself shows the fluidity of boundaries between proto-social sciences at this point, an issue discussed further below (Shephard, 2014). McDougall and Rivers were among the 10 individuals who met to form the BPS in 1901 (Edgell, 1947).

Historians now agree that previous accounts which stressed the significance of shell shock and the Great War for the development of both psychology and psychoanalysis were overstated (Loughran, 2010; Thomson, 2006; cf. Stone, 1985a, 1985b). Nonetheless in professional terms the founding of the BPS's Medical Section in 1919 was a step forward, not least because of the association of psychology with treatment in a medical setting (Edgell, 1947). More generally, after the war there was an increased interest in matters of the mind and Freudian ideas (Thomson, 2006). One instance of how psychological ideas were penetrating the wider society is the work of the Labour politician Evan Durbin. Durbin saw improving citizens' minds as a key component of socialism and social progress and among his prewar publications was a book co-authored with the psychiatrist John Bowlby on personal aggressiveness (Nuttall, 2003). Unsurprisingly, the psychology of aggression featured strongly after the Second World War in investigations into the causes and nature of the recent conflict, and here psychologists were to make important contributions (Eysenck, 1950b). The pre-1939 'psychologising' of society was not confined to the political and cultural elite but rather permeated the whole of society (Thomson, 2006). In so doing it contributed to what one historian has described as the 'morbid age' of the 1920s and 1930s, a period when introspection and 'selfhood' were widespread preoccupations and key components of post-1918 'modernity' (Overy, 2009).

In the policy sphere the 1930 Mental Treatment Act marked a shift to a less judgemental approach to mental illness which was now seen as a public health problem (Jones, 1991) and by the end of the decade, in Hearnshaw's view, a demand had emerged for clinical psychologists in the mental health field (Hearnshaw, 1964). It has to be borne in mind, though, that healthcare provision was divided between the voluntary and municipal sectors and access to any kind of care was determined by factors such as income, employment status, gender, location and age. In the municipal sphere, expenditure in general terms was rising and to this extent mental health services also expanded. But it would be misguided to envisage a comprehensive or curative service beyond a basic minimum. And in any event there was as much concern with, in the language of the times, 'mental defectives' as with mental health itself (Levene et al., 2011). Psychology's claim to scientific status, however, was furthered by developments such as child guidance and the use of psychometric testing and statistical analysis. These had been pioneered by psychologists Cyril Burt, sometimes seen as Britain's first professional psychologist, and Charles Spearman. The development of such 'scientific' techniques chimed with the previously noted point about science's high intellectual and cultural status, and with the desire to establish psychology on a more professional basis (Stewart, 2013).

Nonetheless, it remained unclear what exactly 'psychology' was, not least because its subject matter was ill-defined and there was little of what we would now understand as professional training. The BPS, for instance, down to the late 1940s was open to anyone interested in 'psychology' and not just 'psychologists' and in any event in 1939 it had under one thousand members (Hall, 2007). As Smith points out, while psychology may have attained a distinct identity by the 20th century, nonetheless it remained 'unclear where the boundaries of psychology actually lay'. This was problematic not least with respect to medicine (Smith, 1997, pp.19–20). Such problems were apparent to contemporaries. The Feversham Committee, which investigated mental health services provided by the voluntary sector, noted in 1939 that an 'exact definition, or even a comprehensive description, of the term psychologist offers peculiar difficulty'. The Committee felt on safer grounds, though, with educational psychologists whose task was to assess children's intelligence and to study their behavioural problems. Their further role involved the 'guidance of children, through teachers and parents, in difficulties of adjustment which arise in connection with home and school'. By this account, educational psychologists thus had a treatment role. They also had to have what the Committee rather vaguely described as 'special qualifications' which were 'not necessarily medical', such opacity reflecting the lack of precision then prevalent about training even for such an apparently distinct group as educational psychologists (Feversham Committee, 1939, p.14).

There remained too a tension between psychology as a 'scientific' discipline and one which was 'philosophical'. Writing about shell shock in 1917, J.A. Hadfield felt it necessary to point out that he was using the word 'psychologist' in 'its modern scientific, not in its more familiar philosophical sense' (Hadfield, 1917, pp.41–42). The career, or rather job titles, of Beatrice Edgell further illustrate this point. After her doctorate she was appointed, in 1897, lecturer in philosophy and head of the department of mental and moral science at a college of the University of London, her department being renamed 'philosophy and psychology' a few years later. She then became reader in psychology in 1913 before being appointed Britain's first female professor of psychology in 1927. On her retirement she worked in a child guidance clinic (Lovie & Lovie, 2004). As we shall see, a similar point can be made about McDougall.

This unstable definitional status, however, could work to psychology's advantage as it allowed for dynamic intellectual engagements with other disciplines, notably anthropology. We saw that McDougall, Rivers, and Myers had participated in the Torres Straits Expedition. Another example is Meyer Fortes who took his PhD in psychology at London University under Spearman; worked as a psychologist in the East London Jewish Child Guidance Clinic, publishing important papers on psychology in child guidance; and then refocused on anthropology, eventually becoming professor of that subject at Cambridge (Kuklick, 1991; Stewart, 2013; and, for psychology and its relationship with other social sciences, Smith, 1997). Another outcome of interdisciplinary discussions was an edited volume prompted by meetings of the Social Psychological Discussion Group, which had taken place since 1935 with participants drawn from psychology, sociology, anthropology and social work. Among those present were James Drever, F.C. Bartlett and Mary Collins, all of whom went on to play important roles in the development of clinical psychology (Bartlett et al., 1939). More broadly these individuals clearly all operated in complex but tight-knit professional and intellectual circles – Bartlett, for example, had been taught by Rivers and Myers – and all this might be seen as having positive implications for the development of both psychology in general and clinical psychology.

Psychology was, though, not the only occupation seeking to professionalise in an increasingly crowded field. Again to use the example of child guidance, here psychologists disputed the territory with psychiatrists and the new profession of psychiatric social worker. The Diploma in Mental Health course had been set up at the London School of Economics (LSE) in 1929. This course and the founding shortly afterwards of a professional body, the Association of Psychiatric Social Workers, were crucial in creating a professional identity for this new, psychiatrically oriented, profession. The conflict between psychiatric social workers and psychologists was one which, at least in England, did not go well for the latter prior to the Second World War (Stewart, 2013). Another competitor was occupational therapy with the first training school opening in 1930 and a professional association being formed in 1936 (Hearnshaw, 1964).

It was also the case, at least in England, that psychology only had a weak foothold in institutions such as universities, especially when compared with the United States and Germany. There were, in 1939, only five professorial chairs, one each in Manchester and Cambridge with the remainder in London (Hearnshaw, 1964). Yet, and again to see positive outcomes from an apparently unpromising situation, Ash argues that this allowed 'a wide range of theoretical explanations and practical applications'. Ash also notes Burt's influence on educational policy and practice (Ash, 2003, p.265). Wooldridge has substantiated the argument that one of the few sphere before the Second World War where psychology had policy significance was in its relationship with the Board of Education (Wooldridge, 1994). To further complicate matters, psychology was in a much stronger position in Scotland by virtue of its place in the education system and the work of individuals such as William Boyd and, as a result, child guidance. Psychiatry, by contrast, was very weak (Stewart, 2013). All this was to be of significance in the 1940s.

Educational psychology and industrial and vocational psychology

We now turn to two areas which were important steps in clinical psychology's development and which had made progress before 1939 – educational psychology, particularly its role in child guidance; and industrial and vocational psychology. Child guidance was a form of preventive mental health aimed at children and adolescents. Originating in the United States in the immediate aftermath of the First World War it came to Britain through funding provided by the American philanthropic body the Commonwealth Fund of New York, which channelled its support by way of the Child Guidance Council, the London Child Guidance Clinic, and the LSE mental health course. Child guidance sought to bring 'maladjusted' children to a dedicated clinic where they would be dealt with by psychiatrists, psychologists and psychiatric social workers. The psychiatrist's role was to examine the child mentally and physically. The psychologist would primarily administer psychometric tests, although as we shall see they also took on other roles, while the psychiatric social worker sought to establish the emotional dynamics of the child's family. All three would then contribute to a case conference at which diagnosis and treatment would be established. Much was made of teamwork in child guidance but, at least in the model initially adopted in England, this was hierarchical teamwork with the psychiatrist in charge. This was because the causes of the child's maladjustment were deemed to be pathological rather than behavioural, hence the need for medical intervention. Psychology was to be subordinate to psychiatry, and psychiatrists in England went to considerable pains to assert their self-ascribed dominance. Psychology's role was acknowledged but for the most part this was perceived as reductively 'scientific', that is, concerned primarily with testing, and so of lesser standing than the higher level skills deployed by medically trained clinicians. Psychologists responded by noting that many psychiatrists knew little about child development and that psychiatry was far from being an exact science, unlike psychology. In certain respects these were perfectly reasonable criticisms (Stewart, 2013).

Psychologists were not happy with their supposedly inferior status. James Drever told a child guidance conference in 1935 that, while teamwork was essential, the idea that the psychologist's role be confined to mental testing was 'palpably absurd' and that psychologists had, or should have, a wider clinical role. Again it is important here that Drever worked in Scotland, and indeed ran a psychological clinic in Edinburgh whose clients included children, for in that country psychiatry had established almost no foothold. Scottish child guidance clinics were with few exceptions run by psychologists, so further consolidating their influence on Scotland's educational policy and practice (Stewart, 2013).

Mary Collins noted that in child guidance clinics play was a useful tool, with 'clinical workers (stressing) its value for diagnostic and therapeutic purposes' and as such making an 'important contribution towards child psychology'. But it was 'a method for the highly skilled specialist alone... for in inexperienced hands it may do the child incalculable harm' (Collins, 1939, p.82). Given the way child guidance clinics operated in practice, with psychiatrists having little time to see children and psychologists increasingly promoting techniques such as play therapy, Collins was making a bid here for psychological, rather than psychiatric, expertise. Such trends were noted by the Feversham Committee, which remarked that 'in the field of educational psychology we find less and less emphasis being laid on the mere estimation of intelligence'. The psychologist's role now included investigation into areas such as educational backwardness and helping teachers to address psychological problems in their charges. Among the Committee's recommendations, moreover, was that each local education authority 'appoint a psychologist to advise them on their educational programme'. These psychologists should also 'examine and advise on the treatment of backward children' and those with behavioural and educational problems with 'suitable cases' being referred on to a child guidance clinic (Feversham Committee, 1939, pp.154–155).

It was certainly the case that child guidance, as well as education more generally, had proved an important employment opportunity for psychologists. From just two clinics in the late 1920s, both in London and both using voluntary funding, by 1939 this had increased to over 40 and these were now increasingly run by local education authorities. Almost without exception, these bodies employed psychologists. Psychologists also benefited from fellowships provided by the Child Guidance Council to be held at the London Child Guidance Clinic; and from the funding mechanism the Council provided to support the employment of psychologists by local education authorities. The founding of the *British Journal of Educational Psychology* in 1929 was another important step in the professionalisation of the discipline. However, it remained the case that, in English child guidance at least, psychologists remained subordinate to psychiatrists down to 1939 and not least because Commonwealth Fund support was predicated on the superiority of the medical model (Stewart, 2013).

During the First World War psychologists had been involved in research into problems of fatigue in the munitions industries and officer selection in the armed forces. All this in turn fed into the post-war development of industrial and vocational psychology (Stone, 1985b). Myers was an early powerful advocate of industrial psychology. In 1929 he argued that industrial psychology was 'the most recent application of the youngest of the Natural Sciences', that is, psychology. Again we encounter psychology's claim to scientific status and Myers went on to suggest that psychology was now a branch of biology, having 'emancipated itself from the leading-strings of Philosophy by which it was first nurtured'. Psychology in the course of its development had generated 'several Applied Sciences', these including educational psychology and, now, industrial psychology. The latter had both diagnostic and treatment functions and so in 'treating the industrial, as in treating the human organism' it was necessary to 'systematically reveal and carefully study' the relative importance of various potential causal factors 'before we can hope to apply rational treatment' (Myers, 1929, pp.8–9, 12),

What this might achieve was outlined by Myers and another of industrial psychology's leading exponents, the industrialist Henry Welch. They envisaged a future where large progressive organisations would establish departments staffed by experts trained at the National Institute of Industrial Psychology which had been set up by Welch and Myers in 1921 (again the timing, the immediate aftermath of the First World War, is significant). These psychological experts would select employees, improve training methods, and inform 'the organization of personnel, incentives, layout, design and arrangement both of machines and implements and of products, advertisement – indeed wherever the human factor requires systematic consideration' (Welch & Myers, 1932, pp.133–140). The head of the Institute's Vocational Guidance Department, meanwhile, noted that a vocational adviser had four functions, the last of which was 'to persuade his subject to accept, or, in certain cases to confirm, what appears to be a desirable course of action'. And if the client was seeking a career to which he was clearly unsuitable, then it was the adviser's function to persuade him otherwise (Rodger, 1939, pp.257–258, 269).

We noted earlier the economic and political dislocations of the interwar era and the impact of the First World War on psychology's status. The development of industrial and vocational psychology has to be seen in this broader context. After 1918 American ideas about 'scientific management', or 'Taylorism', spread to Britain. These sought to make industrial capitalism more efficient and, especially in its British variant, to dampen down class conflict and industrial strife. Myers, in a radio broadcast in 1923, suggested that industrial psychology was a key component in a shift from an 'age of mechanism' to an 'age of humanism' although, as

Thomson notes, its actual achievements were rather more modest (Thomson, 2006, pp.142ff, Myers cited p.145). Nonetheless, Myers's comments need to be seen against the background of the rising unemployment and bitter industrial disputes which characterised 1920s Britain.

Psychology, total war, and its aftermath

The Second World War is generally referred to as a 'total' war as it required the full mobilisation of all the resources of the participant nations, with Britain no exception. Experts, including psychologists, came to the fore (Edgerton, 2006). One important social dimension was that around one and a half million people, mostly children, were evacuated from urban areas threatened by aerial bombing and a significant proportion of these were not accompanied by a parent. So, for instance, some 400,000 unaccompanied children left London (Titmuss, 1950, pp.102–103). Concerns had been expressed even before the process started about the psychological impact such separation would have and the evacuees were subject to various surveys in which psychologists, along with psychiatric social workers, played a prominent role (Boyd, 1944; Isaacs, 1941). The actual consequences of evacuation were ambiguous but it did advance the cause of child guidance and the need for familial, and thereby social, stability. The number of child guidance clinics rose during the 1940s. From the psychologists' point of view what was important was that it was to be embedded in the post-war welfare state as an educational and local authority service, and not a medical and NHS one. The1944 Education Act (which applied to England and Wales) recognised, for the first time, 'maladjustment' as a condition which education authorities had to address. This significantly boosted the role of educational psychologists at the expense of psychiatrists. The ubiquitous Drever had emphasised psychology's clinical role to Board of Education investigators during the war. His arguments won the day, and effectively it was the Scottish version of child guidance which was put in place. Psychiatrists, though, continued to argue for their leadership role and this issue remained unresolved well into the post-war era. Nonetheless, here was a very clear instance of psychologists undertaking clinical duties and outflanking their rivals, the psychiatrists (Stewart, 2013).

Psychologists also had a role to play in the armed services in capacities such as personnel selection. As the official report on the subject noted, in the First World War psychologists had been employed in tasks such as officer selection and the psychological problems of employment in the munitions industries. In the recently ended conflict assessment of recruits had again been to the fore with, to take the example of the Royal Navy, five tests being applied to new entrants, including the Raven Progressive Matrices Test. At the War Office, meanwhile, the Director of Selection of Personnel had 19 psychologists at his disposal, supported by over 1000 staff with some level of training in psychology. The report as a whole noted the now recognised importance of psychological understanding in military matters and paid tribute to the work of bodies such as the Industrial Health Research Board (Privy Council Office, 1947). The latter, another product of the First World War, had utilised psychological expertise and in particular engaged with industrial and vocational psychology (Schilling, 1944).

F.C. Bartlett, now head of the Cambridge Psychological Laboratory, further added to such claims by suggesting that recruits to the colonial service should be trained in psychology as well as in language, law, and anthropology. As historian Erik Linstrum notes, it was in this context that Bartlett argued for a 'psychological governor', one who understood that all problems of government were fundamentally to do with how to control 'organised crowd behaviour'. Somewhat less ambitiously, Raven's Matrices were used to assess not only British service personnel but also those in Africa, India and the Middle East before, once the war was over, evaluating students and job applicants in a wide range of imperial situations (Linstrum, 2012, pp.197, 201–202). And although, as we have seen, the actual term was still causing unease in 1945, nonetheless clinical psychology was beginning to consolidate itself in organisational terms. Of particular note here was the creation, in the early 1940s, of a body within the BPS, the Committee of Professional Psychologists (Mental Health). This had its origins in part in the child guidance movement, with the leading figure being Lucy Fildes, by this point a tutor on the LSE's training course for psychiatric social workers. As John Hall suggests, this Committee was both unique within the BPS and in the vanguard of establishing and professionalising clinical psychology (Hall, 2007).

The war, therefore, further contributed both to the psychologising of British society and enhanced opportunities for psychologists themselves. Such trends should be placed in the broader context of plans, fully articulated from the early 1940s onwards, for post-war reconstruction, which resulted in the creation of the 'welfare state'. The aim of the latter was famously captured in William Beveridge's notion of social protection 'from the cradle to the grave' and included reforms such as the creation of the NHS, free and universal secondary education, family allowances and revised forms of social insurance and social assistance. The family was to be the keystone of society and its health, physical and mental, was at least in principle central to social policy. Stable and well-adjusted families would lead to stable and well-adjusted societies, resistant to both individual and social maladjustment and the dangers of what was commonly described, in the growing tensions of the Cold War, as the 'totalitarian mindset'.

So increasing opportunities in education and the NHS opened up opportunities for what was increasingly described as 'clinical psychology' and numbers did appear to rise significantly (Hall, 2007). This was helped by the shortage of trained psychiatrists and underpinned by the identification of the psychologist as an expert who could contribute to individual and national mental well-being (Rose, 1989). Some sense of what this might involve can be found in papers on psychological guidance to parents given in 1946 to a meeting organised by the Committee of Professional Psychologists. Grace Rawlings, soon to play a part in negotiations over psychology's place in the health system, dealt in her contribution with problems encountered by psychologists working in schools or in child guidance clinics. Rawlings outlined which psychological principles had to be understood regarding child-rearing. She then insisted that in acting on these principles psychologists must 'take full responsibility' both in understanding the causes of a child's behavioural problems and in guiding such principles 'towards desirable ends' (Valentine & Rawlings, 1946, pp.99–100). In an upbeat assessment of where psychology stood in 1945 Burt claimed that modern civilisation was 'based on science' and that 'scientific thinking must be applied to man as well as to inanimate nature' if this civilization was to continue. Unsurprisingly, this foregrounded psychology whose discoveries were being employed in education, medicine and business. Educational psychology had 'improved the means by which we train the child at school' while 'vocational psychology will soon be deciding his future occupation and career'. Once in employment industrial psychology was 'introducing more efficient methods into factories, workshops and mines' (Burt, 1945, pp.7–8). Here then was an ambitious programme for psychology and its potential clinical applications.

All occupational groups seeking to establish themselves fully as professions are highly conscious of the need to establish control over, and standards of, training. Clinical psychology was no exception and after the war there came a spate of publications on the subject. Eysenck, for example, acknowledged definitional problems while claiming that clinical psychology was 'among the oldest applications of psychological knowledge to practical problems', dating back to the psychological clinic founded at the University of Pennsylvania at the end of the 19th century. Nonetheless, in England clinical psychology had largely been disguised as educational psychology, for Eysenck another misleading term. But now things were beginning to change (Eysenck, 1950a). Eysenck is central to our story in his role as what Roderick Buchanan describes as a 'clinical partisan'. While never engaged in treatment himself Eysenck drove forward the setting up of training in clinical psychology at the Maudsley Hospital in London in the mid-1940s. This development was supported by the hospital's chief psychiatrist, Aubrey Lewis, although the two men had different intentions. For Lewis, psychologists would be subordinate to psychiatrists, with the latter continuing to carry out treatment, while for Eysenck, at least by his own account, the aim was to free psychology's subordination to medicine in clinical practice. Clearly the Maudsley initiative was an important development in the history of clinical psychology although training was also being instituted, almost contemporaneously, at the Crichton Royal in Scotland and at the Tavistock Clinic in London (see Buchanan, 2010, pp.181–182; for a specific account of the Maudsley, Derksen, 2001; for the Tavistock, Dicks, 1970; for the Crichton Royal, Allan in chapter 23 of this volume).

The psychiatrist H.V. Dicks, after the war Training Secretary at the Tavistock, later recalled how he set up courses in psychiatry and clinical psychology, the latter 'a term which had now come into usage'. He also noted, however, that clinical psychology tended to be focused in the diagnostic and counselling service – as he put it, 'in psychodiagnostics... vocational and educational counselling, and so forth' – rather than in treatment, as continuing patient exposure to the same doctor was deemed important. Nonetheless, clinical psychology had come of age at the Tavistock and in 1947 its staff 'democratically elected' the clinical psychologist J.D. Sutherland as its medical director (Dicks, 1970, pp.168, 175). The timing of the formation of training courses at the Maudsley, the Crichton Royal, and the Tavistock was crucial for it was from 1946 onwards that the National Health Service Acts were being passed, with the service coming into operation in July 1948, the opposition of the British Medical Association notwithstanding. Hall notes the 'highly significant decision' made earlier that year that psychologists be allowed to set up their own committee under the auspices of the Whitley Council machinery. This placed psychologists 'for the first time within a formal structure of the new NHS'. Significant influence was thus effectively granted to the Committee of Professional Psychologists (Hall, 2007, p.42).

So by the mid-1940s clinical psychology appeared to have made considerable professional advances from not always propitious beginnings. Before the Second World War there had been a lack of clear definition of what clinical psychology might involve, there was no systematic or agreed training in the subject, and those seeking a clinical role were confined, for the most part, to services for children. On the other hand, psychology had improved its standing through its claims to scientific status and through its clinical role in Scottish child guidance. More broadly, the psychologising of society had led to heightened interest in psychology's aspirations and potential. These more positive trends had been accelerated by the Second World War and the post-war desire for positive mental health as a means to individual, familial and social stability.

But again the broader context is important. The NHS, for example, was from the outset financially stretched and within the new service mental health was not a priority (Thomson, 2006). A Board of Education's report on maladjusted children, published in 1955, acknowledged that the number of educational psychologists had increased but still sought for this to be doubled in order to avert what it saw as potentially widespread levels of maladjustment. The BPS's evidence on this topic was, intriguingly, the cause of internal division, specifically over the causes of maladjustment and the composition of the child guidance team. This is particularly ironic in the light of Burt's condemnation of psychiatry as 'unscientific' because of its huge range of theoretical and interpretative positions, and was an early indication of a crisis of confidence among psychologists involved in child guidance and more broadly (Stewart, 2013). Clinical psychology had thus 'arrived' by mid-century but not without a struggle and not without potential for further problems.

William McDougall

Thomson (2006), with due cause, refers to the 'The Strange Case of William McDougall'. This is because, as he puts it, McDougall was the 'most celebrated' psychologist for the first half of the last century but since then 'has virtually disappeared from view'. This occurred in part because his was an instinct-driven account of the human psyche, but also because he espoused now unacceptable racial and eugenicist views (Thomson, 2006: 55ff; for other discussions of McDougall see Hearnshaw, 1964; Shephard, 2014; Soffer, 1978; and McDougall's own account of his career, McDougall, 1930). Nonetheless, McDougall's output was prodigious – one obituarist noted a bibliography listing nearly 150 articles and books (Zener, 1939, p.192) – and included a number of best-selling texts which went into multiple editions. His *An Introduction to Social Psychology*, for instance, ran to 29 editions, the last appearing 10 years after his death (McDougall, 1948). He also trained others who were to become important in the early history of British psychology, for example Burt and Hadfield.

McDougall was medically trained but put doctoring aside to focus on psychology. Although care should be taken with his autobiographical writings, McDougall later claimed that he had studied medicine not with the intention of practising it but rather because such training was a 'very desirable part of a thorough education, especially for one who aspires to work in any of the sciences concerned with man' (McDougall, 1930, p.199). On his return from the Far East and prior to the Great War McDougall lectured on psychology at University College London and became Wilde Reader in Mental Philosophy at the University of Oxford. During the war itself McDougall, as a temporary major in the Royal Army Medical Corps, treated shell shock patients, latterly in Oxford. Like Hadfield, who also treated the illness in Oxford, McDougall was convinced that shell shock had psychological and not organic origins and he was to draw extensively on his wartime experiences in subsequent writings (Stewart, 2014).

According to another of his obituarists it was because of his wartime experiences that McDougall became President of the Royal Society of Medicine's Section of Psychiatry (Pattie, 1939, p.303) and his presidential address was entitled 'The Present Position of Clinical Psychology'. McDougall told his audience that he was moving 'outside the boundary of psychiatry' and into the territory of clinical psychology. Implicitly acknowledging that this might be an expression unknown or misunderstood by his listeners he started off by noting that it might be argued that there was not, nor could not be, any branch of psychology which could be so described. This was because 'the clinician deals with his patient as an entire organism' and so in considering 'his mental life' could not separate out any functioning of the mind for sole attention. McDougall in principle agreed with this, observing that when knowledge of the human mind had 'become an adequate and well-established science' then this would be the theoretical foundations for all those 'practically concerned with the working of the mind' – that is, clinicians. Nonetheless it was precisely because previously there had been no such overarching theory that there had recently developed 'a specialised form of mental science which may be conveniently designated *clinical psychology*'. Looking to the future McDougall predicted that from that standpoint 'the present time will be held to be remarkable for the great advances made in our understanding of the mind' and it would be gratefully recognised that 'clinicians have played a great and leading part in this achievement'. McDougall then gave a brief account of the major schools of psychological thought before concluding that clinical psychology was now 'launched upon a great career' (McDougall, 1919).

Clarity of thought or expression were not necessarily characteristics of McDougall's writings. Given his audience, his use of the word 'clinician' could be variously construed, as could the expression 'clinical psychology' itself and much of his speech was actually taken up with attacking 'mechanistic psychology'. But his high status among Britain's small band of psychologists needs to be taken into account, as does his wartime experience of actually treating patients. So here was an eminent figure in psychological medicine anticipating a future where psychologists would have enough 'science' – McDougall clearly had no doubt psychology was by this point such a form of knowledge – to engage fully with the mind's problems. And the very public and insistent use of 'clinical psychology', its ambiguities notwithstanding, was an important landmark in the field's early history.

References

Ash, M.G. (2003). Psychology. In T.M. Porter & D. Ross (Eds.), *The Cambridge history of science: The modern social sciences* (pp.251–274). Cambridge: Cambridge University Press.

Bartlett, F.C., Ginsberg, M., Lindgren, E.J. & Thouless, R.H. (Eds.) (1939). *The study of society: Methods and problems.* London: Kegan Paul, Trench, Trubner and Co.

Boyd, W. (Ed.) (1944). *Evacuation in Scotland: A record of events and experiments.* Bickley, Kent: University of London Press.
British Psychological Society (1945). The usage of certain terms in applied psychology. *British Journal of Psychology, 35*(2), 50.
Buchanan, R. (2010). *Playing with fire: The controversial career of Hans J. Eysenck.* Oxford: Oxford University Press.
Burt, C. (1945). Preface to the second edition. In C. Burt (Ed.), *How the mind works* (2nd edn, pp.7–12). London: George Allen and Unwin.
Collins, M. (1939). Modern trends in child psychology. In F.C. Bartlett et al. (Eds.), *The study of society: Methods and problems* (pp.70–114). London: Kegan Paul, Trench, Trubner and Co.
Derksen, M. (2001). Science in the clinic: Clinical psychology at the Maudsley. In G.C. Bunn, A.D. Lovie & G.D. Richards (Eds.), *Psychology in Britain: Historical essays and personal reflections* (pp.267–89). Leicester: BPS Books.
Dicks, H.V. (1970). *Fifty years of the Tavistock Clinic.* London: Routledge & Kegan Paul.
Edgell, B. (1947). The British Psychological Society. *British Journal of Psychology, 37*(3), 113–132.
Edgerton, D. (2006). *Warfare state: Britain, 1920–1970.* Cambridge: Cambridge University Press.
Eysenck, H.J. (1950a). Function and training of the clinical psychologist. *Journal of Mental Science, 96,* 710–725.
Eysenck, H.J. (1950b). War and aggressiveness: A survey of social attitudes. In T.H. Pear (Ed.), *Psychological factors in peace and war* (pp.49–81). London: Hutchison.
Feversham Committee (1939). *The voluntary mental health services.* London: Author.
Hadfield, J.A. (1917). The mind and the brain. In B.H. Streeter (Ed.), *Immortality: An essay in discovery co-ordinating scientific, psychical and biblical research* (pp.17–74). London: Macmillan.
Hall, J. (2007). The emergence of clinical psychology in Britain from 1943 to 1958 part I: Core tasks and the professionalisation process. *History and Philosophy of Psychology, 9*(1), 29–55.
Hearnshaw, L.S. (1964). *A short history of British psychology, 1840–1940.* London: Methuen.
Hobsbawm, E. (1994). *The age of extremes: The short 20th century, 1914–1991.* London: Michael Joseph.
Isaacs, S. (Ed.) (1941). *The Cambridge evacuation survey: A wartime study in social welfare and education.* London, Methuen.
Jones, K. (1991). Law and mental health. In G.E. Berrios & H. Freeman (Eds.), *150 Years of British psychiatry, 1841–1991* (pp.89–102). London: Gaskell.
Kuklick, H. (1991). *The savage within: The social history of British anthropology, 1885–1945.* Cambridge: Cambridge University Press.
Levene, A., Powell, M., Stewart, J. & Taylor, B. (2011). *Cradle to grave: Municipal medicine in interwar England and Wales.* Bern: Peter Lang AG.
Linstrum, E. (2012). The politics of psychology in the British Empire, 1898–1960. *Past and Present, 215,* 195–233.
Loughran, T. (2010). Shell shock, trauma, and the First World War: The making of a diagnosis and its histories. *Journal of the History of Medicine and Allied Sciences, 67*(1), 94–119.
Lovie, P. & Lovie, A.D. (2004). Beatrice Edgell. *Oxford Dictionary of National Biography.* doi:10.1093/ref:odnb/52394
McDougall, W. (1919). The present position in clinical psychology. *Journal of Mental Science, 270*(LXV), 141–152.
McDougall, W. (1930). William McDougall. In C. Murchison (Ed.), *A history of psychology in autobiography* (Vol. 1, pp.191–223). Worcester, MA: Clark University Press.
McDougall, W. (1948). *An introduction to social psychology* (29th edn). London: Methuen.
Myers, C.S. (1929). Introduction. In C.S. Myers (Ed.), *Industrial psychology* (pp.1–15). London: T. Butterworth.
Nuttall, J. (2003). 'Psychological socialist'; 'militant moderate': Evan Durbin and the politics of synthesis. *Labour History Review, 68*(2), 235–252.
Overy, R. (2009). *The morbid age: Britain between the wars.* London: Allen Lane.
Pattie, F. (1939). William McDougall. *American Journal of Psychology, 52*(2), 303–307.
Perkin, H. (1989). *The rise of professional society: England since 1880.* London: Routledge.
Privy Council Office (1947). *Report of an expert committee on the work of psychologists and psychiatrists in the services.* London: HMSO.

Rodger, A. (1939). The work of the vocational adviser. In F.C. Bartlett et al. (Eds.), *The study of society: Methods and problems* (pp.257–271). London: Kegan Paul, Trench, Trubner and Co.
Rose, N. (1985). *The psychological complex: Psychology, politics and society in England, 1869–1939.* London: Routledge and Kegan Paul.
Rose, N. (1989). *Governing the soul: The shaping of the private self.* London: Routledge.
Rose, N. (1992). Engineering the human soul: Analyzing psychological expertise. *Science in Context, 5*(2), 351–369.
Schilling, R.F. (1944). The work of the Industrial Health Research Board, 1918–1944. *British Journal of Industrial Medicine, 1*(3), 145–152.
Shephard, B. (2014). *Headhunters: The search for a science of the mind.* London: The Bodley Head.
Smith, R. (1997). *The Fontana history of the human sciences.* London: Fontana.
Soffer, R.N. (1978). *Ethics and society in England: The revolution in the social sciences, 1870–1914.* Berkeley: University of California Press.
Stewart, J. (2013). *Child guidance in Britain, 1918–1955: The dangerous age of childhood.* London: Pickering and Chatto.
Stewart, J. (2014, October). *Shell-shock, Oxford, and the Great War.* Paper presented at the Wellcome Unit for the History of Medicine, University of Oxford.
Stone, M. (1985a). Shellshock and the psychologists. In W.F. Bynum, R. Porter & M. Shepherd (Eds.), *The anatomy of madness: Vol. II. Institutions and society* (pp.242–271). London: Tavistock Publications.
Stone, M. (1985b). *The military and industrial roots of clinical psychology in Britain.* Unpublished PhD thesis, University of London.
Thomson, M. (2006). *Psychological subjects: Identity, culture, and health in 20th century Britain.* Oxford: Oxford University Press.
Titmuss, R. (1950). *Problems of social policy.* London: HMSO.
Valentine, C.W. & Rawlings, G. (1946). The psychological guidance of parents in the upbringing of children. *British Journal of Educational Psychology, 16*(2), 96–101.
Welch, H.J. & C.S. Myers (1932). *Ten years of industrial psychology.* London: Pitman.
Wooldridge, A. (1994). *Measuring the mind: Education and psychology in England c.1860–c.1990.* Cambridge: Cambridge University Press.
Zener, K. (1939). William McDougall. *Science, 89*(2305), 191–192.

Chapter 4 The emergence of clinical psychology in the British post-war context

David Pilgrim & Nimisha Patel

This chapter mainly examines the period between the end of the Second World War and the establishment of the Division of Clinical Psychology. This particular period of the mid-20th century is illuminated to outline the conditions of possibility for the emerging character of British clinical psychology. Some of those conditions reflected the legacy of the past. Some were very specific contingent features of life in Britain after 1945. Within the constraints of a short chapter only a general scene setting can be offered to the reader. The fuller implications of points will resonate in several other chapters in this book.

The global setting of Britain

In 1945 Britain was in a parlous state. With its allies having defeated fascism, reconstruction was required urgently and many of the material and social challenges of the prewar years were on hold and still waiting to be solved. The war with Germany was the last spasm of the struggle for hegemony within the colonial powers of Europe. By the time clinical psychology emerged slowly in the post-war period, Britain was presently to become a rapidly declining manufacturing base, relying at home increasingly on cheap and available imported labour. Moreover, its grip on Empire was bit by bit loosening.

After the First World War, Britain ruled around 500 million people and occupied about a quarter of the world's land mass. The whole of the Indian subcontinent was under British domination, as well as a third of Africa in a swathe from Cairo to Cape Town. Military adventurism to govern new territories in Palestine and Iraq coexisted with an episodic but unrelenting defiance in anglophone white-led self-determination movements, in Ireland, Canada, Australia, South Africa and Rhodesia. The end of Empire created a contradiction of a peak in cultural pride before the fall.

All change after the Second World War?

In 1924 the self-aggrandising British Empire exhibition at Wembley stadium could still proudly celebrate the dominion of 58 countries. It set out to reassure its native audience that Empire was Britain's insurance policy for the future. But what a difference two decades was to make. By the end of the Second World War, for the first batch of student clinical psychologists, their recent school atlases would indeed have been colour coded in large pink daubs, indicating the reach of the British Empire. However, battered by the war effort, with food being rationed and children picking their way to school through bomb sites in the big cities, reconstruction was required urgently. And this was only possible in conditions of austerity and diminishing colonial self-confidence. The game was up for the British

Empire, now impoverished by the war and contending with muscular anticolonial independence movements. The most dramatic of these, at the very moment when the first clinical psychology course was established in 1947, was the bloody but successful achievement of Indian independence.

Moreover, the cultural and fiscal legacy of Empire at home was still being played out. British Commonwealth subjects from the Caribbean and the Indian subcontinent, opting to move to the UK, as their passport allowed in the 1950s and 1960s, were embraced for their economic potential. But those very migrants were also scorned by the habitual and casual white racism of many ordinary British people, with landlords openly posting the notice: 'No Blacks, no Dogs, no Irish'. Words like 'darkies', 'coons', 'Pakis' and 'wogs' were to flood the daily discourse of streets and workplaces, especially when the targets of this scorn were physically present.

Populist reactionary politicians soon were seeking to legitimise hostility towards migrants. Enoch Powell, the Minister for Health, who was a significant figure in prompting the run-down of psychiatric institutions in 1963, made his famous 'rivers of blood' speech in Birmingham in 1968 (foreshadowing the more recent anti-immigration politics of the British National Party and UK Independence Party).

'The spirit of 1945' was certainly imbued with a progressive optimism about social justice and economic security. As A.J.P. Taylor, the popular 1960s TV historian with the spotted bow tie, pointed out, 'Imperial greatness was on the way out; the welfare state was on the way in. The British Empire declined; the condition of the people improved' (Taylor, 1965). However, this progressive impulse and policy trajectory was to remain tainted by a pervasive cultural ethnocentricity, stemming from the island status of Great Britain and the residual assumptions of superiority bequeathed by such a vast imperial project for so long. That empire had not only created a land mass of Great Britain, at the centre of a 'UK' with its distinctive identity within Europe; it has also bequeathed an enduring cultural image of a 'Greater Britain'.

Health and welfare after 1945

A more elaborate account of points in this subsection can be found in Webster (1988). A common process shaping the profession and its dominant structure of employment was the rebound post-war optimism after a difficult war, when Britain had been a whisker away from German invasion. The Labour manifesto of 1945 was called *Let Us Face the Future*, signalling an opportunity, a challenge and a shared commitment to moving forwards. A short reductive account of the NHS, the monopoly employer of most clinical psychologists for many decades to come, was that it was a triumph of social democratic reasoning and campaigning in 1945. But this Labourist triumphalism needs to be considered in relation to the following.

First, although throughout the 20th century demands for a nationalised medical service had indeed been associated with Fabian thought (championed, for example, by Sidney and Beatrice Webb), the crisis of organisation brought to the fore by the war effort after 1939 made a more rationalised service a cross-party concern. Plans for the NHS emerged in concrete form, when the serious shortcomings of the Emergency Hospital Service highlighted the problems of the accretions of the British policy habit of 'muddling through'.

Second, despite its later rigidity and proneness to sabotage the NHS in its infancy, the British Medical Association was concerned to improve service planning. This was mainly out of self-interest in relation to the stable income of general practitioners. The British population were only protected from the vagaries of the 'panel' system (exposed by the prewar depression and its extensively associated poverty), when those rich enough to pay and those in employment making their National Insurance contributions were confident in the attendance of their local family doctor for them and their families. Outside of that protected sub-population many ordinary people associated common sickness with anxiety and dilemmas about payment, and they might reluctantly, for lack of funds, eschew what we now call 'primary care'.

Third, since the beginning of the 20th century, the extensive voluntary hospital system had encountered recurring financial crises and these were amplifying in degree and frequency. In 1937 a commission organised by the British Hospitals Association argued for a more sustainable and coordinated regionalised system. This proposal was a priority set by the newly established Nuffield Provincial Hospitals Trust in 1939, just as the war broke out.

Fourth, there was a range of lobbying groups shaping the health policy imagination in the mid-20th century. For example, just before the war some young research-orientated medical practitioners formed a policy lobby ('Medical Planning Research'). This was what we might now call a 'think tank' and it made a number of recommendations to government about improving medical services in terms of both their efficiency and availability. The mass media chipped in with a 'Plan for Britain' in an envisaged victorious scenario (Hopkinson, 1941). The same reformist sentiments were offered by the Ministry of Information in 1942, arguing that there was widespread public support for a state-funded and organised health service.

Thus the post-war Labour government, which eventually settled on a version of these forces of influence, certainly made a reality of its Fabian legacy but this was under conditions of populist and cross-party post-war reconstruction and the wider vision of what we now call 'the welfare state' put forward by a Liberal: William Beveridge; he actually eschewed the phrase 'the welfare state' and preferred instead 'the social service state' (Hennessy, 1992). Socialised medicine may have seemed like a dramatic or even revolutionary new structure in Britain, to be envied or held in suspicion internationally, but in truth it was a product of the shortcomings created by the entrenched national cultural habit of reformist muddling through. The latter was being corrected, for now, by a consensus between Liberal and Labour strategists about welfare reform.

When the first graduates of clinical psychology courses emerged in the early 1950s there was a more specific structural context that can be considered against this backdrop of the new NHS. Most of their work was to be within a subsystem that barely made it into the new health service. 'Mental illness' and 'mental deficiency' services had been quite separate from physical care in a number of ways.

These institutions were not anxiously sought and gratefully received sources of care but instead were feared or held in derision by those who were not 'mental'. They were custodial in function in the main, rather than dealing with their patients in acute states only in a true spirit of voluntarism. After many years, most residents left the institution which had contained them (in both senses of the word) in a coffin. Thus, although the work of psychologists was indeed shaped by the NHS, functionally these new employees were not like the doctors and nurses to be seen daily by the general population in local hospitals or the neighbourhood GP surgery.

Because the residents of 'mental institutions' were there under legal control (such as the Mental Treatment Act of 1930 and the Mental Deficiency Act of 1907), from the outset, clinical psychologists were to occupy occupational niches surrounded by clients who were fairly unusual. Clients were overwhelmingly poor (being unemployed and often unemployable) and their patienthood was created by their social rejection arising from perceived burden or threat. Whereas an 'inverse care law' in the NHS was soon to be noted, with the sharp elbows of the middle classes getting more than their fair share (Tudor-Hart, 1971), the poor were overrepresented in 'mental hospitals'.

Moreover, because these poorer patient groups had an immediate reputation for being chronic and unrewarding, this lessened their social worth in the general population. It would be many years (with the emergence of 'health psychology') before clinical psychologists were to become genuinely familiar with the mainstream hospital system. However, the shift towards psychiatry within district general hospitals began to break this professional association with large institutions, as did the reaction of the psychologists to the impact of medical dominance; a shift to primary care settings to escape the latter was in the offing.

A range of nationally specific structures, pertinent to the new profession's trajectory, was in place then in advance of its infancy in the 1950s. The NHS is the most obvious, which will be clear in a number of chapters in this book. But given that the 'mental illness and mental deficiency' hospitals were included in the NHS as a virtual afterthought then their peculiar organisational forms and institutional habits are pertinent.

Also, some metropolitan initiatives, which were to warrant the status of 'centres of excellence', predated the NHS. The Tavistock Clinic emerged at the end of the First World War, in part in response to the clinical and policy provocation of 'shell shock' (see chapter 3). 'Child guidance' had also emerged between the Wars (Stewart, 2013). By 1920 around 20,000 individuals deemed to be 'mentally deficient' were living in pre-NHS institutions in Britain, and their lives were shaped by families, doctors, voluntary sector bodies and local authorities, which all predated Beveridge. They left an institutional legacy that became the main setting for the work of clinical psychologists in the 1950s and 1960s (Thomson, 1998).

Intellectual legacies in postcolonial Britain

If the NHS and its prior structures are a central consideration about the incipient profession of clinical psychology, then they are not the only one. The ways of thinking common to the British population in general, and its intellectual stratum in particular, were also relevant at the outset. The British habits of pragmatism, 'common sense' and anti-intellectualism meant that to write about British 'intellectuals' even now seems stylistically odd. Nonetheless, these cultural trends needed to be defended in the academy by intellectualised justifications. Historically, these had come from native philosophers like Burke and Bacon, as well as the strong focus on empiricism in the British Isles (Bacon and Locke were English, Berkeley Irish and Hume Scottish). But a paradox of empiricism is that the pre-empirical or non-empirical aspects of life are ignored or are downgraded in importance, which means that those very aspects that are required, in order to reflect philosophically or theoretically, then fall into disuse. That disuse has been compensated for by the importing of intellectual labour in order to rejuvenate British empiricism.

The twin towers of empiricism and eugenics

In his seminal overview of this point, and focusing on the post-war period of relevance to the early days of clinical psychology, Anderson (1968) lists some of the key German, Austrian, Polish and Russian émigrés, in the mid-20th century, who were recruited into this conservative project in the British academy. They included Wittgenstein (philosophy), Berlin (political theory), Malinowski (anthropology), Namier (history), Popper (social theory) and Gombrich (aesthetics). Turning to psychology, we find Hans Eysenck and Melanie Klein as well as Sigmund and Anna Freud. More radical intellectuals, Anderson argues ('red émigrés' like those in the Frankfurt School), went to the US, whereas more conservative ('white') émigrés came to London.

Empiricism is deemed then by Anderson to have an inherent conservatism because of its tendency to validate the visible status quo and not reflect beyond its current possibilities; this is more than a distrust of ideas, it is a distrust of the imagination. Such critical reflection requires some form of idealism; hence the stronger idealist developments in Continental Europe and their more dramatic revolutionary experimentation.

Prior to that, and to support Anderson's point, Britain had never produced intellectuals capable of developing philosophical and theoretical reflections on society as a whole; it had no Marx, Weber, Durkheim, Pareto, Dilthey or Gramsci. But its reformist history, buffered by a short stretch of water in the 'English' Channel, from revolution and violent insurgency on mainland Europe, meant that it could excel in the natural and economic sciences, for example producing Darwin, Ricardo and Malthus. These could provide a self-confident rationale to move from empiricism to empirical research habits, settling on methodological rigour ('methodologism') as the main touchstone of academic legitimacy in Britain.

All of this could develop in splendid ethnocentric isolation from the navel-gazing and bold intellectual experimentation of 'the Continent' with its philosophical idealism. As *The Times* headline of 22 October 1957 noted: 'Heavy fog in Channel – Continent cut off'. The fog of continental philosophical reflection and theory building might get in the way of British pragmatic and methodological priorities. And yet, without theory building, academic respectability for those priorities could be dented: hence the needed list of émigrés noted by Anderson above.

The emergent habits of British clinical psychology may now start to make sense in that longer cultural context. And, adding to that trend of the émigré rejuvenation of the conservative empiricist tradition, a South African cohort came to London in the middle of the 20th century. One of these was Monte Shapiro who from 1947 ran the clinical course at the Institute of Psychiatry (though Eysenck was head of the psychology department). He migrated in the 1930s and came through the war. May Davidson was another key leader who came from South Africa to study at University College London (UCL) before the war. Others like Stanley ('Jack') Rachman and Vic Meyer, both key figures in the development of early British behaviour therapy, came after the war. For a while even Joseph Wolpe, the new doyen of methodological behaviourism from psychiatry, who developed systematic desensitisation, worked at the Maudsley. The socialist and liberal backgrounds of these workers were aligned with the reformist expectation of a 'technological fix' for social problems. This top-down and engineered form of social progress of the 1950s and 1960s preceded later progressive forces from new social movements such as psychiatric survivors, feminists and Black activists (Rogers & Pilgrim, 1991).

The other important intellectual tradition in Britain was eugenics. If the NHS has been the elephant in the room for British clinical psychology in organisational terms, eugenics was its equivalent as a native political philosophy. Without it British clinical psychology would not have started where it was but somewhere else. And where it started was with slavery and colonialism in 19th-century British life. The father of British, and what was to become global, eugenics, was Francis Galton, who bequeathed a Chair in Eugenics to UCL in 1911, which was taken up by Karl Pearson. Pearson was a mathematician and he developed the bulk of what are now the routine methods of 'behavioural statistics' that undergird the British tradition of psychometrics in clinical psychology (Burt, 1912; Pearson, 1904; Spearman, 1904).

Socialism was characteristic of the white South Africans who came to Britain in the mid-20th century, but earlier at the turn of that century many British Fabians and feminists were eugenicists. This was a period before the dark twist of Nazism, when a declining colonial Europe and a (largely) receptive expanding capitalist economy in the US were wary of the impact of 'degeneracy'. In the first quarter of the 20th century, under the intellectual guidance of the Galtonian lineage, willingly waiting in the wings was psychological science. 'Psychometrics' and the 'psychology of individual differences' could now become the technical wing of eugenics to scientifically assess the social, moral and fiscal threat or burden of psychological deviance to the 'British race'.

As Bashford (2013) notes, by the end of the Second World War Britain had enjoyed half a century of eugenics bound up with colonial assumptions abroad and fear of degeneracy of the lower orders at home. Eugenics was an ingrained cultural theme in British life, which had been used to explain both insanity and idiocy since the Victorian period and had guided health and social policy developments (e.g. Down, 1866; Galton, 1881; Mott, 1912; Thomson, 1998). For example, William Beveridge was a proud member of the Eugenics Society (renamed the Galton Institute in 1989), as were Hans Eysenck and Aubrey Lewis at the Institute of Psychiatry.

The racialised postcolonial legacy within British clinical psychology

British clinical psychology developed, indeed it thrived, as part of a social democratic political agenda to ensure free health care to all. At the same time, its workforce, theories, research and services assumed the superiority of indigenous white British people, intellectually and in 'psychological literacy', over New Commonwealth arrivals. The latter came in the 1950s to 1960s from Britain's former colonies in the Caribbean and India, and later from Bangladesh in the early 1970s.

Clinical psychology was anything but 'for all'. Its native version of psychology framed clients and prospective recruits from these minority groups as being intellectually inferior, culturally backward, emotionally limited and prone to 'somatisation', thus stifling the emergence of critical perspectives on 'race' until much later in the mid-1980s. British psychology to all intents and purposes has been seen by the psychologists, and by minority ethnic people in the UK, largely as Eurocentric 'white psychology for white folks' (e.g. Fatimilehin & Coleman, 1998; Howitt & Owusu-Bempah, 1994; McInnis, 2002) and one which pathologises Black people (e.g. Adetimole et al., 2005; Patel et al., 2000) and carefully guards its exclusivity (Fleming & Daiches, 2005).

Within mainstream British clinical psychology, there has been a relative silence about the indigenous history of slavery and then colonialism. And yet clinical psychology, as an applied wing of an academic discipline, has operated within that very postcolonial native context. The latter has included second- and third-generation New Commonwealth immigrants and those of Irish heritage, as well as the presence of asylum seekers and refugees fleeing from war, conflict and persecution. For psychology and other related disciplines two discursive trends began to emerge in response to postcolonial migration and the response of intolerance and racism in British society. The first was one of assimilation, then multiculturalism and recently that of 'embracing and celebrating diversity'. The second was the antiracism of the 1980s and 'tackling institutional racism' within the NHS and other public bodies (since the 1999 Macpherson Report). These two trends reflected liberal adaptive and more critical or oppositional voices in the profession respectively, which together produced the current contested and unresolved 'equality and diversity' legacy.

The first serious and collective challenge to the absence of a critical perspective on racism and cultural blindness and insensitivity within the profession came in the late 1980s. A small group of clinical psychologists formed, including Asad Abbas, Herby Pillay, Aruna Mahtani, Zenobia Nadirshaw, Afreen Huq, Iyabo Fatimilehin, Barbara Daniels, Waseem Alladin, Sue Holland and Nimisha Patel, and requested recognition from the Division of Clinical Psychology (DCP) as a legitimate group with professional and scientific aims. The recognition of this group as a special interest group (SIG) within the DCP came in 1990.

In parallel, a wider multidisciplinary group of health and social care professionals (including clinical psychologists) and service users had formed the Transcultural Psychiatry Society UK, which together with the 'Race' and Culture Special Interest Group in Clinical Psychology (later recognised as a faculty but closed down by the DCP in 2014), fuelled a movement within the profession, and within mental health more widely. This challenged the historical legacy of eugenics. It also drew attention to services that were inappropriate, inaccessible or discriminatory towards clients and staff from minority ethnic backgrounds and disproportionately controlling in relation to black and minority ethnic people, in particular towards African Caribbean men. The continued relative absence of Britain's increasingly diverse and multicultural population within clinical psychology services, and in the profession (there were, in 1989, around 15 clinical psychologists nationally, who defined themselves as from minority ethnic backgrounds, largely from South Asia, Africa and the Caribbean), remained for some 20 years.

Charges of Eurocentricity and racism against the norms of British clinical psychology, in relation to its training curriculum and dominant forms of theory, practices and services grew. However, clinical psychology training remained relatively unchanged and unresponsive to how racism and other forms of structured oppression impacted on the psychological well-being of people. There were persistent calls from the 'Race' and Culture Special Interest Group in the 1990s to revise accreditation criteria for clinical psychology training courses, supported by publications (e.g. Patel et al., 2000).

In the 1990s, the DCP responded in a number of positive ways to these criticisms by adopting recommendations and a key text drafted by the special interest group, calling for a profession which was more accessible to people from black and minority ethnic backgrounds and more able to acknowledge, understand and address social context, racism and culture in clinical psychology practice. Changes were made to DCP professional documents, with contributions from the special interest group, which included changed accreditation criteria for training programmes, changed professional practice guidelines and a briefing paper written by the SIG steering committee. The profession remained still largely unchanged, its workforce and trainees being from the white majority ethnic population, its psychological theories, methods and practice predominantly Eurocentric.

Concerns about access to professional training programmes, and the 'lack of representation' continued (e.g. Williams et al., 2006), but were never named as discrimination within the profession. These concerns became more pressing in the context of the emergent Equality Act in 2010 in the UK, which established the obligations placed on public bodies. In this context, the profession adopted the language of 'equality and diversity' – without also acknowledging inequality and discrimination within the profession. Accordingly, there was an increasing focus on 'diversifying' the profession, by seeking ways to increase access to it by 'BMEs' (used to refer to black and minority ethnic people) (e.g. Turpin & Coleman, 2010). The grouping together of all immigrants and subsequent generations, refugee people, asylum seekers and those 'with difference' (largely colour) with the homogenising acronym of 'BME' drew criticism from psychologists in that amalgam group. This criticism extended to commentaries on the continued eugenic legacy in British psychology and the abiding impact of colonialism in the profession's difficulty in naming racism, not just in relation to recruitment but also in its theories, methods, practices, professional training and forms of service (e.g. Patel, 2010).

Summary: British cultural life in the mid-20th century as a context for the new profession

As E.P. Thompson noted when writing on the cultural history of Britain, with its anglocentric core, the lives of people were played out on 'this empirical island, anchored off Europe'. In the decades after the Second World War, Britain was a nation that had 'lost confidence in itself' and it had inherited an intellectual culture which 'for so long has been insular, amateurish, crassly empirical, self-enclosed and so resistant to international discourse that the damage done is probably irreparable' (Thompson, 1978, p.105).

Thompson, unlike other critical historians, preferred the notion of an 'empirical idiom', as the feature of British life, rather than 'empiricism' as a formal ideology (Thompson, 1965; cf. Anderson, 1968). He may have had a point; empiricism is a philosophical guide for sure-footed academic inquiry but an empirical idiom has been a diffuse feature of British life, including that of the popular consciousness of ordinary people and the orientation of British writers, such as William Hazlitt, George Orwell and, latterly, Ian McEwan.

British society in the post-war years, when the profession of clinical psychology started, as noted earlier, was culturally conservative, ethnocentric, pragmatic, empiricist and eugenic in outlook. But the muddling-through reformism it required and achieved under conditions of reconstruction and imperial turbulence was unevenly played out. London, then as now, dominated the national scene but life went on in a more diversified way in the British Isles. For example, the Scottish traditions of sustained and industrious academicism in the natural and medical sciences were important in shaping goals of the 'technological fix' favoured by British young graduates in the 1950s. The idea that social and psychological problems could be subjected to rational and scientific diagnosis and rectification was commonplace in this period and set a trend – the most recent example being that of Layard's Improving Access to Psychological Therapies (IAPT) initiative.

As far as clinical psychology was concerned this enthusiasm for the technological fix was to be inflected by a number of social processes. First, how was it to position itself in relation to medical dominance in Britain? Second, which version of psychological science should be developed and asserted? Third, was it sufficient to simply be scientific in psychology or should the applications of that science be formally stated in bids for legitimacy within the employment context of the NHS? The fine grain activities in the emerging profession in the 1950s reflected ways of answering these broad questions and is reported in several chapters in this book.

In other words, while the content of the profession was being worked out within an internal logic (of, say, psychometric testing), that logic was being shaped by national traditions and immediate and sometimes parochial opportunities or requirements. Medicine was there to be mollified or challenged (to eat the crumbs off its table or take a slice of its cake). Native eugenic and empiricist tropes in British psychology were being irritated by the contingent post-war presence of psychoanalysis in North London created by one part of the Jewish diaspora (see chapter 15). The NHS as a monopoly employer required that the profession defined itself as part of a workforce, not just as a free-floating applied outcrop of academia.

The legacy of the 1960s counter-culture: a 'disagreement of psychologists'

The British cultural context of the mid-20th century set the scene then for British clinical psychology. As it grew in numbers and confidence during the 1960s and 1970s new particular features emerged in these conditions of possibility. In chapter 15 Pilgrim and Parry describe the emergence of a co-presence of behaviourism, psychoanalysis and humanism within, or affecting, the growing profession. The profession contained mixed views about how to theorise the relationship between experience and behaviour and how to turn that theory into particular client formulations. The arguments were overwhelmingly for a while about theories and models; in other words the content of clinical psychology was a matter of focused disputation. Loose associations of psychologists and non-psychologists like the

Psychology and Psychotherapy Association, set up in 1973, advanced the case for psychology adopting diverse intellectual resources. Also, the counter-cultural aspects of this period (including Marxism and 'antipsychiatry') were reflected in the production of journals like *Red Rat* that reinforced and represented these wider expressions of political dissent in the period.

However, during the 1970s peaceful coexistence with occasional squabbles characterised this point about the content of clinical psychology. Psychologists generally agreed to disagree and a new collective noun emerged: 'a disagreement of psychologists'. The eclecticism of second-wave cognitive behaviour therapy (to be stretched further and later by its 'third wave') was one partial resolution; a sort of syncretism might be possible analogous to that found in religious movements. The mutual tolerance of psychodynamic and humanistic psychologies was to be another symptom of this picture in the 1970s. If psychological theory is considered independently of its particular context then such disagreements and compromise resolutions are inevitable. This is for the very reason that the human sciences perennially exist in the ambiguous spaces between the epistemological planes of the *a priori* sciences (like maths), the *a posteriori* sciences (like biology) and philosophical reflection (Foucault, 1973). To disagree is the normality of the human sciences and today that contestation is both evident and the focus of critical reflection for some clinical psychologists (Cromby et al. 2014; Pilgrim, 2015).

By the end of the 1970s this truism about universal contestation in human science was to find a particular national context in Britain. Not only had it inherited the strong national pattern set by eugenics and empiricism noted above, it had a particular political system: parliamentary democracy. In 1979 the post-war consensus about a cherished welfare state stabilised by Keynesian economics of public investment and gradual growth was disrupted by the election of Margaret Thatcher.

One aspect of Thatcher's new regime, apart from monetarism, was her reform of the NHS, the organisational framework for the great majority of activity in clinical psychology. The NHS was now to be managed, not just administered, and this reflected a contradictory policy with strong resonances still today. It was being both marketised and bureaucratised under Thatcher, creating what is now known in management science as the 'New Public Management' (NPM) model (Pollitt & Bouckaert, 2011). And if the whole system was to be managed then clinical psychology was to be no exception.

Managerialism at the start of the 1980s was defined structurally by the outcome of the Trethowan Report (see chapter 5). In simple terms this meant creating a managed hierarchy of accountability within the profession, with 'area psychologists' being responsible for a part of the clinical psychology workforce on their geographical patch, defined by area health authorities. This geographical definition of structures was to be precarious because reforms of the NHS were soon to alter boundaries. For example, the tier of area health authorities disappeared, leaving smaller and more localised district health authorities (DHAs) as the main functional managed unit. In turn they disappeared with the development of primary care trusts at the turn of this century. However, these geographical revisions did not make managerialism itself an ephemeral aspect of the profession. The logic of NPM carried on like a juggernaut and was reflected in all publicly funded parts of the

British welfare state and in all tiers of education until relatively recently, when it has been augmented and modified by digital governance: the use of computerised systems of surveillance and staff regulation (Dunleavy et al., 2006).

As far as the profession was concerned the first evidence that it was entering this new world of NPM appeared in the mid-1980s in two ways. First some clinical psychologists were intent on becoming general managers in mental health and learning disability services. These were not posts managing clinical psychologists but managing service units (e.g. a mental health service in an area). Second, the DCP agreed to cooperate at a national level with a request from the Department of Health to review the role of psychologists in the NHS. Bearing in mind that only a decade earlier the Trethowan review had been commissioned, this suggested that under the new managerialism, the profession was, according to civil servants and their political masters, in need of further scrutiny.

A final point to note about the legacy of the 1960s was that clinical psychology swelled in a period of second-wave feminism with all of the contradictions that implied. In the post-war period child work was conducted in the main by women and adult mental health work by men. Today the profession is numerically largely female, across all specialisms, and recruitment to training is overwhelmingly of young women (at the time of writing about 85 per cent). This may reflect a wider shift in the health professions, with men eschewing interest in paid caring roles, compared to the past. For example, both human medicine and veterinary medicine were dominated numerically by male applicants in the 1970s but this is no longer the case.

After the 1970s when second-wave feminism peaked, some clinical psychologists offered critiques of both the content of their profession and its patriarchal forms of leadership and knowledge (Nicolson & Ussher, 1992). Some male psychologists in the same period bemoaned the weakening in status and salary justification such a shift to a female dominance would risk (Crawford, 1989). Linking this point about gender balance to other social group memberships, it is clear that the incoming cohorts are predominantly white, female and in their twenties. This poses a challenge for the profession in terms of its weak demographic mirroring to its main client groups.

Conclusion

British culture operating in the middle of the 20th century, when clinical psychology emerged as a profession, was characterised by a number of abiding features, many inherited from the past, which were to have a notable impact. E.P. Thompson's allusion to 'this empirical island, anchored off Europe' gives us a feel for the game about making sense of what is British about British clinical psychology. It is also true that the peculiarities of the British context, for example its empiricism, its faith in eugenics, its policy of 'muddling through' and its obdurate postcolonial casual white racism, were embedded in some universal processes. Psychology, the world over, is contested and so the diverse character of British clinical psychology has been in part about that universal feature of epistemological contestation. However, this chapter has summarised some main features of that universal contestation in the particular cultural and political context of mid-20th-century Britain, when clinical psychology emerged on its shores.

A final particular point to note in conclusion is that as a profession clinical psychology in Britain has changed with the contours, over time, of its embedding organisation, the NHS. Today that linkage has become so precarious that the future of the profession may now need to be understood with reference to newly emerging and maybe quite distinct organisational forms. But from a historical perspective, it is impossible to understand the fate and character of British clinical psychology without understanding the origins, intentions, workings and ethos of the NHS.

References

Adetimole, F., Afuape, T. & Vara, R. (2005). The impact of racism on the experience of training on a clinical psychology course: Reflections from three Black trainees. *Clinical Psychology Forum, 48,* 11–15.

Anderson, P. (1968). Components of the national culture. *New Left Review, 1*(50), 3–57.

Bashford, A. (2013). *Imperial hygiene: A critical history of colonialism, nationalism and public health.* Basingstoke: Palgrave.

Burt, C.L. (1912). The inheritance of mental characters. *Eugenic Review, IV,* 1–33.

Crawford, D. (1989). The future of clinical psychology: Whither or wither? *Clinical Psychology Forum, 20,* 16–17.

Cromby, J., Harper, D. & Reevey, P. (2014). *Psychology, mental health and distress.* Basingstoke: Palgrave.

Down, J.L.M. (1866). *Observations on an ethnic classification of idiots. Lectures and reports from the London Hospital.* London: The London Hospital.

Dunleavy, P., Margetts, H., Bastow, S. & Tinkler, J. (2006). New public management is dead – long live digital governance. *Journal of Public Administration Research and Theory, 16(*3), 467–494.

Fatimilehin, I. & Coleman, P.G. (1998). Appropriate services for African-Caribbean families: Views from one community. *Clinical Psychology Forum, 111,* 6–11.

Fleming, I. & Daiches, A. (2005). Psychologists against racism. *Clinical Psychology Forum, 48,* 7–10.

Foucault, M. (1973). *The order of things: An archaeology of the human sciences.* New York: Viking Books.

Galton, F. (1881). *Natural Inheritance.* London: Macmillan

Hennessy, P. (1992). *Never again: Britain 1945–1951.* London: Jonathan Cape.

Hopkinson, T. (Ed.) (1941, 4 January). A plan for Britain. *Picture Post, 10*(1).

Howitt, D. & Owusu-Bempah, J. (1994). *The racism of psychology.* Hemel Hempstead: Harvester Wheatsheaf.

McInnis, E. (2002). Institutional racism in the NHS and clinical psychology? Taking note of MacPherson. *Journal of Critical Psychology, Counselling and Psychotherapy, 2*(3), 164–170.

Mott, F. (1912). *Heredity and eugenics in relation to insanity.* London: Eugenics Society.

Nicolson, P. & Ussher, J. (1992). *Feminism and clinical psychology.* London: Routledge.

Patel, N. (2010). Plus ça change plus c'est la même chose? Invited commentary on Turpin and Coleman (2010) Clinical psychology and diversity: progress and continuing challenges. *Journal of Psychology Learning and Teaching, 9*(2), 30–31.

Patel, N., Bennett, E., Dennis, M., et al. (Eds.) (2000). *Clinical psychology, 'race' and culture: A training manual.* Chichester: Wiley-Blackwell.

Pearson, K. (1904). On the inheritance of mental and moral characteristics in man. *Biometrika, IV,* 265–303.

Pilgrim, D. (2015). *Understanding mental health: A critical realist exploration.* London: Routledge.

Pollitt, C. & Bouckaert, G. (2011). *Public management reform: A comparative analysis.* Oxford: Oxford University Press.

Rogers, A. & Pilgrim, D. (1991). 'Pulling down churches' – accounting for the British Mental Health Users' Movement. *Sociology of Health and Illness, 13*(2), 129–148.

Taylor, A.J.P. (1965). *English History 1914–1945.* Oxford: Oxford University Press.

Spearman, C.E. (1904). General intelligence objectively determined and measured. *American Journal of Psychology, 15,* 201–299.

Stewart, J. (2013). *Child guidance in Britain, 1918–1955: The dangerous age of childhood.* London: Pickering and Chatto.

Thompson, E.P. (1965). The peculiarities of the English. In R. Miliband & J. Saville (Eds.), *The Socialist Register 1965* (pp.311–362).

Thompson, E.P. (1978). *The poverty of theory and other essays.* London: Merlin Press.

Thomson, M. (1998). *The problem of mental deficiency: Eugenics, democracy, and social policy in Britain c.1870–1959.* Oxford: Oxford University Press.

Tudor-Hart, J. (1971). The inverse care law. *The Lancet, 297,* 405–412.

Turpin, G. & Coleman, G. (2010). Clinical psychology and diversity: Progress and continuing challenges. *Journal of Psychology Learning and Teaching, 9*(2), 17–27.

Webster, C. (1988). *The health services since the war: Vol. I. Problems of health care: The National Health Service before 1957.* London: HMSO.

Williams, P.E., Turpin, G. & Hardy, G. (2006). Clinical psychology service provision and ethnic diversity within the UK: A review of the literature. *Clinical Psychology and Psychotherapy, 13,* 324–338.

Chapter 5 Professional organisation and communication

John Hall & Michael Wang

Introduction

This chapter traces the ways in which clinical psychologists in Britain have organised themselves professionally. From an initial meeting in 1942 the first practitioner psychologists created structures within the British Psychological Society (BPS) which led first to a committee of professional psychologists, then separate divisions of professional psychologists for England and Scotland in 1960, and then to the formation of the Division of Clinical Psychology (DCP) of the BPS in 1966. The chapter outlines the ways in which the DCP and other professional structures have addressed both strategic objectives, and supported members in the challenges they have faced, demonstrated by the two examples of the Trethowan Report and the 'New Ways of Working' initiative. It illustrates the continuing professional preoccupations of clinical psychologists, and the complexities of the internal structures and processes of both the BPS and the DCP.

There is a particular challenge in writing historically and engagingly about a member organisation such as the DCP over several decades. The amount of written material available is vast, including minutes of the main and subsidiary committees and the associated papers, and all the communications sent out to members. The chapter draws from both documents and the recollections of former officers of the DCP, bringing the work of the Division to life.

The pioneers: the work of the Committee of Professional Psychologists (Mental Health)

By 1934 there were an increasing number of members of the BPS who both possessed psychological qualifications, and who were working as psychologists in a professional capacity. The BPS set up a 'Professional Status Committee' to inquire into this issue, and recommended the creation of a 'professional' register, which however would have been nothing more than a list, as being on the register would not have given any idea of the skills of the psychologist.

In 1939 the Feversham Report (Feversham Committee, 1939) recommended that the existing voluntary organisations for mental health should be merged, and at the outbreak of war the three main organisations were amalgamated to form a provisional national association, the National Association of Mental Health (NAMH), heavily funded by the Ministry of Health, which directly employed psychologists working with children in a number of settings. At the NAMH conference in December 1942 the psychologists attending the conference took the opportunity to arrange 'a sectional meeting of psychologists', the first recorded meeting of a group of practising British psychologists for professional purposes. They continued to meet informally, and were first known as the Fildes Committee, from the chair, Dr Lucy Fildes, and were exclusively educational psychologists (CPP(MH) minute, 8 October 1949).

During their meetings in 1943, the suggestion arose that they should form a group within the BPS, and the BPS Council agreed on 4 September 1943 to create the Committee of Professional Psychologists (Mental Health) (CPP(MH)). All psychologists eligible to join formed the Committee proper, but the Minute Books (the main source for this section of the chapter) record the actions of the executive committee, or subcommittee, of CPP(MH). The first formal meeting of the Executive took place on 4 December 1943, and their first act was to inform 'the provisional Council for Mental Health, the Board of Education, the Ministry of Health, and the Local Government Office', of their existence. This set the scene for the negotiations over the next few years between the executive committee of CPP(MH), the BPS Council, through which all formal initiatives had to be channelled, and the government agencies concerned, which were the then Board of Education and Ministry of Health. By the end of their first full year of existence the subcommittee had met eight times – a very high rate of meetings under wartime conditions – and prepared a number of memoranda, which have not survived. Clinical and educational psychologists shared a common organisational history at this point, and emphasis is given in this account to the implications for clinical psychologists of the work of the CPP(MH).

As the possibility of legislation for a national healthcare system became apparent during 1944, and as the NHS Bill was passing through Parliament in 1946, this mix of threat and opportunity absorbed most of the committee's energies. By the last committee meeting of 1947, Grace Rawlings had been invited as a delegate of the Association of Scientific Workers (AScW), the trade union the psychologists had joined, to a conference at the Ministry of Health. In March 1948 an offer was made by the Ministry so that 'psychologists could set up their own (Whitley) committee, which would have representation on Professional and Technical Council Section A'. Although representation of psychologists on Whitley was technically through AScW, as members of the CPP(MH) executive committee were also the AScW representatives no problems arose.

At the 12 June 1948 meeting it was reported that the North West Metropolitan Regional Hospital Board had asked for psychologists to attend meetings of their Psychiatry Advisory Committee – the first record of an invitation of this sort. One co-option to the subcommittee was of a Miss Mellon, 'representing psychologists working in hospitals and other institutions' – the first tacit recognition of psychologists working in those settings. At the meeting on 5 February 1949 there was a long discussion on 'whether other professional committees should be formed within the BPS, or whether our committee's qualifications for admittance should be revised in such a way as to admit the majority of psychologists working in the NHS', raising the possibility that a separate adult committee could have been established.

The 1950 AGM of the BPS recommended the co-option of workers in the adult field to CPP(MH), and the Council approved a subcommittee within the main committee for psychologists working with adults – a cumbersome arrangement. 1952 began with a key event: the first Whitley circular relating to clinical psychologists (P.T.A. Circular No.10) was issued (see chapter 1 for details of the Whitley system). At the first meeting of 1954 on 23 January, it was agreed that the possible regrouping of the committee into health and education sections would be raised at the AGM. At the 12 November meeting a proposal from Dr Gunzburg was received, asking that Monyhull Hospital in Birmingham, for 'mental defectives', be recognised as a training centre: it was agreed as a matter of principle not to recognise single client-group courses.

On 23 June 1956 there was the first note of a proposal that CPP(MH) should become a 'Division' of the Society, rather than the previously considered names of an Association, or Section, of Professional Psychologists. A special working party on the psychologist's role in treatment had been set up, and a letter from Dr Desai was noted at the meeting on 27 April 1957, in which he asked if a special working party was needed to discuss 'the use of conditioning techniques' – the first mention in the CPP(MH) minutes regarding what would become behaviour therapy.

The 1957 set of Whitley circulars (HM (57) 81 and Part II of PTA circular 52) for the first time approved seven named training courses (see chapter 7). In addition to these centres, seven other hospitals at Bristol, Sutton in Surrey, Warwick, Leeds, Manchester, Wickford in Essex, and Oxford were considered to have 'the necessary senior members of staff and facilities' for training. By 1959 there were 147 members of the Adult Section of the CPP(MH): of those 26 gave addresses at hospitals outside London, including psychiatric hospitals (such as the Central Hospital at Warwick), mental handicap hospitals (such as Little Plumstead Hospital in Norfolk) and general hospitals and neurological units (such as the Royal Infirmary at Manchester). There were signs that clinical psychology was establishing a toehold outside the South-East of England.

A number of regional committees had been set up around the country in the late 1950s, with a particular interest in the organisation of regional in-service training. Mahesh Desai, the secretary of the South West Metropolitan RHB committee, was dealing with a large amount of correspondence about the organisation of regional committees, and in April 1960 he convened a meeting at Hull, which agreed to set up a Co-ordinating Committee of Senior Psychologists (CCSP) in the NHS, with two representatives from each region, which as it was outside the BPS did not need to consider matters of concern to educational psychologists. Every NHS region eventually set up a regional committee, except for two where there were too few psychologists (Desai, 1966).

By 1960 the Council of the BPS had at last agreed formal rules for the formation of two Divisions of Professional Psychologists (Educational and Clinical), one for England (EDPP) and one for Scotland (BPS, 1960a, 1960b), committing the BPS irretrievably to be both a professional body as well as a learned society. The continuing mix of both educational and NHS concerns made it obvious that a reorganisation of the structure of the central bodies was required, and so both the English Division of Professional Psychologists and the CCSP agreed that a new Division for clinical psychology only was required. The formal proposal to form the Division was approved at a General Meeting of the BPS on 17 December 1965 and, remarkably quickly for once, the first meeting of the Division took place at the University of Sussex on 10 January 1966 (BPS, 1967, pp.66–68).

At long last a separate Division of Clinical Psychology for the whole UK had arrived, marking the parting of the ways of educational and clinical psychology. Comparing the minutes of the CPP(MH) with the minutes of the BPS Council over the same period, it is noticeable how at a number of points the BPS Council delayed making decisions, and delayed implementation of agreed decisions. Dr

J.P.S. Robertson attended the Council, at their meeting on 12 February 1966, the first time clinical psychologists were directly represented on it.

The structures and functioning of the Division

The first officers of the Division were Dr Mahesh Desai as chair, Dr Pat Robertson as honorary secretary, and Tony Black as honorary assistant secretary, with nine elected and co-opted committee members, and representatives of both the BPS Council and the Educational and Child Psychology Division. The BPS Council elected 159 'foundation' members of the new Division on 8 October 1966. There was plenty of work to do. From 1967 the Committee was preparing evidence for the Society to submit to the Zuckerman Committee on the hospital scientific service. Annual DCP delegate conferences took place at the BPS Annual Conference, and separate summer schools took place annually: in 1968 the lead courses were on repertory grid techniques, computing and on psychophysiology. As in any such organisation, the Division soon developed a number of sub-systems. The training committee continued from the previous EDPP, joined later by a sub-committee concerned with 'clinical services'. By 1968 there were seven branches of the Division, and the Sheffield Committee of Senior Psychologists had become a sub-committee of the regional psychiatric advisory committee.

> *In 1970, just two years after qualifying, I wrote an article in the BPS Bulletin derived from a mini-project my then boss in Norwich, David Castell, had asked me to conduct to work out how many more psychologists were needed in Norfolk (Hall, 1970). This article, primitive as it now looks, was sufficiently daring for me to be co-opted on to the DCP Committee in that year. I had no idea how 'young' the Division then was, but I have very clear memories of climbing the rickety stairs in the old BPS offices in Albemarle Street in London, with the meeting chaired by the ever-smoking May Davidson, and Don Bannister making an immediate impact with his dry wit and incisive comments.* (John Hall)

Members of the Division asked for action on a wide range of issues, and that raised the question of who was to do the work. At the first 1972 meeting of the Division Committee they wanted more Division members to be involved in the affairs of the Division, so it was agreed to set up a number of working parties, membership of each being drawn from regional branches, to save travelling costs (NL 1972 No 9: 1). The Northern Ireland Branch was invited to devise a recruiting campaign for the Division, and the Birmingham branch was invited to produce a comprehensive list of tests and equipment for departments of clinical psychology. At the Open Meeting of the Division in 1983, immediately after the formal AGM, concern was expressed at the 'disappointingly low attendance' at both meetings. In 1992 Ian Wilkinson from Darlington was concerned that 'DCP and MSF [the then incarnation of the trade union] members are spread far and wide, often in small numbers or isolated…and taking on representational roles…and I often find myself in the position of having to give an opinion about the views of members…without any real factual basis' (Wilkinson, 1992, pp.33–34).

A linked concern was achieving a working balance between the central committee, and the range of standing committees, working parties for specific projects, and geographical branches. In 1994 the Yorkshire branch reviewed the relationship between their main groups, which were the regional advisory committee (mostly the more senior psychologists), the postqualification training committee, and the local special interest groups (SPIGs). They completely restructured their branch committee, with more SPIG involvement in organising meetings, with the principle objective of increasing member involvement (Fraise, 1994).

This illustrates a perennial problem for the Division, and for all of the subsystems, where most of the work has been done by a few people, usually in their own time, with some individuals devoting hours a week over many years to the work of the Division. The load on senior officers was heavy. Up to 1985 the chairperson was elected for a three-year term (see Appendix 2), but that year the rules were changed in an attempt to spread the load, so that a person elected would serve one year as chair-elect, one year as chair, and the following year as vice-chair, so building in some continuity in the senior officers. Interestingly this policy was reversed in 2006, and Peter Kinderman was the first chair to be able to be funded part-time for secondment from his employer.

An added complexity began in 1974, when the BPS Council agreed to the formation of two subordinate Boards to the Council, the Scientific Affairs Board and the Professional Affairs Board (PAB), with a system of cross-membership between Boards and Divisions, both to take the load off the Council itself and to encourage collaboration between the different Divisions of applied psychologists. The PAB held its first meeting in January 1974, with May Davidson as the first chair, and, for example, assumed responsibility for the supervision of the assessment of postgraduate training courses in educational and clinical psychology.

The challenge of growth

As the Division grew, with a growing number of branches and special interest groups, all of them having a place on the Division Committee, the Division Committee itself grew. The Division Committee of 6 February 1978 had an extended discussion of the problems that had arisen: 'the Division Committee had all the obligations of the Royal Colleges but with only a fraction of the College's resources' (DCP committee minute 929). The implications were that the Division members might have to pay more to have full-time staff, or meet less frequently, or have a small committee of six to seven people, backed up by a Joint Standing Committee. The honorary secretary's role was 'unmanageable by anyone in full-time employment', as it involved not only taking minutes, but also engaging in day-to-day correspondence and attending a number of meetings. Over 20 years later the problem had not been solved. In 1999 concern was expressed about the unwieldy size of the full committee: the DCP committee meeting on 13 September 1999 was, unusually, nearly a full house with 32 clinical psychologists present from the Executive Committee, Division branches, and Special Interest Groups. This was the situation Mike Wang inherited when he began to attend the DCP Committee.

> *I began to attend DCP committees as Chair Elect in March 2001. What was immediately apparent was the unwieldiness of the committee structure. It felt like walking in treacle. There was a 'full committee' which attempted to be representative of everyone and everything, with more than 40 members. Then there was the Executive Committee which attempted to be strategic and decision-making, but this too comprised at least 30 people, although intended as a senior*

> *subset of the larger full committee. It was clear that neither committee was providing the kind of strategic leadership of the profession needed.* (Michael Wang)

The decision was taken to reorganise the committee structure, and a management consultancy was commissioned to provide some options and recommendations for change (DCP Executive 1/7/02 minute 3.14; Stirling & Eliatamby, 2003). This included the relationship between the DCP and wider BPS, and a survey of the DCP membership offered a number of options, including 'divorce' and the status quo. The majority of members wished the DCP to remain a part of the BPS but with a more 'federated' relationship – in other words, greater autonomy. The deliberations, management consultant reports and opinion surveys culminated in a set of proposals, overseen by Dorothy Fielding as the next DCP chair, for a new, slimmed-down DCP structure with an Executive Committee of only five people, and two new Boards were created, one dealing with professional standards of practice, and one leading on membership services, with an emphasis on what the DCP could provide for individual members. To support this new structure extensive negotiations took place with the newly appointed BPS Chief Executive, Tim Cornford, about increasing support resources for the Division. It was agreed both to significantly increase the number of support staff in the BPS Leicester office and to arrange 'back-fill' payments for the time members were spending on DCP Executive work.

Another action taken at the same time was the creation of a managers' faculty within the Division. A joint meeting took place in 2001 between the Yorkshire and North Eastern Region's Advisory Groups about the absence of any national representative structure for the most senior clinical psychologists within the DCP. Tim Cate and Mike Wang agreed to propose a Managers' Faculty, as a group intended to provide mutual support for heads of service and an opportunity for the DCP to make use of its most senior and experienced members. The inaugural meeting took place at Leeds City Football Club ground at Elland Road with the keynote speaker being Anthony Sheehan, at that time Chief Executive of the National Institute for Mental Health (England).

Publications and communications

In July 1948 the central BPS had improved communications with members by starting a new *Quarterly Bulletin of the British Psychological Society*. It was for all members of the BPS and included short articles, as well as news of appointments of members to new jobs, conference proceedings and obituaries, and it continued for many years to include articles of interest primarily to clinical psychologists. By the second issue of *The Bulletin* there was already an article describing the Psychology Department of the Maudsley Hospital (Crown, 1948). *The Bulletin* became *The Psychologist* in 1988, with a larger and glossier format.

CPP(MH) did not issue a regular newsletter, but the EDPP produced a bulletin during its short six-year life. From the beginning of the Clinical Division, a regular Division *Newsletter* was produced, first cyclostyled on both sides of one sheet of pale blue foolscap-size paper. Issue number 1 was dated February 1967, and the newsletter was produced regularly, with a two-year gap from early 1969. The editor from 1971, John Pinschof, reviewed the major issues of the day, seeing training as a 'constant concern'. Early issues gave information about, for example, the proposed new British Intelligence Scale for Adults, and in January 1968 informed members of the evidence submitted to the Zuckerman Committee. A consortium of editors from Cardiff took over between 1974 and 1981, before Penny Spinks and Jenny West took over. The *Newsletter* reached number 50 by 1985, and that anniversary was celebrated by a special issue (for December 1985), itself of historical interest, with a section on 'Clinical Psychology: Past, Present and Future'.

In 1986 the title was changed to *Clinical Psychology Forum* (CPF), its present title. Craig Newnes, who was editor for 18 years, has been the longest serving editor, moving CPF to a monthly production in 1991, and working with a collective of associate editors. He established an editorial policy semi-independent of the DCP Executive, providing over the years a rich mix of information, articles on service development, and frustration-relieving critical and humorous articles. Graham Turpin has been the most recent CPF editor, holding the office for seven years. Apart from CPF, there is a newsletter for DCP Scotland and for the Special Interest Group on the Elderly. Repeated membership surveys have indicated that CPF is usually the most popular reason why people retain membership of the Division.

The most recent DCP guide to publications (DCP, 2011) illustrates how different categories of other publications have developed, including good practice guidelines, briefing papers, and occasional papers. The briefing papers are often substantial works of scholarship, written by authors with national and international reputations. One example is *Recent Advances in Understanding Mental Illness and Psychotic Experiences,* first published in 2000 (BPS, 2000) and since updated, intended for mental heath service users and mental health professionals and interested members of the public, and providing a guide to the nature of mental illness, causes and treatments, derived from psychological research. There are also the memoranda produced in response to specific calls for evidence from government and other public bodies, one of the most important examples being the evidence given by the BPS to the Trethowan Committee.

Other DCP publications include the mandatory Annual DCP Reports which include reports from all the subsystems of the Division. The relevant peer-reviewed journal of the Society is the *British Journal of Clinical Psychology*, started in 1982 with David Shapiro as its first editor, succeeding the double-decker *British Journal of Social and Clinical Psychology* which started in 1962. And then there are books published by the BPS for a range of readerships, such as the compendium *Professional Psychology Handbook* published in 1995, with information and guidance on a range of topics for practitioner psychologists.

Face-to-face communication is of equal importance to written communication. Business meetings of the Division have often been held in conjunction with 'scientific' or professional updating meetings. For example, in June 1965 a symposium was held at Oxford for psychologists working with children and young people, with three papers in the morning, and the afternoon given over to the inaugural meeting of the SPIG for clinical psychologists working in that field, with an annual subscription of £5. The DCP began an annual series of courses on Management and Organisational Change for District Clinical Psychologists, first held in 1984/85 at the NHS Management Training Centre in Harrogate and organised by Anne Pattie. It was attended by many who went on to be Heads of Service, and still continues as the White Hart Course, an independent management training course for clinical psychologists.

Key events – the Zuckerman and Trethowan processes

One of the most important early issues confronting the Division was the possibility of a governmental review of the functions of clinical psychology. A standard government procedure was to set up a committee with what was considered to be representative and authoritative membership to review an issue, a relevant example being the 1968 Summerfield Report on educational psychology (DES, 1968). Since the Second World War the most rapid percentage growth of health staff had been in scientific and technical staff, such as biochemists and laboratory technicians, but this growth had been uncoordinated, so in 1967 the government appointed a committee, chaired by Sir Solly Zuckerman, to review arrangements for these groups.

The BPS made a submission to the committee (BPS, 1968), proposing that, as graduate scientists, they should be included in the review. What is interesting about the submission is the invocation of 'science' at several points, with references to the 'scientific training' of the psychologists, and their need for 'laboratory-type technicians'. The 1968 Report of the Zuckerman Committee recommended the creation of a hospital scientific service along the lines of the scientific civil service, but considered that the work of clinical psychology did not fit into the scheme they were proposing. The omission of psychologists from Zuckerman gave the BPS leverage to press the government for a separate review.

Accordingly the then Mental Health Advisory Committee convened a working party in 1972 with six medical members (three of whom were psychiatrists) and three psychologists (Alan Clarke, H. Gwynne Jones and May Davidson), with Professor W.H. Trethowan as chair. The BPS evidence (BPS, 1973) was prepared by a 'Working Party' of the Division, which was in fact the whole committee of the DCP, two members of that committee – Michael Berger and John Hall – being involved in this book. An interim consultation document was issued in May 1974 for comment, and the work of the committee was completed in 1974, although the Report was not finally published until 1977 (DHSS, 1977).

The Trethowan Report was the first comprehensive government review of clinical psychology services; its significance lay not only in the specific recommendations, but also as a mandate for the growth of clinical psychology. The recommendations emphasised that psychologists had 'full professional status', and crucially that psychologists could accept direct referrals from GPs. Psychologists should be organised within centralised departments of clinical psychology, and the range of clinical services should be extended beyond the then traditional areas of mental illness, child health, and mental handicap, to the fields of physical handicap, neurological science, geriatrics, primary health care and adolescent services (interestingly distinguished from child health). Detailed attention was paid to personnel, and to the training capacity required to provide those staff. The Trethowan Report was not in any sense an organisational blueprint, as illustrated by the very different ways in which Trethowan was implemented. In two linked articles, David Smail advocated a model for Nottinghamshire based on specialist psychologists with a central base, while David Woolford in rural Dorset proposed a generic model of service, with psychologists attached to localities (Smail & Woolford, 1978).

The wider interest of this 10-year-long process from the beginning of Zuckerman to the publication of Trethowan in 1977 lies in the continual informal and formal lobbying of the government by the BPS and DCP. It illustrates the sheer persistence required in many of the activities of the Division to bring issues to some form of conclusion.

A snapshot in time – 1990–1991

In 1989 and 1990 two linked workforce planning projects had been carried out, both addressing the continuing shortage of clinical psychologists. The independent Management Advisory Service review (1989) had produced a creative model of service delivery, involving the idea of different skill levels contributing to a shared-care model of service delivery. The Department of Health had not expected this outcome from the review, so then separately carried out an internal review, which was essentially a very detailed data-led workforce planning project (MPAG, 1990). These documents meant that following up the 1990 MPAG report was a major goal for the DCP in 1991.

The silver anniversary of the DCP fell in 1991, so is a convenient year to take a snapshot of the committee's work. Peter Wilcock and Malcolm Adams were successive chairs during the year, and their 'Chair's Letter' columns in CPF illustrate the preoccupations of the year. Continuing themes were achieving a balance between the external goals of strategic overview while managing the manifold range of immediate tasks, and the internal goals of being both efficient and a representative and accountable organisation. On 2 October 1990 DCP leads had met with Virginia Bottomley, then Minister of State for Health, one of the first DCP meetings with a government minister. The DCP had realised 'the powerful emphasis on devolution of responsibility to regional level and below...the links between regions and units were obviously being seen as important with less focus on the role of Districts'. In other words, the DCP needed to set their sights on the right target.

Malcolm Adams's first column (CPF, Issue 33, p.34) focused on the impact of the wider health reforms. He recognised that 'strictly speaking the concept of a "District Psychology Department" no longer makes sense in the reformed NHS'. In his next column (CPF, Issue 34, p.32) he reported on the committee's two-day policy meeting in April, which had both reviewed progress on the previous year's goals, thought about the Division's longer-terms aims, and planned work for the forthcoming year: 'a particularly satisfying feature...was the recognition that almost all of the work planned for last year had been successfully accomplished'. Rapid changes in the NHS – including the introduction of the purchasers and providers of health care, and the advent of NHS Trusts and fund-holding GPs – were all making 'the working lives of clinical psychologists full of change, interest and anxiety' (BPS, 1992, p.63).

> I think it was in the 1980s that we really saw the beginning of the continuous political meddling with the NHS that has not ceased since, and it also marked the time when we started to recognise more clearly that we had to look at ourselves and our place in the NHS more proactively. This was a turbulent, and for me an exciting, time to become DCP Chair. All added on to one's everyday workload, which meant that I was literally working seven days a week at that time as DCP Chair,

> clinical practitioner, Head of the District service, and a senior manager with a broader District remit. I had been a member of the Whitley Council PTA Management Working Party on Recruitment and Retention also in 1989, which involved visiting clinical psychology services all over the country to ascertain views about these issues. (Peter Wilcock, DCP Chair 1990–1991, December 2014)

Key events: 'New Ways of Working in Applied Psychology' projects

With both the 'modernisation agenda' across the whole of the NHS, and the formation of the National Institute of Mental Health in England in 1997 to support the delivery of the National Service Frameworks, the Department of Health began to look in more depth at the way the professions were working individually and collectively in the mental health services. This led to the 'New Ways of Working' movement. A steering group was established in 2004 with full professional representation to review the roles of each profession, with Peter Kinderman and Michael Wang nominated by the BPS to represent applied psychology. New Ways of Working for Psychiatrists was the first project to be established, but in 2005 the Department of Health extended the work to include other professions, beginning with clinical and applied psychology. The use of the term 'applied' was important because it recognised the roles in mental health services of BPS Divisions other than the Division of Clinical Psychology. The BPS was approached to be a formal partner in this subsequent project, with Roslyn Hope (a former clinical psychologist) and Tony Lavender (representing the BPS) nominated to co-lead the project (CSIP & BPS, 2007).

Seven sub-projects were included under the 'New Ways of Working in Applied Psychology' umbrella: models of organising, leading and managing psychological services (Tim Cate); training model for applied psychologists (Mike Wang & Jan Burns); new roles of assistants/associates in the future workforce (John Taylor & Tony Lavender); career pathways and the structure of services (Tina Ball & Keith Miller); applied psychology and multidisciplinary team working (Steve Onyett); contribution to Improving Access to Psychological Therapies (Graham Turpin & Roslyn Hope); and statutory roles in new Mental Health Act Legislation (Peter Kinderman & Kate Bailey).

Each group reported separately and the steering group produced a statement on the purpose of applied psychology, namely 'to improve the psychological well-being of the population through working with individuals, teams, organisations and communities'. This project was the most comprehensive review of the work of applied psychologists, with membership of the groups demonstrating the partnership of the Division in the work. As an example of the work of the project groups, the group that looked at the preferred way of organising services considered that guiding principles were more helpful than 'best' models of service organisation. Among these principles were that 'services must be aligned with the vision of future service delivery and the key external drivers for organising Psychological Services', and 'Leaders in service delivery need to be business-minded, politically aware, and demonstrate alignment to the organisation's strategic objectives'.

> *In 2003 Dr Michael Shooter was elected President of the Royal College of Psychiatrists. He had a more progressive influence than his predecessors, and was aware that on top of the chronic shortage of consultant psychiatrists, for the first time the profession was struggling to recruit*

training grades. Dr Shooter approached the Department of Health, who were delighted that the College was interested in rethinking the role of the psychiatrist in the modernised National Health Service. For many years the Department had been trying to break down so-called 'tribal barriers' to increase flexibility of service provision, and to enable less-expensive health care workers to undertake clinical tasks with greater responsibility.

The New Ways of Working project turned out to be a remarkable opportunity not only to have some influence over the future shape of psychiatry, but also to showcase the characteristics and potential contribution of clinical psychology. The New Ways of Working in Psychiatry project was brave and ambitious and its outputs were revolutionary and controversial, including for the first time the debunking of the myth that the consultant psychiatrist was responsible for everything in mental health within his/her geographical patch. Sadly, as soon as a new President of the Royal College took over the reins, the College rowed back on most of its previous commitments to the project.

Some of the good ideas in NWWAP were never properly implemented, largely because economic, national and political events and NHS reorganisation overtook the project's recommendations. With the benefit of hindsight, perhaps there were too many sub-projects and the objectives too ambitious for a single initiative. (Michael Wang)

Relations between the BPS and the DCP

From the 1920 reorganisation of the BPS and formation of the Sections within the Society to form a quasi-federal structure, there was a risk of internal tensions. The problematic relationships between the Medical Section and the Council of the BPS discussed in chapter 8 illustrate how much power the Sections had under this structure. Until the creation of Divisions in 1960, a mere committee of the BPS had little formal influence, but what had not been anticipated, of course, was the rate of growth in size of the Divisions, and in particular the Division of Clinical Psychology. In creating each new interest group, Section or Division, the new subsystem had exactly the same representation and influence as another numbering now nearly 10 thousand, with a history stretching back half a century.

So when in 2003 Mike Wang attended his first Representative Council meeting (until then the most powerful decision-making forum in the Society) he found himself the only formal representative of clinical psychology, in a room with some 60 other psychologists (BPS Representative Council 18/10/03 minutes/ attendance). During his tenure as chair, new Divisions of Counselling and of Health Psychology were consolidated, which had a direct effect on the influence of the Division of Clinical Psychology in relation to the Department of Health. Inevitably these two new Divisions, representing very small numbers of members, were allowed one representative each to sit alongside the DCP representative in all subsequent meetings with the Department of Health (Professional Affairs Board 26/6/02 minute 4.4). This was a serious difficulty, since initially there was little coherence in politics and strategy between the DCP and its two new allies, and some political naivety on the part of the newcomers, compromising the relationships, practices and means of communication with significant figures in government arrangements that the Division had spent many years building up.

On numerous occasions the Division would make representation to administrators and Society senior officers regarding important national issues in the public interest in relation to the

> *promotion of psychology only to be told that what we proposed was 'ultra vires', meaning that it was against the principles and legal framework of charity law and the requirements of the Charity Commissioners, to whom the Society felt beholden (Professional Affairs Board 26/6/02 minute 6.1). The DCP committee often felt that there was overinterpretation of the intentions of charity law given that most of our comparable organisations such as the medical royal colleges (which are also educational charities) have no problem in acting in the way we proposed. Despite DCP intentions, the Society rarely makes public comment on important national developments relevant to the profession of clinical psychology such as the Mid-Staffordshire scandal and the subsequent (2013) Francis Report.* (Michael Wang)

There have been recurring concerns about the relationship between the central BPS and other BPS subsystems, leading to proposals for applied psychologists to hive off from the BPS to form some kind of College of Applied Psychology. May Davidson had raised this in 1976/77 (Kat, 1985), and in 1983 there was a proposal from the Yorkshire branch of the DCP to form a 'professional body for clinical psychologists which would have a wider remit and greater powers than the DCP and would replace it' (Newsletter 41, p.16). Pat Frankish was elected as BPS President for 1999 with this agenda.

This idea has not gone away. Excluding student members, practising clinical psychologists make up over about a quarter of the members of the BPS. As the figures in chapter 1 show, by 2010 the DCP formed around 20 per cent of the membership of the Society, and in a number of ways was carrying out many of the functions of a medical college. A related issue is that the transfer of executive decision-making powers from the Representative Council of the BPS to a small Board of Trustees who are legally responsible, but who appear to some observers to be preoccupied with that personal liability, has caused the Society to behave in a more cautious way.

A view from three perspectives

> Inevitably the DCP and BPS have different views given their membership and concerns. The DCP has a relatively homogeneous group of nearly 10,000 members, until recently linked by shared experiences of employment in the NHS (mostly), good terms and conditions, clear career paths and high quality training. The DCP has always been politically aware given the influence upon it of the Department of Health and the government of the day. The BPS has approximately 50,000 members covering undergraduates, postgraduates, researchers, teachers, other applied psychologists, newcomers and retired people, all with diverse experiences and interests. Some see the BPS as a key part of their lives, whereas for others it is just *The Psychologist* delivered once a month.
>
> Despite their different perspectives the DCP and BPS have much in common. Both want to enhance the usefulness and reputation of psychology, to serve their members and to be responsive to internal and external events. They both have aspirations beyond their resources, carefully consider value for money and rely on volunteers, with BPS staff often forming strong supportive bonds with many of the more active subsystems. My time with both the DCP and BPS was positive: the issues were important, the debates heated, the passion obvious and the people committed.

> Calls for the separation of applied psychology never come with costs identified and the indications are that additional costs would not be welcome to the applied psychology members at present. (Sue Gardner, Chair of DCP 1994/95, Chair of PAB 1996/99, President of the BPS 2009/10, January 2015)

Other organisations

Both the DCP and the predecessor organisations, the CPP(MH) and EDPP, have worked closely with other organisations, the examples already given illustrating the close relationships between the Divisions, the AScW trade union and local NHS groups. Before the Royal Charter was conferred in 1965 there was technically no problem with these arrangements, but in 1967 an AScW National Advisory Committee was set up in parallel with the DCP, creating a clear distinction between DCP and union matters. Eric Bromley and John Pinschof were leading members of the union over many years. John Pinschof recalls joining the union in 1963, when he started training at Manchester: later in the 1960s the Manchester and Liverpool psychologists formed a joint local psychology/scientific branch of ASTMS which organised quarterly meetings discussing union and scientific matters on the same day, probably the most organised area in the country for trade union business (John Pinschof, personal communication, 18 August 2014). A more recent example of DCP and union cooperation was their joint work on Agenda for Change, which led to many clinical psychologists being 'promoted' within the job-matching process. The Regional Advisory Groups of psychologists recommended by the Trethowan Report continued until the establishment of NHS Trusts in the 1990s and the new form of health authority, when the long-standing regional structure disintegrated.

Curiously the group involving heads of training courses was also formally independent of the DCP and their – and later PAB – training committees. Before all training was managed through universities, there had been two separate training bodies, one for university-based courses (CUCPTC), and one for the in-service courses (CORIC) leading to the then BPS Diploma: neither organisation had any connection with the BPS. This amalgamated group, the national Group of Trainers in Clinical Psychology (GTiCP) continues to this day, but it has been difficult to identify the DCP subsystem structures to which it should be allied. With the strong views of many of the GTiCP members they constitute a powerful lobby, and a number of course heads have held prominent positions elsewhere in clinical psychology. Malcolm Adams was head of the University of East Anglia course while also being the consultant adviser to the Department of Health, and Ian Gray and, more recently, Peter Kinderman, Graham Turpin and Michael Wang have been DCP chairs.

Conclusions

Who did all the work?

The early minutes of the CPP(MH) and DCP and other BPS records consistently show a small number of people contributing to all that the CPP(MH) achieved. Lucy Fildes herself inaugurated the Committee, and Grace Rawlings was the first secretary, early on indefatigable in meetings and preparation of memoranda. She was succeeded by May Davidson, who went on to become the first consultant adviser in clinical psychology to the Department of Health. Monte Shapiro worked closely with Herbert Phillipson on both training issues and AScW business, burying their theoretical differences. Mahesh Desai was the driving force behind the establishment of the Committee of Senior Psychologists. H. Gwynne Jones (1969), himself one of the pioneers in behaviour therapy, named Raven, Zangwill, Shapiro, Foulds, Desai, and A.D.B. Clarke as providing 'models to guide the development of the emerging profession'.

Ongoing concerns

From the beginning of the DCP in 1966 a number of issues have continued to preoccupy the Division and other organisations. Some of those continue, such as the promotion of initial and postqualification training, and encouraging communication between members for mutual support. Other issues arise from government initiatives, such as the restructuring of health authorities and the creation of NHS Trusts, and the prescription of forms of practice required by NICE guidance. Despite concerns and predictions to the contrary, and the work by the Division they involved, government-endorsed national reports such as Trethowan, MAS/MPAG and New Ways of Working, have all enhanced the standing of the discipline and profession.

There are three major historical challenges to cohesive professional organisation of the profession of clinical psychology. One recurrent problem is the increasing complexity of the organisation, with the multiplication and growth of what are now faculties, and the associated balance between them and the central committee structures of the Division, leading to periodic reorganisation to revise unwieldy and ineffective decision-making structures. For example, the Faculty for Children, Young People and their Families had 1054 members in 2010 – larger than the entire DCP in 1980. The second challenge is managing the conflicts and tensions between the encompassing BPS and its concerns as a learned society and the professional structures within it, whether that is seen as all professional branches of psychology together, or only those branches working primarily in health care, or clinical psychologists alone. And lastly, there is the question of how to encourage able people to take up the real challenge of doing this work, demanding, rewarding and frustrating as it is.

The roll of those who have been chairs of the Division (see Appendix 2) does not begin to do justice to all the work done by other Division, Committee, Faculty and Branch officers and members – as well as often their secretaries and BPS staff. Many have held multiple offices, some over many years. Without them none of this would have happened.

Primary sources

The main sources for 'The pioneers' section of the chapter are the three bound minute books of the Committee of Professional Psychologists (Mental Health) held in the BPS archive, covering the period from 1943 to January 1958: BPS/002/02/06/08/01; BPS002/02/06/08/02: and BPS002/02/06/08/03. A fuller version of this section is in Hall (2007). NL refers to material from the *DCP Newsletter*, CPF to material from *Clinical Psychology Forum*, and PAB to Professional Affairs Board minutes.

References

British Psychological Society (1960a). English Division of Professional Psychologists (Educational and Clinical). *Bulletin of the British Psychological Society, 41*, 33–36.

British Psychological Society (1960b). Scottish Division of Professional Psychologists (Educational and Clinical). *Bulletin of the British Psychological Society, 42*, 88–91.

British Psychological Society (1967). *Annual report.* London: Author.

British Psychological Society (1968). Memorandum to the Zuckerman Committee. *Bulletin of the British Psychological Society, 21*, 79–82.

British Psychological Society (1973). Report on the role of psychologists in the health services. *Bulletin of the British Psychological Society, 26*, 309–330.

British Psychological Society (1992). *Annual report 1991–1992.* Leicester: Author.

British Psychological Society (2000). *Recent advances in understanding mental illness and psychotic experiences. A report by the Division of Clinical Psychology.* Leicester: Author.

Care Services Improvement Partnership & the British Psychological Society (2007). *New ways of working for applied psychologists in health and social care: The end of the beginning.* London: Department of Health.

Crown, S. (1948). The psychology department – Maudsley Hospital. *Bulletin of the British Psychological Society, 2*, 57–58.

Department of Education and Science (1968). *Psychologists in education services (Summerfield Report).* London: HMSO.

Department of Health and Social Security (1977). *The role of psychologists in the health service (Trethowan Report).* London: HMSO.

Desai, M.M. (1966). The Co-ordinating Committee of Senior Psychologists in the National Health Service: 1960–1966. *Bulletin of the British Psychological Society, 19*(65), 21–24.

Division of Clinical Psychology (1985, December). *50th Anniversary Newsletter, 50.*

Division of Clinical Psychology (2011). *A guide to DCP publications.* Leicester: Author.

Feversham Committee (1939). *The voluntary mental health services.* London: Author.

Fraise, J. (1994). DCP branches and SIGs: A strategy for closer liaison. *Clinical Psychology Forum, 70*, 38–39.

Francis, R. (2013). *Report of the Mid Staffordshire NHS Foundation Trust Public Inquiry.* London: HMSO.

Hall, J.N. (1970). Psychological manpower in the health service: Use or misuse. *Bulletin of the British Psychological Society, 23*, 219–222.

Hall, J.N. (2007). The emergence of clinical psychology in Britain from 1943 to 1958, part I: Core tasks and the professionalisation process. *History and Philosophy of Psychology, 9*(1), 29–55.

Gwynne Jones, H. (1969). Clinical psychology. In B.M. Foss (Ed.), *Supplement to the Bulletin of the British Psychological Society* (pp.21–23). London: British Psychological Society.

Kat, B. (1985). The May Davidson Award Lecture: The emergence of clinical psychology as a profession. *DCP Newsletter, 50*, 20–29.

Management Advisory Service (1989). *Review of clinical psychology services.* Cheltenham: Author.

Manpower Planning Advisory Group (1990). *Manpower Planning Advisory Group report on clinical psychology.* London: Department of Health.

Smail, D. & Woolford, D. (1978). Implementing Trethowan. *DCP Newsletter, 21*, 13–19.

Stirling, S. & Eliatamby, A. (2003). *Office for Public Management: Review of the functions and structures of the Division of Clinical Psychology.* Leicester: British Psychological Society.

Whitley Council Professional and Technical Council A (1952). *RHB (52) 11, HMC (52) 11 & BG (52) 10 Clinical Psychologists.* London: NHS.

Whitley Council Professional and Technical Council A (1954). *HM (54) 17 & PTA circular 27 Clinical Psychologists.* London: Whitley Council for the Health Services.

Whitley Council Professional and Technical Council A (1957). *HM (57) 81 & part II of PTA circular 52 post-graduate training and study of clinical psychologists.* London: Whitley Council for the Health Services.

Wilkinson, I (1992). A survey of opinion among clinical psychologists. *Clinical Psychology Forum, 46*, 33–34.

Zuckerman Report (1968). *Hospital scientific and technical services.* London: HMSO.

Chapter 6 The historical political and NHS context

Anne Richardson

As a profession, clinical psychologists take pride in their stance as 'scientist practitioners', as professional, applied scientists in health and social care. But it is axiomatic that evidence of effectiveness by itself is insufficient to determine effective practice. A variety of apparently extraneous factors commonly play an important part, and it would be difficult to overestimate the impact of the National Health Service (NHS) which has sustained, constrained, frustrated and nurtured members of the profession since its inception in 1948. This chapter describes some of the most significant events in the historical, political and NHS context informed by my own perspective, first as a clinical psychologist working in the NHS and then as a senior civil servant and lead for mental health policy at the Department of Health (DH).

It includes direct effects upon the profession, such as specifically targeted statutory or policy change, as well as indirect effects such as NHS reorganisation, the consequences of which, while they may have been unintended, have been highly significant. I will describe briefly some of the most important historical events for the profession in the years since 1948, and then describe a few of the most salient themes in mental health policy development between 1995 and 2010 when I worked at the DH. I hope to make an argument concerning the overarching importance of understanding the political and NHS context for the development of the profession and about the importance of managing it actively.

Employment

Probably the most important influence – without it, it is unlikely that there would have been a formal profession of clinical psychology – is the National Health Service (NHS), which Aneurin Bevan described in 1948 as 'the biggest single experiment in social service that the world has ever seen or undertaken'. From that point forward, hospitals, their management boards and all their employees were effectively nationalised. This meant a standardised approach to pay, terms and conditions, as well as more uniform arrangements for accountability and focus. Clinical psychologists as NHS employees were inevitably required to align their interests with those of the NHS and although it is difficult to believe now that, on balance, the consequences were not broadly beneficial for the profession, it certainly has not always felt comfortable.

Pay is a good example. The Whitley Council arrangements (see chapter 1) were adopted for the NHS as a basis for agreement about terms of employment. The impact of Whitley arrangements in standardising the pay of clinical psychologists meant that for many years pay compared very favourably with, and was often better than, academic salaries or the salaries of those in the prison service and other applied settings. As with many other NHS employees included under Whitley, psychologists' pay grew faster than price inflation would predict. In 1952, for example, a psychologist might earn £530 per annum at the bottom of the scale and a minimum of £1300 for a post carrying 'exceptional responsibility'. In 2014, a trainee could earn up to £25,000, more than double the salary predicted by price inflation and those at the very top of the scale could earn over £80,000, almost three times as much as in 1952. In the years that followed, in defining clear levels of responsibility in association with grades and salary points, Whitley arrangements also meant rapid movement through the pay scale at times of high demand. This was particularly true in the 1980s, as individual clinical psychologists at a relatively young age were quickly promoted to posts with higher levels of responsibility and a higher level of pay.

Whitley arrangements, albeit with many adaptations, were to remain largely unchanged for the next 50 years and it was not until 2004 that *Agenda for Change* (Department of Health, 2004a) harmonised grading and pay for all non-medical, non-dental, and most management staff in the NHS. Agenda for Change has had an impact upon the profession about which many have been critical. Some argue, for example, that it has led to a bottleneck at the more senior end of the salary spectrum; it is said that opportunities for promotion have been curtailed. However, there are other factors operating, including the fiscal climate which is currently restricting pay for most groups. Furthermore, as clinical psychologists now find themselves in the company of a much larger and much more diverse group, they effectively 'compete' for the more generically defined management responsibilities that define pay grades under Agenda for Change. Lastly, as there are many more clinical psychologists in the workforce than formerly, promotion *within* a job is now much less likely than it was at times of rapid growth in the profession and at times when the economy was strong.

Politics

Much has been written about the influence of politics upon the NHS, and a detailed discussion of this goes beyond the scope of a short chapter. Suffice to say that those working in the NHS are powerfully aware of the fact that politics and public opinion drive policy in health and social care more than is sometimes evident in other government departments. Politics has also driven a significant volume of organisational change. The second decade of the NHS, the 1960s, illustrates this very well. In 1961, for example, Enoch Powell's 'water tower' speech marked the beginning of the concept of care in the community as he announced the need to set 'the torch to the pyre of old mental hospitals' and a programme began of hospital closures that would last for at least the next 20 years.

For clinical psychologists, it was a period of great expansion in the scope and application of their skills and also of their professional identity. In 1965 the British Psychological Society was granted its Royal Charter, and 1966 saw the creation of the Division of Clinical Psychology (DCP). For many years, owing to its largely scientific origins, debate had centred upon whether the clinical psychologists' role should be considered as predominantly 'scientific' or 'applied', and upon the implications for organisation, pay, terms and conditions. The Zuckerman Report (1968) recommended that hospital scientific services should be organised at regional level to facilitate the organisation of training and supervision, but it sat on the fence in respect of clinical psychologists, apparently uncertain about which categorisation should apply.

> *My own first job in 1977 at one large long-stay hospital on the outskirts of London was concerned, in large part, with the assessment of long-stay psychiatric in-patients – many of them resident there for over 25 years - who were being prepared for life in the community in what were then 'group homes' or warden-supervised accommodation developed in partnership with local housing associations. Needless to say, the hospital has now been converted to luxury flats and it is notable that few of the profits from the sale of what was prime land were returned to the NHS for the benefit of those who had lived there formerly.*

At the same time in the NHS, a series of scandals and subsequent inquiries, for example Ely (Howe, 1969), Farleigh (Watkins, 1971), Normansfield (Sherrard, 1978), and the Seebohm Report (Seebohm, 1968) lifted the lid on poor practice in institutional care for people with severe mental illness (SMI) and/or learning disabilities. In the past 10 years inquiries seem no less frequent than they were, but there is some evidence that we may be habituating to their findings and they arguably have less impact than they did (Walshe, 2003).

Roles, accountability and responsibility

As clinical psychology expanded beyond mental ill health and learning disabilities into new roles including paediatrics, geriatrics and primary care, the Trethowan Report (DHSS, 1977), published eight years after Zuckerman, was hugely significant for clinical psychologists in legitimising the view that they held about themselves as a functionally independent profession able to develop without medical supervision. Furthermore, it endorsed growth and expansion. After much lobbying by the profession, by the trade union representing psychologists and by May Davidson – the first psychologist to act as an adviser to the Department of Health – the Department was persuaded to publish it and for many years it stood as the clinical psychologist's organisational 'bible' – the first formal report solely concerned with the professional practice of clinical psychology in the NHS and a milestone in the development of direct referrals to clinical psychology services from primary care (see chapters 5 and 17).

Unsurprisingly, as the profession became more clearly focused upon its applications in health care rather than upon its beginnings in science, it was also during the 1970s that the campaign for statutory registration – primarily as a means to protect the public rather than to reinforce professional identity – began to gather momentum. In 1987 the Privy Council granted an Order in Council which amended the British Psychological Society's Royal Charter and Statutes and authorised the Society to maintain a voluntary Register of Chartered Psychologists. However, it was not until 2009 that the formal statutory register of practitioner psychologists opened under the auspices of (what is now) the Health and Care Professions Council (HCPC). A Private Members Bill brought before the House of Lords by Lord Alderdice in 2007 had failed to gain support from the government, not least because of a climate of suspicion about what was seen as professional 'special pleading'. So it was only in partnership with a process designed to simplify the regulation of many other healthcare professionals together that registration for practitioner psychologists could proceed. Now, HCPC (the regulator) oversees just over 20 thousand practitioner psychologists and protects seven psychology titles: clinical psychologist, educational psychologist, occupational psychologist, health psychologist, forensic psychologist, counselling psychologist and sport and exercise psychologist – a huge milestone for the profession although not a development that was welcomed uniformly by a small section of mainly academic psychologists.

Organisation in a shifting landscape

Growth in the scope as well as the number of trained clinical psychologists has been a leading consequence of their employment within the NHS (see chapter 7). However, like other NHS employees, clinical psychologists have also had to deal with an ever-changing organisational landscape. From the inception of the NHS in 1948 to 1974 – the longest period of organisational stability in its history – the NHS was managed within a relatively simple model consisting of hospital boards and local management committees, and psychologists employed in the NHS were mostly working in hospitals. However, in 1974, following the NHS Reorganisation Act brought in by the former Conservative government led by Edward Heath, the incoming Labour government oversaw the first major health service reorganisation.

Service planning, management and delivery were divided into three tiers: 14 regions, 90 Area Health Authorities (AHAs) and 200 local District Management Teams. For the Trethowan Report, published only two years afterwards, it was therefore ambitious to recommend that a very small profession like clinical psychology should be organised at Area level while working towards District organisation in the longer term. With just under 1500 psychologists employed at that time, and most of these concentrated in London and the South East, very few AHAs could boast a full complement. But by the time the Labour government lost the election in 1979 and Margaret Thatcher had taken the helm, all was not well with the NHS and another reorganisation was on the way. By 1982, plans were implemented to abolish the Area tier of the NHS and create 200 new District Health Authorities (DHAs). For many in a profession whose star was clearly rising, this had a beneficial impact upon opportunities for growth in levels of responsibility, promotion and pay.

> *As a new young 'principal' psychologist in 1982 – my second job – and the only psychologist employed in one of the newly created DHAs – I arrived to find they had forgotten I was coming. There was no office, no budget, no computer, no clarity about management arrangements and no more than a brief job description which suggested 'service development' should be the primary task. Within three years our service boasted 13 staff and a strong presence in both primary care and for people with long-term needs. We also developed a very amicable relationship with colleagues employed in local authority social care: the pioneering Mike Bender and his small team of community psychologists albeit working to a very different model (see chapter 17).*

The third major NHS reorganisation within 10 years came in the form of Sir Roy Griffiths' 'general management inquiry' (Griffiths, 1989) whose recommendations were subsequently enshrined in the National Health Service and Community Care Act (1991). Griffiths' report resulted in another new set of NHS changes, among the most important of which was the introduction of an internal market in heath care, known as the 'purchaser–provider split'. The reforms had a relatively minor impact upon clinical psychologists, although fundamental changes were made to the way that training places were commissioned (see chapter 7).

Not for the first time, new working relationships with commissioners had to be established and the case for investment in the profession had to be restated. As demand for qualified clinical psychologists continued to grow, the DCP was successful in lobbying the Manpower Planning Advisory Group (MPAG) of the Department of Health, who then appointed Derek Mowbray to produce his Management Advisory Service Report (MAS, 1989). In addition to recommending an increase in the size of the profession (to 4000 by the year 2000), he outlined three 'levels' of psychological skill, highlighting awareness of what the report called the 'sapiential authority' exclusive to qualified psychologists. However, the Department of Health failed to support the report's recommendations – already there were signs that government ministers wanted to devolve the detail of decision making to local level – but it did serve to reinforce the profession's distinct identity within health care and it portended the development of new roles for the application of psychological skills in health.

Needless to say, the BPS took every opportunity to press government to address the continuing major shortfall in the supply of trained clinical psychologists and the Department's Steering Group on Health Services Information was sufficiently persuaded by the arguments to commission the University of Bath to gather information on staffing levels and the organisation of services. The report (Scrivens & Charlton, 1985) showed that, of the 188 Districts employing psychologists, 82 provided services beyond their district boundary and the number of psychologists employed per District varied between 1 and 20 (with an average of seven to eight) – fewer even than Trethowan (see chapter 5), let alone Mowbray, envisioned. The following year, the Chair of the Regional NHS Planners agreed to meet with representatives of the BPS and this, in turn, prompted the Manpower Planning Advisory Group (MPAG) in December 1987 to agree a programme of work which focused both upon the numbers of psychologists and the desired skill mix. The final report of the MPAG contained detailed workforce planning information and, importantly, presented a coherent account of the unique role occupied by clinical psychologists in health. Furthermore, it offered great clarity of vision concerning the application of clinical psychology beyond mental health and learning disabilities – a 'milestone' in the history of the profession.

Further organisational reforms – what Alan Maynard (Maynard & Sheldon, 2002) called an 'evidence-free re-disorganisation' of the structure of the NHS – were introduced in 1994 to further streamline management, and to create a clear line of accountability for the delivery of the government's 1992 'Health of the Nation' targets to the NHS Management Executive. Fourteen Regional Health Authorities were replaced by eight Regional Offices; new commissioning bodies were established (again) for education and training, and DHAs and Family Health Service Authorities were merged. Service reorganisation, which almost always slows progress to some degree, did mental health services few favours. Furthermore, in mental health, where most clinical psychologists could still be found, there was very limited new investment. Legislation was out of date; there had been no White Paper on mental health for over 20 years, and reform of the Mental Health Act was long overdue. But perhaps the most notable feature of the NHS environment at this point in its history was the frugality of its funding and, when the Labour Government came into power in 1997, the percentage of gross domestic product (GDP) spend on health had fallen to about 6 per cent, well behind the European average, despite modest growth in the UK economy. In combination with an observably inefficient use of resources, inequities in access to care and a strengthening economy, the scene was set for radical change.

New Labour 1997–2010

The general election of 1997 marked the end of 18 years of Conservative Party politics in Britain and 'New Labour' came into office formulating policy for health that built on what was called 'The Third Way' (Blair, 1998). The approach set the scene for more active standard-setting by government, and for decentralisation of responsibility for delivery to local level, where closer partnerships could be made with, for example, providers in the charitable and other non-statutory sectors ('Leverage, not size, is what counts', Blair, 1998). As the economy had grown, it was also possible to invest. This helped Britain to keep up with the European 'Joneses' (Maynard & Sheldon, 2002), and 'The New NHS: Modern, Dependable' (Department of Health, 1997) contained a commitment to invest an extra £1.5 billion in the NHS. The significant population drivers for this change included waiting times, a concern about inequalities in health care, and unhappiness about access to services for people with unmet needs, including people with mental ill health who were increasingly vocal about wanting better access to 'talking treatments'. The New NHS set out an intention to develop new national standards, National Service Frameworks (NSFs), for local delivery, placing new Primary Care Groups (the forerunner of Primary Care Trusts) firmly in charge.

Astonishingly for some, the Adult Mental Health NSF (Department of Health, 1999) was given equal priority for early development with the NSF for coronary heart disease. The surprise was at least in part because mental health had for many years been seen as the poor relation of health care. There were accusations of underresourcing, problems associated with old poorly maintained buildings, difficulties with recruitment and staff retention, inequities in provision that particularly affected people with mental health problems from black and minority ethnic communities and widespread dissatisfaction with the impact of hospital closures. This was a fertile environment in which to begin my own 15-year spell of work at the Department of Health and an exciting time to be involved in the development of mental health policy.

Ministers were also expressing an interest in mental health services, some undoubtedly for personal and/or family reasons; 'everyone was aware that care in the community was failing' (Paul Boateng, personal communication, 11 March 2014) and all were very affected by the events surrounding the death of Jonathan Zito, a musician who was tragically killed by stabbing in 1992 by a homeless 'care in the community' patient, Christopher Clunis, who had ceased to take his medication. Paul (now Lord) Boateng, then a junior Minister for Health with responsibility for mental health, led development of a mental health White Paper following an official visit to Australia in the summer of 1998 – a visit I was fortunate enough to join – to explore the operation of standards in Australia. The White Paper

(Department of Health, 1998) followed and then the Mental Health National Service Framework was published a year later. 'Without political prioritisation, change of the magnitude subsequently seen in mental health could never have been achieved. There was a conjunction of the stars' (Paul Boateng, personal communication, 11 March 2014).

Along with reform of the 1983 Mental Health Act, the NSF was a major plank in the agenda to modernise health care. It set out the service models, supported by the evidence, that were necessary to deliver effective treatment and care, and improve access to and outcomes from services. Standards Two and Three, which concerned primary care, made it clear to commissioners that psychology services were fundamental to routine care. Indeed, access to psychological therapies was formally included as an element of local performance assessment of services for people with 'common mental disorders'. Together with the establishment of new roles for approved non-medical practitioners, including clinical psychologists, in the delivery of care for people detained under the reformed Mental Health Act, the profile of applied psychology in health care was rising and numbers employed in the NHS rose from just over four thousand to just over seven thousand in the seven years between 1997 and 2004 – growth of more than 70 per cent (Appleby, 2004). However, on a less positive note, Graham Thornicroft (2011) argued that the strategy failed to address the real problem that perhaps only a quarter of those needing treatment actually received any. Need was (and is) still outstripping supply.

New Labour had inherited high levels of poverty and inequality and the themes of social exclusion and unemployment had been major drivers of policy change (Hills & Stewart, 2005). But the second and third terms of the Labour government (2001–2010) were characterised by competing themes as the economic recession began, and as politicians became concerned about the rising care costs for an ageing population with 'long-term conditions'. It was becoming clear, as spending restrictions began to be imposed, that the position could only worsen over the next 20 years as patients became 'better educated and more affluent, less deferential to authority and professionals…and want more control and more choice' (Wanless, 2001).

Inevitably, it seems, NHS reorganisation was again seen as a potential solution. Constitutional reform with separate assemblies for Scotland and Wales had already marked the start of action to implement the principles of 'devolution and subsidiarity' which were governing development of policy in Europe and, by 2001, it was the turn of the NHS. Within a year, 'Shifting the Balance of Power' (2001b) meant abolition of England's 95 health authorities, a shift of their responsibilities to 300 Primary Care Trusts, and the creation of 28 new health authorities, set to become Strategic Health Authorities, which replaced what had formerly been 'regional offices'. By these means, local clinicians and managers working in Primary Care Trusts and NHS Trusts were empowered to ensure that local services reflected the needs of the local community and to commission them accordingly – a step that represented the implementation of what had always been a central plank of the 'Third Way' – to shift responsibility for delivery of services away from central government towards front line staff and patients. This development also saw the beginnings of improved connections between health and social care which had always been separately funded and organised within local rather than national government.

The dismantling of the old architecture was a blow to those concerned with delivery of the mental health NSF published just six years before, because new staff in new jobs always take time to settle in. New organisational arrangements inevitably meant delays in commissioning and developing services. However, the National Institute for Mental Health in England was established in 2001 under the leadership of Professor Louis Appleby, National Director for Mental Health, to 'coordinate research, disseminate information, facilitate training and develop services'. Its first publications were 10 documents ('Cases for Change') containing guidance for new commissioners in primary care who would not necessarily have skills in or knowledge about mental health. The documents were published to mixed reviews, the more scathing of which concerned their lack of scientific rigour: 'If it's not in a randomised controlled trial, I don't believe it's true' (Glasby, 2011).

Talking treatments

But lack of scientific rigour was not a criticism levelled at those writing at the time about evidence-based talking treatments, which were a tremendously important driver of interest in clinical psychology. Public awareness of, and demand for, such services, particularly for counselling and psychotherapy delivered by trained practitioners as alternatives to medical (drug) treatments, had risen significantly, yet few understood such treatments or how best to provide them (see chapter 13).

At the end of the previous administration, Glenys Parry, the second clinical psychologist (after Ed Miller) to work as policy adviser within the Department of Health, had been responsible for the development of the first review of strategic policy on psychological therapies (NHS Executive, 1996). This was distributed to NHS Trusts and local authorities as a guide to which 'talking treatments' to commission and how to organise them. There followed a series of DH publications which served to raise the profile of evidence-based 'talking treatments' (Department of Health, 2000, 2001a, 2001c, 2004b). But importantly, and perhaps as a portent of things to come, Parry's review acknowledged the fact that effective treatments might be offered by other than clinical psychologists. As demand for clinical psychologists had continued to grow and vacancy rates were high, policy makers had started to ask where else they could look if there were not enough clinical psychologists being trained. There were two very clear examples.

First, attention had already been focused by the NSF on ways to strengthen access to effective treatments for people with common mental disorders. In a few areas (see chapter 17) service models involving multidisciplinary delivery of effective treatments for common disorders were being developed and appeared to be working. Some of these were visited by Professor Louis Appleby, then National Director for Mental Health, who was impressed. A conversation with senior policy officials after this about the very high numbers (around 9000) of good quality graduate psychologists seeking to obtain a place on a clinical psychology training course (almost 25 applicants for every place on a clinical training course in London at that time) made it a very short step to include a commitment in the 2000 NHS Plan to train 'One thousand new graduate primary care workers, trained in brief therapy techniques of proven effectiveness, [who] will be employed to help GPs manage and treat common mental health problems in all age groups including children'.

A discussion paper (Richardson, 2002) for the providers of one-year postgraduate courses that would initially be funded to the tune of £15m by the Department of Health, was then circulated, followed by guidance on how to recruit and use the graduate workers (Department of Health, 2003). A national evaluation undertaken just five months after the programme began (Harkness et al., 2006) showed high levels of job satisfaction among the almost 360 staff then in post and a reasonably close match between practice and the policy intention (see chapter 17). Although several of the appointees were clearly wanting to use their role as graduate primary care workers as a stepping stone to clinical psychology training, it was clear that there were more graduates waiting in the wings to fill posts.

The second example has its origins in a somewhat different set of circumstances. In a meeting in the Cabinet Office of experts from a variety of backgrounds (Professors David Clarke, David Nutt and Lord Layard) and representatives from the Department of Health (Professor Louis Appleby and myself), as well as the Department for Work and Pensions, HM Treasury and the Cabinet Office, evidence was presented concerning the impact upon individuals and the economic impact of untreated common mental disorder. Compelling statistics were discussed, including that a very significant proportion of sickness absence due to untreated mental ill health (up to 38 per cent of those claiming incapacity benefit) was costing the economy dearly. Richard Layard, an economist, estimated that the UK was spending £7–10bn on benefits payments to people with mental health problems: 'there are more people on incapacity benefit due to mental problems (850,000) than the total number of people on job seekers allowance. If unemployment was once the most prominent source of misery, it has been replaced by mental illness' (Layard, 2005).

Notwithstanding the complexity of the chain that would lead to a return to work for the individuals concerned, it was too important an opportunity to miss. The 'Improving Access to Psychological Therapies' (IAPT) programme was formally established in 2006 with significant new investment to ensure that trained staff would be available to deliver evidence-based talking treatments. Two demonstration sites were initially established, one in Doncaster and one in Newham. Focused on cognitive behaviour therapy (CBT) where the evidence of effectiveness was clearer, the programme ensured that by 2011 147 of the 151 primary care trusts in England could claim to have a service in at least part of their area covering approximately 60 per cent of the population. Although there have been concerns about the programmes' reliance upon CBT, it was largely regarded as a success. In addition to delivering 'talking treatments', clinical psychologists also became more actively involved in supervising the staff delivering 'low intensity' interventions as part of stepped care, for managing the system of care, and for what has been a complex process of measuring outcomes: 'Evidence based practice has arrived and the IAPT programme is built on it; psychologists should embrace the opportunity it provides and build alliances in primary care to ensure that they have a central role in its provision' (Pilling & Roth, 2008).

Of course, not everyone was content with the direction of travel: 'Trailing along for most of its career as a minor profession in the shadow of medicine, clinical psychology has often been tempted to sacrifice integrity to expediency' (Smail, 2006) and the debate continued about whether clinical psychology was neglecting its scientific roots in favour of a pragmatic application of skills to health care.

More reorganisation

In 2006 and again in 2011, significant NHS reorganisations had major effects upon clinical psychologists, as upon other NHS employees. In 2006, local health authorities were replaced by 150 Primary Care Trusts (PCTs) and 152 local (social services) authorities. Eight regional offices became 10 Strategic Health Authorities (SHAs). And by 2011 the Health and Social Care Act had replaced PCTs with Clinical Commissioning Groups (CCGs), 10 SHAs became five, and the Department of Health separated itself from the NHS Commissioning Board (now NHS England). For trainers of clinical psychologists (see chapter 7) the need to negotiate with another new set of commissioners was wearing. At local level, with primary care commissioners working in partnership with local authorities to whom public health doctors were now accountable, there were (and still are) challenges associated with a widespread lack of knowledge about what to commission for whom. For example, a report by the Audit Commission (2006) showed clearly that commissioning decisions owed less to population need than to long-term historical pattern of spend, that is, to habit. It argued that mental health trusts (and hence their commissioners) lacked the breadth and depth of information available to acute trusts and did not have the information to understand fully what they were doing.

Now, both the structures and the processes of commissioning are more clearly aligned to population needs. Local Health and Wellbeing Boards now draw up local 'Joint Strategic Needs Assessments' to inform the development of 'Health and Wellbeing Plans' and new CCGs carry responsibility to secure an appropriate level of services. There are, therefore, positive signs of a more 'joined-up' approach between health and social care. However, the early signs suggest that there is a long way to go before commissioners get beyond the point that 'habit' (Audit Commission, 2006) or the current need for cost savings govern their decisions.

Future directions

Clinical psychologists as professional applied scientists working in health and social care have mostly thrived and diversified over the almost 70 years since the inception of the NHS in 1948. More psychologists are employed in a wider range of clinical settings than was envisaged in 1948 (when only mental health and learning disabilities were considered) and the history arguably shows that there has been a fairly good 'fit' between the skills and interests of the profession, their clients, and the NHS architecture even if, for some clinical psychologists, there have been developments (graduate workers, IAPT or statutory registration) which exemplify the way that compromise and political expediency, albeit informed by evidence from diverse sources can hold sway. It is also true that knowledge has not always translated into patient benefit, or certainly not as quickly as one might like (Michie et al., 2010; Tansella & Thornicroft, 2009; Thornicroft et al., 2011).

What matters in the future is that we learn from this, that we take our knowledge of systems, structures and behaviour change, and understand where, why and how decisions are taken. There are implications for a profession wanting to develop further in health and social care to understand more about local population needs, financial flows, the annual planning cycle, the people in positions of local responsibility and how to engage with them. In addition, there seem to be a number of important current themes to consider.

First, it is difficult to see how a focus on mental ill health and upon 'talking treatments' will not continue to drive change (Department of Health, 2011a, 2011b). Even if the hoped-for impact upon mental ill health-related incapacity benefit of IAPT has not fully been realised (Griffiths & Sheen, 2013) funding has been continued by the current coalition government (£400 million between 2010 and 2014) and it has been extended to children and older people, providing significant opportunities for development. 'The only way to truly contain costs in health care is to improve outcomes: in a value-based system, achieving and maintaining good health is inherently less costly than dealing with poor health' (Porter, 2009).

Second, and particularly while concerns remain about the cost of health and social care, there is an opportunity for clinical psychologists to extend their roles in the measurement of public health outcomes (see e.g. Barkham et al., 2010) and guidance on outcomes published by the Department of Health (2011a, 2011b) and the NHS Confederation (Richardson & Cotton, 2011).

Third, it is also clear from the history of clinical psychology in the NHS that leadership is critical, not only from within the profession where some exceptional figures (May Davidson, Glenys Parry) have significantly influenced policy, but also outside it (William Trethowan, Derek Mowbray). However, the roles occupied at the DH first by May Davidson, then David Hawks, Ed Miller, John Hall, and Malcolm Adams, and subsequently by internal advisers Ed Miller, Glenys Parry, and myself, have now gone. Now, with a much slimmed-down Department of Health and with oversight for commissioning held by NHS England effectively 'at arm's length' from government, opportunities for the profession to further its interests on a national scale have simultaneously broadened (potentially to every CCG) and narrowed (to an executive non-departmental body). 'The fundamental problem is not a lack of good stuff to push, it's a lack of good people to pull' (Graham Thornicroft, personal communication, March 2011).

Last but by no means least, it is important to remember that change in the NHS doesn't always start at what we usually call 'the top' with the service managers, planners and commissioners. Service users and carers can have very different priorities from those of politicians and clinicians (see chapter 2) and they can be very powerful, as can members of the public affected by mental care concerns. For example, Jayne Zito, the wife of the young man killed by 'care in the community' patient Christopher Clunis, had a profound influence upon the plans drawn up to reform the Mental Health Act when New Labour came to power in 1997. Alliances with service users as full partners in the delivery and evaluation of healthcare services arguably matter as much as alliances with ministers once did.

References

NB Department of Health documents are held in the government archive: http://webarchive.nationalarchives.gov.uk

Appleby, L. (2004). *The National Service Framework five years on.* London: Department of Health.

Audit Commission (2006). *Managing finances in mental health: A review to support improvement and best practice.* London: Author.

Barkham, M., Hardy, G.E. & Mellor-Clark, J. (Eds.) (2010). *Developing and delivering practice-based evidence: A guide for the psychological therapies.* Chichester: Wiley.

Blair, T (1998). *The third way: New politics for the new century. Pamphlet 588.* London: The Fabian Society.

Department of Health (1997). *The new NHS: Modern, dependable.* Cm 3807. London: Author.

Department of Health (1998). *Modernising mental health: Safe, sound and supportive.* London: Author.
Department of Health (1999). *Modern standards and service models. The Mental Health National Service Framework.* London: Author.
Department of Health (2000). *Psychological therapies: Working in partnership.* London: Author.
Department of Health (2001a). *Choosing talking therapies.* London: Author.
Department of Health (2001b). *Shifting the balance of power within the NHS: Securing delivery.* London: Author.
Department of Health (2001c). *Treatment choice in psychological therapies and counselling: Evidence-based clinical practice guideline.* London: Author.
Department of Health (2003). *Fast forwarding primary care mental health: Graduate primary care mental health workers. Best practice guidance.* London: Author.
Department of Health (2004a). *Agenda for change.* London: Author.
Department of Health (2004b). *Organising and delivering psychological therapies.* London: Author.
Department of Health (2011a). *Healthy lives, healthy people: Transparency in outcomes, proposals for a public health outcomes framework.* London: Author.
Department of Health (2011b). *No health without mental health: A cross-government mental health outcomes strategy for people of all ages.* London: Author.
Department of Health and Social Security (1977). *The role of psychologists in the health service (Trethowan Report).* London: HMSO.
Glasby, J. (Ed.) (2011). *Evidence, policy and practice: Critical perspectives in health and social care.* Bristol: The Policy Press.
Griffiths, R. (1989). *Working for patients.* London: Department of Health.
Griffiths, S. & Sheen, S. (2013). Improving Access to Psychological Therapies (IAPT) programme: Scrutinising IAPT cost estimates to support effective commissioning. *Journal of Psychological Therapies in Primary Care, 2,* 142–156.
Harkness, E., Bower, P., Gask., L. & Sibbald, B. (2006). *National evaluation of graduate primary care workers.* York: National Primary Care R & D Centre.
Hills, J. & Stewart, K. (Eds.) (2005). *A more equal society? New Labour, poverty, inequality and exclusion.* Bristol: The Policy Press.
Howe, G. (1969). *Report of the committee of inquiry into allegations of ill-treatment of patients and other irregularities at the Ely Hospital, Cardiff.* Cmnd 3975. London: HMSO.
Layard, R. (2005, January). *Mental health: Britain's biggest social problem.* Paper presented at No. 10 Strategy Unit Seminar on Mental Health. http://eprints.lse.ac.uk/47428/
Management Advisory Service (1989). *Review of clinical psychology services.* Cheltenham: Author.
Maynard, A. & Sheldon, T. (2002, 17 August). Funding for the National Health Service. [Letter to the editor]. *The Lancet, 360,* 576.
Michie, S., Webb T.L. & Sniehotta F.F. (2010). The importance of making explicit links between theoretical constructs and behaviour change techniques. *Addiction, 105,* 1897–1898.
NHS Executive (1996). *NHS psychotherapy services in England: Review of strategic policy.* London: Department of Health.
Pilling, S. & Roth, A. (2008). Commentary on 'Improving access to psychological therapy: The Doncaster demonstration site organisational model' by Richards and Suckling. *Clinical Psychology Forum, 181,* 41–43.
Porter, M.E. (2009). A strategy for health care reform – Toward a value-based system. *New England Journal of Medicine, 361,* 109–112.
Richardson, A. (2002). *Graduate primary care workers: The content and process of one-year full-time training. A discussion paper distributed to HE establishments in England.* London: Department of Health.
Richardson, A. & Cotton, R. (2011). *No health without mental health: Developing an outcomes based approach.* London: NHS Confederation.
Scrivens, E. & Charlton, D. (1985). *The nature and size of clinical psychology. Bath Social Policy Papers No.6.* Bath: University of Bath.
Seebohm, F. (1968). *Report of the Committee on Local Authority and Allied Personal Social Services.* Cmnd 3703. London: HMSO.
Sherrard, M.D. (1978). *Report of the Committee of Inquiry into Normansfield Hospital.* Cmnd 7357. London: HMSO.
Smail, D (2006). Is clinical psychology selling its soul (again)? *Clinical Psychology Forum, 168,* 17–20.

Tansella, M. & Thornicroft, G. (2009). Implementation science: Understanding the translation of evidence into practice. *British Journal of Psychiatry, 195*, 283–285.
Thornicroft, G. (2011) A new mental health strategy for England. *British Medical Journal, 342*, 1346.
Thornicroft, G., Lempp, H. & Tansella, M. (2011). The place of implementation science in the translational medicine continuum. *Psychological Medicine, 41*, 2015–2021.
Walshe, K. (2003). *Inquiries: Learning from failure in the NHS?* London: The Nuffield Trust.
Wanless, D. (2001). *Securing our future health: Taking a long-term view.* London: Public Inquiry Unit.
Watkins, T. (1971). *Report of the Farleigh Hospital Committee of Inquiry.* Cmnd 4557. London: HMSO.
Zuckerman Report (1968). *Hospital scientific and technical services.* London: HMSO.

Chapter 7 The development and training of the clinical psychological workforce: From probationers to practitioner doctorates

Tony Lavender & Graham Turpin

Introduction

The origins of the profession of clinical psychology are inextricably linked to the creation and subsequent development of the National Health Service (NHS). Most key developments within the profession have been in response to demands from its major employer: the NHS. Training and workforce planning, the subject of this chapter, have been determined in the main by NHS requirements. Moreover, the NHS has itself been determined by a variety of sociopolitical and economic forces (see chapters 1, 4 and 6). This symbiotic relationship between the NHS and the profession is unique to the UK.

The chapter is constructed around what we consider to be three distinct historical phases in the development of clinical psychology training within the UK. The first concerns the early history during the middle of the 20th century (1946–1964) and the emergence of a profession of clinical psychology. It describes the origins of probationer training (i.e. psychology apprenticeships) together with the establishment of the first formal training courses. The second phase (1964–1978) involves the evolution of two competing models of training comprising on the one hand three-year inservice (NHS) courses and two-year university-based programmes on the other. The third phase (1979 –2007) focuses on the reconciliation of these different models of training, the emergence of clinical doctorates, and the key NHS drivers that established the current training structures. Within each of these phases, we also briefly describe the then state of NHS workforce planning activities and processes. Finally, we conclude with a discussion of some unresolved issues and challenges for the future. We should also like to direct the reader to the appendices at the end of this volume (Appendix 4), where further detailed information is recorded about workforce numbers within the NHS and the dates when individual training programmes commenced.

The birth of the NHS and clinical psychology (1946–1964)

Origins of the profession

Although the idea of a clinical psychologist (or rather a psychologist working in the mental health field) had existed from the start of the First World War, it did not become a reality until after the Second World War. It is important to note that up to 1930 the majority of people with mental health problems were treated compulsorily in large mental health hospitals (see chapters 1, 3 and 17). There was, however, a growing awareness (Royal Commission, 1926) of a need for more outpatient work and community care, populated by a variety of health workers. With respect to mental health, there were two institutions which had a significant influence on psychological work: the Tavistock Clinic and the Maudsley Hospital. The Tavistock Clinic was established in 1920 and it aimed to promote the modern psychological treatment of adults and children, and thereby embrace all methods of psychotherapy (see chapters 13 and 15).

The other key institution was the Institute of Psychiatry (formerly Maudsley Medical School), which was established in 1948, and unlike the Tavistock Institute (formed in 1946/7), mainly employed mainstream psychiatrists (see chapter 9). Edward Mapother, the first superintendent, in liaison with Charles Spearman at UCL, began to appoint psychologists at the Maudsley in the 1930s. A Miss Steadman and W.H. Pinard were appointed half time mainly to work clinically with children and on research with adults (see chapter 16).

Origins of training and formalised courses

According to a 1962 briefing paper (copy in the May Davidson papers held at the Wellcome Library, London: catalogue reference PSY/DAV), when the NHS was established it was estimated that there were around 70 clinical psychologists and many were working part-time. Most of these, although possessing a degree in psychology, were trained as teachers (e.g. Graham-White; see chapters 2 and 16), and several had trained as educational psychologists associated with child guidance clinics (e.g. Grace Rawlings). Some of these psychologists would have been employed as probationer psychologists and supervised by a senior psychologist working either within the locality or more usually just within their own hospital. Hence the origins of training lay with supervised apprenticeships rather than the establishment of formal courses such as those at the Tavistock or Maudsley.

With respect to courses, it is not absolutely clear which was the first clinical psychology training course in the UK. There is evidence that in the 1930s a Miss Simmons developed training in psychology for staff working in the Child Guidance section of the Tavistock Clinic (Dicks, 1970). Certainly by 1945 courses for psychologists (i.e. educational, medical/clinical) were established at the Tavistock, and by 1951/1952 there was a prospectus (copy in the John Raven papers held at the Wellcome Library: catalogue reference PSY/RAV/2/8) for a two-year programme that described a first year working with children (educational) and a second year with adults (clinical).

In parallel with these developments, work to establish the first clinical psychology programme at the Maudsley Hospital began in 1946 (Buchanan, 2010). Chapter 9 deals specifically with the emergence of clinical training at the Maudsley Hospital and the particular contributions of Hans Eysenck and Monte Shapiro. We will only consider the headlines, since they set the scene for developments elsewhere in the UK. Eysenck saw the role of a clinical psychologist as principally conducting research as an independent professional, although there was much pressure to perform assessment as directed by a psychiatrist (Derksen, 2000). This support role was frequently referred to as a 'pseudopsychiatrist' (Yates, 1970). Moreover, Aubrey Lewis, the Professor of Psychiatry, was strongly opposed to psychologists being directly involved in therapy: a view that was conveniently and initially echoed by Eysenck (see chapter 9).

The planning for the course started in 1946 and Monte Shapiro was appointed as head of the Clinical Section within the Psychology Department in 1947 (Buchanan, 2010). The course did not actually lead to a University of London Diploma until 1952 because of the efforts of Cyril Burt to block this development. According to Ann Clarke (as reported by her nephew David Shapiro, personal communication, November 2014), who together with her husband Alan, were both PhD students at the Institute of Psychiatry and had originally come to be supervised by Eysenck, Burt considered Eysenck a rival and did everything he could do to limit his and the Maudsley's influence within the University of London.

The Maudsley course went through a number of rapid changes, which reflected the diverse influences controlling its future. In 1949, the intake on the Route 'A' or the 12-month course doubled to 12. An additional 'B' route was also proposed lasting an extra two years and leading to a PhD (Eysenck, 1949). Also in 1949, Eysenck spent six months at the University of Pennsylvania observing the development of the profession in the US; his trip was supported by a scholarship organised by Lewis. His experiences led him to develop a vision for the UK profession (Eysenck, 1949), which stressed assessment and research skills versus therapy as the major roles of prime importance to the profession (see also chapters 9 and 14).

Divergent views of training at the Institute of Psychiatry

During the 1950s, Eysenck focused on those students completing their PhDs and seldom, if ever, saw patients or took part in ward rounds. Shapiro, on the other hand, was responsible for delivering a clinical service within the Maudsley, as well as for directing the Diploma, and he encouraged the Diploma students to apply their psychological skills and knowledge to the understanding of the individual patient or client (Derksen, 2000). Hence Shapiro's teaching represented the UK version of the scientist-practitioner (Shapiro, 1957, 1966, 1967; see also chapter 24).

It is clear from correspondence between Shapiro and Eysenck, held by Monte's son David Shapiro, that their relationship was frequently fractious and they held very different aspirations for the future of the profession. Indeed, at one time (Autumn 1961) Eysenck appears to challenge Shapiro's leadership of the Diploma. It was perhaps inevitable that Eysenck withdrew from direct involvement with clinical training, leading him to quit the Committee of Professional Psychologists in 1953. The Institute course continued to develop and supported the study of behaviour therapy and its applications (Shapiro, 1964; Yates, 1970): a therapeutic approach which Eysenck now championed for clinical psychologists (see chapters 9 and 14). In 1955, Shapiro published a detailed description of the 13-month Diploma of the University of London in Abnormal Psychology within the *BPS Bulletin* (Shapiro, 1955). In 1966, the course became a one-year MSc and a decade later was extended into a two-year MPhil degree (Payne, 2000; Yule, 2011). While Eysenck had prepared the ground for the birth of formal training in the UK, it was very much Shapiro who developed the Institute of Psychiatry training scheme and had more generally advanced the profession through his work with the BPS and other contemporary psychologists such as May Davidson, Mahesh Desai and Grace Rawlings.

Other developments elsewhere in clinical psychology training

The Institute of Psychiatry had been very influential in developing clinical psychology training both within the UK and also the Commonwealth (i.e. Australia and Canada) and this has been documented elsewhere (Dabbs & Newnes, 2000; Yule, 2011). Indeed, the third of the earliest courses was established in 1952 at the Crichton Royal Hospital, Dumfries and was led by John Raven, an Institute graduate. The course was for three years and based within the hospital, which had close links with Glasgow University (see chapter 23). The first year concentrated on psychometric tests with adults and children, while the second and third years were spent on research-intensive investigations, feeding into ward rounds and offering psychotherapeutic and rehabilitation work alongside other staff. It appears that this course operated through organising the experiences of probationer psychologists within the NHS and could claim to be the first inservice training programme.

Impact of the NHS and Whitely Council on the profession

With the creation of the NHS, it became clear that the roles and employment of both educational and clinical psychologists would need to be formalised (see chapter 1). A new negotiating machinery for pay and conditions within the NHS, known as the Whitley Council, was created in 1952 and stipulated the NHS requirements for a psychologist to hold a British or Irish honours degree in psychology or 'equivalent', to be normally 25 years old and to have one of the following trainings:

- Completed an approved clinical psychology training course (full time) plus one year supervision (University course route).
- Served for three years under supervision to the satisfaction of the employer (Independent Probationer route).
- Completed two years' training, and left to the discretion of employers about whether a third supervised year was needed (Inservice course route).

In 1957, part II of PTA circular 52 was published which recognised 'approved training courses' including the Institute of Psychiatry, the Crichton Royal and the Tavistock.

BPS guidance on training and standards of practice

The Whitley Council summarised only the minimum requirements for training and entry into employment within the NHS. This left a large demand for supporting administration and guidance as to how the profession would agree the details of these arrangements. The British Psychological Society (BPS) led on this work, although much of the practical negotiations were conducted by professional members of the then relevant trade union, the Association of Scientific Workers.

During the early 1950s the training of professional psychologists was overseen by the (Steering) Committee on Training in Psychology (CTP), whose minutes from the early 1960s are available within the BPS archives held at the Wellcome Library (catalogue reference PSY/BPS/1/4/6) The CTP also sought advice from the Committee of Professional Psychologists (CPP), which was formed by the BPS during the war to progress applied professional psychology. A key member of the CPP was Grace Rawlings. It is interesting to note that various members of staff from the Maudsley Hospital (e.g. M.H. Himmelweit and M.B. Shapiro) attended these early committees, and indeed Eysenck was a member of the CPP but rarely attended and resigned in 1953. The CPP had developed various subcommittee structures, including one for mental health (CPP(MH)). The names of these committees were frequently prefixed by 'English', due to divisions between the English and Scottish educational psychologists.

Perhaps the most important of the CPP subcommittees was a working party formed in 1952 to address concerns about training of psychologists in the education and health services in England and Wales. The working party sought to flesh out the details of the Whitley Council P.T.A. Circular No. 10. The Report (BPS, 1955) describes the role of clinical psychologists and focuses on diagnosis and assessment. With regard to treatment the Report (p.4) states that 'the psychologist does not engage directly in psychotherapy, he participates in the re-education of patients and influences treatment by helping to assess…'.

Roles for rehabilitation, research and teaching are also heavily emphasised. The guidance recommends the nature, length and content of various trainings and effectively documents the first set of BPS accreditation criteria for training courses for professional psychologists (educational, clinical and prison). The report also recommended the range of training experiences and techniques to be acquired during training. It noted particular concerns about the independent probationer route and suggested that very few hospitals had sufficient senior staff to offer the experiences recommended by the new guidance.

From the late 1950s onwards one of CTP's major roles was the scrutiny and approval of courses. These recommendations were then approved by the BPS Council and would form the basis for the Whitley Council circulars recognising approved programmes of training (Whitley Council, 1952, 1957). This process of course approval was the start of the accreditation process for clinical training programmes overseen by the Committee for Training in Clinical Psychology (CTCP), which held its first recorded meeting in 1982. However, the DCP had a training committee, which reported to the Professionals Affairs Board during the early 1970s and was the forerunner of CTCP. It would appear that the first reported onsite visit of a clinical programme was at the University of Birmingham in 1974. Detailed accreditation criteria have continually been produced and revised on approximately a five-year cycle up until the most recent version in 2013.

Inservice training

Alongside the CTP there was also the Co-ordinating Committee of Senior Psychologists (CCSP) in the NHS, which was active in the 1960s. It was chaired by May Davidson and the secretary was Mahesh Desai. This was an extremely important committee since it represented the views of practising clinical psychologists working within the various hospitals and asylums across the English and Welsh (and later Scottish) Regional Boards. Again, together with the CPP(MH), it was a predecessor to the Division of Clinical Psychology, and perhaps more importantly the network of Regional Advisory Committees that were to advise Regional Health Authorities (established in 1974) across the next few decades. From the minutes, it had a number of aims: establishing a network of regional committees of senior psychologists that would be recognised by their respective local regional boards and medical committees, discussing professional matters associated with the Whitley Council and beyond (e.g. private practice, professional liability insurance), establishing a national framework for policing the quality of inservice training and probationers, and lobbying for substantial increases in the numbers of trainees and psychologists employed (see also chapters 1 and 8).

In 1962 the CCSP drafted a document on inservice training, which was subsequently approved by both the CPP and the CTP. A particular focus was to improve the quality of training and supervision for lone probationers who were not associated with a regional course.

Early attempts to estimate numbers of qualified staff and the demand for psychologists

With the recognition of the profession of clinical psychology in the 1950s by the CTP and CPP (BPS, 1955), a key question had become 'What was the size of this newly recognised profession?'. Indeed, this issue featured within the correspondence in 1956 between the CPP and the CTP (reported later by Mahesh Desai in the minutes of the CCSP in NHS, Wellcome Library catalogue reference PSY/BPS/1/4/5) suggesting a meeting with the Ministry of Health through the Mental Health Advisory Committee. The Ministry of Health were originally resistant to a meeting, but finally met with May Davidson in the early 1960s. The 1962 briefing paper in the May Davidson papers at Wellcome Library, referred to above, was drawn up for that meeting. In the 1960s the CCSP also organised various surveys of NHS psychologists about their involvement in training and supervision. The Committee again commits in 1962 to deriving lists of senior psychologists and their locations.

Similar activities were also undertaken by other BPS committees. The Training Committee undertook a 'Survey of the Users of Psychologists' to canvass the views of employers. At its meeting in July 1962, there is a request from the English Division of Professional Psychologists (EDPP or CPP) to circulate a report on the 'Establishment and Accommodation of Psychologists in General Hospitals' to relevant ministerial and NHS regional committees. In 1965, again following a request from the EDPP about the shortage of clinical psychologists within the NHS, the Society requested a meeting with the Minister of Health. In July 1965 the request for an inquiry into demand for psychologists within the NHS met a familiar rebuttal: 'Ministry is not in favour of a survey on the demand for clinical psychologists, but if other methods of ascertaining the information failed, they would consider this'. There appears to have been a follow-up meeting in June 1968 attended by May Davidson, H. Gwynne Jones, Grace Rawlings and Sheila Chown following a request from the Ministry of Health to discuss 'Clinical Psychologists in the NHS'. A new feature of the discussions is the issue of psychologists qualified overseas being employed within the NHS.

The 1962 briefing paper held within May Davidson's papers is entitled 'Notes on Psychologists in the National Health Service' and has familiar headings such as 'What is a clinical psychologist?', 'What do they do?', 'How many are there?', 'How many are needed?', and 'How are they trained and recruited?'. Within this document, it is estimated that there were originally 70 posts at the inception of the NHS. By December 1956, there were 130 psychologists within the NHS, with 10 per cent employed part-time. By 1959 this figure had increased by 50 per cent to 190 and it was estimated to continue to rise by 50 per cent per annum. However, only a minority of hospitals actually employed a senior psychologist during the first decade of the NHS (see also chapters 1, 8 and 17).

The emergence of clinical psychology services (1964–1978) and the two training routes

Two routes to training are consolidated

The publication of criteria for inservice training (both organised courses and lone probationers) in 1962 by the CCSP in the NHS drew attention to the quality of these training routes. There were particular concerns about the range of clinical experience that most probationers were exposed to, especially if they were based in a hospital with a single client group (e.g. psychiatric asylum, 'mental handicap' hospital), and also the quality of supervision. These concerns culminated in a Training Conference at the University of Sussex held by EDPP (Clinical Section) in 1966. This was a crucial year in that the Royal Charter had been granted, the Division of Clinical Psychology was to be newly formed, and a committee had been established to introduce a BPS Diploma in Clinical Psychology. Key themes at the conference were the problems of probationers and poor supervision, as was the balance between research/academic approaches and clinical skills. In addition, the perceived elitist and selective nature of university training courses was discussed, since married and more mature candidates, or those with third class honours degrees, were finding it increasingly difficult to access training. It looked as if university courses might become the only qualifying route and people questioned the wisdom of introducing a BPS Diploma. Nevertheless, the eventual outcome was the establishment of the BPS Diploma in Clinical Psychology in 1968 and the formalisation of three-year inservice training programmes.

By 1979 training courses were divided into either two-year university-based masters programmes or three year inservice schemes leading to the Diploma in Clinical Psychology. The inservice schemes that developed were set up to train people specifically for their local service. Six such schemes were established between 1968 and 1988 (see Table 7.1). The courses were only made possible by the establishment of the Society's Diploma in Clinical Psychology and overseen by the influential Board of Examiners. Since BPS was not a higher education institution, it could only award diplomas and did not have the power to offer Master's qualifications. For a more detailed account of the start of the South East Thames Salomons scheme see Lavender and Squier (2000).

NHS reorganisation and the emergence of more formal professional structures through the BPS

The NHS had largely remained untouched until the reorganisation of 1974 that saw the 700 individual hospital boards replaced with a regional framework of area and district management teams. At the same time, clinical psychology started to expand and gain recognition as a new emergent professional group. Instead of just considering the role of individual psychologists, discussions were under way as to how psychological services comprising teams or departments of psychologists should be organised, and what services they might offer to a range of patients within the NHS. These considerations exposed massive underprovision of psychological services (see chapter 1). Other client groups, apart from adults, became identified as having important unmet psychological needs and began to be

Table 7.1 Chronology of clinical psychology training courses

We have only indicated the start dates of programmes and the date of any transfer or name change from an inservice course to a university. Many university courses started as two-year Master's programmes but then evolved into three-year doctorates. For simplicity, we have omitted these dates and the exact titles of the academic awards.

1947	Maudsley Hospital Medical School
1952	Tavistock Institute (closed in the 1960s)
	Crichton Royal Hospital
1959	Queen's University Belfast
1960	Edinburgh University
	Glasgow University
1962	Liverpool University
1964	Newcastle University
1965	Leeds University
1966	Birmingham University
1968	Wessex Inservice (moved to University of Southampton in 1999)
1971	University of Surrey
1972	South East Thames Inservice (moved to Salomons: Canterbury Christ Church University in 1996)
1973	North East London Polytechnic (renamed University of East London from 1994)
1975	North West Thames Inservice (moved to University College London in 1987)
	South Wales Inservice Course (moved to Cardiff University in 1993)
1975	University of Exeter (original degree in Community and Clinical Psychology)
1976	Aberdeen University (closed in 1989)
	Lancashire Inservice Course (moved to Lancaster University in 1993)
	Oxford University (closed in 1979)
1981	Oxford Inservice Course (awarded Open University Doctorate from 1993 and moved to Oxford University in 2000)
1982	University of Leicester
	University of Plymouth
1986	University of Hull (integrated six-year undergraduate/postgraduate programme; the first cohort had commenced their undergraduate degree in 1983/84)
1987	University College London
1988	Cambridge University (closed 1994; trainees in second and third years transfer to the University of East Anglia)
	North Wales Inservice Course (moved to Bangor University in 1991)
1990	University of Sheffield
1991	Bangor University
1993	Lancaster University
	Cardiff University
1994	University of East Anglia (with transfer of Cambridge University trainees; first new cohort 1995)

1996	Teesside University
	Salomons: Canterbury Christ Church University
1997	Royal Holloway, University of London
1998	Coventry/Warwick Universities
1999	University of Southampton
2000	Oxford University
2001	University of Bristol (closed in 2011, contract awarded to the University of Bath)
	University of Hertfordshire
2004	Staffordshire/Keele Universities
	University of Essex/Tavistock Institute
2005	Universities of Lincoln/Nottingham
2010	University of Bath

included in training (see chapters 16 –22). In addition, it marked the expansion of community care, as heralded by Enoch Powell and the new Mental Health Act (Powell, 1961).

It was also during this period that the Trethowan Report (DHSS, 1977) was published and had a major impact on the development of the profession and its training over the next decade or so (see chapter 1). With respect to training, it identified the need for more trainees, a widening of the curriculum beyond just adult mental health and the end of the independent probationer route, and recommended that qualified psychologists should be supported by psychology technicians.

Growth in the clinical psychology workforce but inability to meet demand

In 1966, the issue of workforce planning was taken up by the newly formed Division of Clinical Psychology. In a paper by P.T. Brown, read at the British Association for the Advancement of Science (1973), on the training of clinical psychologists as clinical scientists, he estimated that there were 583 NHS posts within the UK and these were equivalent to 557 full-time posts. Of these, 33 per cent were training probationers and around 20 per cent were basic grades or newly qualified. He goes on to describe the numbers entering training (66 university and 18 diploma places), together with estimates of need ranging from 1:60,000 to 1:35,000 psychologists to the population. He concludes that the workforce shortage in 1972 ranges between 366 and 1030 qualified staff. He also quotes a survey by Kear-Colwell (1972) that suggests nearly half of clinical psychologists that moved to a new post left the NHS despite their grade. Further data are provided by region in the October 1976 *DCP Newsletter*. There is a count of qualified staff by region for 1973 (i.e. not trainees or those employed by universities), including the relative population size of each region, and the total had reached 509 staff. It soon became apparent that the growth in the profession envisaged by Trethowan would be severely limited by the available supply of qualified psychologists working within the NHS and the relatively scarce numbers of training places.

Major changes to NHS (1979–2007)

NHS reorganisation, the BPS Register of Chartered Psychologists, and implementing the Trethowan Report

In summer 1979, the Royal Commission published its report into the NHS, which led to further reforms (see chapters 1 and 6). This all culminated in the White Paper *Working for Patients* in 1989, together with 10 working papers, including Working Paper 10, which specifically addressed the training of health professionals within the NHS. A major change in the arrangements for education and training was introduced: purchasers of training were to be Regional Health Authorities and the providers the university courses.

A major preoccupation for the BPS at this time was the introduction of a scheme of registration of psychologists, which would require an amendment to the Royal Charter. The impetus for registration coincided with pressure brought about by the publication of the Sieghart Report in 1978, which was concerned with the need to create a register of psychotherapists following the Scientology scandal of the early and mid-1970s. In 1987 a voluntary charter was established requiring three years' postgraduate training to join the Register and become a Chartered Psychologist. The creation of the Register would have unintended consequences on the development of training in the subsequent decade.

Demand outstrips supply: MPAG and MAS

During the mid-1980s there was ever-increasing recognition post-Trethowan of the shortage of clinical psychologists (see chapters 1 and 17). The DCP urged the Department of Health and Social Security, and its main committee responsible for workforce issues, the Manpower Planning Advisory Group (MPAG), to advise regional general managers about increasing the numbers of training posts. Its response was to commission a 'greenfield review' of clinical psychology known as the MAS/MPAG reports (see chapters 1, 5 and 6). The MPAG report was published in September 1989 and among other recommendations it suggested an increase in the workforce from just under 2500 (1989) to 4000 by year 2000. Bernard Kat had been responsible for a survey of courses seeking to establish both local demand for training and course capacity. It recommended that the number of training places went from 173 (in 1990) to 300 by 2000. Unfortunately, the Department of Health's response was neither to endorse the report, nor to recommend policy changes – rather to wait and see how this would all work following the implementation of the wider policy reforms.

Consolidating length of training to three years and the growth of the profession

There had, since the inception of formal training in the UK, been debate about the appropriate length of training. Eysenck (1949) had suggested a three-year PhD but only for an elite few of the best researchers. The original Whitley Council Circulars had allowed both two- and three-year routes. The establishment of the BPS Diploma and the acceptance of three-year inservice schemes had formally endorsed this route. At the same time the BPS accredited two-year university courses (see Table 7.1). With the creation of the BPS Register, it was necessary to revisit the optimum length of training.

Three key issues were to determine the future pattern of training. First, changes to the BPS accreditation criteria had always added to course requirements (e.g. the 1989 changes required the addition of placement/experience with older people) but never reduced what was expected. Second, the adoption of the Charter and associated Register meant that the duration of training leading to Chartership was three years. In negotiations to establish the Charter it was clear that it was untenable to say training should last either two or three years. Third, the Regional Health Authorities (RHAs) had always hosted regional inservice schemes, but with the emergence of the purchaser–provider divide, and Strategic Health Authorities (SHAs) now being the purchasers of training, there was pressure for inservice regional schemes to move into universities or non-NHS organisations.

The above arguments reinforced the view of the inservice trainers that three years was now the appropriate length of training generally but created tension between inservice and university staff. These were discussed frequently at meetings of the two groups of training staff, the Committee of Regional Inservice Courses (CORIC) and Committee of University Clinical Psychology Training Courses (CUCPTC).[1] Change appeared inevitable, leading to some kind of standardisation of training at three years. However, there were also significant forces aligned against such a move, and perhaps the greatest opposition was from both the NHS and within the profession itself. Since Trethowan, it had become recognised that there was a great shortage of clinical psychologists. As Trethowan pointed out, this was despite the fact that there was a plentiful supply of psychology graduates who were keen to train (see chapter 1). The DCP and BPS had approached the DHSS on numerous occasions to pressure Regional Health Authorities into supporting an expansion of clinical psychology training. The MAS/MPAG reports had placed the shortage of staff and the vacancy rate of the profession as somewhere within the region of 10 to 20 per cent. Such a high vacancy rate, as Bernard Kat stressed on numerous occasions with DHSS staff, led to inadequate psychology services for the public, together with inflated salaries for those staff who were already in post. Neither situation should be preferable to the DHSS. Clearly, one solution was to invest more in clinical psychology training. Unfortunately, calls for extending training from two to three years for university courses amounted to a 50 per cent increase in costs when the name of the game was increased training numbers.

The emergence of clinical doctorates

The profession's interest in doctorates had been reawakened in the mid-1980s when the University of Birmingham offered its two-year Master's graduates in clinical psychology an opportunity to register for a further two years for a PhD. Similarly, many senior NHS clinicians would register part-time for PhDs, although it should be stressed that the successful completion rates for these part-time clinicians was said to be low. The recognition of a clinical doctorate had become popular in the US, with the research-based PhD, as advocated by the Boulder Conference in 1949 (Chiszar & Wertheimer, 1988) but being supplemented by the PsyD at the Vail Conference in 1972 (see chapter 24). At the same time, professional or practitioner doctorates were gaining academic respectability within both

[1] Minutes for these two organisations have been located and are about to be archived by the BPS.

the US (e.g. PsyD, MD, DPharm, DOrthoptics) and also in the UK with several institutions offering practitioner doctorates within Education (DEd), Engineering (DEng) and other professional disciplines. In the UK it was Tony Carr, the course director at Plymouth Polytechnic, who, following a visit to examine US PsyD and clinical PhD programmes, first proposed to CTCP on 31 October 1986 the start of a new three-year doctoral degree to start in September 1987 and to be approved by the Council for National Academic Awards (CNAA).

Chris Cullen, who was CTCP Chair at that time, published an influential discussion paper about doctoral degrees in applied psychology in *The Psychologist* (1988) where he sought feedback on the various arguments for and against, and the varieties of doctoral degrees proposed (e.g. PhDs, DClinPsys, MDs). Letters in response duly arrived at *The Psychologist.* These consisted of support for the US PsyD model (Delroy, 1988; Mollon, 1989); specific support for the Plymouth proposals (Jerrom, 1988; Koch, 1989); and the use of MD and 'doctor' titles (Grieve & McGuire, 1989; Parker, 1989). However, perhaps the most important correspondents were Bernard Kat, who initially judged the Plymouth proposals to be ill-timed (Kat, 1989a), followed by a robust response from Tony Carr detailing the evolution of the Plymouth proposals from 1985 and its apparent approval by a CNAA validation panel in March 1987, which unfortunately was then kicked into the long grass within the CNAA hierarchy (Carr, 1989). Kat acknowledges that he was unaware of the timing of the Plymouth proposals and the delays and political obstacles put in its way (Kat, 1989b). The final letter is from Malcolm Adams (1989) representing the BPS's Membership and Qualifications Board (MQB) informing the readership about the one-day conference that took place in May 1989 to discuss clinical doctorates, and the production of a BPS consultation paper. The BPS concluded from both the conference and consultation that there was insufficient support for the clinical doctorate generally or for it to endorse specifically the Plymouth proposals with CNAA.

It was perhaps unfortunate that the first professional doctorate within clinical psychology should have been proposed at a polytechnic and so was subject to the overall jurisdiction of the CNAA. Had it been presented at an existing university, it would have been within the institution's own gift to recognise the new degree. Although the CNAA was said to have been generally sympathetic to practitioner doctorates, it was reluctant to go ahead with approval within a single subject (i.e. clinical psychology) without some indication of professional support. The BPS Council and MQB and Scientific Affairs Board papers from this time indicate a reluctance to support the introduction of clinical doctorates. There were a number of issues that prevented the type of unqualified support required by the CNAA. First, the BPS was more concerned with the generic criteria for chartered psychologists than specific qualifications. With the recent introduction of the voluntary register it was important that the public and other professionals should seek the prestige and significance of the title 'Chartered Psychologist' rather than a particular academic award or qualification. Academics were also concerned about devaluing the PhD award. There was also a great deal of support for the Society's Diploma to become a Master's degree awarded either by the Society or some external body such as the CNAA.

By the 1990s, the position surrounding three years of training was becoming unsustainable. At a one-day conference in York in 1990, Graham Powell (outgoing Chair of CTCP) announced, in response to the need to provide a length of training consistent with the three-year period of Chartering, that all courses should be three years by 2000. Unfortunately, three years of training was totally inconsistent with existing university qualifications (i.e. Master's degrees). Indeed, due to the Bologna regulations (www.ehea.info), and the introduction of systems of module credits within UK universities, the duration of a standard Master's degree in the future would actually reduce to between nine months and one year.

The pressures on universities to move from two-year Master's degrees (or in the case of the University of East London, three-year Master's degrees) to three-year doctorates were overwhelming. Plymouth's proposals unfortunately were on hold awaiting the dissolution of the CNAA and the establishment of the University of the Southwest (Plymouth), an independent award-granting institution under the auspices of the New Education Act (1994). The first clinical doctorate was announced in the *Times Higher Education Supplement* in May 1992, and was launched by the University of Wales. Professor Mark Williams had been appointed a year earlier with the specific brief to introduce the clinical doctorate to Wales and the UK.

The changes to the Education Act also threatened the ability of the BPS to offer the Diploma, so it had to find a new home for its award. The Board of Examiners (especially Toni Whitehead and Gerry Greene) were extremely keen to introduce a clinical doctorate through CNAA's successor, the Open University Validation Services. Thus the BPS, together with the Salomons scheme (Tony Lavender, South East Thames Inservice Scheme), set about securing institutional accreditation and establishing a new Doctorate in Clinical Psychology as an Open University Degree.

With the above changes, all universities began to see the doctorate as the future. The momentum was such that by 1995, all courses were offering doctorates,[2] together with 'top-up doctorates' for existing qualified staff (Turpin, 1995). The financial cost of moving from two to three years was absorbed in part because the improving economy, and the approach of an election, meant the Conservative Government was able to increase NHS funding by 6.6 per cent in real terms in 1991. In many respects, the widespread adoption of three-year doctorates could be seen as a resounding success for the profession. Unfortunately, its advent did not address the workforce shortages. The challenges inherent in supplying an adequately sized and trained clinical psychology workforce is described below.

Reviewing the workforce and estimating demand and training numbers

In a special training issue of the DCP's newly titled *Clinical Psychology Forum*, Whitehead and Parry (1986) provide an overview of workforce and training needs, based mainly on the recently published report by Scrivens and Charlton (1985). The overall UK establishment then stood at 1615 but the argument was now expressed in terms of the difficulties in filling advertised posts. The NHS was creating posts to meet demand for services, but the supply of psychologists is such that many of

2 Courses varied in the exact title of the clinical doctorate (DClinPsy, PsyClinD, etc.) and indeed some, such as the University of Exeter, awarded a Doctorate in Clinical and Community Psychology up until 2011.

these existing and newly created posts went unfilled following advertisement. For example, around 900 new posts were advertised in the Bulletin of the BPS in 1985. They calculated how the current number of training places (120) would need to be expanded if the vacancies were to be filled. Finally, Brown and Loftus (1988) draw attention to other problems other than the overall number of staff or vacancies. Again using the Scrivens and Charlton (1985) data, they pointed to the fact that 70 per cent of NHS Districts had fewer than nine psychologists in post, and that 30 per cent of Districts had fewer than four posts. They questioned whether such small numbers could provide a sufficient critical mass in order to deliver a clinically comprehensive and effective service.

The focus on vacancies and the inadequate supply of trained staff to fulfil expectations of expansion and improvement in psychology services throughout the NHS led to the already reported commissioning of the MAS report and subsequent steps to increase the training numbers of the clinical psychologists within the system (see subsection on MPAG and MAS above).

Option appraisals and alternative funding models, bursaries and investment in training

For a number of years (1989 until 1997), trainees on the University of Birmingham course had been in receipt of a bursary instead of a trainee salary. Education and training leads from the West Midlands started to discuss with local Regional Health Authorities (RHAs) (i.e. Trent) the possibility of rolling out the bursary scheme to encompass all courses. Indeed, despite vehement objections from the profession, local courses and supervisors, Trent RHA attempted to introduce bursary funding to the 1994 intake of the University of Sheffield course. However, by the end of the summer the scheme was withdrawn since clinical supervisors had withdrawn their support for the course. The profession had also lobbied the Department of Health about adverse effects of bursary funding on attracting a diverse range of students into the profession since they might prove to be disincentives for working-class men and people from ethnic minority backgrounds (BPS, 1988, pp.1–3).

The BPS was still trying to pressurise the NHS Executive about its failure to increase training numbers following the publication of the MPAG report in 1990. It was decided to form a Society working group in October 1994, cochaired by Graham Turpin and Malcolm Adams, to perform an options appraisal about the future demand for clinical psychology, and how such a demand might be met through consideration of different training and funding models. The report *Clinical Psychology Training: Meeting Health Service Demand* was published in September 1995 and made a number of recommendations about expanding training rapidly so as to realise the economies of scale that expansion might bring (BPS, 1995). It emphasised the very low attrition rate from clinical training and the contributions that trainees and qualified staff make to the service. Essentially the report suggested the expansion of training places from 186 (1994/1995) through to 300 (1996/1997) within three years. Eventually this was endorsed and by 2000, there were annually 500 training places throughout the UK.

National Service Frameworks, workforce surveys and planning

The publication of the options appraisal in 1995, as described above, represented the continuing efforts of the Society to work cooperatively with the Department of

Health/NHSE in planning the commissioning of training and the development of workforce planning. A major impetus for this was the introduction of further reforms to the NHS introduced by a newly elected Labour Government in 1997. Within the psychology community there was considerable support for these reforms and particularly with the announcement of a National Service Framework for Mental Health (see chapters 6 and 17). In 1999 a Mental Health Workforce Action Team was established and the BPS nominated Tony Lavender as its representative; he later chaired the subgroup tasked with estimating the number of staff that would be required to deliver the mental health services detailed in the Framework. In parallel, estimations carried out by Boardman and Parsonage (2005) at Sainsbury Centre and by Lavender and Paxton (2004), identified a similar supply-side shortage in staff. The Department of Health also agreed to jointly survey the numbers of applied psychologists within the public sector (Lavender et al., 2005).

Regular meetings were also established with the National Workforce Review Team in 2000, which provided national guidance to the SHAs about workforce demand and supply, constituting additional leverage to increase supply. In 1997 there were approximately 300 training places but by 2005 this had risen to almost 600 and by 2009 to 628, a doubling of training places in a decade. This was achieved by expanding the size of existing training programmes as originally recommended by the BPS (1995) rather than creating many more new courses (see Table 7.1).

A major preoccupation of courses was adapting to the increased numbers but also tackling the major barrier to expansion, which was the availability of placements. Bottlenecks existed in specialties with limited supervisor capacity (i.e. older adults and learning disabilities) that resulted from the rigid application of the existing CTCP criteria. These criteria were revised and clinical experience replaced placements, which meant that trainees could gain experience of working with people with disability and ages across a range of placements. Supervisors were also encouraged to supervise more than one trainee at any one time.

Mental Health Service Review, New Ways of Working and IAPT

The Department of Health and the National Institute of Mental Health (established in 1997 to support the delivery of the NSF) began to look in more depth at the way the professions were working individually and collectively in the mental health services. This gave rise to the New Ways of Working (NWW) movement. A Steering Group was established in 2004 with full professional representation to review the roles of each profession. New Ways of Working for Psychiatrists was the first to be established but New Ways of Working for Applied Psychologists was shortly to follow and was jointly chaired by Tony Lavender and Roslyn Hope. This is discussed in greater detail in chapter 5. Unfortunately, the implementation of NWW for Applied Psychologists (BPS, 2007) was overshadowed by a major new initiative, Improving Access to Psychological Therapies (see chapter 14).

Conclusion and unresolved issues

While researching and writing this chapter we were both struck by the existence of major issues concerning the clinical psychology workforce and its training that have yet to be satisfactorily resolved. Some of these issues concern the profession generally and will be taken up in the final chapter. Nevertheless, we wish to draw attention to what we consider to be the most salient issues, which require resolution, hopefully in the near future.

Professional identity and recognition

In order to plan rationally for a health profession, it has to be recognised and acknowledged within the NHS. Ever since 1967, when the Zuckerman Committee failed to decide whether clinical psychologists were scientists or clinicians, there has been uncertainty as to how clinical psychology should be recognised and represented within the Department of Health and the government. At various times and in the different nations, psychology has been associated with medicine and dentistry, professions allied to medicine and clinical scientists. Failure to identify psychology with these major professional groupings or to secure recognition of psychologists as an independent group has often resulted in the profession not gaining government recognition nor benefiting from professionally focused developments concerning training. Two examples are recent major initiatives in the last decade focusing on developing clinical academic careers and the Darzi Workforce reviews (Department of Health, 2008) where clinical psychology as a profession was omitted from the process and not considered. Indeed, even today there are calls for psychology to be represented at the highest levels of government through the creation of a Chief Psychologist (Karpur, 2014). This lack of recognition has also resulted in significant problems in collecting reliable workforce data about the profession either for actuarial purposes or for future workforce planning.

Understanding our professional roles and contributions

An issue related to the failure to recognise the existence of psychology within the NHS is the degree to which our role and contribution is understood. A common misconception is that psychologists mainly work with adults providing psychological therapies, and that they are remunerated well above other counselling or psychotherapy providers. A challenge has been for the profession to effectively market itself and, in the terms of May Davidson's 1962 briefing paper, explain who we are and what we do. Indeed, we need to promote our contribution, especially for consultant psychologists, to innovation and leadership within the health service, as well as our specialised therapy skills. Many of these issues were examined in some detail within *New Ways of Working for Applied Psychologists* (BPS, 2007; see also chapter 5).

Skill mix and psychology roles and contributions

Trethowan recognised the popularity of psychology and the large numbers of psychology graduates produced each year from our universities. Since then there have been various initiatives (e.g. Graduate Mental Health Workers, IAPT Psychological Well-being Practitioners) to expand access to psychological services by the utilisation of psychology graduates within services in addition to fully trained or qualified clinical psychologists. Despite recommendations made by NWW for Applied Psychologists, the profession generally has yet to harness the contribution to be made by psychology graduates. In Northern Ireland and Scotland (see chapter 23), there have been innovative programmes to formally train either psychology assistants or associates but these have not been introduced into England and Wales. The status and training psychology assistants, or technicians as described by Trethowan, requires our urgent attention.

Acknowledgements

Particular thanks should go to Lucy Horder and Keren Gilbert from the BPS Partnership and Accreditation Team for their research into course accreditation dates. Similarly, we would also like to thank members of the Group of Trainers in Clinical Psychology who commented on earlier drafts and also supplied much missing documentation from the past. We are also grateful to David Shapiro for sharing copies of Monte Shapiro's papers and correspondence. Finally, we would like to dedicate this chapter to the memory of Malcolm Adams, who helped to implement many of the developments in training in the last 30 years.

References

Adams, M. (1989). Doctorates in clinical psychology. [Letter to the editor]. *The Psychologist, 2,* 521.

Boardman, J. & Parsonage, M. (2005). *Defining a good mental health service.* London: Sainsbury Centre for Mental Health.

British Psychological Society (1955). Post-graduate training in educational and clinical psychology. *Bulletin of the British Psychological Society, 25,* 1–19.

British Psychological Society (1988). *Implications of adopting the bursary model of funding training in clinical psychology. A policy statement. Membership and Qualifications Board and the Division of Clinical Psychology.* Leicester: Author.

British Psychological Society (1995). *Clinical psychology training: Meeting health service demand.* Leicester: Author.

British Psychological Society (2007). *New ways of working for applied psychologists.* Leicester: Author.

Brown, P.T. (1973, August). *Training clinical psychologists.* Paper presented at the 135th Annual Meeting of the British Association for the Advancement of Science, Canterbury.

Brown, P. & Loftus, M. (1988). Clinical psychology in crisis. *The Psychologist, 1,* 393–395.

Buchanan, R.D. (2010). *Playing with fire: The controversial career of Hans J. Eysenck.* Oxford: Oxford University Press.

Carr, T. (1989). Development of the D.Clin.Psy. [Letter to the editor]. *The Psychologist, 2,* 212.

Chiszar, D. & Wertheimer, M. (1988). The Boulder Model: A history of psychology at the University of Colorado. *Journal of the History of the Behavioral Sciences, 24,* 81–86.

Cullen, C. (1988). Doctoral degrees in applied psychology. *The Psychologist, 1,* 395–396.

Dabbs, A. & Newnes, C. (2000). Special issue: Histories of clinical psychology training. *Clinical Psychology Forum, 145,* 1–50.

Delroy, S. (1988). Doctor of Psychology (Psy.D) in clinical psychology. [Letter to the editor]. *The Psychologist, 1,* 440– 441.

Department of Health (2008). *A high quality workforce: NHS Next Stage Review (Darzi Workforce Review).* London: HMSO.

Department of Health and Social Security (1977). *The role of psychologists in the health service (Trethowan Report).* London: HMSO.

Derksen, M. (2000). Clinical psychology and the psychological clinic: The early years of clinical psychology at the Maudsley. *History and Philosophy of Psychology, 2,* 1–17.

Dicks, H.V. (1970). *Fifty years of the Tavistock Clinic.* London: Routledge, Keegan & Paul.

Eysenck, H.J. (1949). Training in clinical psychology: An English point of view. *American Psychologist, 4,* 173–176.

Grieve, R. & McGuire, R. (1989). Doctoral degrees in applied psychology. *The Psychologist, 2,* 71.

Jerrom, B. (1988). Doctoral degrees in applied psychology. [Letter to the editor]. *The Psychologist, 1,* 497.

Karpur, N. (2014, 7 November). Why the Health Secretary should see a psychologist. *The Health Service Journal,* 18.

Kat, B. (1989a). D.Clin.Psy. [Letter to the editor]. *The Psychologist, 2,* 25–26.

Kat, B. (1989b). Keeping us up-to-date. [Letter to the editor]. *The Psychologist, 2,* 284.

Kear-Colwell, J.J. (1972). A study of clinical psychologists' job movements during the period 1.11.67 to 30.9.70. *Bulletin of the British Psychological Society, 25,* 25–27.

Koch, H. (1989). D.Clin.Psy. [Letter to the editor]. *The Psychologist, 2,* 103.

Lavender, A., Gray, I. & Richardson, A. (2005). *English survey of applied psychologists in health and social care and in the probation and prison service.* Leicester: BPS.

Lavender, A. & Paxton, R. (2004). *Estimating the applied psychology demand in adult mental health.* Leicester: BPS.

Lavender, A. & Squier, R. (2000). South East Thames Regional Clinical Psychology Training Scheme: In the beginning. *Clinical Psychology Forum, 145,* 22–26.

Management Advisory Service (1989). *Review of clinical psychology services.* Cheltenham: Author.

Manpower Planning Advisory Group (1990). *Manpower Planning Advisory Group report on clinical psychology.* London: Department of Health.

Mollon, P. (1989). D.Clin.Psy. [Letter to the editor]. *The Psychologist, 2,* 25.

Parker, A. (1989). When is a psychologist a doctor? [Letter to the editor]. *The Psychologist, 2,* 243–244.

Payne, R.W. (2000). The beginnings of the clinical psychology programme at the Maudsley Hospital, 1947–1959. *Clinical Psychology Forum, 145,* 17–21.

Powell, E. (1961). *Water tower speech.* http://studymore.org.uk/xpowell.htm

Scrivens, E. & Charlton, D. (1985). *The nature and size of clinical psychology services within health districts in England.* Policy Papers No. 6. Bath: University of Bath.

Shapiro, M.B. (1955). Training of clinical psychologists at the Institute of Psychiatry. *Bulletin of the British Psychological Society, 26,* 15–20.

Shapiro, M.B. (1957). Experimental method in the psychological description of the individual psychiatric patient. *International Journal of Social Psychiatry, III,* 89–102.

Shapiro, M.B. (1964, November). *Behaviour therapy. Principles of treatments for psychosomatic disorders.* Proceedings of a conference held at the Royal College of Physicians, London.

Shapiro, M.B. (1966). The single case in clinical-psychological research. *Journal of General Psychology, 74,* 3–23.

Shapiro, M.B. (1967). Clinical psychology as an applied science. *British Journal of Psychiatry, 113,* 1039–1042.

Turpin, G. (1995). Practitioner doctorates in clinical psychology. *The Psychologist, 8,* 356–358.

Whitley Professional and Technical Council. (1952). *PTA circular 5. RHB (52) 11, HMC (52), BG (52).* London: Ministry of Health.

Whitley Professional and Technical Council. (1957). *PTA circular 52, Part II, HM (58).* London: Ministry of Health.

Whitehead, T. & Parry, G. (1986). National training needs in clinical psychology. *Clinical Psychology Forum, 6,* 7–10.

Yates, A. J. (1970). *Behaviour therapy.* New York: Wiley.

Yule, W. (Ed.) (1997). *50th Anniversary of the Maudsley Clinical Psychology Course: 1947 to 1997.* William Yule Archive, King's College London. (Copy available in the BPS Archive, London AUD/003/OHP 55)

Chapter 8 Colleagues, competitors and offspring: Relationships with other professions

John Hall

Introduction: The central issues

The work of most clinical psychologists has brought them into day-to-day ongoing relationships with their immediate clinical colleagues, who have typically included a doctor, and members of other healthcare professions such as nurses, therapists and social workers, each with their own practice assumptions. This chapter explores the shifting kaleidoscope of multidimensional organisational and professional relationships between psychologists and other clinical professionals in different settings, and how those relationships have changed over time. Relationships with non-clinical colleagues, such as hospital administrators, are discussed in chapter 12.

Phases of development

These shifts in organisation and settings, and hence in immediate colleagues, can be seen as a number of sequential phases, which are only roughly determined by date. They have been affected both by local levels of staffing, and by the variable rates of implementation of changed patterns of institutional and professional working.

From 1948 to the late 1960s, the psychologists in child guidance settings worked mainly with doctors and social workers. Psychologists, most with little prior experience, began to work from the late 1940s and early 1950s in the large mental illness and mental handicap hospitals that had never previously employed psychologists. Their most common work experience would be working on their own – up to the 1970s it was not uncommon for there to be only one or two psychologists in a hospital – engaging with other therapeutic professionals such as nurses and occupational therapists.

Between the late 1960s and the late 1970s the numbers of psychologists in individual hospitals grew so that some hospitals employed several psychologists. They were managed within individual hospital management committees so that it was difficult for psychologists working in the same locality, but with different client groups, to collaborate with each other. In the late 1970s to 1990, following both the reforms of health service administration in 1974 and the implementation of the 1977 Trethowan Report, Area, and then District, departments of clinical psychology were established. These brought together all the psychologists within one locality, usually with a common base (proudly labelled at the entrance to a hospital as 'Psychology Department') and providing each psychologist with a room of their own, giving psychologists some control of the allocation of their time to different areas of work. The continuing reduction in size of the large hospitals was associated with a move of psychologists to non-hospital bases and the expansion of community-based work, associated with closer contact with primary care and other community colleagues, including workers in voluntary agencies, and multidisciplinary teamwork began to be a reality. From 1948 there was a slow increase in the provision of psychological services in clinical areas other than mental health and learning disability.

From 1990 the introduction of general management and NHS Trusts meant that direct managerial relationships through a trust head psychologist could move to the management of psychologists by general managers, with the disappearance of a separate psychology department and working in an open office. From 1997 a series of National Service Frameworks were published that made service delivery through specified forms of specialist teams mandatory. New groups of primary-care staff were created, including some who were relatively briefly trained. From the late 2000s increasing numbers of psychological services were taken over by for-profit and charitable agencies, with greater likelihood of psychologists being again the only one in a unit, and further increase in numbers of non-psychologists carrying out psychological procedures through Improving Access to Psychological Therapies (IAPT) programmes.

Most of the working time of psychologists has been spent, directly or indirectly, with 'patients', alongside their families and friends. This has been associated with an evolving range of teaching, training, supervisory and consultancy relationships, including training and supervising members of other professions in psychological therapy procedures. Over the past 40 years there has been a substantial growth in the range of other professions offering psychological interventions, most significantly those working as counsellors and psychotherapists (see chapter 13).

Working relationships before the NHS

From the start of the Tavistock Clinic in 1920, in 1925 at the East London Child Guidance Clinic, and in Edinburgh and Glasgow from the early 1920s, there were psychologists working with children. These clinics were an important site for psychologists seeking to establish themselves as scientific professionals, but they were 'disputed territory' for psychologists, both with respect to team leadership and the possibility of restrictions in their roles (Stewart, 2013). There were four other areas where psychologists worked with people with psychological problems. From the 1930s a handful of psychologists were working in mental or mental handicap hospitals, primarily as researchers. The National Institute of Industrial Psychology (NIIP), which fostered a semi-clinical approach, was the largest single employer of psychologists in Britain between the wars (Richards, 1983). The provisional National Association for Mental Health set up early in the Second World War directly employed a small number of psychologists, and during the war a number of psychologists worked in military settings carrying out a range of tasks (Privy Council, 1947). So when the NHS began in 1948, any models of interprofessional relationships were based on these varied experiences in educational and charitable settings, as researchers, or as colleagues in 'organisational' work in either the pre-war NIIP or the armed forces.

The central role of doctors in the early growth of clinical psychology

Most jobs for psychologists depended on decisions made directly by doctors, or were indirectly influenced by medical recommendations. Psychologists were employed because doctors wanted them. Relationships between doctors and psychologists are often characterised – and caricatured – as battles between psychiatrists and psychologists en bloc, but this view simplifies a complex set of relationships, which were differentiated between groups of doctors, including between groups of psychiatrists, and by the settings in which they worked.

NHS and local authority psychiatrists

From 1948 there were three main subgroups of NHS and local authority clinical psychiatrists. Psychiatrists in child guidance settings worked with psychologists whose immediate boss was either the county or borough chief education officer or medical officer. The largest subgroup were the psychiatrists working with adults, nearly all in mental hospitals, with some outpatient clinics. Psychiatrists working with people with learning difficulties were mostly based in mental handicap hospitals, which often included child patients. Both of these forms of underfunded and understaffed institutions continued much as before, with a lay hospital administrator and senior nurses working alongside the medical superintendents who were both the lead clinicians and effectively the chief executives of the hospitals. It was their clinical interests and managerial concerns, supported by the then Royal Medico-Psychological Association, that dictated who was employed by the hospital and what they did, in the absence of any national guidance about which professional staff, other than nurses, should be employed. A further complication was the relatively poor standard of psychiatric training, with the attendant risk of a narrow outlook in their attitudes. The official history of the Royal College of Psychiatrists acknowledges that as late as the 1960s 'many junior [psychiatrist] posts were isolated and most psychiatric units and mental hospitals had totally inadequate libraries. ... Many juniors could spend several years doing the same work in an isolated hospital with no postgraduate teaching facilities' (Bewley, 2008, p.62). A survey of reasons for the high wastage rates of psychologists from the late 1960s suggested that the main reasons were likely to be poor relationships with other professions (naming doctors), poor status within the hospital services, and poor communication with senior officials (Kear-Colwell, 1972, p.27).

In 1958 Peter Mittler took up post at Fairmile Hospital in Berkshire. He was expected to provide services to three institutions caring for three different client groups: Fairmile itself, a typical county mental hospital; Borocourt Hospital, for people with intellectual impairments; and Smith Hospital for severely autistic children; and his 'community' work was a weekly child psychiatric clinic. When he first took up post he was the only clinical psychologist for the entire county of Berkshire. (Mittler, 2010).

Academic psychiatrists and doctors

Academic psychiatry in Britain before the Second World War had lacked the leadership of the university-led clinics in Germany or the well-funded American institutions such as the Johns Hopkins Hospital, where the influential psychiatrist Adolf Meyer worked, adopting an empirical 'psychobiological' approach that was influential in Britain. The opening of the Maudsley Hospital in London in 1922 as the first research hospital for treatable cases was then a landmark for academic psychiatry in Britain (see chapter 9). During the war the hospital was evacuated to Mill Hill in north London, and after it returned to the Maudsley site, Aubrey Lewis became Professor of Psychiatry in 1946. In 1948 the Institute of Psychiatry was formed on the Maudsley site as part of the Postgraduate Medical Institute of London University, and became the leading training establishment for psychiatrists in the country, and also the largest centre of clinical psychology research and training in Britain.

Lewis appointed Hans Eysenck as head of psychology, as well as other leading research psychologists, notably Jack Tizard and Neil O'Connor, at what was to become the Social Psychiatry Research Unit (see Shepherd, 1961). John Raven, who had also worked at Mill Hill, was appointed in 1943 as Director of Psychological Research at the Crichton Royal at Dumfries in Scotland, at the instigation of William Mayer-Gross, appointed there in 1937 as Director of Clinical Research. Both of these early appointments illustrate the expectations of research-minded psychiatrists of fruitful collaboration with psychologists.

A high proportion of the new generation of academic psychiatrists trained at the Maudsley, and when they in turn moved to newly created academic departments of psychiatry outside London they looked for a contribution to both research and teaching from psychologists. For example, Max Hamilton trained at the Maudsley after wartime service in the RAF, and when Professor of Psychiatry at Leeds (and later the last medically qualified President of the BPS), supported the new clinical psychology training course started there in 1965 by Ralph McGuire. But most clinical psychologists were probably unaware of the bitter internal debate within the Royal Medico-Psychological Association (RMPA) between 1968 and 1972, essentially between the 'old guard' medical superintendent-dominated Council of the RMPA and younger trainees wanting to improve training standards, which led to the Royal College of Psychiatrists being founded from the RMPA in 1971, with a more demanding membership examination (Howells, 1991).

A later stimulus to the appointment of clinical psychologists in teaching centres arose from the growth in teaching of psychology to medical students, following the Todd Report (Royal Commission on Medical Education, 1968). This recommended the teaching of psychology to all medical students, and led to the appointment of psychologists (usually clinical psychologists) to lecturing posts in medical schools (Griffiths, 1976). Most of these appointments were initially within university departments of psychiatry, so the psychologists contributed not only to the teaching of medical students, but also to the training of psychiatrists and to the wider world of the medical school, and hence to general medicine and surgery.

Medical and surgical consultants

Before the Todd Report the personal accounts of early psychologists (e.g. Ralph Hetherington, 1969) specifically mention the early expectations of physicians and surgeons of help from psychologists. Neurologists, often working in one of the elite teaching hospitals, were among the first group of physicians with whom clinical psychologists worked. Oliver Zangwill had worked closely with neurosurgeons during the Second World War, and after his appointment as Professor of

Box 8.1 Where did all of this happen?

The growing numbers of psychologists from the early 1950s were working mostly in one of the large mental hospitals built throughout Britain from the early 19th century onwards, some housing 2000 or more patients. These hospitals were always purpose-built, either as a block of buildings linked by corridors, or later as a group of separate villas. The mental handicap hospitals could be large houses with purpose-built villas added later. Over my career I have visited over 50 of these hospitals. Very often the psychologists' offices were in marginal spaces in the hospitals, either in buildings on the periphery of the hospital site, or off a main corridor, up some stairs to a suite of rooms that had been junior doctors' accommodation.

An odd recurring feature of psychologists' recollections of working in these places is the importance attached to where they ate lunch, illustrating the hierarchical milieu in them. In 1958 Pat Kingerlee went to work in a mental hospital in Portsmouth: 'It was a very enjoyable place to work, although in retrospect there were some strange aspects. Our chief had lunch in the Medical Officers Mess so we never met informally as one might do in the staff canteen.' In 1970 she took a post in Northampton: 'my first office was rather well situated on the main corridor opposite that of the Medical Director. As staff joined we were given a group of gloomy rooms, recently vacated by EEG, at the end of the female admission ward at the hospital's perimeter' (Pat Kingerlee, personal communication, 4 October 2014). Alan Smith, in his unique diary-based autobiography, describes his experience in 1970 where there was a 'Doctors Table' with a linen tablecloth, and the nurses sat at plastic tables. When he moved to another hospital 'a nice lady psychiatrist with a grand manner' took him under her wing to the doctors' own dining room through a door off the main canteen (Smith, 2011, pp.26–30).

For well over 30 years these hospitals were the main base for most clinical psychologists. While they have been rightly criticised for their neglect by government, and for the callous treatment at some, many clinical psychologists have positive memories of them, and of the friendships made there. Peter Mittler, working in Oxford in 1954, said: '...the work of all professions was warmly welcomed, and the atmosphere was friendly and positive. I later learned that other hospitals resonated with territorial tensions between psychiatrists and psychologists' (Mittler, 2010, p.88).

Psychology at Cambridge continued to visit Queens Square Hospital in London, where his prestige was of great value and wider influence (Zangwill, 1965). Another early example of collaboration with physicians is the 1956 paper by John Graham-White on a case of ulcerative colitis.

Doctors as administrators, managers and others

Each Regional Hospital Board (RHB) had a regional medical officer and colleagues who translated Ministry of Health policy into local strategy. One of the RHB medical officers would usually have responsibility for mental health, and so for clinical psychology. The calibre of the senior officers in the RHBs varied significantly, as discussed by Welshman (2005) in his comparison of the Sheffield and Oxford RHBs, but it was these senior RHB doctors who took a step of faith in funding the new regionally financed clinical psychology training courses from the

1960s: little attention has been paid to their role. Following the 1974 reorganisation of the NHS, each Area and District had a lead medical officer, often from a community medicine background, and very rarely from a psychiatric background, whose responsibilities meant that they were more open to making clinical psychology accessible beyond the mental health services, and they made major decisions directly affecting the work of psychologists as the 1977 Trethowan Report was implemented.

Of individual interest are the few medically qualified members of the BPS who were doubly qualified as psychologists, or the few doctors who were thinking primarily as psychologists in part of their role. For example, Russell Davis moved from being Reader in Clinical Psychology at Cambridge to be Professor of Psychiatry at Bristol in 1962. Some psychiatrists, such as the rehabilitation psychiatrist Douglas Bennett, were shrewd in their ability to select and support outstanding psychologists. He appointed successively David Griffiths (who went on to head the first clinical psychology training course in Wales), Fraser Watts (who became both Chair of the BPS Division of Clinical Psychology and President of the BPS), Geoff Shepherd (a leading figure in mental health service development) and Isobel Morris (who moved into management at the Maudsley Hospital and was appointed OBE).

Other professional colleagues

Nurses

The generic title 'nurse' encompasses a number of groups which historically have been completely separate in both their training and work. For example, the then Medico Psychological Association introduced in 1891 a Certificate of Proficiency in Mental Nursing, preceding by nearly 30 years the standardisation of training for general and other nurses and others achieved by the 1919 Nurses Registration Act, which created the General Nursing Council. Psychologists have not usually been closely involved in ward-based practice, but the centrality of the ward as the base for care and treatment emphasises the importance of hospital nurses as a group.

Some therapeutic approaches in mental health settings have led to closer involvement with nurses, including therapeutic communities, introduced from the 1950s and applying the principles of small groups and social psychiatry, where psychologists could be a member of the community (see Kennard, 1988). The theoretically very different ward-based operant conditioning programmes were developed from the late 1960s for long-stay psychiatric patients or with people with learning disabilities – in 1972 there were 28 such programmes running in Britain (Hall, 1973).

The Jay Committee (Department of Health and Social Security, 1979) proposed that mental handicap nurses required educational, psychosocial and community skills, and questioned whether 'nurses' were needed at all in this field. An important report on their function, seeing their fundamental role as promoting the autonomy of people with learning disabilities, was written by Chris Cullen (later a President of the BPS) (Cullen, 1991). From the commencement of the run-down in numbers of the large psychiatric hospitals, nurses who knew the patients had often supported them on discharge, and this major shift in mental nursing practice led to new formalised roles as community psychiatric nurses (CPNs; Nolan, 1993), and psychologists were more widely concerned about the work of nurses in the community (Llewelyn & Trent, 1987). The first training course for CPNs was set up at Chiswick College by the early 1990s, and over that decade they began to work in general practices, accepting referrals from other agencies (Simmons & Brooker, 1990), and becoming immediate colleagues for psychologists working in those practices.

Social workers and the therapeutic professions

The Younghusband Report recommended in 1959 the creation of a single profession of social work from the then different groups of social workers, each with their own separate training (Ministry of Health, 1959). In 1962 a unified profession of social workers was finally created, based on one common minimum qualification standard, which led to the formation in 1970 of the British Association of Social Workers. Although social work has been unified as a profession, the training and functions of social workers have been subject to repeated change (Payne, 2005). As far as early clinical psychologists were concerned, the group of social workers with whom they worked most closely were the psychiatric social workers, who since 1930 had trained at university-based courses, and were the best trained of all the early social worker groups (Timms, 1964). Unusually at least three clinical psychologists – Derek Jehu, Martin Herbert and Douglas Hooper – became professors of social work.

The two largest therapeutic professions in Britain are physiotherapy and occupational therapy, and with speech and language therapists are the therapists with whom psychologists have worked most closely. The first professional body for physiotherapists in Britain was formed in 1894, and the first body for occupational therapists (the Scottish Association) was founded in 1934, 40 years later. They and other therapeutic professions were essentially unregulated until the passing of the Professions Supplementary to Medicine Act in 1960. The number of professions regulated through this route grew to 12 until replaced in 2002 by the Health Professions Council, which became the Health and Care Professions Council in 2012 – the body which now also registers practitioner psychologists.

> *In 1970 I worked at Stanley Royd Hospital, Wakefield – an early Victorian asylum – on a research project on the effectiveness of token economies. In this 1500-bedded hospital there was then no qualified occupational therapist; the only social worker was a recently retired senior nurse, and the only previous psychological input had been from a psychologist from Wakefield Prison who came in two evenings a week to do psychometric testing.*

Major developments in relationships with others

Three developments have had a major impact on the relationship between psychologists and other groups. The shift in educational role from being solely class-room teachers to being trainers of others (initially nurses) in therapeutic skills; moves from institutional bases remote from the communities they served to bases nearer to those communities and hence to the staff working there, usually working as a member of a multidisciplinary team; and the growth in other groups outside the NHS providing psychological services.

From formal teaching...

A major commitment of the early psychologists in most mental and mental handicap hospitals was classroom teaching of both student mental health nurses in the hospital nurse training school, and of trainee psychiatrists for the then Diploma in Psychological Medicine (DPM). The DCP established working parties to provide guidance on teaching psychology to other groups, such as the working party on teaching psychology to nurses (Division of Clinical Psychology, 1974). With the teaching of medical students already mentioned, this led to the publication of books by clinical psychologists explicitly designed for this educational market. The BPS strongly supported this by publishing from 1980 a series, *Psychology for Professional Groups*, which included texts for physiotherapists, occupational therapists, doctors, nurses, social workers and speech therapists. Four of the authors were clinical psychologists – Fay Fransella, David Griffiths, John Hall and Martin Herbert. The editorial foreword common to all the books spoke of the texts as encouraging 'practitioners to improve their skills', as part of a rhetoric of 'giving psychology away'.

From 1990, under the rubric of 'Project 2000', nurse education was transferred to the higher education sector, viewing trainee nurses as learners and not apprentices. From the same period, training of the therapeutic professions was moved from the either stand-alone or hospital-based training schools into the higher education sector, with these groups offering degree-level qualifications from the early 1990s. These moves have led to the creation of multiprofession faculties of healthcare studies, with staff who may be both psychologists and members of one or other of these professions, occupying senior professional posts: a past President of the College of Occupational Therapists, Jenny Butler, has a first-class honours degree in psychology.

...to training others in psychological skills

A key publication by Marks et al. (1975) reported the outcome of a training programme for mental health nurses to carry out behavioural therapies with adult neurotic disorders, in which they achieved outcomes comparable to those obtained by psychologists. In 2004 the Department of Health planned to recruit 1000 new graduates to assist in the treatment of depression and anxiety in primary care. They were termed primary care graduate mental health workers (PCGMHWs), a cumbersome title clearly implying that they were not to be seen as offering counselling. As with the nurse therapists, early publications again demonstrated good outcomes after relatively brief training (Gilbert & Russell, 2006). Within the IAPT framework, PCGMHWs can also undertake further training to work as 'high intensity therapists'. In all of these roles, a range of interventions based on psychological concepts and research are being provided by non-psychologists, and occupational roles have been very rapidly established as second-level practitioners.

Further developments in the range of learning relationships have moved beyond didactic classroom teaching to skill sharing, and to supervisory and consultancy relationships, as illustrated by Joyce Scaife's 2001 volume on supervision in mental health settings. In practice these different elements of education, training and supervision may be combined, as illustrated in the range of interactive training programmes (up to diploma level), shorter courses, online video training modules and clinical supervision (face-to-face, by telephone or via internet links) in CBT provided by the Oxford Cognitive Therapy Centre (www.octc.co.uk), established by Joan Kirk in 1992. Similar suites of well-organised postqualification training in a range of therapeutic modalities are widely available to healthcare staff from a wide range of backgrounds, establishing psychologists as major providers of clinically relevant training way beyond the early classroom teaching in the old asylums.

Moves from institutions to the community, primary care and team working in the later growth of clinical psychology

David Hawks (1975) addressed the conceptual complexity of 'community care', pointing out that the implementation of a policy of community care involved a number of then rarely examined assumptions, including the nature of community and the burden on the community, and had many of the attributes of a moral enterprise. Certainly the implications of these policies for staff relationships were not considered.

Two major practical and interlinked steps in implementing these policies were first the moves to community settings of specialist services, often with some form of community-based day services, essentially as an outreach form of specialist secondary care. Secondly, closer links with primary care and other community agencies developed, bringing psychologists for the first time into direct relationships with general medical practitioners and their colleagues. The crucial consequence was that general practitioners were then able to access psychologists directly, since pre-Trethowan all referrals of patients by GPs had to be made to a named medical consultant. The first report of a psychologist's experience of actually working at this level by McAllister and Philip (1975) concluded that there was a 'useful role for psychologists'! Together with the current arrangements for commissioning services, these changes have made GPs of more central significance to clinical psychologists.

Teams and networks

The opinion of the Trethowan Report in 1977 was that relations between psychologists and other professions should be based on multidisciplinary teamwork. Their statement was carefully worded: they were aware that this was 'a growing practice', clearly implying that it was not widespread in the mid-1970s (Department of Health and Social Security,1977), and implying some development from simple parallel working or co-working. It has been suggested that informal team working 'arose spontaneously', and that no one needed to instruct doctors and nurses in the 1960s to work together with routine meetings to monitor patients, and establish links between GPs and in-patient units (Burns, 2004, p.viii). But from that period team working has developed in most areas of clinical practice in which clinical psychologists work, raising issues of team leadership, clarity of purpose of each team member, and the ability of each team member to contribute effectively.

Many psychologists will be members of several formally constituted multidisciplinary teams, alongside numerous and regular committees which come together to achieve a task. Over the past 20 years co-working and team-working objectives and processes have been formalised, prescribed and specialised. A key purpose of the practice of case management, first introduced in the 1970s, was to coordinate the care provided to service users by different staff, leading to the emergence of case manager and key worker roles which could be assumed by any worker irrespective of their profession of origin. The practice guidance from the National Service Frameworks promulgated from 1999 for several client groups required the creation of separate teams with specific functions, such as early intervention teams focusing on younger adults in their first episode of care. 'Superspecialised teams' have been formed to address the needs of rare problems that cannot be economically provided by each local healthcare system. The importance of teamwork for psychologists is illustrated by the detailed work over many years of Steve Onyett, who led the work on the team-working section in the New Ways of Working programme (Onyett, 2007).

Growth in other groups outside the NHS providing psychological services

There is a long tradition in Britain of both counselling and psychotherapy carried out by lay people and professionals, as described by Paul Halmos (1965) in his sociological overview of the 'coming of the counsellors'. Before the Second World War the Freudian psychoanalysts were the largest and most influential group of psychotherapists, organised as members of the British Psychoanalytical Society, first founded in 1913, and the next largest group were the Jungian psychotherapists. The Marriage Guidance Council (MGC, Relate since 1988), formed in 1938, was one of the most respected counselling organisations in Britain after the war, selecting volunteer counsellors who then underwent training, among the psychologists involved being Douglas Hooper, who was for a number of years vice-president of Relate.

The development of counselling as a distinct profession in Britain is more recent. Hugh Lytton thought in 1969 that 'counselling, in its professional sense a relative newcomer in Britain, is likely to spread and increase in importance' (Lytton, 1969, p.278). His words were well timed, as the Standing Conference for the Advancement of Counselling (SCAC) was set up in 1971 to bring together the existing statutory and voluntary counselling organisations, including the MGC, and now continues as the British Association for Counselling and Psychotherapy, with over 40,000 members in 2014. There has been an explosive growth in counselling, and counselling training is now widely available throughout Britain at a number of levels, up to three-year courses leading to a Master's degree. These courses can be based on a number of therapeutic models, and for counsellors with a psychology degree there is now a BPS Division of Counselling Psychology, with training standards meeting HCPC registration requirements.

Box 8.2 What have *they* made of *us*?

Most psychiatrists have a very imperfect understanding of the origins of clinical psychology. We are not generally aware that it is such a new profession – most of us imagine it started around the time of William James. We are aware, however, of its recent very rapid growth both in numbers and confidence, and our relationship is complex and sometimes uncomfortable. Most of our interactions with clinical psychologists in the day-to-day clinical arena are positive and fruitful. But we have all seen the occasional CMHT [community mental health team] with a second-rate consultant lording it over psychologists who are markedly brighter, with bags of social intelligence and often a more appropriate (in the 21st century) approach to patient care. Another reason is a profound misunderstanding (or simply ignoring) of the enormous differences in our training, culture and roles. I see you as scientists applying your skills to human problems; we are a craft, trained via a sophisticated apprenticeship that borrows the fruits of science. – Tom Burns CBE, Professor of Social Psychiatry, October 2014

I found clinical psychologists generally exceptionally helpful, and indeed in principle much the most important element in the team, whatever other assessments and inputs were needed. We have all worked hard to establish ourselves within our various professional organisations and to progress along separate career paths, but find ourselves funded and supported to work in disciplinary silos. When I was Professor of Rehabilitation, in all that time I never succeeded, despite many attempts, to get the heads of therapy and clinical psychology round the same table at the same time to discuss collaborative working. Individual members of our team were keen and intuitively very good at it but the heads of service seemed to feel threatened and disapproving. There are some problems we need to solve together, and there are also other problems that complicate joint working. – Lindsay McLellan, Professor of Rehabilitation Medicine, October 2014

Many psychologists are shocked to find that senior CBT training staff, supervisors and managers of services (such as IAPT) are nurse therapists. Many nurse therapists now don't think of themselves as nurse therapists, but call themselves 'cognitive behavioural psychotherapist' and while some have kept their core profession in their job description and title, others have only too quickly moved to psychotherapist. Some psychologists tend to look down on nurses, and we know of instances where they don't want to be managed by them. Many of the therapists at the Maudsley Hospital are nurses, but people often assume that they are clinical psychologists. In the day-to-day working of a service this is not a problem, but when senior posts become available they are often only advertised as being for 'psychology' only, even though many nurse therapists are doing similar jobs at the same banding – and may have supervised the psychologists previously! – Simon Darnley, Cognitive Behavioural Nurse Therapist, October 2014

Conclusions

Most of the few psychologists in post in the new NHS were relatively inexperienced, with very few more experienced from their earlier work in child or military settings. Most of them worked alone, with less than adequate training: in 1966 less than half of the members of the new Division of Clinical Psychology had a formal training (BPS, 1967). In the segregated and hierarchical mental hospitals or mental handicap hospitals of the period they functioning essentially as technical psychometrists with uncertain status. They were usually subordinate to doctors, and team work in the hospitals in any meaningful collaborative way was virtually unknown: any form of shared care could only be an aspiration.

An underlying dynamic to all of the subsequent changes has been the increased numbers of formally trained and experienced psychologists working in increasingly specialised roles, with an increase in the relative experience of the psychologists, to the point where a psychologist may be the most experienced member of a team, and the person with the most knowledge and skills in particular areas of the team's work. But there are continuing tensions between the demands of being an individual clinician, and being a 'firm' or team member, with potentially divided loyalties. The range of settings where psychologists work has increased over the past 70 years, including service-providing charities, for-profit businesses, independent private practice, and highly technical fields of acute medicine. The single most important change was the move from closed institutions to both general healthcare and community-accessible settings, where psychiatrists are no longer the single most important group of doctors for psychologists, now replaced by GPs.

Some professional groups have experienced their own struggles to achieve formal recognition within the NHS (as with the therapeutic professions in 1960) and with university links have now acquired their own postgraduate training and evidence base for practice. Others have had their own internal power battles (as with the creation of the Royal College of Psychiatrists in 1971), or major role transformation (as with nurse therapists from 1975), or been subject to continuing legislative revision of their function (as with social workers). All doctors and other healthcare professions now learn some applied psychology in their training. Some have studied psychology to degree level, many have acquired considerable psychological skills and competencies comparable to clinical psychologists, so there is a now a market for psychological services, completely absent from the early NHS, both within the NHS and directly from the public, who will seek the provider of those services who they see as most competent and most cost-effective.

Every profession has its own historical story to tell, with their own distinct value systems, skill sets and expectations, with substantive interprofessional conceptual differences. It is easy to be so preoccupied with change in our own profession that we do not take time to understand change in others.

Many psychologists form life-long friendships with their colleagues, based at least in part on common values and shared experiences. But all of these changes have transformed core patterns of interprofessional relationships for clinical psychologists. Differentials of length of experience, knowledge and competence, status and power, and not least remuneration are more complex. To long-standing concerns about the competence and authority of colleagues are now added concerns about possible abuse by them, raising uncomfortable issues of confrontation and becoming a whistleblower. The consequences of poor relationships and their contribution to work-related stress characterised by, for example, lack of mutual respect or harassment, have long been recognised (Winefield, 1984).

Doctors had many different reasons for wanting clinical psychologists, but the early expansion of clinical psychology was dependent on their hopes for the nascent profession: what the psychiatrists got may not have been what they expected. A retiring President of the Royal College of Psychiatrists foresaw in 2000 a scenario where 'an increasingly large and self-confident profession of clinical psychology...might seem before long both to general practitioners and to the Health Departments to be the most important source of therapeutic skills and professional advice in the mental health field' (Kendell, 2000, p.9). Colleagues can also be potential competitors.

References

Bewley, T. (2008). *Madness to mental illness: A history of the Royal College of Psychiatrists.* London: RCPsych Publications.

British Psychological Society (1967). *Annual report of the British Psychological Society 1966/67.* London: British Psychological Society.

Burns, T. (2004). *Community mental health teams: A guide to current practice.* Oxford: Oxford University Press.

Cullen, C. (1991). *Mental handicap nursing in the context of 'Caring for People': Report commissioned by the four chief nursing officers.* London: Department of Health.

Department of Health and Social Security (1977). *The role of psychologists in the health service (Trethowan Report).* London: HMSO.

Department of Health and Social Security (1979). *Report of the Committee of Enquiry into Mental Handicap Nursing (Jay Report).* London: HMSO.

Division of Clinical Psychology (1974). Teaching psychology to nurses. *Bulletin of the British Psychological Society, 27,* 272–283.

Gilbert, T. & Russell, G. (2006). Primary care graduate mental health workers: An evaluation of the contribution of a cohort of graduate workers in their first year. *Primary Care Research and Development, 7*(3), 230–240.

Graham-White, J. (1956). The psychologist's contribution to clinical method: A case of ulcerative colitis. *Journal of Psychosomatic Research, 1,* 160–166.

Griffiths, R.D.P. (1976). The teaching of psychology in medical schools: A pat on the back or a kick in the pants? *Bulletin of the British Psychological Society, 29,* 269–273.

Hall, J.N. (1973). Ward behaviour modification projects in Great Britain. *Bulletin of the British Psychological Society, 26,* 199–201.

Halmos, P. (1965). *The faith of the counsellors.* London: Constable.

Hawks, D.V. (1975). Community care: An analysis of assumptions. *British Journal of Psychiatry, 127,* 276–285.

Hetherington, R. (1969). Twenty years of psychology at the Crichton Royal, Dumfries: A personal account. *Bulletin of the British Psychological Society, 22,* 303–306.

Howells, J.G. (1991). Re-establishment of the Royal College of Psychiatrists. In G.E. Berrios & H. Freeman (Eds.), *150 years of British psychiatry* (Vol. 1, pp.117–134). London, Gaskell.

Kear-Colwell, J.J. (1972). A study of clinical psychologists' job movements during the period 1.10.67 to 30.9.70. *Bulletin of the British Psychological Society, 25,* 25–27.

Kendell, R.E. (2000). The next 25 years. *British Journal of Psychiatry, 176,* 6–9.

Kennard, D. (1988). *An introduction to therapeutic communities* (2nd edn). London: Jessica Kingsley.

Llewelyn, S.P. & Trent, D. (1987). *Psychology for community nurses.* London: British Psychological Society.

Lytton, H. (1969). Counselling and psychology in Britain. *Bulletin of the British Psychological Society, 22,* 273–279.

Marks, I., Hallam, R.S., Philpott, R. & Connolly, J.C. (1975). Nurse therapists in behavioural psychotherapy. *British Medical Journal, 3,* 144–148.

McAllister, T. & Philip, A.E. (1975). The clinical psychologist in a health centre: One year's work. *British Medical Journal, 4,* 513–514.

Ministry of Health (1959). *Report of the Working Party on Social Workers in the Local Authority Health and Welfare Services (Younghusband Report).* London: HMSO.

Mittler, P. (2010). *Thinking globally, acting locally: A personal journey.* Milton Keynes: AuthorHouse.

Nolan, P. (1993). *A history of mental health nursing.* London: Chapman & Hall.

Onyett, S. (2007). *New ways of working for applied psychologists in health and social care – working psychologically in teams.* Leicester: British Psychological Society.

Payne, M. (2005). *The origins of social work.* Basingstoke: Palgrave.

Privy Council. (1947). *Report of an expert committee on the work of psychologists and psychiatrists in the services.* London: HMSO.

Richards, B. (1983). *Clinical psychology: The individual and the welfare state.* Unpublished PhD thesis, North East London Polytechnic.

Royal Commission on Medical Education (1968). *Report of the Royal Commission on Medical Education 1965–1968 (Todd Report).* London: HMSO.

Scaife, J. (Ed.) (2001). *Supervision in the mental health professions: A practitioner's guide.* Hove: Brunner-Routledge.

Shepherd, M. (1961). Department of Psychiatry at the Institute of Psychiatry, University of London. *Bulletin of the British Psychological Society, 44,* 29–35.

Simmons, S. & Brooker, C. (1990). *Community psychiatric nursing: A social perspective.* London: Butterworth-Heinemann.

Smith, A. (2011). *From tests to therapy.* Leicester: Troubador.

Stewart, J. (2013). *Child guidance in Britain, 1918–1955.* London: Pickering & Chatto.

Timms, N. (1964). *Psychiatric social work in Great Britain 1939–1962.* London: Routledge & Kegan Paul.

Welshman, J. (2005). Hospital provision, resource allocation, and the early National Health Service: the Sheffield Regional Hospital Board, 1947–1974. In M. Pelling & S. Mandelbrote (Eds.), *The practice of reform in health, medicine and science, 1500–2000: Essays for Charles Webster* (pp.279–301). Aldershot: Ashgate.

Winefield, H.R. (1984). The nature and elicitation of social support: Some implications for the caring professions. *Behavioural Psychotherapy, 12,* 318–330.

Zangwill, O.L. (1965). In defence of clinical psychology. *Bulletin of the British Psychological Society, 20*(69), 29–39.

Chapter 9 Clinical psychology at the Institute of Psychiatry and the Maudsley Hospital: The early years

William Yule

The Institute of Psychiatry course at the Maudsley Hospital in London was the first university-based and accredited course in clinical psychology in the UK. It resulted from the vision of two men (Aubrey Lewis and Hans Eysenck) being developed by a third (Monte Shapiro). Its origins are not well documented and this chapter relies greatly on the recollections of early staff and trainees.

Henry Maudsley donated money in 1908 to found a hospital 'for the early treatment of patients with curable mental illness, and for research and teaching in psychiatry at university level' (Jones et al., 2007). The hospital was used as a military hospital during the First World War, and became a school of the University of London in 1924. Edward Mapother was appointed as first Professor of Psychiatry in 1936. With the outbreak of war in 1939, the hospital services were split, with most being relocated to a school in Mill Hill, north London. This time, the buildings were again used for returning soldiers with wounds and shell shock.

Mapother died in 1940. One of his junior psychiatrists, Aubrey Lewis, was appointed in charge at Mill Hill and was eventually appointed to the Chair of Psychiatry in 1945. Staff returned to the Maudsley site on Denmark Hill in South London after the war. In the year of the founding of the National Health Service, the academic functions were incorporated into the Institute of Psychiatry as one arm of the British Postgraduate Medical Federation of the University of London. The Maudsley Hospital was itself amalgamated with the Bethlem Royal Hospital ('Bedlam') which had been resited on the outskirts of Croydon. So the Bethlem-Maudsley was formed. At that time, psychology was a subsection of the psychiatry department.

Aubrey Lewis and the Social Psychiatry Research Unit

Aubrey Lewis's father was an English Jewish watchmaker who emigrated to Australia and settled in Adelaide, where Lewis was born in 1900. Lewis had wanted to study psychology but for reasons unknown was prevented from doing so. He trained in Australia and the US in medicine, anthropology and psychiatry. However, he always saw scientific psychology as being the underpinning of psychiatry. He was truly a polymath with a fierce intellect and indeed a fierce demeanour. He demanded accuracy and clear presentation from his trainees, many of whom were reduced to tears when trying to present findings to him. He joined the staff at the Maudsley, and moved to the Mill Hill site in 1939. A number of 'stars' were on the staff there – Maxwell Jones (of therapeutic community fame), Annie Altschul (a psychiatric nurse from Austria who had fled the Nazis), John Raven (of Matrices and Mill Hill Vocabulary fame), Felix Post (a German refugee who went on to develop psychogeriatrics) and others. Eric Trist was a psychologist who moved up to Mill Hill from the Maudsley. However, he soon moved on to the war office selection boards (WOSB) and so Lewis asked advice from Philip Vernon about a replacement.

Vernon had been appointed in 1935 by London County Council to the Child Guidance Clinic at the Maudsley. He did little but testing and writing reports on up to five children a day. He was given freedom of the Maudsley doctors' common room and wore a white coat. He had little to do with Aubrey Lewis, but they got on well. The clinic had no contact with Cyril Burt. Vernon moved to Glasgow in 1935 but had something to do with the wartime appointment of psychologists.

> Lewis consulted me, and I suggested Eric Trist, who was a bit haphazard, but nevertheless liked by the psychiatrists. When he left for WOSB, Lewis asked again, and I suggested Eysenck, who was unemployable as an alien except as a fireman, but was glad to be rescued. Many people have blamed me for giving him a start; but I'm sure that he deserved it, and would have made his mark in any case. (P. Vernon, personal communication, December 1981).

Despite having these luminaries, in fact there was a shortage of staff which shaped the style of work they could do in the face of huge demands. Many patients presented with war-related stress – called 'effort syndrome' by them. There were too many to offer much by way of individual interventions so large group psychotherapy was introduced. Lewis was unhappy about how badly that was evaluated. ECT was also introduced to treat severe depression, although Lewis baulked at using leucotomies.

Lewis was wedded to multidisciplinary team working, but not as it later developed. He sought critical input from members of different disciplines, but always on the understanding that the medically trained psychiatrist was supremo. He was firm in his view that other disciplines, including psychology, should not have responsibility for treatment. Thus he encouraged Eysenck and others to undertake research relevant to mental health. Lewis insisted on detailed and complete clerking of all patients, so Eysenck had access to these 'item sheets' which permitted him to undertake complex data analyses that were crucial in the development of his measures of the personality traits.

Lewis's commitment to psychology is evidenced by the research unit he formed when he returned to the Denmark Hill site after the war. Lewis had a very broad view of the origins of mental disorder and was particularly interested in social factors. In 1948, he was made director of the first MRC unit to be headed by a psychiatrist – the Occupational Psychiatry Research Unit. He appointed a number of very bright independent-thinking researchers, many of them psychologists. Lewis encouraged them to develop their own projects and there was lively debate with people like Jack Tizard, Neil O'Connor, Beate Hermelin, Peter Venables, John Wing, George Brown and Michael Rutter. By 1958 the unit was renamed the Social Psychiatry Research Unit to reflect its enlarged areas of investigation and application.

A number of the staff of the immediate post-war generation were fired by ideals of social justice and so were active members of the Communist Party. These radical thinkers greatly influenced the work of the Institute of Psychiatry as a whole, and the emerging psychology department in particular.

Hans Eysenck

Hans Eysenck fled Germany in the 1930s. He wanted to study physics but was not accepted on a course so he enrolled in 1935 to study psychology at University College London where Cyril Burt was head of department. He graduated with first class honours in 1938. He was one of Burt's brightest students, so much so that Burt organised for him to appear on television in 1937 – probably one of the first psychologists to appear on the new medium. Eysenck was a clear populariser from the very beginning. He went on to enrol for a PhD which was again regarded as outstanding.

As a German now living in London, while Britain was at war with Germany, it was difficult for Eysenck to get employment. He could not join the armed forces and Gibson (1981) notes that Burt seemed 'curiously unwilling to come to Eysenck's aid'. Whether this was related to an earlier incident where Burt had reworked a paper Eysenck had written so that it gave more prominence to Burt's views than had the original is not known. Burt also admonished Eysenck for publishing too many papers while still an undergraduate. He saw this as bad form and un-British for a foreigner. Whatever the origins, from then on Burt opposed Eysenck's professional development on many crucial occasions. Eysenck got a job at the Islington Air Raid Precautions station where staff corrupted his name to 'Helsinki'. All changed when Aubrey Lewis appointed him to a research post at Mill Hill. The post was funded by a Rockefeller Grant to Lewis and also supported Hilde Himmelweit and Asenath Petrie. Eysenck also started to work with Desmond Furneaux on aspects of hypnosis.

The survey and experimental work undertaken at Mill Hill led to the publication of Eysenck's first and influential book *Dimensions of Personality* in 1947. When the war ended, many of the staff at Mill Hill returned to the Maudsley although some, like John Raven, left for other pastures. But then, as now, research grants come to an end and only funds from other sources including the Bethlem Hospital Foundation kept the psychology service alive. Eysenck is unique in British psychology – not just clinical psychology – in being the only person to both publish their own autobiography (Eysenck, 1990) and be the subject of two biographies (Buchanan, 2010; Gibson, 1981), the former giving a lot of detail on other psychologists at the Maudsley, and Eysenck's own use of research funds.

The developing department of psychology

When the Maudsley returned to South London after the war, psychology was a subsection of the department of psychiatry. Its remit was to undertake research basic to advancing psychiatry, as well as to teach psychiatrists and psychologists. At that time, there was no university-based postgraduate training in psychology to equip people to work in mental health. As described elsewhere (see chapter 7), there was training in what was referred to as 'clinical' psychology in the US, but by the early 1940s there was already a great deal of unease at what was taught. The gap between the findings of scientific psychology and the uncritical practice of dubious therapies was already clear.

In Britain, there had been psychologists working with 'patients' for many years, without advanced training to do so. Some psychologists worked in industry and organisations; some worked with children, advising on intellectual problems and remedial educational needs. The then independent Bethlem Royal Hospital also had some psychologists working there, including R.J. Bartlett ('Daddy' Bartlett) who also taught part-time at UCL in 1936 when Eysenck was an undergraduate. He is not to be confused with Frederick Bartlett who headed the university department at Cambridge. Much later, after amalgamation, animal laboratories were established at the Bethlem where the Maudsley strains of 'neurotic' and 'stable' rats were bred.

Years later, in an unpublished memo on the future of the department following his retirement, Eysenck wrote:

> The Department of Psychology was set up in the early 50s after considerable discussion between Sir Aubrey Lewis and Professor Eysenck, agreement having been reached on certain fundamental points. The major points were the following: (1) The Department would have three main functions, namely teaching, research and clinical work. (2) Teaching would be of three groups: Clinical psychologists in training for the MPhil (or its predecessor); PhD students; and psychiatrists as part of the DPM or other qualification. (3) Clinical teaching and clinical work done for the Hospital(s) would be a joint activity, and would in part be paid for by the Hospital(s) reimbursing the University. (4) The division of functions implied by the recognition of research and clinical duties was not to divide the Department into two independent halves; it was clearly agreed on both sides that clinical work depends for support, innovation and theoretical justification on an active research side, and that in turn clinical work can provide problems for the research side, and opportunities for testing predictions made on theoretical grounds. (5) Similarly, as far as teaching was concerned, it was clearly recognised that such teaching depended for its excellence on an active research side, and an active and innovative clinical side, and that both sides should work together in harmony in order to obtain the best results... Broadly speaking it may be said that these guidelines have been followed.

This blueprint set the scene for the milieu in which clinical psychology as an applied science developed at the Maudsley. Initially Eysenck saw the need for clinical psychologists to be trained to a doctoral level. But first they needed to have experience of work with patients, so he envisaged a one-year supervised clinical experience followed by a high level research training. It took many years to achieve this in full.

Thus in 1947 the first clinical psychology course was started with three students – Barbara Kay, Sydney Crown and Joy Pickard. The course was not then accredited by the University of London. The clinical work done for the joint hospitals was to come from the university department with suitable reimbursement. The staff and trainees were to be accountable to the head of the department, and not to any hospital personnel – clinicians or otherwise. That mode of virtual professional independence lasted until the advent of general management many years later.

What was not foreseen in the original agreement was the dramatic increase in the demand for clinical psychology services. By the time the Institute was officially founded in 1950 there were fewer than 11 staff, including full-time research staff. By 2014 the total number of clinical psychologists working in the South London and Maudsley NHS Trust was 466. The Higher Education Funding Council for England teaching budget did not keep pace with this explosion and in many ways there was an imbalance within the established department.

Eysenck and Lewis

Although the Maudsley Hospital had been recognised as a Medical School of the University of London in the 1930s, its main purpose was to improve the training of psychiatrists. When staff moved back after the war, Aubrey Lewis was now head of the enterprise and was made Professor of Psychiatry in 1945. Despite funding difficulties, Eysenck and some of the psychologists who had worked with him at Mill Hill also returned, and initially Eysenck was appointed as a senior psychologist to the Maudsley Hospital in October 1946. The group of psychologists formed a subdepartment within Lewis's department of psychiatry. In October 1947, Eysenck was appointed to a readership within the Medical School, which became the Institute of Psychiatry within the newly created British Postgraduate Medical Federation in 1948, almost coincidentally with the founding of the National Health Service. The psychology section became a full department in 1955 when Eysenck was made professor.

These developments occurred with Eysenck and Lewis agreeing on an agenda to develop psychology as applied for psychiatry. Lewis was intractably opposed to nonmedical personnel providing 'therapy'. Initially Eysenck is on record as agreeing with this stance. At that time, Lewis and many of the Maudsley psychiatrists were opposed to psychodynamically based psychotherapy. Eysenck was critical of the application of unvalidated interventions – a view that was further strengthened when he saw how clinical psychology was developing in the United States. However, as better evidence-based psychological therapies developed in the 1950s, Eysenck argued strongly that since psychologists had developed them on the basis of psychological theories and studies, then psychologists should be the ones to use them to treat patients. This led to a rift with Lewis who tried to persuade the Committee of Management of the Maudsley Hospital to ban psychologists from giving therapy, or at least from giving it other than under the direct supervision of a medical practitioner.

The Eysenck–Burt dynamic

Eysenck had attempted to get the course officially recognised and accredited by London University. Regulations were in place to provide postgraduate diplomas in a number of emerging specialisms. A case was made to the Board of Studies in Psychology to have the Maudsley course recognised as preparing students for the Diploma in Psychology (Section D: Abnormal). This seemed straightforward and was approved by the Board. However, when the minutes were circulated, the opposite conclusion was minuted. According to Gibson, the regulations really applied to courses at UCL and Cyril Burt strongly opposed his former protégé using them. He pressurised the secretary of the committee – a lecturer in his own department – to 'amend' the record (certainly not for the last time as later events were to demonstrate). It took the combined objections of Eysenck and Lewis to have the record set straight, thereby permitting graduates of the Maudsley course to obtain the first university-approved postgraduate qualification in clinical psychology in Britain (for many years, the Diploma also qualified those with teaching experience to become educational psychologists).

It is still a mystery why Burt was so obstructive. Earlier, he had been very supportive of Eysenck but that support began to fade during the war. Burt is on record as making disparaging references to 'the Jewish gang' at the Maudsley, presumably assuming that all German émigrés of the time were Jewish. Later, he actively opposed Eysenck's promotion to a chair.

From the earliest days, there had been schisms within British psychology. In the immediate post-war days, the big divide was between Burt's approach to psychology at UCL and Frederick Bartlett's at Cambridge. At least both were 'Oxbridge' graduates. Neither Eysenck nor Lewis were, and some remarked that had it not been for the war, neither would have advanced as far as they did. Much later, both Shapiro and Eysenck failed to be honoured by the British psychological establishment, much to the shame of the BPS. Shapiro was not accepted into membership of the Experimental Psychological Society despite Eysenck's appealing to them; Eysenck's achievements were ignored at his retirement and beyond.

Some of the antagonism may stem from Eysenck's challenge to the BPS to become more democratic (Eysenck, 1949). He contrasted the way the BPS conducted its business with the way the APA did, the latter being more democratic and involving more membership participation. In October 1949 (BPS Council, 1949) the suggestion was deemed to be expensive and time-consuming. There is little evidence of cordial relations ever being re-established. The attempts by later Maudsley staff to get the BPS Medical Psychology Section to become more psychological and less medical (or at least less psychodynamic) did not help to heal the gap in differences between South and North of the River Thames.

The start of the clinical psychology course

Monte Shapiro was not in charge of the first course, which was mainly taught by Hilde Himmelweit and Victor Kantor. However, he did teach on it. Eysenck later said he had considered Himmelweit should lead the course but thought she would not stand up to the psychiatrists, and so appointed Shapiro instead. In a letter from Bob Payne to Alan Dabbs in October 1994 after the publication of Eysenck's autobiography, Payne notes a number of contradictions and inexactitudes in the account of the early days of the course. He wrote:

> the psychology department on 1949 when I arrived was quite a large one, taking up two complete floors of the old private patients building [now Mapother House] and with labs and offices elsewhere both at Maudsley and Bethlem. The clinical section was by then also quite large. It had already graduated two courses in 1947–48 and 1948–49... When I arrived, Monte was the senior lecturer in charge of the clinical teaching section.

He lists members of staff involved in his course, most of whom he says were involved in running the two previous courses.

During his absence in the US, Eysenck had left Sidney Crown in charge of the department, but it was clear that Monte Shapiro acted independently in running the clinical teaching section, and had done so for two years. Crown published a brief report on the psychology department at the Maudsley Hospital in volume one of the BPS Bulletin (Crown, 1948). In addition to Eysenck the staff were: M.B. Shapiro (doing research on parent attitudes), H. Himmelweit, J.E.M. Stephen (educational psychologist), M. Israel (specialist on the Rorschach test), and Ardie Lubin, who taught statistics. There were four students – J. Ingham, J. Sandler, S. Cox and S. Crown. Payne had listed F. Talland (Newcombe), J. Ingham and M. Israel as lecturers and E. Stephen, B. Hopkins, J. Pickard and S. Cox as assistant lecturers, with again Ardie Lubin as teaching statistics.

Monte Shapiro and the clinical course

Monte Shapiro played a crucial role in establishing clinical psychology at the Maudsley and influencing it in the UK. He studied psychology in Rhodesia and completed his Master's degree at Rhodes University in South Africa. His studies were interrupted by the war, during which he trained and served as a navigator in the RAF. That training convinced him of the need for proper training in all complex procedures. He was shot down in a raid over Amsterdam in 1943, was wounded in his arm and did not receive proper treatment while a prisoner of war. In the POW camp he managed to get some psychology texts and set out to help his fellow prisoners of war. He tried to use some psychodynamic ideas but did not find them helpful or effective, and found more useful application from some Pavlovian ideas. Then, as later, he saw his calling to be using psychology to help others. Like other young people who had confronted the realities of war, he joined the Communist Party to help form a more egalitarian society, but left it after the Hungarian uprising of 1956.

Returning to the UK, he attended the Annual Conference of the BPS in Exeter to scope the opportunities for working in psychology. He went to hear a paper on the reasons for the problems of absenteeism in the coal mines – a very serious problem in the immediate post-war years – and (as he said in a recorded conversation with Mike Berger and Bill Yule in September 1979, to be found in BPS audio archive at AUD/001/45) he was horrified by what he heard. The speaker seriously said that when men went down the mines this was tantamount to entering mother earth and so evoked the Oedipal complex. Fortunately, he then met Desmond Furneaux and was very impressed with his harder scientific approach to psychology. Furneaux recommended that he contact Hans Eysenck, recently returned to the Maudsley.

Eysenck offered Shapiro a part-time post in the Children's Department, where he became one of two psychologists employed directly by the hospital. Immediately he was expected to test a child using the Stanford–Binet test of intelligence. He carefully read the manual and with some misgivings carried out the testing. He immediately saw many problems with the validity of such measurement and set about teaching himself psychometrics. As he was employed only part-time, the rest of the week saw him reading voraciously in the library.

Eysenck was sent by Aubrey Lewis to the US to see how mental health services in general, and psychology in particular, were developing there. Eysenck spent six months visiting many mental health facilities while based as Visiting Professor at the University of Pennsylvania in 1949. Contrary to some accounts, he did not participate in the influential Boulder Conference that tried to establish the nature of clinical psychology in the US, but was undoubtedly aware of the issues and arguments and came back more determined than ever that British clinical psychology would be an applied science and not descend into uncritical, evidenceless psychotherapy.

Thus, while not in charge of the very first course, Monte Shapiro became more involved in the later ones and was clearly heading the emerging course in 1949, as recorded by Bob Payne among others who enrolled on it. Also around this time, Shapiro moved from working with children to working with adult patients. He saw much of the work in the hospital as being based on ignorance and misconception. He recognised rubbish when he saw it and so he set about being more systematic and evidence-based.

While child psychiatrists demanded intelligence testing, adult psychiatrists demanded Rorschach testing. Once again, Shapiro had to get out the manual and try to teach himself what to do. Yet again, he saw more problems than answers. However, the paymasters wanted Rorschach tests, so it was decided to employ an expert to teach this to students and improve the service to the hospital, and this was done by Maryse Israel (later Metcalf) who had completed an advanced training in the application of the Rorschach in Switzerland.

By this time, members of the department were holding series of seminars to teach themselves about the new techniques and instruments of their trade. A member of staff would summarise the literature on a topic and present it to the group. The discussions would be minuted and decisions would be taken about whether to incorporate the measure or technique in the work of the department. Maryse Israel reviewed the evidence for the validity of the Rorschach as a diagnostic tool and convinced first herself and then the rest of the psychology staff that it had insufficient validity to warrant its continued use. That decision remains more than 60 years on. A set of Rorschach cards can be seen in the Science Museum as being on loan from the Institute's psychology department.

Monte Shapiro's philosophy of science

Shapiro was the first to acknowledge when he did not have a skill that mattered. His reaction to having to administer a Binet or a Rorschach was the same. He read the manual and thought hard about it. In both instances, he quickly concluded that neither test had sufficient evidence to justify its use. He set about learning and teaching psychometrics and classical test theory. Thus he, and his staff and trainees, were able to argue with psychiatrists and give detailed reasons for refusing to undertake meaningless testing. This approach was thoroughly approved by Lewis, who saw it as a vital part of the education of psychiatrists. Instead of ordering a test (as in a laboratory test), the referring doctor had to complete a form setting out a problem for which they were seeking the psychologist's advice.

In other words, the combined approach of Lewis, Eysenck and Shapiro was to apply the methods as well as the findings of psychology for the benefit of the patient. Thus was the scene set for the intensive experimental investigation of the single case. Shapiro developed this into identifying critical components of the presenting problems and attempting to bring the psychological process under experimental control, thereby leading to a fuller understanding of the patient's subjective experiences. In retrospect, he came within a whisker of founding new therapies, since bringing the 'symptoms' under experimental control meant changing them for the better. But psychologists were then not supposed to undertake treatment, and so 'experimental investigations' continued for many years.

All of the first three course members joined the staff the following year when Shapiro assumed responsibility for the teaching. This set the pattern for many years, when a few of the newly qualified clinical psychologists were appointed to assistant lectureships and passed their new knowledge and skills to the following group.

An additional reason for ensuring that trainees could both administer psychological tests and interpret them related to the conditions under which they had to work. The 'testing rooms' in the psychology department were previously patient bathrooms with the claw-footed baths still in situ. A sagging piece of plywood was placed over the top and patient and psychologist had to sit 'side-saddle' on opposite sides of the bath. Before being let loose on a patient, the trainee had to read up the manual, observe a live demonstration (no such things as videos then), practise on a fellow trainee and finally demonstrate their new skill in a live 'pass out'. The supervisor watched closely and noted whether any major or minor errors were made in the administration or the later interpretation of the results. Such pass outs were rigorous and often stressful.

While Eysenck and his research group were pioneering multivariate statistics to help develop measures of personality, staff on the clinical side of the department were also devising new statistical procedures to assist in understanding the meaning of test results. In all this, Shapiro initially had great support from Ardie Lubin, an American psychologist who had studied under Burt at UCL soon after Eysenck. He was as much a polymath as Lewis and brought an understanding of research methodology and statistics to bear on his wide knowledge of psychology. Detailed discussion with Lubin helped shape Shapiro's quest for better ways of understanding the unique presentations of patients.

Since clinicians were always concerned to track changes in patients' performances or to compare their standing on different measures so as to identify any unusual presentation, so staff such as Payne and H. Gwynne Jones developed sophisticated statistics to be applied to the scores of single cases. In turn, the trainees had to master such statistical techniques, and be able to interpret results according to the evidence presented in manuals and subsequent independent scientific papers. Later, A.E. Maxwell joined the department to teach statistics; later still he founded the independent department of biostatistics.

So how did Shapiro guide all these developments? He kept up a steady flow of thoughtful papers on the role of the clinical psychologist, but the published corpus of his work is relatively sparse and does not do justice to his thinking (Shapiro, 1955, 1962). There are now many memoirs from past trainees who clearly were greatly influenced by his approach and who hold him in fond esteem. But they also acknowledged the frustration of being taught by him. At a memorial service held in 2000 (see video recording in the BPS visual archive: PHO/002/01/13), Janet Carr elegantly described just how muddled Shapiro could be. In 1949 he would begin a lecture, be seized by some thought the first words sparked off, and then go off on a different direction. He was still doing that in 1962 when I trained. But we tolerated that style because of the uncompromising integrity he showed and taught us in working with patients: Listen and observe. Think. Always justify your opinions. Where is the evidence for that statement? Go and read all about it and come back to discuss later.

Shapiro's scientific thinking had been greatly influenced by Claude Bernard's (1865/1927) *Introduction to the Study of Experimental Medicine.* Both were concerned with applying the methods of natural science to understanding individuals. Bernard wrote:

> Experimenters must doubt, avoid fixed ideas, and always keep their freedom of mind. The first condition to be fulfilled by men of science, applying themselves to the investigation of natural phenomena, is to maintain absolute freedom of mind, based on philosophic doubt…and that the theories we hold are far from embodying changeless truths. (1865/1927, p.35)

He went on to say: *'Even when we have a theory that seems sound, it is never more than relatively sound, it always includes a certain proportion of the unknown'* (p.162). To paraphrase Bernard, he taught that averages conceal what they are supposed to reveal. In other words, the average is a statistic applied to a group or population; the metric may not necessarily describe the attributes of a particular individual. It was the pursuit of understanding the unique aspects of the thinking and feeling of a patient that lay behind Shapiro's model of single case investigation.

Payne emphasised the need for more experimental investigations of the single case. He pointed out that by the 1950s, biochemists could act as applied scientists in so far as they could apply scientific knowledge and method to answer questions posed by a physician. The psychologist first needed to have a science to apply: 'it is doubtful whether there *exists* what might be called a science of abnormal psychology at the present time which we can apply routinely' (Payne, 1957, p.189). Thus, as Shapiro frequently argued, the role and duty of the psychologist was to amass information and to formulate the problems presented. 'Formulation' was alive and well at the Maudsley in the 1950s, although a bowdlerised form appears to have been reinvented by others more recently.

So we have Shapiro wedded to scientific method and constantly wary of theories, constantly questioning the basis for techniques espoused by others, while remaining open to ideas from many sources. Through discussion with Ardie Lubin and others he developed a new method to track the changes in a patient's daily adjustment. He drew on the well-established psychological approach of using paired comparisons, not dissimilar to Stephenson's Q-sort. Rather than present a series of propositions and ask patients to rate them, he would develop statements from the patient's own description. By getting comparisons across all combinations and applying detailed arithmetic, the new 'Personal Questionnaire' (or PQ) allowed people to measure daily fluctuations in mood. Once measured, mood could then be manipulated.

This was the time that Osgood's Semantic Differential and Kelly's Personal Construct Repertory Grid were being used in clinical practice. In fact all three are virtually identical in mathematical terms, allowing the placement of a construct in n-dimensional space and permitting the estimation of the distance between constructs. Certainly by 1962 (when I trained) Kelly's text was a mainstay of the curriculum. Seeing the patients as being their own scientist fitted well with Shapiro's overall approach. Later, in the 1960s, Monte held a series of staff seminars to examine the ideas of Charles Truax and Robert Carkhuff, in which he actively obtained tapes from the originators and had staff undertake blind ratings to establish whether the qualities of empathy and so on could really be reliably rated.

Shapiro's role in establishing behaviour therapy at the Maudsley has been well documented. The first case of applying Pavlov's ideas to treating anxiety in a ballerina arose from a discussion between Shapiro, H. Gwynne Jones and a registrar enthused by their lectures. However, Shapiro is on record as having toyed with Pavlov's ideas while he was imprisoned in Germany. He was supportive of the revolution heralded by the appointment of Jack Rachman to the clinical staff in 1961 when Wolpe's systematic desensitisation was first used with patients. However, he never totally bought in to behaviour therapy alone.

The advent of the behaviour therapies

The arrival of these new 'conditioning' techniques caused alarm among some of the psychiatrists. Attempts were made at the ruling medical committee of the hospital to limit their use to medically qualified personnel. This was debated at the

> **Box 9.1 Audit**
>
> From the beginning, psychology reports contained an account of the total time spent on a particular investigation. Audrey Davis, the sometimes fierce course secretary, recorded all the procedures and times on her punch cards, clipping out a hole for each test. Thus she could slip a knitting needle into the pack of cards and tell how many patients were seen for which procedures or how many tests were done. All that before computers and before Körner data!

medical committee in 1960 and while it was proposed 'That the treatment of patients shall only be carried out by medically qualified staff or duly registered medical auxiliaries working under their direction', this was amended to omit 'duly registered medical auxiliaries working under their direction' and substitute 'under adequate medical supervision'. Inevitably, the numbers of patients being treated by clinical psychologists using a rapidly expanding range of interventions led to a re-examination of this resolution.

In late 1967, Eysenck and the new Professor of Psychiatry, Dennis Hill, put a joint paper to the medical committee that recognised the legal responsibilities of the physicians but also accepted that clinical psychologists could deliver the treatment. The floodgates were opened, but there was a slight problem. Members of the clinical psychology section were not informed of this decision until 1972 when they had to battle for some amendments. Out of this came the request that psychology

Box 9.2 Psychology and the courts

For many years, psychology reports were used by psychiatrists when addressing the courts. This hearsay activity was brought to a halt. After the capsize of the car ferry Herald of Free Enterprise in March 1987, I was asked by a consortium of lawyers acting for survivors and their families to arrange to evaluate them. Many of the department were involved in developing a standardised format which presented the evidence from the clients and separated hard information from clinical opinion. These reports were used in the first 'class action' in the UK courts and the contribution of psychologists was warmly welcomed by the courts. The vague stranglehold of woolly opinions was broken.

should be represented on the medical committee so that such omissions would not be repeated. When Rachman took over responsibility for the clinical section he was invited to attend. He quickly had it agreed that he could send a deputy, and so for the following 15 years or so I sat on that committee.

Later, psychologists won the right to have patients registered under their own names, without having the supervision of psychiatrists. For the most part, there were very good working relationships between psychologists and psychiatrists. It was just more difficult to make progress when there were so many psychiatrists practising in the one place.

The Institute's legacy

Many of the early trainees and staff went on to found clinical psychology courses elsewhere – Reg Beech at Manchester, Doug Savage at Newcastle, Phil Feldman at Birmingham and David Griffiths at Cardiff. Others, such as Vic Meyer and H. Gwynne Jones, moved elsewhere in London, and others outside London, Don Kendrick to Hull, and later Gwynne Jones moving on to become professor of psychology at Leeds. Others greatly influenced developments in the NHS, most notably Don Bannister in Kent, who had parted company with Shapiro but continued to support the course.

Thus, from the serendipitous collaboration of two outsiders (Lewis and Eysenck), each determined to move psychiatry from alienist to scientist, and the appointment of a dogged scientist in the form of Shapiro, the profession of clinical psychology was established at the Maudsley Hospital on the lines of an applied science. Not just applying 'science' in the sense of formulaic recipes, but in applying scientific method to the problems presented by individual patients. That philosophy and practice shaped many bright young psychologists, many of whom went on to leading teaching, research and NHS posts throughout the UK.

A celebration of the 50th anniversary of the Maudsley Clinical Psychology Course was held on 4/5 July 1997, and the contributions have been compiled as Yule (2011).

References

Bernard, C. (1927). *Introduction to the study of experimental medicine* (H.C. Greene, Trans.) London: Macmillan. (Original work published 1865)

British Psychological Society Council (1949). Notes from Council meetings. *Quarterly Bulletin of the British Psychological Society, 1*(6), 203–205.

Buchanan, R.D. (2010). *Playing with fire: The controversial career of Hans J. Eysenck.* Oxford: Oxford University Press.

Crown, S. (1948). The psychology department – Maudsley Hospital. *Bulletin of the British Psychological Society, 1*(2), 57–58.

Eysenck, H.J. (1947). *Dimensions of personality.* London: Routledge and Kegan Paul.

Eysenck, H.J. (1949). Correspondence with BPS Council. *Quarterly Bulletin of the British Psychological Society, 1*(4), 156–157.

Eysenck, H.J. (1990). *Rebel with a cause: The autobiography of Hans Eysenck.* London: W.H. Allen.

Gibson, H.B. (1981). *Hans Eysenck: The man and his work.* London: Peter Owen.

Jones, E., Rahman, S. & Woolven, R. (2007). The Maudsley Hospital: Design and strategic direction, 1923–1939. *Medical History, 51*, 357–378.

Payne, R.W. (1957). Experimental method in clinical psychology and practice. *Journal of Mental Science, 103*, 189–196.

Shapiro, M.B. (1955). Training of clinical psychologists at the Institute of Psychiatry. *Bulletin of the British Psychological Society, 26*, 15–20.

Shapiro, M.B. (1962). A two-year course for the training of clinical psychologists at the Institute of Psychiatry, Maudsley Hospital, Denmark Hill, London SE5. *Bulletin of the British Psychological Society, 48*, 30–32.

Yule, W. (Ed.) (1997). *50th Anniversary of the Maudsley Clinical Psychology Course: 1947 to 1997.* William Yule Archive, King's College London. (Copy available in the BPS Archive, London AUD/003/OHP 55)

Part 3
Psychological Roles

Chapter 10 Psychologists as testers

Katherine Hubbard & Dougal Hare

> *[I]f you are not like everybody else, then you are abnormal, if you are abnormal, then you are sick. These three categories, not being like everybody else, not being normal and being sick are in fact very different but have been reduced to the same thing.*
>
> (Michel Foucault, interview 1975, Foucault, 2004, p.95)

The ways in which psychologists have deduced whether people are 'normal' or not have changed dramatically throughout the last century. One tool that psychologists use to do this is the psychological test. Yet psychological tests themselves have also changed historically. Tests like the Word Association Test (WAT) and the Rorschach, which were developed in Switzerland in the first decades of the 20th century, are very different to the cognitive tests of today and self-report methods such as the Beck Depression Inventory. The changes in test preference and use illustrate the sociohistorical shifts and cultural understandings of psychological tests throughout psychology's past.

The altering contexts of the 20th and 21st centuries have shaped the discipline of psychology, and the tests psychologists adopt. Throughout this chapter we draw reference to certain historical events and contexts which have influenced both the use of testing and which tests have been used. Of course, some tests are considered nowadays as relics from the past which are only suited to the cabinets of museums. For example, the Rorschach plates currently sit in two displays at the Science Museum. Some tests remain relatively unknown and forgotten in the backs of the filing cabinets of psychologists, whereas others continue to be in everyday use in Britain. The pattern of tests which are used, forgotten and displayed as historical objects is revealing of the contexts and perspectives we are currently influenced by in psychology.

In this chapter we outline the history of tests in British psychology and pay particular attention to the Rorschach and cognitive tests. We adopt a particularly critical perspective in doing so. As authors, we have a particularly distinctive frame of experience as the first author is a historian of psychology and the second is a qualified clinical psychologist engaged in professional training and research. In our history of testing in Britain we illustrate the socially constructed nature of testing practices and tests themselves.

First, we outline the constructed nature of testing and draw reference from the problematic work of Francis Galton. We then go on to describe the patterns of testing in Britain from around the 1930s, paying attention to societal shifts and contexts. Next, we describe the often ignored history of the Rorschach and projective testing in Britain. In relative contrast we then outline the history of cognitive and intelligence testing which gained popularity as the popularity of projective tests decreased. We pay particular attention to the use of intelligence tests in the diagnosis of intellectual and developmental disabilities. Finally, we consider contemporary perceptions of the relationship between psychologists and tests.

The constructed nature of the psychological test

Tests are evidently constructed, in the sense that they are developed and created by psychologists. They do not grow on trees nor can they be hunted down; they are also statistically analysed to ensure they have 'construct validity'. Therefore, arguing that tests have a socially constructed nature may appear strange. However, what we mean by this is that tests are developed and, in turn, often also contribute to the construction of mental disorder. For example, as discussed more in depth later in the chapter, intellectual disabilities are often defined by a person's score on an IQ test. The test, therefore, constructs what it means to have an intellectual disability, despite the test's own constructed nature. One reason tests are so convincing in this manner are the statistics used to demonstrate that they have validity. For this reason, we begin this section by discussing the work of Francis Galton. Galton's development of statistical approaches to intelligence illustrate how context can influence even the most concrete-looking constructs in psychology.

Galton (1822–1911) is one of the central figures when considering psychometrics and testing. He was influenced by the work of his cousin Charles Darwin and developed a similar evolutionary approach. Galton established what is now understood as the basis for statistical work in psychology, including the idea of normal distribution. He argued *a priori* that traits and human characteristics were hereditary and promoted statistical and experimental approaches to investigate this. In his 1869 book *Hereditary Genius* he argued that genius was inherited and that intelligence was structured according to race (white men being the most intelligent). Later, he coined the term 'eugenics' and believed marriages between more desirable people should be promoted in order to better society. Galton's work on eugenics is evidence for his sexist and racist views, and the eugenics movement provides us with a clear example of scientific elitism and racism in psychology's history (see Richards, 2010). Galton's work on testing is just one example of testing being used to support highly problematic societal beliefs about the world (see chapter 3).

The sometimes hegemonic use of tests in research and clinical work gives the impression that this use is unbiased. Such methods are trusted as they are viewed as empirical and scientific. However, as the above description of Galton's work shows, science is not strictly without motive or influence. In fact, tests are not mere objects but embody ideals which can be powerful and dangerous. They may be inanimate but that is not to say that they cannot be used to 'do' things (Daston, 2004). Hacking (2000) argues that mental illness is a good example of where 'human kinds' are constructed – that is, negotiated classifications of people. Hacking references the historically situated examples of hysteria, anorexia, the 'feeble-minded' and schizophrenia to argue, not that these illnesses are not 'real' – although some have argued that to be the case (Boyle, 2002) – but that they are situated and constructed in specific contexts. They are situated in times and places not transhistorically and globally constant.

The use of tests on symptoms or experiences can lead to the construction of them as permanent and ubiquitous 'human kinds', meaning the tests themselves are important contributors to such constructions. In this way mental illnesses (and the concept of mental illness itself) become reified according to specific social and historical contexts in which they are meaningful. For example, the experience of hearing voices has been understood very differently historically and culturally. For those following the guidelines of the *Diagnostic and Statistical Manual of Mental Disorders* (DSM), hearing voices may be viewed as a symptom of schizophrenia; for others it may be a comforting experience during bereavement (Ritsher et al., 2004). The voices themselves may also be perceived differently according to culture (Luhrmann et al., 2014). Therefore, the same experience can be constructed in different ways and one of the ways is symptomatic of schizophrenia. But that is not to say because it is constructed the experience is any less meaningful, rather that it is one understanding of its meaning within a certain context.

Drawing on the work of Foucault (1975/1991, 1961/2001), the use of tests can be seen as an exercise of power, used in surveillance, control and the classification of people. Tests act as a method of further legitimising the dichotomy of the 'mad' and the 'sane'. Psychology has grown in influence and is a force within Western society with significant power especially via diagnosis, in which testing has played a central role.

One example where testing has been highly influential and has responded to social contexts is the Second World War (see Bourke, 2001). The war acted as a catalyst for applied psychology, and the subsequent NHS Act of 1948 had a major impact on the growth of psychology (see chapters 4 and 6 for full discussion). Therefore, a range of factors including historical events, institutional bodies, changing scientific standards of testing and societal beliefs have influenced how tests are used and why and what kinds of tests are popular. Yet despite these influences, tests are often viewed as unbiased measures of innate characteristics. This attitude, along with the unrecognised power of tests, has historically led to the application of tests in discriminatory ways (see Hegarty, 2003).

Patterns of test use in Britain

Perhaps surprisingly to some contemporary practitioners and researchers projective tests used to be relatively popular in Britain. The *Fifth Mental Measurements Yearbook* (Buros, 1959), an important text for test evaluation, was divided according to a projective–objective dichotomy. In fact, despite their differences, projective and objective tests were sometimes used in conjunction (see Buchanan, 1997, for a history of the Rorschach and the Minnesota Multiphasic Personality Inventory (MMPI)). From the 1930s onwards, projective tests were very popular. The WAT had been developed by Carl Jung in 1910, and the Rorschach by Hermann Rorschach in 1921. The Thematic Apperception Test (TAT) was published by Christiana Morgan and Henry Murray in 1935 in the United States and some tests were being developed by British psychologists, for example, Herbert Phillipson and Margaret Lowenfeld. The popularity of projective methods throughout this period corresponds with the additional adoption of psychoanalysis in British psychology. The Tavistock clinic was a psychoanalytic and psychodynamic institution and so the use of projective methods particularly appealed to the psychologists working there.

In contrast, following the work of Galton, some psychologists were keen to develop psychometrics using statistical approaches. Hearnshaw (1964), in his review of the development of British psychology, argued that the widespread use and faith in psychometrics was especially characteristic of British psychology (see

Box 10.1 Books on projective methods

There were several very popular projective methods developed by British psychologists. Here are two books, one by Herbert Phillipson who developed the 'Objects Relations Technique' (1955) and one by Margaret Lowenfeld who developed the 'Mosaic Test' (1954).

The
Object Relations
Technique

A projective method of personality assessment derived from theoretical constructs of psychotherapy, and linking interpersonal and perceptual approaches

HERBERT PHILLIPSON, M.A.
Clinical Psychologist, The Tavistock Clinic, London

Foreword by J. D. Sutherland,
Medical Director, The Tavistock Clinic, London

THE LOWENFELD MOSAIC TEST

Full Colour Supplement with Index

Margaret Lowenfeld

chapter 3 for a full discussion of British empiricism). However, Hearnshaw also believed that the emphasis on these types of tests had declined since the retirement of Cyril Burt in 1951 but was later resurrected and maintained by Hans J. Eysenck and Philip Vernon. Eysenck was particularly preoccupied with statistical, experimental and psychometric forms of psychology and developed his own test, the Eysenck Personality Inventory, in 1975.

Overall, the use of projective methods declined from around the mid-20th century. In contrast, more objective standardised tests (named according to the *Mental Measurements Yearbook* projective–objective dichotomy), such as cognitive and IQ tests, increased in use. This can be somewhat attributed to increasing concerns surrounding validity, reliability and the statistical nature of tests from the 1950s. The development of the DSM from 1952 (Grob, 1991), and attempts by the American Psychological Association in 1954 to standardise tests such as the Rorschach, indicate the increased emphasis on validity and statistical approaches. Works such as Meehl's *Clinical Versus Statistical Prediction* (1954) further evidence this cultural shift in psychology towards more 'testable' tests. Also from the 1950s there was an additional concern regarding the ethics of testing and the appropriateness of psychologists' reliance on tests (Hetherington, 1981). In Britain, the more experimental approach based on the Maudsley, where Eysenck and Vernon worked, became more dominant, though the Tavistock continued to support projective testing.

The rising social movements, including the antipsychiatry movement, in the 1960s and 1970s indicate major shifts in cultural understandings of testing and its relation to diagnosis (Richards, 2010). Testing was also criticised for reliability issues, misapplications, privacy issues and for use in discriminatory research regarding race and culture. The reliance psychologists had on testing also had repercussions as to what the role of the psychologist was perceived to be. In 1964 Hearnshaw noted:

> The psychological test, a standardised measure of human performance, has been an indispensable tool of applied psychology in all its main branches, educational, occupational and clinical, so much so that psychologists working in applied fields have sometimes erroneously been regarded simply as testers. (Hearnshaw, 1964, p.249)

Hetherington (1981) later echoed this point and said the use of tests in clinical psychology led to the belief that psychologists were mere assessors of people's strengths and weaknesses. Porteous (1986) reflected that the previous overreliance on testing gave the impression of psychology being an underdeveloped profession.

In 1980, the Standing Committee on Test Standards was established by the BPS. This group instigated a survey of BPS members regarding their attitudes towards tests, the frequency they were used and which named ones were utilised. According to Poortinga et al. (1982), who later published the results, this was done in reaction to the anti-test attitudes from the 1950s and 'societal discontent about psychological assessment'.

An initial questionnaire was circulated with the *BPS Bulletin* in May 1980. The first questionnaire was returned by 1425 psychologists and 567 respondents returned the second questionnaire. Most respondents were clinical and educational psychologists. Some 60 per cent of respondents said the purposes of test use was 'selecting assessment' or diagnosis for more than half the time, or for 'selecting treatment goals'. Cognitive/intelligence tests were the most commonly used, followed by achievement/attainment tests (unsurprisingly most popular among educational psychologists). In third place were personality tests (which were more popular among clinical psychologists) and finally developmental tests. For personality, questionnaires were the most popular measure, with attitudes measures and personal construct measures following a close second. Projective tests came in third place.

The tests that were used most were the WAIS (Wechsler, 1955), WISC (Wechsler, 1949), and the Stanford–Binet. Clinical psychologists often used Cattell's 16 PF for personality but researchers tended to use Eysenck's Personality Inventory. For those clinical psychologists who did use projective methods, the Bene Anthony, the Rorschach and the TAT were the most commonly used. However, the Rorschach and the MMPI were criticised by respondents more than they were supported. The BPS members also echoed some of the growing concerns about testing. For example, 84 per cent had reservations about the norms for testing and others commented about doubtful reliability and validity. The final report was published by the BPS Professional Affairs Board in 1986 (Tyler & Miller, 1986).

From the 1990s there was a greater emphasis in assessing the test users as well as the tests themselves. Bartram (1996) identified that 'Underlying the problem of test abuse and misuse are two issues: inadequate tests and incompetent tests users' (1996, p.62). He also argued that the BPS had concerns regarding the problems of testing especially within industry and commerce. Focusing mainly on occupational psychology, Bartram describes the implementation by the BPS of a certification procedure. This was done to ensure that testing was up to standard and to protect people from the misuse of tests. This was especially important, Bartram argued, because: 'Psychometric testing has probably had more impact on society than any other single development in psychology.' (1996, p.70).With that in mind, that psychometrics have arguably had the biggest impact on society, we next explore the history of a test which has had a great influence on society, especially in popular culture.

Rorschach: A blot on the history of testing?

The history of the Rorschach test in Britain and the British projective test movement has been neglected to date. This is despite there being a British Rorschach Forum and a British journal devoted to projective methods from 1952 to 1997. By comparison, the British projective test movement was smaller than that of the United States and France where the Rorschach and other projective tests continued to remain popular (see Hegarty, 2003; Lemov, 2011). Although this account has not received as much attention from historians, it has been documented by those who actually use the Rorschach (most recently by McCarthy Woods, 2008).

The test was originally developed by Hermann Rorschach in 1921 in his book *Psychodiagnostik.* The test consists of 10 ink blot 'plates' upon which the person 'projects' what they can 'see'. In the same way that one can look up at the sky and 'see' a dinosaur in the clouds, one can look at the ambiguous ink blot stimuli and say what one 'sees'. These methods of playing with perception in ambiguous stimuli like clouds is not new and are said to have been part of games for centuries, although Hermann Rorschach was the first person to develop the idea into a test of apperception. However, unlike looking at clouds, Rorschach argued that it was not *what* you saw which was most informative, rather it was *how* you saw it, for example, whether you used the whole ink blot in your answer (e.g. a bat), or just one part of it (e.g. this bit looks like a bird). Or whether you attributed movement to the blot (e.g. two people stirring a big pot) or noticed colour in the blots (e.g. a colourful rose bush). If a person gave a lot of movement responses to the blots Rorschach argued it was indicative of being 'introversive', while many colour response indicated 'extratension' (Rorschach, 1921; see also Akavia, 2013).

A small amount of literature from the Cambridge Psychological Laboratory appeared in the early 1930s, including a three-part paper by Philip Vernon in the *British Journal of Medical Psychology.* However, the Rorschach is said to have really taken off in Britain from 1933 from when Theodora Alcock 'discovered' the test. It was Alcock who continued to work on the Rorschach, unlike the previously enthusiastic Vernon who later became more critical of its use. Theodora Alcock was one of the founding members of the British Rorschach Forum established in 1948. The other members were C.J. Earl, a psychiatrist who tried to popularise the Rorschach within medical circles, and Eric Trist, a clinical psychologist who worked at the Maudsley until 1942 when he left and his position was filled by Hans J. Eysenck. From then onwards all of the founding members were working at the Tavistock, which acted as the institutional centre for the Rorschach, in its decades of relative popularity in Britain.

In 1952 the group of founding members of the Rorschach Forum launched *The Rorschach Newsletter* (later renamed *British Journal of Projective Psychology and Personality Study* from 1968 and *British Journal of Projective Psychology* from 1986). The journal was dedicated to the Rorschach and other projective methods and was developed to 'enable all members of the Rorschach Forum to keep in touch with work that is being done'. Rorschach interest in Britain increased and by the 1960s summer schools, biannual conferences and Rorschach courses were all popular. The Rorschach had already come under some criticism but was enjoying popularity within institutions such as the Tavistock and child guidance clinics (see chapter 16). 1968 was a very important year for the projective test moment in Britain. The British Rorschach Forum was renamed the British Rorschach Forum and Society for Projective Techniques (and changed again in 1970 to the British Society for Projective Psychology and Personality Study). It was also in 1968 that arguably the most important event in British Rorschach history occurred – the International Rorschach Congress in London. The congress was attended by Rorschach enthusiasts from all over the world and in many ways put Britain on the map for the international Rorschach scene (McCarthy Woods, 2008).

However, following this great success, criticisms of the Rorschach and projective methods began to take hold. Criticism had emerged early in the British Rorschach history. For example Audrey Lewis, who was Chair of Psychiatry at the Maudsley, described the Rorschach as of 'limited or doubtful value' in 1934. It was at the Maudsley that most of the criticisms of the Rorschach emerged and then abounded. This was of course in contrast to the support provided by the Tavistock (see chapter 15 for a full discussion of the battles between the two institutions). Eysenck, working from the Maudsley, was one of the most influential critics of the Rorschach. In the Mental Measurements Yearbook, Eysenck likened the Rorschach to phrenology – the debunked and highly problematic science of measuring head bumps. Eysenck also called upon the work of Lee Cronbach, who had used statistical analysis to illustrate the Rorschach's lack of reliability. In fact the more statistical and experimental approach adopted by the Maudsley became the predominant way to 'do' psychology and the use of the Rorschach and other projective tests accordingly decreased.

There have been efforts to revive the Rorschach. For example, the work of John Exner (1969), has proved revolutionary for Rorschach workers in some places such as the United States (though the work of Exner continues to be criticised, see Wood et al., 2003). Such revival has not occurred to the same extent in Britain. In 1988 Zahid Mahmood conducted a survey on members of the British Rorschach Forum and Society for Projective Techniques, and it was reported that 90 per cent of members recognised that use of the Rorschach and projective testing had declined (Mahmood, 1988). Mahmood concluded that the Rorschach had fared badly but that other tests that were developed by Britons, like Herbert Phillipson's 1955 Object Relations Test and the tests developed by Margaret Lowenfeld, were still in relative use. Despite some optimistic outcomes – for example, Lowenfeld's World Technique is still in use in the form of Sand Play – the projective test movement has all but finished in Britain. The journal and the society ended in 1997, much later than many would have predicted. Nowadays, unlike in France, trainee clinical psychologists in Britain are not taught the Rorschach.

The Rorschach remains, despite its lack of attention in clinical psychology, an inherently interesting and appealing test. As a psychological object, it behaves in ways which throughout history have been controversial and simultaneously alluring. After all, we still look up at the clouds to see what we can 'see'. The Rorschach may be long gone from professional British clinical psychology, but because of the appealing nature of the test and its presence in popular culture, it may still come to mind in the public imagination about clinical psychology.

Intelligence testing

Intelligence is what the test tests. (Edwin Boring, 1923, p.35)

If the Rorschach remains as a half-forgotten historical curiosity, there is another form of assessment that apparently retains the scientific credentials the Rorschach seemingly lacked. This currently dominates, and even defines, the practice of many clinical psychologists in Britain, namely the intelligence quotient (IQ) test. That IQ testing is still undertaken by British clinical psychologists in the early 21st century is surprising given that the underlying notion of intelligence followed a similar arc to that of projective testing. Like projective testing, both the practice and study of IQ testing also peaked in the mid-20th century, albeit with a lingering senescence to the present day in the form of the assessment technology.

The assessment, or rather assessments, in question are the family of related test batteries collectively known as the Wechsler Intelligence Scales (WIS). These include the WAIS (Wechsler, 1955), the WISC (Wechsler, 1949), the Wechsler Preschool & Primary Scale of Intelligence and the Wechsler Abbreviated Scale of Intelligence. Fundamental to all of these scales is the inherent assumption of the validity of Galton's 1869 notion of general ability or 'g'. This was subsequently codified by Charles Spearman as long ago as 1904 as a single general ability, defined as the ability to learn. It is important to note that IQ cannot and should not be taken as being synonymous with human intelligence (Morton, 2005). Theorists such as Byrne (1995) regard intelligence itself as an evolutionary adaptation to flexibly identify and implement idiosyncratic and effective solutions to novel problems. This stands in contrast to the conceptualisation of intelligence based on g/IQ that posits intelligence as a genetically determined and fixed property of the brain. This distinction is relevant because the clinical use of psychometric testing by British clinical psychologists is intrinsically bound up with the history of the concept and study of intelligence in Britain in the 20th century. This in turn was derived from 19th-century eugenic theory and ideology (see chapter 4).

In particular, the presumption of IQ as an innate biological fact that is embodied in and measurable by the WIS is a stance that has historically excluded other concepts of intelligence. This has resulted in the more developmentally and socially orientated notions of Jerome Brunner and Jean Piaget or Lev Vygotsky not being operationalised and used by clinical psychologists. Rather, British clinical psychology has largely remained faithful to a hierarchical conceptualisation of intelligence that was essentially worked out in the mid-20th century through the work of Thurstone (1938) and Vernon (1950). In this model of human intelligence, a varying number of factors, usually identified as being verbal or nonverbal, verbal-educational or spatial-mechanical (Vernon, 1950) or as 'fluid' or 'crystalline' (Cattell, 1971), are regarded as accounting for differing amounts of variance in a single overarching factor of general intelligence (in other words, 'g'). Interestingly, Raven's Matrices, first published 1938 (revised 1956), which have been the longest standing indigenous competitor to the WIS, were designed from the outset as a measure of general ability, and the nonverbal nature of Raven's test ensures a niche survival as it facilitates IQ testing of people with impaired or absent language abilities.

Later theorists such as Anderson (1992) have proposed that IQ is essentially an index of working memory and/or processing speed – both obvious metaphors from computing. Such a reference to computer technology leads to another question that can be asked when considering the history of IQ testing: Is g/IQ a scientific concept or is it, in effect, a technology? The latter notion is supported by the fact that the first workable cognitive tests were developed by Alfred Binet and Théodore Simon in the early years of the 20th century for the purposes of identifying children in need of special educational support. This was later appropriated by the followers of Galton in the US in their search for the hitherto elusive 'g'. Thus it would appear that IQ testing has been essentially a technological project that has driven both science and practice and, as will be discussed below, this is particularly the case when intellectual (learning) disability is considered.

Looking back, it can be seen that for much of the 20th century, the scientific study of intelligence via statistical methods, rather than by the study of actual cognitive and neurological processes and data, has provided the primary technology of applied psychology in educational and clinical settings. This is not to say that other approaches cannot be identified in the history of psychological testing in Britain. Mention should be made of two very different approaches, namely Hudson's (1967) attempts to reframe intelligence as creative thinking and the development of the British Ability Scales (BAS) (Elliot et al., 1978). The latter has its origins in a British Psychological Society initiative to develop a test to effectively replace the WIS.

Richardson (1991) reported the aims of the BAS project as being the development of a scale of general mental capacity adapted to 'British intelligence' and standardised on a British population, and the extension of said scale to provide a measure of special abilities. Explicit in the design of the BAS was the concept of intelligence as comprising a range of measurable skills, such as verbal ability, verbal fluency, numerical ability, spatial ability, inductive reasoning and memory (Richardson, 1991). A distinctive feature of the BAS was not only that its five-factor model resulted in a wider range of cognitive skills being assessed, bringing the BAS more in line with neuropsychology and developmental psychology, but that it was ostensibly developed on an objective and empirical, rather than subjective, basis and utilised the then new techniques of Rasch (1961). In contrast, Hudson's work was a bold attempt to reframe intelligence as creativity and the ability to cope with the unexpected, the novel and the contradictory, an endeavour that in many ways predated more recent thinking about intelligence as being an evolutionary adaptation. Although Hudson's work can now be seen to have relevance to a number of clinical issues, including the assessment of executive functioning and of autism spectrum disorders, it nonetheless failed to have any significant impact on the practice of clinical psychologists. Their practices remain linked to early theoretical assumptions about 'g' and are shaped mainly by utilitarian considerations about formal testing in organisational settings like the NHS. A similar fate of non-adoption seems to have befallen the BAS.

Outside of the field of mainstream education and the significant contribution of psychologists such as Cyril Burt to the development of selective education in the UK (Board of Education, 1938), the group of people whose lives have been most directly affected by psychological testing are the 2.25 per cent of the population who have been variously described as having 'intellectual and developmental disabilities'. Although the physical reality of developmental disorders had already been delineated by John Langdon Down (1866), the notion of a distinct population of people who could be categorised by their failings in inherent intellectual ability only emerged from the work of the early exponents of mental testing in Britain in the early years of the 20th century. Identification of the 'feeble-minded' developed from the intense interest in and promotion of eugenic ideas by Pearson and later Burt. The main instrument for enacting these eugenic assumptions was the adoption of Terman's (1916) Stanford–Binet test, imported from the US. What the Stanford–Binet and the subsequent Raven's Matrices and WIS all shared was that their designs were derived from a mixture of intuition and *post-hoc* statistical manipulation.

With the technology available to undertake such mental testing, the concept of mental deficiency/handicap emerged in the late Edwardian period, seemingly based on empirical data developed from the earlier underdefined concepts of 'idiocy' and 'feeble-mindedness'. This created an indispensable role for psychologists. The Mental Deficiency Act of 1913 mandated the institutionalisation of those deemed to be 'feeble-minded' and in some manner lacking mental abilities. Given the often arbitrary nature of the 'diagnosis' of 'feeble-mindedness', the emergence of apparently scientific IQ testing was taken up and recommended by the Board of Education in 1924. The use of IQ tests to define intellectual disability eventually subsumed the older categories, with those people formerly described as 'idiots', 'imbeciles' and 'severely subnormal' being presumed to have IQ scores under 50 and the 'feeble-minded' and 'mildly subnormal' being placed in the 50–70 range (e.g. Kushlick & Cox, 1973). Although the provision for people with intellectual disabilities (ID) has changed markedly since the mid-1950s, the actual definition of ID has continued to be based on IQ (Leyin, 2010) despite the BPS developing a three-factor definition based on IQ, adaptive functioning and age of onset. Like the inertia about one version of intelligence noted above in practical testing, the same can be said of the role of IQ still wholly or predominantly defining disability.

The perceptive reader will have noted that the formative period of intelligence testing not only predates the emergence of neuropsychology and developmental psychology, as they are currently understood, but also predates the development of clinical psychology as a distinct profession in the UK. Yet the demand for IQ testing remains essentially the same as it was in the 1920s and 1930s, with forms of assessment technology originally developed outside of the UK nearly a century ago. The survival of IQ testing and the use of the WIS by British clinical psychologists in the 21st century is interesting. Although it has now largely disappeared from adult mental health practice it still forms the basis of much practice in intellectual disabilities and child and adolescent mental health. The history of British clinical psychology as a whole is to a greater or lesser degree bound up with the post-imperial history of the UK (see chapter 4). Given the historical cultural context, it was perhaps inevitable that optimistic attempts to develop a distinctly British psychometric technology, such as the BAS, were fostered but also that they failed in the same optimistic post-war social democratic welfare state. It would seem that such a social democratic political reform failed to cut its attachments to older eugenic assumptions; remember that the Fabian British tradition contained its own robust advocates of eugenics.

Conclusion

To conclude, we would like to provide two anecdotes which highlight continued perceptions of psychologists using tests. The first is recalled by the second author:

> *I was asked a few years ago by a senior registrar in psychiatry whether he, the registrar, could see 'it being done'. When questioned further, the registrar replied somewhat tetchily that he wanted to see what clinical psychologists did, which seemed an odd request as all parties had been part of an autism assessment clinic that very morning. The exasperated registrar finally demanded to see an IQ test as that was what psychologists do (for psychiatrists to interpret).*

This interprofessional 'misunderstanding' seems to encapsulate the relationship of clinical psychologists to what is essentially obsolete technology. Therefore, the conceptualisation of clinical psychologists as mere testers remains in some areas.

However, it is not only important to recognise how psychologists are viewed by other professionals, but also how the relationship between psychologists and tests are perceived by those individuals undergoing therapy and intervention. The first author recalls:

> *During my time working at a child and adolescent mental health service I distinctly remember a young adolescent boy look with terror at the clinical psychologist approaching him down a corridor with the large briefcase of IQ tests. The young boy simply ran and absconded from the building.*

The perceptions of psychologists utilising tests therefore has resonances for both professionals and for those who are undergoing (or are threatened with) the test.

What these anecdotes show, and the history outlined above illustrates, is that an essential point about such tests is the context in which they are embedded at any given time. That includes the contexts in which they were developed, and the contexts they are used at present. It is therefore important also to retain an understanding of one's present sociohistorical context and why a test is being used.

Tests, whether from the perspective of the registrar in the first anecdote, or the adolescent in the second, continue to be perceived as powerful, either as the main 'tool' of psychologists, or as a terrifying thing from which to run. This is also historically true in that tests are powerful in that they are used to 'do' things and are not necessarily the passive objects they appear to be in psychologist's cabinets and museum displays. It is therefore important that those who continue to wield the test, namely clinical psychologists, recognise both the inherent power and the constructed nature of such in order to avoid further misuses of testing.

References

Anderson, M. (1992). *Intelligence and development: A cognitive theory.* Oxford: Blackwell.

Akavia, N. (2013). *Subjectivity in motion. Life, art and movement in the work of Hermann Rorschach.* New York: Routledge.

Bartram, D. (1996). Test qualifications and test use in the UK: The competence approach. *European Journal of Psychological Assessment, 12*(1), 62–71.

Board of Education (1938). *Report of the consultative committee on secondary education with specific reference to grammar schools and technical high schools.* London: HMSO.

Boring, E. (1923). Intelligence as the tests test it. *New Republic, 36,* 35–37.

Bourke, J. (2001). Psychology at war 1914–1945. In G. Bunn, A.D. Lovie & G.D. Richards (Eds.), *Psychology in Britain: Historical essays and personal reflections* (pp.133–149). Leicester: British Psychological Society.

Boyle, M. (2002). *Schizophrenia: A scientific delusion?* New York: Taylor & Francis.

Buchanan, R.D. (1997). Ink blots or profile plots: The Rorschach versus the MMPI as the right tool for a science-based profession. *Science, Technology & Human Values, 22,* 168–206.

Buros, O.K. (Ed.) (1959). *Fifth mental measurements yearbook.* Highland Park, NJ: Gryphon Press.

Byrne, R.W. (1995). *The thinking ape: Evolutionary origins of intelligence.* Oxford: Oxford University Press.

Cattell, R.B. (1971). *Abilities: Their stricture, growth and action.* Boston, MA: Houghton Mifflin.

Daston, L. (Ed.). (2004). *Things that talk: Object lessons from art and science.* New York: MIT Press.

Down, J.L.H. (1866). Observations on an ethnic classification of idiots. *London Hospital Reports, 3,* 259–262.

Elliot, C.D., Murray, D. & Pearson, L.S. (1978). *The British Ability Scales.* Windsor: NFER.

Exner, J.E. (1969). *The Rorschach systems.* New York: Grune & Stratton.

Foucault, M. (1991). *Discipline and punish* (I. Sheridan, Trans.). Harmondsworth: Penguin. (Original work published 1975)

Foucault, M. (2001). *Madness and civilisation: A history of insanity in the age of reason* (R. Howard, Trans.). London: Routledge. (Original work published 1961)

Foucault, M. (2004). Je suis un artificier. In Roger-Pol Droit (Ed.), *Michel Foucault, Entretiens* (pp.89–136). Paris: Odile Jacob.

Grob, G.N. (1991). Origins of DSM-I: A study in appearance and reality. *American Journal of Psychiatry, 148,* 421–431.

Hacking, I. (2000). *The social construction of what?* Cambridge, MA: Harvard University Press.

Hearnshaw, L.S. (1964). *A short history of British psychology: 1840–1940.* London: Methuen.

Hegarty, P. (2003). Homosexual signs and heterosexual silences: Rorschach research on male homosexuality from 1921 to 1969. *Journal of the History of Sexuality, 12*(3), 400–423.

Hetherington, R. (1981). The changing role of the clinical psychologist. *Bulletin of the British Psychological Society, 34,* 12–14.

Hudson, L. (1967). *Contrary imaginations: A psychological study of the English school-boy.* Harmondsworth: Penguin.

Kushlick A. & Cox, G.R. (1973). The epidemiology of mental handicap. *Developmental Medicine and Child Neurology, 15,* 748–759.

Lemov, R. (2011). X-rays of inner worlds: The mid-twentieth century American projective test movement. *Journal of the History of the Behavioral Sciences, 47,* 251–278.

Leyin, A. (2000). Psychometric assessment, learning disabilities and the law: Response to Murray & McKenzie (1999). *Clinical Psychology Forum, 135,* 3–4.

Luhrmann, T.M., Padmavati, R., Tharoor, H. & Osei, A. (2014). Differences in voice – hearing experiences of people with psychosis in the US, India and Ghana: Interview-based study. *British Journal of Psychiatry, 206*, 41–44.

Mahmood, Z. (1988). The projective science in the world at large: A blot on the landscape. *British Journal of Projective Psychology, 33*(2), 55–66.

McCarthy Woods, J. (2008). The history of the Rorschach in the United Kingdom. Rorschachiana: *Journal of the International Society for the Rorschach, 29*, 64–80.

Meehl, P. (1954). *Clinical versus statistical prediction.* Minneapolis: University of Minnesota Press.

Morton, J.J. (2005). Difficult questions about g. *Cortex, 41*, 232–233.

Poortinga, Y.H., Coetsier, P., Meuris, G. et al. (1982). A survey of attitudes towards tests among psychologists in six western European Countries. *Applied Psychology, 31*(1), 7–33.

Porteous, M.A. (1986). A survey of Irish psychologists' attitudes towards tests. *International Review of Applied Psychology, 35*, 231–238.

Rasch, G. (1961). On general laws and the meaning of measurement in psychology. In *Proceedings of the Fourth Berkeley Symposium on Mathematical Statistics and Probability, IV* (pp.321–334). Berkeley: University of California Press.

Raven, J.C. (1956). *Progressive Matrices: A perceptual test of intelligence.* London: H.K. Lewis.

Richards, G.D. (2010). *Putting psychology in its place. Critical historical perspectives* (3rd edn). London: Routledge.

Richardson, K. (1991). *Understanding intelligence.* Buckingham: Open University Press.

Ritsher, J.B., Lucksted, A., Otilingam, P.G. & Grajales, M. (2004). Hearing voices: Explanations and implications. *Psychiatric Rehabilitation Journal, 27*, 219–227.

Rorschach, H. (1921). *Psychodiagnostics: A diagnostic test based on perception* (P. Lemkau & B. Kronenberg, Trans.). New York: Grune & Stratton.

Terman, L.M. (1916). *The measurement of intelligence: An explanation of and a complete guide for the use of the Stanford Revision and Extension of the Binet-Simon Intelligence Scale.* Boston, MA: Houghton Mifflin.

Thurstone, L.L. (1938). Primary mental abilities. *Psychometric Monographs*, No. 1. Chicago: University of Chicago Press.

Tyler, B. & Miller, K. (1986). The use of tests by psychologists: Report on a survey of BPS members. *Bulletin of the British Psychological Society, 39*, 405–410.

Vernon, P.E. (1950). *The structure of human abilities.* London: Methuen.

Wechsler, D. (1949). *Wechsler Intelligence Scale for Children.* New York: Psychological Corporation.

Wechsler, D. (1955). *Wechsler Adult Intelligence Scale.* New York: Psychological Corporation.

Wood, J.M., Nezworski, M.T., Lilienfeld, S.O. & Garb, H.N. (2003). *What's wrong with the Rorschach? Science confronts the controversial inkblot test.* San Francisco: Jossey-Bass.

Chapter 11 Psychologists as researchers

Susan Llewelyn, Gillian Hardy
& Katie Aafjes-van Doorn

Introduction

Undertaking, applying and consuming research has been positioned as a core component of clinical psychology practice since its inception as a profession in the UK. This chapter describes the evolution of British clinical psychologists' engagement with research as a source of inspiration, direction and professional acumen, and how it has significantly developed as an activity and source of ideas over time. We demonstrate how the evolving maturity of the discipline can be traced through the growing breadth of the type of topics addressed, and through the sophistication and variety of theories and methodologies employed. Research is not immune to larger contextual influences, so we also show how the evolution of the practice and application of research has reflected the wider concerns of the profession and of the problems that it has been trying to help to resolve. We argue that on the whole the diversity of topics and research methodologies have been, and continue to be, important for the profession.

The chapter opens with definitions, followed by analyses of published research, and a closer look at the emphasis on scientific research in the early days. The role of psychological research in assessment and treatment is then considered, before an examination of the developments in methodology, training and contextual issues facing the profession.

What do we mean by 'research'?

Within psychology more generally, a distinction has commonly been drawn between 'pure', 'basic' or 'fundamental' research and 'applied' research. In pure or basic research, theoretically proposed mechanisms are examined as they occur in controlled settings, as far as possible independently of context or impact, often (but not always) using experimental methodology with the aim of expanding our understanding. By contrast, applied research is concerned with the systematic investigation of the practical application of knowledge. Hence the effects of a condition, process or intervention are examined, sometimes using less tightly controlled designs including correlational or observational analyses, but nevertheless basing the study on theory. An example of fundamental (although clinical) research would be an experimental study involving the manipulation of cognitions held by people with eating disorders using a Stroop test to examine the characteristics of those cognitions. An example of applied research would be an investigation of the impact on people with auditory hallucinations of a package of interventions based on cognitive principles. A further type of research is 'audit' or 'service evaluation', which is usually not theory-based, but carried out with the intention of documenting a condition or service, or assessing an intervention's impact. In an audit or service evaluation the numbers of those attending a type of clinic might be recorded, describing their features and evaluating intervention-related outcomes.

Clinical psychologists have long been engaged in these three types of research, all seen as central to the role (and training) from the early days. Another important distinction, however, is between the psychologist as 'researcher' or as 'consumer' or 'user' of research. It has been claimed, for example, that most clinical psychologists are not active researchers postqualification, such that the modal number of research publications for clinical psychologists is effectively zero (Milne et al., 2000). We argue, however, that clinical psychologists have always been active consumers and users of research, and have based much of their work on the research traditions of academic psychology. A helpful concept here is that proposed by Cooper and Graham (2009, p.46) of 'research as a state of mind' which has informed many of the core activities of clinical psychology.

Dimensions of change: Analysis of published research

Following methodology used by Clarke (1979), we conducted an analysis of papers published between 1952 and 2012 by the *British Journal of Medical Psychology* (which became *Psychology and Psychotherapy: Theory, Research and Practice* in 2002) and the *British Journal of Social and Clinical Psychology* (*British Journal of Clinical Psychology* since 1981). This revealed a number of significant changes in emphasis over the years (see Table 11.1).

Additionally, from Clarke's (1979) editorial on the first 75 years of the *British Journal of Psychology* (1904–1979) we have abstracted some of the key markers in clinical psychology research publications. The early years tended to focus on measurement and psychological tests, although there were also discursive articles on, for example, the relevance of psychoanalysis to art criticism. Statistical developments became common, while by 1954 many articles concerned 'abnormal psychology'. Hearnshaw (1964) noted that UK psychology before the Second World War emphasised methods above theory, particularly on experimental methodology in Cambridge, and statistics in London. There was a widespread faith in psychometrics and a tendency to regard psychology as a biological rather than social science.

According to Hearnshaw, the post-war period then saw a shift towards environmentalist explanations in areas where previously hereditary ideas tended to pass unquestioned, and increasingly articles focused on the application of knowledge. By the 1960s, there was a wide range of experimental studies and papers on topics such as autism and 'subnormality'. Papers on cognition emerged by the 1970s, becoming dominant towards the end of the century, together with reports on clinical trials of interventions for a wide range of conditions. Recent years have witnessed a huge expansion of publications on clinical psychology as applied outside psychiatry, for example in physical health and community contexts, and the use of more qualitative methodologies.

Early days of research in practice: The centrality of scientific psychology

Given that until the 1950s, treatment and care of people with 'abnormal behaviour' was very largely under the control of medical staff, a key opportunity for psychologists interested in mental health was to apply knowledge and methodologies drawn from psychology principally as research tools, to see how and where psychology could be useful in understanding those with mental health problems. Many early psychologists originally saw themselves, and were seen by others, as the scientists and researchers within the organisation, who would provide evidence to underpin and support the work of medical doctors, nurses and others working particularly in mental health care. Indeed, when clinical psychologists were first appointed in the mental hospitals from the late 1940s, for at least some, their core role was research. Many other psychologists had 'research' included in their job descriptions, particularly those in senior roles.

The scientific role practised by many early clinical psychologists involved making use of what they already knew theoretically from academic research about, say, personality, motivation, leaning, or child development, and applying this, together with knowledge of research methodology, to help in the assessment and diagnosis of individual patients. Their professional contribution therefore required familiarity with and understanding of appropriate measures to use, and knowledge of issues such as validity and reliability, distribution of scores and the limits of prediction, as well as of specific domains of function.

Subsequently others became involved in audit and service evaluation. Parry (1992), for example, reviewed a number of service-based evaluative methods and clarified the distinctions between service evaluation, operational research, professional audit, service audit, quality assurance and total quality management. Examples of service level research include an evaluation of mental health outcome at a community-based psychodynamic psychotherapy service for young people (Baruch & Fearon, 2002), and the comparison of psychiatric admission patterns before and after out-patient psychotherapy in three different treatment programmes in a district service setting (Pearson et al., 2002).

In addition to knowing what academic research had to say about assessing people or mental health care organisations, many early clinical psychologists also wanted to push this knowledge further, and to ask critical questions about the applicability of their academic knowledge in clinical settings dominated by psychiatry. Their aim was to bring the approach of the laboratory psychologist into the confusing world of mental health care and to enhance the work of psychiatry in a more psychological direction. Nevertheless, most research was initially conducted at the direction of psychiatrists, and indeed only with the permission of psychiatrists for 'their' patients to be seen. Sometimes this work was primarily psychiatric in nature: for example, there are a number of publications from the 1950s authored by clinical psychologists which essentially researched the impact of the new psychoactive drugs. Other well-respected clinical psychologists, such as Ralph McGuire (Leeds and Edinburgh)and Roger Baker (Leeds), and statisticians such as Graham Dunn (Institute of Psychiatry), spent much of their time providing advice on design and the choice of appropriate statistical analysis for their medical colleagues, being nominally credited as authors way down in the list of study contributors. Note, however, that there was also a different and more independent research role for clinical psychologists working outside psychiatry, for example in neurology, and there is a well-respected strand of research working with the learning disabled (e.g. Alan and Ann Clarke and Jack Tizard), in epidemiological

Table 11.1 Changing themes in clinical psychology research publications (from literature review conducted by authors)

Themes	Past publications	Recent publications
Type of research publication	Theoretical, conceptual General opinions and ideals.	Empirical (scientific). Specific/applied (experience of real life patients/practice).
Focus	Development/psychometrics of cognition/personality assessment tools.	Evaluation of process and interventions/services outcome.
Sample	Case studies of patients in long-term therapy.	Brief, evidence-based, cost-effective interventions for large (non)clinical samples recruited in universities and online.
Measures	Longer comprehensive administered test batteries.	Brief self-report used regularly in clinical practice.
Patient focus	One- or two-person psychology.	Inclusion of family, carers, systems and cultural context.
Theory	Psychoanalytic theories.	Cognitive/behavioural theories. Integration of complementary theories (cognitive, behavioural and dynamic theories)
Method	Unspecified methods of data selection/analyses. No control groups.	Specified quantitative/ qualitative research methods. Use of active and no-treatment control as the norm.
Targeted problems	Psychosomatics, physical symptoms, medical illness and rehabilitation	Mental health and adjustment to non-medical life changes.
Diagnoses	Psychodiagnostics (defining, operationalising and measuring conceptual categories).	Mental health continuum, functional analyses. Transdiagnostic formulations.
Professional role	Clinical psychologist's role to conduct assessments and help with medical problems/ treatments.	Wider roles of conducting research, assessments, supervision, offering specific treatments for mental health problems and service audits.

studies (e.g. Isle of Wight study) and with children (e.g. Uta Frith, Simon Baron-Cohen, Dorothy Bishop).

As documented elsewhere in this book, there were many competing demands on the early clinical psychologists' time, with no statutory guidelines regarding how that time should be spent, and some general ambiguity about what clinical psychologists were 'for' anyway. Nevertheless it was widely acknowledged that with psychologists' academic psychology qualification, research should be a key component of their workload. For example, the Zuckerman Report (Zuckerman, 1968) suggested that the psychologist's task was to apply the principles of science for the assistance of clinicians, while the Trethowan Report (Department of Health and Social Security, 1977) recommended that a part of their week should be devoted to research. Likewise the Medical Research Council saw psychology as a key source of research skill, such that up until the 1970s, it provided funding for some trainee places, underscoring the position of psychologists as research contributors to the NHS.

The importance of the research role can further be seen in the terms of employment of most British clinical psychologists. From 1952 NHS psychologists were employed as scientists within the Whitley Council pay grouping. Psychologists were seen as providing the scientific 'back-up' particularly for psychiatry, just as biochemists did for physicians. It was not until the redesign of pay scales under Agenda for Change (implemented across the UK in 2004), that this designation of psychologists as scientists was formally discontinued.

Assessment-related research

The application of research competence from academic psychology into the applied setting is particularly evident in the primary involvement of most early clinical psychologists in the assessment and classification of individuals, either those in receipt of mental health care or those resident in the institutions where psychologists were first employed. The research role initially involved applying psychological models (e.g. the idea of intelligence as an inherited characteristic) and developing instruments (e.g. concerning verbal and nonverbal intelligence) for purposes of categorisation of the behaviour or abilities of the individuals in receipt of care. This was done largely to support the work of the organisations providing care, and the need for accurate ways of categorising people (see also Chapter 10). Our analysis of two key journals across the decades (see above) shows that a high percentage of published research in the 1950s, 1960s and early 1970s concerned the development of measures, and examination of their psychometric properties, for example the assessment of intelligence in people diagnosed as schizophrenic or investigation of cognitive deficits in the elderly (e.g. Kendrick, 1972). As researchers, many clinical psychologists were seeking to improve the utility and robustness of such measures, gathering and publishing research studies on their psychometric validity and reliability.

Alongside requests for assessment of intelligence, requests were often received for 'personality'. Projective tests such as the Thematic Apperception Test and Rorschach tests, often used by psychiatrists, were subjected to research scrutiny, and progressively a range of other personality traits and personality inventories and batteries of tests were developed, aimed at creating a complete profile of a patient's psychological status. Some of this work used an essentially psychological nomothetic framework, understanding personality in dimensional terms (e.g. Claridge & Broks, 1984; Eysenck, 1952), while others used models such as personal construct theory (Bannister, 1970). Shapiro (1966) also devised an innovative idiopathic measure for understanding individuals.

The research contribution on assessment has continued since the 1970s, albeit making up a less dominant proportion of studies. More recently psychologists have tended to focus on the development of categorical measures that complement the psychiatric or medical system, and also on reaffirming the role of interviews as providing a chance to review the patient's problems collaboratively before deciding what tests might be worth administering.

Treatment-related research

The growing involvement by psychologists in the management and subsequently the treatment of those with mental health difficulties (described elsewhere in this book) meant that the focus of research activity progressively broadened to include questions about the effectiveness of therapeutic efforts. As with assessment, psychologists drew upon the models currently used within the parent discipline, which then led to the application of psychological interventions, together with research investigating the effectiveness of these interventions, in a mental health context. As outlined in Table 11.1, a substantial proportion of the early published research on treatments used psychodynamic models (e.g. Sandler, 1972). Over the decades this changed, initially to more behavioural interventions and then to cognitive approaches. Questioning the efficacy of psychodynamic models, Eysenck (1952) proposed the application of learning theory-based approaches to treatment of abnormal behaviour, and much subsequent research in the 1950s and 1960s focused on behavioural interventions, including the use of functional analysis and the effects of the application of learning theory to so-called abnormal behaviour, for instance Baker and colleagues (1977) on the use of token economies with patients in long-stay psychiatric hospitals, and behaviour modification with those with obsessive-compulsive behaviour (e.g. Hodgson & Rachman, 1977). The growing importance of cognitive models within academic psychology in the 1960s and 1970s can be seen in the increasing numbers of research studies, and range of mental health conditions studied, that employed this model, reflecting growing confidence in psychological understanding of mental illness. Much of this research also questioned the medical model of mental health problems.

A good example is research concerning psychosis, which has developed very significantly over the last 50 years, largely resulting from psychologists listening to their patients' accounts of psychotic experiences, and systematically applying both their clinical and psychological research skills. 'Above all else, actually giving patients time to talk about their psychotic experiences has led to a transformation in how we understand and treat psychosis' (D. Freeman, in interview 20 August, 2014). Initially, in the 1950s and 1960s, research about psychosis by psychologists was limited, since mentally ill patients as a group were not thought of as particularly amenable to or worthy of systematic psychological assessment or intervention. Furthermore, research psychologists were not encouraged to talk to people with schizophrenia for fear of reinforcing their abnormal symptoms. By the end of the 1960s, however, attention shifted to the context of the observed 'abnormal' behaviour, and how the psychiatric environment was itself maintaining abnormality. Examples include research based on behavioural approaches such as token economies, or sociologically informed studies of long-stay hospital wards (e.g. Caine & Smail, 1968). Meanwhile the move to community care grew, and psychologists were involved in new residential home developments (e.g. Shepherd, 1995). A number of single-case studies were published (e.g. Fowler & Morley, 1989) and these described models for treating nonresponders to medication, showing some unexpectedly positive changes. This work helped demonstrate the potential for psychological therapy in psychosis. Psychologists such as Bentall et al. (1989), and Garety and Freeman (1999) challenged the orthodoxy, and published evidence undermining the idea of a discreet disease entity called 'schizophrenia'. Subsequent research on the relevance of family communication, life events and expressed emotion (e.g. reviewed by Onwumere et al., 2011), have all shown that family environments and trauma influence the onset, progression and course of psychosis. All of this demonstrated how psychological researchers could contribute very significantly to understanding and treating what had previously been considered an untreatable medical problem.

Other examples include research with children (Uta Frith), autism (Simon Baron-Cohen), eating disorders (Zafra Cooper) and anxiety (David Clark). Work on autism has been based on theoretical developments of theory of mind, while cognitive behavioural therapy (CBT) has drawn heavily on cognitive psychology. According to the International Benchmarking Review of UK Psychology (Economics & Social Research Council, 2011), CBT is now used all over the world for the treatment of many forms of psychological disorders, such as post-traumatic stress, anxiety and depression, and its research foundation has been central to its successful adoption.

Treatment trials, examining both process and outcome questions, have attempted to understand not only if interventions work, but also how and why (e.g. the Sheffield studies, D. Shapiro et al., 1995). Barkham and others have developed methods for interrogating very large naturalistic data sets derived from UK service settings, comparing these with large international data sets on costs and outcomes, benchmarking outcomes against data from controlled clinical trials and understanding these services in the wider context of public mental health and well-being (Barkham et al., 2001).

Growing sophistication of research design and statistical analysis

Huge changes have been seen in the research methods applied to mental health problems. These include sample size, from an N of one to several thousands (as the field has grown in confidence and has been able to attract serious funding); awareness of the importance of a wide range of psychological variables; growing use of technology (e.g. virtual reality labs in the study of paranoia); and the increasing involvement of service users and the general public in shaping research questions (e.g. the Hearing Voices network). Also, there has been an increase in collaboration with other professional groups, such as behavioural geneticists, psychiatrists, neuroscientists or statisticians. Although these collaborations have been beneficial, it has again potentially created the problem of invisibility of the specific contributions of our profession.

The last 50 years have also seen research studies become more varied and complex in their research questions, design and analytic approaches. This includes the use of single-case design, the introduction of systematic reviews and the development of complex statistical methods. In the past decade or so, the use of qualitative methods has grown. In particular in the UK, interpretative phenomenological analysis (Smith & Osborn, 2003) has become increasingly popular. Another recent trend has been the use of mixed methods in research, where both quantitative and qualitative data are collected and analysed in a single study.

Research and clinical psychology training

As has been discussed elsewhere in this volume, the Boulder model of clinical psychology accorded a central place to research in the training of clinical psychologists, as did the early model and practices developed at the Maudsley Hospital by Monte Shapiro and Hans Eysenck. Shapiro in particular considered that the research role was critical; according to Payne (2011, p.10), Shapiro

> had a very pure conception of science... [the aim of which should be] to bring the observed abnormality under experimental control. The theory was only satisfactory when it allowed you to specify the conditions under which the abnormality could be made to come and go, so that it could be controlled experimentally by manipulating the relevant variables.

Eysenck also considered that research should take a central place in training rather than the provision of therapy, proposing that clinical psychologists should not be diverted into providing treatment. He also argued that two years was the minimum time needed for trainees to develop the research and statistical analysis skills necessary for the role. Training on statistical techniques was famously rigorous at the Maudsley:

> The course issued clinical data handbooks (findings of research relevant to clinical work with individuals)... and fundamental papers on stats for the individual case. You had to know how to work with such data in relation to the performance on tests. And a lot of the critique of papers in seminars and tutorials focused on statistical and study design issues /psychometric problems, etc. (M. Berger, personal communication, 27 September 2014)

Clinical psychologists have been well placed to participate in all aspects of research excellence, not least because they were and are the only healthcare professionals to receive extensive training in research design and methodology as well as having a basic knowledge of psychological processes. More specifically, training at Master's level and subsequently at doctoral level meant research methods teaching has long been a required part of the curriculum, and training culminates in a substantial piece of independent research thesis (i.e. a substantial and original piece of clinically relevant research). Trainees are also expected to display research-mindedness through essays, case reports and projects. In 1991, the Board of Examiners' research curriculum of the BPS Diploma in Clinical Psychology identified areas of research where trainees needed to become competent, including: understanding the role of research in a professional context, framing research questions, research design including ethical issues, test construction, multivariate designs, process-outcome measurement and methods of analysis. This was supported by key texts on research methodology for trainees, for example, Parry and Watts (1996). Interestingly, these requirements have stayed reasonably consistent over time and across various developments in other training requirements. The major change has been the addition of qualitative methodologies.

Over the last decade, clinical psychology training programmes in Britain have reaffirmed the scientist-practitioner model: describing explicit identities of both 'researcher' and 'practitioner', and viewing psychologists as both conductors and consumers of research, who apply research findings to practice.

Contextual and professional issues

According to the International Benchmarking Review of UK Psychology (ESRC, 2011), research completed by British clinical psychologists has been, in numerous areas, world-leading. Compared to the US, there has been a relatively strong emphasis on transdiagnostic processes, that is, on phenomena that cut across various mental disorders, for example the biased processing of affective information. The theoretical understanding and resulting therapeutic interventions are being taught worldwide to students and clinicians as state-of-the-art clinical psychology. Basic research has also been highly influential (e.g. Holmes et al., 2004).

At some universities clinical psychology has been associated with medical schools, helping to foster links between clinical psychology and psychiatry, while in others it has been associated with departments of psychology, fostering interactions with other subdisciplines such as cognitive psychology and social psychology. After the Second World War, several research units were set up focusing on applied research, of which the Applied Psychology Unit at Cambridge is the largest and best known (Hearnshaw, 1964). Psychological research from these units, as well as from psychologists working in the NHS, has had very important societal pay-offs in the form of evidence-based treatment manuals and guidelines, including those for children, people with a learning disability (e.g. the Hester Adrian Research Unit for learning disabilities at Manchester) and the elderly (published by the National Institute for Health and Clinical Excellence). Patients have increasingly demanded greater accountability and monitoring of the effect of services, requiring mental health services to demonstrate results with audits and evaluations. At a national level this has meant sifting through the evidence and evaluation research to create guidelines.

Overall this research has provided a sound evidence base for a range of psychological therapies and has helped to support carer and service user involvement, and service development in the NHS (Cooper & Graham, 2009). There have also been critical contributions from clinical psychologists to the work of the UK Government's National Treatment Agency, for example the provision of psychotherapy for long-term prisoners, and to the work of the charity known as Beat, which provides help for people with eating disorders. The creation of the nationwide large-scale programme Improving Access to Psychological Therapies (IAPT) was heavily based on the evidence on the cost-effectiveness of psychological treatments.

Secondary research skills have also become particularly important in recent years. These include regular consumption and evaluation of other people's research work to inform clinical practice and to stay up to date with the most recent evidence base; and the provision of teaching and supervision for other clinical psychologists, mental health professionals and service users.

Despite the support on political, policy and training levels, not all aspects of research in clinical psychology in the UK have been positive. Within the profession, as noted, research activity has been relatively low (Milne et al., 2000). Various reasons have been suggested, including the fact that due to increased clinical demands and limited resources, NHS practitioners have found it hard to prioritise research time. It has become more and more difficult for clinical psychologists to obtain research grants in the UK, although senior figures continue to be funded for larger scale multiprofessional clinical trials. Consequently, research is being increasingly restricted to small-scale applied studies (e.g. those carried out by clinical psychology trainees) or other more applied studies funded by the NHS, rather than large original psychological research studies (collection of new data). Recent reviews suggest that the majority of clinical psychology doctoral theses are left unpublished (approximately 75 per cent, according to Cooper & Turpin 2007), calling into question the extent to which the 'researcher' identity is being modelled for trainees by trainers and qualified staff (see Gelso, 2006; Holttum & Goble, 2006). It is possible that anxiety and lack of confidence among trainees and qualified clinical psychologists, as well as negative experiences with ethics or research and development processes, play a part in this, although note that a lack of (original) publications does not necessarily mean that research has not been conducted or consumed. Lastly, there have been some significant tensions within the profession about the role of research. These include rivalries over psychological models, the pressure of providing 'evidence-based' treatments, concern about the (sometimes lacking) importance of social context. All of these issues have led to questions about the value of research, its type and focus, and how to apply findings in clinical practice.

Ethics and service user involvement

Several major shifts can be traced across the years concerning the relationship between those being studied and those carrying out the research. First, social changes since 1945, and the progressive growth of awareness of the personhood and rights of the mentally ill patient, or service user, can be observed in the choice of language used in research papers from 'research subject' to 'research participant'. These terms evoke different meanings and demonstrate an attitudinal shift, although the wholesale unreflective adoption of the term 'participant' might also be inappropriate. A more recent change focuses on how to determine the circumstances in which the terms 'subject', 'participant' and, for example, terms like 'activist', should legitimately be used (Corrigan & Tutton, 2006).

Second, there has been a huge change regarding awareness of the importance of research ethics, and the rights of those being studied to receive protection from harm, to have a choice about their participation, and to retain some degree of control over the use of their own data. The standards in research are not new; ethical standards to protect people have been around for over 60 years (Nuremberg Code 1947; Declaration of Helsinki 1964; International Conference of Harmonisation of Good Clinical Practice 1996, Medical Research Council Good Clinical Practice 1996; European Directive, transposed into UK law 2004; Research Governance

Framework 2005). But only since 2004 has all research carried out in the NHS with patients or staff, or on NHS premises, required approval from an NHS research ethics committee. These requirements have undergone various changes, for example the creation of a national R&D application form and the National Research Ethics Service in 2007. This has been paralleled by the progressive evolution of NHS control over the organisation and conduct of research and development (R&D) functions carried out in the NHS, and the appointment of R&D directors, some of whom were clinical psychologists, in Trusts.

Third, the involvement of those being studied in the research process itself has dramatically changed. While data from patients or mental health service users have of course comprised the overwhelming majority of research studies carried out, the notion that participants themselves might have a view on what should be studied, or how the research should be conducted, has only evolved gradually. From 2002 onwards, more attention has been paid to questions about the acceptability of self-report measures to users, beyond their use in traditional psychometric evaluation. Also, until recently, very little service user involvement in research on mental health issues had been reported in the academic literature. Pilgrim and Waldron (1998, p.95) captured the spirit of service user involvement in research in the context of the planning of mental health services: 'This paper…attempted to take users beyond the role of passive suppliers of opinion and encouraged their role as active negotiators of change'. Mental health service users may be involved in any or all of the stages of research, from defining the priorities for research through commissioning, designing and carrying out research, to the dissemination of the findings.

Involvement of individuals with personal experience of mental distress in planning and providing mental health services has grown internationally over the past three decades. First-hand direct experience supports service user contributions from an epistemological perspective that differs from 'professional' researchers (Beresford & Evans, 1999). This can lead to research outcomes that are different and more relevant to service users and providers. With increasing evidence demonstrating the benefits of involving service users in research, successive UK governments have prioritised service user involvement in planning and delivery of care and in the design, conduct, analysis and reporting of studies (see also chapter 2).

Research achievements

Over the years there have been many positive outcomes produced or supported by British clinical psychology researchers. These include:

- inclusion of sound psychological perspectives and procedures into the assessment of children, adults and older people, especially for those with disabilities or in receipt of psychiatric services;
- the extension of research from fundamental and applied research to treatment development and service evaluations;
- the increasing sophistication of research methods, designs, quantitative and qualitative analyses;
- development of our understanding of many areas including, for example, psychosis, trauma, eating disorders and autism, and their treatments;
- development and evaluation of CBT treatments, now being taught and

implemented throughout the world;
- the general impact of this research on changes in public attitudes towards mental health, national policies, evidence-based practice guidelines;
- inclusion of service users and their perspectives in all parts of research;
- application of ethical standards and committees for the benefit of service users;
- the development of the profession, and diversity of views about research, which have been and continue to be important for the discipline.

As already noted, there have also been conflicts and areas of disappointment, including the relative lack of active involvement in gathering new data, difficulties in implementing research findings, rivalries about the strength of evidence for specific psychological models, the scarcity of work addressing pre-empirical and nonempirical research concerns (see also chapter 4) and the relative lack of awareness of social context. There has also been unease about the lack of evidence for some of what psychologists do in their daily clinical practice.

Conclusion

The research component of the clinical psychologists' role, albeit a core part of professional (self-promoting) rhetoric, has fundamentally driven up the standards of care for service users, and has by and large led to improved services, innovation and to a more 'reflective' profession. Both the contributions from clinical psychologists historically and the potential for further work are immense. Clinical psychologists, by virtue of their extensive research training, are well placed in health care to conduct successful research. The research skills of the clinical psychologist will become even more crucial for the future survival of the profession, in an era of reduced funding for the NHS, in that these skills distinguish psychologists from other 'therapists' who may offer other cheaper clinical interventions. This means that research skills, initiatives and publication should change from a 'nice-to-have' to a 'must-have', and deserve more attention among clinical psychologists in the future. In particular the role of basic fundamental research based on core psychological principles is critical, since it is that which underpins the profession's unique contribution.

Acknowledgments

Grateful thanks to Susan Killoran, Fellow Librarian, Harris Manchester College, Oxford University, for her considerable help in sourcing journals.

References

Baker, R., Hall, J.N., Hutchinson, K. & Bridge, G. (1977). Symptom changes in chronic schizophrenic patients on a token economy: A controlled experiment. *British Journal of Psychiatry, 131*, 381–393.

Bannister, D. (1970). *Perspectives in personal construct theory.* Waltham, MS: Academic Press.

Barkham, M., Margison, F., Leach, C. et al. (2001). Service profiling and outcomes benchmarking using the CORE-OM: Toward practice-based evidence in the psychological therapies. *Journal of Consulting and Clinical Psychology, 69*(2), 184–196.

Baruch, G. & Fearon, P. (2002). The evaluation of mental health outcome at a community-based psychodynamic psychotherapy service for young people: A 12-month follow-up based on self-report data. *Psychology and Psychotherapy: Theory, Research and Practice, 75*(3), 261–278.

Bentall, R.P., Claridge, G.S. & Slade, P.D. (1989). The multidimensional nature of schizotypal traits: A factor analytic study with normal subjects. *British Journal of Clinical Psychology, 28*(4), 363–375.

Beresford, P. & Evans, C. (1999). Research note: Research and empowerment. *British Journal of Social Work, 29*(5), 671–677.

Caine, T.M. & Smail, D.J. (1968). Attitudes of psychiatric patients to staff roles and treatment methods in mental hospitals. *British Journal of Medical Psychology, 41*(3), 291–294.

Claridge, G. & Broks, P. (1984). Schizotypy and hemisphere function – I: Theoretical considerations and the measurement of schizotypy. *Personality and Individual Differences, 5*(6), pp.633–648.

Clarke, A.D.B. (1979). Editorial: Seventy-five years of the *British Journal of Psychology* 1904–1979. *British Journal of Psychology, 70*(1), 1–5.

Cooper, M. & Graham, C. (2009). Research and evaluation. In H. Beinart, P. Kennedy & S. Llewelyn (Eds.), *Clinical psychology in practice* (pp.46–58). Oxford: Oxford University Press.

Cooper, M. & Turpin, G. (2007). Clinical psychology trainees' research productivity and publications: An initial survey and contributing factors. *Clinical Psychology & Psychotherapy, 14*(1), 54–62.

Corrigan, O. & Tutton, R. (2006). What's in a name? Subjects, volunteers, participants and activists in clinical research. *Clinical Ethics, 1*(2), 101–104.

Department of Health and Social Security (1977). *The role of psychologists in the health service (Trethowan Report).* London: HMSO.

Economics & Social Research Council (2011). *International Benchmarking Review of UK Psychology.* Swindon: RCUK.

Eysenck, H.J. (1952). The effects of psychotherapy: An evaluation. *Journal of Consulting Psychology, 16*(5), 319–324.

Fowler, D. & Morley, S. (1989.) The cognitive-behavioural treatment of hallucinations and delusions: A preliminary study. *Behavioural Psychotherapy, 17*(3), 267–282.

Garety, P.A. & Freeman, D. (1999). Cognitive approaches to delusions: A critical review of theories and evidence. *British Journal of Clinical Psychology, 38*(2), 113–154.

Gelso, C.J. (2006). On the making of a scientist-practitioner: A theory of research training in professional psychology. *Training and Education in Professional Psychology, 5*(1), 3–16.

Hearnshaw, L.S. (1969). Psychology in Great Britain: An introductory historical essay. In B.M. Foss (Ed.), *Supplement to the Bulletin of the British Psychological Society* (pp.3–9). London: British Psychological Society.

Hodgson, R.J. & Rachman, S. (1977). Obsessional-compulsive complaints. *Behaviour Research and Therapy, 15*(5), 389–395.

Holmes, E.A., Brewin, C.R. & Hennessy, R.G. (2004). Trauma films, information processing, and intrusive memory development. *Journal of Experimental Psychology: General, 133*(1), 3–22.

Holttum, S. & Goble, L. (2006). Factors influencing levels of research activity in clinical psychologists: A new model. *Clinical Psychology & Psychotherapy, 13*(5), 339–351.

Kendrick, D.C., (1972). The Kendrick battery of tests: Theoretical assumptions and clinical uses. *British Journal of Social and Clinical Psychology, 11*(4), 373–386.

Milne, D., Keegan, D., Paxton, R. & Seth, K. (2000). Is the practice of psychological therapists evidence-based? *International Journal of Health Care Quality Assurance, 13*(1), 8–14.

Onwumere, J., Bebbington, P. & Kuipers, E. (2011). Family interventions in early psychosis: Specificity and effectiveness. *Epidemiology and Psychiatric Sciences, 20*(2), 113–119.

Parry, G. (1992). Improving psychotherapy services: Applications of research, audit and evaluation. *British Journal of Clinical Psychology, 31*(1), 3–19.

Parry, G. & Watts, F.N. (1996). *Behavioural and mental health research: A handbook of skills and methods.* Hove: Psychology Press.

Payne, R. (1997). The early years – some personal recollections. In W. Yule (Ed.), *50th Anniversary of the Maudsley Clinical Psychology Course: 1947 to 1997.* William Yule Archive, King's College London. (Copy available in the BPS Archive, London AUD/002/OHP 55)

Pearson, S.W., Tillett, R.I. & Lloyd, K.R. (2002). Study of psychiatric admission patterns before and after out-patient psychotherapy in a district service setting. *Psychology and Psychotherapy: Theory, Research and Practice, 75*(4), 437–443.

Pilgrim, D. & Waldron, L. (1998). User involvement in mental health service development: How far can it go? *Journal of Mental Health, 7*(1), 95–104.

Sandler, J., Dare, C. & Holder, A. (1972). Frames of reference in psychoanalytic psychology. *British Journal of Medical Psychology, 45*(2), 133–142.

Shapiro, D.A., Rees, A., Barkham, M. et al. (1995). Effects of treatment duration and severity of depression on the maintenance of gains after cognitive-behavioral and psychodynamic-interpersonal psychotherapy. *Journal of Consulting and Clinical Psychology, 63*(3), 378–387.

Shapiro, M.B. (1966). The single case in clinical-psychological research. *Journal of General Psychology, 74*(1), 3–23.

Shepherd, G. (1995). The 'ward-in-a-house': Residential care for the severely disabled. *Community Mental Health Journal, 31*(1), 53–69.

Smith, J.A. & Osborn, M. (2003). Interpretative phenomenological analysis. In: J.A. Smith (Ed.), *Qualitative psychology: A practical guide to research methods* (pp.51–80). London: Sage.

Zuckerman, S. (1968). *Hospital scientific and technical services.* London: HMSO.

Chapter 12 Psychologists in organisations

Bernard Kat

Deinstitutionalisation

When the NHS was created in 1946, it inherited a stock of old asylums, some dating from the 1845 County Asylums Act, and increasing numbers of patients for whom those hospitals had become their homes. Psychologists' contributions to the care and management of those patients came as the aim of government policy was moving towards 'deinstitutionalisation'. In 1962 Enoch Powell, then Minister of Health, announced his plan to cut the number of 'mental illness' beds in the UK, increase the number of 'mental handicap' beds, and considerably increase the number of short-stay psychiatric units in general hospitals. Powell's Hospital Plan, together with excessive optimism about the powers of new drug treatments, created pressure to resettle long-stay patients out of the former asylums and into various forms of community care. The pressure was only intensified by a series of official reports between 1967 and 1972 about scandalous mismanagement of care in some hospitals.

At that time UK clinical psychologists, of whom there were only about 450 in the whole NHS, were beginning to foresee the changes in their roles implied by the development of behaviour therapy. Through the work of Ayllon and Azrin (1968) some were also becoming aware of an American behaviour modification programme known as the 'token economy', one of a number of psychological procedures for promoting rehabilitation into community care, another being social skills training (Spence & Shepherd, 1983). There are a number of contemporary reviews of working as a psychologist in institutions at that time (Cullen, 1985; Hall, 1987, 1992; Lavender, 1985).

The idea that patients' behaviour and experiences are shaped as much by the environment in which they are living as the disorder from which they are suffering has a long history, typically traced back to William Tuke, who set up The Retreat in York in 1796 (Tuke, 1813/1996). That early regime of 'moral treatment' was developed by lay managers, before the asylums came under medical control during the later part of the 19th century, and foreshadowed the therapeutic communities established during the Second World War (Kennard, 1998). Whereas behaviour modification programmes relied on staff power and control for their implementation, a therapeutic community was a deliberate attempt to create a society with a democratic, even egalitarian, culture. It was a society in which therapeutic decisions and functions were shared by the whole community and where the status differences between staff and residents were greatly reduced, if not completely abandoned. Following their research on the Claybury Hospital community, Caine and Smail (1969) concluded that the basic beliefs and personalities of those involved were critical to whatever success the community achieved.

Clinical psychologists also began to address the broader question of what constitutes good psychological care in general hospitals and community settings. Nichols (1984) developed and explained the defining features of good 'psychological care' and promoted a culture-based approach to creating a caring environment through the behaviour of the clinical staff.

The psychological care of people suffering from dementia provides another example of cultural shift. The 'reality orientation' approach to reducing confusion and increasing the engagement of such patients had been developed in the US in the mid-1970s. The first UK guide to implementing such programmes was Holden and Woods (1982). What they advocated was not a set of techniques but a systematic approach to the 'whole person' built on cultural change within the ward and staff group.

Community psychology

Sometimes 'the community' and 'the population' can be synonyms, generic terms for the largest organisation of all. Bender (1976) and Koch (1986), the first major UK publications concerning psychological work in community settings, were 'home grown' without reference to developments on the other side of the Atlantic, prompted by the deficiencies in the implementation of 'community care'. The *Journal of Community and Applied Social Psychology* was first published in 1991, followed shortly by the first edition of Orford's influential book (Orford, 1992), which acknowledged its debt to Rappaport's pioneering work (Rappaport, 1977). Orford's description of community psychology's aims, 'to correct the individualistic bias [of psychology] by aiming always to consider people within the contexts of their social settings and systems of which they are parts or which influence them' would serve just as well as a statement of the aims of psychologists in organisations.

Populations and public health psychology

The introduction of an 'internal market' in health care in 1991 (described at the time as the 'purchaser–provider split') had a profound consequence for psychology, about which there has been relatively little discussion. The 1974 reorganisation had brought with it the idea of 'district' professional posts with, at least in principle, a responsibility to advise on the population's need for the profession's services and the developments required. That idea largely survived the introduction of Unit management in 1982. To give an example from my own career, when I was appointed to a district psychologist post in 1984 I was part of the district medical officer's team, along with the district health promotion officer and two registrars in public health medicine. We were all aware of the impact of beliefs, attitudes and behaviour on health and illness and we could see that a public health psychology could make an effective contribution to the broader field of public health, but our team did not survive the introduction of general management in 1985. Academic and clinical health psychologists later began to develop some of the conceptual tools required, for example Hepworth (2004) and Wardle and Steptoe (2005). Smail's analysis of the relationship between individual distress and societal power and interest also has implications for public health (Smail, 2005).

The idea of professional input to the assessment of population need for services survived in a weakened form until 1991 when needs assessment and service specification were taken off into separate 'purchasing' organisations, very few of which had any psychologists involved. But on top of the loss of budgetary control and service management to general managers, for the time being NHS psychologists had also lost the opportunity to innovate a public health psychology through day-to-day practice. In 2003 the Society's Division of Health Psychology and the Department of Health (DH) created a part-time consultancy post for a senior health psychologist to work in the DH Division of Public Health (Abraham & Michie, 2005) and the DH New Horizons consultation (Department of Health, 2009) prompted innovative thinking (Hanna, 2009). But it was not until 2012, when Public Health England and Health and Wellbeing Boards were set up, that there were public organisations through which applied psychologists might be able to create population-based interventions for the prevention of ill health and promotion of well-being, and the Applied Psychology and Public Health Network was set up in 2013 to facilitate developments.

Once the 'internal market' was in operation, few psychologists were permitted by their general and contract managers to negotiate directly with 'purchasers', later renamed 'commissioners'. But the BPS Division of Clinical Psychology did invest in projects to support those members who were in a position to do so, for example Kat (1992), the creation of the BPS Centre for Outcomes Research and Effectiveness in 1995, and the *Introductory Guide to Commissioning* (DCP, 2012). The next time that population-needs assessment was addressed in relation to psychological therapy services was as part of launching the Improving Access to Psychological Therapies (IAPT) project.

Organisational relationships and the management of staff to achieve them

It is a truism that all clinical staff need to learn some psychology, but purposeful use of the clinical environment implies much more thorough design and management of the human and social resources required. Multidisciplinary teamwork and internal consultancy provide two examples of applied psychologists' contributions.

The policy of 'care in the community', which aimed to help people with special needs (e.g. people with mental health problems, learning disability or physical disability, and frail older people) to live independent lives in their own homes or sheltered accommodation, led to the creation of various types of multidisciplinary clinical teams. It had been assumed that the work of such teams would be more efficient and effective than the sum of the work undertaken by their constituent individual professionals. Unfortunately such teams often ran into serious problems even if they started off functioning as a team. Overt problems, such as lack of cooperation between members' employers, inadequate facilities and absence of agreed roles and organisational relationships, were easily stated but very difficult to overcome. However, in some teams other problems created rivalries and conflict that made team functioning almost impossible; for example, a team which included a psychiatrist with a strong commitment to biological explanations of mental illness and a psychologist with an equally strong commitment to social and developmental explanations of the same phenomena.

John Ovretveit, a Chartered Psychologist who became Director of the Health and Social Services Management programme at Brunel University, sought to clarify the problems and the steps that might be taken to prevent them (Ovretveit, 1986). The Division of Clinical Psychology published a widely cited report, *Responsibility*

Issues in Clinical Psychology and Multidisciplinary Teamwork (DCP, 1986). Onyett (1992) and Onyett et al. (1997) provided detailed guidance on the use of case management as a way of increasing the flexibility, continuity and responsiveness of mental health services by assigning clear responsibilities to individual members of staff working in teams. The Division published a revised version of its 1986 document in 2001 entitled *Working in Teams* (BPS, 2001), the third section of which presented 28 scenarios in which a clinical psychologist faced a problem in teamworking and discussed the best course of action to take following the principles set out earlier in the document.

Management consultancy is now a substantial industry in the UK. Typically, the client organisation seeks external (and supposedly objective) advice about management and change from companies with the requisite expertise. Some of that expertise derives from pioneering work and systemic thinking by psychologists (Campbell et al., 1989). In the past 30 years psychologists, particularly in the public sector, have received consultancy requests from within their own employing organisations leading to the practice of 'internal consultancy'. The BPS published *The Change Directory* (Brunning et al., 1990) as an introductory guide to organisational development and the management of change. There followed a series of publications on internal consultancy based primarily on the work of David Campbell (Bor & Miller, 1991; Campbell et al., 1994; Huffington & Brunning, 1994). The model of clinical psychology practice on which the Manpower Planning Advisory Group (MPAG, 1990) based its recommendations was a form of internal consultancy which assumed that NHS organisations would want and use such consultancy and did not address the question of what should happen if they did not.

Service design and clinical pathways

The emerging discipline of 'service design' is said to have originated from the marketing and management of service industries, initiated by Shostack (1984). Motivated by the need to ensure that commercial services attract and satisfy customers, it sees itself as a specialism within the field of design. However, service design thinking has already been applied to health care in the US, for example Stickdorn and Schneider (2011). The concept of a clinical pathway (also known as a care pathway) was given impetus by the 1997 White Paper *The New NHS: Modern, Dependable* (Department of Health, 1997). Unlike service design thinking, which starts from the customer's experience, pathways are now seen as one of the best tools for managing the quality and outcomes of health care by standardised evidence-based care processes (Johnson, 1997). The publication of a review of strategic policy concerning psychotherapy services (Department of Health, 1996) was a landmark event in the organisation and provision of psychological therapies. Led by a clinical psychologist, the review anticipated some aspects of service design and clinical pathways by identifying the purposes of those services and characteristics which commissioners should seek to ensure. This was followed in 2004 by more detailed guidance, again coordinated by a clinical psychologist, on 'organising and delivering psychological therapies', which included 'issues of access to psychological therapy services, waiting times and how to improve care pathways' (Department of Health, 2004).

At the same time as the DH 1996 publication, Roth and Fonagy published the first edition of their review of psychotherapy research *What Works for Whom?* Their conclusions included some proposals about the ways in which psychological therapy services should be provided. For example:

> We have found evidence to suggest that patients with relatively mild and acute disorders without comorbidity may be amenable to briefer treatments, and perhaps to more generic – though usually theory-based – therapies. In contrast, more severe and chronic disorders seem to require more specialised and possibly more lengthy treatments. In the light of these observations, we see some merit in a 'cascade' model of treatment, which employs broad criteria for assigning patients to care at primary, secondary, and tertiary levels, and within secondary and tertiary care might guide factors such as appropriate treatment length.

By comparison with the 'stepped care' model on which the IAPT initiative has been based (NICE, 2011), the cascade model implied an initial expert assessment to assign patients to the correct level of intervention, not unlike the consultant-led diagnostic procedures used in medicine and surgery.

Service systems

Psychologists have contributed to determining whether services achieve their quality standards and intended outcomes. Berger (1996) and Sperlinger (2002) pioneered work on defining the outcomes of psychology services. Barkham et al. (2010) developed the widely used CORE (clinical outcomes in routine evaluation) system. Ovretveit (1992) and Dickens (1994) addressed questions about what constitutes quality in human services. Clifford and Damon (1988) reviewed the evaluation of community-based services. Firth-Cozens (1993) wrote a monograph on the use of audit in mental health services. More recently, within that tradition Lueger and Barkham (2010) have provided guidance on the use of benchmarking to improve the quality of practice and services.

Apart from this tradition of organisational audit within the profession, some clinical psychologists have been called upon to participate in the work of NHS research ethics committees. For example, as a member of one of these committees for some years up to 2000, I found that other members often looked to me for advice from a psychological perspective. Topics included whether a research question was important enough to put subjects to the trouble of participating, whether participants would understand the information leaflets they would be given, whether procedures for obtaining consent were reasonable and transparent (particularly when participants were young or disadvantaged in some way), and whether the deception involved in the use of a control or placebo group was necessary and acceptable.

Professional competence

This chapter has reported examples of psychologists' work in and with organisations. The achievements speak for themselves, but is it reasonable to claim that clinical psychologists in general have adequate expertise in the systems and organisational aspects of health and social care? (For a fuller discussion of professional expertise see Cheshire and Pilgrim, 2004.) The professional competences of a newly qualified practitioner are defined by the Standards of Proficiency for Practitioner Psychologists, published by the Health and Care Professions Council (HCPC, 2012b).

- Paragraph 2a2 requires clinical psychologists to be able, in the context of selecting and using appropriate assessment techniques, to 'assess social context and organisational characteristics'.
- 2b1 requires them to 'be able to conduct service evaluations'.
- 2b2 requires them to 'be able to draw on knowledge of development, social and neuropsychological processes across the lifespan to facilitate adaptability and change in individuals, groups, families, organisations and communities'.
- 3a1 requires them, in relation to understanding psychological models, to 'understand change processes in service-delivery systems; understand social approaches such as those informed by community, critical and social constructivist perspectives; and understand leadership theories and models, and their application to service-delivery and clinical practice'.
- 3a2 requires them to 'know how professional principles are expressed and translated into action through a number of different approaches to practice, and how to select or modify approaches to meet the needs of an individual, groups or communities'.

These competences are the products of a three-year postgraduate training that is likely to have included an introduction to systemic family therapy; this will have been preceded by a three-year undergraduate degree usually with a social psychology component, and which may also have included other aspects of environmental and community psychology.

However, although clinical psychologists have a strong record as system-level problem solvers and innovators, at the time of writing their training courses rarely teach service design, development and evaluation as a topic. That may change as more clinical psychologists work outside NHS employment, freelance or for commercial companies. Nonetheless, it does raise a question about why training seems to have been so focused on the assessment and therapy of individual patients and their immediate contacts. And why is it that commissioners and managers of health and social care organisations have not seen applied psychologists as the 'go-to' profession for innovation, problem solving and service design and development, inadvertently depriving their organisations of much needed skill and expertise?

Those questions have been around almost since the Trethowan Report was published. Clinical psychology was one of the professions studied by Ovretveit (1984). Using the concept of levels of work (Jaques, 1978) he observed:

> There is a need to distinguish between the level of work which a person is capable of doing, the work which they actually do, and the work which they are expected and paid to do and for which they are accountable. Many organisational problems can be explained by disparities between these three aspects. For example, many psychologists have the experience and ability to carry out Level 4 comprehensive service provision. They sometimes find that their proposals are blocked or ignored or they are experienced as a nuisance, and it becomes apparent that they are not

actually expected to undertake significant developments. In addition they may not be provided with the necessary budgetary and personnel authority to implement and manage the changes, and in fact only actually undertake Level 3 systematic service provision.

The discrepancy between NHS postholders' duties and their capacity to undertake much more responsible and demanding work also emerged in another way. In 1984 the Körner Committee's recommendations concerning the statistical information to be collected by the NHS in order to monitor its work, known as 'Körner data', began to be implemented. The main measure selected to quantify psychologists' workload was face-to-face contacts between psychologists and their individual patients. That decision created problems which were never fully resolved: how was 'indirect' work such as professional supervision of other staff, psychologists' research as scientist-practitioners, and their service development and evaluation activities to be quantified? The problem became more acute from 1991 onwards when 'purchasers' and 'providers' sought to establish unit costs for the purposes of service contracts.

Meanwhile, whatever lack of agreement there may have been between psychologists and NHS management about the work that psychologists should be undertaking, by the middle of the 1980s the demand for psychologists had seriously outstripped supply, creating unfillable vacancies. The profession was, therefore, one of the first to be reviewed by the Department of Health Manpower Planning Advisory Group (1990). The MPAG report was advised by a consultancy report by Derek Mowbray's Management Advisory Service (MAS, 1989). Neither the MAS report nor the final MPAG report anticipated that clinical psychologists would continue to work primarily as 'face-to-face' clinicians except as training experience.

The MAS report preferred the title 'health care psychologist' because it was more descriptive of the intended role, and recommended that psychologists should 'become fully independent professional practitioners, accorded equal status with medical practitioners and assuming responsibility for the psychological well-being of individuals served by and providing health care'. The report proposed a model of service delivery based on the principle of 'shared care' (i.e. working in partnership with medical practitioners to ensure the quality and effectiveness of all aspects of patient care) 'through the provision of direct and indirect patient care, management and organisational advice and training and research (service evaluation)'. The MPAG's final report concurred with much of what the MAS had recommended but presented the proposals in the form of accountable actions. In response to the question 'What do clinical psychologists do?' the report observed: '…the key words are "enabling" and "problem-solving". Whether the problems are those of individuals, families or institutions, applied psychologists use their scientific understanding of behaviour and experience to help people find a way out of their difficulties.' The report went on to identify the responsibilities of clinical psychologists as:

(a) undertaking more complex clinical duties where the problems encountered require a clinical psychologist's understanding of the processes involved;
(b) planning clinical programmes concerned with psychological aspects of patient care (in any aspect of health care);

(c) promoting and supporting programmes of early intervention for patients whose psychological problems have been presented as physical ill health or whose physical ill health is exacerbated by psychological problems;
(d) providing support, advice and consultancy to other staff concerning the psychological aspects of care;
(e) helping other staff develop their psychological knowledge and skills through joint case work and training;
(f) supporting the setting, measuring and monitoring of standards in relation to the psychological aspects of care; and
(g) developing new systems, procedures and techniques in response to service requirements (e.g. methods of needs assessment in relation to community care).
(MPAG, 1990)

The immediate reason why the MPAG report was not widely discussed was that it was published just when the quasi-market for NHS services was being introduced in April 1991. Not only were managers preoccupied with setting up the new systems, but 'purchasers', especially fund-holding GP practices, were soon seeking to contract for psychologists' highly valued assessments and therapies for their patients and putting pressure on contract managers to reduce long waiting times for appointments. An opportunity to build capacity into the organisational fabric of the NHS to respond to the growing understanding of the behavioural and psychological elements of health care had been lost.

But there were other deeper reasons why the MAS and MPAG proposals were not acted upon, some relating to the NHS but others relating to the profession's own weaknesses in promoting the work and achievements of psychologists.

Reflecting on the research undertaken on the therapy professions between 1968 and 1990 (in which he included psychology), Ovretveit (1993) noted that over these years there had been 'a decline in the management and prescribing authority of the medical profession over the therapy professions, and a replacement of top-level profession management with general management'. He distinguished between 'management autonomy' and 'practitioner autonomy'. The former referred to the extent of the service head's authority to manage the budget for the service and determine how the staff should spend their time. The management autonomy of the heads of professions was degraded first by the introduction of general management from 1985 onwards and then by the introduction of contracted services from 1991 onwards. 'Practitioner autonomy' was the freedom of practitioners to decide what cases they would take and what other kinds of work they would undertake 'without those decisions being questioned or overridden unless policies or contract is infringed' (Ovretveit, 1984). As management autonomy was lost in the course of successive reorganisations and restructuring, so practitioner autonomy was also lost. But as Jaques's (1989) theory of the development of working capacity would predict, practitioners' personal capacity for autonomy was not lost. Psychologists are, after all, highly selected for their ability to conceptualise problems and plan interventions. Innovative work with systems and employing organisations may have continued but it became, at best, the result of personal initiatives by individual psychologists and, at worst, covert activity undertaken without the knowledge, authority or approval of senior management.

The difficulties in contracting psychology services may also have accounted for an apparent change in the public perception of psychologists, particularly among NHS managers. On the one hand there were neither enough qualified psychologists to meet demand for services, nor was the 'clinic' model of service provision challenged appropriately by 'purchasers' and managers. On the other hand, owing to changes both in the universities and in NHS personnel agreements, grand-sounding titles like 'doctor', 'highly specialised' and 'consultant' had come into widespread use. Psychologists became used to being told that they were expensive, although compared to what or whom, or in terms of what unit cost, was rarely discussed. The possibility that the NHS was not using psychologists, a skilled and scarce resource, to best effect was not discussed again at national level until the New Ways of Working project (BPS, 2007b).

It was not just an NHS problem. Despite the achievements in organisational research and innovation described earlier, the profession itself did not do much to publicise or promote its work in and with NHS organisations. The concept of the clinical psychologist as 'scientist practitioner' was imported from the US by Hans Eysenck in the late 1940s when he was setting up the first UK clinical psychology training course. An important element is training in research skills. Research, in the sense of creating new knowledge, has higher status within psychology as a discipline than developing and providing services based on psychology applied to real-life problems; that can be deduced from the fact that the British Psychological Society publishes professional journals concerned with the former, but not with the latter. Further, creating value for an organisation like the NHS by innovating and evaluating procedures and services does not create new knowledge as normally understood. It is the function of an 'applied psychologist', not a 'scientist practitioner', and the entrepreneurial nature of the activity does not fit easily with an 'evidence-based practice' conception of professional work. In the absence of a BPS journal concerned with the design and provision of psychologists' professional services, *Clinical Psychology Forum* (which is circulated only to members of the Society's Division of Clinical Psychology) was the de facto journal for reporting such work until the worldwide web facilitated communication. Some non-Society journals, such as *Health Service Journal* and the *Journal of Mental Health*, also carried publications. The first – and for a time the only – book describing the day-to-day reality of psychologists' work was West and Spinks (1988) which included seven case studies about service development and working with organisations. One of the New Ways of Working reports (BPS 2007a, Appendix4) also included vignettes of such work.

The legacy of ambiguity

This chapter about the work of psychologists in organisations is also about the organisational context of the work of the profession, and the efforts that some members of the profession have made to analyse and change that context. The chapter thus far has used the notion of 'profession' without question and accepted that it can be applied to clinical psychology. Yet the very use of the word 'profession' in relation to clinical psychology invites the sociological and political analyses developed by David Pilgrim (Cheshire & Pilgrim, 2004; Pilgrim & Treacher, 1992). The implied conclusions of this chapter, that psychologists are problem solvers, innovators and service developers, and that those activities permit the profession's purpose to be identified, conflicts with one of clinical psychology's clearest and most uncomfortable characteristics: role ambiguity. It also raises further questions about who or what legitimises that purpose and who ultimately benefits from it. Over 10 years before Pilgrim and Treacher (1992), David Hawks (1981, p.11) wrote: 'Clinical psychologists confront a peculiar dilemma. If they acknowledge the problems which present themselves to them they must concede the paucity of their role in intervening in them. Faced with such a dilemma, clinical psychologists have reacted in a number of ways', most of which he went on to argue were demonstrably inappropriate. He supported the idea of 'corporate clinical practice' focused on system-level projects; the example he gave was resettlement of people with learning disabilities into community accommodation, and it was he who wrote the foreword to Koch's seminal 1986 book *Community Clinical Psychology*. In the same volume, Sutton and McPherson (1981, p.167) reported an emerging reconstruction of psychological practice

> by moving away from what is happening 'within' the individual and his immediate environment and raising the intention to incorporate how individuals are affected by organisations and social systems. Psychological practice is thus to be reconstructed by analysing and influencing the ways in which these wider phenomena function… Psychological practice in the public sector is to be more of a social psychology than hitherto and in making this suggestion some of those involved turn (paradoxically, it may appear) to the private sector of organisational and industrial psychology for their conceptual tools).

However, a desire to modify the impact of organisations and social systems on those affected by them inevitably raises difficult ethical problems for the psychologists concerned. Codes of professional ethics tend to focus on redressing the imbalance of power between professional and client and the presumed conflict of loyalty between the psychologists' own needs and the needs of their clients. But many psychologists have other obligations which also need to be taken into account. Psychologists may not be responsible for assessing the needs for their services in the population served, but service commissioners may want to maximise the number of people who are offered the service and may do so by limiting the work that can be undertaken with any one client to less than the psychologist believes is therapeutically effective. Further, psychologists in health and social care are usually managed employees, typically of employers who are providing the very same organisation that the psychologist is seeking to change on behalf of the organisation's clients. The challenge for the psychologist is to find a way of prioritising those potentially conflicting loyalties.

The Health and Care Professions Council's Standards of Conduct, Performance and Ethics (HCPC, 2012a) seem to imply that priority must be given to professional conduct over any responsibilities that psychologists may have to their employer or commissioner of their services. The British Psychological Society's Code of Ethics and Conduct (BPS, 2009) tries to take account of the complexity of professional practice by leaving much to individual judgement: 'This code uses the word "should" rather than the more coercive "must" or the permissive "asks" to reinforce the advisory nature of the code as a framework in support of professional judgement'. Francis (1999) went a helpful step further by identifying sequences of questions to be asked and answered in difficult situations.

It is normally assumed that the health and social care organisations in which psychologists work are benevolent and operate in the best interests of their clients or residents. However this chapter is being written shortly after a series of public scandals concerning quality of care, at Winterbourne View (Department of Health, 2012) and Mid Staffordshire (Francis, 2013). To whom should psychologists who find themselves in such organisations be most loyal: their employer? Should they become 'ethical informants' (Francis, 1999), commonly known as 'whistleblowers', thereby risking their jobs and their careers? Some psychologists have courageously taken the risk of doing so, with variable results. In 1968 the psychologist newly appointed to head the psychology department at Whittingham Hospital helped to precipitate the public inquiry into ill-treatment of patients (DHSS, 1972). In 1991 a principal psychologist at Ashworth Special Hospital disclosed serious abuse of female patients to the inquiry led by Louis Blom Cooper (Department of Health, 1992). But in 2014 the motives of a psychologist who exposed poor patient care and staff welfare at West London Mental Health Trust were questioned by the industrial tribunal to which she appealed after she lost her job (Whistleblowing claimant 'not acting in good faith', 2014).

This chapter is written at a time when the boundaries between the domains of applied psychology are becoming ever more fluid because the boundaries between public services are shifting rapidly as a result of government policies. When I qualified as a clinical psychologist, psychology in health care and clinical psychology were synonymous and very few were not employed by the NHS. Now more different kinds of psychologists are contributing to health care and at the same time the boundaries between health and social care, between public and commercial services, between employed and independent practice, are also changing. Psychologists' strength is in their capacity to innovate and develop services; their weakness is in their propensity to fragment into small specialised groups with separate identities which mean little if anything to those wanting their services. Work at system level with employing and contracting organisations, with the aim of ensuring benefit to the 'person in context', may provide a unifying theme for the next stage of applied psychologists' development.

References

Abraham, C. & Michie, S. (2005). Contributing to public health policy and practice. *The Psychologist, 18*, 676–679.

Ayllon T. & Azrin N.H. (1968). *The token economy: A motivational system for therapy and rehabilitation.* New York: Appleton-Century-Crofts.

Barkham M., Mellor-Clark, J., Connell, J. et al. (2010). Clinical outcomes in routine evaluation (CORE) – The CORE measures and system. In M. Barkham, G.F. Hardy & J. Mellor-Clark (Eds.), *Developing and delivering practice-based evidence* (pp.257–284). Chichester: Wiley-Blackwell.

Bender, M. (1976). *Community psychology.* London: Methuen.

Berger, M. (1996). *Outcomes and effectiveness in clinical psychology practice.* Leicester: Division of Clinical Psychology of the British Psychological Society.

Bor, R. & Miller, R. (1991). *Internal consultation in health care settings.* London: Karnac Books.

British Psychological Society (2001). *Working in teams. A report by the Division of Clinical Psychology of the British Psychological Society.* Leicester: Author.

British Psychological Society (2007a). *New ways of working for applied psychologists in health and social care – Career pathways and roles.* Leicester: Author.

British Psychological Society (2007b). *New ways of working for applied psychologists in health and social care – Final report of the New Roles Project Group.* Leicester: Author.

British Psychological Society (2009). *Code of ethics and conduct.* Leicester: Author.

Brunning, H., Cole, C. & Huffington, C. (1990). *The change directory.* Leicester: British Psychological Society.

Caine, T.M. & Smail, D.J. (1969). *Treatment of mental illness.* London: University of London Press.

Campbell, D., Caldicott, T. & Kinsella, K. (1994). *Systemic work with organisations: A new model for managers and change agents.* London: Karnac Books.

Campbell, D., Draper, R. & Huffington, C. (1989). *A systemic approach to consultation.* London: Karnac Books.

Cheshire, K. & Pilgrim, D. (2004). *A short introduction to clinical psychology.* London: Sage.

Clifford, P. & Damon, S. (1988) Evaluating community-based services. In F.N. Watts (Ed.), *New developments in clinical psychology* (Vol. 2, pp.226–244). Leicester: British Psychological Society.

Cullen, C. (1985). Working with groups of mentally handicapped adults. In F.N. Watts (Ed.), *New developments in clinical psychology* (Vol. 1, pp.84–95). Leicester: British Psychological Society.

Department of Health (1992). *Report of the Committee of Inquiry into Complaints About Ashworth Hospital, 1991–1992.* Cm 2028-1. London: HMSO.

Department of Health (1996). *NHS psychotherapy services in England. Review of strategic policy.* London: Author.

Department of Health (1997). *The new NHS: modern, dependable.* Cm 3807. London: Author.

Department of Health (2004). *Organising and delivering psychological therapies.* London: Author.

Department of Health (2009). *New horizons: Towards a shared vision of mental health (consultation).* London: Author.

Department of Health (2012). *Transforming care: A national response to Winterbourne View Hospital.* London: Author.

Department of Health and Social Security (1972). *Report of the Committee of Inquiry into Whittingham Hospital.* Cmnd 4861. London: HMSO.

Dickens, P. (1994). *Quality and excellence in human services.* Chichester: Wiley.

Division of Clinical Psychology (1986). *Responsibility issues in clinical psychology and multidisciplinary teamwork.* Leicester: British Psychological Society.

Division of Clinical Psychology (2012). *Introductory guide to commissioning.* Leicester: British Psychological Society.

Firth-Cozens, J. (1993). *Audit in the mental health service.* London: Psychology Press.

Francis, R. (2013). *Report of the Mid Staffordshire NHS Foundation Trust Public Inquiry. Executive summary.* London: HMSO.

Francis, R.D. (1999). *Ethics for psychologists.* Leicester: British Psychological Society.

Hall, J. (1987). Psychological work in institutions. In J. Marzillier & J. Hall (Eds.), *What is clinical psychology?* (pp.62–84). Oxford: Oxford University Press.

Hall, J. (1992). Psychological work with longer-term problems. In J. Marzillier & J. Hall (Eds.), *What is clinical psychology?* (2nd edn, pp.60–82). Oxford: Oxford University Press.

Hanna, J. (2009). *Connecting communities: A New Horizons strategy for local well-being service networks.* Leicester: British Psychological Society.

Hawks, D. (1981). The dilemma of clinical practice: Surviving as a clinical psychologist. In I. McPherson & A. Sutton (Eds.), *Reconstructing psychological practice* (pp.11–20). London: Croom Helm.

Health and Care Professions Council (2012a). *Standards of conduct, performance and ethics.* London: Author.

Health and Care Professions Council (2012b). *Standards of proficiency for practitioner psychologists.* London: Author.

Hepworth, J. (2004). Public health psychology: A conceptual practical framework. *Journal of Health Psychology, 9,* 41–54.

Holden, U.P. & Woods, R.T. (1982). *Reality orientation.* Edinburgh: Churchill Livingstone.

Huffington, C. & Brunning, H. (Eds.) (1994). *Internal consultancy in the public sector.* London: Karnac Books.

Jaques, E. (1978). *Health services: Their nature and organisation and the role of patients, doctors and the health professions.* London: Heinemann.

Jaques, E. (1989). *Requisite organisation: The CEO's guide to creative structure and leadership.* Arlington, VA: Cason Hall.

Johnson, S. (1977). *Pathways of care.* Oxford: Blackwell.

Kat, B. (1992). *On advising purchasers.* Leicester: Division of Clinical Psychology of the British Psychological Society.

Kennard, D. (1998). *An introduction to therapeutic communities.* London: Jessica Kingsley.

Koch, H. (1986). *Community clinical psychology.* Beckenham: Croom Helm.

Lavender, T. (1985). Quality of care and staff practices in long-stay settings. In F.N. Watts (Ed.), *New developments in clinical psychology* (Vol. 1, pp.70–83). Leicester: British Psychological Society.

Lueger, R.J. & Barkham, M. (2010) Using benchmarks and benchmarking to improve quality of practice and services. In M. Barkham, G.E. Hardy & J. Mellor-Clark (Eds.), *Developing and delivering practice-based evidence* (pp.223–256). Chichester: Wiley-Blackwell.

Manpower Planning Advisory Group (1990). *Report on clinical psychology.* London: Department of Health.

Management Advisory Service (1989). *Review of clinical psychology.* Cheltenham: Author.

National Institute for Health and Clinical Excellence (NICE) (2011). *Commissioning stepped care for people with common mental health disorders.* London: Author.

Nichols, K.A. (1984). *Psychological care in physical illness.* Beckenham: Croom Helm.

Onyett, S. (1992). *Case management in mental health.* London: Chapman & Hall.

Onyett, S., Standen, R. & Peck, E. (1997). The challenge of managing community mental health teams. *Health and Social Care in the Community, 5*(1), 40–47.

Orford, J. (1992). *Community psychology: Theory and practice.* Chichester: Wiley.

Ovretveit, J. (1984). *Organising psychology in the NHS.* London: Brunel Institute of Organisation and Social Studies.

Ovretveit, J. (1986). *Organisation of multidisciplinary community teams.* London: Brunel Institute of Organisation and Social Studies.

Ovretveit, J. (1992). *Health service quality.* Oxford: Blackwell Scientific.

Ovretveit, J. (1993). *Therapy services: Organisation, management and autonomy.* Reading: Harwood Academic.

Pilgrim, D. & Treacher, A. (1992). *Clinical psychology observed.* London: Routledge.

Rappaport, J. (1977). *Community psychology: Values, research and action.* New York: Holt, Rinehart & Winston.

Roth, A. & Fonagy, P. (1996). *What works for whom? A critical review of psychotherapy research.* New York: Guilford Press.

Shostack, G.L. (1984). Designing services that deliver. *Harvard Business Review, 62,* 133–139.

Smail, D. (2005). *Power, interest and psychology.* Ross-on-Wye: PCCS Books.

Spence, S. & Shepherd, G. (1983). *Developments in social skills training.* London: Academic Press.

Sperlinger, D. (2002). *Outcome assessment in routine clinical practice in psychosocial services.* Leicester: British Psychological Society.

Stickdorn, M. & Schneider, J. (2011). *This is service design thinking.* Amsterdam: BIS Publishers.

Sutton, A. & McPherson, I. (1981). Psychological practice in a social context. In I. McPherson & A. Sutton (Eds.), *Reconstructing psychological practice* (pp.165–172). London: Croom Helm.

Tuke, S. (1996). *Description of the Retreat: An institution near York for insane persons of the Society of Friends.* London: Process Press. (Original work published 1813)

Wardle, J. & Steptoe, A. (2005). Public health psychology. *The Psychologist, 18,* 672–675.

West, J. & Spinks, P. (1988). *Clinical psychology in action.* Bristol: Wright.

Whistleblowing claimant 'not acting in good faith', tribunal finds. (2014, 10 November). *Health Service Journal.*

Chapter 13 Psychologists as therapists: An overview

Glenys Parry

Introduction

This and the following two chapters focus on clinical psychologists as psychological therapists. The layperson might easily assume that this was and is the main purpose of the whole profession; on the contrary, the development of a therapeutic role was gradual, fraught with tensions and difficulties, and remains ambiguous. It has never been the only role played by clinical psychologists, nor were they ever the only practitioners of psychological therapy. When the fledgling profession began to treat patients in the NHS in the 1960s, it was treading on the toes of another, far more powerful, profession that saw psychotherapy as its prerogative – psychiatry. Within two decades, other therapy practitioners were nipping at the heels of the clinical psychology profession: mental health nurses were trained in behaviour therapy and later cognitive behaviour therapy; counselling in primary care expanded rapidly and a range of other mental health practitioners – social workers, occupational therapists and NHS psychotherapists – laid claim to psychological therapy expertise. Boundary disputes between professions were (and remain) commonplace in multidisciplinary health care, and it is important to understand the pre-existing context of psychotherapy into which psychologists as therapists were assimilated.

At every stage, the development of psychologists as therapists was part of the enormous expansion of training and major developments in clinical psychology roles more generally. Clinical psychology has grown at an extraordinary rate, from a small group of technicians or scientists supporting medical doctors, mainly within psychiatric and learning disability services, to a much larger, independent profession providing assessment and formulation, programme design, psychological therapies, rehabilitation, service evaluation, managerial services and organisational consultancy across the whole spectrum of hospital and community health and social care.

Psychologists as therapists must span two boundaries: in common with the whole profession, that between academic psychological science and the realities of psychological practice but also the boundary between clinical psychology and wider psychotherapeutic practice. This has always been an uneasy and unstable position to hold. Some personal reflection seems appropriate here to establish the perspective from which this chapter is written.

In my own career I have been involved with, and reflected upon, these issues since 1970. My first engagement with clinical psychologists as therapists was an oppositional one, as an undergraduate psychologist very active in the emergent gay movement, protesting to Reg Beech (head of clinical psychology services for South Manchester from 1973) and at BPS conferences against the use of aversion therapy to 'treat' homosexuality. I mentioned my role in the

Campaign for Homosexual Equality (CHE) on my application form when applying for clinical training. At my first interview I was simply asked whether or not I would be 'able to treat a homosexual'. The next interview by contrast asked how my experience of working in CHE could be useful in the NHS. Needless to say I accepted this offer and rejected the first.

I was completely convinced of the virtues of the scientist-practitioner as a model for good practice. I felt, and still feel, that applying psychological science and skills to health care was an honourable endeavour, but compared with medicine, there were (and are) few ready-made career paths for psychologists to pursue both research and practice. I worked on the psychosocial causes of depression and as a psychotherapy researcher at an MRC unit for six years, during which I founded Changes, *the journal of the Psychology and Psychotherapy Association, with Jenny Firth-Cozens. Not wanting to become a career academic without enough NHS engagement, in the early 1980s I became academic director of an NHS clinical psychology training course and clinical psychologist in Child and Adolescent Mental Health Services (CAMHS) and in adult psychotherapy. During this time I worked in the BPS on accreditation of clinical training courses and with the Manpower Planning Advisory Group during their review of clinical psychology. In the 1980s I was editing a psychotherapy series for Wiley and was sent a manuscript for review. It turned out to be the draft of a book by Anthony Ryle on a new development: cognitive analytic therapy. I remember taking the manuscript to bed with me, and a few hours later 'eureka!' was echoing in my mind. I'd been trained in both CBT and short-term psychodynamic therapy and valued both, but was always struggling with which to use with whom, since I distrusted mishmash eclecticism. I started practising CAT under Tony Ryle's supervision and became a founder member of ACAT and a CAT trainer and supervisor.*

In 1990 I moved into NHS management as head of a District psychology service, developing the 'trading agency' model as a way of protecting a coherent psychology service. This job included a three-year stint in the Department of Health as psychology and psychotherapy policy adviser, initiating a major strategic review of psychotherapy services. After this I took on the role of R&D Director of a mental health Trust to foster NHS-based research, continuing with clinical work and my own research, before tiring of the bureaucratic monster research governance was becoming and moving to a job in a new area: chair of psychological services research, combining methods from psychotherapy research and health services research. Throughout these years I've continued psychological therapy practice and teaching, wrestling with how best to span the boundaries of psychology as a science and psychological practice, between being a clinical psychologist and being a psychotherapist. It's been an interesting and unusual career trajectory and my experience in these roles underpins my approach to this chapter.

The early context: 1948–1969

In the early post-war years, clinical psychology had not emerged as a separate discipline or profession. Psychiatrists, psychoanalysts and doctors who had undertaken research in psychological topics had been, since 1919, eligible to be members of the BPS. Freud was honoured as a psychological scientist, being awarded honorary membership of the BPS on 13 March 1926; the certificate is still on display in his apartment in Berggasse, Vienna. Indeed it was a group of BPS psychoanalysts who provided lectures, seminars and personal analyses for the Hampstead Child Therapy Course and Clinic, which Anna Freud founded in 1947 and which opened to patients in 1952. Psychoanalysis was influential, although primarily available in London. The Tavistock Clinic, founded in 1920, became part of the new National

Health Service in 1948, providing clinical services under the administration of the North West Metropolitan Regional Hospital Board. By the 1950s the Tavistock Clinic was offering a prospectus of training courses including a two-year training in clinical psychology, whose aim, as laid out in its *Prospectus of Courses of Training 1952/1953* (copy held in the BPS archives at the Wellcome Library, catalogue reference PSY/RAV/2/8) was 'to equip psychologists to take part, as a member of a psychiatric team, in diagnosis, vocational guidance and remedial work with patients suffering from behavioural disorders in hospitals, out-patient departments or (where the psychologist is experienced in working with children) in child guidance clinics'. The approach was largely based on 'psycho-analytic principles and the field theories of Gestalt psychologists'.

At the same time, London's Maudsley Hospital medical school was renamed the Institute of Psychiatry, Hans Eysenck was in post and Monte Shapiro was heading the team of staff offering the first postgraduate training in clinical psychology. The emphasis here was in sharp contrast to psychoanalytic theory and practice – it trained people in applied abnormal psychology and the scientific method, gleaned from the laboratory rather than the consulting room. Eysenck never overcame his intense dislike of psychotherapy, which he reviled as unscientific and ineffective (Eysenck, 1952). However, this critique was as much an attack on poor research methods and data quality as on psychological treatment; he concluded that these shortcomings 'highlight the necessity of properly planned and executed experimental studies into this important field' and indeed his 1952 paper, although repeatedly rebutted (e.g. Strupp, 1963) provided a spur for advances in psychotherapy research methods in the next two decades. Monte Shapiro, unlike Eysenck, was a practising clinician who, while sharing Eysenck's distaste for obscurantist and doctrinaire psychoanalysis, had a profound influence on clinical psychology's developing paradigm of the pragmatic scientist practitioner.

In parallel with these metropolitan developments, across the rest of the country clinical psychologists were employed in the NHS, mainly to administer tests, and probationer psychologists began to receive formal training in the 1950s. Here too the competence of the psychologist was primarily in administering a wide range of tests, interpreting the results and providing a report to the consultant psychiatrist. A typical request was 'IQ please', although tests of personality, and projective tests such as the Rorschach, were also used. Projective testing, now widely seen as 'unscientific', was of great importance in this period, used by clinical psychologists even at the Institute of Psychiatry and studied assiduously in scientific journals. The therapeutic role was not yet a mainstay of professional psychology practice.

In contrast, psychoanalysis and psychiatry ruled the therapeutic roost. In the former, the British object relations school was becoming influential, moving from the work of Melanie Klein to emphasise the importance of mental representations of relationships rather than drives derived from animal instincts. Psychoanalytic training became influential within psychiatry, as psychoanalytic psychiatrists became the psychiatric establishment and medical doctors were practitioners of 'the talking cure'. By 1963, the BPS felt the need to tighten the rules on membership offered to medical practitioners, adopting a points system. The BPS agreed (BPS Council Minute 3934, January 1963) that in order to be granted graduate membership, future medical applicants would have to score three points on a scale which granted two points for membership of the Society of Analytical Psychology (Jungian) or Membership of the Institute of Psychoanalysis (Freudian). The remaining point could be obtained by an MD on a purely medical topic. The BPS *British Journal of Medical Psychology* (the precursor of *Psychology and Psychotherapy: Theory, Research & Practice*) was edited by medics and many of the contributors were psychoanalysts, including Klein, Ronald Fairbairn and Harry Guntrip. Social work too was at that time a therapeutic profession, with psychodynamic casework a main activity.

The 1960s was the decade when the therapies based on behavioural science became widely disseminated by clinical psychologists. In the 1950s Joseph Wolpe, a South African psychiatrist, laid the experimental foundations for the concept of reciprocal inhibition and the therapeutic technique of systematic desensitisation (Wolpe, 1954), developed at the Institute of Psychiatry through Jack Rachman, Vic Meyer and others. This was quite separate from the US tradition of Skinnerian behaviourism, which was resisted here, although in the 1960s there were attempts at rapprochement. The Maudsley group, despite internal tensions, crewed the flagship for developing a therapeutic mandate for clinical psychology, based on a new tradition of psychological laboratory science rather than scholarly theorising grounded in individual case reports. Although those early therapeutic adventures were undoubtedly naive, reductionist and of dubious effectiveness (Marzillier, 2010), they laid the foundations for clinical psychology's claim to specialist expertise, an essential 'rhetoric of justification' for any profession, and formed the basis for a burgeoning range of therapies in later decades.

New therapies, new roles: 1970–1990

The 1970s and 1980s were heady times for clinical psychologists practising psychological therapies. In the 1970s behavioural treatments were changing the role of clinical psychology to a therapeutic one, both in mental health and learning disabilities services. They included systematic desensitisation for phobic anxiety, aversion therapy to treat alcoholism and homosexuality (then seen as a psychiatric disorder, although this was being vigorously challenged by the emergent gay rights movement), and token economies attempting to change patients' behaviour in psychiatric wards. Behaviour modification and behaviour therapy were well established methods and the British Association for Behavioural Psychotherapy (BABP) was inaugurated in 1972, after considerable debate over whether to use the term 'psychotherapy' (Lomas, 1991).

During the 1970s clinical psychologists were being influenced by theorists such as Albert Bandura, Marvin Goldfried, Donald Meichenbaum and Walter Mischel, who were integrating cognitive and social learning theory to move beyond classical and operant conditioning models in behaviour therapy. Thus, before Beck's formulation for cognitive treatment of depression broke onto the scene in 1979, cognitive behaviour therapy was well developed. Indeed, it continued to develop in parallel with Beck's cognitive therapy, although the distinction between CBT and CT, important to some (e.g. Goldfried, 2003), has been blurred by others (e.g. Kuyken & Beck, 2007) and is too esoteric for most practitioners.

Although there are always exceptions to generalisations, clinical psychologists have generally been the ultimate pragmatists, drawing on a range of psychological theories in both research and practice, rather than doggedly adhering to a specific theoretical or therapeutic school. Thus in the 1970s and 1980s, a smorgasbord of theory was available across cognitive, behavioural, constructivist, humanistic, experiential and psychodynamic schools, all of which had influence on professional therapy practice to a greater or lesser extent. These are explored in more detail in the following two chapters, but summarised briefly here.

In addition to the developments outlined above, CBT-linked methods included Albert Ellis's rational emotive therapy, Arnold Lazarus's multimodal therapy, and Martin Seligman's work on learned helplessness and attribution theory.

Psychoanalytic therapy had not ceased to innovate during these decades, with the emergence of brief focal psychodynamic therapies in the 1970s, championed by David Malan at the Tavistock Clinic. Malan made a major contribution to counteracting the insular, obscurantist and antiscientific aspects of much of the psychoanalytic establishment, which was still hugely powerful in London-based training institutes holding sway over the psychotherapeutic training of psychiatrists. Malan was committed to the empirical investigation of psychodynamic therapy, despite having few research resources at his disposal. A different psychodynamic method was developed by Bob Hobson, a Jungian psychiatrist and psychotherapist, whose 'conversational model' was later renamed 'psychodynamic interpersonal therapy'. Other developments applied Bowlby's attachment theory to adult psychological functioning, and towards the end of the 1980s, mentalisation-based therapy emerged from the collaboration of Peter Fonagy and Anthony Bateman.

Influential humanistic and experiential approaches included client-centred (later person-centred) therapy grounded in Carl Rogers's work, Gestalt therapy (Fritz Perls), existential therapy (Irvin Yalom), psychodrama (Jacob Moreno) and transactional analysis (Eric Berne). Humanistic methods were used in individual therapy but also in groups, such as 'encounter groups' and throughout the 1970s were widely offered in an unregulated, quasi-professional environment.

A separate stream of cognitive clinical theory and therapy was widely but separately influential among clinical psychologists, linked to constructivism, an epistemological stance that humans cannot directly experience reality but construct their experiential world. It also emphasises human intention (teleology) as well as meaning-making. The first such approach was from George Kelly, who introduced personal construct theory in 1955. UK clinical psychologists Don Bannister, Fay Fransella and Miller Mair championed his approach, developing repertory grid techniques as an ideographic form of therapy-linked assessment. Cognitive constructivism did not begin and end with Kelly, however, with Michael Mahoney making important contributions in these decades.

Kelly's personal construct theory influenced Anthony Ryle in developing cognitive analytic therapy (CAT), which sought to reframe some key concepts in object relations theory within a cognitive model. Ryle was trained in the psychoanalytic tradition but had been influenced by George Kelly and by the classic 1960 cognitive psychology text *Plans and the Structure of Behavior* by Miller et al. (1960). Ryle was an integrationist seeking to create a pragmatic, structured, effective, researchable, time-limited therapy for the UK NHS. CAT offered an alternative to 'mishmash' eclecticism – eclectic use of methods within a clear theoretical framework. Possibly because of this integration and because of his emphasis on a psychological formulation shared with the patient, while CAT is practised across all mental health professions, his work proved particularly attractive to clinical psychologists.

A self-professed 'eclectic' therapy developed in these decades, although more widely practised in the UK only later, is Gerald Klerman and Myrna Weissman's interpersonal therapy. The provenance of this method is unusual in that it was developed explicitly by researchers as a comparison treatment in a randomised controlled trial of medication, and for many years was only practised by research therapists until adopted by some clinical psychologists in routine practice. Usually it is the other way round.

As well as the dazzling array of therapeutic methods which clinical psychologists attempted to incorporate into their therapeutic practice, there were huge developments afoot within psychological therapies more generally, both within and outside the BPS. While clinical psychologists began to occupy new ecological niches within the healthcare system, as consultants, programme designers, managers, clinical health psychologists and neuropsychologists, other groups staked their claims to psychological therapy expertise. These decades were characterised by a struggle to define the unique role of clinical psychologists compared with other psychological therapy practitioners and other psychologists. Justification of the privileges of a professional role (and any legitimacy for policing entry into it), rests on the unique contribution made by that profession. Psychological therapists competing with clinical psychologists for NHS territory included psychiatrists practising as psychotherapists, nurse behaviour therapists, primary care counsellors, and lay-trained adult and child psychotherapists. Leaving aside whether such threats were real or whether the defensive responses served their protectionist purpose, we see considerable time and effort going into defining and defending the therapeutic role of clinical psychologists.

The pioneer for training psychiatric nurses in behaviour therapy was Isaac Marks, South African by birth and a Maudsley-trained psychiatrist, who in the 1970s saw the need for a much larger workforce of behaviour therapists. He argued that training nurse therapists would take less time and money than training psychologists and psychiatrists and that the pool of suitable trainees was much larger. This development was perceived as a threat by many within clinical psychology who opposed the idea, attempting to protect its recent status as a therapeutic profession by laying claim to behaviour therapy and later cognitive behaviour therapy, as methods grounded in psychological theory and formulation and so distinctly the province of clinical psychology. This defensive protectionism was a doomed enterprise.

Counselling developed from the Marriage Guidance Council (later renamed Relate) and student counselling. The first university service began in 1963 in Keele and the Association of Student Counsellors in 1970. In the same year, the Standing Conference for the Advancement of Counselling was inaugurated at the instigation of the National Council for Voluntary Organisations. From this the British Association for Counselling emerged in 1977 as an organisation open to individual membership, providing a framework for the professionalisation of counselling, both in terms of promoting its role and regulating its standards. In 1979, as a result of pressure from graduate psychologists practising as counsellors, the BPS Professional Affairs Board set up a working party to consider the relationship between psychology and counselling. It recognised counselling as a legitimate activity for psychologists as it was based in the understanding of psychological processes, and recommended that the BPS establish a Section of Counselling Psychology as a focus for scientific interest. This was created in 1982, although full professional recognition within the BPS was not attained until the next decade.

The practice of psychotherapy had not been regulated, either by a professional body or by statutory registration. Government concern over Ron Hubbard's Church of Scientology in the 1960s led to Sir John Foster's report in 1971. He recommended statutory registration of psychotherapists, but not psychologists.

> I have become convinced that it is high time that the practice of psychotherapy for reward should be restricted to members of a profession properly qualified in its techniques. ... The dangers inherent in an incompetent assessment of someone's intellectual capabilities or his fitness for a particular employment, albeit regrettable, do not appear to me to be of a comparable order with those resulting from an abuse, or an incompetent use, of a system of therapy which operates by a deliberate intervention in the patterns of people's irrational emotions. (Foster, 1971)

A Joint Professions Working Party on the Statutory Registration of Psychotherapists was set up with BPS representation, and reported in 1978 (Sieghart, 1978) but although members of this working party met DHSS officials in 1981 to lobby for statutory regulation, they were sent away until psychotherapists could 'speak with one voice'.

There followed strenuous efforts to find a way for psychologists, psychiatrists, counsellors and 'lay' psychotherapists to agree a structure for the regulation of psychotherapy. From 1982 a standing conference of psychotherapy organisations was held in Rugby, courtesy of the British Association for Counselling. In 1989 this became the UK Standing Conference for Psychotherapy and in 1992 the UK Council for Psychotherapy (UKCP).

As well as these multidisciplinary developments, the role of psychotherapists within the BPS and the DCP was under continuous review. In 1973, the BPS set up a working party on psychotherapy to consider the professional interests of psychotherapists within the Society and ways in which the development of psychotherapy could be fostered within the Society. Despite the concept of 'behavioural psychotherapy' adopted by BABP – renamed British Association for Cognitive and Behavioural Psychotherapy (BABCP) in 1992 – at that time most people (including said working party) spoke of 'psychotherapy' in contradistinction to 'behaviour therapy', seeing the former as exploratory, emotionally expressive, influenced by psychodynamic theory, and the latter as prescriptive, task-oriented and grounded in experimental science. The use of psychotherapy in the more generic sense of any psychological therapy was only just beginning to emerge by the end of the 1980s.

As part of the long journey towards establishing the BPS Register of Chartered Psychologists the question of the psychotherapeutic role of psychologists was again discussed. A 'Charter Guide' published by the BPS in April 1988 considered the distinction between psychologists and psychotherapists, noting that many non-psychologists practise 'psychotherapy or counselling' but distinguishing this from competence in the psychology of psychotherapy or counselling. However, the document does not attempt to specify what characterises a distinctly psychological approach to counselling or psychotherapy, suggesting that further discussion would be needed to establish criteria. It refers to the BPS Professional Affairs Board criteria for postqualification courses, which include a critical evaluation of comparative effectiveness of psychological therapies based on research, experience and supervision accompanied by a programme of relevant postqualification academic teaching, and a formal method of assessing competence.

Hence a new idea emerged, of psychotherapy as a subspecialty within clinical psychology, rather than a role that all clinical psychologists were qualified to undertake. Unsurprisingly, this evoked some intraprofessional rivalry over who could claim such specialist expertise. This whole development was influenced by the aspirations of 'lay' psychotherapists to establish a recognised profession with registers of accredited practitioners. In particular some clinical psychologists were anxious that the emergence of a separate 'adult psychotherapy' profession (which was looking very likely in the 1980s) would be under the influence and training of psychiatrists, and that clinical psychology would lose out. In 1990, under the leadership of Adele Kosviner, the BPS published a policy paper *Psychological Therapy Services: The Need for Organisational Change* (BPS, 1990). A companion paper (Part 2) from the DCP (BPS DCP, 1990) outlined recent developments and recommendations for training and career structure in clinical psychology. These argued the case for the unique contribution of clinical psychologists to psychotherapy services and stated that clinical psychology should not remain passive in the face of the many developments towards establishing an independent profession of psychotherapy, but should provide scope for a specialist practitioner role within clinical psychology. They challenged the notion that medical psychotherapists should be the leaders in this psychological field, asserting the need for psychologists with specialist expertise in psychotherapy to have leadership roles. They recommended that basic clinical training and postqualification training should be improved to maintain standards of expertise within the profession. They saw a danger that the delivery and development of formal psychological therapies would leave the profession.

From this, there was a new attempt to establish a subregister of psychologists qualified as psychotherapists within the BPS. Again, although much work was undertaken to define appropriate training requirements and to formalise recognised qualifications, the attempt was ultimately unsuccessful.

From margins to mainstream: Since 1990

For a while, some people's dream (other people's nightmare) of a unified psychotherapy profession seemed within grasp; in 1993 the Department of Health was minded to support the launch of the UKCP voluntary register as a way of introducing some safeguards against unethical and exploitative practice. However, such unity was short-lived. Even before the UKCP register was established, the psychoanalytic establishment felt ill-served by its structures. It was outvoted in a proposal to form a separate section of psychoanalytic psychotherapy to distinguish the long-established psychoanalytic institutes from the more recent grouping of organisations practising variants of psychodynamic therapy (Balfour & Richards, 1995).

Box 13.1 Psychotherapy within the BPS

1919 BPS Medical Section established by doctors with interests in psychodynamic theory and psychotherapy, who had been involved with treating 'war neurosis'.

1921 *British Journal of Medical Psychology*, journal of BPS Medical Section, launched.

1952 Eysenck writes to the BPS *Quarterly Bulletin* complaining that the editorial policy of the *British Journal of Medical Psychology* favoured ideographic psychoanalytic papers at the expense of scientific abnormal psychology. This triggered a six-year struggle within BPS between the Council and the Medical Section on the appropriate basis for psychotherapeutic psychology.

1958 BPS Council asks the Medical Section to formulate a broader definition of its purpose, beyond psychodynamic theory and therapy.

1963 More stringent criteria established for medical doctors to become BPS members.

1970 BPS Council declines to support the Royal Medico-Psychological Association (precursor of the Royal College of Psychiatrists) in a proposal for the statutory regulation of non-medically qualified psychotherapists and hypnotherapists by extending the Professionals Supplementary to Medicine Act, 1960, and instead proposes a joint working party to consider the issue.

1971 Sir John Foster published his report on 'The Practice and Effects of Scientology', recommending statutory registration of psychotherapists. Fifty-three BPS Fellows and Associates propose setting up a BPS Division of Therapeutic Psychology. BPS Council rejected this proposal as unacceptable and instead agreed to set up a working party on psychotherapy to consider the issues.

1973 BPS Working Party on Psychotherapy convened to consider the professional interests of psychotherapists within the Society and ways in which the development of psychotherapy can be fostered within the Society.

1974 BPS declined to support the British Psychoanalytical Society in its proposal to government seeking statutory regulation of the practice of psychotherapy for gain.

1975 BPS Working Party on Psychotherapy reports, recommending a standing committee on psychotherapy.

1981 Joint Working Party on the Statutory Registration of Psychotherapists met Department of Health officials to lobby for statutory regulation, and were sent away until psychotherapists could 'speak with one voice'.

1982 BPS is represented at the Rugby Conference of psychotherapy organisations.

1983 DCP Psychological Therapies Special Interest Group established.

1988 BPS documentation on registration of psychologists recognised the distinction between non-psychologists practising 'psychotherapy or counselling' and competence in the 'psychology of psychotherapy or counselling'.

1990 BPS policy statement on the need for organisational change in NHS psychotherapy services. DCP recommendations published for psychotherapy training and career development within clinical psychology.

Within a year of the UKCP register launch, they established a separate register under the British Confederation of Psychotherapists (now the British Psychoanalytic Council). In 2006, the cognitive behavioural therapists withdrew from the UKCP register. BABCP, their regulatory body, remained as an institutional member until 2009 when it finally severed all links.

A further attempt to regulate a unitary profession of psychotherapy was made in 2010 with a proposal to place psychotherapists under the Health Professions Council (now the Health and Care Professions Council, HCPC), the body that regulates practitioner psychologists. Six psychoanalytic psychotherapy organisations mounted a legal challenge during which the Department of Health remained neutral, but the matter was resolved when the proposal for statutory regulation was dropped and instead the Professional Standards Authority took on the role of accrediting various voluntary registers as a form of 'light touch' regulation.

Officials in the Department of Health were always well aware that there are two aspects to professional regulation. While those arguing for such registers always emphasise the protection of the public against harm from unregulated practice, official recognition through an accredited register is also a vehicle for professional aspiration. It enables the aspirants to join the club of what Bernard Shaw called 'conspiracies against the laity'; professional status brings undoubted rewards. A good example of this, when I was policy adviser in the Department of Health, was a brief flurry of interest in establishing a register of stage hypnotists, when there was a press scare that members of the public were being harmed by participation in their shows. The evidence for harm was so sparse and the dangers of according official recognition of the performers as professional practitioners so real, that the proposal was dropped.

This is not to say that psychological therapies are harmless. Medicine has long recognised that most effective treatments carry a degree of toxicity and the problem of adverse effects of therapy has been noted in the research literature for decades (Barlow, 2010; Bergin, 1963). However, it is only as psychotherapy becomes part of mainstream provision that the fact that it is potentially harmful attracts serious attention among practitioners.

What the history of these four decades (1960–1990) shows is that the practice of psychological therapy is so diverse, so riven with factional strife, that all attempts to force it into a unitary professional framework have failed. Whether this gallimaufry of psychotherapeutic practice can ever become a coherent profession remains an open question. The position of clinical psychologists in relation to these developments has been both ambiguous and ambivalent.

Counselling psychologists finally achieved divisional status within the BPS in 1994 after fierce resistance and delaying tactics from other Divisions, sceptical of the justification or need for a new professional group of psychologists and, naturally, perceiving the development as a threat to their own professional status. Despite this, from 1994 graduates of the Diploma in Counselling Psychology, or those with the Statement of Equivalence to the Diploma, were able to use the professional title 'chartered counselling psychologist'. It can be argued that the key distinction between clinical and counselling psychology is its grounding in the psychology of well-being rather than of illness or disorder. Other claimed distinctions, such as its grounding in humanistic values and human rights, rejection of positivist science as the only valid route to knowledge, the study of subjectivity, and eschewing the role of the 'expert' (Orlans & Van Scoyoc, 2009) are perhaps of more rhetorical than factual value, since these beliefs are shared by many clinical psychologists.

Official recognition of psychological therapies, or 'talking treatments', came in the 1990s, with the Department of Health 1996 review of psychotherapy services in England (see Box 13.2). This laid the groundwork for work on psychological therapy guidelines (Department of Health, 2001) and directly influenced the routine inclusion of psychological therapies alongside medical interventions in NICE guidance for specific conditions. Following this, psychological treatments were included in the National Service Framework for Mental Health Services in 1999 and the 2002 mental health service mapping exercise included psychological therapies services. In 2004, a five-year review of the National Service Framework for Mental Health reinforced the importance of psychological therapies after a consultation revealed that psychological therapies were a high priority for service users and their poor availability a major source of dissatisfaction.

These developments set the stage for the next step change in the policy profile of psychological therapies. Richard Layard, a Labour life peer and founder-director of the Centre for Economic Performance at the London School of Economics, had been publishing on the economics of happiness and argued for the importance of mental health in labour economics. His alliance with David Clark, a distinguished academic clinical psychologist, produced a powerful lever for promoting a new development, the Improving Access to Psychological Therapies (IAPT) programme (Centre for Economic Performance, 2006; Layard & Clark, 2014). This was launched in two demonstration sites in 2006 and was quickly rolled out. It built on the earlier initiative of primary care graduate mental health workers, in training a new workforce, termed 'psychological well-being practitioners' providing high-volume, low-intensity guided self-help and simple CBT-based interventions, combined with newly trained cognitive behavioural therapists offering CBT proper. Clinical psychology as a profession was immensely supportive of the IAPT initiative and worked in collaboration with the programme at every stage, despite the misgivings of many psychologists that the new arrangements would undermine their role as therapists by offering a less expensive alternative.

As part of the continued growth in provision of psychological therapies since 1990, clinical psychologists have often been innovators in new applications of therapy and influential in teaching and supervising others in these methods. For example, over the last two decades psychologists' therapeutic role extended beyond anxiety and depression to work in psychosis and personality disorder, through CBT for psychosis, dialectical behaviour therapy, cognitive analytic therapy, mentalisation-based therapy and 'third wave' cognitive therapies, such as compassion-focused therapy, and mindfulness-based cognitive therapy. Clinical psychologists have also been influential in NICE expert reference groups for psychological therapies and, most recently, the development of competence frameworks for NHS staff working with different client groups.

Conclusion

In trying to overview nine decades of development of clinical psychologists as therapists, this chapter inevitably misses many details. I have tried to sketch the bigger

Box 13.2 National strategic review of psychological therapies 1996

As a personal reflection, in 1992 I was seconded to work in the Department of Health mental health policy branch, as a Senior Medical Officer, a senior civil service grade at that time. I followed in the footsteps of Ed Miller, who in 1990 had been the first clinical psychologist in this role, having earlier been the consultant adviser to the Chief Medical Officer. I was responsible for policy advice on both psychology and psychotherapy, including medical psychotherapy. Within a short time of taking up my post I was invited to represent the Department at a conference in Washington, organised by the US National Institute of Mental Health, which had been asked to feed into Hillary Clinton's ill-fated review of the US healthcare system. I was asked to present the UK position on the provision of psychological therapies in health care. Having only just arrived, I asked my Department colleagues for a quick briefing on policy for NHS provision of psychotherapy. I was nonplussed to be told that there was no policy.

This demonstrated the need for a consistent and formal policy position to give psychological therapies some legitimacy as evidence-based treatments which should be provided as part of mental health care. I commissioned Tony Roth and Peter Fonagy to review the evidence on psychological therapy effectiveness (later published as Roth & Fonagy, 1996), convened an expert advisory group and undertook a survey of psychological therapy provision in NHS Trusts in England. The results showed a patchy, fragmented, disorganised, poorly resourced and confusing service, neither evidence-based nor responsive to need (Department of Health, 1996).

One clear finding was that the word 'psychotherapy' was being used in many different ways and there was no consensus on it. It was recognised that many mental health professionals were using psychological methods as part of their roles, but not as a stand-alone treatment and often with minimal training or supervision. Most psychological therapy delivered by clinical psychologists was pragmatic and eclectic, based on sound psychological principles but drawing on a range of methods. Specialist practitioners in clinical psychology and from different core professions offered formal psychotherapy within specific therapy schools. This third group would characterise themselves as 'psychotherapists'. The review distinguished between these three types of work, seeing a need for each. It also balanced evidence-based practice (offering therapies shown to be effective) with practice-based evidence (monitoring outcomes routinely). It was the first time clinical psychologists' role as psychological therapists was unequivocally supported by an NHS policy.

picture of the profession's struggle for recognition and its repeated attempts to define a unique role for psychologists in psychological therapies. The success of the profession in establishing the value and effectiveness of psychological treatments as part of a publicly funded NHS is outstanding, but to quote Teresa of Avila, there are more tears shed over answered prayers than over unanswered prayers. The inevitable consequence of recognising the need for greater access to psychological therapies is the need to deliver them on an industrial scale. The requirement to contain costs demands reduced skill mix, with stepped care, managed care and low-intensity interventions within the IAPT initiative. Just as in the industrial revolution, the therapist becomes a technician within the prespecified machinery of delivery rather than a cottage industry of artisan practitioners, customising interventions for each individual. Some in the profession see this as a threat, but clinical psychology has always succeeded in adapting to new contexts, evolving to respond to the needs of the healthcare system through innovation and reinvention. My own view is that it will continue to do so.

References

Balfour, F. & Richards, J. (1995). History of the British Confederation of Psychotherapists. *British Journal of Psychotherapy, 11*, 422–426.

Barlow, D.H. (2010). Negative effects from psychological treatments: A perspective. *American Psychologist, 65*(1), 13–20.

Bergin, A.E. (1963). The effects of psychotherapy: Negative results revisited. *Journal of Counseling Psychology, 10*(3), 244–250.

British Psychological Society (1990). *Policy statement: Psychological therapy services: The need for organisational change.* Leicester: Author.

British Psychological Society Division of Clinical Psychology (1990). *Psychological therapy services: The need for organisational change, Part 2: Recent developments and recommendations for training and career structures in clinical psychology.* Leicester: BPS.

Centre for Economic Performance (2006). *The depression report. A new deal for depression and anxiety disorders.* London: Author.

Department of Health (1996). *NHS psychotherapy services in England: Review of strategic policy.* London: Author.

Department of Health (2001). *Treatment choice in psychological therapies and counselling: Evidence-based clinical practice guideline.* London: Author.

Eysenck, H.J. (1952). The effects of psychotherapy: An evaluation. *Journal of Consulting Psychology, 16*(5), 319–324.

Foster, J. (1971). *Enquiry into the practice and effects of Scientology.* London: HMSO.

Goldfried, M.R. (2003). Cognitive-behavior therapy: Reflections on the evolution of a therapeutic orientation. *Cognitive Therapy and Research, 27*, 53–69.

Kuyken, W. & Beck, A.T. (2007). Cognitive therapy. In C. Freeman & M. Power (Eds.), *Handbook of evidence-based psychotherapies: A guide for research and practice* (pp.15–39). Chichester: Wiley Blackwell.

Layard, R. & Clark, D. (2014). *Thrive: The power of evidence-based psychological therapies.* London: Allen Lane.

Lomas, H. (1991). The development of the BABP. *Behavioural Psychotherapy, 19*(2), 211–215.

Marzillier, J. (2010). *The gossamer thread: My life as a psychotherapist.* London: Karnac Books.

Miller, G. A., Galanter, E. & Pribram, K.H. (1960). *Plans and the structure of behavior.* New York: Holt, Rinehart and Winston.

Orlans, V. & Van Scoyoc, S. (2009). *The social and historical context of counselling psychology. A short introduction to counselling psychology.* London: Sage.

Roth, A.D. & Fonagy, P. (1996). *What works for whom? A critical review of psychotherapy research.* New York: Guilford Press.

Sieghart, P. (1978). *Statutory registration of psychotherapists: The report of a professions joint working party.* London: HMSO.

Strupp, H.H. (1963). Psychotherapy revisited: The problem of outcome. *Psychotherapy: Theory, Research & Practice, 1*, 1–13.

Wolpe, J. (1954). Reciprocal inhibition as the main basis of psychotherapeutic effects. *Archives of Neurology and Psychiatry, 72*(2), 205–226.

Chapter 14 Psychologists as therapists: The development of behavioural traditions in clinical psychology

Sarah Marks

In terms of endurance, institutional funding and support, behavioural approaches have perhaps been the most dominant and successful of the traditions in British clinical psychology, all the more so since the development of cognitive behavioural therapies. This chapter will trace the origins of behavioural approaches in the British context beginning in the 1950s, the key role of clinical psychologists in their development, and the subsequent integration of behavioural modification with cognitive therapy traditions from the 1960s, leading up to the present context of Improving Access to Psychological Therapies.

The key centre for the development of behaviour therapy was a group of clinical psychologists and psychiatrists at the Institute of Psychiatry and the Maudsley Hospital in London, providing the foundations for an evidence-based therapeutic movement that underpinned the later development of cognitive-behavioural therapies. The institutional setting of the newly amalgamated Bethlem and Maudsley Hospitals, forming a home for the University of London Institute of Psychiatry, headed by Sir Aubrey Lewis, provided a professional and experimental space for the development of psychotherapeutics in post-war Britain. The imperative for critical experimentalism in research, along with a broad education in the philosophy of science, laid the foundations for a move away from traditional psychoanalytic approaches in Britain. This emergence of behavioural therapy as an experimental science at the Maudsley has been credited as one of the single most important developments in the international psychology community for facilitating the development of behaviour therapy as a distinct movement (Krasner, 1971). But how did this space emerge?

The creation of state-funded hospital psychiatry resulted in a widening of hospital services for individuals suffering from distress categorised under the label of 'neuroses', who would previously been treated by their family doctor and would not have been referred for secondary or tertiary care (Busfield, 1998). The need for a training centre for the newly nationalised profession soon became apparent, which is how the Institute of Psychiatry originally came into being, with research being essentially secondary to its role as a teaching hospital (Waddington, 1998). Keir Waddington asserts that a significant outcome of the organisation structure of the Institute, split as it was over the Maudsley and Bethlem Royal Hospitals, was the ability to nurture a truly multidisciplinary approach to the treatment of mental distress, allowing the resources and scope for research across the full breadth of interventional techniques (Waddington, 1998). Thus both a department of psychiatry and a separate department of clinical psychology were established.

The institutional state of mental health services in the immediate post-war period was unfavourable to the recently professionalised clinical psychologist (Hall, 2007), who was viewed primarily as a diagnostic assistant to the psychiatrist, operating within a traditional framework which regarded behavioural disorders within a medicalised disease model (Fishman & Franks, 1992). Cyril Franks, a psychologist who trained at the Institute of Psychiatry, has argued retrospectively that the dissatisfactory status of the psychological profession was one of the catalysts for the shift towards a new theoretical basis for psychotherapeutics (Fishman & Franks, 1992).

The name that is perhaps most commonly associated with the early years of the development of behaviour therapy is Hans Eysenck, the German émigré clinical psychologist at the Maudsley who was the founding editor of the journal *Behaviour Research and Therapy*. His interest in behaviourist, and particularly Pavlovian, approaches, was initially triggered by his growing opposition towards psychoanalytic psychotherapy, as detailed by Glenys Parry and David Pilgrim in chapter 15. A landmark publication was Eysenck's 1952 paper 'The Effects of Psychotherapy: An Evaluation', published in the *Journal of Consulting Psychology*. Looking to dispute this 'social need', Eysenck sought to question the efficacy of the psychoanalytic approach through an examination of data from various other studies, concluding that the evidence did not support the efficacy of therapy, to the extent that there actually appeared to be 'an inverse correlation between recovery and psychotherapy; the more psychotherapy, the smaller the recovery rate' (Eysenck, 1952, p.322). With this interest in the scientific evidence for recovery and improvement of symptoms, a number of practitioners at the Maudsley looked towards Pavlov and methodological behaviourism, with a Pavlov reading group coming into existence at the hospital in the late 1950s (R. Rawles, in interview with author, 8 December 2014). One advantage of behaviourism was its materialistic, anti-dualistic approach; another was the possibility of testing the conditioning techniques in experimental settings. Explicitly breaking with psychoanalysis, the emphasis shifted from treatment of the mind to treatment of the nervous system (Wolpe, 1963). For Eysenck: 'there is no neurosis underlying the symptom but merely the symptom itself. Get rid of the symptom and you have eliminated the neurosis' (Eysenck, 1960, p.3). To quote Jan Ehrenwald's summary:

> Behaviour modification as a therapeutic tool is an offspring of a philosophy and a technique. The philosophy is frankly materialistic, positivistic, causal-reductive, and is based on Pavlovian, Watsonian, and Skinnerian principles of conditioned reflexes, operant reinforcement, and learning theory... Behaviour is determined by genetic and environmental factors such as operant reinforcements, aversive or punitive interventions, and their consequences. The self – or the sense of self – is merely a product of our sociocultural environment generating self-knowledge and self-control. Freedom and dignity are illusions and autonomous man is a mythical animal. (Ehrenwald, 1991, p.445)

Although, as Stanley Rachman argues, Eysenck was crucial for the institutional development, promotion and popularisation of behaviour therapies, his personal profile has somewhat overshadowed other key figures in the historical literature.

Eysenck had eschewed treatments by psychologists in favour of research, especially within personality. Monte Shapiro, on the other hand, was influenced by theories of learning (i.e. both Pavlovian and Hullian) and keen to apply them to understanding the patient's experiences, and by doing so hoped to intervene with an appropriate psychologically based treatment. Together with A.T. Ravenette and H. Gwynne Jones, he began to publish a series of papers demonstrating the promise of behaviour therapy within the single case (Gwynne Jones, 1956; Shapiro & Ravenette, 1959). The first paper to be published in the tradition was Gwynne Jones's 1956 article 'The Application of Conditioning and Learning Techniques to the Treatment of a Psychiatric Patient'. The patient in question, a dancer, was treated for an emotional disorder that had resulted in anxiety and a disabling increased need for urination during work and when in public places. The treatment involved gradual exposure and 'graded re-education' to reduce symptoms and reduce the anxiety response in everyday situations (Gwynne Jones, 1956). Shapiro saw this work as providing scientific evidence of the effectiveness of behaviour therapy; this was in marked contrast to Joseph Wolpe's claims for desensitisation, which Shapiro considered unsubstantiated (Shapiro, 1964), much to Eysenck's annoyance.

Rachman himself, a doctoral student of Eysenck's, contributed substantially to techniques in the treatment of anxiety, phobias and obsessive compulsive disorder (OCD), and is one of the few psychologists thus far to have written historically on the development of behavioural techniques (Rachman, 2015). While experimentation was being carried out in the psychology department of the Institute of Psychiatry, Aubrey Lewis was simultaneously encouraging members of the department of psychiatry to clinically evaluate the efficacy of the methods being carried out by the psychologists (Gelder, 1968). This analysis began with J.E. Cooper's small-scale control study of deconditioning treatments published in *The Lancet* (Cooper, 1963), and was soon followed by an extended collaborative study by Cooper with Isaac Marks and Michael Gelder (Cooper et al., 1965). This paper suggested that patients suffering from phobias responded more rapidly to desensitisation techniques than patients suffering from other neurotic disorders, and that desensitisation, along with psychotherapy, could offer a significant improvement in patients' symptoms across the anxiety disorders (Gelder et al., 1967).

As Maudsley behaviourists began to move to other institutions, behaviour modification began to be employed at other hospitals across the country. One of the first to transfer was Victor Meyer, who began developing therapeutic interventions for OCD at the Middlesex Hospital, where he founded a Behavioural Psychotherapy Unit in 1962 (Bruch, 2002). Meyer developed exposure-and-response-prevention therapy for patients suffering from OCD by exposing them to the stimuli which provoked their anxieties and preventing them from performing their anxiety-reducing rituals. For example, one of Meyer's first patients to undergo this treatment had a severe fear of dirt: she was gradually exposed to dirty objects while being denied access to water and cleaning agents over a period of eight weeks, and her anxiety and compulsive cleaning behaviour began to wane (Meyer, 1966). Stanley Rachman cites this research as a key turning point for psychotherapeutic practice:

> What he did was very brave. Dr. Meyer applied to humans what studies had shown applied to frightened animals: if they were exposed to what scared them for a

> prolonged period of time and prevented from leaving the situation, they became less scared. Therapists were scared to do it with patients...he had broken the ice. (Rachman, 2005)

Given the budget constraints of the post-war nationalised health care service, investment into the rates of efficacy of treatments in psychology and psychiatry can be seen in part as a rational consequence of the economics of health care. As a result of this shared interest in the evidence base of psychotherapeutic treatments, clinical psychologists working on behaviour therapies were able to make a strong case for the use of their approaches over others in the NHS, even at such an early stage in the service's development.

The first textbook for training in behaviour therapy in Britain was authored by Eysenck and Rachman in 1965, *The Causes and Cures of Neurosis.* Victor Meyer and Edward Chesser established a formal training course in behaviour therapy at the Middlesex Hospital in the 1970s, which later became a higher degree diploma course in 1979 (Bruch, 2002). Meyer and Chesser also produced one of the key textbooks in the field, *Behaviour Therapy in Clinical Psychiatry* (Meyer & Chesser, 1970).

With the quantity of publications in the field rising, and the number of qualified practitioners in both psychiatry and clinical psychology increasing by the early 1970s, a professional association was founded in 1972 in the form of the then British Association for Behavioural Therapy (BABP), after a meeting of various interested delegates at the Middlesex Hospital in London (Lomas, 2008). The following year the association founded its own journal, initially the *BABP Bulletin,* later to become the journal *Behavioural Psychotherapy.* Four years later, the European Association for Behaviour Therapy was officially founded, but there had already been an informal association between the BABP with its analogues in the Netherlands and Germany for several years (see http://eabct.eu/about-eabct).

While early research at the Maudsley and Middlesex hospitals concentrated on treatment of neurotic disorders, in the 1970s behavioural approaches began to be used with patients with schizophrenia. A pioneer of this was H. Gwynne Jones, who took up a professorship at the University of Leeds in 1969. A key area of research conducted at his initiative at Leeds related to the treatment of institutionalised patients with chronic schizophrenia, carried out by Roger Baker, John Hall and Keith Hutchinson using a token economy system. A group of seven patients were moved to a smaller, improved ward, then gradually given daily activities, followed by free (non-contingent) tokens, then a contingent token system based on reinforcement of appropriate behaviours. Although the reinforcement phase was not associated with significant improvement in itself, patients did show improvement overall in terms of initiative, dressing, and symptoms such as withdrawal and thought disorder (Baker et al., 1974), and a later better controlled study confirmed the improvement produced by the token regime.

Reflecting back on the process, John Hall states that at the time, although the process was clearly therapeutic, they would not necessarily have described it as therapy in itself, but rather as rehabilitation (John Hall, in an interview with the author, 11 November 2014). This rehabilitative treatment of chronic psychiatric patients is a reminder that psychological interventions should not be overlooked as an enabling factor in the history of deinstitutionalisation, which has often been narrated instead as a consequence of the introduction of antipsychotic pharmaceuticals (Tansey, 1998).

While behaviour therapy and modification are recognised as having had significant therapeutic successes, there have been other aspects of their use which have gained significant criticism. One of the more controversial has been the use of aversion therapies for the purposes of the 'social normalisation' of 'undesirable behaviours' such as transvestism and homosexuality in the 1960s and 1970s. Methods included the use of the emetic apomorphine, or mild electric shocks applied to the arm, administered at the same time as the patient was shown an image of themselves in women's clothing (Gelder, 1968). Simon LeVay has also documented the work of clinical psychologist Philip Feldman and his collaboration with psychiatrist Malcolm MacCulloch and their use of aversion therapy in the 'treatment' of homosexuality, a project which became surrounded in controversy both in terms of ethics and the quality of the research itself (LeVay, 1996).

Behavioural approaches have also been adopted across a number of other spheres outside of the health services, including criminal justice, education and social work. The latter in particular has not been without controversy, after the 'pindown' scandal in the 1980s in which children in residential care in Staffordshire were physically restrained for long periods of time, with the perpetrators justifying their actions as a form of behaviour training (Levy & Kahan, 1991). This example is one used in the training of contemporary practitioners to reflect upon the ethical aspects of cognitive and behavioural interventions in their work, encouraging students to examine the boundaries between intervention and coercion with vulnerable service users, particularly in relation to 'punishment' and 'reward' techniques (Wilson et al., 2008, p.358).

From behaviour modification to CBT

CBT as it is practised now in Britain is by no means an unmediated product of the behaviour therapies developed at the Maudsley in the 1950s and 1960s. The 1960s saw the development of new 'cognitive therapy' approaches in the US, which a number of British clinical psychologists took an interest in, seeking to gain copies of key papers and books to inform their practice in the UK (W. Dryden, personal communication, 24 September 2010).

The invention of the cognitive therapies is attributed to two psychotherapists: Albert Ellis and psychiatrist Aaron Beck. Ellis's first work on rational emotive behaviour therapy dates to 1955, when he first began to practise it after conducting a systematic review of available forms of psychotherapy (Ellis, 2007). For Ellis, the personal story of the patient was crucial to understanding the formation of the neurosis; in direct contrast to Eysenck's dismissal of the personal lives of patients having any significance to their treatment (Ramon, 1985, p.198). The psychoanalytic notion of suppression was also seen as flawed: instead of the effects of childhood being manifested through unconscious processes, rational-emotive therapy identified a conscious, active 'self-indoctrination' process, in which the patient reiterates pathogenic thoughts and inner monologues born out of childhood experiences (Ellis, 1962). Aaron Beck's most widely read book, *Cognitive Therapy and the Emotional Disorders*, was first published in 1976 and provides a step-by-step targeted approach to the specific problem areas associated with depression. These techniques primarily involve deconstructing and challenging the client's 'maladaptive' beliefs (Beck, 1991). The therapist's primary role, then, is to explore how the client's belief system came to be so, and gradually pull these beliefs apart, providing alternative, more positive ways of thinking, which are then reinforced through 'cognitive rehearsal'. This latter technique – the role-playing of difficult situations and preparing a positive reaction, then rewarding oneself for accomplishing the positive reaction when the situation actually arises – does have similarities with behavioural conditioning, but the explicit exploration of the origins of the emotional disorders as a fundamental part of the therapeutic process itself is at odds with the approaches of more traditional behaviour therapies.

At first glance, it appears difficult to see how the behavioural and cognitive worldviews could be compatible – the former, after all, frequently rejects the relevance of the latter in the aetiology of psychopathology. As G. Terence Wilson states, in traditional behaviour therapy

> cognitive approaches are rejected as improper targets of experimental study or relegated to the status of epiphenomenal events that are merely the by-products of physical actions in the body and/or the external environment; they exert no causal effect on a person's behaviour or subjective state. (Wilson, 1978, p.8)

Further incompatibilities are apparent in the interest of cognitive psychologists in how experience becomes organised and structured by the mind, whereas traditional behavioural psychologists rejected the possibility of the mind possessing innate organisational ability (Schulz & Schulz, 2004, p.492). The most significant disparity between the two theoretical systems is perhaps their view of volition: for behaviourists, free will is purely epiphenomenal, whereas cognitive psychology allows for volition, and ascribes volition agency in particular cognitive processes, such as the selection of experiences to commit to memory (Schulz & Schulz, 2004, p.493). However, therapeutic integration did occur, and it has indeed been argued that the cognitive revolution came about as a development within behavioural therapy, or was to some extent 'implicitly' influenced by it (Hoffman, 1984).

The extent to which cognitive processes could be completely excluded from explaining the efficacy of behavioural therapy was doubtful – the effect of the patient's expectation of positive results, for example, is a cognitive process as distinct from a behavioural one (Hoffman, 1984). Therapeutic strategies such as verbal conditioning, as developed by Luria (1961) and Staats (1963), and subsequently taken up in Britain by Michael Gelder (1965), are particularly similar to a cognitive approach, to the extent that it seems peculiar to categorise it as a solely behavioural intervention (Eifert, 1987). Self-instruction techniques, in which 'clients are taught to emit self-statements that are incompatible with, and opposite in emotional content to, the negative self-statements they have employed previously' (Eifert, 1987, p.176), had marked similarities to the semantic reinforcement techniques in Beck's cognitive therapy for emotional disorders (Beck, 1991).

The boundaries between the categories of cognitive and behavioural interventions are evidently unclear, yet the incorporation of cognitive models remained highly contentious for many self-professed behavioural therapists. From a practical perspective, Hoffman argues persuasively that the integration of cognitive and behavioural techniques was in part a result of consideration of time and economics: in vivo treatment of neuroses was a long and costly process whereas simulation thereof, through use of symbolic stimuli and through verbally induced 'cognitive rehearsal', can reduce the time required for treatment to take effect (Hoffman, 1984).

While Ellis, and particularly Beck, have been very influential in British clinical psychology, the tradition of cognitive therapeutics developed on this side of the Atlantic remained closely linked with the pre-existing behavioural tradition. John Teasdale, for example – a key figure in the development of cognitive approaches to depression such as the theory of 'learned helplessness', and later a codeveloper of the integrative cognitive subsystems approach and mindfulness-based CBT – initially began work in behaviour therapy approaches at the Maudsley, with a PhD on the process of habituation in relation to desensitisation and fear (Dalgleish, 2004; Rachman, 2004). This was also the case for Paul Salkovskis and David Clark, whose work is discussed further below.

Transatlantic connections remained important, however. A key text which brought together behavioural and cognitive approaches was the US psychologist Albert Bandura's work on self-efficacy, which dealt with the cognitive aspects of fear alleviation and their impact upon patients' behaviour modification – challenging the traditional behavioural models of the treatment of phobia (Bandura, 1977). It is important to reiterate that this development, as with most of the significant texts which contributed towards the cognitive shift in psychotherapy, came about through the clinical observations by therapists of their patients, rather than a 'trickle-down' diffusion of applied methods from the theoretical developments in cognitive science.

In terms of charting the rise of the integrated 'cognitive behavioural' approach in psychotherapy, it is worth identifying instances of the term in the literature. According to David Clark and Christopher Fairburn, 'cognitive behaviour therapy' can be found (although they state this without reference) in the first instance in the literature of the mid-1970s, with the first clinical trials coming at the end of the same decade (Clark & Fairburn, 1997). This is a roughly accurate pronouncement: an inaugural conference on 'cognitive behaviour therapy' was held in New York in 1976 (Wilson, 1978), with Mahoney's (1974) *Cognition and Behaviour Modification* having appeared two years earlier. A 1978 book, published in the US and edited by Foreyt and Rathjen, includes the rather amusingly titled introduction: 'Cognitive Behaviour Therapy: Paradigm Shift or Passing Phase?' (Wilson, 1978). Arguably, the first serious 'cognitive behaviour' text came as far back as 1969 with Bandura's *Principles of Behaviour Modification*, which argued that certain therapeutic processes, such as covert modelling, were better conceived of as cognitive processes rather than behavioural conditioning (Bandura, 1969).

Philip C. Kendall and Steven D. Hollon, in the introduction to their 1979 *Cognitive-Behavioural Interventions: Theory, Research and Procedures* emphasise that CBT

> is not yet another new exotic therapy. Rather it is a purposeful attempt to preserve the demonstrated efficiencies of behaviour modification within a less doctrinaire

> context and to incorporate the cognitive activities of the client in the efforts to produce therapeutic change. (Kendall & Hollon, 1979, p.1)

The same authors argue that the 'hyphenation' of the two terms came about through a bilateral movement, as behaviour therapists turned their research to mediation techniques (such as symbolic stimuli, as discussed above), and a certain degree of interest shown by cognitive therapists towards the more established field of behaviour modification (Kendall & Hollon, 1979, p.2).

In terms of institutional integration in Britain, the key turning point did not occur until the 1990s, when the alliance of the cognitive and the behavioural approaches became institutionally recognised through the renaming of the BABP to the British Association of Behavioural and Cognitive Psychotherapies in 1992. In the same year the authors of the *Handbook of Psychotherapy and Behaviour Change* documented that:

> Most of the people who used to consider themselves behavioural therapists now identify themselves as cognitive-behavioural. Also, most people who once considered themselves strictly cognitive practitioners are now willing to take on the cognitive-behavioural label as well. Although many influences have produced these changes, it is pleasing to note that the effect of the research has been substantial. (Bergin & Garfield, 1994, p.824)

Cognitive behaviour therapy research and training in the UK

As mentioned above, the Maudsley Hospital and Middlesex Hospital pioneered early research and training in behaviour therapy, but Michael Gelder's move to Oxford led to a further research group being founded at the University of Oxford's Department of Psychiatry in 1970, initially specialising in research on agoraphobia and depression. In later years, with the addition of David Clark, Paul Salkovskis and Anke Ehlers to the centre's staff, research expanded to the application of CBT approaches to post-traumatic stress disorder, the anxiety disorders, hypochondriasis and obsessive compulsive disorder (Gelder & Mayou, 1997). After the retirement of Isaac Marks from the Institute of Psychiatry at King's College London, Salkovskis and Clark were appointed as professors of clinical psychology there, perhaps symbolising the more dominant role of clinical psychologists, as opposed to psychiatrists, within cognitive and behavioural approaches.

One of the key areas of research in CBT in the UK, which has perhaps been more highly developed than anywhere else in the world, is the development of CBT for psychosis. Originally drawing from the development of family interventions such as behavioural family therapy and the concept of 'expressed emotion' (Pilling et al., 2002), researchers became interested in exploring how patients' coping skills might be enhanced using cognitive techniques that were being used in the treatment of depression (Barrowclough & Tarrier, 1992). These approaches have been further developed since the 1990s, with Richard Bentall and Peter Slade's work on desensitisation of hallucinations (Bentall et al., 1994), Max Birchwood and Paul Chadwick's work on delusions (Chadwick et al., 1996), and Anthony Morrison and Gillian Haddock's techniques for coping with voices and intrusive thoughts (Morrison et al., 1995). Central to CBT approaches to psychosis has been the development of a cognitive model of positive symptoms, which looks at the role of cognitive factors such as emotional reasoning, schemas and attribution biases in the formation of symptoms such as delusional beliefs (Fowler et al., 1995). CBT for psychosis has been the subject of scepticism, exemplified by a Maudsley Debate held in April 2014 titled 'This house believes that CBT for psychosis has been oversold'. The continuing debate over CBT and psychosis is perhaps indicative of a broader professional dispute in which clinical psychology has explicitly challenged some of the assumptions and practices of mainstream biological psychiatry (Bentall, 2004).

CBT in practice: Mental health policy and IAPT

Writing in the early 21st century, it has been evident for at least 20 years that, although still controversial, CBT has become one of the most internationally popular forms of therapy, and recent policy developments have rendered it by far the most dominant form of psychotherapy now available through the National Health Service. The advent of the Labour government's Improving Access to Psychological Therapies (IAPT) scheme in 2007 is one of several policy attempts to improve mental health services, and one which has been continued by the coalition government (HM Treasury, 2010).

One avenue of explanation is the rise of evidence-based medicine in British health care, followed shortly after by a growth in evidence-based psychology. The term was coined in the early 1990s. According to the MEDLINE database of international publications in the life sciences, collated by the US National Library of Medicine, the term was cited only once in 1992, rising to 2957 citations by February 2000 (Straus & McAlister, 2000, p.837). Those lobbying for an increase in funding for CBT services readily engaged with the evidence-base agenda. David Clark, along with many other academic psychologists, and specifically those who speak in favour of CBT in policy, underlines its evidence base as demonstrated through randomised control trials, review articles and meta-analyses. This is by no means a new trend in clinical psychology, as the early behaviour therapy control trials at the Maudsley illustrate (Buchanan, 2010).

In England and Wales, evidence-based practice became institutionalised with the foundation of the National Institute for Clinical Excellence (NICE) in 1999 (now National Institute for Health and Clinical Excellence), which provides guidelines to NHS practitioners for best clinical practice, and evaluates the cost-benefits of particular treatments within the framework of a state-funded healthcare system (Dobson, 1999). The NICE guidelines on depression and anxiety, published in December 2004, advised that 'When considering individual psychological treatments for moderate, severe and treatment-resistant depression, the treatment of choice is CBT' (NICE, 2004, p.27). CBT was also recommended in the NICE guidelines for treatment of schizophrenia, particularly in cases with a history of relapse (NICE, 2003).

Evidence-based medicine is not without its cogent critiques, however. Concerns have been raised that published evidence is skewed towards positive outcomes because negative results tend not to be published. This problem, referred to as publication bias, is a long-term feature of publishing in science and medicine. It occurs when journals with a particular editorial agenda in favour of a treatment reject negative results for publication and, in terms of authorial selection as to which studies are or are not included in meta-analyses, this results in negative results not being included in studies, biasing overall statistical results towards the agenda of the author (Begg & Berlin, 1988). Pim Cuijpers has argued that the efficacy of psychotherapies, CBT included, is 'considerably overestimated' in the treatment of depression in adults as a consequence of publication bias in meta-analyses (Cuijpers, 2010, p.178).

Even representatives of the CBT community itself have demonstrated reservations about the effects of the guidelines on effective practice. Clinical psychologist Paul Salkovskis, editor of *Behavioural and Cognitive Psychotherapies*, published an article criticising NICE's guidelines, arguing that their explicit focus on the randomised control trial as the fundamental knowledge base for governance did not reflect the true developmental process which had underpinned cognitive behavioural therapy. He argued that the implementation of the guidelines would lead to a narrowing of the scope of cognitive behavioural therapy in practice, which would counteract the productive developments gained through the pluralist integrative approach which had developed in the 1990s (Salkovskis, 2002).

Despite the recommendations contained within the NICE guidelines, it took at least three years for the cause to be taken up by politicians, and then only as a result of considerable lobbying. The key figure for initiating this process was the Labour peer, Lord Richard Layard of Highgate. An economist and director of the LSE's Centre for Economic Performance, Layard had been the primary policy architect of the New Deal under the Labour Government after 1997. His motivations for improving access to psychotherapies were, in part, in keeping with the wider project of the New Deal, as it recognised the detriment caused to the national economy by incapacity through mental distress. Layard has a longer standing interest in mental health, having later become interested in the economics of subjective well-being. This is illustrative of a wider intellectual shift towards a concern with subjectivity in the late 20th century, growing out of the overall problem of the disparity between increased economic wealth and the incongruous lack of growth in individuals' happiness in Western society. Layard's book, *Happiness: Lessons from a New Science*, is a popular exemplar of such concerns, combined with a simplified explication of recent neurobiological sciences demonstrating the 'reality' of subjective emotion through use of imaging technologies that demonstrate positive and negative affect in brain function (Layard, 2005).

Concerted efforts to implement the NICE guidelines began with Layard's success in getting a pledge to improve care for mental illness included in the Labour Party Manifesto for the 2005 general election (in which, through accident, the pledge was to improve 'behavioural, as well as drug therapies'). Layard was advised that expert confirmation of the evidence base for the efficacy of psychotherapeutics would be required in order to persuade policy makers of the importance of investment. Consequently, David Clark, Professor of Clinical Psychology at the Institute of Psychiatry, was called in to conduct a question and answer session. Clark has continued to play a key role in authoring policy documents and acting as a national adviser to the IAPT initiative (Layard, in interview with author, 5 July 2009).

The integration of psychotherapy into an NHS framework has raised particular tensions with regard to the imposition of a medical model of governance, which practitioners see as misplaced. This is echoed again in Paul Salkovskis's critique of evidence-based medicine as a means of selecting treatments:

> Evidence Based Medicine may be appropriate as a way of making coherent sense of dozens of studies in which thousands of patients are administered identifiable doses of medication, or in treatments such as most psychotropic medications, which have been stumbled upon rather than developed and refined. It seems unlikely that it will ever be appropriate to exclusively consider the management of psychosocial problems in this way; to do so would be to endorse a one-dimensional approach to science. CBT has thrived because, from the earliest days, it has been both evidence based and empirically grounded. This grounding is in a range of different types of evidence, including but definitely not confined to randomised controlled trials. (Salkovskis, 2002, p.9)

With regard to the clinical psychology profession, IAPT has been perceived both as a success and a potential threat. On the one hand, investment in psychological services has been consistent with the case made by clinical psychologists over several decades. On the other hand, the stepped nature of the IAPT programme, divided as it is between low- and high-intensity interventions that can be administered by professionals other than clinical psychologists, offers a challenge to the supremacy of clinical psychologists in service provision (Turpin, 2009). The presence of both IAPT services and clinical psychology services in parallel has potentially put them in competition with each other, with IAPT services sometimes being favoured for funding or perceived as more legitimate (M. Wang, in interview with author, 7 January 2015). While clinical psychologists were central to developing these approaches, arguably the ascendancy of CBT in the health service has counterintuitively resulted in the profession being somewhat marginalised.

Conclusion

Behavioural – and later cognitive-behavioural – approaches have arguably formed the most influential tradition in British clinical psychology, in part because of the role that clinical evidence has played in the context of a state-funded healthcare service. They have also had a significant part to play in rehabilitation and deinstitutionalisation, and the conceptualisation of disorders such as depression, anxiety and psychosis. These approaches have become increasingly popular within healthcare service delivery, as well as in broader social settings through self-help materials and popular psychological literature. Yet they continue to be omitted from histories of mental health care in the 20th century, which often focus instead on the role of psychiatry, and the rise of psychopharmaceuticals in particular. Given the contemporary importance of cognitive and behavioural approaches it is crucial, therefore, to understand its origins, and consequently to turn historical attention to the role of clinical psychology in the history of mental health.

Note: Some of the material in this chapter has previously appeared in Marks (2012).

References

Baker, R., Hall, J.N. & Hutchinson, K. (1974). A token economy project with chronic schizophrenic patients. *British Journal of Psychiatry, 124,* 367–384.

Bandura, A. (1969). *Principles of behaviour modification.* New York: Holt, Rhinehart & Winston.

Bandura, A. (1977). Self-efficacy: Toward a unifying theory of behavioural change. *Psychological Review, 84,* 191–215.

Barrowclough, C. & Tarrier, N. (1992). *Families of schizophrenic patients: Cognitive behavioural intervention.* London: Chapman Hall.

Beck, A.T. (1991). *Cognitive therapy and the emotional disorders.* London: Penguin.

Begg, C.B. & Berlin, J.A. (1988). Publication bias: A problem in interpreting medical data. *Journal of the Royal Statistical Society, 151*(3), 419–463.

Bentall. R.P. (2004). *Madness explained: Psychosis and human nature.* London: Penguin.

Bentall, R.P., Haddock, G. & Slade, P.D. (1994). Cognitive behaviour therapy for persistent auditory hallucinations: From theory to therapy. *Behaviour Therapy, 25,* 51–66.

Bergin, A.E. & Garfield, S.L. (1994). *Handbook of psychotherapy and behaviour change.* Chichester: Wiley.

Bruch, M.H. (2002). *Edward Stuart Chesser.* http://munksroll.rcplondon.ac.uk/Biography/Details/5231

Buchanan, R.D. (2010). *Playing with fire: The controversial career of Hans J. Eysenck.* Oxford: Oxford University Press.

Busfield, J. (1998). Restructuring mental health services in twentieth-century Britain. In M. Gijswijt-Hofstra & R. Porter (Eds.), *Cultures of psychiatry and mental health in post-war Britain and the Netherlands* (pp.9–28). Amsterdam: Rodopi.

Chadwick, P., Birchwood, M. & Trower, P. (1996). *Cognitive therapy for delusions, voices and paranoia.* Chichester: Wiley.

Clark, D.M. & Fairburn, C.G. (1997). *Science and practice of cognitive behaviour therapy.* Oxford: Oxford University Press.

Cooper J.E. (1963). A study of behaviour therapy in thirty psychiatric patients. *The Lancet, 1*(7278), 411–415.

Cooper J.E., Gelder, M.G. & Marks, I.M. (1965). Results of behaviour therapy in 77 psychiatric patients. *British Medical Journal, 1*(5444)1222–1225.

Cuijpers, P. (2010). Efficacy of cognitive-behavioural therapy and other psychological treatments for adult depression: Meta-analytic study of publication bias. *British Journal of Psychiatry, 196,* 173–178.

Dalgleish, T. (2004). Interfacing basic science with clinical practice: A Festschrift special issue for John Teasdale. *Behaviour Research and Therapy, 42,* 971–974.

Dobson, F. (1999). *The National Institute of Health and Clinical Excellence (Establishment and Constitutional) Order. Statutory Instruments no. 220.* London: NHS England and Wales.

Ehrenwald, J. (Ed.) (1991). *The history of psychotherapy.* Northvale, NJ: Jason Aronson.

Eifert, G.H. (1987). Language conditioning: Clinical issues and applications in behavioural therapy. In H.J. Eysenck & I. Martin (Eds.), *Theoretical foundations of behaviour therapy* (pp.167–193). New York: Plenum Press.

Ellis, A. (1962). *Reason and emotion in psychotherapy.* New York: Lyle Stewart.

Ellis, A. (2007). *Overcoming resistance: A rational emotive behaviour therapy integrated approach.* New York: Springer.

Eysenck, H.J. (1952). The effects of psychotherapy. *Journal of Consulting Psychology, 16,* 319–324.

Eysenck, H.J. (1960). *Behaviour therapy and the neuroses.* New York: Pergamon Press.

Eysenck, H.J. & Rachman, S. (1965). *The causes and cures of neurosis: An introduction to modern behaviour therapy based on learning theory and the principles of conditioning.* London: Routledge.

Fishman, D.B. & Franks, C.M. (1992). Evolution and differentiation within behavior therapy: A theoretical and epistemological review. In D.K. Freedheim (Ed.), *History of psychotherapy: A century of change* (pp.159–196). Washington, DC: American Psychological Association.

Fowler, D., Garety, P. & Kuipers, E. (1995). *Cognitive behaviour therapy for psychosis: Theory and practice.* London: Wiley.

Gelder, M. (1965). *Verbal conditioning in psychiatric patients.* Unpublished DM thesis, University of Oxford, Oxford.

Gelder, M. (1968). Psychological treatments. In M. Shepherd & D.L. Davies (Eds.), *Studies in psychiatry* (pp.110–118). London: Oxford University Press.
Gelder, M., Marks, I. & Wolff, H.H. (1967). De-sensitisation and psychotherapy in the treatment of phobic states: A controlled enquiry. *British Journal of Psychiatry, 113*, 53–73.
Gelder, M. & Mayou, R. (1997). The Oxford University Department of Psychiatry. *The Psychiatrist, 21*, 328–330.
Gwynne Jones, H. (1956). The application of conditioning and learning techniques to the treatment of a psychiatric patient. *Journal of Abnormal and Social Psychology, 52*, 414–420.
Hall, J. (2007) The emergence of clinical psychology in Britain from 1943 to 1958, Part 1: Core tasks and the professionalisation process. *History and Philosophy of Psychology, 9*(1), 29–55.
HM Treasury (2010). *Spending review 2010.* London: HMSO.
Hoffman, N. (1984). Cognitive therapy as the result of a turnabout from psychoanalysis. In N. Hoffman (Ed.), *Foundations of cognitive therapy: Theoretical methods and practical applications* (pp.2–4). New York, London: Plenum Press.
Kendall, P.C. & Hollon, S.D. (1979). *Cognitive-behavioural interventions: Theory, research and procedures.* New York: Academic Press.
Krasner, L. (1971). Behaviour therapy. *Annual Review of Psychology, 22*, 483–532.
Layard, R. (2005). *Happiness: Lessons from a new science.* London: Penguin.
LeVay, S. (1996). *Queer science: The use and abuse of research into homosexuality.* Cambridge, MA: MIT Press.
Levy, A. & Kahan, B. (1991). *The pindown experience and the protection of children: The Report of the Staffordshire Care Inquiry 1990.* Stafford: Staffordshire Social Services Department.
Lomas, H. (2008). *The development of BABCP.* www.babcp.com/About/Development.aspx
Luria, A. (1961). *The role of speech in the regulation of normal and abnormal behaviours.* New York: Liveright.
Mahoney, M.J. (1974). *Cognition and behaviour modification.* Cambridge, MA: Ballinger.
Marks, S. (2012). CBT: The historical context and present situation. In W. Dryden (Ed.), *Cognitive behaviour therapies* (pp.1–25). London: Sage.
Meyer, V. (1966). Modification of expectations in cases with obsessional rituals. *Behaviour Research and Therapy, 4*, 273–280.
Meyer, V. & Chesser, E.S. (1970). *Behaviour therapy in clinical psychiatry.* Harmondsworth: Penguin.
Morrison, A.P., Haddock, G. & Tarrier, N. (1995). Intrusive thoughts and auditory hallucinations: A cognitive approach. *Behavioural and Cognitive Psychotherapy, 23*, 265–280.
National Institute for Health and Clinical Excellence (NICE) (2003). *Schizophrenia: Core interventions in the treatment and management of schizophrenia in adults in primary and secondary care.* London: Author.
National Institute for Health and Clinical Excellence (NICE) (2004). *Depression: Management of depression in primary and secondary care.* London: Author.
Pilling, S., Bebbington, P., Kuipers, E. et al. (2002) Psychological treatments in schizophrenia: I. Meta-analysis of family intervention and cognitive behaviour therapy. *Psychological Medicine, 32*, 763–782.
Rachman, S. (2004). A tribute to John Teasdale. *Behaviour Research and Therapy, 42*, 975–976.
Rachman, S. (2005, July). Keynote address to the 12th Annual OCF Conference, San Diego.
Rachman, S. (2015). The evolution of behaviour therapy and cognitive behaviour therapy. *Behaviour Research and Therapy, 64*, 1–8.
Ramon, S. (1985). *Psychiatry in Britain: Meaning and policy.* London: Croom Helm.
Salkovskis, P. (2002). Empirically grounded clinical interventions: Cognitive behavioural therapy progresses through a multi-dimensional approach to clinical science. *Behavioural and Cognitive Psychotherapy, 30*(1), 3–9.
Schulz, D.P. & Schulz, S.E. (2004). *A history of modern psychology.* Belmont, CA: Thomson.
Shapiro, M.B. (1964, November). *Behaviour therapy. Principles of treatments for psychosomatic disorders.* Paper presented at conference held at the Royal College of Physicians, London.
Shapiro, M.B. & Ravenette, A.T. (1959). A preliminary experiment of paranoid delusions. *Journal of Mental Sciences, 105*, 295–312.
Staats, A.W. (1963). *Complex human behaviour.* New York: Holt, Rinehart & Winston.

Straus, S.E. & McAlister, F.A. (2000). Evidence-based medicine: A commentary of common criticisms. *Canadian Medical Association Journal, 163*(7), 837–41.

Tansey, E.M. (1998). 'They used to call it psychiatry': Aspects of the development and impact of psychopharmacology. In M. Gijswijt-Hofstra & R. Porter (Eds.), *Cultures of psychiatry and mental health in post-war Britain and the Netherlands* (pp.79–102). Amsterdam: Rodopi.

Turpin, G. (2009). The future world of psychological therapies: Implications for counselling and clinical psychologists. *Counselling Psychology Review, 24*, 23–33.

Waddington, K. (1998). Enemies within: Post-war Bethlem and the Maudsley Hospital. In M. Gijswijt-Hofstra & R. Porter (Eds.), *Cultures of psychiatry and mental health in post-war Britain and the Netherlands* (pp.185–202). Amsterdam: Rodopi.

Wilson, G.T. (1978). Cognitive behaviour therapy: Paradigm shift or passing phase. In J.P. Foreyt & D.P. Rathjen (Eds.), *Cognitive behaviour therapy: Research and application* (pp.7–32). New York: Plenum Press.

Wilson, K., Ruch, G., Lymbery, M. & Cooper, A. (2008). *Social work: An introduction to contemporary practice.* Harlow: Pearson.

Wolpe, J. (1963). Psychotherapy: The non-scientific heritage and the new science. *Behaviour and Research Therapy, 1*(1), 23–28.

Chapter 15 Outside the behavioural tradition: Psychodynamic, humanistic and constructivist therapies in clinical psychology

David Pilgrim & Glenys Parry

Introduction

If the core orthodoxy of British clinical psychology was emerging at the Institute of Psychiatry during the 1950s, then this was not the whole picture. At a time when psychoanalytic ideas were a strong cultural influence, for a while the Maudsley development of clinical psychology as an applied psychometric science looked set to debar the first British clinical psychologists from becoming therapists. In 1949, Hans Eysenck argued that 'the psychologist has sufficient scope in the fields of diagnostic testing and clinical research to make it undesirable for him to become a "Jack-of-all-trades" by also providing therapy' (Eysenck, 1949, 1950).

Eysenck considered that therapy was value-led (he was correct) and that this was not compatible with the 'disinterested' role that a proper applied scientist should adopt: a dubious point he went on to query himself and probably for opportunistic reasons (see below). At that time, the dominant method of therapy was psychoanalytic, and Eysenck's student Peter Hildebrand moved to the Tavistock Clinic soon after completing his doctorate at the Institute of Psychiatry in 1953. The enmity that developed between them (and with Joseph Sandler who followed a similar path to Hildebrand) was grounded in Hildebrand's PhD data, which challenged Eysenck's personality dimensions. In 1952 Eysenck attacked the whole enterprise of psychotherapy, by claiming that the effects of therapy could be accounted for wholly by spontaneous remission (Eysenck, 1952). Despite his argument being refuted later, his paper remained influential and was still being cited in the 1970s. The matter of the dominance of a form of traditional British empiricism represented by the Maudsley psychologists is considered in Chapter 3 and in this case set a trajectory for the orthodoxy of both first and second wave CBT.

Another factor shaping the initial antitherapy position for psychologists at the Maudsley was that its first medical director, Aubrey Lewis, made it clear to Eysenck that a therapeutic role for the newly emerging profession would not be countenanced by the medical profession (Derksen, 2001). However, Eysenck's purist line on assessment did not last during the 1950s and his imminent change of direction about the legitimacy of therapy in part implied an ambition for professional autonomy, in defiance of Lewis's warning.

Well before the decade was out Eysenck was arguing that psychologists should be the professional experts to treat neurosis, using behaviour therapy. This stance eschewed both the psychodynamic traditions that he held in contempt and Skinner's radical behaviourism that he dismissed, in favour of Hullian and

Pavlovian psychology (Eysenck, 1955; Eysenck & Gwynne-Jones, 1958). In turn the Skinnerians were understandably critical of the Maudsley contentment with methodological behaviourism (see chapter 14) and the deleterious impact this was to have on the intellectual competence of clinical psychologists (Blackman, 1979).

The opposition from the Maudsley psychologists (and psychiatrists) to psychodynamic psychology was also now well on record and this was culturally in tune with the British preference for empiricism driven by a mixture of pragmatism and common sense. However, Britain was also the home to the very target of this contempt, for peculiar historical and political reasons. In North London from the 1920s an international and prestigious presence was evident. Melanie Klein, Sigmund Freud and his daughter Anna Freud were to become the focus both of influential schools of therapy and of internationally famous disputes within psychoanalysis.

The Continental presence in North London and the Tavistock Clinic

Klein had settled in London voluntarily in 1926 (following an invitation to work there from Ernest Jones). Freud and his loyal daughter Anna, again aided by Jones, were part of the Jewish diaspora in flight, under duress, from Nazi persecution in 1938. All were surrounded by devotees in and around Hampstead. Given British cultural traditions (see chapter 4) London would not seem a propitious last resting place for this ageing psychoanalytical group. Despite this, North London became an international focus for its lively, or even notorious, ideological debates and schisms during the 1940s and 1950s.

Before the Klein–Freud dispute took hold in the 1940s, psychoanalysis was a marginal force but it was not invisible or absent in Britain. In 1911 David Eder (for a while designated by Sigmund Freud as his key ambassador in England, even before Ernest Jones) had presented an outline of psychoanalysis to the Neurology Section of the British Medical Association. The Chair and all of the audience stood up and walked out in protest at what they probably felt was an offensive Continental discussion of our dark instinctual life (Hobman, 1945). The following year, a popular account of Freudian concepts appeared (Hart, 1912) which was reprinted 15 times before 1940. James Glover was offering psychoanalytic therapy sessions as early as 1913, when the London Society of Psycho-analysts was founded and papers on Freudian themes were presented to the British Association meeting (Hearnshaw, 1964).

By 1919 military doctors struggling to comprehend and treat 'shell shock' (Salmon, 1929; Stone, 1985) had come home to set up the first section of the BPS, the Medical Section, to act as a forum for debate in psychopathology and psychotherapy. By 1920 Hugh Crichton-Miller established an Institute of Medical Psychology in Tavistock Square, with Field Marshal Haig and Admiral Beatty as honorary vice-presidents. It focused on treating war veterans (though its first recorded patient was actually a child) and its initial approach was not singularly psychodynamic. Armstrong noted the eclectic orientation of the Tavistock Clinic, which:

> with its associated Institute of Medical Psychology, promoted a unified psychosomatic approach to diagnosis and treatment. Crichton Miller, the Clinic's founder

> published his views on aetiology [which included the notion that] the emotions, sepsis, the endocrines and blood circulation all had inter-dependent effects on mental stability. (Armstrong, 1980, p.294)

This tentative eclectic step (reminding us again of the cautious attitude in British culture towards wholesale intellectual positions) was found alongside more vehement rejections of psychoanalysis within the medical profession after, not just before, the First World War. For example, Armstrong-Jones (1921) argued that psychoanalysis might be 'relevant to life in an Austrian or German frontier but not relevant to ordinary English life'. Similarly Crichton-Browne (cited in Turner, 1996) suggested that 'Freud resembled Socrates as much as a toadstool does a British oak'.

Despite the deeply rooted British cultural contempt for psychoanalysis, by the outbreak of the Second World War in and around Hampstead there was the Tavistock Clinic and a small community of psychoanalysts, some British and some Continental. As an indication of the prestige that had built up rapidly about psychodynamic psychology by 1939, when hostilities returned again with Germany, J.R. Rees, the Director of the Tavistock Clinic since 1934, was appointed as chief psychiatrist to the British army. Rees was not a trained psychoanalyst, though he had had a Jungian analysis.

Two important and influential developments in British psychology emerged from the tensions between the Freudians and the Kleinians. The first was British object relations theory, which eventually would become associated, in radicalised form, with both 'anti-psychiatry' and feminist therapy (e.g. Eichenbaum & Orbach 1982; Laing, 1967) and would be one basis for the development of cognitive analytic therapy (Ryle, 1990). The second was attachment theory, with both John Bowlby and Mary Ainsworth working at the Tavistock Clinic (Bowlby et al., 1956).

The training role of the Tavistock is not as clear historically as that documented about the Institute of Psychiatry and we are grateful to Helen Oliver, the current librarian at the Tavistock Clinic, for her help in tracing this history. Training in clinical psychology began in 1953 but petered out in the mid-1970s. The Clinic ran a two-year course for most of the period, and it expanded into an advanced course for a further two years, which gave training and experience in psychotherapy for clinical psychologists. The course in this format was still listed in the 1974/1975 Tavistock prospectus, but by 1976 only the advanced training was offered, with Fred Balfour and Paul Upson as its leaders.

The demise of the core clinical course probably reflected two processes, First there was the marginalisation of psychodynamic psychology within the British cultural tradition of pragmatism and empiricism, with its distrust of Continental idealism. Second, the psychodynamic model in Hampstead was being privileged over clinical psychology's nationally developing norms of training and clinical practice. The Tavistock graduates were likely to go on either to train as psychoanalysts or as specialist psychodynamic therapists; this was a model-driven form of professionalisation, rather than one based on one emergent wing of applied psychology. For example, Phil Mollon describes in detail how for him in the 1980s the identity of psychodynamic therapist outweighed the core professional role of being a clinical psychologist (Mollon, 1989).

Thus the impact of the psychodynamic tradition upon British clinical psychology can be summarised in the post-war period as being about its considerable influential background presence. Its *direct* role in clinical psychology was marginal compared to the emerging character of medical psychotherapy within the Royal Medico-Psychological Association (which became the Royal College of Psychiatrists in 1971). By the 1980s, British medical psychotherapy was dominated by a psychodynamic orientation (Pilgrim, 1986). Clinical psychology, by contrast, was much more eclectic and dominated more by methodological behaviourism and its revisions.

Graduates of the Tavistock course included Sue Holland, who went on to develop a radical community psychology programme in White City with poor women (Holland, 1979), and Joan Busfield, who became a well-regarded academic medical sociologist at the University of Essex (Busfield, 1985). However, no training course in Britain was led by a Tavistock graduate; this was in contrast to the Maudsley psychologists, who dominated these leadership roles in the 1970s.

This relative absence of a psychodynamic leadership role was in part linked to the point noted above, about the psychotherapeutic orientation being privileged for Tavistock trainees over their core profession of clinical psychology. However, the demise of the Tavistock course did not erase the significance of psychoanalysis in the profession. Some NHS psychology departments developed a reputation for their psychodynamic orientation, especially some linked to the in-service courses of the NHS, which also might use local medical psychotherapy units as placements.

Some clinical psychologists went on to pursue psychoanalytical training or postgraduate courses in psychodynamic therapy at the Tavistock Clinic and other courses at the Universities of Leeds (in the case of the first author) and Edinburgh, where Hampstead-trained staff in psychoanalytical working had settled (the medical psychoanalysts, Ron Markillie and Jock Sutherland respectively). A recent indication of the irrepressible psychodynamic influence in British clinical psychology has been the emergence of a training course at the University of Essex in 2005, linked once more to the Tavistock Clinic.

Thus when we consider psychoanalysis in Britain there is a paradox. On the one hand it has been inimical to traditional British cultural values and philosophical emphases, at odds with those of the idealism of mainland Europe. On the other hand, it has remained a hardy perennial in the British mental health industry, in adult psychotherapy, as well as those working with families and children.

The presence of psychoanalysis inside the BPS had been strong since the inception of the Medical Section in 1919. As its name suggested, it was effectively a medical society and its leaders saw it as such (Rickman, 1938). Moreover, the doctors involved were by and large psychoanalysts. Given that Eysenck had launched British empiricist clinical psychology in part in opposition to this pre-existing therapeutic authority, the position of the Medical Section and its journal, the *British Journal of Medical Psychology*, proved a political obstacle to the hegemony of the Maudsley group. Accordingly, the latter set about trying to join the Section and alter its traditional ways. In response the psychoanalysts in charge of the Section tried to block the Maudsley putsch. This dispute became so intemperate that the Council of the BPS had to suspend the business of the Section in 1958 (Pilgrim & Treacher, 1992).

American humanism in the British context

British clinical psychology has produced a number of champions of what we broadly might call a 'humanistic approach', although Don Bannister felt that for psychologists to become 'humanistic' was rather like a group of sailors deciding they ought to be interested in ships (Bannister & Fransella, 1970). More specifically, from the 1960s there was an increased interest in constructivist approaches, especially that of George Kelly and his personal construct theory (PCT) (Kelly, 1955).

The 'big four' of the British Kellyans in the 1960s and 1970s were Don Bannister, Fay Fransella, Miller Mair and Phillida Salmon (Neimeyer, 1985). The first three were clinical psychologists and the last one a child psychologist with a strong interest in psychotherapy. Bannister and Mair were hostile to the narrow behavioural orthodoxy of the Maudsley. Both Bannister and Fransella trained there, with the former having a particularly irritable relationship with Eysenck but a mutually respectful one with Shapiro. Another advocate of PCT in British clinical psychology, who focused on challenging a reductionist biomedical view of depression, was Dorothy Rowe, an Australian who had settled in Britain (Rowe, 1983).

Kelly's theory had its origins in the work of William James and James Dewey in the US (Butt, 2008). It was not merely a radical form of subjectivism or phenomenology but it also provided a form of idiographic assessment, with the availability of the repertory grid technique (e.g. Bannister, 1962). Compared to the open-ended humanism of Carl Rogers' work, PCT was both underpinned by a pragmatic orientation (hence its alignment with an aspect of British culture) and it sought to take personal experience seriously, without emphasising the unconscious.

After the Second World War, American humanism (including PCT) became associated with a 'Third Force' in psychology, carving a way between behaviourism on one side and psychoanalysis on the other (Wann, 1964). It reflected a broader shift in one part of US culture towards holism in the arts and humanities, which was reflected in the mental health industry of the time (Halliwell, 2013). Kelly was extending the work of Carl Rogers (his immediate predecessor as professor of psychology at the Ohio State University) and although both were championing 'humanistic' psychology, it was Rogers, Abraham Maslow and Rollo May whose names became associated with this term. By contrast, Kelly's preference for ideographic measurement, and the intensive statistical analysis of the role repertory test, possibly marked him out as being more compatible with British empirical psychology.

At the centre of PCT therapy was a pragmatic way of having collaborative conversations with patients in order to help them reconstrue their world. That cognitive emphasis anticipated and prefigured a key feature of later second (and some third) wave CBT. From the outset the British PCT group did not deny that behaviour therapy might work some of the time to help people to change their lives; the objection was to the mechanistic reductionism of behaviourism (Bannister & Fransella, 1970). PCT put human agency central to its concerns.

It is also worth noting that Monte Shapiro at the Maudsley was sympathetic to the Rogerian tradition of person-centred work, despite his wider commitment to aggregate evidence (chapter 9). Shapiro explicitly embraced the 'helping others' position (prefiguring and confirming Bannister's wry observation about sailors taking an interest in ships) and was not sympathetic to Eysenck's pre-1958 position of psychologists being purely 'disinterested' scientists.

However, the narrow confines of the Maudsley approach to therapy invoked opposition from the humanists, despite the softening role of Shapiro. In 1972 Bannister and Mair collaborated with the academic social psychologist John Shotter and another clinical psychologist David Smail to set up the Psychology and Psychotherapy Association, which was a pluralistic forum for psychotherapists from any professional background. Smail single-handedly produced a newsletter for a while, before this chapter's second author became editor, when it became the *Journal of the Psychology and Psychotherapy Association*; later, with another clinical psychologist, Jenny Firth-Cozens, she produced it, more professionally, as *Changes*. Eventually it morphed into the *Journal of Critical Psychology, Counselling and Psychotherapy* (at the time of writing edited by a clinical psychologist, Craig Newnes).

Miller Mair was director of psychological services and research at the Crichton Royal hospital in Dumfries from 1975. A reflection of his concern about the adequacy of core clinical training was his establishment and maintenance of a post-graduate course, which explored critical alternatives to the orthodoxy of British behaviour therapy. In 1968 he had organised the first international symposium on PCT in London. In the same year, with Bannister he produced *The Evaluation of Personal Constructs* (Bannister & Mair,1968). With Fay Fransella, Bannister and Mair organised a second international PCT conference in Cambridge. Mair in particular wanted to encourage clinical psychologists to explore the creative two-way relationship between psychology and psychotherapy (Mair, 1989). That same curiosity led Smail to come to question whether the therapy relationship was of any substantial humanistic impact, as his work shifted from therapy itself to the social conditions affecting mental health (Smail, 1987; cf. Smail 2005).

The reasons why the work of Kelly, rather than Rogers, took greater hold in British clinical psychology are not completely clear, even with hindsight. One possibility highlighted by Butt (2008) is that Kelly focused on 'man the scientist' and his approach was highly cognitive and pragmatic. By contrast Rogers believed that warm relationality will in and of itself ensure positive personal change. Kelly's work could more easily be incorporated into the scientific humanism already evident as the professional identity of British clinical psychology (Richards, 1980). This left the more full-blooded humanism of Rogers to be embraced by the counselling and 'human potential' movements internationally (not just in Britain). A comparison of the training curricula of counselling courses with those of clinical training in the past 50 years highlights this point. Ironically Rogers's point about the central role of benign relationality has continued to be a motif of the core conditions of efficacy in psychological therapy, through decades of work on the therapeutic alliance (Martin et al., 2000). Despite his passion for humanistic values, his legacy to empirical psychotherapy research is seemingly secure.

From Kelly to CAT in Britain

One enduring influence of Kelly in clinical psychology was the role that personal construct theory played in the development of a new psychotherapeutic method in the 1980s: cognitive analytic therapy (CAT). This approach, while practised by therapists of different core professions, has found particular favour within clinical psychology.

It was developed by Anthony Ryle, a medical practitioner who came to psychotherapy via the less-travelled route of general practice and student counselling, rather than psychiatry. Although trained psychoanalytically, he was interested in cognitive psychology and developed a novel method of using Kelly's repertory grids to map cognitive representations of relationships (Ryle, 1975, 1990).

Dissatisfied with many aspects of psychoanalytic theory and practice, he aimed to design a pragmatic, short-term therapy suitable for the NHS and applicable to a wide range of problems. He did it by translating key concepts from object relations theory into cognitive terms, and by using Kelly's constructivist ideas; people are neither pushed by instinctual forces or governed purely by external contingencies, but are purposefully making sense of the world through aim-directed action. His integration of cognitive and psychoanalytic concepts was later developed further through the influence of Mikael Leiman, a Finnish clinical psychologist who imported influences from the work of Vygotsky and Bakhtin (Leiman, 1997).

CAT is notable for two features that fit well with both the theory and practice of clinical psychology: an emphasis on psychological formulation developed collaboratively and the pragmatic application of a range of psychological principles. While both psychodynamic and CBT methods can (and do) claim to be formulation-based, the former often disdains to share the formulation with the client and the latter is increasingly treated as a technical process in the delivery of a standard protocol for a particular diagnosis, on an industrial scale. It could be argued that within British clinical psychology, CAT has inhabited the space that humanistic psychology opened for psychodynamic therapies and CBT.

Discussion

The abiding presence of psychodynamic, humanistic and constructivist ways of working within British clinical psychology reflects the pragmatic eclecticism of the profession. The core scientism that was associated with Eysenck's initial insistence on a 'disinterested' approach to the assessment of patients failed to hold in two senses.

First he abandoned his own stricture within a few years. His change of direction in 1958 now placed psychologists in the driving seat of a (narrowly permitted) version of psychological therapy: behaviour therapy. Second, that subsequent stricture about behaviour therapy itself only held until the mid-1970s, when 'second wave CBT' began to incorporate cognitivism, thereby undermining the initial scientistic rhetoric of methodological behaviourism and its rejection of inner life. A wariness about, or even antipathy towards, subjectivism was now brought back in from the cold on pragmatic grounds, when behaviour therapy morphed into 'cognitive-behavioural therapy' and thoughts and feelings were suddenly conceded as being as important, psychologically, as behaviour.

Moreover, Shapiro's impact during the 1960s on the actual practice of behaviour therapy (Eysenck did not see patients) from the outset had Rogerian resonances (Shapiro, 1963). He was concerned to take individual patients and their complaints very seriously in their idiosyncratic detail. He reflected and emphasised the humanistic impulse to help others in his work, an impulse mirrored in the common motivation of those entering clinical psychology, both then and now. Thus from the outset what we now think of as scientific 'first wave' CBT has had its 'soft' side, and the recent consensus in the profession about the importance of a unique psychological formulation, rather than a psychiatric diagnosis, can be traced both to Shapiro at the Maudsley and to those who critiqued that orthodoxy (such as Bannister, Fransella, Mair, Salmon and Smail) (Johnstone & Dallos, 2006).

By the time that the 1970s arrived we can see that a range of hybrids were emerging and so pluralism and syncretism characterised the profession. Apart from second and then third wave CBT reflecting this point, we also witnessed a particular way in which psychodynamic and humanistic ideas merged in the British context, with the emergence of CAT.

If we review the above picture we can discern a pattern over time. Initially, core cultural assumptions arising from the orthodoxy of British empiricism settle centre stage at the Maudsley. However, there was the co-presence of the psychodynamic tradition, drawing its impetus not from the Second World War (in the case of the neophyte profession of clinical psychology) but from the First World War. The 'Great War' created the conditions of possibility for the Medical Section of the BPS, the British Psychoanalytical Society and the Tavistock Clinic.

The staff in these organisations coalesced into a self-assured, medically led, metropolitan elite that was well established by the time that the Maudsley culture exerted its own version of scientific self-confidence. The undignified spats and chicanery which came to characterise the politics of the Medical Section of the BPS in 1958 was a conflict waiting to happen. The serendipity of Sigmund and Anna Freud spending their final years in Hampstead added to this explosive mixture.

With hindsight, we can also speculate on the niche of legitimacy that was created by the Kellyans. PCT was not a particularly strong movement at the time in its native US, where other humanists, such as Rogers and Maslow, were better known and regarded. What was it about British culture that permitted its seeding and then growth, when nurtured by Bannister and Mair in the 1960s and 1970s? Clearly the punch trading in the Medical Section between two heavyweight competitors was not going to be the whole picture. Humanistic psychology, broadly conceived, was finding its place in the competition as well.

One factor in the popularity of PCT in Britain might have been that it was open-minded about how personal change took place and thus could contest two different forms of rigidity on each side. The behaviour therapists, limiting themselves during the 1960s to a few techniques, such as flooding and systematic desensitisation, limited their range of applicability. Indeed by the end of the 1960s they had to confess that only a small minority of psychiatric problems could be treated with behaviour therapy (Yates, 1970). As for psychoanalysis, and as a separate matter from its efficacy, its expense and duration meant that its role in the NHS was always going to be limited.

PCT, in advance of second wave CBT, offered an approach that respected subjectivity and human agency fully but without any fixed set of strictures about its therapeutic applications. Once patients and their experience had been attended to seriously, then whatever could be negotiated with them helpfully in relation to their existential complaints could be tried out.

This matter of collaboration or coproduced change was both pragmatic (suiting the British culture of therapists and their patients) and was democratically open to all (suiting the typical needs of ordinary NHS patients who would not be able to pay for prolonged therapeutic explorations).

Shorn of its full original folksy optimism from George Kelly in the mid-West of the US, PCT found a niche in the lives of ordinary British people in the NHS. Its cognitive emphasis also meant that later it could become another form of 'cognitive therapy', though its advocates might still distance themselves from CBT (e.g. Winter, 2009). At the same time, the libertarianism of PCT was in tune with the countercultural period of the 1960s. Note, for example, that Bannister made his own libertarian socialist views explicit to his colleagues in conversations.

If the young were aspiring to 'do their own thing in their own time' to use a hippy cliché of the time, then PCT was a fairly good starting point. With its emphasis upon unique personal construing and few methodological prescriptions about how reconstruing could be facilitated in the self and others, it was in tune with the countercultural ethos of the 1960s and 1970s, just as much as say the work of Ronald Laing and David Cooper. As part of the same zeitgeist, many clinical psychologists in the 1970s were influenced by, and participated in, personal 'experiential' training and continuing professional development through encounter groups, Fritz Perls's Gestalt therapy, psychodrama, bodywork, transpersonal therapy and so on.

Finally we need to remember that there were experiments with therapeutic psychology in Britain in the 20th century outside of the academy and the clinic (Cheshire & Pilgrim, 2000). In the same year that the BPS was formed (1901), so too was the London Psycho-Therapeutic Society. Psychological matters had been at the centre of currents it incorporated, including spiritualism, theosophy and Christian Science. These spiritual origins were secularised in the Society and Continental influences about hypnotism and autosuggestion were added to the eclectic mix.

By the 1920s, just when the Tavistock Clinic was formalising what was to become a form of professionalised therapy, the Federation of Practical Psychology Clubs emerged. By the outbreak of the Second World War there were over 50 of these scattered across England and Scotland. Practical psychology, outside of what was still a weakly developed discipline of psychology in the academy, and even weaker in the clinic, offered sensible help and self-help to the masses. The latter could buy and receive mail-order manualised exercises and practical guidance in systems such as the complete life guide of Pelmanism.

All of these self-help initiatives and commercial projects made a claim (sometimes grandiosely) about both their practical applicability and scientific integrity or insights. And yet few made sense to, or were endorsed by, university-educated psychology graduates. What this copresence of different forms of psychology signalled though was that the general public often might be at ease with expertise that lay outside of the ambit of orthodox academic respectability.

Professionalised psychology might have favoured a sombre and earnest consensus among like-minded and like-trained peers (whether this was about psychoanalysis or behaviourism) but the wider masses, quite happily, favoured alternatives. This trend remains today in the extensive self-help genre of books. Moreover, as the tensions and reconciliations between behaviourism, psychoanalysis and humanistic psychology were to reveal in all the anglophone countries, whatever 'scientific psychology' was, it was by no means a unitary whole and it did not speak with one voice. Given this, then as now, what were the public to make of psychology as a respectable academic discipline? Some degree of public scepticism was understandable and predictable.

Thus when we consider the sectional interests of psychodynamic, behavioural and humanistic forms of clinical psychology in Britain, we also need to take into account how those forms might have adapted to this tradition of practical psychology and populist versions of self-help, and the expectations that it encouraged in the public imagination. And that public imagination and the expressed need it encouraged would be placed in a new organisational structure entailing mass access after 1948: the NHS. As was noted in chapter 4, that organisational structure did not determine the content of psychology in Britain but as a context its determining effect was profound.

Finally we can note that the non-behavioural traditions we overview in this chapter (as well as the behavioural tradition they have tended to dissent from) are overwhelmingly Eurocentric in origin, even if they were modified as bodies of knowledge across the Atlantic (i.e. variants of US humanism) or were derived in part from the 'near' East (such as the Russian psychology of Bakhtin, Pavlov and Vygotsky). This trend contains a relative silence about forms of psychological understandings of distress, and assumptions about personal stasis and change, from elsewhere, such as Africa and Asia. This point is noted in chapter 4 and has a bearing on the content of this chapter. The indirect incorporation of those other forms of understanding can be found though, for example in the traces of Buddhism which are present in many therapeutic currents inside and outside of clinical psychology.

References

Armstrong, D. (1980). Madness and coping. *Sociology of Health and Illness, 2*(3), 393–413.

Armstrong-Jones, R. (1921) Discussion of psychoanalysis. *Journal of Mental Science, 67*, 107.

Bannister, D. (1962). The nature and measurement of schizophrenic thought disorder. *Journal of Mental Science, 108*, 825–42.

Bannister, D. & Fransella, F. (1970). *Inquiring man*. London: Penguin.

Bannister, D. & Mair, J.M.M. (1968). *The evaluation of personal constructs*. London: Academic Press.

Blackman, D. (1979). Behaviour modification: Control and counter-control. *Behavior Analysis, 1*(2), 37–50.

Bowlby, J., Ainsworth, M., Boston, M. & Rosenbluth, D. (1956). The effects of mother-child separation: A follow-up study. *British Journal of Medical Psychology, 29*, 211–247.

Butt, T. (2008). *The psychology of personal constructs*. Basingstoke: Palgrave Macmillan.

Busfield, J. (1985). *Managing madness*. London: Hutchinson.

Cheshire, K. & Pilgrim, D. (2000). *A short introduction to clinical psychology*. London: Sage.

Derksen, M. (2001). Science at the clinic: Clinical psychology at the Maudsley. In G.C. Bunn, A.D. Lovie & G.D. Richards (Eds.), *Psychology in Britain: Historical essays and personal reflections* (pp.267–89). Leicester: BPS Books.

Eichenbaum, L. & Orbach, S. (1982). *Outside in...inside out: Women's psychology – a feminist psychoanalytic approach*. Harmondsworth: Penguin.

Eysenck, H.J. (1949). Training in clinical psychology: An English point of view. *American Psychologist, 4*, 173–6.

Eysenck, H.J. (1950). Functioning and training of the clinical psychologist. *Journal of Mental Science, 96*, 710–25.

Eysenck, H.J. (1952). The effects of psychotherapy: An evaluation. *Journal of Consulting Psychology, 16*(5), 319.

Eysenck, H.J. (1955). A dynamic theory of anxiety and hysteria. *Journal of Mental Science, 101*, 28–51.

Eysenck, H.J. & Gwynne-Jones, H. (1958). *The psychiatric treatment of neurosis.* Paper presented at the Royal-Medico Psychological Association, London.

Halliwell, M. (2013). *Therapeutic revolutions: Medicine, psychiatry and American culture 1945–1970.* London: Rutgers University Press.

Hart, B. (1912). *The psychology of insanity.* Cambridge: Cambridge University Press.

Hearnshaw, L.S. (1964). *A short history of British psychology: 1840–1940.* London: Methuen.

Hobman, J.B. (1945). *David Eder: Memoirs of a modern pioneer.* London: Gollancz.

Holland, S. (1979). The development of an action and counselling service in a deprived urban area. In M. Meacher (Ed.), *New methods of mental health care* (pp.95–106). London: Pergamon.

Johnstone, L. & Dallos, L. (2006). *Formulation in psychology and psychotherapy: Making sense of people's problems.* London: Taylor & Francis.

Kelly, G. (1955). *The psychology of personal constructs.* New York: Norton.

Laing, R.D. (1967). *The politics of experience and the bird of paradise.* Harmondsworth: Penguin.

Leiman, M. (1997). Procedures as dialogical sequences: A revised version of the fundamental concept in cognitive analytic therapy. *British Journal of Medical Psychology, 70*(2), 193–207.

Mair, J.M.M. (1989). *Between psychology and psychotherapy: A poetics of experience.* London: Routledge.

Martin, D.J., Garske, J.P. & Davis, M.K. (2000). Relation of the therapeutic alliance with outcome and other variables: A meta-analytic review. *Journal of Consulting and Clinical Psychology, 68*(3), 438–450.

Mollon, P. (1989). Some narcissistic perils for clinical psychologists learning psychotherapy. *British Journal of Medical Psychology, 62*(2), 113–122.

Neimeyer, R.A. (1985). *The development of personal construct psychology.* Lincoln, NE: University of Nebraska Press.

Pilgrim, D. (1986). *NHS psychotherapy: Personal accounts.* Unpublished PhD thesis, University of Nottingham.

Pilgrim, D. & Treacher, A. (1992). *Clinical psychology observed.* London: Routledge.

Richards, B. (1983). *Clinical psychology, the individual and the state.* Unpublished PhD thesis, Polytechnic of North East London.

Rowe, D. (1983). *Depression: The way out of your prison.* London: Routledge.

Rickman, J. (1938, 7 September). The Medical Section of the British Psychological Society. *Medical Press and Circular, 197*, 188–192.

Ryle, A. (1975). *Frames and cages: The repertory grid approach to human understanding.* Brighton: Sussex University Press.

Ryle, A. (1990). *Cognitive analytic therapy: Active participation in change.* Chichester: Wiley.

Salmon, T. W. (1929). Care and treatment of mental diseases and war neurosis ('shell shock') in the British army. In T. W. Salmon & N. Fenton (Eds.), *The Medical Department of the United States Army in the World War: Vol. 10. Neuropsychiatry* (pp.497–547). Washington, DC: US Government Printing Office.

Shapiro, M.B. (1963). A clinical approach to fundamental research with special reference to the study of the single patient. In P. Sainsbury & N. Kreitman (Eds.), *Methods of psychiatric research. An introduction for clinical psychiatrists* (pp.123–149). London: Oxford University Press.

Smail, D. (1987). *Taking care: An alternative to therapy.* London: Dent.

Smail, D. (2005). *Power, interest and psychology: Elements of a social materialist understanding of distress.* Ross-on-Wye: PCCS Books.

Stone, M. (1985). Shellshock and the psychologists. In W.F. Bynum, R. Porter & M. Shepherd (Eds.), *The anatomy of madness: Vol. II. Institutions and society* (pp.242–271). London: Tavistock.

Turner, T. (1996). James Crichton-Browne and the anti-psychoanalysts. In H. Freeman & G. Berrios (Eds.), *150 years of British psychiatry: Vol. 2. The aftermath* (pp.144–155). London: Athlone.

Wann, E.T. (1964). *Behaviorism and phenomenology: Contrasting bases for modern psychology.* Chicago: University of Chicago Press.

Winter, D.A. (2009). Cognitive-behaviour therapy: From rationalism to constructivism. In R. House & D. Loewenthal (Eds.), *Against and for CBT: A constructive dialogue?* (pp.137–147). Ross-on-Wye: PCCS Books

Yates, A. (1970). *Behavior therapy.* New York: Wiley.

Part 4
Work with Client Groups

Chapter 16 Towards a history of clinical child psychology

Michael Berger

Clinical child psychologists (CCPs) are clinical psychologists (CPs) specialising in work with pre-adult age groups after qualification. Although preponderantly in NHS Child and Adolescent Mental Health Services (CAMHS), they have a significant presence in child health, social care, services for young people with learning difficulties, and the criminal justice services, or they work independently. In these diverse settings, services include direct client and family contact, working with staff, prevention, improving service delivery, clinical and service research, and providing legal reports. Underpinning this diversity are substantial theoretical and empirical advances in knowledge and understanding of typical development, psychological adaptability and difficulties, with a repertoire of skills in assessment, formulation and intervention. In 2014 there were well over 900 CCPs in the British Psychological Society's Division of Clinical Psychology (DCP) Faculty for Children, Young People and their Families, probably an underestimate of the numbers working as CCPs in the UK.

About 24 per cent of the UK population – 15 million individuals – are aged 0 to 19 years (ONS, 2012). Extrapolations from prevalence studies give estimates of multiple hundreds of thousands of children and young people (hereafter, younger people) with 'mental disorders' (Young Minds, 2014). The numbers who do not meet thresholds for a 'disorder', but who might benefit from psychology services, cannot be estimated because of the absence of epidemiological research with a psychology remit.

This chapter highlights an eventful period in the history of child clinical psychology, from the start of the DCP in 1966 to the end of 2001 when child practitioners established a Faculty of the DCP following many years as a Special Interest Group (SIG). The SIG replaced the first group to focus on child psychology in the DCP, the Sub-Committee on Psychology Services for Children (SCPSC), established 12 years after the founding of the DCP. This early history is interesting and instructive because of its persisting themes and long-term consequences. As psychological services for children and families long pre-dated the DCP, an outline of that history is introduced as a context for the later developments. This chapter is an abridged account of some of the history, with more detailed coverage and related topics given in an extended version (Berger, 2015).

Foundations of child clinical psychology practice

Development occurs across the lifespan, but the pre-adult years are notable for their rapid qualitative and quantitative changes and for the profoundly influential settings that younger individuals encounter: families, peer groups, school, post-school and the wider community. Knowing about developmental processes and life-experience interactions is fundamental to child clinical psychology practice.

Younger people are not small adults or initially undifferentiated beings: from birth they have diverse capacities and rapidly emerging and changing competencies that shape and are shaped by their experiences, transformations that are among the most remarkable of human phenomena. Hence, when there is a need for psychology involvement, younger people and their families will require suitably tailored and developmentally sophisticated services. Practitioners, as a minimum, must also have skills that enable them to understand and work with the strengths and needs of younger people, parents, families, carers, other adults, professionals and different agencies, and be able to work in and across the multiple and varied settings and cultures that are part of the lives of children. Consequently, CCPs must also be competent in many aspects of understanding and working with adults, from when they were younger, and as adults, parents and as brokers of power. Recognising and working with the various power imbalances – sometimes wielded by the young person – are critical, as they can be in other areas of clinical (and other psychology) practice. These CCP perspectives and others derive from the complex interplay of many influences, historical and current. Complexity for child clinical psychology in particular includes the fundamental development, dependency and context interplay interactions that exert a profound influence on the nature and outcomes of practice, elaborated in Berger (2015).

Scope of this chapter

A brief note about methodology is followed by an account of child practice prior to 1966, the early history of child clinical psychology in the DCP, the changing nature of clinical practice, the diversification of services and concluding comments. National, regional and local histories and practice variations are among many omissions that will need to be accommodated in future histories. Children with intellectual disabilities are discussed in chapter 18.

Methodology

Much of the information here derives from signed minutes of the DCP from its first meeting in February 1966 to March 1998, which are held in the BPS archives (http://archives.bps.org.uk). Signed DCP minutes from then to the end of 2002 are untraceable. Minutes of most meetings of the predecessors of the Child Faculty to the end of 2002 were inaccessible, presumed lost. However, a small collection of assorted papers, including some minutes, is available, as are updates describing Faculty developments in April 2001 and 2002. Specific references to minutes and a discussion of the strengths and weaknesses of this approach are in Berger (2015). My involvement in early child clinical psychology developments assists interpretation, tempered by the usual limitations of recall. Some information comes from interviews (face-to-face or telephone), and email correspondence with a number of colleagues involved at the time.

Prior context

Children with behaviour difficulties, learning problems and the like – at one time labelled as 'maladjusted' or 'delinquent' – came into prominence as social changes introduced compulsory state education in Western societies. Standardised psychological tests, derived from Binet's researches, aided the identification of children requiring special education. 'Difficult' children and their families, usually the mother, began to be seen in special 'clinics' in the US and subsequently the UK, where services were influenced and funded by the US child guidance movement, notable for its underlying social and moralistic drivers, the labelling of the children and families, and the notion that they, and not the circumstances of their lives, were primarily responsible for their 'maladjustment'. Seen as akin to a 'disease', they were referred to medically led clinics to be 'cured'. Sampson (1980) and Stewart's (2009) accounts are basic historical sources about these developments. Jack Tizard mounted a powerful critique of the child guidance clinics (CGCs) in 1973. An impressive Maudsley Lecture by the American child psychiatrist Leo Kanner (1959) gives an enlightening account of the development of child psychiatry and child guidance in the US. Accounts by UK child psychiatrists Kenneth Cameron (1956) and Wilfred Warren (1971), among others, are valuable because of the influences of psychiatry on clinical psychology and child clinical psychology.

For many years most CGCs were run by local education authorities (LEAs), with educational psychologists (EPs) providing clinical input and school liaison (Cashdan, 2013, describes the work of an English EP – the Scottish and other nations arrangements differed, if not initially, certainly subsequently). The London Child Guidance Training Centre began training of EPs for work in schools and CGCs in 1928, with employment in LEAs eventually 'restricted' to those with teaching qualifications and classroom experience. Services established in the NHS child psychiatry clinics used the CGC model (psychiatrist, social worker and EP). Thus, well before the advent of the DCP, there were EPs working 'clinically' with children in the NHS as were CPs, the latter trained in recognised generic training programmes following the introduction of clinical courses (see chapter 9). There were, however, issues regarding the use of the term 'clinical'.

'Clinical' psychology

Concerns about using the term 'clinical' are discussed by Derksen (2000). As a term it probably originated in CGCs to avoid using 'medical', reserved for doctors. The 'clinical' work of EPs comprised work undertaken in the CGC, including psychometric testing, with the educational element being school-based. The initial brochure for the Institute of Psychiatry course used the term 'clinical psychology' (Payne, 1997) and graduates saw themselves as 'clinical psychologists' (Payne, 1997, p.10), even though the qualification then was a Diploma in Psychology (Section D. Abnormal) of London University.

The 1949 Institute course brochure stated that each student would investigate 'about 40 adult and 40 child cases' (Payne, 1997, p.8), giving scope for generic practice. It is not clear just when 'being a CCP' emerged. My own appointment (before 1966) to the Institute and to the Maudsley Hospital Children's Department and Bethlem Hospital Adolescent Unit involved working exclusively with children and adolescents. Most of my predecessors probably worked across the age spectrum. Bill Yule joined me in the Children's Department some years later, also to work exclusively with children. Most likely too, CPs elsewhere, for instance in paediatric settings in the UK, worked solely with younger people. Whatever the precise origins, there were CPs working clinically and exclusively with children in the NHS when the DCP began. However, the situation was complicated because of the pre-existing employment of EPs in NHS clinics. Essentially, psychologists working with children in the NHS could do so via two routes, through a clinical psychology qualification or educational psychology training and NHS employment, although most were LEA-employed in CGCs. Hence, when the DCP came into being, there were immediate, child-services-related problems to contend with. Also prior to the DCP, there had been a fundamental shift in the clinical roles of psychologists in both child and adult services.

Developing roles

The early NHS work of CPs – primarily psychological testing – serviced psychiatry needs. The shift from testing, less pronounced for children's services, came about through dissatisfaction with the tests, the advent of the behaviour therapies, the emergence of Shapiro's higher-level conceptualisation of clinical practice and his emphasis on formulation (see Derksen, 2000; see also chapter 9). The use of tests with children persisted for clinical reasons. Involvement in therapy took some years to become established but was becoming fully embedded by the time the DCP started. In becoming 'therapists', CCPs moved into the 'psychiatric territory' of medical/psychiatric disorders, and likewise 'doing clinical work with children' intruded in the presumed (by them) 'province of EPs', areas in which they were not necessarily welcome.

The pre-DCP professional context also needs noting: essentially, CPs and EPs came under the English Division of Professional Psychologists (EDPP) and the Scottish equivalent (SDPP). Clinically trained members were supported by a Health Sub-Committee of the EDPP. Why the DCP, and later the Professional Affairs Board (PAB), were introduced are dealt with in chapter 5.

The DCP begins

At its first meeting, on 4 February 1966, the DCP encountered challenges arising from child services. One was defining the equivalent qualification to that already enabling individuals to work as a CP in the NHS, subsequently encompassed by 'lateral transfer', the requirements to be met by EPs and others wanting employment or to progress in NHS posts. It had been agreed that CPs in the NHS working with children could join the EDPP while remaining members of the DCP. By the second meeting, on 18 March 1966, the head of the EP training at London Child Guidance Training Centre requested the establishment of a joint (DCP and EDPP) working party on work with children in the NHS '...to explore all the problems relating to psychological work with children in the N.H.S.' The underlying concern became apparent at the first meeting of the Joint Working Group on 2 April 1966: the EDPP honorary secretary stated they were becoming 'the Division of Educational and Child Psychology' – clearly, a territorial grab and *fait accompli*, with a particular message: child psychology territory and practice 'belong' to the DECP/EPs (like the colonisation of the 'clinical' by the DCP perhaps). Some in the DECP clearly had a problem with CPs working with children, an issue that persisted, colouring professional relationships for many years.

Other problems arose: for instance, proposals for courses training child psychologists that circumvented CP or EP entry qualifications. In 1967 the DCP was asked to consider a course at Nottingham University for training psychologists to work with children that had been rejected by the DECP. As it was not intended for CPs, it was not considered a DCP matter. Subsequent events demonstrated otherwise. In 1974 the Scottish DECP rejected a Diploma in Applied Child Psychology at Stirling University. Three previously recognised courses for working with children in the NHS were considered unsuitable, and the DCP requested their withdrawal. The message was very clear, repeated over the years: no professional training courses were recognised that did not satisfy DCP or DECP requirements.

A belief that there was substantial overlap in the training of CPs and EPs led to proposals in the Underwood Committee Report (Ministry of Education, 1955) for dedicated child psychology training. This theme recurred in the Summerfield Report (DES, 1968), set up to report on EP training and services. The conclusions of the Trethowan Report, *The Role of Psychologists in the Health Services* (DHSS, 1977), also referred to this but were inconclusive, which was unfortunate because Trethowan was looked to for guidance in several other reports, including the Court Report on Child Health Services, *Fit for the Future* (Court, 1976).

The Trethowan Report and child psychology

Trethowan was a major transformative event in the history of clinical psychology, considered in a number of chapters here. Of the 34 recommendations in the Committee's 1974 Consultation Document, the last three concern child services. These note the debates about the kinds of psychology services children need in the context of scarce resources and increasing demand from teachers and social workers who would normally use EPs.

Witnesses had proposed a 'new discipline of child psychology' combining child clinical psychology and educational psychology, a historical distinction whose continuation remained artificial. Trethowan anticipated EPs spending less time in CGCs and more in schools dealing with children with difficulties, advising teachers and prevention. The Committee, therefore, remained undecided about a new profession, leaving it to the professions to make the decision but convinced that closer liaison at an individual level was needed to achieve comprehensive services. There was an injunction for CCPs and EPs to recognise and understand each other's expertise and areas of overlap, especially regarding pre-schoolers, the 'mentally handicapped' and in centres providing comprehensive assessment. Also, GPs and social workers involved with children should have close links with both. Finally, it recommended that LEA psychologists should sit on area psychological advisory committees to facilitate some of the changes.

The BPS Council's memorandum on the Trethowan recommendations (BPS Council, 1974) was prepared by a working party of 14 representatives, including EPs from England and Scotland, CPs (including the Chair), and me as a CCP. It was considered at a special meeting of the PAB in May 1974. The Council accepted that greater collaboration between CPs and EPs in 'mental handicap' was needed. The Society congratulated Trethowan 'on their explicit recognition of the important contribution made by Psychologists to child care' (BPS Council, 1974, p.9), emphasised the need for 'flexibility in the field of health care for children' (p.9), and that EPs be involved in higher level services planning. The 'highly relevant comments on integration and planning' between EPs and CPs were recognised, and it was noted that closer links in training were being explored. These comments were the spur to a range of other PAB and Division activities.

Responding to Trethowan

In November 1974 the PAB asked the DCP to prepare a paper mapping out an 'ideal' training scheme for child psychologists and the criteria for acceptability into specialised services. In a paper 'Clinical Psychology Services for Children' presented at the April 1974 BPS Annual Conference, I argued that the field was mature enough to support a post-qualification specialisation for work with children (Berger, 1975). A paper to this effect was submitted to the DCP by Berger and Yule in 1975.

This was followed in 1975 by the first of several PAB working parties on training in child psychology that I was asked to convene, with Yule the DCP nominee. In November 1975 the DECP restated the entry criteria for courses for educational *and child psychologists* (my emphasis) and, in an obvious reference to the Nottingham course and possibly the Berger and Yule (1975) paper, stated 'a generic form of training in "applied child psychology"...would be premature'. The PAB invited Professor Jack Tizard to chair the new working party that included Professor John Newson (founder, with his wife, Elizabeth, of the Nottingham course), and an EP Union observer. The Tizard recommendations (that Yule and I accepted) were published a year later, held up because of two dissenting minority reports: Peter Pumfrey (DECP) accepted that there were unmet service needs but this did not necessitate 'the establishment of a widely based field of applied child psychology' or alternative forms of training equivalent to current courses. An equally dismissive report was submitted by the observer from the Association of Educational Psychologists (AEP, the EP union founded in 1962). The DCP accepted the minority reports in 1977, insisting on initial generic training. The Secretary General of the Society was informed of the grave concerns of the DCP about the main report. In a survey of CPs and EPs at that time, most agreed that work with children should be developed post-qualification.

A PAB report from an ad hoc committee on child psychological services, specially convened, included the Secretary General of the Society, probably reflecting the disquiet that something proposed by eminent Society members (Tizard and Newson) had been rejected. Their recommendations included another PAB working party (led by an EP, Klaus Weddell) to determine whether the present grouping was the most appropriate for the delivery of child psychology services. Any proposed changes were not to be rushed. The ad hoc committee report cited the preliminary results of a DECP survey on which it based its views. This study had clear limitations, making its conclusions questionable. The new Weddell working party in 1978 included DCP representatives, but the DCP rejected AEP representation. By this time the DCP had established the Sub-committee on Psychological Services for Children (SCPSC) to assist with child-related matters.

The Weddell committee issued a draft report in late 1980, but it was rejected by the DCP. It resurfaced and the SCPSC identified factual errors, with the DCP blocking circulation until corrected in 1981. The PAB circulated the report anyway, resulting in a major spat. The DCP then wanted the report circulated to assess the support of local CPs. The PAB set up a Standing Committee on Psychological

Services for Children (different to the DCP equivalent). The responses of CCPs and EPs to the PAB 1981 proposals were published (Lindsey & Cogill, 1983), a paper devoid of data and, to me, having its own agenda.

The DECP's continuing problem

In that eventful time (within the world of the Divisions) Geoff Lindsey (Honorary Secretary, DECP and PAB member) stated that CCPs 'should' join the DECP, and proposed a letter to that effect to be sent to all CCPs. The initial letter was rejected because of inaccuracies and the implied need for CCPs to move to the DECP. The wording of the 'invitation' was discussed at a meeting in 1982 and eventually issued. Several meetings later, the minutes note that DECP recruitment exercise had 'limited success': one application (I confess – albeit remaining in the DCP).

This attempt to get CCPs to move revisits 'problems' troubling the DECP in 1966: that all child practitioners had to be in the DECP and/or only EPs should work with children. Exemplifying this, in response to a suggestion that in training, CPs should become familiar with schools and other education settings, 'some [EPs] argued that as only educational psychologists *should* work with children, such a development was unnecessary' (Lindsay & Cogill, 1983, p.157). Whether or not this opinion was widespread among EPs and reflected an ignorance of CCPs and their work, compounded by arrogance or otherwise, is not known. That it was not universal is evidenced by ongoing positive and constructive relationships between CCPs and EPs in many services.

No further overtures between then and 2001/2, the end of this history, are known, partly because of missing minutes. The DECP focus shifted radically following the Warnock Committee Report (DES, 1978) on special educational needs, leading eventually to EPs becoming engrossed in such work. My recollection from that time is of EP territoriality assertively shifting to 'statementing' – determining entitlement to special education provision – with CCPs being 'allowed' to contribute on behalf of their clients, provided they did not make recommendations. A reconfiguration of CCPs relationship around that time embedded them fully in the DCP, lessening even further, if that were possible, the likelihood of any switch of Division loyalties.

Child clinical psychology in the DCP: Reconfiguring the relationship

Going back to 1966, I am not aware of the newly-formed DCP committee having a CCP among its members but the DECP was represented. Clearly, from the foregoing, child psychology issues were prominent and diverting. A 'CCP perspective' became available following my joining the DCP in 1971, continuing until 1973, and I represented the DCP on the DECP from November 1972. Later, I represented the BPS Council on the DCP and PAB. Yule joined the DCP Training Committee in 1972 and the DCP in January 1975. Hence, during those years there was some child clinical psychology input to the DCP, but no mechanism to ensure continuity. Possibly we were unduly influential in the DCP and PAB, but the DCP had a wide membership they could have canvassed, a prerogative they did not exercise then but did later. In 1978 I asked the DCP to establish a standing subcommittee on child psychology. A formal proposal was requested – but not my presence – for the next meeting. The proposal detailed the ways a subcommittee could help the DCP.

I was then asked to convene a working party and report on psychological services for children, lateral entry of EPs, and Council of Europe pronouncements. The working party eventually became SCPSC, giving advice and responding to DCP requests but was not represented on the DCP Committee. My term ended in April 1981, with the SCPSC now being 'regarded as essential'. A new convenor, Stephen Cogill, was appointed in 1982 and co-opted to the DCP Committee, representing the Division on the DECP, and the group was retitled to include adolescents (SCPSCA). Clearly services for younger people had arrived in the DCP.

The business and achievements of the SCPSCA

The SCPSCA responded to a wide range of matters. Noteworthy was the inclusion of members (J. Smith, and Marion Levick as alternate) on the Health Advisory Service group that produced *Bridges over Troubled Waters* (HAS, 1986), an influential report on inpatient services for adolescents. The SCPSC was superseded in 1985 by a Special Interest Group (SIG).

A Special Interest Group takes over

The first SCPSCA Colloquium aimed at reaching out to practitioners occurred in 1982. Organised by Keith Turner, it was successful, followed by similar annual events. During the 1984 Colloquium, setting up a Special Interest Group (SIG), the third in the DCP, was discussed, and it was eventually established in September 1985. Described as a resource for 'kindred spirits' by its first Chair, John Richer (personal communication, 22 September 2014), it took time to become fully embedded due to constitutional amendments required by the DCP, with failure to comply resulting in disaffiliation and loss of the right to represent the Division/Society. The changes were accepted. Concerns about the SIG's autonomy also arose because transition arrangements imposed a handover period of a year to 'maximise the transfer of political skills in the area' (as reported in a minute from 1986). Jean Sambrooks made the SIG's dissatisfaction clear in a letter in November 1985, resulting in two SIG Committee members joining the SCPSCA in 1986. Despite some protests, SCPSCA was eventually declared redundant, holding its last meeting in March 1987. The SIG took over, created an Advisory Committee and became responsible for training and practice, the DCP retaining control of policy. The SIG became fully established in 1989.

Unhappiness in all SIGs about the lack of representation on the DCP was resolved in 1986 by SIGs being treated as Branches, with communications channelled through the Branch Representative. For complex issues, a SIG member could attend the DCP Executive. The children's SIG also had difficulty with its public image and offered a bottle of champagne to the creator of the best logo submitted at the 1991 AGM. A logo was selected (see Figure 16.1, upper left), but its suitability for signifying a professional organisation, hoping to be taken seriously at higher levels in the NHS and elsewhere, is a moot point.

The PAB eventually assumed a 'higher level' responsibility for dealing with child-related issues, its policy formulated in the context of an in-built EP majority (as recorded in minutes of 1990 and of the first Executive Committee in 1992). When relevant matters reached the DCP, transmission to SIGs was poor, even five years after the SIG took over. The SIG could only receive signed minutes. Persisting concerns led to Irene Sclare, Child SIG Chair, being appointed the first all-SIGs representative in 1992. When SIGS eventually achieved individual representation, an Executive Committee alternating with the Full Committee had been set up, with SIGs attending only the latter. Issues in the relationship between the DCP and the SIGs remained, still evident in 2002.

There were difficulties too getting the SIG's views into external bodies and at government level. By 1995 some child matters emanating from the PAB were passed directly to the SIG and representatives began involvement in various groups. However, not all potentially pertinent matters reaching the DCP (Executive) got through to the SIG. Nevertheless, some CCP views were heard where it mattered: Helen Beinart (SIG) and Gill Evans (DECP) representing the PAB, gave evidence to the House of Commons Health Select Committee inquiry into child mental health (Beinart & Evans, 1996). This was one of a number of achievements at that time, culminating in 1998 in the NHS Health Advisory Service (HAS) requesting links with the SIG for future reference, a sign that the SIG was 'getting there'.

Had they been available, minutes of SIG meetings for the period 1993 onwards would certainly have dealt with a major transformative event for CAMHS: the publication of the HAS (1995) report *Together We Stand.*

The HAS investigations and report

CCPs were making a clear impact in clinical services, sufficient to lead the HAS report, in a double-edged endorsement, to recognise that CCPs 'are skilful and entrepreneurial professionals with attributes that can be harnessed within a multidisciplinary context to ensure imaginative and innovative service delivery' (p.94).

The report, with some exceptions, identified major problems across CAMHS. Their vision to overcome these comprised comprehensive, effective and seamless services, sensitive and locally responsive, delivered through a four-tier service model that, while not intended as prescriptive, turned out to be so. Tier 1 covers primary care services, dealing with low severity difficulties; Tier 2 focuses on community services that may involve specialists for difficulties of greater severity, with possible input from Tier 3 specialist services, such as CAMHS multidisciplinary teams; Tier 4, highly specialist provision, includes inpatient services (see NHS England, 2014, pp.10–11).

The report introduced tiered thinking, language and, importantly, tiered service structures into the NHS that still persist. Whether or not the model produced the many changes needed is questionable. Apart from the tiered model, not always properly implemented, other aspirations were not widely realised for various reasons, including insufficient funding (CAMHS Review, 2008; Cottrell & Kraam, 2005). Some important features of the HAS Report were also troubling. I argued (Berger, 1966) that the HAS case and one of the feeder epidemiological studies were biased against CCPs, motivated in part to contain them – why else 'harnessed' in the quote above? Further, the model of tiered services could be articulated in different ways that might be more helpful to CCPs and consequently, beneficial to service users.

The SIG moves on

Papers, minutes and copies of the newsletter *SiG NET* demonstrate the SIG commitment to enhancing practice (see Box 16.1). Given the brief time frame, the work and practitioner focus of successive SIG committees are impressive: minutes from the period 1990–91 and a report in April 2001, prepared for the DCP's Strategy Meeting, are evidence of the SIG's policy and practice initiatives and commitment to training through day meetings, sessions at DCP summer schools and the SIG annual conferences. The contribution is also evident in *SiG Net*, illustrated by the November 2000 issue edited by Jo Douglas which carries specially

Box 16.1 SIG Publications

Purchasing Clinical Psychology Services for Children, Young People and their Families, 1993 (Draft tabled March 1993. Printed version not seen)
Clinical Child Psychology Supply, November 2000
Managing Litigation Arising in Clinical Work with Children and Families: Some Practice Guidelines for Clinical Child Psychologists, July 2000
Position Paper: Issues for Child Clinical Psychologists in Relation to Working in Interagency and Multi-agency Projects, November 2000
Position Paper: Minimum Standards for Evaluating Outcome in Clinical Practice, 2000
Guidelines for Commissioning and Purchasing Child Clinical Psychology Services, March 2001
Promoting User Participation in Clinical Psychology Services for Children and Young People: How to Hear the Voice of the Child, October 2001
Practice Guidance on Consent for Clinical Psychologists Working with Children and Young People, October 2001

Faculty (Drafted by the SIG (SIG minutes 2 April 2001))
Briefing paper: Child Clinical Psychologists Working with Children with Medical Conditions, April 2003

written articles and briefings on current policy and other relevant developments. The SIG was also updated through a feature on recent internet-published policy and other documents.

It is clear that the SIG was realising some of its aspirations but there were concerns about its reach and influence, reflected in objectives agreed at the annual strategy meeting in November 2000. Interestingly, a discussion in the DCP Service Development Subcommittee in June 2001 concerned renaming SIGs to reflect their status. The committee agreed a change was necessary but was uncertain about the use of 'Faculty'. Regardless, the SIG renamed itself the Faculty for Children and Young People in 2001 with a new logo and letterhead, a change of style and approach, with *SiG NET* replaced by *Service and Practice Update* (see Figure 16.1).

The Faculty issued an impressive report on its progress for the 2002 DCP Strategy Meeting evidenced by the papers in Box 16.1 and its membership of various policy groups (workforce, the Children's National Service Framework), joint groups with psychiatry and paediatrics, a successful publication *Drawing on the Evidence*, and its revamped newsletter, *Service and Practice Update*.

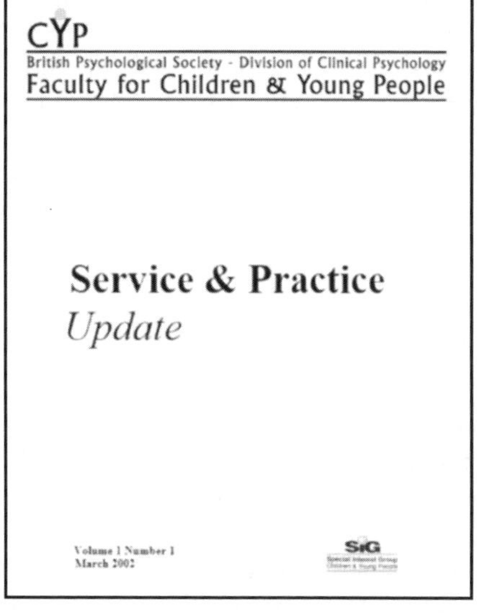

Figure 16.1 SIG and Faculty logos and periodical covers (*Update* cover recreated from original design)

DCP–Faculty relationship

Why name changes were considered necessary, and how they came about, are detailed elsewhere (see Berger, 2015), but rebranded, the Faculty title and new image survived to 2014. Did this make a difference? It would be naive to think that it did, given the complex environment in which it operated. But perhaps the cognitive shift entailed led to a better starting place for CCPs. Certainly, the Faculty felt that 'the change in title had made a positive difference in communicating with external agencies'(minutes from meeting in April 2002). However, they remained dissatisfied with their relationship with the DCP and proposed a changed Division structure with 'greater representation…in the leadership and strategy of the Division' (minutes July 2002). The DCP included this proposal in briefing an external consultant examining the long-term strategy for the Division.

The underlying issue seems essentially to be about being taken seriously within and beyond the DCP. Yet even when mechanisms were established, DCP minutes reflect continuing dissatisfaction. Why did this persist? In part the answer is in DCP strategy day minutes for 2001 and 2002: these show a potential attendance of over 50 people, the majority of whom represented the multiple facets of the DCP's activities. While some represented internal subcommittees (finance, membership, etc.), representatives preponderantly came from the many subsystems, the SIGs, Faculty, Branches and groups representing other parts of its remit, with each also wanting to be taken seriously. The DCP was not, and probably is still not, geared up effectively to manage the needs and expectations of all these groups. That being the case, it is a systemic issue needing to be addressed, something beyond the scope of this chapter.

The preceding sections have looked at some of the issues, political and structural, for CCPs. What remain to be covered, again going back in time, are the changing nature of practice and the diversification of services.

From child guidance in the NHS and onwards – developing clinical roles

Testing

The CGC model began to include other professionals, although not uniformly. Inpatient unit equivalents included nursing and teaching staff, and possibly other therapists. Testing remained part – albeit smaller – of the standard contribution of CCPs in multidisciplinary work, still aimed at identifying developmental difficulties that might be clinically relevant. (For adults, testing – apart from use in neuropsychology and some other areas – is less of an issue.) A fuller account of testing, exemplified by work with children and families at the Maudsley and other settings, is given in Berger (2015). Here it is sufficient to note that training in test evaluation and use remained a part of clinical training and practice for at least some courses and for some practitioners, and still remains as an important part of the CCP clinical contribution (see chapter 10).

Therapies

Psychologists had been 'forbidden' to engage in therapy in the pre-1960s Maudsley although the treatment of night-time bed-wetting (Young & Turner, 1965) and remedial work in reading, spelling and related difficulties were exempt, as were some controlled single-case experiments (see chapter 9). Inevitably, the prohibition was relaxed: my training in 1963/64 for instance included 'doing' therapy. The acceptance was not necessarily widespread or wholehearted, indicated by the comment 'Is this one for puppy-training then?' addressed to me by the consultant psychiatrist at a diagnostic intake meeting (Yule, 2009, p.51): I was, as a staff psychologist, being given 'permission' to do behaviour therapy in the Children's Department, a context in which the 'patient' and all clinical work came under the 'responsible' consultant psychiatrist.

Behavioural work with children developed from innovative intervention studies (see Rachman, 1962), in parallel with evidence that outcomes of psychotherapy-treated children were no better in control groups (Levitt, 1963). Studies in the US inspired many developments, with clinical work stimulating systematic studies. For instance, interventions with the language difficulties of children with autism (Yule & Berger, 1972), based on the work of Lovaas (1966), led to collaborative research with psychiatrists (Michael Rutter and Lionel Hersov), using behavioural interventions in the home-based treatment of children with autism (Howlin et al., 1973). Our early behavioural work with classroom difficulties is a further example. The Teacher–Child Interaction Project (Berger, 1972; Wigley et al., 1985) was probably the first such project using behavioural approaches in British mainstream schools (Wheldall, 1987, p.xv). While keen to pass on behaviour management skills to others, we began to appreciate the complexities involved (Berger, 1979). Nevertheless, behavioural therapies flourished, attested to by texts such as Martin Herbert's (1981) *Behavioural Treatment of Problem Children* and *Behaviour Problems in Young Children* by Jo Douglas (1989).

A major benefit of these assessment and therapy skills is their generality: where psychological factors are important, the principles can be adapted to varied problems in diverse settings.

Widening scope

As evidence of the attraction of a CCP career, by early 2001 membership of the Child Faculty approached 500 (reported in the Children and Young People SIG Report to the DCP strategy meeting, April 2001). SIG practice guidance (see Box 16.1) encouraged diversification and the tiered service model facilitated CCP involvement in social services and community work, especially with young people in local authority care. This included assessment and interventions with young people and carers, consultation and training programmes for social workers (Lukeman, personal communication, 26 November 2014), expert reports for court proceedings and early intervention community-based family interventions (e.g. Day & Davis, 1999). Services in general practice surgeries allowed GPs to refer directly to CCPs. Other services offered consultation and support for community paediatricians and health visitors as well as direct work probably introduced before the advent of the HAS tiers.

A significant development, 'paediatric psychology', stemmed in part from psychiatric input to child health departments in general and children's hospitals (Wrate & Kolvin, 1978). The contribution of CCPs in these settings grew and diversified. The SIG/Faculty issued a paper on working in health settings (Box 16.1). There are many areas, if not most, where CCP input contributes: pain management, adherence to treatments, staff training and support, among others in the many different branches of paediatrics, the aim being to adapt psychological interventions to improve the quality of care and outcomes, as it is in all areas.

Concluding comments

Readers with knowledge of past and current child clinical psychology will know how much of the journey from first beginnings in the DCP to Faculty has not been covered, especially national and local services, practice innovations and many other contributions. Such a history cannot be encompassed in a single chapter. Instead, the intention here has been to give some sense of the history and document the time from when child clinical psychology emerged to a pragmatic end point. In part this arises because I was intimately involved with several aspects of these early stages and this book is a special opportunity to recount a story that might not otherwise have been written. I am also aware of the many major achievements and challenges that have occurred since 2002, but have avoided venturing into these.

Psychologists regarding themselves as CCPs were around possibly before the DCP began but emerged professionally and politically in an established DCP, and have since then increased in numbers, knowledge and skills, and in the scope of practice. This chapter has attempted to document some of the early struggles and successes in establishing and developing the CCP identity. The growth and diversification of child clinical psychology have arisen against a background of service reorganisations, financial constraints and cuts, professional rivalries, the sometimes uncomfortable relationships with the DCP, and other challenges. Most important among these perhaps is how best to achieve a relationship within the BPS and particularly the DCP – and maybe outside of these organisations – that will allow the contributions and aspirations of CCPs to progress in the interests of their service users and services. These issues and themes will hopefully resonate with current practitioners, as will the aspirations and achievements of the earlier generations. At the forefront of all this and driving the development of CCP is the belief in what is being offered: the relevance and value of the contributions of child psychology and the commitment of CCPs to the development, well-being, social care and education of children, young people, their families and carers. This belief sustained and motivated us in the past and will hopefully continue to energise and guide services and innovation.

Acknowledgements

Thanks to Helen Beinart, Jo Douglas, Diane Lukeman, Marion Levick, Mike Maskill (BPS Archivist), John Richer, Irene Sclare, Graham Turpin, Miranda Wolpert and William Yule, for their time and information, and to my wife Judith Berger (Middleton) for her tolerance, for listening and for her perspectives.

References

Beinart, H. & Evans, G. (1996). *Health committee: Child and adolescent mental health services.* Minutes of evidence, 7 November 1996. London: HMSO.

Berger, M. (1972). Modifying behaviour at school. *Special Education, 61,* 18–21.

Berger, M. (1975). Clinical psychology services for children. *Bulletin of the British Psychological Society, 28,* 102–107.

Berger, M. (1979). Behaviour modification in education and professional practice: The dangers of a mindless technology. *Bulletin of the British Psychological Society, 32,* 418–419.

Berger, M. (1996). Divided we stand! Issues for clinical psychology services for children and young people: A personal view. *Clinical Psychology Forum, 88,* 40–46.

Berger, M. (2015). *Towards a history of clinical child psychology.* Manuscript in preparation.

Berger, M. & Yule, W. (1975). *Proposals for training child psychologists.* London: Division of Clinical Psychology. (Copy available in the BPS Records Archive, London, BPS/001/3/11/07)

BPS Council (1974). Memorandum on the consultation document of the sub-committee of the D.H S.S. (The Trethowan Committee) Standing Mental Health Advisory Committee. *Agenda papers of the Professional Affairs Board,* 11 May 1974 (BPS/001/3/11/07). London: BPS Records Archive.

Cameron, K. (1956). Past and present trends in child psychiatry. *British Journal of Psychiatry, 102,* 599–603.

Cashdan, A. (2013). Halfway between Cyril Burt and the present day: A lone educational psychologist in the late 1950s. *Educational & Child Psychology, 30*, 107–113.

Child and Adolescent Mental Health Services Review (2008). *Children and young people in mind: The final report of the National CAMHS Review.* London: Department for Children, Schools and Families and the Department of Health.

Cottrell, D. & Kraam, A. (2005). Growing up: A history of CAMHS (1987–2005). *Child and Adolescent Mental Health, 10*(3), 111–117.

Court, W.D.S. (1976). *Fit for the future: Report of the Committee on Child Health Services (Court Report).* Cmnd 6684. London: HMSO.

Day, C. & Davis, H. (1999). A community child mental health service: A framework for the development of parenting initiatives. *Clinical Child Psychology and Psychiatry, 4*, 475–482.

Derksen, M. (2000). Clinical psychology and the psychological clinic: The early years of clinical psychology at the Maudsley. *History & Philosophy of Psychology, 2*(1), 1–17.

Department of Education and Science (1968). *Psychologists in education services (Summerfield Report)* London: HMSO.

Department of Education and Science (1978). *Special educational needs. Report of the Committee of Enquiry into the Education of Handicapped Children and Young People (Warnock Report).* London: HMSO.

Department of Health and Social Security (1977). *The role of psychologists in the health service (Trethowan Report).* London: HMSO.

Douglas, J. (1989). *Behaviour problems in young children: Assessment and management.* London: Routledge.

Health Advisory Service (1986). *Bridges over troubled waters: NHS Health Advisory Service report on services for disturbed adolescents.* London: HMSO.

Health Advisory Service (1995). *Child and adolescent mental health services: Together we stand.* London: HMSO.

Herbert, M. (1981). *Behavioural treatment of problem children: A practice manual.* London: Academic Press.

Howlin. P., Marchant, R., Rutter, M. et al. (1973). A home-based approach to the treatment of autistic children. *Journal of Autism and Childhood Schizophrenia, 3*(4), 308–336.

Kanner, L. (1959). The thirty-third Maudsley Lecture: Trends in child psychiatry. *British Journal of Psychiatry, 105*, 581–593.

Levitt, E.E (1963). Psychotherapy with children: A further evaluation. *Behaviour Research and Therapy, 1*, 45–51.

Lindsey, G. & Cogill, S. (1983). Psychological services for children: Grass roots opinion. *Bulletin of the British Psychological Society, 36*, 155–158.

Lovaas, I.O. (1966). A programme for the establishment of speech in psychotic children. In J. K. Wing (Ed.), *Early childhood autism: Clinical, educational and social aspects* (pp.115–144). Oxford: Pergamon Press.

Ministry of Education (1955). *Report of the Committee on Maladjusted Children (Underwood Report).* London: HMSO.

NHS England (2014). *Child and adolescent mental health services (CAMHS) Tier 4 report.* London: Author.

Office for National Statistics (2012). *2011 Census: Population and household estimates for the United Kingdom. Table 3a: Usual resident population by five-year age group, local authorities in the United Kingdom.* London: Author.

Payne, R. (1997). The early years – some personal recollections. In W. Yule (Ed.), *50th Anniversary of the Maudsley Clinical Psychology Course: 1947 to 1997.* William Yule Archive, King's College London. (Copy available in the BPS Archive, London, AUD/003/OHP 55)

Rachman, S.J. (1962). Learning theory and child psychology: Therapeutic possibilities. *Journal of Child Psychology and Psychiatry, 3*, 49–63.

Sampson, O. (1980). *Child guidance: Its history, provenance and future.* Leicester: Division of Educational and Child Psychology, British Psychological Society.

Stewart, J. (2009). The scientific claims of British child guidance, 1918–1945. *British Journal for the History of Science, 42*, 407–432.

Tizard, J. (1973). Maladjusted children and the child guidance service. *London Educational Review, 2*, 22–37.

Warren, W (1971). 'You can never plan the future by the past': The development of child psychiatry in England and Wales. *Journal of Child Psychology and Psychiatry, 11*, 241–257.

Wheldall, K. (Ed.) (1987). *The behaviourist in the classroom.* London: Allen & Unwin.

Wigley, V., Yule, W. & Berger, M. (1985). Helping withdrawn children in school. *British Journal of Special Education, 12*, 159–162.

Wrate, R.M. & Kolvin, I. (1978). A child psychiatry consultation service to paediatricians. *Developmental Medicine and Child Neurology, 20*, 347–356.

Young, G.C. &Turner, R.K. (1965). 'CNS' stimulant drugs and conditioning treatment of nocturnal enuresis. *Behaviour Research and Therapy, 3*, 93–101.

Young Minds (2014). *Mental health statistics.* www.youngminds.org.uk/training_services/policy/mental_health_statistics

Yule, W. (2009). Therapeutic developments in child psychology: Behaviour therapy to cognitive behaviour therapy. In P. Graham, H. Minnis & M. Nicholson (Eds.), *The development of child and adolescent psychiatry from 1960 until 1990* (pp.49–54). www.gla.ac.uk/media/media_196525_en.pdf

Yule, W. & Berger, M. (1972). Behaviour modification principles and speech delay. In M. Rutter & J.A.M. Martin (Eds.), *The child with delayed speech* (pp.204–219). London: Heinemann.

Chapter 17 Clinical psychology in adult mental health services

Gillian Bowden, Fabian Davis, Kathy Nairne & Geoff Shepherd

Introduction

To understand the evolution of British clinical psychology and its role in adult mental health, we first consider psychologically informed initiatives to manage 'madness' within hospitals and asylums and the factors contributing to disillusionment with the institutional approach. During a period of rapid de-institutionalisation after the Second World War, clinical psychologists found receptive ground for psychological ideas. In its next phase, clinical psychology continued to promote and adapt service developments towards comprehensive models of care, including care coordination and community service systems, alongside the diversification of service provision and delivery to meet local needs. Mental health services in primary care developed partnership working with GPs and some of these initiatives are described. Latterly, the NHS programme 'Improving Access to Psychological Therapies' (IAPT) has been a major influence on the provision of psychological therapies in primary (and more recently secondary) care in England. It has also shaped a more general view of the profession's contribution. Finally, we suggest some recurring themes and tensions that have affected these developments, and raise some questions. Fundamentally, these concern the extent to which psychologists are prepared to acknowledge broader social perspectives and to share responsibility and influence with other professions and with service users and communities. Responding to these questions would mean radical changes to our profession and how it currently operates.

Working with people in asylums

Before the 18th century, care of people with mental health problems was mainly a family and community responsibility. The only institutional provision consisted of a small number of private madhouses and the workhouses (designed to manage the indigent or 'undeserving poor'). In response to scandals in private madhouses where inmates were subject to harsh or inhumane treatments, a group of Quakers established the 'York Retreat' in 1796, attempting to create a respectful and compassionate atmosphere in which people with mental health problems could be treated (see Digby, 1985; Tuke, 1813/1996). This 'moral treatment era', as it became known, was arguably the first psychologically informed approach for dealing with madness in an institutional context. It inspired the building of local asylums across Britain and Europe in the first half of the 19th century.

Initial optimism waned as asylums became larger and overcrowded due to increasing numbers of people coming through their doors fuelled by large-scale migration from rural areas. The founding principles and values of moral treatment – humanity, understanding, compassion – became more difficult to sustain and less influential in these new institutions. Scientific developments also shifted attention away from compassionate principles of management towards the search for a biological 'cure' (e.g. the spirochete basis of syphilis). There was also an increasing interest in identifying and cataloguing varieties of madness (diagnosis).

Two world wars, and the advent of psychoanalysis, reopened an interest in psychological approaches in institutions, specifically for the treatment of 'war neurosis' (or 'shell shock'), which had been first identified in the First World War. It was estimated that between 20 and 50 per cent of all military discharges resulted from psychological trauma (Bourke, 2001). During World War II, psychologists also became involved in selection and training of military personnel and the detection and prevention of malingering (Bourke, 2001). Several hospital settings were used to treat what would now be regarded as 'post-traumatic stress disorder', one being Mill Hill Emergency Hospital, where in 1942 Hans Eysenck was appointed as a research psychologist.

The beginning of clinical psychology in the NHS

After the war Mill Hill was reconstituted at Camberwell and became the new Institute of Psychiatry with Eysenck as Head of Psychology (see chapters 8 and 9). Eysenck and Raven at the Crichton Royal Hospital in Dumfries developed personality and psychometric tests (see chapter 10) which were framed as the application of psychology to clinical work and essentially 'objective' and 'scientific' approaches to the study of human behaviour. They formed the start of clinical psychology in the NHS.

By the 1950s British clinical psychology's psychometric phase was acceding to a new interest in 'therapy', this time not using psychodynamic ideas, but established learning theory which became known as 'behaviour therapy' (see chapter 14). Eysenck, Shapiro, Gywnne Jones, Vic Meyer and others argued there was an established body of objective, scientific knowledge based on learning principles available to support these new therapies.

Eysenck, and later figures such as S. 'Jack' Rachman and Andrew Mathews, developed other behavioural treatments – desensitisation, flooding, response prevention and aversion therapy (e.g. Mathews, 1978) – which students were duly trained to administer. These early behaviourists, led by Eysenck, also began a fierce criticism of existing psychological treatments (i.e. psychodynamic approaches) as being 'unscientific', arguing that they must be replaced by these new treatments (see chapter 14) and be evaluated using the highest experimental research (randomised controlled trials). Concurrently, Shapiro and others were developing a much more phenomenological approach, using a single case methodology, with idiopathic outcome measures. Shapiro believed in the role of clinical psychologists as 'applied scientists' (e.g. Shapiro, 1966). His approach was based on a belief that people were unique and that psychology's job was to find what helped each individual. Interventions would be highly personalised and related to the individual's particular difficulties and circumstances. This was the beginning of very divergent views on the most appropriate direction for applied clinical psychology. While Shapiro was advocating for individual uniqueness and clinical psychology's role to help tailor individual approaches, Eysenck, Rachman and colleagues (later including David Clark and Paul Salkovskis) were establishing standardised approaches with fidelity to generalised treatment models.

De-institutionalisation – moving out of the mental hospital

Meanwhile there were significant changes happening in the pattern of psychiatric services based in the old institutions. After 1945, an emphasis on human rights and collective responsibilities facilitated the development of the welfare state and the NHS itself. When the NHS was established in 1948 the mental hospitals were included in its provisions (in fact they only just avoided being part of the new local social services departments).

In 1954 there were 154,000 patients in long-stay mental health institutions, comprising about 40 per cent of NHS inpatient beds yet receiving only 20 per cent of hospital funding. The Mental Health Act 1959 identified the community as the most appropriate place of care for people with mental health problems and in 1961 the Health Minister, Enoch Powell, gave his famous 'water tower' speech in which he announced his intention to halve the number of beds for people with mental health problems within the next 15 years. The 1962 Hospital Plan advanced a vision for developing acute inpatient units for people with mental health problems on district general hospital sites, proposing that local authorities should provide a range of services to support people in the community. These views were based on an ideological consensus that the old institutions were not fit places for people to live and that patients could have better, more fulfilling, and higher quality lives in the community. At the time there was actually little evidence to support this view.

However, evidence was soon forthcoming. Wing and Brown (1970) studied patients in three long-stay hospitals between 1960 and 1968 and found their lives were severely limited by the institutionalised nature of their environments, in particular the lack of meaningful activity. Investigations into the ill-treatment of patients in asylums in England and Wales including Ely, Farleigh and Whittingham (DHSS, 1969, 1971, 1972) gave further impetus for closing the old asylums. Thus by 1974 there were 100,000 residents in asylums, 50,000 fewer than 20 years previously. Many of those people who remained were elderly, with a mix of physical and mental health problems. However, community services had not yet developed significantly and the first large-scale planned hospital closures, with associated community service provisions, did not take place until the 1980s. Clinical psychologists were often at the forefront of these developments (see Box 17.1).

One of the next big influences was a psychiatrist – Douglas Bennett. He came to the Maudsley in 1962 and became interested not only in improving the quality of day-to-day interactions between staff and patients, but also the organisation of long-term care settings to include greater emphasis on individual care planning and structured activities. His views were essentially psychological and social, and were summarised in a classic textbook on psychiatric rehabilitation coauthored with a clinical psychologist, Fraser Watts (Watts & Bennett, 1983). Both his ideas and practice had a profound influence on a generation of clinical psychologists, beginning with David Griffiths and Fraser Watts and going on to include Isobel Morris, Geoff Shepherd, Rachel Perkins and Philippa Garety.

In 1977 the 'ward-in-a-house' scheme was established at 111 Denmark Hill. Evaluations demonstrated that people with severe and long-term mental health problems could benefit from a carefully structured, therapeutic environment, rather than the passive custodialism that characterised the old institutions.

Around the same time there was also an interest in the application of behav-

Box 17.1 From Shepherd (1984)

...people gradually became interested in shifting the balance of care for the long-term mentally ill back towards the community and away from the hospital. Care in the community thus consists of attempting to provide as many services as possible, for as many as possible, from a community rather than a hospital base. Hence, we should be careful to distinguish between 'care in the community' and 'care by the community'. The community must not be expected to provide care by itself. This would place an unrealistic responsibility on families, voluntary organisations, etc., and while it is necessary, indeed desirable, that informal care-givers should make a significant contribution to the care of the long-term mentally ill they should not be asked to accept intolerable burdens. (G. Shepherd, 1984)

Box 17.2 111 Denmark Hill

One other scheme which I am proud to have been involved in was 111 Denmark Hill, a ward-in-a-house for patients needing a longer hospital stay than is usual today. Its operation owes most to Herman Afele and Sue Lewis who were the senior nurses and to Isobel Morris and Philippa Garety, the psychologists. There have always been psychologists in charge of the day to day working of the unit, although its operation was my responsibility. Together we devised a plan with a view to providing for the non-institutional operation of what is essentially an institution. The psychologists looked back to the work of King, Raynes and Tizard and adopted their principles for countering institutionalism. The second step was to institute rehabilitation programmes; having discussed the patient's problems with the staff and having agreed an order of priority, members of the staff sought to deal with only two patient problems at a time and to make charts on which the patient's compliance with the programme was recorded four times a day. The third step was to recognise that the staff were the only form of therapy and that this unrewarding work put them under great strain in terms of their relationships with other staff and patients. We took account of their needs in a weekly meeting taken by a psychotherapist from outside the unit who acted as a referee and elucidated some of the conscious and unconscious causes of our discontents. The psychologists also prepared graphs to show whether the daily charts were or were not demonstrating any progress in our rehabilitation programme. We never really established why the programme was so successful; was it the diffusion of conflict or the feedback of results or was it the staff involvement in all decisions or was it a combination of all three? (Bennett, 1994)

ioural principles of reinforcement to change behaviour and improve functioning of patients on long-stay wards in institutions. This was known as the 'token economy'. Psychologists were involved in setting up, running and evaluating these programmes (e.g. Hall & Baker, 1973; and Box 17.3).

Token economies were popular in the 1960s and 1970s but fell out of favour from the 1980s as services became more community-based (see also Chapter 14). Reflecting now, they are an uncomfortable reminder of a period in which most psychologists thought entirely of doing things 'to' patients, rather than 'with'

Box 17.3 Powick Hospital in Worcestershire

Then one of the psychiatrists asked me to set up a token economy in one of the long stay wards. This is a system in which patients showing good behaviours are given tokens, which they can save up to get real rewards. Some of these patients have gradually become mute over the years, possibly because they don't have any need to speak. The institution provides all their needs whether they ask for them or not. From now on these patients will be given tokens for any words (or even grunts) uttered. After collecting a few tokens, their prize will be a cigarette.

Giving them cigarettes would never have occurred to me, but the nurses insist that this is the only realistic option. *They will do anything for a cigarette.* (Smith, 2011)

them. Recovery-based ideas of today place patients at the centre of the process and emphasise the importance of helping them identify their goals and then assisting them towards these, while encouraging as much choice and control as possible.

The growth of the profession

By 1974, of 585 psychologists employed in the NHS, 470 were working in mental hospitals. In *Better Services for the Mentally Ill* (DHSS, 1975) their significant contribution to the treatment of mentally ill patients was acknowledged and an increase in activity and numbers recommended. This report acknowledged the existence of separate psychology departments, but also called for psychologists to act as full members of the mental health multidisciplinary team, retaining contact with both primary care and social services staff.

The Trethowan Report (DHSS, 1977; see chapters 1, 6 and 23) was a milestone influenced by Frank MacPherson's Tayside Area Clinical Psychology Service. It focused exclusively on the role of clinical psychologists in health services and pointed to the shift in role from assessment to treatment provision with reference to behaviour therapy and token economies.

Subsequent recommendations covered the organisation and relationships of psychologists to other professions, in particular where they should work (hospital vs. community) and from whom they should take referrals (psychiatrists vs. GPs). The role of psychology in teaching other professions, including medical practitioners, was prominently endorsed, as was psychologists' contribution to research. Clinical psychologists were recognised for the first time as having full professional status and being responsible for their own practice. With the ensuing transfer of mental health services into district general hospitals in the latter half of the 1970s a variety of psychology services were developed. Increasing numbers of psychologists gradually formed themselves into departments taking on management and governance functions. Meanwhile, in addition to the psychologists who continued to work in the asylums, new contributions were developed. These included psychological and psychotherapeutic group therapy programmes in day hospitals, support for newly emerging specialist services like 'mothers and babies' units in acute ward settings and eating disorder units. 'Therapeutic communities' (which used many of the principles of moral treatment) also developed, based in hospital wards and other residential settings (Kennard, 2004). These organisationally based interventions contained an overriding aspiration to use all kinds of psychological knowledge to support and develop services at the individual level, but also at the levels of services and communities.

By the late 1970s and early 1980s community mental health centres (CMHCs) had started to be established, often in advance of a planned hospital closure. These early CMHCs arose out a recognition of the dangers of new community provisions neglecting previous long-stay patients which had been identified in the 'de-institutionalisation' movement in the US. CMHCs were only ever partially successful, partly because of the tension between prioritising the needs of relatively small numbers of people with the most severe problems over very large numbers with lesser problems (Patmore & Weaver, 1991).

In the 1970s CMHC developments were coupled with the desire to provide a much wider range of mental health services at a local level and promote less stigmatised access. Many psychologists took advantage of these opportunities to provide both a psychological therapies service to primary care and ongoing support for people who had previously lived in an institution and were often now living in supported housing on the periphery of the old hospital sites, or in local group homes. Many people also found their way into accommodation in the private sector, albeit often insecure and of dubious quality. At this time, psychologists working in social services settings created their own national network and shared innovative practices regarding social integration and community participation in day centres set up as part of hospital reprovision programmes.

Again, with a backdrop of running down the old institutions and increasing numbers of reprovision programmes, a variety of inter-professional collaborations came about, such as the Interdisciplinary Association of Mental Health Workers formed in 1983. This was one of the first explicit alliances with the growing service user movement. The latter saw its more public beginnings with groups like 'Survivors Speak Out' and 'Mad Pride' which, for the first time, recognised that professionals might have mental health issues themselves. Some psychologists worked in partnership with these groups, especially those who were involved in deinstitutionalisation (see also chapter 2). In one area (Bromley) the reprovision programme funded a local service user-led group as early as 1987. These initiatives resulted in hospital patients' parents, spouses and siblings being supported and genuinely involved in the closure programme. Psychologists participating in reprovision planning teams also engaged in educational work with families within the increasing number of multidisciplinary rehabilitation and resettlement teams. Research by George Brown had demonstrated the paradoxical finding that patients resettled from the old institutions and into their families had poorer outcomes than those resettled to non-familial settings. This gave rise to research on psychosocial factors contributing to relapse in schizophrenia and the concept of expressed emotion (Vaughn & Leff, 1976).

Many of these teams came to be formally led by clinical psychologists who had gained their experience and expertise in the earlier, less systematic closure programmes and in some of the more pioneering CMHC settings. This work was facilitated by increasing interest in psychological approaches to managing psychotic symptoms for individuals and families, led by the work of Ian Falloon in Buckingham, Philippa Garety and Elizabeth Kuipers in London, Max Birchwood and Jo Smith in Birmingham, Christine Barrowclough and Nick Tarrier in Manchester and Richard Bentall in Liverpool, among others.

By 1985 the principles of effective care in the community were beginning to be established while clinical psychologists used the experience gained from the process of institutional closure to inform their contribution to the development of community services. Planned and systematic hospital closure programmes were being established with reprovision teams (rehabilitation and resettlement) set up in every region. The models mentioned above all had their place, as did recommendations on employment support, housing and increasing emphasis on effective teamwork to support people with both long-term mental illness in the community and in primary care. This was a time of enormous enthusiasm and creativity among many mental health professions with clinical psychologists, alongside colleagues, often becoming team leaders in resettlement programmes.

These early developments in community care were influenced by theoretical developments in the social disability field, notably the ideas of Wolf Wolfensberger on 'normalisation' and 'social role valorisation' (Wolfensberger, 1983). Multidistrict reprovisions such as Darenth Park in Kent, serving several London and Kent boroughs, acted as organisational precursors to the later mental health closure programmes and demonstrated important lessons which informed adult mental health services. They were supported by many of the same planning and development staff in the regional offices of the time, including some psychologists who transferred between client groups. In these early experiments in small group housing, many of the models later championed by mental health psychologists were taken straight from learning disability services. The contribution of psychologists working in learning disability to the development of services for adults with long-term and severe problems, therefore, needs to be clearly acknowledged.

Psychologists working in these new settings needed good support systems because they were often operating as 'sole practitioners'. This was provided by local and regional groups and, around this time (1987), the BPS DCP Special Interest Group in Psychosocial Rehabilitation was established with 150 members countrywide. This group went on to become the Psychosis and Complex Mental Health Faculty of the BPS in 2003 with, by then, more than 500 members. The importance of these voluntarily organised professional networks cannot be underestimated. In London the notes of the local group from 1987 show the presence of 10 members, now leading psychologists, all involved in rehabilitation and resettlement clinical roles, who later took leadership roles in managerial and research activities. Similar gatherings across other regions provided mutual support and facilitated the flow of 'practice-based evidence' which could then be critiqued and shared. This contributed to the thinking and evidence used in policies to create specialised teams – crisis resolution and home treatment, assertive outreach, early intervention – which later became the key building blocks of the National Service Framework (NSF) for mental health (Department of Health, 1999).

As these teams developed, clinical psychologists took on varying roles from individual clinicians to team leaders. One of the most important was to develop the team's capacity to produce psychological formulations of patients' difficulties, that is, a psychological and social understanding of the range of factors influencing course and outcomes. They also helped with teamwork (Onyett, 2003) and case management (Onyett, 1998). Psychologists were also influential in facilitating practices in specific teams. For example, Cupitt et al. (2013) describes the model workings of assertive outreach teams, her own position on this having been derived from experience as a psychologist in one of the first voluntary sector organisations to provide support for vulnerable people with long-term mental health problems living in West London. Similarly, Birchwood (1995) developed early intervention in psychosis services based on the example of Pat McGorry in Australia. This was an early example of CBT for psychosis in the British context. As indicated earlier, there was also a growing interest in services for families, such as the Somerset Family Service (Burbach & Stanbridge, 1998) and the Meriden family programme in Birmingham (Fadden & Birchwood, 2002).

Once the NSF was established the creation of the National Institute for Mental Health in England (NIMHE) and subsequently the Care Services Improvement Partnership (CSIP) afforded opportunities for psychologists to take part in further innovation. These included 'New Ways of Working' (Onyett, 2007); employment (e.g. Perkins & Rinaldi, 2002; Perkins et al., 2009); social inclusion (e.g. Davis & Turpin, 2004); and most recently, recovery (e.g. Perkins & Slade, 2012; G. Shepherd et al., 2008). These approaches are now becoming fully incorporated into service developments and, despite the threats from current austerity policies, they are increasingly recognised as essential components of modern mental health care.

Diversification

Work with primary care

Increased interest during the 1970s in engaging directly in the community led to work in GP surgeries and health centres. Early reports highlighted the advantages of individual therapy in this setting, with psychologists operating as the first point of contact between service user and doctor (e.g. Broadhurst, 1972). The first published record of a clinical psychologist being appointed to a primary care post was in 1975 (McAllister & Phillip, 1975). The role of a psychologist was in an integrated health team, seeing both adults and children who often had behavioural and emotional problems resulting from physical illness or disability. It also suggested a role for psychologists in improving doctor–patient communication and in training other members of the team to use psychological methods (Broadhurst, 1977).

An emerging dilemma was the tension between an 'individual' versus 'organisational' focus. Should work be about providing specialist psychological therapy in a more accessible, nonstigmatising environment? Or should it aim to increase the effectiveness of the primary health care team, through collaborative work with GPs, district and practice nurses and health visitors, providing consultation, training, supervision and joint work? Salmon (1984) argued that there were dangers in adhering to a 'specialist' model of treatment in which the primary care team transferred responsibility for treatment to the psychologist. Scarce clinical psychologists would only be able to treat a small subset of all the people who could benefit. A second problem was the loss of opportunity for psychologist and GP to learn from each other's differing knowledge of a service user's history. A wider group of people would benefit from psychological knowledge if GPs and nurses could be trained to draw on a psychological approach in their own work.

Many psychologists saw their role in primary care as being a 'generalist' one, acting as the first point of assessment for those presenting with a mental health problem, sometimes seeing people across the life span and helping those with psychological problems related to physical illness. Psychologists could mirror the GP's role, by working to a short timescale with service users on particular aspects of their difficulties, with the opportunity for them to return when needed to work on another aspect. This provided valuable continuity rather than a 'complete' treatment in the short term. Many GPs felt supported by the relationship with clinical psychologists as on-site professional colleagues.

By the 1990s primary care psychology was becoming established as a specialty in its own right. In 1991 the first English Primary Care Psychology Conference was convened following regular meetings between the Tower Hamlets and Bexley services. A steering group was set up to establish a Special Interest Group and the production of a primary care psychology newsletter. Regular special interest meetings took place in some local areas, such as South London, in which ideas for good practice were shared. The opportunity for networking was significant at a time when primary care psychology services were not always seen as being part of core mental health work and potentially vulnerable.

In 1994 a special edition of *Clinical Psychology Forum* featured primary care and described how psychologists had developed their role to be 'responsive to the context, wanted by GPs, and not heavily dependent on large numbers of psychologists' (Day & Wren, 1994). Again, the emphasis not only focused on treatment of individual service users, but also on providing consultation to the whole primary care team in relation to clinical cases and other areas such as organisational issues and communication skills (Casey et al., 1994). A 'partnership model' addressed joint work and liaison with GPs and other members of the primary health care team (Donnison & Burd, 1994) and service developments were described that were racially and culturally appropriate (Mahtani & Marks, 1994).

For Mary Burd, a pioneer of primary care clinical psychology from the 1970s onwards, it was clear that partnership with GPs was crucial (Box 17.4). The psychologist became a mental health member of the primary care team, for whom patients were 'a joint venture...they weren't "my patients"' (Mary Burd, personal communication, 23 October 2014). Many service users whose problems were often no less severe or complex than those seen in secondary care could be contained within a primary care setting (see Box 17.4).

In the 1980s and 1990s many practices employed counsellors to work on site, so 'primary care counselling' developed alongside primary care psychology. Although this situation presented some challenges (e.g. Miller, 1994) most psychology services collaborated with their counsellor colleagues to increase the range of therapeutic approaches and to support GPs with standards of clinical governance and monitoring the effectiveness of psychological interventions in primary care (e.g. M. Shepherd et al., 2005, 2007).

The NHS Plan in 2000 proposed two new groups of mental health workers in primary care: gateway workers (GWs) and graduate mental health workers (GMHWs). The aim was for 1000 new GMHWs to be appointed by 2004 to receive training and provide brief interventions for people with mild to moderate mental health problems in primary care, with a community resource and enablement

Box 17.4 Tower Hamlets Primary Care Psychology and Counselling
From its inception, this service has been driven by a clear model and vision based around partnerships with GP practices and primary care staff, as well as the local community. In the early 1980s Mary Burd's vision was that the psychologist became an integral part of primary care, where the task was providing advice about how to understand and, therefore, manage patients. The key was using regular presence in the practice to raise the profile of mental health issues. Mary retired shortly before IAPT came to Tower Hamlets when Lucy Marks and Maria Casey integrated IAPT into the existing primary care psychology and counselling service as Compass Wellbeing Community Interest Company, a social enterprise (Lucy Marks, personal communication, 30 November 2014).

focus (see chapter 8). Many primary care trusts directly employed the GMHWs and, predictably, the implementation of GMHWs and GWs was variable across England. Seeing the potential to improve access to psychologically informed approaches within primary care, many clinical psychologists took on lead roles and often provided clinical supervision (M. Shepherd & Rosairo, 2008). Services recognised for good practice included those in Salford, Gloucestershire (DH, 2007) and Great Yarmouth and Waveney, which reduced onward referral to secondary services by 85 per cent and acute admissions by 40 per cent (DH, 2006).

Meanwhile services were developing a range of ways to provide help for psychological and psychosocial problems in the local community which went well beyond a focus on individual therapy. One of the best known examples of this is the STEPS service in Glasgow (White, 2008). This began in November 2004 and made use of a stepped care model, with a menu of self-selection services that users could access, including a stress control class, advice clinic, First Steps Support Group, advice phone line, Steps out of Stress (self-help booklet series), website, book prescribing and healthy reading, as well as opportunities for brief individual therapy, group therapy and single contacts with a therapist. Partnership working was seen as very important.

The 2004 NICE guidelines for depression and anxiety problems recommended that evidence-based therapies should be provided for all people suffering from depression and anxiety, much of this in a primary care setting, using a stepped care model. Clinical psychologists took on significant roles advising on guideline implementation and were creative in developing plans for group work and self-help in order to increase the availability of therapy, particularly cognitive behavioural therapy. From this point onwards there was a shift towards the idea of 'evidence-based practice' driving service development, rather than local service developments supported by 'practice-based evidence'.

IAPT

David Clark, Head of Psychology at the Institute of Psychiatry, and the economist Richard Layard, presented an internal briefing paper to the Cabinet Office in 2004 arguing that society would benefit if more resources were available for psychological therapies for anxiety and depression, as recommended by the NICE guidelines. This, together with other arguments, led to the 2005 Labour election manifesto pledge to increased access to psychological therapies. The Layard report on depression and anxiety was then presented to the Department of Health (Centre for Economic Performance, 2006) and paved the way for IAPT. It envisaged benefits, mainly in terms of reduced personal distress, but also the cost-effectiveness of returning people to employment through treating their psychological symptoms (see chapters 6 and 14 for more details). Rolled out gradually from 2008, IAPT has secured unprecedented investment in psychological approaches with clear standards on training, supervision and outcomes monitoring.

For existing local psychology services, well integrated with primary care, it was challenging to be asked to conform to a 'top-down' prescriptive model. IAPT seemed an almost entirely 'symptom-based' approach – a psychological version of the 'medical model' – with the emphasis on standardised approaches to 'treatment' and 'cure' and little attention to the influence of social issues on aetiology or outcomes. It also stood in sharp contrast to a broader vision of primary care psychology involving close collaboration with the primary health care team and a flexible approach to the provision of therapy. However, most lead primary care psychologists, particularly trained cognitive behavioural therapists, pragmatically decided to work with this new approach in order to access the increase in resources.

Many led on implementation and acted in a supervisory and training role for this new workforce of 'high intensity' cognitive behaviour therapists and 'low intensity' workers ('psychological well-being practitioners'), providing guided self-help. Important innovations included the introduction of the stepped care service model, use of telephone triage and telephone therapy, session-by-session outcome monitoring and, in many cases, a system for self-referrals together with active outreach to facilitate access for black and minority ethnic groups.

A notable service, grounded in community psychology values and principles, was established by Liz Howells. The 'LIFT psychology' service in Swindon and Wiltshire was developed some years before the IAPT initiative but has now become a leading IAPT service. LIFT continues to be user-centred and steered, offers open access psychological therapies and, importantly, links with local groups and communities to develop ways of supporting people to deal effectively with common mental health problems.

In 2011 the Department of Health published *Talking Therapies: A Four-year Plan of Action* (DH, 2011) for completion of the roll-out of IAPT for adults with depression or anxiety disorders, with a greater emphasis on accessibility for older adults and people with long-term physical conditions and medically unexplained symptoms. It included expanding access to psychological therapies for people with severe mental illness.

Applications of community psychology approaches

Alongside the structural and procedural innovation of the 1980s onwards many clinical psychologists took part in service development and community engagement, often using approaches derived from community psychology, liberation psychology, social disability theory and empowerment models. Building on values expressed during the period of de-institutionalisation from earlier influences beyond the UK, community psychology developed practices of enabling choice and self-determination, enhancing empowerment, consciousness raising, community organising and building social capital. These developments have been very important. This chapter cannot do justice to the full history of community psychology in Britain which, by definition, concerns itself with communities rather than groups or individuals, and the interested reader is referred to Burton et al. (2007) for a thorough overview of the history of UK community psychology.

A notable example, though, of a community psychology approach which influenced many clinical psychologists was Sue Holland's work with depressed women on the White City estate in London (Holland, 1988). Holland's approach was grounded in feminism and began with individual psychotherapy 'psychic space', progressing to involvement in groups 'social space' and then to collective social action 'political space'. Mental health was reframed so that instead of being seen as private individual distress it came to be seen in a societal context. David Smail was another key figure and an early pioneer of therapeutic communities. As head of Nottingham clinical psychology department from 1969 he sought to expose the damaging psychological effects of an increasingly competitive and unequal society (see Box 17.5). During the Thatcher years, Smail became increasingly vocal about the toxic effects of the misuse of power and disillusioned with what he saw as hubristic claims made for talking therapies (e.g. Smail, 1995, 2005). In 2002 he founded the Midlands Psychology Group of academic and therapeutic psychologists who consider distress from a socialist materialist perspective.

Another influential figure promoting community psychology concepts was Jim Orford, who worked from a clinical base in mental health and addictions (e.g. Orford, 2008). Orford offered encouragement, advice, support and legitimacy for many of those trying to work community psychology, often in isolation. In a review of Orford's book on community psychology (Orford, 2008), David Smail described community psychology as 'the only credible destination for the applied discipline of clinical psychology' (Smail, 2010).

At an organisational level, community approaches were successfully developed by Bender (1972) and Tully et al. (1978). Michael Bender established a whole department of mostly clinically trained psychologists in the London Borough of Newham's Social Services Department. This offered an alternative to the NHS way of working and made psychology accessible to communities. After Bender left in 1988 there was a move of colleagues into the NHS in Newham, Tower Hamlets, Hackney and Haringey but in many cases the emphasis and approach continued. In Newham, it remained a contractual obligation for all staff to spend half a day a week on community psychology. Despite these inspiring initiatives, community psychology approaches have been difficult to legitimise in mainstream health services.

Working with people in complex systems

Throughout these developments a number of continuing tensions have emerged. One is the conflict between trying to keep up with the needs of individuals in distress with limited psychology resources versus trying to do something to develop

Box 17.5 Community psychology in Nottingham (extract from Bostock et al., 2015, p.7)

Designated Community Psychology roles in Nottingham enabled us to work with people in the communities where we also had clinical responsibilities, for example a women's action for health group inspired by working with Sue Holland (Fenner, 1999) and a men's health action project (Melluish & Bulmer, 1999). Participatory action research was effective for working with others to influence developments (Bostock & Beck, 1993). This method set the scene for later work in Northumberland which involved young people (Bostock & Freeman, 2003) and women who had experienced domestic abuse (Bostock et al., 2009). The qualitative research with women who had experienced domestic abuse identified the importance of social processes and found that systems actively reinforced abuse through ineffective protection; failing to address the costs of leaving abusive relationships; and not recognizing the unacceptability of abuse. Services which took the victim's side, offered a common bond and effective, practical help enabled the abuse to be challenged.

Collaborations with African Caribbean parents led to an examination of the implications of power and control in mental health service provision, and of the impact of migration and community self-reliance on the development and amelioration of psychological distress (Fatimilehin & Coleman, 1999). This work informed the development of a culturally competent service for African Caribbean children and families in Nottingham, and several years later, the development of the 'Building Bridges' service in Liverpool that was strongly grounded in community psychology principles (Fatimilehin, 2007).

the 'psychological capital' within the wider community through teaching, coaching, facilitation, research and development work. Many psychologists have tended to try to resolve this conflict by generating 'practice-based evidence' through small-scale research projects to bolster their (and others') arguments for increased resources or greater access to effective care. For the individual practitioner, this may provide a positive solution, but the tension often remains.

An example of how the profession tackled this tension at a systemic level is the transformation of the BPS's Psychosocial Rehabilitation Special Interest Group (SIG) into the Psychosis and Complex Mental Health Faculty. In the late 1990s the attempt to provide high quality therapeutic approaches was reinforced by a growing evidence base reflected in the publication of the NICE guidelines for schizophrenia (NICE, 2002). This focused on the implementation of evidence-based practice in the scientist practitioner mould. The risk seen by the SIG committee at the time was that their hard-won place in being influential in championing the position of severely mentally ill people in service developments might be compromised if delivering evidence-based interventions was seen as the only role for psychologists.

This led to the creation of the Faculty. Led by Fabian Davis, the committee set out to find all the various subgroups of psychologists that were emerging around the country, some of which were already SIG-affiliated and others that were new and related to the NSF's functional teams. The Faculty then brought them together in an alliance that endures to this day. The new Faculty is the largest in the DCP with over 500 members active across all the functional areas mentioned above, including working groups on services for people diagnosed with a personality disorder, family work, assertive outreach, rehabilitation and recovery, small-scale research, increasing diversity, early intervention, social inclusion and latterly home treatment, acute and crisis care. The Faculty was set up by leaders in each of the functional areas and two service user consultants working at a national level, Peter Campbell and Jan Walcraft.

Faculty committee members have since formed alliances with DCP divisions and professional groups and worked across boundaries on socially inclusive practice. Developments since 2010 have focused on implementing the NICE guidelines for schizophrenia and the leadership roles taken by clinical psychologists in the extension of IAPT for SMI (severe mental illness) and stepped care for people with complex mental health problems. The Psychosis Faculty has, therefore, attempted to bridge the gap between individual treatments and organisational change.

Recovery approaches

A second tension underlying the service developments described above is the relationship between professionals delivering evidence-based interventions and the development of roles within mental health services where people can use their lived experience of mental distress to enhance their own and others' recovery. This approach has an increasingly strong evidence base (Repper & Carter, 2011; Trachtenberg et al., 2013) and has raised some fundamental questions about the role of professionals in mental health services. It came to the fore with support and leadership from a range of professionals – nursing, occupational therapy, psychiatry and clinical psychology – and many of these have been prepared to declare their personal experience as an example to others (e.g. Rachel Perkins, Rufus May). At the time of writing, the right balance between 'experts by experience' and 'experts by profession' remains open to debate. It seems likely that the most effective resolution will be to combine both professional and 'user-led' perspectives, with an equal respect for both, in the coproduction of new services. This is the position advocated by organisations like ImROC (Implementing Recovery through Organisational Change; www.ImROC.org) which have supported local services in coproducing a range of new developments – peer support workers, recovery colleges, 'safety planning' – to improve both quality and effectiveness of mental health services.

Themes and persistent questions

This brief and selective history of the work of clinical psychologists with adults has identified some recurring themes and questions.

Should clinical psychologists be concerned with the social context as much as with psychological processes? The period of de-institutionalisation felt a very positive time to be in the profession. Clinical psychology had a lot to say about social change and reintegration into community settings. There was a hope that we could begin a new narrative about mental health in the community with less emphasis on 'mental deficiencies' and hospital treatments, and clinical psychologists were engaged in articulating these ideas. Many felt that the broader agendas of inequality, human rights and social inclusion were consistent with their own broader interests in the factors influencing mental distress and the power of social and cultural factors to shape personal outcomes. These ideas were also consistent with a vague value base of 'wanting to make a positive difference' which had underpinned many peoples' entry into the profession. With a few exceptions, this no longer seems to be the case. Psychologists seem to have been asked to take a narrowly psychological, more medical, view of mental health problems. How does this sit with our basic views of ourselves as applied social scientists with a commitment to social change?

Should clinical psychologists be 'applied scientists' or simply 'technically competent practitioners'? As clinical psychologists have become increasingly encouraged simply to respond to the symptoms of people with mental health issues in the community, so they have become more like 'technicians' – narrowly trained to deliver a narrow range of standardised treatments. Clearly, there is a need for both paradigms. But where is the capacity for innovation, applying new ideas to social and psychological problems, creating new interventions and developing capacity within systems to come from? Have we got the balance right?

Should we concentrate on implementing 'evidence-based practice' or collecting 'practice-based evidence'? Traditionally, clinical psychologists used their scientific skills to research what they did in everyday practice. Somehow this activity seems to have been taken from them by a system of research funding that concentrates research in a few centres, and a system of central audit of practice that determines what will be examined and who will decide what constitutes good outcomes. Of course, everyone benefits from the efforts of expert researchers and well-informed regulators, but surely there is also a place for experienced clinicians, with research training, to look at what they do and see if it meets standards of quality and effectiveness? As a profession, we need to reassert our claim to be capable of critically examining what we do and how it can be improved by being prepared to evaluate local outcomes using good locally collected data.

Can psychologists use leadership skills to increase the capacity of whole systems to manage distress? We need to address the issue of our role in leadership for improvement. Working at a systemic level we could increase capacity of whole systems. There are many examples of this throughout this chapter. We can apply our basic psychological understanding (much acquired prior to clinical training) to the nature of change, how to develop effective relationships, evaluation, the importance of social identity and groups, to help services develop in ways that promote social capital, for example with genuine user involvement and improved care pathways (see Onyett, 2012, for further discussion).

Do psychologists pay enough attention to basic therapeutic skills? We all know that approximately 50 per cent of the variance in any study of the effectiveness of psychological treatments is accounted for by so-called 'non-specific' or relationship factors (Lambert, 1986). No psychological therapist can be effective without being able to create good therapeutic relationships. At the recent launch of the BPS Clinical

Division document on *Understanding Psychosis* (Cooke, 2014) there was a considerable amount of moving testimony from service users about what was important to them in terms of their encounters with professionals, and these centred on very basic relationship factors – an ability to listen, a willingness to understand different perspectives, respect, honesty, a non-judgemental approach, and so on. These skills are certainly not the monopoly of trained clinical psychologists. Indeed, there is some evidence that professional training makes no difference in this respect (Strupp & Hadley, 1979). We certainly have had dramatic instances of failures in these basic skills among some caring professionals in the health service (Francis, 2013). So as psychologists are we comfortable that we pay enough attention to these skills? Do we set them out clearly? Do we select trainees according to these skills as well as research or intellectual skills? Do we audit them routinely in our own practice by asking the people we work with? Do we identify the working conditions that make it more or less likely that they will be squeezed out of our practice? Finally, there is now growing evidence that peer workers – service users with lived experience of mental distress – can be extremely effective in supporting others' recovery. They can't do everything, but working alongside traditional professionals they can bring experience that is uniquely valuable. As psychologists are we prepared to meet this challenge? That would require a really radical transformation in our roles.

Conclusions

Partly because this chapter needed to be relatively brief and partly because of our own, inevitably limited and biased, experience, we have only managed to mention a small selection of the considerable contributions that clinical psychologists have made to services for adults with mental health problems in Britain over the past 50 years. There are many more outstanding examples across all four nations and we apologise for our omissions. A striking feature which is common across all the examples mentioned is the ability to connect with and empathise with people in distress, to demonstrate leadership in this and, by applying basic psychological understanding, to promote capacity within systems to understand and create conditions which enable people to become and give of their best. These are the basic values of our profession. In the current context of austerity and cutbacks they are difficult to hold on to: perhaps that is why they are needed more than ever.

Acknowledgements

Particular thanks to Jan Bostock, Mary Burd, Steve Onyett, Annie Mitchell, Lucy Marks and Melanie Shepherd for their significant contributions to this chapter.

References

Bender, M.P. (1972). The role of the community psychologist. *Bulletin of the British Psychological Society, 27*, 211–218.

Bennett, D. (1994). Interview with Greg Wilkinson, August 1993. *Psychiatric Bulletin, 18*, 622–626. Available at http://pb.rcpsych.org/content/18/10/622.full.pdf

Birchwood, M. (1995). Early intervention in psychotic relapse: Cognitive approaches to detection and management. *Behaviour Change, 12*(1), 2–19.

Bostock, J. & Beck, D. (1993). Participation in social enquiry and action. *Journal of Community and Applied Social Psychology, 3*, 213–224.

Bostock, J., Fatimilehin, I. & Godsi, E. (2015, February). A tribute to David Smail: From Nottingham and beyond. *Clinical Psychology Forum.* David Smail special issue, pp.5–7.

Bostock, J. & Freeman, J. (2003). 'No limits': Doing participatory action research with young people in Northumberland. *Journal of Community and Applied Social Psychology, 13,* 464–474.

Bostock, J., Plumpton, M. & Pratt, R. (2009). Domestic violence against women: Understanding social processes and women's experiences. *Journal of Community and Applied Social Psychology, 19,* 95–110.

Bourke, J. (2001). *The Second World War: A people's history.* Oxford: Oxford University Press.

Broadhurst, A. (1972). Clinical psychology and the general practitioner. *British Medical Journal, 1,* 793–79.

Broadhurst, A. (1977). What part does general practice play in community clinical psychology? *Bulletin of the British Psychological Society, 30,* 305–309.

Burbach, F.R. & Stanbridge, R.I. (1998). A family intervention in psychosis service integrating the systemic and family management approaches. *Journal of Family Therapy, 20,* 311–325.

Burton, M., Boyle, S., Harris, C. & Kagan, C. (2007). Community psychology in Britain. In S. Reich, M. Riemer, I. Prilleltensky & M. Montero (Eds.), *International community psychology: History and theories* (pp.219–237). New York: Kluwer Academic Press.

Casey, M., Harris, R. McDonald, K. & Todd, G. (1994). Opportunities for consultation. *Clinical Psychology Forum, 64,* 36–38.

Centre for Economic Performance (2006). *The depression report. A new deal for depression and anxiety disorders.* London: Author.

Cooke, A. (2014). *Understanding psychosis and schizophrenia: Why people sometimes hear voices, believe things that others find strange, or appear out of touch with reality, and what can help.* Leicester: British Psychological Society.

Davis, F. & Turpin, G. (2004). *DCP evidence presented to the Social Exclusion Unit's enquiry into Social Exclusion and Mental Health.* Leicester: British Psychological Society.

Day, C. & Wren, B. (1994). Journey to the centre of primary care: Primary care psychology in perspective. *Clinical Psychology Forum, 64,* 3–6.

Department of Health (1999). *National service framework for mental health: Modern standards and service models.* London: Department of Health.

Department of Health (2006). *Practice-based commissioning: Early wins and top tips.* London: HMSO.

Department of Health (2007). *Commissioning a brighter future: Improving access to psychological therapies.* London: HMSO.

Department of Health (2011). *Talking therapies: A four-year plan of action.* London: HMSO.

Department of Health and Social Security (1969). *Report on Ely Hospital: Report of the Committee of Inquiry into allegations of ill-treatment of patients and other irregularities at Ely Hospital, Cardiff.* Cmnd 3795. London: HMSO.

Department of Health and Social Security (1971). *Report of the Farleigh Hospital Committee of Inquiry.* Cmnd 4557. London: HMSO.

Department of Health and Social Security (1972). *Report of the Committee of Inquiry into Whittingham Hospital.* Cmnd 4861. London: HMSO.

Department of Health and Social Security (1975). *Better services for the mentally ill.* London: HMSO.

Department of Health and Social Security (1977). *The role of psychologists in the health service (Trethowan Report).* London: HMSO.

Digby, A. (1985). *Madness, morality and medicine: A study of the York Retreat 1796–1914.* Cambridge: Cambridge University Press.

Donnison, J. & Burd, M. (1994). Partnership in clinical practice. *Clinical Psychology Forum, 64,* 15–18.

Fadden, G. & Birchwood, M. (2002). British models for expanding family psychoeducation in routine practice. In H.P. Lefley & D.L. Johnson (Eds.), *Family interventions in mental illness: International perspectives* (pp.25–41). Westport, CT: Praeger.

Fatimilehin, I.A. (2007). Building bridges in Liverpool: Delivering CAMHS to black and minority ethnic children and their families. *Journal of Integrated Care, 15*(3), 7–16.

Fatimilehin, I.A. & Coleman, P.G. (1999). 'You've got to have a Chinese chef to cook Chinese food!' Issues of power and control in the provision of mental health services. *Journal of Community & Applied Social Psychology, 9*(2) 101–117.

Fenner, J. (1999). Our way: Women's action for mental health (Nottingham). *Journal of Community & Applied Social Psychology, 9,* 79–91.

Francis, R. (2013). *Report of the Mid Staffordshire NHS Foundation Trust Public Inquiry.* London: HMSO.

Hall, J. & Baker, R. (1973). Token economy systems: Breakdown and control. *Behaviour Research and Therapy, 11,* 253–263.

Holland, S. (1988). Defining and experimenting with prevention. In S. Ramon & M. Giannichedda (Eds.), *Psychiatry in transition: The British and Italian experiences* (pp.125–137). London: Pluto.

Kennard, D. (2004). The therapeutic community as an adaptable treatment modality across different settings. *Psychiatric Quarterly, 75*(3), 295–307.

Lambert, M.J. (1986). Implications of psychotherapy outcome research for eclectic psychotherapy. In J.C. Norcross (Ed.), *Handbook of eclectic psychotherapy* (pp 436–462). New York: Brunner Mazel.

Mahtani, A. & Marks L. 1994). Developing a primary care service that is racially and culturally appropriate. *Clinical Psychology Forum, 64,* 27–30.

Mathews, A. (1978). Fear-reduction research and clinical phobias. *Psychological Bulletin, 85*(2), 390–404.

McAllister, T.A. & Phillip, A. (1975). The clinical psychologist in a health centre: One year's work. *British Medical Journal, 4,* 513–4.

Melluish, S. & Bulmer, D. (1999). Rebuilding solidarity: An account of a men's health action project. *Journal of Community & Applied Social Psychology, 9,* 93–100.

Miller, R. (1994). Clinical psychology and counselling in primary care: Opening the stable door. *Clinical Psychology Forum, 64,* 11–14.

National Institute for Clinical Excellence (NICE) (2002). *Schizophrenia: Core interventions in the treatment and management of schizophrenia in primary and secondary care.* London: Author.

Onyett, S.R. (1998). *Case management in mental health.* Cheltenham: Stanley Thornes.

Onyett, S.R. (2003). *Teamworking in mental health.* London: Palgrave

Onyett, S.R. (2007). *New ways of working for applied psychologists in health and social care: Working psychologically in teams.* Leicester: British Psychological Society.

Onyett, S.R. (2012). 'Leadership challenges for clinical psychologists' – challenge or opportunity? *Clinical Psychology Forum, 238,* 10–17.

Orford, J. (2008). *Community psychology: Challenges, controversies and emerging consensus.* Chichester: Wiley.

Patmore, C. & Weaver, T. (1991). *Community mental health teams: Lessons for planners and managers.* London: Good Practices in Mental Health.

Perkins, R., Farmer, P. & Litchfield, P. (2009). *Realising ambitions: Better employment support for people with a mental health condition.* London: HMSO.

Perkins, R. & Rinaldi, M. (2002). Unemployment rates among patients with long-term mental health problems. A decade of rising unemployment. *Psychiatric Bulletin, 26,* 295–298.

Perkins, R. & Slade, M. (2012). Recovery in England: Transforming statutory services? *International Review of Psychiatry, 24*(1), 29–39

Repper, J & Carter, T. (2011). A review of the literature on peer support in mental health services. *Journal of Mental Health, 20*(4), 392–411.

Salmon, P. (1984). The psychologist's contribution to primary care: A reappraisal. *Journal of the Royal College of General Practitioners, 34,* 190–193.

Shapiro, M.B. (1966). The single case in clinical-psychological research. *Journal of General Psychology, 74*(1), 3–23.

Shepherd, G. (1984). *Institutional care and rehabilitation.* London: Longman.

Shepherd, G., Boardman, J. & Slade, M. (2008). *Making recovery a reality.* London: Sainsbury Centre for Mental Health.

Shepherd, M., Ashworth, M., Evans, C. et al. (2005). What factors are associated with improvement after brief psychological interventions in primary care? Issues arising from routine outcome measurement to inform clinical practice. *Counselling and Psychotherapy Research, 5,* 273–280.

Shepherd, M., Evans, C., Ashworth, M. et al. (2007). Making CORE-OM data work for you and your service: A primary care psychology and counselling team's experience of routine outcome measurement. *Clinical Psychology Forum, 176,* 10–13.

Shepherd, M. & Rosairo, M (2008). Low-intensity workers: Lessons learned from supervising primary care mental health workers and dilemmas associated with such roles. *Mental Health in Family Medicine, 5*(4), 237–245.

Smail, D. (1995). Power and the origins of unhappiness: Working with individuals. *Journal of Community and Applied Social Psychology, 5*, 347–356.

Smail, D. (2005). *Power, interest and psychology. Elements of a social materialist understanding of distress.* Ross-on-Wye: PCCS Books

Smail, D. (2010) Book reviews. *Journal of Community & Applied Social Psychology, 20*, 433–434.

Smith, G. (2011). *From tests to therapy: A personal history of clinical psychology.* Leicester: Matador.

Strupp, H.H. & Hadley, S.W. (1979). Specific vs. non-specific factors in psychotherapy: A controlled study of outcome. *Archives of General Psychiatry, 36*(10), 1125–1136.

Tuke, S. (1996). *Description of the Retreat: An institution near York for insane persons of the Society of Friends.* London: Process Press. (Original work published 1813)

Tully, B., Doyle, M., Cahill, D. et al. (1978). Psychology and community work in mental health. *Bulletin of the British Psychological Society, 31*, 115–119.

Trachtenberg, M., Parsonage, M., Shepherd, G. & Boardman, J. (2013). *Peer support in mental health care: Is it good value for money?* London: Centre for Mental Health.

Vaughn, C.E. & Leff, J.P. (1976). The influence of family and social factors on the course of psychiatric illness. A comparison of schizophrenic and depressed neurotic patients. *British Journal of Psychiatry, 129*, 125–137.

Watts, F.N. & Bennett, D.H. (1983). *Theory and practice in psychiatric rehabilitation.* Chichester: Wiley.

White, J. (2008). Stepping up primary care. *The Psychologist, 28*, 844–847.

Wing, J.K. & Brown, G.W. (1970). *Institutionalisation and schizophrenia: A comparative study of three mental hospital, 1960–1968.* Cambridge: Cambridge University Press.

Wolfensberger, W. (1983). Social role valorization: A proposed new term for the principle of normalisation. *Mental Retardation, 21*(6), 234–239.

Chapter 18 Intellectual disability: Making sense and making a difference

Jennifer Clegg

Largely in the aftermath of the Second World War a small group of genial, razor-sharp psychologists became involved in intellectual disability (ID),[1] among them Jack and Barbara Tizard and Ann and Alan Clarke. Alan Clarke underlined that Ann, his wife and fellow psychologist, was awarded her PhD at 21. Both the Clarkes and Barbara Tizard got PhDs at the Maudsley, benefitting from challenging weekly seminars but effectively without any supervision. Jack Tizard had studied both psychology and philosophy in New Zealand, the latter with Karl Popper who later maintained that Jack was the best student he had had. Patterns of Residential Care (King et al., 1971), one of the many projects which Tizard planned and got funded, was described by Mittler (2010) as having influenced government thinking for the next 25 years.

Segal (1991) observed that many pioneers in ID had been displaced or were in some way strangers. Herbert Gunzburg was a refugee before the war, Peter Mittler and Beate Hermelin during it. Mittler travelled to England alone aged eight after Kristallnacht and was most grateful to be welcomed into an English family. Much later, he reported choosing to study psychology instead of anthropology because Frederick Bartlett opened the department's door and made him feel welcome.

Others came from New Zealand or Australia to study at British universities, including psychologists Neil O'Connor and Jack Tizard, and Aubrey Lewis the Maudsley psychiatrist who appointed them to research ID. Some experienced unorthodox upbringings. Jack Tizard was an orphan brought up by aunts who were committed Christians, both parents having died of TB by the time he was three. Alan Clarke's mother died as a result of medical negligence when he was 14, 'a bitter blow'. Ann Clarke described her childhood as 'exotic and happy': her parents were teachers in India and her Danish mother was also a Quaker missionary. Ann was home-schooled in Madras by a Danish governess, returning to England to matriculate from an English school so that she could attend university.

These psychologists were committed to changing society by improving the lot of the marginal: fortunately, they chose to do so by working with people who have ID.

---

[1] Intellectual disability is the current international term for people with significantly lower cognitive abilities and adaptive skills who require support. They have been referred to previously using many different terms, including 'mental handicap', 'mental retardation' and 'learning difficulties', and they continue to be referred to with the term 'learning disability' in UK policy documents. ID is used throughout unless citing or quoting.

Scope and sources

This chapter addresses the development of ID clinical psychology from the Second World War up to publication of the five National Development Group pamphlets (DHSS, 1976–1977) under Peter Mittler. It is grounded in interviews with ID psychologists selected for the BPS History of Psychology Centre's oral history project: Barbara Tizard, Peter Mittler, Ann and Alan Clarke. It is informed by autobiographies (Mittler, 2010; B. Tizard, 2010), biographies and festschrifts (A.D.B Clarke and B. Tizard, 1983; B. Tizard and Varma, 1983; Segal and Varma, 1991), and obituaries of A.D.B. Clarke, Cliff Cunningham, Herbert Gunzburg, Beate Hermelin, Neil O'Connor and Jack Tizard. It considers how psychology features in histories of (largely) British ID written by historians. It draws on BPS Council Minutes 1960–1974 in Wellcome Archives and Manuscripts PSY/BPS/1/3/8a; 9, 9a, 10, 10a, 106; on the Wellcome archive on Raven PSY/RAV/2/; on the timeline of events related to abnormal and clinical psychology abstracted and updated from Geoff Bunn's BPS chronology (Appendix 1); and on these early psychologists' key publications.

Following orientation to people, places and practices the chapter considers the different kinds of people who have been in and out of the social-administrative category currently called ID, and how different historians of ID see clinical psychology and what the implications of these are. It concludes by looking at one of the ways that these early psychologists made a difference.

Early clinical psychologists

Before the Second World War the Physician Superintendent of Monyhull Hospital in Birmingham, Dr C.J.C. Earle, employed Herbert Gunzburg after he had left Vienna: Gunzburg already had a PhD in psychology. In an address to the Royal Medico-Psychological Association (RMPA) in 1943, Earle apparently argued that hospitals should employ what he called 'clinical psychologists' (reported by Gunzburg, 1992, who believed he was at that time the only psychologist so employed in ID) and give them equal status to doctors. From the outset Earle considered psychologists should not just be testers but also address education, training and social adaptation.

John C. Raven, whose 1936 MSc was carried out with people with ID in London, became Lionel Penrose's research assistant. He administered the Stanford–Binet to all parents and siblings of children identified as 'mentally deficient' in East Anglia. This led to Raven's development of his Standard Progressive Matrices and Coloured Progressive Matrices.

Jack Tizard initially took an academic post in psychology at the University of St Andrews. He was unhappy there, not least because he was separated from his new wife Barbara, who was completing her PPE degree in Oxford. Barbara went on to study psychology as a postgraduate before her PhD at the Maudsley. Jack met Eysenck and Monte Shapiro who recommended him to Aubrey Lewis as he was setting up what became the MRC Social Psychiatry Research Unit at the Maudsley. In 1948 Jack and Neil O'Connor were appointed to research occupational aspects of ID, igniting Jack's commitment to address 'the administrative problems of providing adequate services to meet the needs of the mentally subnormal and their families' (J. Tizard, 1964).

After the Clarkes finished their PhDs, family illness delayed them from taking up Alan's Rockefeller research fellowship in social psychology. Meanwhile, McCarthy set up the Committee on Un-American Activities, so when they went to revalidate their visas their Communist party membership was revealed and the visas cancelled (Clarke & Clarke, 2008). Unemployed, they accepted two vacant clinical psychology posts at the Manor Hospital for people with ID, from which their predecessors had 'bailed out'. Only 16 research papers on ID had been published worldwide by 1948 (B. Tizard, 1983) so their friends were concerned this would ruin promising academic careers. They dug deeply into this potentially demoralising situation for 12 years, applying intelligence, integrity and methodological rigour. Ann said that they just spoke to one another and the patients at Manor, stimulated only by the weekly Maudsley seminars. Barbara Tizard (B. Tizard & Varma, 1992) lauded their willingness to pursue an idea over a long period of time, so bringing immense knowledge to each theme they considered. The Clarkes defied convention by preparing patients for work, not only by finding jobs and teaching job skills, but also by teaching them how to duck questions about where they lived until people got to know them.

Peter Mittler pursued a number of false starts before being appointed probationer clinical psychologist under May Davidson at the Warneford Hospital, Oxford. From there a visit to the Clarkes at the Manor Hospital persuaded him that ID rather than adult mental health was where exciting work was being done that could assuage the social reformer in him (Mittler, 2009). He obtained a clinical psychology post that involved working in a 500-bed ID hospital, very satisfied by working with patient-oriented nurses who were keen to develop rehabilitation programmes.

Places

In parallel with developments in London, a significant locus for ID unfolded in the West Midlands where physician superintendents founded the Midland Mental Deficiency Society in 1952. Gunzburg (1992) described their inaugural meeting as taking the revolutionary step of including nonmedical professionals, further emphasised when he became its second chairman and editor of its *Journal of Mental Subnormality* (eventually the *British Journal of Developmental Disabilities* in 2012).[2] Gunzburg provided a thoughtful and challenging editorial to every issue (Mittler, 1995) during his 40-year editorship.

Nearby, in Worcestershire, Gerry Simon, Medical Director of Lea Castle Hospital, launched the Institute of Mental Subnormality in 1971 (now British Institute of Learning Disabilities). This ran conferences, courses and workshops, publishing good practice guidance and a research digest. Liz Perkins (now Hensel), who worked there from 1972, recalls that publications and training courses were mainly developed by the psychologists who all became tutors to the Institute, and were all behaviourists (Liz Hensel, personal communication, 22 December 2014). At one time about a quarter of all UK clinical psychologists working in ID were estimated to have worked at Lea Hospital or Lea Castle. Behavioural approaches were also promulgated by Janet Carr in London and, for a period, at the Hester Adrian Research Centre (HARC) in Manchester (but see below).

[2] Data tracked by Tony Simmonds, librarian, University of Nottingham.

Aberdeen was also significant for ID. The University had appointed one of the founders of modern psychology, Alexander Bain, Regius Professor of Logic in 1860, and created the UK's first full lectureship in psychology in 1896 (Hearnshaw, 1964). This framed David F. Clark's situation in 1966 when he returned north to Ladysbridge Hospital. There he became top grade clinical psychologist and also clinical senior lecturer in the Department of Mental Health at the University of Aberdeen,[3] with research interests that are remarkably contemporary. His 1984 book summarises a 1966 paper on behaviour therapy for Tourette's syndrome, now highly pertinent to current inclusion of neurodevelopmental disorders within ID services (Clegg et al., 2013). His 1975 PhD on body image and motor skill foreshadowed the current turn towards embodied therapies, for example in psychomotor therapy which makes a significant contribution to challenging behaviour services for ID in continental Europe (see Kay et al., in press). Throughout the 1970s Clark also contributed to BPS working parties concerning clinical psychology in ID.

Aberdeen also hosted two significant ID studies. Voysey-Paun (1975/2006) researched the way mothers respond to discovering their child has ID in a classic qualitative study, A Constant Burden. This showed how their protests about this tragedy die out for want of an audience. Instead, these mothers acquired a narrative which demonstrated their acceptance of an official though implicit ideology: 'I have discovered the true meaning of life' and 'it has made my other children better people'. Around the same time a longitudinal cohort study of children with ID in Aberdeen started to publish its results. Jack Tizard appears to have been midwife to this influential study. He knew that US epidemiologists were looking for a database that could facilitate prospective research so brought a population database established in 1951 in Aberdeen to the attention of a personal friend, Dr Herbert Birch. Birch made funds from the (American) Association for the Aid of Crippled Children available to facilitate follow-up research between 1961 and 1977 that tracked how children with ID entered adulthood. Its authors, Stephen Richardson and Helene Koller (1996), found that the number of children identified as having ID varied significantly over time. Their study must be unique in finding few problems during the transition into adult services, which was attributed to ID having high priority and good funding in Aberdeen at the time.

Another US influence on British ID was the American Association on Mental Deficiency's collaboration with the RMPA and the BPS in the development of a London interdisciplinary conference in 1960. Harvey Stevens in the US planned it with the UK's Alec Shapiro and Alan Clarke: it was the forerunner of the International Association for the Scientific Study of Mental Deficiency (IASSMD) (Clarke, 1991). Now the International Association for the Scientific Study of Intellectual and Developmental Disabilities (IASSIDD), this remains ID's most significant forum for international exchange about research, and for influencing the WHO through congresses and publications (Parmenter, 2004). British psychologists have been significant contributors to it. Alan Clarke was its first Secretary-General in 1964 and then President; Ann and Alan Clarke were jointly honoured with IASSMD's Distinguished Achievement Award in 1982; while from 2004 to 2008

[3] David Findlay Clark, authorised biography, Debrett's, downloaded 15 November 2014.

David Felce (University of Cardiff) and from 2008 to 2012 Glynis Murphy (University of Kent) were IASSIDD presidents.

Manchester was another significant location for ID psychology. The UK's National Association of Mental Health (NAMH) planned a memorial to the late President Jack Kennedy after his assassination in 1963. He had funded Kennedy Centres for research into ID at leading American Universities and the NAMH wanted to raise funds for a similar Kennedy Institute in the UK. However, when NAMH identified Manchester as the site and sought permission from the family to use the Kennedy name it received no reply. Around the same time the chair of the fund-rasing committee, the mental health worker Baroness Adrian, died so it was named the Hester Adrian Research Centre, instead. Peter Mittler was HARC's first Director, from 1968 to 1982: he regarded his clinical experience as essential to its success. HARC aimed to conduct research into psychological, social and educational aspects of services for people with ID, and to disseminate research to staff and parents (Mittler, 2010). It opened during a period of unprecedented political attention to ID led by a Labour Secretary of State, Barbara Castle. In 1975 she created the National Development Group and invited Peter Mittler to chair it. His ability to develop cooperative and problem-solving meetings and to write succinctly resulted in five pamphlets (DHSS, 1976–77) that were very influential.

Practices

These post-war clinical psychologists were idealists who aimed to reveal competencies, resilience and the possibilities of people with ID. Barbara Tizard had been a communist from an early age and she and Jack hosted the Maudsley Communist Party in their flat. This consisted largely of her and Jack, Neil O'Connor, Monte Shapiro, and Ann and Alan Clarke, and was as likely to discuss Pavlov as Marx (B. Tizard, 2010).

They worked hard for their ideals. Jack Tizard's research days were followed by him writing his PhD in the evenings and weekends, while contributing to BPS working parties and advising the National Council for Civil Liberties during its 1947–50 campaign to release patients from ID hospitals. He maintained that pace throughout his life. 'He wanted to change the world, or more specifically to change the lot of underprivileged groups of all kinds. He believed deeply that social science should work for human betterment.' (B. Tizard, 2008). Similarly, after work Ann and Alan Clarke ran evening classes, one of which persuaded Beate Hermelin to study psychology and then devote her life to researching cognitive impairments in children with sensory impairments and autism (Frith, 2009). For Peter Mittler, lectures to social workers at the LSE and teaching in Manchester provided a vehicle for him to convey his 'messianic' approach to ID.

Far from being crushed by doing 1400 IQ tests in their first year, the experience fired Ann and Alan Clarke's curiosity about whether IQs change, and if so under what circumstances. The fact that they knew intimately how long it takes to do an IQ test properly was put to good use when the Clarkes investigated what turned out to be fraudulent research by Cyril Burt. Their suspicions were raised in part by his implausible claim to have done 200 Binet tests in one month (Clarke & Clarke, 2007).

As well as being significant intellectuals and researchers, Barbara Tizard was the primary parent to her five children (two adopted from care), and Ann Clarke to her two. This was before the women's movement changed expectations: while both Jack Tizard and Alan Clarke supported their wife's career, neither provided any childcare. Alan Clarke, Peter Mittler and Jack Tizard all held significant positions within and on behalf of the BPS, Clarke and Tizard as President. Clarke was also heavily involved in the creation and running of IASSMD before he moved directly from clinical practice to a chair at the University of Hull, where ultimately he became its sole pro-vice-chancellor. Tizard and Mittler worked with the WHO and UN, writing position papers and frequently travelling the world to lecture on ID. Mittler observed that while these papers were not explicitly psychological, if he had not been a psychologist he would not have been in a position to write these papers, which he considered to be his greatest contribution. Towards the end of his career, Tizard turned back to research by establishing the Thomas Coram Research Unit in London, which he directed until his death. Barbara reported that Jack was always able to persuade people to give him funds for research: his lively rhetoric and directive conclusions probably helped.

Box 18.1 Inspiring rhetoric: Jack Tizard

In the best studies...the methodological problems have been competently tackled in a way that is scarcely possible in most other branches of psychiatry at present... Though we do not know the answers to many of the problems...we have an idea how to find them. From the expenditure of quite modest sums a rich harvest could be gathered. (J. Tizard, 1964, p.13)

The truth as I see it is, however, that none of our social and health services today are working very well... More clear-cut lines of responsibility, more autonomy, different orientations, better staff training and better staff deployment would do much to change this situation. A continuation of the present system doesn't, I think, offer so much for the future. (J. Tizard, 1973, reprinted in Clarke & B. Tizard, 1983, p.156).

All of these psychologists were clear, persuasive and productive writers. They wrote positively and realistically about people with ID and the iniquitous conditions under which they lived and staff worked, inspiring research and funding. One example is Jack Tizard and Jacqueline Grad's (1961) survey of the families of people with ID in the 1950s, which described nearly half of these children as 'sluggish' (9 per cent), 'restless' (25 per cent), or 'uncontrollable' (9 per cent). Such language sits uncomfortably with today's lexicon, but would be welcomed by parents who object to contemporary euphemisms that fail to acknowledge their difficulties.

A very significant publication affecting clinical practice was Ann and Alan Clarke's magisterial *Mental Deficiency: The Changing Outlook* (1958), which went into four editions (for a review of the huge significance of this work see Hall, 2008). It established a tradition of careful data collection and thoughtful analysis, shifting ID away from the descriptions provided by medical textbooks and towards evidence about interventions that could make a difference.

Mittler (2009) emphasised the importance of working alongside parents and other professionals: 'The really interesting thing about psychology is its intersection with other disciplines.' The Thomas Coram Research Unit was similarly multidisciplinary: '[Jack] was less a psychologist, perhaps, than someone who worked on the boundaries of psychology, medicine, education and the social sciences' (B. Tizard, 1983, p.5). He was also an early exponent of qualitative research, arguing that detailed observational studies of children carried out by skilled people had produced more valuable results than formal experiments (J. Tizard, 1964).

Regular rigorous examination from Lewis and Eysenck made these psychologists value difference and debate. The acknowledgements to an early book display this somewhat gleefully: 'I can think of scarcely a single topic upon which all of these people would be likely to agree' (J. Tizard, 1964, p.3). Despite the appalling conditions they encountered in post-war hospitals and the huge need, these psychologists made sense of the situation of people with ID in ways that made a difference. They did it by finding a problem, researching it, and taking action, but differed widely about what constituted 'a problem'. The Clarkes and Barbara Tizard investigated intriguing differences between received wisdom and what they observed. For Jack Tizard, problems emerged from seeing bad situations he wanted to change, but you could not solve a problem without first really understanding it. Once you did, demonstration projects could show and evaluate how it can be improved but only when they resulted in sustained changes in context. Mittler also focused on problems that needed an agent of social change but his preferred solutions were educational, both for people with ID and for parents and professionals. He lamented that current psychologists are less political and less outspoken than we should be.

A moving target

Alan Clarke observed that nine different terms had been used to describe the ID client group just during his career. Both a psychotherapist (Sinason, 1992) and a historian (Stiker, 1982/1999) have argued that this continual process of euphemism allows people to avoid acknowledging the impact that ID has on personhood. Hacking (2007) noted that different kinds of people are referred to when classification schemes change.

Many classic texts (e.g. J. Tizard, 1964) start by explaining the meaning and implications of different terms. Wright's glossary of words that 'vex and confuse scholars in the field' (2011, p.187) describes how changes in terminology create problems for historical analysis.

'Intellectual disability' is becoming the international term. To date it does not feature in DH policy statements, nor has it spread to nurses specialising in ID whose professional affiliation has always been more contested (Mitchell, 2000). Nevertheless, clinical psychologists are now members of the BPS DCP Faculty for People with Intellectual Disabilities, psychiatrists are now members of the Royal College of Psychiatry's Faculty of the Psychiatry of Intellectual Disability, and a version of this term appears or will appear in current revisions of the diagnostic manuals DSM-5 (APA, 2013) and ICD-11 (expected 2015).

While DSM-5 de-emphasises IQ<70 but still mentions it, the upcoming ICD-11 may make no mention of IQ<70 at all. Its working group proposed the following:

'Replacing mental retardation with intellectual developmental disorders, defined as "a group of developmental conditions characterized by significant impairment of cognitive functions, which are associated with limitations of learning, adaptive behaviour and skills"' (Salvador-Carulla et al., 2011, p.177). They argue that referencing ICD-11 as a disorder rather than a disability is a radical acknowledgement of the limited reliability of IQ scores.

Box 18.2 ID name change in DSM-5

By removing IQ test scores from the diagnostic criteria, but still including them in the text description of intellectual disability, DSM-5 ensures that they are not overemphasized as the defining factor of a person's overall ability, without adequately considering functioning levels. ...In DSM-5, intellectual disability is considered to be approximately two standard deviations or more below the population, which equals an IQ score of about 70 or below. (APA, 2013)

British history invites a little wariness. As the 1913 Mental Deficiency Act was enacted, a minority of Liberal MPs objected that this legislation would target and affect the poor disproportionately, not least because the category 'moral imbecile' allowed for persistent moral misdemeanour to be regarded as a sign of mental defect (Thomson, 1998). Jack Tizard found that this legislation did indeed incarcerate the poor.

Tizard's (1950) study of 'feeble-minded' defectives in three hospitals found that they had a mean IQ of 76 (SD 10). The National Council for Civil Liberties (NCCL) waged a campaign from 1947 against detaining people with borderline and normal levels of ability in ID hospitals, with the support of Tizard and Alan Clarke. The NCCL (1951) report *50,000 Outside the Law* included their data. This provoked a review of legislation to which the BPS (largely informed by Alan Clarke and Neil O'Connor) gave evidence, arguing that an upper IQ limit to mental deficiency established by competent psychological assessment was necessary to stop oppressive incarceration on purely social grounds (Royal Commission on the Law Relating to Mental Illness and Mental Deficiency, 1955). Fellow communist and psychiatrist B.H. Kirman also argued, ironically, that psychiatrists were locking up as mentally deficient people who were 'obviously that type belonging to a low class, the scum of society – somebody you didn't like the look of' (unpublished address cited in Toms, 2013, p.121). As a result the Mental Health Act (1959) specified that people with 'arrested or incomplete development of mind' were those with IQs under 70. This should make WHO pause before removing statements of maximum IQ from the definition of ID in ICD-11: while IQ is of course fallible, history indicates that doing away with it is not the radical move current exponents believe.

Clarke and Clarke (1958) observed ID to be a social-administrative category; Lewis (1960) considered the cardinal problem for ID research was that its object of study had 'a fuzzy outline and an unsteady basis'. Whether people with borderline levels of ability should or should not be included was an issue for NCCL and Tizard: currently solutions differ from country to country, and across services that specialise respectively with people who have ID, mental health problems, or forensic services. Whether this porous boundary is leaking people out or in almost certainly tells us more about the state of services than about the people so categorised.

To see ourselves as others see us

British historians of ID offer three broadly different accounts of clinical psychology's role in ID. Some focus on medicine and the law, making scant mention of psychology. Others are strongly critical. A third group accords psychology a place alongside more traditional professions.

The first type is exemplified by Thomson (1998), who covers British ID services from 1870 to 1959, during which prominent psychiatrists such as C.J.C. Earle (see Gunzburg, 1992) and Lewis (1960) were positive about clinical psychology's contribution to ID. According to Hall (2007), this period includes the recognition of clinical psychology as a profession within the new NHS, with BPS and subsequently Ministry of Health approval of the first three training courses. Publications such as the Clarkes' (1958) textbook and J. Tizard and O'Connor's (1952) paper about the employability of thousands of people labelled as feeble-minded 'challenged almost all aspects of then current practice, and produced considerable turmoil in the field' (B. Tizard, 1983, p.11). Jack Tizard was clearly influential. He had advised NCCL's successful campaign to release patients from mental handicap hospitals, was an adviser to the UK government on handicapped children, gave evidence to the Royal Commission that influenced the 1959 Mental Health Act, and from 1953 was a consultant to WHO, OECD, and CERI. Yet clinical psychology is entirely absent from Thomson's analysis. Attention to psychoanalysis and psychiatric social work, but not clinical psychology, is also a feature of Thomson's (2007) *Psychological Subjects.* David Pilgrim, in an unpublished analysis of Thomson (2007) (personal communication, 27 October 2014), wondered whether to attribute Thomson's silence to ignorance of extensive, relevant and available documentation about clinical psychology, to mental health historians' disproportionate interest in psychoanalysis and psychiatric social work, or to poststructuralists' lack of interest in professions, but found none of these wholly convincing.

In similar vein, Wright's (2011) social history of Down's syndrome tracks the way that parents and doctors sought to balance individual and parental rights. In summarising the way that research into prenatal screening has resulted in very significant reductions in the number of children born with Down's syndrome in many countries, Wright's history illuminates the awkward space occupied by people with disabilities who are positioned within conflicting social, ethical and scientific imperatives. Yet his conclusion contains a puzzling observation: 'Medical science has failed to make any appreciable progress in curing or even moderating the Down's phenotype' (2011, p.186). If his criterion for studying contributions to Down's rests on that expectation, few are likely to feature.

Health, learning and well-being were the broader concerns of two longitudinal research projects led separately by psychologists Janet Carr and Cliff Cunningham. Cunningham worked at HARC where he followed 90 per cent of the babies born with Down's syndrome in Greater Manchester during 1973, publishing his findings both in academic papers and in an introductory text for parents and carers that went into three editions (2006). Carr (1995) studied a cohort of Down's babies from six weeks to 50 years. A regional tutor to the clinical psychology course at St George's Hospital London up to 1992, she continued to receive international invitations to discuss this research for another 20 years. Did these monumental research projects really have nothing to contribute to Wright's social history of Down's?

In contrast to such baffling absence, other historians treat psychology as one of the excessively powerful 'psy' professions. Foucault (1975/1977) described a 19th-century shift away from recording the lives of the wealthy, powerful and holy to focus on the least powerful: criminals, the insane and defective. According to this Foucauldian lens, the gaze of the psychologist fell on the powerless to discipline difference. This critical perspective is most visible in Goodey's (2011) history of ID. His argument rests on a selective list of what he considers to be psychology's subdisciplines, which bears no resemblance to psychology's core topics identified by Danziger (1997). Could there be a connection between his odd selection and Goodey's stated intention to demonstrate the spuriousness of psychology as a discipline, in order to dissolve intelligence as a concept and so dissolve ID as a category?

Jansz and van Drunen (2004) argue that while applied psychologists' engagement with social management does require historical scrutiny, perspectives range from positivist accounts that emphasise psychology's contribution to general welfare to critical accounts that see psychology as a pernicious tool of social control. They conclude that any nascent profession has to negotiate with power, but that clinical psychologists have not merely been its servant: they have also enabled oppressed groups to acquire a voice of their own that has transformed social agendas.

The most explicit challenge to a Foucauldian history of ID is given by Toms (2010, 2013) in his history of the mental hygiene movement, a US amalgam of William James, James Dewey and psychoanalysis. It focuses on emotionality and the subjective life. Mental hygiene was crystallised in Britain by the Curtis Report (Care of Children Committee, 1946) but, as Toms points out, its findings were not applied to those who were mentally deficient. He singled out different responses to bedwetting to illustrate the gulf.

The Curtis Report regarded bedwetting as an unconscious expression of distress that was outside the child's conscious control. Punishment was liable to exaggerate the problem, so children evacuated away from their families should have affection, security and appropriate mother substitutes to meet their psychological needs. Yet children with mental deficiency were excluded from the report's remit; they were sent not to families but to boarding schools, where bedwetting was frequent. It was punished by referring to such children as 'offenders' who were reported to the 'camp commandant'. One register of 'offenders' listed more than half of the children in that school (Toms, 2010). Toms concludes that continuing lack of attention to emotions in people with ID has historical roots: 'Intellectual deficiency has been used to dismiss the relevance of emotional life and experience' (Toms, 2010, p.25).

In both 2010 and 2013 Toms highlights Gunzburg and Jack Tizard as having done a great deal to combat the authoritarian, emotionally unsupportive and often punitive care experienced by people with ID. Concern about the aridity of the care provided to people with ID was echoed by Mittler (2009). He described having brought a long flirtation with behaviour modification to an end, despite its incredible power, because he became disillusioned with its mechanistic aspects that took no account of feelings.

In sum, how should clinical psychologists make sense of histories that ignore, attack, or accord psychology a place within the history of ID? Hearnshaw (1964) noted that psychology excites a variety of reactions and prejudices, while Aubrey Lewis (1958) observed that some psychiatrists would rather walk the plank than take an excursion in psychology's direction. When these reactions are moderated a more important history is able to emerge, that focuses our attention onto dehumanising impulses and forces in ID: their origins, and how people from different disciplines have cooperated to challenge them.

Making sense in order to make a difference

Expanding our conceptual vocabulary is necessary if we are to avoid being constrained by the sense that things already make. As Richards (1996) points out, nobody was conditioned before Pavlov. Similarly, nobody received either institutionally or child-oriented care before King et al. (1971). History helps us to see that things could be other than they are. This final section draws on a metaphysician, Gilles Deleuze (1968/1994), who argued that new concepts do not emerge by rejecting or defeating what exists. They emerge out of reflection by people who are or become able to see differently.

One of the issues that has dogged ID services is criticism of a moralistic and judgemental attitude towards parents and staff. It was a major issue taken up by Peter Mittler, the Tizards and the Clarkes whose complexities may benefit from some unravelling.

Box 18.3

On the whole there is a power gulf between professionals and parents...[that] gets in the way of the human being involved. (Mittler, 2009)

In our comments we are sometimes critical of the manner in which establishments function. We should, however, be distressed if this were taken as a personal criticism of the staffs themselves. *It would indicate that the main point of our studies had not got across* – namely that institutions differ in their patterns of care because they are differently organised, and because the structure of the organisation acts as a constraint on what can be achieved...no-one who has watched nursing staff and child care staff at work can fail to be impressed by what they see. (King et al., 1971, p.vii, italics added).

The Clarkes challenged criticism of mothers in Bowlby's (1951) earliest statement of what became attachment theory, not least because it resulted in a WHO expert committee (1951) concluding that day nurseries and crèches caused permanent damage to the emotional health of future generations. The Clarkes assembled a formidable argument against Bowlby, drawing on their own research and that of 11 other contributors to conclude that children are more resilient than had been accepted, that there is a 'need for greater recognition of the possibility of personal change following misfortune' (Clarke & Clarke, 1976, p.271), and that 'the whole of development is important, not just the early years' (p.272). Rutter (1976) offered a more nuanced analysis, arguing that researchers need to go beyond simple questions such as whether separation is a good or bad thing for children. He concluded that a complex understanding of what influences child temperament was needed, and how and why family discord interacts with it. Yet it was the Clarkes' rejection of Bowlby which influenced British psychology. Burman subsequently argued that 'psychology played its part in post-war celebration of home and hearth which defined and regulated women's fitness as mothers' (1994, p.78), 'attachment theory thus naturalises class and cultural privilege' (p.85), and 'exploitation and oppression suffuse the structure of developmental psychology' (p.188).

A characteristic of challenges to attachment theory has been almost exclusive focus on the very first statement about 'maternal deprivation' published by Bowlby (1951). Only the chapter by Rutter in the Clarkes' (1976) book referred to any of Bowlby's other publications, remarkable considering that his main theoretical statement *Attachment and Loss* (1969) had been published seven years earlier. Burman (1994) also referred only to Bowlby's 1951 monograph, with scant reference to subsequent attachment research by other scholars. This shows not only a determination to critique statements that Bowlby went on to moderate in the face of criticism, but also maintains focus on family relationships to the exclusion of that large number of people with ID cared for by staff. From King et al. (1971) onwards the importance of reducing staff 'churn' and supporting stable relationships that allow for emotional attachments has been identified repeatedly (Buntinx, 2008; Schuengel et al., 2013) but gets no hearing. Jack Tizard observed in 1976 that governments should stop dabbling in short-term interventions and instead research how to devise and maintain environments that promote well-being. Just like Voysey-Paun's protesting mothers we too are in danger of giving up saying what gets no hearing; woe betide us if we are taught to reproduce the official ideology instead.

Conclusions

First, the intellectual independence and political commitment of early ID clinical psychologists made an extraordinary difference to people with ID, for which they were recognised and honoured nationally and internationally. This stands in sharp contrast to the steady increase in professional regulation since that time, for example in the Care Quality Commission's imposition of particular types of intervention and its lack of interest in innovative interventions. This hugely constrains the difference that current clinical psychologists are able to make.

Second, a history of ideas rather than professions allows a more important history to emerge, one that focuses our attention onto the origin of dehumanising impulses in ID and shows how they have been challenged by cooperation.

Finally, in his 1976 presidential address to the BPS Jack Tizard argued that clinical psychologists should focus on original research, and be protected within university-based units. He also said that governments should not distract them by commissioning examinations of particular topics, nor waste their time and energy disseminating such findings into practice: instead, they should draw on their knowledge and their unique ways of looking at problems. Yet recently the Department of Health (2012) required the BPS to promulgate one particular intervention, positive behavioural support, and university-based clinical research departments and posts in ID are under considerable threat. The intellectual tradition established by the first ID clinical psychologists is in dire need of protective action.

References

American Psychiatric Association (2013). *Intellectual disability.* DSM-5 factsheet. www.dsm5.org/documents/intellectual%20disability%20fact%20sheet.pdf

Bowlby, J. (1951). *Maternal care and mental health.* Geneva: World Health Organization.

Bowlby. J. (1969). *Attachment and loss: Vol. 1. Attachment.* London: Hogarth Press.

Buntinx, W. (2008). The logic of relations and the logic of management. *Journal of Intellectual Deficiency Research, 52*(7), 588–597.

Burman, E. (1994). *Deconstructing developmental psychology.* London: Routledge.

Care of Children Committee (1946). *Report of the Care of Children Committee (Curtis Report).* Cmd 6922. London: HMSO.

Carr, J. (1995). *Down's syndrome: Children growing up.* Cambridge: Cambridge University Press.

Clarke A.D.B. (1991). A brief history of the international association for the scientific study of mental deficiency. *Journal of Intellectual Deficiency Research, 35,* 1–12.

Clarke, A.M. & Clarke, A.D.B. (1958). *Mental deficiency: The changing outlook.* London: Methuen.

Clarke, A.M. & Clarke, A.D.B. (1976). *Early experience: Myth and evidence.* Shepton Mallet: Openbooks.

Clarke, A.M & Clarke, A.D.B. (2007, 29 August). *Interview by M. Wang* [Audio recording]. BPS History of Psychology Centre Oral History Project (AUD/002/OHP 25). J.C. Kenna Audio Archive, BPS, London.

Clarke, A.M. & Clarke, A.D.B. (2008). Discovering human resilience. *The Psychologist, 21*(12), 1084–1086.

Clarke A.D.B. & Tizard, B. (Eds.) (1983). *Child development and social policy: The life and work of Jack Tizard.* Leicester: British Psychological Society.

Clark, D.F. (1984). *Help, hospitals and the handicapped.* Aberdeen: Aberdeen University Press.

Clegg, J.A. Gillott, A. & Jones, J. (2013). Conceptual issues in neurodevelopmental disorders: Lives out of synch. *Current Opinion in Psychiatry, 26,* 289–294.

Cunningham, C. (2006). *Down's syndrome: An introduction for parents and carers* (3rd edn). London: Souvenir Press.

Danziger, K. (1997). *Naming the mind.* London: Sage.

Department of Health (2012). *Transforming care: A national response to Winterbourne View Hospital.* London: Author.

Department of Health and Social Security (1976–1977). *National development group for the mentally handicapped.* NDG pamphlets 1–5. London: Author.

Deleuze, G. (1994). *Difference and repetition* (P. Patton, Trans.). London: Athlone. (Original work published 1968)

Frith, U. (2009). The avengers of psychology. *The Psychologist, 22*(8), 726–727.

Foucault, M. (1977). *Discipline and punish* (A. Sheridan Trans.). New York: Pantheon. (Original work published 1975)

Goodey, C. (2011). *A history of intelligence and 'intellectual disability'.* Farnham: Ashgate.

Gunzburg, H. (Ed.) (1992). *Despite mental handicap: Learning to cope with adult daily life.* Stratford-upon-Avon: British Society for Developmental Disabilities.

Hacking, I. (2007). Kinds of people. *Proceedings of the British Academy, 151,* 285–318.

Hall, J. (2007). The emergence of clinical psychology in Britain from 1943 to 1958, part II: Practice and research traditions. *History and Philosophy of Psychology, 9*(2), 1–33.

Hall, J. (2008). Mental deficiency – changing the outlook. *The Psychologist, 2*(11), 1006–1007.

Hearnshaw, L.S. (1964). *A short history of British psychology 1840–1940.* London: Methuen.

Jansz, J. & van Drunen, P. (Eds.) (2004). *A social history of psychology.* Oxford: Blackwell.

Kay, J. Clegg, J.A. Emck, C. & Standen, P.J. (in press). The feasibility of psychomotor therapy in acute mental health services for adults with intellectual disability. *Journal of Intellectual and Developmental Disabilities.*

King, R. Raynes, N. & Tizard, J. (1971). *Patterns of residential care.* London: Routledge.

Lewis, A. (1958). The study of defect. *American Journal Psychiatry, 117,* 289–304.

Lewis, A. (1960). Between guesswork and certainty in psychiatry. *The Lancet, 1,* 171–175.

Mitchell, D. (2000). Parallel stigma? Nurses and people with learning disabilities. *British Journal of Learning Disabilities, 28,* 78–81.

Mittler, P. (1995). Herbert Gunzburg: Obituary. *Journal Intellectual Disability Research, 39*(1), 1.

Mittler, P. (2009, 30 November). *Interview by J. Perks* [Audio recording]. BPS History of Psychology Centre Oral History Project (AUD/002/OHP 54). J.C. Kenna Audio Archive, BPS, London.
Mittler, P. (2010). *Thinking globally, acting locally.* Milton Keynes: Authorhouse.
NCCL (1951). *50,000 Outside the law.* London: Author.
Parmenter, T. (2004). Contributions of IASSID to the scientific study of intellectual disability. *Journal of Policy and Practice in Intellectual Disabilities, 1,* 71–78.
Richards, G.D. (1996). *Putting psychology in its place.* London: Routledge.
Richardson, S. & Koller, H. (1996). *Twenty-two years: Causes and consequences of mental retardation.* Cambridge, MA: Harvard University Press.
Royal Commission on the Law relating to Mental Illness and Mental Deficiency (1955). *Minutes of evidence: Seventeenth day, witnesses B.P.S. and S.M.O.H.* London: HMSO.
Rutter, M. (1976). Parent-child separation: Psychological effects on the children. In A.M. Clarke & A.D.B. Clarke (Eds.), *Early experience: Myth and evidence* (pp153–186). Shepton Mallet: Openbooks.
Salvador-Carulla, L., Reed, G.M., Vaez-Azizi, L.M. et al. (2011). Intellectual developmental disorders: towards a new name, definition and framework for 'mental retardation/intellectual disability' in ICD-11. *World Psychiatry, 10,* 175–180.
Schuengel, C. de Schipper, J.C. Sterkenburg, P. Kef, S. (2013). Attachment, IDs and mental health: Research, assessment and intervention. *Journal Applied Research Intellectual Disability, 26,* 34–46.
Segal, S. (1991). Introduction: Peter Mittler. In S. Segal & V. Varma (Eds.), *Prospects for people with learning difficulties* (pp.1–19). London: David Fulton.
Segal, S. & Varma, V. (Eds.) (1991). *Prospects for people with learning difficulties.* London: David Fulton.
Sinason, V. (1992). *Mental handicap and the human condition.* London: Tavistock Publications.
Stiker, H-J. (1999). *A history of disability* (W. Sayers, Trans.). Ann Arbor: University of Michigan Press. (Original work published 1982)
Thomson, M. (1998). *The problem of mental deficiency.* Oxford: Oxford University Press.
Thomson, M. (2007). *Psychological subjects: Identity, culture and health in twentieth-century Britain.* Oxford: Oxford University Press.
Tizard, B. (1983). Jack Tizard: A brief memoir. In A.D.B. Clarke & B. Tizard (Eds.), *Child development and social policy: The life and work of Jack Tizard* (pp.1–6). Leicester: British Psychological Society.
Tizard, B. (2008, 14 March). *Interview by H. Barrett* [Audio recording]. BPS History of Psychology Centre Oral History Project (AUD/002/OHP 28). J.C. Kenna Audio Archive, BPS, London.
Tizard, B. (2010). *Home is where one starts from.* Edinburgh: WordPower Books.
Tizard, B. & Varma, V. (Eds.) (1992). *Vulnerability and resilience in human development.* London: Jessica Kingsley.
Tizard, J. (1950). The abilities of adolescent and high grade mental defectives. *Journal Mental Science, 96,* 889–907.
Tizard, J. (1964). *Community services for the mentally handicapped.* London: Oxford University Press.
Tizard, J. & Grad, J. (1961). *The mentally handicapped and their families.* London: Oxford University Press.
Tizard, J. & O'Connor, N. (1952). The occupational adaptation of high-grade mental defectives. *The Lancet, 2,* 6–20.
Toms, J. (2010). Mind the gap: MIND, and mental hygiene movement and the trapdoor in measurements of intellect. *Journal of Intellectual Disability Research, 54,* supp.1, 16–27.
Toms, J. (2013). *Mental hygiene and psychiatry in modern Britain.* Basingstoke: Palgrave MacMillan.
Voysey-Paun, M. (2006). *A constant burden.* Aldershot: Ashgate. (Original work published 1975)
World Health Organization (1951). *Expert committee on mental health. Technical report series No. 31.* Geneva: Author.
Wright, D. (2011). *Down's: The history of a disability.* Oxford: Oxford University Press.

Chapter 19 Neuropsychology

Alan Collins, Tom McMillan & Peter Rankin

Conditions of emergence

As a term, 'neuropsychology' first gained some prominence when used by the physician William Osler in 1913 and by Karl Lashley in the title of his chair at Harvard in 1937 (Bruce, 1985), although there is an earlier use by James Mark Baldwin in his *Fragments in Philosophy and Science*, published in 1902. However, it was not until the second half of the 20th century that it became fully established as an area within the academic discipline and within clinical psychology. In many ways this is hardly surprising in the British context. As has been much rehearsed, prior to the Second World War psychology in Britain was a small affair and clinical psychology did not exist as a profession (Hearnshaw, 1964). Of course, the areas of interest and practice encompassed by neuropsychology and clinical psychology did not spring from nowhere in the 1940s. The legacies of earlier interests and practices were a number of conditions crucial for the emergence of neuropsychology and of clinical neuropsychology. In no order of priority, these were conceptual debates around materialism and localisation, the increasing prominence of neurology and psychiatry as legitimate medical specialisms, the growth of neurosurgery, the creation of a range of technologies including EEG and psychological tests, the existence of powerful elite networks of medical professionals working with people with brain injuries, and the establishment of units dedicated to head injury interventions. We cannot do full justice to these here but these conditions allow us to understand why the opportunities provided by the Second World War and the establishment of the National Health Service did combine to allow a clinical neuropsychology (CNP) to emerge.

By 1939, earlier often complex debates over materialism probably seemed anachronistic to most. While dualism might persist in various more subtle forms, and there were influential idealists writing, for many the issue was largely resolved: there was no separate mind substance, and mental matters were ultimately grounded in the body and in the brain in particular (Smith, 1997). The situation on localisation was more uncertain. The well-known investigations by the likes of Broca, Wernicke and Ferrier had persuaded most that the architecture of the brain was one where localised function was the norm (Young, 1970). However, in the 1920s Karl Lashley's work and his ideas of equipotentiality had sown some doubt about whether all higher mental functions were localised (Lashley, 1929; for contemporary reservations, see Hunter, 1930). Consequently, for some at least, localisation was not a settled matter.

Localised function gave neurosurgery a particular rationale: identify the location of the tumour in order to conduct safer and more effective surgery with as little detrimental effect as possible on subsequent functioning. Identifying the location of a tumour or brain damage was difficult with noninvasive techniques. Hans Berger had introduced EEG in the late 1920s but while EEG could help to identify areas of abnormal activity, particularly in epilepsy, it did not measure function, whereas psychological tests promised to do just that (Gross, 2008). The potential and range of application of psychological tests had increased enormously since the end of the First World War (Sokal, 1987). During that war Germany was much better prepared to deal with soldiers with head injuries than Britain was, and German neurologists such as Kurt Goldstein and Walther Poppelreuter promoted the idea that the impact of brain injury could be assessed using psychological tests (Poser, 1996). They also showed that tests were not limited to tests of intelligence, and by the Second World War there was a growing acceptance that a logic of testing and measurement could be applied to a vast array of psychological functions (Sokal, 1987). These developments were part of the expansion of psychological inspection of citizens and an increasing tendency to govern ourselves and others through psychological practices (Rose, 1985).

By the mid-20th century, neurology and psychiatry were small but recognised medical specialties (Weisz, 2006). In neurology in particular, elite networks were powerful and a period working at what was then the National Hospital for Nervous Diseases, or more briefly ‘Queen Square’, was seen as invaluable in pursuing a career in neurology (Casper, 2014). The elite and networked nature of neurology was epitomised by the Hexagon Club. Founded in 1930, this was a dining club created by and for neurologists working at Queen Square. It had six members: Charles Symonds, Russell Brain, Hugh Cairns, McDonald Critchley, Derek Denny-Brown, and George Riddoch. All of them were major figures in British neurology in the 20th century. As we shall see, some of these neurologists and their students or protégés were of crucial importance in facilitating the emergence of CNP. Without their cooperation, and that of some psychiatrists, involvement of psychologists with brain-damaged patients would have been delayed or made impossible.

Without access to people with brain damage any human neuropsychology is impossible. It was this access, and the development of formal professional roles, that finally led to CNP becoming established in Britain, with the final impetus coming from three directions: the formation of head injury units run by medical doctors sympathetic to psychology and psychologists, the challenges of the Second World War and the establishment of the National Health Service.

An embryonic specialism

Before the Second World War, neurologists such as Hugh Cairns lobbied hard and effectively for the establishment of dedicated head injury units and the concentration and development of expertise that these allowed. One of the units was established in Oxford and in 1940 the unit became a Military Head Injuries Unit staffed by Cairns and Charles Symonds, Ritchie Russell, Denny-Brown and Russell Brain. Such units were important not only because the concentration of patients and doctors fostered the development of greater expertise but also because war injuries were often focal and the patients had no prior history of brain damage. Later the Oxford unit was to be particularly important for neuropsychology but during the war at least, another such unit in Edinburgh and the activities there of Oliver Zangwill was more important for the emergence of neuropsychology (Collins, 2006).

The Cambridge psychologists Andrew Paterson and Oliver Zangwill were offered posts at the Brain Injuries Unit of the Royal Edinburgh Infirmary shortly after the outbreak of war. It is clear that the medical doctors wanted particular things from them especially: advice on whether the presenting problems were organic or functional in origin, a profile of the patient's abilities and some indication of what kinds of things a patient might and might not cope with in everyday life. In producing such assessments, Paterson and Zangwill used standardised psychological tests but they also created individually tailored tests to examine particular abilities in a particular patient. They also introduced experimental procedures and technologies (including a tachistoscope to test distance perception). As well as scores on tests, Zangwill continued to see a place for qualitative comment in assessment. While the creation and selection of tests might require expertise, they were increasingly designed so that using them did not. But if judgement too was required, as Zangwill maintained, then the psychologist's role in clinical settings involved techne, that is, skill, craft and judgement, and these qualities were not reducible to a body of knowledge about tests (Porter, 2009). From early on it was also clear that Zangwill did not see the role of psychologist as limited to assessment: rehabilitation, or re-education as he labelled it, could also form part of the psychologist's role. He published examples of this in work on dysphasia (Butfield & Zangwill, 1946; Zangwill, 1947). Paterson and Zangwill's work highlighted possible roles for psychology but his work at the Royal Infirmary also alerted Zangwill to the great potential such work had for psychology.

The intimate relations between the establishment of the National Health Service (NHS) and the emergence of a British clinical psychology are explored elsewhere in this volume. While a clinical neuropsychology could hardly be said to be at the centre of these developments, the wartime work of the likes of Zangwill and Paterson and the connections they forged, helped to identify a possible circumscribed role for psychologists working with patients with brain damage. Equally importantly, Zangwill's subsequent high profile academic career, first at Oxford then as head of department at Cambridge, facilitated links between key medical professionals and a few well-placed academic psychologists.

Shortly after the war, a number of psychologists were working in medical settings and, as described elsewhere in this volume, clinical psychologists managed to gain recognition within the newly founded NHS and representation on the important Whitley councils. Several psychologists who found themselves in medical settings working with brain-damaged patients were to become renowned and respected neuropsychologists and, by contrast with medical specialisms such as neurology and neurosurgery, several were women. One might speculate about why this was the case, such as the difficulties facing a woman wishing to enter a medical career and the possibilities offered by clinical psychology as a new profession still linked to care. But whatever these wider reasons, in the 1950s, Moyra Williams, Maria Wyke, and Elizabeth Warrington were all in posts working with brain-damaged patients, and in the early 1960s, one of the earliest graduates of the clinical psychology programme at the Institute of Psychiatry, Freda Newcombe, was appointed by Ritchie Russell at Oxford to work as a psychologist with patients who had received missile wounds to the head (Marshall, 2001). Each of these women made major contributions to a clinically oriented neuropsychology over the following decades.

As noted previously, the approach to psychological assessment developed in Britain by the likes of Warrington, Williams, Wyke and Newcombe contrasted with that being developed in the US (Beaumont, 1983). In the US, the practice of using a 'battery' of tests standardised on the same normative data, which could 'map' strengths and difficulties, became established from the late 1940s and is most closely associated with the work of Ward Halstead and his student Ralph Reitan. The idea was to develop a set of tests that evaluated a full range of psychological functions and which could be applied to all patients. By contrast in Britain there was less systematicity and less reference to formal batteries of tests but more attention to selecting tests according to the presenting problems of the patient, although some tests, most notably the Wechsler intelligence scales, were almost routinely applied because of their qualities (Crawford, 1992). The reasons for the emergence of the British approach and its similarity to a typical neurological investigation are often attributed to the particularly close links between British neuropsychology and neurology, as explored earlier in the chapter. It was also consistent with the approach in clinical psychology emphasised by Monte Shapiro, who was head of the influential Clinical Section at the Maudsley and who promoted a model of intervention whereby assessing the individual patient was treated as a form of tailored experiment (Shapiro, 1951).

In the January 1968 BPS Division of Psychology *Newsletter*, it was estimated that there were some 400 full-time and part-time clinical psychologists in post in the UK. The number engaged primarily in assessment of patients with neurological disorders is likely to have been extremely small, with psychologists like Warrington, Williams, Wyke, and Newcombe making up a substantial proportion of them, although there were others, such as Malcolm Piercy (another Zangwill student) who worked at the Maida Vale and Royal Free hospitals (Hécaen & Piercy, 1956). It is clear that, for neuropsychology at least, the notion that clinicians were 'cold-shouldered' by academics is difficult to sustain (Derksen, 2001). On the contrary, several academics were keen to work with clinicians in this area and several who were to become major figures, such as Lawrence Weiskrantz, Marcel Kinsbourne and Tim Shallice, were active collaborators and brought with them considerable expertise in experimental psychology (e.g. Kinsbourne & Warrington, 1962; Warrington & Shallice, 1969; Warrington & Weiskrantz, 1968). A cynical view of these collaborations would be that they existed mainly because clinicians were a means by which academics could gain access to patients, but this underestimates the major contribution to studies made by the clinicians themselves. It also underestimates the role of clinical experience and insight: psychologists such as Warrington, Wyke and Newcombe saw very large numbers of patients and developed a sense for when a pattern of difficulties was unusual or challenging.

Not all neuropsychological assessments were directed at identifying the consequences of brain injury. Assessment could also contribute to localising impairments prior to neurosurgical intervention. The neurosurgeon Murray Falconer used neuropsychological assessment when considering temporal lobectomy for epilepsy. Such examinations also allowed pre-operative and post-operative comparisons in cognitive function (Powell et al., 1985) and in this way assessment of the consequences of neurosurgical intervention. While the case of H.M., investigated by Brenda Milner (who studied with Zangwill) following surgery by William Scoville, was perhaps the most famous individual case study on a patient affected by neurosurgical intervention, psychologists or psychological tests were involved in examining the effects of other major procedures such as leucotomy and electroconvulsive therapy. For example, the psychiatrist Sidney Crown, then at the Institute of Psychiatry, reviewed the effects of leucotomy as measured by such tests and concluded that while there were detrimental effects on verbal intelligence some studies suggested a decrease in neuroticism (Crown, 1951). Conclusions were often equivocal and, as one might expect given the wide range of factors feeding into the use of treatments, rarely definitive in deciding whether a technique should be abandoned or retained.

While we have concentrated on the British context, the nascent neuropsychology had an international dimension. In 1951 the first International Neuropsychological Symposium (INS) was held at Mondsee in Austria (Zangwill, 1984). Attendance was by invitation only and the meeting was arranged by Klaus Conrad from Hamburg, Hans Hoff from Vienna, Henry Hécaen from Paris, and Oliver Zangwill from Oxford. It was one of the first occasions on which an international group used the term 'neuropsychological' to describe their activities. The meetings of the INS continued annually and in 1963 the select group launched the journal *Neuropsychologia*. Although the symposium initially had an exclusive and elitist ethos, later organisations such as the more American-focused International Neuropsychological Society were much less elitist, and international exchange was an important element in the subdiscipline from the outset.

Theoretical interpretations of the effects of brain damage began to change in the 1960s. Topics such as imagery, attention and memory had remained areas of psychological investigation in Britain, but there is no doubt that the theoretical language of cognitive psychology shifted in the 1950s and 1960s (Greenwood, 1999; Lovie, 1983). In Britain developments in engineering, and the emergence of cybernetics and information theory, were important to this theoretical language (Collins, 2012). In the late 1950s Donald Broadbent adopted ideas from engineering and information theory to explain psychological abilities in terms of information flow and processing (Broadbent, 1958). Similar information-processing models were developed by some neuropsychologists and were often expressed as diagrams, something that resonated with the much earlier German diagram tradition and drew on a different intellectual tradition to clinical models revolving around learning theory. A major attraction of this type of cognitive model was that it appeared to fulfil the long-held ambition of developing theoretical accounts that simultaneously explained both normal and impaired function. For academic psychologists this was a rich vein, and during the 1980s it led to highly influential findings and publications (Shallice, 1988, gives an influential overview).

From the work of Zangwill and Paterson onwards, neuropsychology in Britain was concerned with practical matters. These concerns were not limited to localisation of damage: they extended to wider questions of identifying the cause of deficits, obtaining an understanding of a person's abilities, predicting their ability to function in everyday life, and improving that functioning. Thus, although CNP may have been dominated by assessment, it was never only assessment, and in more recent years rehabilitation has become more prominent in the neuropsychologist's role.

The development of neuropsychological rehabilitation

Early historical accounts of neurorehabilitation track major developments in the rehabilitation of soldiers in Germany and Austria during the First World War

(Boake, 2003). These centres followed attempts to match a compensatory (rather than restitutive) approach to rehabilitation that focused on daily routine after discharge via vocational models following a hospital-based residential programme. Kurt Goldstein, a neurologist and psychiatrist in Frankfurt, was influenced by Gestalt teachings. He developed a holistic rehabilitation model that has subsequently held great international currency. Key issues from that time continue to be recognised including problems associated with insight, adaptation and fatigue. There was a decline in interest then until the Second World War, with significant developments as a result of work with head injuries by Luria. As has already been briefly mentioned, in the UK Zangwill carried out a study on aphasia therapy, using techniques developed by Goldstein, and went on to propose that neurorehabilitation could use strategies of 'substitution' or 'direct training'.

Following the Second World War there was expansion of neurorehabilitation facilities in the UK. In the NHS, this largely followed a disability-focused medical model of rehabilitation, which increasingly included 'multidisciplinary' teams with occupational therapy, physiotherapy, speech and language therapy, psychology and medical leadership from backgrounds in rheumatology, neurology and psychiatry. Intervention was based on a programme of therapy 'sessions' often involving a single therapist and a single patient. By the 1980s, clinical psychologists were becoming increasingly interested in the rehabilitation of patients with brain injury (Miller, 1980; Powell, 1981). In the same decade several centres in the NHS emphasised and supported the linking of research and clinical practice, with neuropsychologists seen as critical to research, often in a leadership role. These rehabilitation centres included the Rivermead Centre in Oxford (Barbara Wilson), the Wolfson Centre in London (Michael Oddy, Andy Tyerman, Tony Coughlin, Rodger Weddell, Tom McMillan) and the Astley Ainslie in Edinburgh (Ian Robertson). This linkage between research and practice served to publicise current thinking and drive forward clinical practice at a time when the model of the clinician researcher was actively supported by the NHS. By now, the concept of rehabilitation had extended to include psychosocial effects of brain injury taking account of the role of the family, including work in Glasgow and Wimbledon (Brooks et al., 1987; Oddy et al., 1985). The shift in the scope of rehabilitation further strengthened the claim that neuropsychology was concerned with more than psychometric assessment. There was an increasing perception of the relevance of clinical psychology training, and with this the potential for developing or adapting psychological interventions for people with brain damage, including for challenging behaviour, disorders of mood and cognitive impairment. Specialist centres developed to treat challenging behaviour after brain injury, such as the Kemsley Unit at St Andrews Hospital in Northampton where early neurobehavioural perspectives on rehabilitation were developed by Rodger Wood and Peter Eames (Wood & Eames, 1981) and later by Nick Alderman.

At the prestigious MRC Applied Psychology Unit in Cambridge there was recognition of the importance of developing clinical research in rehabilitation with the appointment of the clinical (neuro)psychologists Barbara Wilson and Ian Robertson as senior scientists in the early 1990s. Alan Baddeley, who then led the unit, promoted the idea that good theoretical accounts should have practical implications (Baddeley, 1990). He collaborated with many leading clinical neuropsychologists, including Nick Alderman (dysexecutive function), Neil Brooks (procedural memory), Ian Robertson (attention), Alan Sunderland (meta-memory), Faraneh Vargha-Khadem (developmental amnesia), Elizabeth Warrington (amnesia) and Barbara Wilson and Jon Evans (errorless learning). Barbara Wilson had much significant collaboration with Baddeley, and sought to link academic research on cognitive impairment with practical intervention that was relevant to daily life. For example, the Rivermead Behavioural Memory Test was explicitly oriented towards assessing everyday functioning, such as remembering a route, rather than more abstracted measures of memory such as digit span.

Goldstein's 'holistic' model of rehabilitation was developed in the US in the 1970s by Yehuda Ben-Yishay and later by George Prigatano (Ben–Yishay, 1996; Prigatano, 1989), incorporating the importance of dealing with the 'whole' person, including the impact of emotional changes after brain damage and changes in lifestyle (Goldstein 1959), and with less of the focus on associations between impairment and function, that had preoccupied many neuropsychologists. Individuals were seen in their totality and a core principle of rehabilitation was working on goals throughout the 24-hour period in a 'therapeutic milieu', with physical environment and responses from staff or family to behaviour outside formal treatment sessions geared towards the achievement of adaptation and change. In the early 1990s in the UK, Rodger Wood developed a psychology-led series of neurorehabilitation units with the Disabilities Trust in the UK with a 'holistic' neurobehavioural focus, that provided an alternative to the medical model (Wood & Worthington, 2001). A research practice-linked NHS day patient unit that followed holistic principles was developed in Ely by Barbara Wilson. The centre was named after Oliver Zangwill and opened in 1996. The importance of these clinical and research developments should not be underestimated; with them came a gradual acceptance in the UK that clinical (neuro)psychologists could and should be in charge of rehabilitation hospitals where the main focus is psychosocial rehabilitation. This was actively supported by the development of formal training in CNP at that time (discussed below). The development of an evidence base for 'holistic' neurorehabilitation has continued to grow (Cicerone et al., 2011).

Extending the field: The case of paediatric neuropsychology

The scientific context

Following a similar professional pattern to adult and paediatric neurology, paediatric neuropsychology developed some decades after adult neuropsychology became established. Paediatrics did not have a large population of war veterans with specific brain lesions to learn from or requiring clinical support in the 1940s. The first international articles referring to paediatric neuropsychology did not appear until the 1980s (e.g. Fletcher & Taylor, 1984; Gaddes, 1980). Indeed, when clinical paediatric neuropsychology started to establish itself, misconceptions appeared to be widely held about childhood brain injury. For example, the plasticity studies of Margaret Kennard which demonstrated a negative linear relation between age at brain injury and a primate's functional motor outcome, were often overgeneralised to all cognitive functions, albeit not by Kennard herself (Dennis, 2010). Therefore, in clinical practice it was often assumed that the 'Kennard principle' meant that brain-damaged children had a more favourable prognosis than adults due to greater neural plasticity and this had unfortunate implications for clinical planning and resource allocation (Johnson et al., 1989). Such misconceptions about the consequences of childhood brain injury were probably reinforced by clinical observations that children with unilateral lesions did not present with specific enduring 'adult-like' neuropsychological deficits (Rankin & Vargha-Khadem, 2008).

It was not until the mid-1980s and 1990s that significant technological advances made it possible to measure brain integrity in development directly, resulting in the President of the US declaring the 1990s to be the 'decade of the brain' (Jones & Mendell, 1999). Subsequently there was an exponential growth in scientific investigations that could elucidate mechanisms of synaptic transmission and learning and measure effects of injury and recovery prenatally and across childhood and adolescence. Hebb's original postulate about learning and the organisation of behaviour in development (Hebb, 1949) was opened to empirical investigation with significant implications for understanding effects of different lesions on different cognitive systems at different ages.

Studies of neural memory and learning in particular dampened the nature–nurture debate as it became apparent that experience and learning affected gene expression and neural architecture throughout development so that an interactional bio-psycho-social model became more relevant for understanding developmental psychopathology (Pennington, 2002).

UK clinical practice

In terms of UK clinical practice, Peter Griffiths first documented in 1989 the 'potential emergence' of a fully individuated clinical specialty known as 'paediatric neuropsychology' (Griffiths, 1989). Griffiths trained as a clinical psychologist, and developed his interest in paediatric neuropsychology when he moved to the Fraser of Allander Neurosciences Unit at the Royal Hospital for Sick Children in Glasgow in 1973. In the early 1980s, Griffiths spent a sabbatical at the University of Victoria, Canada, with Bill Gaddes who had published seminal work on learning disabilities and brain function. This experience greatly influenced Griffiths' approach to clinical work and he went on to publish several case studies (e.g. Griffiths & Hunt, 1984).

During the 1980s Oliver Chadwick worked with Michael Rutter at the Institute of Psychiatry and produced several papers on the epidemiology and characteristics of children following head injury (e.g. Chadwick et al., 1981). Given the investigations possible at that time, these focused on cognitive and behavioural rather than neural functioning but raised awareness of children's neuropsychological needs.

Faraneh Vargha-Khadem took up a research post at the Institute of Child Health (ICH) in 1983 and in 1986 a joint clinical post at Great Ormond Street Hospital for Children, London. She had been influenced by the teachings of Hebb as an undergraduate in Montreal and when starting work in the UK, together with Elizabeth Isaacs, published influential studies on the effects of unilateral lesions in childhood (e.g. Isaacs et al., 1997). They collaborated with many influential scientists at ICH including David Gadian, a professor of biophysics who developed novel neuroimaging paradigms for studying childhood brain lesions. Over subsequent decades Vargha-Khadem and her team published hundreds of influential studies demonstrating some of the key issues now taken for granted in paediatric neuropsychology practice, including ontogenetic cerebral lateralisation, cortical reorganisation, crowding effects, sleeper effects, epilepsy effects and neurosurgery, and the potential for compensation/remediation. Vargha-Khadem has remained at these institutions to the present time, developing one of the largest clinical and research departments in paediatric neuropsychology outside North America.

Judith Middleton helped develop one of the UK's first child head injury rehabilitation units at Tadworth Children's Trust in 1986 and went on to have a major role in establishing professional paediatric neuropsychology in the UK. Middleton became the director of the rehabilitation programme at Tadworth, and developed a dedicated multidisciplinary team delivering 24-hour rehabilitation. As part of the programme families could stay with children and learn support skills and strategies to use following discharge. To extend this knowledge and support nationally, she cofounded the Children's Brain Injury Trust charity in 1991, which supports over 5000 families in the UK a year. Middleton moved to the Radcliffe Infirmary, Oxford, in 1992 where she developed a paediatric neuropsychology service. In 1995, she set up the first BPS CPD child neuropsychology training course at Charney Manor, Oxfordshire. This two-week residential course was later directed by Arleta Starza-Smith and Shauna Kearney. It continued for 16 years and helped foster a professional identity for child neuropsychology, creating a network of UK psychologists who increasingly embraced this area. Throughout the 1980–1990s the UK's regional paediatric neuroscience centres started to create specialist paediatric neuropsychology posts; what is notable during these decades is that there were in total about 25 practitioners in these specialised posts. Although other child psychologists in neurodevelopmental, educational and community mental health settings were developing the field, the numbers with such specialist competencies were extremely small.

In 1997 the first UK textbook specifically on paediatric neuropsychology was produced (Temple, 1997). Christine Temple was an academic who studied cognitive neuropsychology at UCLA, completed her PhD with John Marshall and Freda Newcombe at Oxford studying children with reading difficulties, and went on to establish the Developmental Neuropsychology Unit at Royal Holloway in 1985 and later at the University of Essex from 1991.

When the BPS Division of Neuropsychology (DoN) developed a formal paediatric training route in 2004, the clinical psychologists Judith Middleton, Avron Moss, Arleta Starza-Smith and Annette Schwartz, and educational psychologists Tony Baldwin and Steven Whitfield developed the initial curriculum. This curriculum was delivered by the University of Nottingham alongside their adult neuropsychology training programme until 2007. Consequently Peter Rankin and Faraneh Vargha-Khadem developed the programme at UCL ICH/Great Ormond Street Hospital that also runs international symposia that are broadcast online, raising the international profile of the UK profession. The field was further consolidated by the establishment of the DoN Faculty of Paediatric Neuropsychology, in October 2011 and has subsequently been chaired by Ingram Wright, Liam Dorris and Cathy Grant.

In summary, paediatric neuropsychology became established in the UK in the 1980s and 1990s and remains a small specialism although it has grown exponentially in recent years. A formal training programme is now available with a strong international profile. Clearly, paediatric neuropsychology will have a critical role to play in explaining developmental psychopathology for decades to come with significant practice implications for all professional psychologists.

The development of professional training in clinical neuropsychology

In the 1970s and 1980s, psychologists who worked clinically with people with neurological disorders tended to have gained skills and experience through mentorship and supervised practice, or were clinical psychologists who had received basic training including in psychometric assessment and then similarly sought supervised practice. At the Institute of Psychiatry in London in the late 1980s, Maria Wyke and Tom McMillan talked about a need for a formal professional training route for neuropsychologists. Accreditation of professional psychology training in the UK was by the British Psychological Society, via its Divisions and their substructures. The route to divisional status was through the initial step of establishing a Special Interest Group with 100 members. The inaugural meeting of the Special Group in Clinical Neuropsychology (SGCN) took place on 7 June 1991 with Tom McMillan as the founder. The original committee comprised Graham Beaumont (secretary), Neil Brooks, Laura Goldstein, Tom McMillan (chair), Michael Oddy (treasurer), Graham Powell, Peter Wilcock (DCP observer), Andy Tyerman and Barbara Wilson. Graham Beaumont, a past President of the BPS, provided insights and understanding of the BPS structures and processes.

The SGCN developed draft rules and terms of reference for the Division and formed a Committee for Training that developed a training syllabus and draft terms of reference for both the training committee and the Board of Examiners. The SGCN also organised training events and joint meetings with the British Neuropsychology Society (which was formed in 1989 and had an academic focus) and promoted the need to expand neuropsychological services. The formal training model developed for CNP in the UK was that of a postqualification specialism, somewhat akin to allied medical fields of neurology, neurosurgery and psychiatry. Key considerations in choosing this model were facilitation of clinical neuropsychologists in leadership or 'consultant' roles and review of the content of other professional psychology courses. This led to the view that much of clinical psychology training would need to be replicated in a CNP qualification that should emphasise principles and practice of psychological interventions as much as assessment of impairment. There were practical issues when deciding about the training model, including difficulty in accessing new funding for a qualification course and avoidance of unhelpful competition with existing clinical psychology courses, including for clinical supervisors (then a growth limiter for clinical psychology training). These factors weighed towards a postqualification training model that would provide a 'gold standard' for neuropsychology (with an intention that students might be part funded by employers) and away from an initial qualification model in CNP as found, for example, in Australia. Hence the CNP candidate had first to qualify in clinical psychology or educational psychology (the latter for the paediatric CNP qualification only) and then 'in clinical practice' to demonstrate the knowledge base by BPS examination or via an accredited university course. In addition, there was a requirement for supervised clinical practice with a range of conditions and for research. In 2010 the DoN published a competency framework for both the adult and paediatric training, and in turn this has given education providers greater flexibility in how they may develop CNP training according to changing demands.

Almost exactly eight years after its inaugural meeting, the SGCN became the Division of Neuropsychology, following a meeting of the BPS Council in 1999 attended by Michael Oddy (first Chair of the Division) and Tom McMillan. The SGCN membership grew by more than tenfold over the next 20 years to almost 1400, outstripping growth rates in neurology and neurosurgery during that time.

Conclusion and reflections

By 2000 neuroscience was a burgeoning area and there was a growing cultural acceptance that many personal difficulties could be explained in terms of brain processes. Partly as a consequence, by the end of the 20th century it would have been difficult to imagine a clinical psychology without a neuropsychological component. However, this was not the case when clinical neuropsychology emerged in Britain after the Second World War. While it risks anachronism to call this activity clinical neuropsychology, as this designation came into general use later, it is clear that by the mid-1940s, individuals trained first and foremost as psychologists were using their skills in a professional, clinical capacity to work with people who had suffered brain damage. The nature of their role was initially shaped by the demands of medical doctors and wartime clinics. After the war the existence of a tightly knit elite network of medical doctors who saw a role for psychology and psychologists in assessment of those with brain injury ensured that a small number of psychologists entered posts in the newly founded NHS.

From early on there was resistance to seeing neuropsychology as being concerned solely with assessment and the negative connotations of being a 'mere technician' that that implied. By contrast, the potential contribution to rehabilitation was promoted from the beginning and while it took some decades before the promise was realised, we would argue that its realisation has been the major historical shift within clinical neuropsychology since its emergence in post-war Britain. Together with tailored assessments, incorporation of techniques from experimental psychology and the emergence of a rich theoretical language for describing dysfunctions, the idea of neuropsychological expertise developed a particular character both for adults and children. What emerged was an approach to rehabilitation that meshed with the much promoted idea of clinician-scientist, with psychologists often seen as leading research and offering particular expertise in that regard. The development of other formal structures, notably professional training courses, confirmed the wider area, and neuropsychology became what it currently is: a specialised area of applied psychology.

References

Baddeley, A.D. (1990). *Human memory: Theory and practice.* Hove: Lawrence Erlbaum.

Beaumont, J.G. (1983). *Introduction to neuropsychology.* Oxford: Blackwell.

Ben-Yishay, Y. (1996). Reflections on the evolution of the therapeutic milieu concept. *Neuropsychological Rehabilitation, 6,* 327–43.

Boake, C. (2003). Stages in the history of neuropsychological rehabilitation. In: B.A. Wilson (Ed.), *Neuropsychological rehabilitation: Theory and practice* (pp 11–21). Lisse: Swets & Zeitlinger.

Broadbent, D.E. (1958). *Perception and communication.* Oxford: Oxford University Press.

Brooks, D.N., McKinlay, W., Symington, C. et al. (1987). Return to work within the first seven years of severe head injury. *Brain Injury, 1*(1), 5–19.

Bruce, D. (1985). On the origin of the term 'neuropsychology'. *Neuropsychologia, 23*(6), 813–814.

Butfield, E.D.N.A. & Zangwill, O.L. (1946). Re-education in aphasia: A review of 70 cases. *Journal of Neurology, Neurosurgery, and Psychiatry, 9*(2), 75–79.

Casper, S.T. (2014). *The neurologists: A history of a medical specialty in modern Britain, c.1789–2000.* Manchester: Manchester University Press.

Chadwick, O., Rutter, M., Brown, G. et al. (1981). A prospective study of children with head injuries: II. Cognitive sequelae. *Psychological Medicine, 11*(1), 49–61.

Cicerone K. D., Langenbahn, D.M., Braden C. et al. (2011). Evidence-based cognitive rehabilitation: Updated review of the literature from 2003 through 2008. *Archives of Physical Medicine and Rehabilitation, 92*(4), 519–530.

Collins, A.F. (2006). An intimate connection: Oliver Zangwill and the emergence of neuropsychology in Britain. *History of Psychology, 9*(2), 89–112.

Collins, A.F. (2012). England. In D. Baker (Ed.), *Oxford library of psychology: History of psychology* (pp.182–210). Oxford: Oxford University Press.

Crawford, J.R. (1992). Current and premorbid intelligence measures in neuropsychological assessment. In J.R. Crawford, D.M. Parker & W.W. McKinlay (Eds.), *A handbook of neuropsychological assessment* (pp.21–50). Hove: Lawrence Erlbaum.

Crown, S. (1951). Psychological changes following prefrontal leucotomy: A review. *British Journal of Psychiatry, 97*(406), 49–83.

Dennis M. (2010) Margaret Kennard (1899–1975): Not a 'principle' of brain plasticity but a founding mother of developmental neuropsychology. *Cortex, 46*(8), 1043–1059.

Derksen, M. (2001). Science in the clinic: Clinical psychology at the Maudsley. In G.C. Bunn, A.D. Lovie & G.D. Richards (Eds.), *Psychology in Britain: Historical essays and personal reflections* (pp.267–289). Leicester: BPS Books.

Fletcher, J.M. & Taylor, H.G. (1984). Neuropsychological approaches to children: Towards a developmental neuropsychology. *Journal of Clinical Neuropsychology, 6*, 39–56.

Gaddes, W.H. (1980). *Learning disabilities and brain function.* New York: Springer-Verlag.

Goldstein K. (1959). Notes on the development of my concepts. *Journal of Individual Psychology, 15*, 5–14.

Greenwood, J.D. (1999). Understanding the 'cognitive revolution' in psychology. *Journal of the History of the Behavioral Sciences, 35*(1), 1–22.

Griffiths, P. (1989). Investigative methods in paediatric neuropsychology. In J.R. Crawford & D.M. Parker (Eds.), *Developments in clinical and experimental neuropsychology* (pp.247–258). New York: Plenum.

Griffiths, O. & Hunt, S. (1984). Specific spatial defect in a child with septo-optic dyplasia. *Developmental Medicine and Child Neurology, 26*, 391–400.

Gross, A.G. (2008). The brains in Brain: The coevolution of localization and its images. *Journal of the History of the Neurosciences, 17*, 380–392.

Hearnshaw, L.S. (1964). *A short history of British psychology: 1840–1940.* London: Methuen.

Hebb, D.O. (1949). *Organisation of behavior.* New York: Wiley.

Hécaen, H. & Piercy, M. (1956). Paroxysmal dysphasia and the problem of cerebral dominance. *Journal of Neurology, Neurosurgery, and Psychiatry, 19*(3), 194–201.

Hunter, W.S. (1930). A consideration of Lashley's theory of the equipotentiality of cerebral action. *Journal of General Psychology, 3*(4), 455–468.

Isaacs, E., Christie, D., Vargha-Khadem, F. & Mishkin, M. (1997). Effects of hemispheric side of injury, age at injury, and presence of seizure disorder on functional ear and hand asymmetrics in hemiplegic children. *Neuropsychologia, 34*(2), 127–137.

Johnson, D., Uttley, D. & Wyke, M.A. (1989). *Children's head injury: Who cares?* London: Taylor & Francis.

Jones, E.G. & Mendell, L.M. (1999). Assessing the decade of the brain. *Science, 284*(5415), 739.

Kinsbourne, M. & Warrington, E.K. (1962). A variety of reading disability associated with right hemisphere lesions. *Journal of Neurology, Neurosurgery, and Psychiatry, 25*(4), 339–344.

Lashley, K.S. (1929). *Brain mechanisms and intelligence: A quantitative study of injuries to the brain.* Chicago: University of Chicago Press.

Lovie, A.D. (1983). Attention and behaviourism – fact and fiction. *British Journal of Psychology, 74*(3), 301–310.

Marshall, J.C. (2001). In memory of Freda Newcombe. *Neuropsychologia, 39,* iii–iv.

Miller, E. (1980). Psychological intervention in the management and rehabilitation of neuropsychological impairments. *Behaviour Research and Therapy, 18*(6), 527–535.

Oddy, M., Coughlan, T., Tyerman, A. & Jenkins, D. (1985). Social adjustment after closed head injury: A further follow-up seven years after injury. *Journal of Neurology, Neurosurgery & Psychiatry, 48*(6), 564–568.

Pennington, P. (2002). *The development of psychopathology: Nature and nurture.* London: Guilford Press.

Porter, T.M. (2009). How science became technical. *Isis, 100*(2), 292–309.

Poser, U. (1996). Historical review of neuropsychological rehabilitation in Germany. *Neuropsychological Rehabilitation, 6*(4), 257–278.

Powell, G.E. (1981). *Brain function therapy.* Aldershot: Gower.

Powell, G.E., Polkey, C.E. & McMillan, T. (1985). The new Maudsley series of temporal lobectomy. I: Short-term cognitive effects. *British Journal of Clinical Psychology, 24*(2), 109–124.

Prigatano, G.P. (1989). *Principles of neuropsychological rehabilitation.* New York: Oxford University Press.

Rankin, P.M. & Vargha-Khadem, F. (2008) Neuropsychological evaluation – children. In J. Engel & T.A. Pedley (Eds.), *Epilepsy: A comprehensive textbook* (2nd edn, pp.1067–1076). London: Lippincott Williams & Wilkins.

Rose, N.S. (1985). *The psychological complex: Psychology, politics, and society in England, 1869–1939.* London: Routledge & Kegan Paul.

Shallice, T. (1988). *From neuropsychology to mental structure.* Cambridge: Cambridge University Press.

Shapiro, M. (1951). An experimental approach to diagnostic psychological testing. *Journal of Mental Science, 97,* 748–764.

Smith, R. (1997). *Fontana history of the human sciences.* London: Fontana.

Sokal, M.M. (1987). *Psychological testing and American Society: 1890–1930.* New Brunswick, NJ: Rutgers University Press.

Temple, C. (1997). *Developmental cognitive neuropsychology.* Hove: Psychology Press.

Warrington, E.K. & Shallice, T. (1969). The selective impairment of auditory verbal short-term memory. *Brain, 92,* 885–896.

Warrington, E.K. & Weiskrantz, L. (1968). A study of learning and retention in amnesic patients. *Neuropsychologia, 6*(3), 283–291.

Weisz, G. (2006). *Divide and conquer: A comparative history of medical specialisation.* Oxford: Oxford University Press.

Wood R.L.I. & Eames, P.G. (1981). Applications of behaviour modification in the rehabilitation of traumatically brain injured patients. In G. Davey (Ed.), *Applications of conditioning theory* (pp.81–101). London: Croom Helm.

Wood R.L.I. & Worthington, A. (2001). Neurobehavioural rehabilitation: A conceptual paradigm. In R.L.I. Wood & T.M. McMillan (Eds.), *Neurobehavioural disability and social handicap following traumatic brain injury* (pp.1–28). Hove: Psychology Press.

Young, R.M. (1970). *Mind, brain and adaptation in the nineteenth century: Cerebral localisation and its biological context from Gall to Ferrier.* Oxford: Oxford University Press.

Zangwill, O.L. (1947). Psychological aspects of rehabilitation in cases of brain injury. *British Journal of Psychology. General Section, 37*(2), 60–69.

Zangwill, O.L. (1984). Henry Hécaen and the origins of the International Neuropsychological Symposium. *Neuropsychologia, 22*(6), 813–815.

Chapter 20 Clinical psychology with older people

Bob Woods & Cath Burley

The last 50 years have seen dramatic changes in the position of older people in society, and the emergence of dementia as a global challenge. In the UK, clinical psychology with older people has gone from non-existent to being at the heart of policy development and practice. This chapter charts this growth, highlighting external factors that have influenced this development, and the significance of a powerful group identity.

Older people – the changing picture

The specialism developed during a period of profound social and demographic change. Fifty years ago, 'the elderly', born around 1890 onwards, had grown up with Victorian values and belief systems. Emotional reticence, respecting their elders and being able to cope were long-held values. Two world wars had a major impact on gender roles, as well as on social and family relationships. Developing resilience and coping with change were key themes for this population. The 'elderly' are not a homogeneous group. The 'baby boomers' have different life experiences to earlier cohorts. For each successive cohort, later life is uncharted territory.

Census figures from the Office of National Statistics indicate that by 2011 one-in-six people were aged 65 or over (16.4 per cent of the population). Life expectancy at birth increased from 45 for men and 49 for women in 1901 to 76 for men and 81 for women in 2001. Between1911 and 1914, 63 per cent died before the age of 60; this reduced to 12 per cent by 2011. In 1911 there were 13,000 people over 90 years old. There are now 33 times as many 90-year-olds as there were 100 years ago, with 13,780 people over 100-years-old.

These changes have influenced how both government and the population plan for retirement. Retirement and pension provision, once legally fixed at 65 for men and 60 for women, have become more flexible. Many people choose to work for as long as health and motivation persist, some for financial reasons or changes in marital circumstances. Others engage in caring roles, second careers, education or active volunteering. Physical health gains and improved pensions have made later life a time of social and educational opportunity, a time to celebrate successes and family, a time to reflect. Age discrimination continues, but is increasingly challenged by older people themselves.

Before the NHS, state provision for older people centred on the workhouse and the 'lunatic asylum'. There were fears from the inception of the NHS about the rapid rise in numbers of older people, concerns about managing dementia, institutional provision and bed blocking. Local authorities were given the duty under Part III of the 1948 National Assistance Act to provide residential homes. In contrast with the workhouses they replaced, these residential homes were intended to be small and comfortable, with the previous 'master–inmate' relationship replaced by one akin to that of 'a hotel manager with a guest'. Townsend's (1962) national survey of old people's homes showed that progress in moving away from the workhouse model was slow, and the quality of new homes varied greatly.

In the NHS, the development of geriatric medicine, led by pioneers such as Marjory Warren, appointed as one of the first consultant geriatricians in 1949, introduced concepts of multidisciplinary assessment and rehabilitation (Kong, 2000), and the establishment of geriatric units. The parallel development of old age psychiatry in the 1940s and 1950s (Hilton, 2005), with an emphasis on assessment and treatment in the community, began to have an impact on the large number of older people who were patients in the former asylums, now serving as mental hospitals. By the 1970s, long-stay geriatric wards and long-stay wards for people with dementia remained commonplace, often in unsuitable, poorly maintained and poorly located facilities. Policy documents such as the discussion document *A Happier Old Age* (DHSS, 1978) and the subsequent White Paper *Growing Older* (DHSS, 1981) increasingly emphasised fulfilling the desire of older people to live independently in their own homes, by use of existing resources, and a greater contribution from the community, including voluntary and private sectors (Tinker, 2014), a theme that continues to underpin policy.

The early years

The Trethowan Report, *The Role of Psychologists in the Health Services* (DHSS, 1977), provides a clear watershed in the history of clinical psychology with older people in the UK (See chapter 6), although older people received little mention in the long-awaited document. The British Geriatrics Society provided evidence to the sub-committee, highlighting the need:

> We were told that the involvement of psychologists in the clinical management of geriatric patients is at present minimal or non-existent. The British Geriatric Association (sic) told us they would welcome more participation by psychologists in this field, in particular in helping to develop a therapeutic milieu in wards and day hospitals and in developing programmes to help elderly people in adjusting to their failing functions. (DHSS, 1977, p.8)

Geriatrics is included in the illustrative list of eight specialist groupings that would potentially be found in a fully developed area psychological service, each headed by a senior psychologist, setting the scene for a distinct specialism to emerge, separate from mental illness, neurological sciences and primary health care. For example, in Newcastle-upon-Tyne in 1979, an area psychological service was established and Bob Woods was appointed as head of the Specialist Grouping for the Elderly (a 'grouping' of one).

Evidence for clinical psychologists working with older people prior to Trethowan comes mainly from research publications, so may not fully reflect the extent of clinical practice. At Tooting Bec Hospital – a former workhouse infirmary accommodating around 2000 'elderly mentally ill patients' – there was a Laboratory for Clinical Research on Ageing in the 1940s (Hilton, 2005). Psychologist Margaret Eysenck worked in the laboratory and published a study where 20 psychological tests (including Raven's Matrices, later widely used with older people) were given to 84 men with senile dementia (average age 73), and repeated four months later (Eysenck, 1945).

In subsequent decades psychologists developed cognitive tests to differentiate older patients with 'organic' problems from those with 'functional' disorders, or dementia from depression. The Institute of Psychiatry produced several tests; for example, Monte Shapiro (1956) published a study of 102 patients aged 60 and over, carried out with the pioneering old-age psychiatrist Felix Post and clinical psychologist, James Inglis. They found that many of the clinical and psychological tests commonly used at that time were of limited usefulness for differentiating those clinically categorised as 'organic', 'functional' or 'doubtful'. Inglis (1959) went on to publish his own memory tests, assessing paired-associate learning, while a lecturer at the Institute in the 1950s. The Modified Word Learning Test (MWLT) developed by Don Walton at Winwick Hospital, Warrington, was used with older patients to detect brain damage and 'organicity', with the aim of 'detecting cases of early dementia' (Walton & Black, 1957). Don Kendrick developed the original Kendrick Battery of cognitive tests at the Bethlem and Maudsley Hospitals (Kendrick, 1972), following an attempt to further modify the MWLT (Kendrick et al., 1965). Antonia Whitehead worked with Felix Post at the same hospitals on one of a series of studies which sought to compare older people with depression with those experiencing dementia (Hemsi et al., 1968), leading to several other related publications.

The Newcastle studies, carried out between 1963 and 1971 (Savage et al., 1973), assessed community samples of older people for comparison with psychiatric samples, using intelligence tests developed in the US such as the WAIS, together with the MWLT and Inglis's paired-associate learning tests. The authors stated that 'intellectual difficulties associated with functional disorder in the aged may be quite different from those in the young' and expressed a hope to bring together psychological and psychiatric perspectives on ageing in their work. They worked with an old-age psychiatry research group which at this time was establishing that 'senile dementia' was in fact, in the majority of cases, equivalent, in terms of brain changes, to Alzheimer's disease, which had been thought to be a condition mainly seen in younger people (Blessed et al., 1968).

Perhaps the first study to offer hope that psychosocial approaches could make a therapeutic difference was co-authored by Moyra Williams, a clinical psychologist in Oxford. This pioneering evaluation of activity and stimulation for older people in hospital was led by Lionel Cosin (Cosin et al., 1958), a geriatrician. Inglis (1962) reflected upon psychological practice in 'geriatric problems', contrasting two approaches – one focusing on assessment, the other on behaviour change, following manipulation of key variables. He warned that testing to support diagnosis might be more complex and not as valuable as then often thought, and argued for a more experimental psychology approach, which could potentially ameliorate disorders.

Development of a specialism

The evidence of psychologists expressing a special interest in working with older people emerges in the late 1970s. Around 1977, a small group of psychologists in

Scotland began to meet for peer support and exchange of ideas. This became 'PACE – Psychology Applied to the Care of the Elderly'. The group included Mary Gilhooly at Aberdeen University, investigating family care-giving for people with dementia, and Ian Hanley, who was researching reality orientation at Edinburgh. They met regularly and by 1979 had 17 members and a newsletter. The group went on to produce an edited book (Hanley & Hodge, 1984), the chapters reflecting the diversity of work being undertaken in Scotland. These included a range of assessment approaches, going beyond cognitive testing to encompass rating and observing behaviour and behaviour analysis, two chapters on reality orientation and a chapter on understanding and treating depression.

A PACE member, Kate Johnson, compiled a UK-wide list of interested psychologists, which by 1978 had 16 responses. The following year, the BPS *Bulletin* had articles and letters raising the profile of working with older people. Mumford and Carpenter (1979) described the need for 'Psychological services and the elderly'; Jeff Garland, based in Oxford, invited interested people to contact him with a view to forming a similar group to PACE and John Hodge, a member of PACE, wrote outlining the aims and functions of the Scottish group. It was in this context that Age Concern England requested a meeting with the BPS Division of Clinical Psychology to explore how the development of clinical psychology with older people might be supported. The meeting was held on 24 November 1979, at the Middlesex Hospital, London. Age Concern representatives included Sally Greengross,[1] then deputy director, with the DCP represented by David Mulhall, the then DCP secretary. Jeff Garland and Bob Woods attended on behalf of psychologists working with older people.

This positive meeting identified as a priority action bringing together psychologists working with older people early in 1980. Although the DCP would have liked to offer an organisational home for such 'special interest groups', it was not constitutionally possible. An article by Bob Woods in the DCP Newsletter in 1980, entitled 'Sans psychologists, sans everything' makes explicit the then perceived mythology regarding work with older people:

- Few are interested in the specialty and even fewer work in it.
- Trainee psychologists will resist having to carry out placements with older people.
- There will be a dearth of applicants for new posts.
- Training courses provide little training in work with older people.
- There is little point anyway – older people are demented or are too rigid to change or have only a short time to live.

Psychologists, typically working single-handed with older people, felt the need to come together and challenge the ageism they encountered from colleagues in the services in which they worked. 'Ageism' was a recently coined term (Butler, 1969), but was certainly evident, for example in well-meaning career advice not to work exclusively with older people.

The 'Inaugural meeting of a special interest group for psychologists working with the elderly' was held at Corbett Hospital, Stourbridge, West Midlands

[1] Now Baroness Greengross, President of the International Longevity Centre.

(arranged by Anne Broadhurst, from Birmingham University) on 23 May 1980. The agenda for the meeting included discussion of a newsletter, regional subgroups, links with other organisations and appointment of officers, possible sources of finance, and the compilation of a register of members. Una Holden was appointed the group's first chair, with Bob Woods, vice-chair, Jeff Garland, secretary and Cath Burley, treasurer.

The first AGM (10 October 1980), at the Warneford Hospital, Oxford, included a scientific meeting on 'Assessment of residential care settings for the elderly', with presentations from John Hall (Oxford) and Anne Pattie (York). The first newsletter appeared in 1980, edited by Jack Dykes and Barry Greatorex, and included an article by Una Holden on 'Tricks of the trade', as well as the draft constitution.

The first residential conference was held at Leicester University, on 1–3 July 1981. Around 35 people attended from the 106 on the membership list. There were four sessions: 'The non-demented elderly', 'Environment and the elderly', 'Incontinence' and 'Community emphasis'. The community session introduced a focus on support for relatives, and the 'non-demented elderly' session included talks on normal ageing and on death and dying. The speakers included several members of other disciplines, such as Dr Brian Lodge, a geriatrician from Leicestershire talking on community services, and Janet Blannin, a continence nurse. The constitution was ratified and the name 'PSIGE' was formally adopted, an acronym for 'Psychologists' Special Interest Group on the Elderly'.

PSIGE streams at successive autumn British Society of Gerontology conferences enabled psychologists to meet nationally (in Hull in 1982 and Exeter in 1983) as the 16 regional groups were in their infancy. An extraordinary general meeting at Exeter discussed joining the DCP, which was now able to accommodate special interest groups.

This created some controversy, with concerns that PSIGE would become less inclusive of other disciplines or nonclinical psychologists. In a DCP subsystem, these would be excluded from voting or becoming committee members (as would non-BPS members). It was also suggested that 'the elderly' and ageing were not simply a matter for clinical psychology, and that a broader BPS subsystem should be established, such as a Section on Ageing. The counterargument was that if PSIGE remained outside the BPS and DCP, it would not be in a position to influence the development of the profession or be consulted on government and other policy documents. Eventually, the motion was carried, and commitments made to explore associate membership for members of other professions, and to co-opt members to the committee to enable it to reflect the range of interests. PSIGE became a BPS DCP special interest group in 1983, incorporating PACE soon afterwards. The DCP asked the group to consider changing its name but it was 30 years later that the name formally changed to the 'Faculty of the Psychology of Older People' (FPOP).

Despite the formation of PSIGE, the influence of psychology on care of older people remained limited. Few members worked full-time with older people, and there was variable geographical coverage (with concentrations around London and Manchester). In 1982, two leading old-age psychiatrists commented: 'Despite the enthusiasm of a few individuals, psychology has not yet established itself as a regular contributor to psychogeriatric services…it is fair to say that it is more a case of potential than of clearly defined roles' (Arie & Jolley, 1982, p.237). The specialism had been formed, but had yet to make its mark.

Therapeutic approaches

In the late 1970s and early 1980s the widespread adoption of a therapeutic role by clinical psychologists, largely related to the development of the behavioural therapies, coincided with the specialism's growth. Behavioural modification and behavioural psychotherapy were seen as key components of the psychologist's role in both old-age psychiatry (Leng, 1982) and geriatric settings (Larner & Leeming, 1984), with the 'cognitive' dimension soon also explicitly included (Woods & Britton, 1985, pp.198–203), thanks to American trials of cognitive therapy for older people with depression being published (e.g. Gallagher & Thompson, 1983).

Although older people were excluded from most of the early research studies on cognitive behaviour therapy (CBT) for depression and anxiety, limiting the evidence base, CBT was widely adopted as a core element of psychological therapy for older people, with lively discussions regarding possible adaptations. This was assisted by visits in the mid-1990s from Dolores Gallagher-Thompson and Larry Thompson (key-note speaker at 1998 PSIGE Conference, Edinburgh), who led the major US research group on CBT for older people, and from Bob Knight, whose book *Psychotherapy with the Older Adult* (1996) was an inspiration for many. Ken Laidlaw worked with these US pioneers and has been at the forefront of encouraging the application of CBT to older people in the UK, placing the approach in a model incorporating lifespan characteristics. The importance of sharing dysfunctional beliefs and fears about the ageing process, laid down early in life and sometimes causing profound problems, was relevant both for older people and for the psychologists who worked with them. A range of practical suggestions such as slower pacing, adapted homework-setting and compensations for sensory loss have been advocated (Laidlaw et al., 2003). The chronicity of problems and the presence of comorbid health difficulties also need to be taken into account in applying CBT with older adults (Barrowclough et al., 2001).

A wide range of psychological therapies have been adapted and applied with older people, including cognitive analytic therapy (CAT) and more recently third-wave CBT therapies. Psychodynamic approaches have been spearheaded by Rachael Davenhill and colleagues at the Tavistock Institute, London (Davenhill, 2007), with specific courses and resources having been offered for some years. Systemic approaches – typically developed in services for children – have had particular applicability, with many problems experienced by older people embedded within family or other systems (including care homes). Workshops on this topic have been a consistently popular feature of PSIGE conferences down the years, with contributions from Chris Gilleard, Alison Roper-Hall, Marion Dixon and others (see, for example, Gilleard, 1996; Roper-Hall, 1993). Family therapy clinics for older adults have been established in some areas, but more frequently psychologists have integrated the approach into their practice.

Specific approaches to the developmental phase of later life include life review, a psychotherapeutic form of reminiscence work (Butler, 1963), and therapy for loss and grief. A lifespan approach in both assessment and therapy helped older people connect with the contexts in which they had lived and worked, the role transitions experienced and the attachments, successes and losses of their lives. As this lifespan could cover two world wars, themes also included separation, evacuation and coping with change. Veterans of both world wars came into therapy for the first time in later life when the coping strategies they had been able to use, such as keeping physically active or using distraction, became harder to sustain so that post-traumatic stress disorder became evident (Davies, 1997).

The potential for therapeutic interventions in the dementias was noted as early as the late 1970s (Miller, 1977b; Woods & Britton, 1977). 'Reality orientation' (RO), the first formalised approach, was described at length by Holden and Woods (1982). This comprised both small group work (with a cognitive focus) and environmental adaptation and was evaluated in a number of small-scale UK research projects in the 1970s and 1980s. Placing the person with dementia in the position of 'expert' and using their relatively preserved remote memory meant that reminiscence groups offered an attractive alternative to RO (Norris, 1986). By the early 1990s RO was less fashionable, having become too often a form of 'reality confrontation', despite embracing 'validation therapy' techniques of responding to the feelings expressed by the person with dementia rather than correcting facts (Feil, 1993). RO re-emerged, repackaged, with a clear value base, as cognitive stimulation therapy (Spector et al., 2003). Its relatively strong evidence base gained recognition in practice guidelines, such as those issued by NICE and the Social Care Institute for Excellence (SCIE) (NCCMH, 2007). Reminiscence therapy continued in a variety of forms, with a more recent focus on individual life story work (Subramaniam & Woods, 2012). Prominent clinical psychologists, such as Una Holden and Mike Bender, helped to create a range of visual and auditory prompts and triggers, manuals and training aids in the 1980s through the publisher Winslow Press, assisting the implementation of these approaches.

Winslow Press also published a series of brief manuals written by Graham Stokes, each focusing on a specific 'problem behaviour' such as aggression (Stokes, 1987), using the 'A-B-C' (antecedents – behaviour – consequences) behavioural approach. Psychologists questioned the term 'problem behaviour', asking for whom the behaviour was a problem – frequently not those with dementia themselves. 'Challenging behaviour' was coined, with the medical term 'behavioural and psychological symptoms of dementia' resisted as misleading and inaccurate. Although some crossover of practice from learning disability services was evident, applied behaviour analysis approaches have been less prevalent in the dementia field. Esme Moniz-Cook advocated functional analysis in recognition of the hidden nature of some of the antecedent influences. Mike Bird's application of highly individualised approaches, based on a formulation, has been influential (Bird & Moniz-Cook, 2008). Ian James in Newcastle pioneered a highly regarded psychology-led challenging behaviour team, including outreach to care homes. There has also been recognition that people with dementia might benefit directly from psychotherapeutic approaches, in relation to adjustment and symptoms of anxiety and depression, in group and individual contexts (e.g. Cheston, 1996) and that CBT might be feasible in the early stages of dementia. Group and individual approaches for family carers – including psychoeducation, CBT for depression and so on – have been widely practised since the late 1970s.

Neuropsychological assessment

Cognitive assessment (for diagnostic purposes) was the very earliest focus of psychological work with older people in the UK and, although at times overshadowed by the development of therapeutic work, has remained a core feature. The emphasis quickly shifted from deficit-based diagnostic assessment to an assessment of the person's profile of abilities, strengths and weaknesses (Volans & Woods, 1983), to inform rehabilitation and coping strategies and to evaluate change over time. This was challenging, as it typically required comparison with normative data on a number of tests of different abilities, rather than against cut-off scores as employed in diagnostic assessment. For example, the original Wechsler Memory Scale had norms only up to age 49, and a variety of sources needed to be consulted to identify more age-appropriate norms. Development of assessments covering a wider range of cognitive domains with age norms often available up to age 89, and greater ecological validity, has made assessment more sensitive and comprehensive.

Depression and dementia were no longer seen as mutually exclusive diagnoses, and depression was identified from mood assessment rather than cognitive profile. Neuropsychological assessment was still seen as valuable in supporting a diagnostic process where there was uncertainty as to whether cognitive problems being experienced were consistent with a dementia diagnosis or for differentiating atypical dementias. Memory clinics were developed in the 1980s initially to identify people with early-stage dementia who might participate in drug trials. Early clinics at the Maudsley Hospital and at Bristol had neuropsychological input from the outset. These clinics gave the potential to offer prediagnostic assessment counselling and a range of interventions, as well as medication. The psychological role was championed in a special issue of the *PSIGE Newsletter* in January 1998. In the late 1990s, fuelled by the availability of anti-dementia drugs, the focus of many memory clinics became assessment and prescription rather than psychosocial intervention. Brief cognitive screening tools, such as the Mini Mental State Examination (MMSE), were often used with simplistic diagnostic cut-off points by non-psychologists. In many clinics in-depth psychological assessment became rare. Esme Moniz-Cook, in Hull, developed psychology-led memory clinics, based in primary care, but this was an atypical service model.

Many psychologists developed postqualification skills in neuropsychology, and made contributions to the understanding of specific neurodegenerative conditions, including those occurring earlier in life (which were often seen in old age services), as well as the consequences of strokes. For example, Una Holden (1995) drew attention to less common dementias and Robin Morris built on the earlier contributions of Ed Miller, in expanding neuropsychological understanding of Alzheimer's disease (Miller, 1977a; Miller & Morris, 1993).

Many old-age psychologists are also neuropsychologists, some recognised through the 'grandparenting clause' when the Division of Neuropsychology (DoN) formed, some gaining the Qualification in Clinical Neuropsychology since. Neuropsychological assessment continues to be a core area of work, and FPOP works closely with the DoN to enable this to be sustained as training and qualification models develop further.

Dementia – the change of culture

A significant change during the period covered by this chapter has been the 'discovery of the person with dementia' (Woods, 2001), the placing of the person at centre stage, an active participant in assessment, treatment and decision making. Linguistically, the transition has been from 'senile dement' through 'dementia sufferer' to 'person living with a dementia'. Psychology has had a key role in this dramatic change. In the early 1980s, it was realised that 'normalisation' principles, which had proved so transformational in learning disability services, could also be applicable to dementia care. The principles of 'social role valorisation' emphasised the value, individuality and rights of the person living with, in this case, dementia. The King's Fund, an independent think tank, brought together a working group (including Bob Woods) to produce a working paper which spelled out how these principles could be applied in dementia care (King's Fund, 1986). Several national conferences, including psychologists such as Christine Barrowclough and Ellie Stirling, took the work forward (Stirling, 1996).

Independently, Tom Kitwood, a social psychologist at Bradford University, was asked to advise a local old-age psychiatry unit. He spent considerable amounts of time observing people with dementia in the unit and their interactions with other patients, relatives and staff. From his observations, aiming to capture the perspective of the person with dementia, he evolved his 'person-centred theory of dementia care' (summarised in Kitwood, 1997), which identified factors enhancing and reducing the personhood of the person with dementia. A structured observational method, dementia care mapping (DCM), was developed, enabling the observation and quantification of the well-being of the person with dementia, and the influence of the care environment.

Kitwood's work transformed the world of dementia care, in the UK and internationally, far beyond the influence of normalisation. It struck a chord with many, with the need for 'person-centred care', valuing the person as an individual, becoming the accepted benchmark for good practice, and the value base for all other dementia care interventions. Kitwood went on to work with a number of clinical psychologists, and spoke at PSIGE conferences, before his untimely death in 1998. Dawn Brooker took forward his work at Bradford, revising and extending DCM, expanding its international profile. In a landmark *British Medical Journal* paper, a team led by Jane Fossey (Fossey et al., 2006) were able to demonstrate that staff training in person-centred care reduced antipsychotic medication use in nursing homes. DCM is an invaluable marker for well-being for those people with dementia who cannot express their views. More recently people with dementia have been supported to present their own perspectives, with their own voice. With earlier diagnosis, those living well with dementia are likely to become a major force for social and political change.

Training

The conundrum faced when the specialism was formed was how to grow in a context of negative attitudes and expectations. The solutions adopted were to offer (hopefully) lively and engaging teaching sessions on training courses, and to offer as many placement opportunities as possible, to increase initially the pool of potential candidates for older adult posts, to become the supervisors of the future.

As the accreditation criteria for clinical psychology training courses evolved, the importance of all trainees receiving teaching on, and some experience with, older adults began to be explicitly stated. The input to training courses increased dramatically in these early years, from a zero baseline. In 1983, a survey showed an average of 15 hours teaching on older people, and in 1985 the first UK textbook appeared (Woods & Britton, 1985). Requirements to have 'some experience' on placement sometimes appeared to be interpreted as seeing one person aged 65 or over – perhaps for a cognitive assessment. This tokenistic approach concerned older adult supervisors, who saw the value of a full six-month placement as transforming the trainee's attitudes to older people and the potential for the breadth of psychological work with them, over and above development of specific skills. PSIGE argued for work with older people to become a compulsory placement – to achieve this required older adult supervisors to have the highest supervision load of any specialism, but such was the passion felt for this endeavour that this was indeed achieved for several years in the mid to late 1990s.

Ultimately, the rapid growth in training places and the arguments for developing core competencies made a compulsory older adult placement difficult to sustain, with DCP accreditation criteria since 2002 emphasising core transferable skills rather than specific experiences with different client groups. The emphasis is for all trainees to gain experience across the lifespan, but not necessarily to have a specific older adult placement. In response, guidelines for good practice were developed by the PSIGE Training Subgroup (PSIGE, 2006). They aim to ensure that trainee clinical psychologists, upon qualifying, are able to meet the needs of older people, in whatever setting or context they come into contact with them. It provides a model curriculum as well as guidance on placement experience. Although some training programmes still support core older adult placements, there is not equity nationally.

Maturation of a specialty

In limited space, it is impossible to do justice to all strands of psychological work with older people, or to the many individuals who have contributed to the development of the specialism. Since the early years PSIGE has continued to grow – from 106 members in 1981, to 314 members in 1998, to 651 members in 2014. Importantly, it has been well served by a succession of talented and enthusiastic officers and committee members. Internal communication has been strong, with annual conferences well attended, despite pressures on training budgets, task groups focusing on producing papers on key areas of interest (e.g. primary care in the November 1998 *Newsletter*) and a regular newsletter (128 issues to end of 2014) that has become increasingly professional in appearance, while retaining a mix of articles that are relevant and close to the breadth of practice.

Externally, contributions to policy documents and guidance have been a growing feature. Major contributions were made to the 2001 National Service Framework for Older People by Lindsay Royan and Charles Twining, to the 2006 NICE–SCIE guidelines on the management of dementia, to the 2009 National Dementia Strategy for England, and to the comparable documents in post-devolution Wales and Scotland. PSIGE has been proactive in, for example, producing a suite of dementia-related documents in 2014 and advice for commissioners (latest version, 2006),[2] and has benefited from its status as a DCP subsystem in this respect. It has forged good working relationships with groups with similar interests, such as the Royal College of Psychiatrists, as well as third sector organisations such as Age Concern (now Age UK) and Alzheimer's Society.

Perhaps the greatest future challenge relates to the whole basis on which the specialism is defined. Age is an arbitrary index, and to use it to define a specialism might be seen as a form of age discrimination. Yet how else to define the essence? Working with older people requires a lifespan developmental context, which is less of a feature in other areas. The interrelationship of mood with multiple and chronic physical health difficulties, together with a greater risk of cognitive impairment in the 'old old' requires a breadth of specific competencies. The 2007 Age Concern Inquiry into Mental Health and Well-being in Later Life indicated that many older people do not want to be referred to specialist older people services – they see themselves simply as adults, and want the best services that are available for adults. However, those living in age-specific care settings need psychologists who can train and support staff in maintaining quality of life and help prevent the abusive incidents highlighted so frequently.

In some areas, there have been moves to develop all-age adult mental health services, sometimes alongside all-age dementia services. From a psychological perspective, if clinical psychologists have been trained to apply their skills across the whole range of problems and conditions encountered, this appears to make good sense. It avoids the difficulty of transition, when a person is deemed to require an older adult mental health service, having previously received the service from 'adult mental health'; it appears to avoid age discrimination, as required by legislation. Is resistance to it any more than a desire to build up the specialism, which has developed its 'PSIGE mentality' (Woods, 2005) through having to battle for older people to receive a fair share of psychological resources, having to group together against external forces, devaluing and diminishing work with older adults? There are suspicions that such a development is actually a cost-cutting exercise rather than an effort to improve service quality. Above all though is the consistent data indicating that older people are less likely to receive psychological input than any other age group. While a fit and previously active 69-year-old with depression may be best served by an all-age service, what of the frail older person, who has developed depression following a stroke, and who is facing a decision regarding entering a care home? There is a shortage of organisations providing advocacy for older people with mental health difficulties other than the dementias, and it is the passion for older people that has driven PSIGE from the start that makes us want to be certain that individuals in such circumstances are not overlooked and their psychological needs neglected. The challenge for the specialism is to provide a clear message regarding why there is a need for specialist input, and where this is required.

---

[2] See FPOP website www.psige.org/info/member+publications.

References

Arie, T. & Jolley, D. (1982). Making services work: Organisation and style of psychogeriatric services. In R. Levy & F. Post (Eds.), *The psychiatry of late life* (pp.222–251). Oxford: Blackwell,.

Barrowclough, C., King, P., Colville, J. et al. (2001). A randomised trial of the effectiveness of cognitive-behavioral therapy and supportive counseling for anxiety symptoms in older adults. *Journal of Consulting & Clinical Psychology, 69*, 756–762.

Bird, M. & Moniz-Cook, E. (2008). Challenging behaviour in dementia: A psychosocial approach to intervention. In R. T. Woods & L. Clare (Eds.), *Handbook of the clinical psychology of ageing* (2nd edn, pp.571–594). Chichester: Wiley.

Blessed, G., Tomlinson, B.E. & Roth, M. (1968). The association between quantitative measures of dementia and of senile change in the cerebral grey matter of elderly subjects. *British Journal of Psychiatry, 114*, 797–811.

Butler, R.N. (1963). The life review: An interpretation of reminiscence in the aged. *Psychiatry, 26*, 65–76.

Butler, R.N. (1969). Age-ism: Another form of bigotry. *Gerontologist, 9*, 243–246.

Cheston, R. (1996). Stories and metaphors: Talking about the past in a psychotherapy group for people with dementia. *Ageing & Society, 16*, 579–602.

Cosin, L.Z., Mort, M., Post, F. et al. (1958). Experimental treatment of persistent senile confusion. *International Journal of Social Psychiatry, 4*, 24–42.

Davenhill, R. (Ed.) (2007). *Looking into later life.* London: Karnac Books.

Davies, S. (1997). The long-term psychological effects of World War Two. *The Psychologist, 10*(8), 364–367.

Department of Health and Social Security (1977). *The role of psychologists in the health service (Trethowan Report).* London: HMSO.

Department of Health and Social Security (1978). *A happier old age. A discussion document on elderly people in our society.* London: HMSO.

Department of Health and Social Security (1981). *Growing older.* London: HMSO.

Eysenck, M.D. (1945). An exploratory study of mental organisation in senility. *Journal of Neurology, Neurosurgery, and Psychiatry, 8*, 15–21.

Feil, N. (1993). *The validation breakthrough: Simple techniques for communicating with people with 'Alzheimer's type dementia'.* Baltimore: Health Professions Press.

Fossey, J., Ballard, C., Juszczak, E. et al. (2006). Effect of enhanced psychosocial care on antipsychotic use in nursing home residents with severe dementia: Cluster randomised trial. *British Medical Journal, 332*, 756–758.

Gallagher, D.E. & Thompson, L.W. (1983). Effectiveness of psychotherapy for both endogenous and non-endogenous depression in older adult out-patients. *Journal of Gerontology, 38*, 707–712.

Gilleard, C.J. (1996). Family therapy with older clients. In R.T. Woods (Ed.), *Handbook of the clinical psychology of ageing* (pp.561–573). Chichester: Wiley.

Hanley, I. & Hodge, J. (Eds.) (1984). *Psychological approaches to the care of the elderly.* London: Croom Helm.

Hemsi, L.K., Whitehead, A. & Post, F. (1968). Cognitive functioning and cerebral arousal in elderly depressives and dements. *Journal of Psychosomatic Research, 12*, 145–156.

Hilton, C. (2005). The origins of old age psychiatry in Britain in the 1940s. *History of Psychiatry, 16*(3), 267–289.

Holden, U. (1995). *Ageing, neuropsychology and the 'new' dementias: Definitions, explanations and practical approaches.* London: Chapman & Hall.

Holden, U.P. & Woods, R.T. (1982). *Reality orientation: Psychological approaches to the 'confused' elderly.* Edinburgh: Churchill Livingstone.

Inglis, J. (1959). A paired-associate learning test for use with elderly psychiatric patients. *Journal of Mental Science, 105*, 440–443.

Inglis, J. (1962) Psychological practice in geriatric problems. *Journal of Mental Science, 108*, 669–674.

Kendrick, D.C. (1972). The Kendrick battery of tests: Theoretical assumptions and clinical uses. *British Journal of Social and Clinical Psychology, 11*, 373–386.

Kendrick, D.C., Parboosingh, R. & Post, F. (1965). A synonym learning test for use with elderly psychiatric subjects: A validation study. *British Journal of Social and Clinical Psychology, 4*, 63–71.

King's Fund (1986). *Living well into old age: Applying principles of good practice to services for people with dementia.* London: Author.

Kitwood, T. (1997). *Dementia reconsidered: The person comes first.* Buckingham: Open University Press.

Knight, B.G. (1996). *Psychotherapy with the older adult.* Thousand Oaks, CA: Sage.

Kong, T.K. (2000). Dr Marjory Warren: The mother of geriatrics. *Journal of the Hong Kong Geriatrics Society, 10,* 102–105.

Laidlaw, K., Thompson, L.W., Dick-Siskin, L. & Gallagher-Thompson, D. (2003). *Cognitive behaviour therapy with older people.* Chichester: Wiley.

Larner, S.L. & Leeming, J.T. (1984). The work of a clinical psychologist in the care of the elderly. *Age and Ageing, 13,* 29–33.

Leng, N. (1982). Behavioural treatment of the elderly. *Age and Ageing, 11,* 235–243.

Miller, E. (1977a). *Abnormal ageing: The psychology of senile and presenile dementia.* Chichester: Wiley.

Miller, E. (1977b). The management of dementia: A review of some possibilities. *British Journal of Social and Clinical Psychology, 16,* 77–83.

Miller, E. & Morris, R. (1993). *The psychology of dementia.* Chichester: Wiley.

Mumford, S. & Carpenter, G. (1979). Psychological services and the elderly. *Bulletin of the British Psychological Society, 32,* 286–288.

National Collaborating Centre for Mental Health (2007). *Dementia: A NICE-SCIE guideline on supporting people with dementia and their carers in health and social care.* National Clinical Practice Guideline No. 42. London: BPS and Royal College of Psychiatrists.
(Available at www.scie.org.uk/publications/misc/dementia/dementia-fullguideline.pdf)

Norris, A. (1986). *Reminiscence.* London: Winslow Press.

PSIGE (2006). *Good practice guidelines for UK clinical psychology training providers for the training and consolidation of clinical practice in relation to older people.* Leicester: BPS.

Roper-Hall, A. (1993). Developing family therapy services with older adults. In J. Carpenter & A. Treacher (Eds.), *Using family therapy in the nineties* (pp.185–203). Oxford: Blackwell.

Savage, R.D., Britton, P.G., Bolton, N. & Hall, E.H. (1973). *Intellectual functioning in the aged.* London: Methuen.

Shapiro, M.B. Post, F., Loefving, B. & Inglis, J. (1956) 'Memory function' in psychiatric patients over 60: Some methodological and diagnostic implications. *Journal of Mental Science, 10,* 232–246.

Spector, A., Thorgrimsen, L., Woods, B. et al. (2003). Efficacy of an evidence-based cognitive stimulation therapy programme for people with dementia: Randomised controlled trial. *British Journal of Psychiatry, 183,* 248–254.

Stirling, E. (1996). Social role valorization: Making a difference to the lives of older people? In R.T. Woods (Ed.), *Handbook of the clinical psychology of ageing* (pp.389–422). Chichester: Wiley.

Stokes, G. (1987). *Aggression.* Bicester: Winslow Press.

Subramaniam, P. & Woods, B. (2012). The impact of individual reminiscence therapy for people with dementia: Systematic review. *Expert Reviews in Neurotherapeutics, 12*(5), 545–555.

Tinker, A. (2014). *Older people in modern society.* London: Routledge.

Townsend, P. (1962). *The last refuge.* London: Routledge & Kegan Paul.

Volans, P.J. & Woods, R.T. (1983). Why do we assess the aged? *British Journal of Clinical Psychology, 22,* 213–214.

Walton, D. & Black, D.A. (1957), The validity of a psychological test of brain damage. *British Journal of Medical Psychology, 30,* 270–279.

Woods, R.T. (2001). Discovering the person with Alzheimer's disease: Cognitive, emotional and behavioural aspects. *Aging & Mental Health, 5*(Supplement 1), S7–S16.

Woods, R.T. (2005, July). *Still crazy after all these years? An examination of the PSIGE mentality.* Keynote address presented at the PSIGE Conference, Chester.

Woods, R.T. & Britton, P.G. (1977). Psychological approaches to the treatment of the elderly. *Age & Ageing, 6,* 104–112.

Woods, R.T. & Britton, P.G. (1985). *Clinical psychology with the elderly.* London: Croom Helm/ Chapman Hall.

Chapter 21 Clinical health psychology

Paul Bennett

Introduction

The beginnings of clinical health psychology in the UK in the late 1970s and early 1980s can be compared to the 'big bang' in physics, in the nature of their development, if not magnitude. In the beginning, there were no physical health services, then a sudden expansion of services within physical health settings occurred across the country apparently spontaneously and in a relatively brief time span. While there may have been some common stimuli that triggered these developments (including classic texts on health psychology from both within and without the UK; e.g. Broome, 1989; Matarazzo et al., 1984; Stone et al., 1979), and some informal links between the emerging departments, their development was often piecemeal and relatively isolated. Despite this separation, a key driver to this expansion among many of those involved was a desire to move from what was seen as an atomised model of working in mental health to one that encompassed working with other professionals and whole healthcare systems. For others, the ability to engage with a more theoretical perspective to their work, and to produce theoretically informed research was a key driver. The desire to work with people who had physical health problems was important, but other factors were clearly relevant to this expansion.

Any history of clinical health psychology, delivered in a relatively short chapter, has, to some degree, to be partial, and this chapter highlights a number, but not all, of the early developments in the field to give a flavour of key developments and the factors and people that drove them. As an early career clinical health psychologist in the 1980s, working first in Cardiff in elderly medicine and to a lesser extent in pain and tinnitus services, and then in Birmingham on a heart disease prevention project, I saw many of the early developments in clinical health psychology. I also became involved in the Health Psychology Section in 1986 after being accidently voted onto its first national committee,[1] and have been a member of that committee on and off for a number of years since, including at the time the Division of Health Psychology was established, with its implications for the professionalisation of health psychology. The tension between health and clinical health psychology has been an important issue since then (more so perhaps for health rather than clinical health psychologists) and is likely to continue into the future. This chapter reflects some of those interests and speculates as to how these differing strands of professionals may achieve some degree of rapprochement.

---

[1] In an unexpected reciprocal action, after proposing my then head of department (Louise Wallace) as a member of the committee, she then proposed me. As membership of the committee was determined by a vote at the meeting, and as there were several of my colleagues at the meeting who voted for me, I was duly elected onto the committee, despite being a complete unknown to the majority of the meeting.

A false dawn: Medical psychology in the BPS

Early developments in what was termed 'medical psychology' within the British Psychological Society (BPS) were described by what has become an 'underground' (i.e. unpublished) paper by Burton and Kagan (2007). This account describes how the BPS was organised in 1919 to include three specialist sections: educational, industrial, and medical. The Medical Section included people who had been active in treating war neurosis, and became a forum for discussion of psychodynamic theory and psychotherapy. Indeed, by the early 1950s it had become a kind of 'psychodynamic interest group' including many medical doctors. In parallel to the medical section, a Committee of Professional Psychologists (Mental Health) was established in 1943 by educational psychologists to deal with issues affecting the professional status of its members. In 1951, an adult division of this committee, focusing on mental health of adults was formed, and gained representation on the Council of the BPS (see also chapter 5).

In 1952 Hans Eysenck wrote to the BPS *Quarterly Bulletin* complaining about the editorial policy of the *British Journal of Medical Psychology*. He considered it to be publishing increasingly 'speculative papers'. In correspondence with Eysenck the editor of the journal noted that the focus of the journal was primarily related to 'the dynamic interactions of the forces of individual personality and its development'. Both Eysenck and, subsequently, the BPS Council considered this to be inappropriate. Nevertheless, the journal editors resisted change, and for the following six years the Medical Section and BPS council engaged in a dispute in which the Section defended a position against experimental and idiographic approaches at the same time as the BPS asked for an outlet for experimental and statistical research. In 1953, the BPS established a publications committee to administer the policy of the Society's journals. This, and the General Secretary of the BPS, required the Medical Section to widen the scope of the *British Journal of Medical Psychology* to include papers not only from medical psychologists (i.e. medically qualified individuals working with a psychodynamic perspective) but to include also psychotherapy, neuropsychiatry, clinical and experimental research. The medical section refused to make such changes, and despite meetings of a joint committee between BPS Council and the Medical Section (in which the Council requested that the journal include all applications of psychology to medical problems, biological as well as psychological), the Medical Section refused to make such changes.

In response to this intransigence, the BPS Council took action to reduce the power of the so-called 'psychodynamic clique' that was considered to be in control of the Section and its publishing, including establishing a postal vote for committee members in 1955 and Council taking responsibility for the vetting and appointment of all its journal editors in 1957. In addition, the journal was required to publish in accordance with principles formulated by the publications committee (which had been approved by Council). By 1958, although the Medical Section had made some rule changes concerning membership (such as excluding medical practitioners), the orientation of the Section and publishing policy of the journal had changed very little. And there the matter seems to have come to a somewhat shuddering halt, partly because more behaviourally and scientific psychologists established a section more appropriate to their training and orientation (the

English Division of Professional Psychologists, educational and clinical), and partly because of the establishment of the *British Journal of Social and Clinical Psychology*, the development of which began in 1956, and which was first published in 1962.

The Medical Section remained within the BPS, largely focusing on psychodynamic therapies, and the *British Journal of Medical Psychology* transmuted to *Psychology and Psychotherapy: Theory, Research and Practice* in 2002, reflecting the potential confusion between the term 'medical' (which continued to reflect a psychodynamic perspective) and the emerging field of (clinical) health psychology and the publication of the *British Journal of Health Psychology* which began in 1996.

The emergence of modern clinical health psychology

The clinical health psychology that emerged in the UK during the late 1970s and early 1980s was clearly distinct from the psychodynamic or psychosomatic models which placed unconscious psychodynamic processes at the heart of 'somatic' disorders. It also differed from, but is related to, behavioural medicine, which is an interdisciplinary field combining both (para-)medical and psychological perspectives to the study and treatment of illness. Finally, it was seen as distinct from the mental health psychology seen as the dominant paradigm at the time by many of its practitioners. Although clinical health psychologists continued to have an interest in what may be termed 'abnormal' emotional or cognitive states, they also began to consider and adopt very different types of psychological interventions and settings for their work. The change in perspective involved a significant shift from what they saw as the dominant 'illness model' (i.e. working with distressed individuals) of mental health to include among others: a focus on behavioural change as a means of preventing illness (e.g. heart disease prevention); the psychology of rehabilitation and coping with long-term health conditions (e.g. asthma, renal disease, spinal injury, pain); understanding and support of 'normal' emotional responses to serious illness or physical trauma; working in primary care and other preventive settings; and working with systems: changing patterns of care provided by healthcare systems and subsystems

Clinical health psychology as a specialty within broader clinical psychology departments emerged at this time relatively independently in a number of innovative centres, including Leeds, London, Birmingham, and Manchester. But its origins were not confined entirely to the major clinical psychology centres. In fact, centres such as Dudley and Gloucester provided an equally strong impetus for the development of the emerging specialism. It is difficult to determine how many psychologists were working as clinical health psychologists at this early time. However, a somewhat frustrating survey of British clinical psychologists (Norcross et al., 1982) presents some tantalising evidence. They reported that 23 per cent of those who participated in the survey were working in psychiatric hospitals, while a surprisingly large 22 per cent (222 respondents) were working in general hospitals. Of course, many of these individuals would have been engaged in working in mental health, and respondents' area of specialism was not reported. Nevertheless, even at this relatively early time, clinical psychology had a presence in general medical settings. There was also support for this new role in clinical training courses. By the early 1990s, training courses were catching up with developments in the field. Kennedy (1992), for example, reported that around 45 per cent of clinical training courses were providing between 10 and 19 hours of input relevant to clinical health psychology, over 20 per cent were providing between 20 and 39 hours of training, while one course was providing over 40 hours of training in clinical health psychology. Placements were perhaps less well covered, with four courses providing no placements in clinical health psychology at this time. But eight courses provided between 5 and 20 per cent of their placements within clinical health psychology, and one course provided up to 30 percent of its placements in this area. Although the course is not named in the paper, anecdotal evidence suggests the leading teaching and training course at the time was in Leeds. Since then, at least two courses have been established (in Bristol and Bath) which have had a leading focus on clinical health psychology.

A Yorkshire powerhouse

Yorkshire did, and still does, have significant strength in clinical health psychology, and the related discipline of health psychology (see below). Departments in Sheffield and Leeds arose in similar timeframes and with similar subsequent developments. Two key clinical health psychologists in the early 1980s in Sheffield, who have subsequently dominated their fields, are Clare Bradley in diabetes and Pauline Slade in women's health. Both were clinical psychologists with a strong emphasis on applied clinical research. Bradley has also been part responsible with Christopher Brewin for an important shift in the evaluation of psychological therapies, incorporating the element of patient choice into the design of treatment outcome studies (Brewin & Bradley, 1989).

The Leeds clinical health services benefited from being a separate clinical psychology service, not linked to mental health services, within St James's Hospital (Leeds East Health Authority). Originally a disparate group of clinical psychologists working in areas as diverse as paediatric oncology, elderly medicine, plastic surgery and trauma, diabetes and cardiac, renal, assisted conception, and pain, they were melded into a flourishing Department of Physical Health Psychology by Dorothy Fielding in the late 1970s. This department, while venturing into primary care, had no input into mental health services, which were provided by psychologists in the Leeds West Health Authority. In common with many developing services, the role of psychologists within the hospital shifted from the provision of individual therapy with referred patients to being more embedded in medical teams and offering consultancy and training, with a strong emphasis on communication skill training (Latchford & Unwin, 2009). From a total of six psychologists in the 1980s the department had in 2014 a total of 45 clinical health psychologists, similar in size to the present Sheffield service. This development has been supported by strong links with health psychologists on the Leeds clinical psychology training course, and in particular the pain expertise of Stephen Morley. In the early 1990s it was estimated that one third of placements on the Leeds course were in physical health services.

The Midlands and South West

One of the first clinical health services to emerge from a more generic psychology service did so in a somewhat unprepossessing area. Annabel Broome, working in Dudley in the West Midlands, used her personal contact with medical power brokers (including the health authority's chief medical officer) to develop a service providing input into cardiac, renal, chronic pain and maxilla-facial surgery services. As in Leeds, emphasis was placed on working with systems of care as well as with individual patients and with helping people cope with challenging health problems, including disfigurement, in the absence of diagnosable mental health problems. Broome was later to edit one of the most influential UK texts of the time (*Health Psychology: Processes and Applications*, 1989), providing a template for interventions in health care across a range of clinical areas and intervention approaches.

One of Broome's junior colleagues, Louise Wallace, facilitated further development in the Midlands. Rejecting the mental health model then dominant in Birmingham, Wallace moved to Dudley before moving back to South Birmingham Psychology Services in 1984. These services were one of the first to be independent of mental health provision in the UK, and allowed the development of a range of entrepreneurial specialisms, including physical health. She established a range of specialties including burns, chronic pain, and cardiac services. The service was the first to involve a psychologist working with healthy individuals to reduce risk for heart disease, as part of the South Birmingham Coronary Prevention Programme, and to work in areas of physical disability. Wallace wrote an early BPS report (1989) on the contribution of psychology to the care of people with physical disabilities.

Separately, but parallel to these developments, Peter Harvey (who later became the Chair of the DCP) worked in oncology and the newly developing HIV/AIDS services in Central Birmingham. He wrote an influential book, *Health Psychology*, in 1989. He was also one of the first clinical health psychologists to delineate how clinical health psychologists differed from health and clinical psychologists (Harvey, 2009). He drew a clear line between clinical health and psychoanalytic approaches: 'we are not the new somatisers'. He also separated the discipline from psychiatry and liaison psychiatry, which he argued have medical and diagnostic approaches. He considered clinical health psychology to embrace the understanding and facilitate the entirety of the interaction between (medical) clinician and patient, and to support and improve it. He saw it as having a critical role in enhancing health-related communication at all levels. It also offered a humanising counterweight to those he termed the 'biologisers' of behaviour. Finally, he considered that it supported individuals in managing their illness. This emphasis on systems of care as the purview of clinical health psychologists is a common theme.

One of the more unexpected, yet influential, early centres of clinical health psychology was in Gloucester, where a clinical neuropsychologist, Louise Earll, separated from the Gloucester clinical psychology department based on a local mental health hospital to establish a health psychology department in the general Gloucester Royal Hospital. This separation was not just managerial/bureaucratic, since the department also adopted a very different way of working. Although the psychologists within the department continued to see individual patients (in particular working in the context of pain, cardiac rehabilitation, chronic neurological conditions, and renal patients), their work also included the provision of research and consultancy (to whichever medical specialties would pay) across the hospital. Driven by the need to seek funding as well as a more general revised model of working, the team worked with outpatient services to provide a more patient-oriented service as well as other projects. This new way of working, perhaps inadvertently, provided a template for the training and job role of a profession yet to emerge: health psychologists.

London and beyond

London, inevitably, was also central to the early development of clinical health psychology. A number of individuals in the London hospitals were responsible for development of clinical health services and the empirical basis of the emerging profession. Clare Philips, working at the Maudsley Hospital, provided a strong early impetus for its development, arguing along with Stanley Rachman for a much stronger relationship between medicine and psychology than then existed (Rachman & Philips, 1978). A second clinical health psychologist working at the Maudsley, Myra Hunter, has worked there and at King's College, London, since 1988, focusing on women's (and now men's) health. She has published seminal research (e.g. Hunter, 1990) and clinical guidance in these areas, as well as being involved in medical specialisms including cardiology and oncology. Another early pioneer, Maggie Watson, joined the Royal Marsden Hospital and Institute of Cancer Research in 1986 as a research fellow. She conducted seminal studies related to psychological therapies, psychological response and survival (e.g. Watson et al., 1984), screening and quality of life in cancer patients before qualifying as a clinical psychologist in 1988 and being appointed consultant clinical psychologist at the Royal Marsden Hospital in 1991.

A further key individual is frequently cited as an influence on many others establishing clinical health psychology services around the country. Marie Johnston, the head of psychology services at the Royal Free Hospital, with support from other clinical psychologists including John Weinman, Susan Michie and Theresa Marteau, established a model clinical health psychology service. Johnston did not initially train as a clinical psychologist, but was an academic working in Oxford University with people who had physical health problems largely in primary care. She was subsequently asked by May Davison to establish a similar service in London, where in 1977 she moved to an academic post at University College, London, while simultaneously engaging in clinical research, studying for her BPS Diploma in clinical psychology and providing a small clinical service. After qualifying she followed Fay Fransella as head of clinical psychology in both the university and the Royal Free Hospital. At this time a clinical psychology service was already established, providing input into neuropsychology, older adults, child and adult mental health. Johnston developed this further by establishing a 'self-management' clinic which accepted patients from a range of medical disciplines including cancer, palliative care, coronary heart disease and transplants, and also accepted staff referrals. This service received no unique funding, but was run by cross-funding from the other psychology specialties, and become less 'workable' as funding became more tightly linked to them over the years. The service was highly committed to teaching medical students and other health professionals. It also adopted a strong research ethos, providing a model of clinical research within a service context, particularly through the use of single case studies.

The London group of which Johnston was a part was highly entrepreneurial, research-focused, and influential. Over time, however, many of its early practitioners who were trained clinical psychologists moved into academic posts established under the rubric of health psychology and developed early postgraduate programmes in health psychology, a discipline tangential to clinical health psychology and considered later in the chapter. A very different strand of work emanating from London drew inspiration from both the emerging discipline of health psychology and clinical neuropsychology services such as those at the Rivermead rehabilitation centre at Oxford and the National Hospital for Neurology and Neurosurgery in London.

Focusing on the very specific discipline of rehabilitation following spinal injury, Paul Kennedy was based in London at the Royal National Orthopaedic Hospital in Stanmore from 1984 and then moved to the National Spinal Injuries Centre in Stoke Mandeville in 1988. In London he was the first and only psychologist to be involved in the care of patients with spinal injuries in the UK, and was then the first psychologist to be employed at Stoke Mandeville Spinal Injuries Unit. He built strong links with a number of US programmes, which were even then well established, and his approach involved working both directly with patients and developing psychologically sophisticated models of care. He established an assessment and goal-planning process that has become a model for spinal units throughout the UK and which remains central to the care of patients in the unit. Although Kennedy was the first psychologist to be working at what may be considered the premiere, certainly the best known, spinal injuries centre in the UK, other centres, some of which may not have been considered the traditional 'centres of excellence', were also beginning to incorporate the work of psychologists. These included Salisbury (Eileen Griffiths) and the Northwest Regional Spinal Injuries Centre in Southport (Clive Glass) (see Wilson et al., 1993).

Forces beyond

Much of the work that clinical health psychologists became involved with in the early days were driven by local conditions: clinicians and managers that were sympathetic to the psychological needs of patients within their care, local research showing need, and so on. But one external force contributed in itself to a significant rise in the number of psychologists working in health-related areas. The arrival of HIV/AIDS in the mid-1980s caused a significant rise in the number of psychologists working in the context of sexual health. A key player in this process was Lorraine Sherr, who was advantageously placed to take this role following her doctoral thesis assessing the impact of the government's 'Don't die of ignorance' early intervention through television adverts to reduce transmission of HIV (Sherr, 1987).

Showing some of the entrepreneurial approach common to many developing health psychology services, input into working with people with HIV/AIDS was a surprisingly pragmatic decision. An embryonic clinical health psychology service was already established in St Mary's (University College London) Hospital in the early 1980s, but despite providing a service to medical specialties such as the Special Care Baby Unit and oncology was struggling to gain significant traction within the larger hospital. The arrival of AIDS and the clear psychological problems faced by individuals facing this challenge provided the impetus for the development of such services and led to a significant increase in the number of employed clinical health psychologists.

The opportunity was also taken to adopt a different way of working than the traditional role of clinical psychologists, with support from key health psychologists in the US (Martin Fishbein) and Australia (Philip Ley). A model of integrated care was established in which psychosocial ward rounds were led by clinical psychologists, but involved whole medical care teams, increasing the holistic care of patients and reducing the need for individual consultations with clinical psychologists. Significant effort was also given to teaching and training appropriate communication and other psychological skills to all staff involved in care of these people. A second, and necessary, innovation was to ensure the service had a significant research basis. The challenges faced by people who were HIV-positive or had AIDS were as yet poorly understood, as were the best means of providing psychological care for them. In the absence of such information, a key driver for the service was to research the relevant evidence and to publish, facilitating the understanding of psychosocial factors associated with HIV/AIDS to a wider audience. This process was facilitated by Sherr's early editorship of the journal *AIDS Care* from 1989 and work published by others, such as Robert Bor (e.g. Bor et al., 1988) from the Royal Free Hospital.

The care of people with HIV/AIDS was initially focused on centres with large gay populations (it was initially believed that the condition was confined largely to the gay population, and this group certainly suffered its highest prevalence at this time), with London providing significant early services, and then Brighton (led by Heather George). Its link to intravenous drug use also led to the early development of services in places such as Edinburgh where there was high IV drug use and HIV prevalence rates. Reflecting how demand follows need, however, the increasingly sophisticated and successful treatment of HIV infection has meant that since the mid-1990s psychology services have been 'somewhat challenged' and had a diminished role in this area of care. Nevertheless, psychological care of those with HIV is still seen as central to their overall care, and clinical health psychology services have a significant input to these individuals. Sherr herself went on to have a significant role at an international level, working for the World Health Organization, among others, in its fight against the devastating psychosocial impact of AIDS across the world.

The problem of pain

UK clinical research and practice in the management of pain is world class, and has been since the 1980s. Following a Winston Churchill Travelling Fellowship, Chris Main, working in the Manchester and Salford Pain Clinic, established the first UK low back pain management programme in 1982 and went on to lead a multidisciplinary Department of Behavioural Medicine. Other centres in London, Bath and Leeds later become world leaders, both in terms of the development of pain management programmes and in theoretical perspectives on the experience of pain (e.g. Eccleston et al., 1997; McCracken & Morley, 2014; Philips & Rachman, 1996). One of the most influential services, in Bath, was established in 1994. Showing its somewhat small beginnings, Christopher Eccleston and Kiki Mastroyannopoulou (1995) described how they established a three-week cognitive behavioural inpatient chronic pain management programme in the Royal National Hospital for Neurological Diseases, with the first group of six patients completing the programme in July that year. As with virtually all other early services identified in this chapter, this programme explicitly involved training others in the process of psychological care. In addition, it provides an early example of a clinical health psychologist and health psychologist working together within a larger multidisciplinary team. The centre did not arise completely isolated from others around it, however, and had explicit roots and links with the Gloucester Pain Management programme, established in the earlier 1990s (Gloucestershire Royal Hospital, 1994).

The formalisation of clinical health psychology

The Division of Clinical Psychology is a strong advocate for clinical psychology across a range of organisations and settings. Its large membership and its ability to fully cost its key honorary committee members renders it the most powerful entity supporting professional psychologists within the BPS. However, it cannot provide support for particular specialties within the broader discipline. This stems from a range of 'faculties' within the wider organisation. The Faculty of Clinical Health Psychology is a special interest group for all clinical psychologists practising in physical health settings. It came into being in December 1998, following on from the Forum for Clinical Psychologists working in Physical Disability and Rehabilitation, led by Richard Pemberton. The Faculty's first chair was Tony Wells. Its goals include: (a) promoting the professional and scientific work of Division members, (b) fostering effective clinical services and support of services users, (c) providing advice to psychologists working in physical health and disability, (d) advising on training of psychologists at all levels of training, (e) advising the Society and other relevant organisations about psychological needs and role of psychology in relation to them.

The family cousins

The clinical health psychology faculty is, however, not the only entity representing psychologists working in physical health settings; nor are clinical health psychologists the only psychologists that do so. Following the findings of a working group established by the American Psychological Society (APA) in 1973, areas of research and practice related to physical health were recognised as a specific discipline additional to clinical health psychology (APA Task Force on Health Research, 1976) and in 1977 the APA established its Section 38: health psychology. Matarazzo famously defined the discipline as:

> the aggregate of the specific educational, scientific and professional contributions of the discipline of psychology to the promotion and maintenance of health, the prevention and treatment of illness, the identification of diagnostic and etiologic correlates of health, illness and related dysfunction, and the analysis and improvement of the health care system and health policy formation. (Matarazzo, 1980, p.815)

Partly influenced by these developments, the failure of the medical section to shift from its psychoanalytic stance, and her work as a corresponding contributor to the APA report, Marie Johnston along with John Weinman (see Johnston et al., 2011) argued in a letter to the *BPS Bulletin* that the BPS should establish a similar entity.

A working party was subsequently established to consider establishing a BPS Health Section (focused around a common research interest), and in December 1986, following an inaugural meeting at the annual BPS London Conference, the Section was formally established with Marie Johnston as founding chair. The committee consisted almost entirely of clinical psychologists both in academic and applied settings, who were seeking an alternative voice to the DCP through which to explore their interest in aspects of psychology relevant to physical health.

The motivation to form the Section was driven by a number of factors, including a desire to engage with scientific and theoretical areas typically beyond the remit of clinical health psychology at the time, including research into the relationships between behaviour and health, the role of social cognition models in determining health-related behaviours, models of behavioural change, and psychobiological (psychophysiology and psychoneuroimmunology) models of health. It was also driven by more pragmatic imperatives including the need to support individuals involved in teaching behavioural sciences in medical schools and teaching and training health professionals in a range of health-related issues related to communication skills, adherence and so on. As a Section, its aim was to provide a forum for discussion and support for those involved in both research and practice related to health psychology. Its members included clinical psychologists as well as academics engaged in health psychology research and teaching.

The shift from a largely academic group to one aspiring to practitioner status followed debates held in St Regent's College in 1990 and the Section's annual conference (held in conjunction with the European Health Psychology Society) in 1991. At this conference a general members' meeting was held which included a debate focusing on the benefits and costs of remaining a section or moving towards divisional status. Speaking in support of change, moving toward divisional status and the professional development of health psychology, were Theresa Marteau and Stephen Wright, and in support of maintaining the status quo, a scientific discipline-based entity, were Paul Kennedy and Malcolm Adams. The meeting voted overwhelmingly for a movement towards divisional (and hence, practitioner) status. Interestingly, all the key speakers in the meeting were clinical psychologists.

The Section became a Special Group in 1993 (a sign of progress towards divisional status) and was awarded divisional status in 1997. This change in status was not without controversy. The awarding of divisional status meant that the individual training needs and professional practice of health psychologists were recognised, and members were able to obtain chartered status with the BPS. At the time of its inception, there was significant unease within the DCP at the development of a profession with potentially overlapping skills and work areas. As a consequence, the DCP placed strong pressure on the Council to ensure that practitioners within the newly formed Division were not trained in therapeutic skills. The skill set of the new profession therefore focused on research, teaching, and consultation skills. They did not include any form of psychological intervention.

A marriage made in heaven?

Over time, this clear delineation between the roles of health and clinical health psychologists has become less clear. The BPS acknowledged, or even supported, the fuzzy boundaries between the competencies of the two disciplines by including behaviour change interventions as one of the core competencies of health psychologists in 2009 (BPS 2009). These became: generic professional skills as well as specific skills in (a) behaviour change interventions, (b) research, (c) consultancy and (d) teaching and training. Even more changes occurred when the Health and Care Professions Council (2012) determined the proficiencies of health psychologists to include: (a) the ability 'to develop and apply effective interventions to promote psychological well-being, social, emotional and behavioural development', (b) the ability 'to implement psychological interventions appropriate to the presenting problem and to the psychological and social circumstances', and (c) the ability, 'on the basis of psychological formulation, to implement psychological therapy or other interventions appropriate to the presenting problem'. The differences between clinical health and health psychology became less clearly defined although the training of health psychologists has, at the time of writing, yet to include interventions to influence emotional consequences of physical health problems.

The future?

Psychology, if not psychologists, has now become central to the care of physical ill individuals. There are several guidelines for the care of physically ill individuals which specify the need for appropriate psychological care, and referral to psychologists if various criteria are met. Even the general NICE guidelines for the treatment of acutely ill patients in hospital (www.nice.org.uk/guidance/cg50) specify the need for high quality communication, information provision and informed decision making, all areas central to health psychology teaching and training.

Clinical health psychology interventions are not only effective, they have the potential to be cost-effective: a highly prized quality in an increasingly cash-strapped healthcare system. They also fit within the zeitgeist of present government proposals for increasing levels of self-management of disease and a shift to patient responsibility for care (www.gov.uk/government/policies/improving-quality-of-life-for-people-with-long-term-conditions). Despite this potential, clinical health psychologists face a number of challenges. First, how (and indeed whether) health and clinical health psychologists can work together to provide effective services. As the two disciplines' core skills appear to merge, a clear delineated role for each becomes more difficult to determine. At present, the lack of training in intervention approaches beyond behaviour change suggests that health psychologists' role may be limited to behaviour change interventions in individuals experiencing relatively low levels of emotional distress. However, as health psychologists gain training and experience in managing distress this clear delineation of roles may become less clear. An equally simple split may be that health psychologists focus on prevention and public health, while clinical health psychologists work with people and in primary and secondary care systems where this prevention has not been achieved. While this is appealing, public health programmes have not been particularly welcoming to health psychologists. More work is needed here. A more radical approach may be to remove the separation of training programmes and to foster commonalities between them rather than focusing on differences, perhaps along the lines suggested by Kinderman (2005).

Some rapprochement needs to be achieved between the two professions because both also face competition from external forces. Psychologists are frequently seen as expensive, and fulfilling roles that other, less expensive, professionals can undertake. Consultant nurses, counsellors and others have been seen as equally effective and cheaper alternatives to psychologists. This is not necessarily a 'bad thing' and clinical psychology has a long history of sharing relevant skills. However, we have also learned that such a process should be proportionate. Many basic psychological interventions or psychologically sophisticated interactions with service users should not involve professional psychologists. However, psychologists need to be at the heart of preparing other health professionals for such encounters and themselves engage in more psychologically complex activities. The boundaries between these differing skill levels may be fuzzy, but the profession needs to ensure that the voice of psychology is listened to when services are planned and developed. Much has been achieved over the past three decades. Medical practitioners, service managers, and even government policies are now more receptive to the role of psychology than at any previous time. NICE guidelines frequently include psychological interventions in physical healthcare settings and there are even NICE guidelines on the practice of behavioural change (www.nice.org.uk/guidance/ph49). We, collectively, need to work to ensure that psychologists remain at the heart of clinical care.

Acknowledgements

Enormous thanks to busy professionals who gave their time to be interviewed in preparation for this chapter, and who often exceeded what could reasonably be asked for by sending original papers of suggested readings: Patrick Hill, Gary Latchford, Louise Wallace, Paul Kennedy, Lorraine Sherr, Marie Johnson.

References

APA Task Force on Health Research (1976). Contributions of psychology to health research: Patterns, problems, and potentials. *American Psychologist, 31*, 263–274.

Bor, R., Miller, R. & Goldman, E. (1988). *Theory and practice of HIV counselling: A systemic approach.* London: Routledge.

Brewin C. & Bradley C. (1989). Patient preferences and randomised clinical trials. *British Medical Journal, 299*, 313–315.

British Psychological Society (2009). *Qualification in health psychology (stage 2). Candidate handbook.* Leicester: Author.

Broome, A.K. (1989). *Health psychology processes and applications.* Colchester: Chapman & Hall.

Burton M. & Kagan, C. (2007). *British clinical psychology in historical perspective. The genesis of a profession.* www.compsy.org.uk/British%20Clinical%20Psychology%20in%20Historical%20Perspective.pdf

Eccleston, C. & Mastroyannopoulou, K. (1995). The development of an in-patient chronic pain management service: Some reflections on training and teamwork. *Clinical Psychology Forum, 77*, 22–24.

Eccleston C., Williams A.C. de C. & Stainton Rogers, W. (1997). Patients' and professionals' understandings of the causes of chronic pain: Blame, responsibility and identity protection. *Social Science and Medicine, 45*, 699–709.

Gloucestershire Royal Hospital (1994). *Pain management manual: Handouts and materials.* Gloucester: Author.

Harvey, P. (1988). *Health psychology.* London: Longman.

Harvey, P. (2009). From behavioural medicine to health psychology. *Clinical Psychology Forum, 199*, 12–17.

Health and Care Professions Council (2012). *Standards of proficiency. Practitioner Psychologists.* London: Author.

Hunter, M.S. (1990). Psychological and somatic experience of the menopause: A prospective study. *Psychosomatic Medicine, 52,* 357–67.

Johnston, M., Weinman, J. & Chater, A. (2011) A healthy contribution. *The Psychologist, 24,* 890–892.

Kennedy, P. (1988). Clinical services for spinal cord injured people. *Clinical Psychology Forum, 15,* 16–18.

Kennedy, P. (1992). Health psychology input to clinical psychology training course. *Clinical Psychology Forum, 46,* 7–9.

Kinderman, P. (2005). The applied psychology revolution. *The Psychologist, 18,* 744–746.

Latchford, G. & Unwin, J. (2009). Clinical health psychology: An introduction to the special issue. *Clinical Psychology Forum, 199,* 9–11.

Matarazzo, J.D. (1980). Behavioral health and behavioral medicine: Frontiers for a new health psychology. *American Psychologist, 35,* 807–818.

Matarazzo, J.D., Weiss. J.M., Herd. J.A. et al. (Eds.) (1984). *Behavioral health: A handbook of health enhancement and disease prevention.* New York: Wiley.

McCracken, L.M. & Morley S. (2014) The psychological flexibility model: A basis for integration and progress in psychological approaches to chronic pain management. *Journal of Pain, 15,* 221–234.

Norcross, J.C., Brust, A.M. & Dryden, W. (1982). British clinical psychologists: II, Survey findings and American comparisons. *Clinical Psychology Forum, 40,* 25–29.

Philips, C. & Rachman, S. (1996). *The psychological management of chronic pain: Patient's manual.* London: Springer.

Rachman, S. & Philips, C. (1978). *Psychology and medicine.* London: Penguin.

Sherr, L. (1987). An evaluation of the UK government health education campaign on AIDS. *Psychology and Health, 1,* 61–72.

Stone, G.C., Adler, N.E. & Cohen, F. (1979). *Health psychology – A handbook: Theories, applications, and challenges of a psychological approach to the health care system.* San Francisco: Jossey-Bass.

Wallace, L.M. (1989). BPS working party report on psychology and physical disability. *Clinical Psychology Forum, 17,* 36–37.

Watson, M., Greer, S., Blake, S. & Shrapnell, K. (1984). Reaction to a diagnosis of breast cancer. Relationship between denial, delay and rates of psychological morbidity. *Cancer, 53,* 2008–2012.

Wilson, C., Kennedy, P. & Glass, C. (1993). The development of psychological services following spinal trauma. *Clinical Psychology Forum, 55,* 17–19.

Chapter 22 Forensic clinical psychology

Gisli H. Gudjonsson & Susan Young

Introduction

This chapter will focus on the pioneering work conducted in the UK that is relevant to the practice of forensic clinical psychology. It will highlight both the importance of research and innovative professional practice.

Court work: Professor Lionel Haward

Lionel Haward pioneered forensic psychology in the UK from the early 1950s; it was his experience with forensic work in the Royal Air Force between 1939 and 1946 that stimulated his interest in forensic psychology. He first published on the topic in 1953, but most of his innovative work occurred between the mid 1960s and late 1970s. In 1965 he started teaching forensic psychology to trainee clinical psychologists, as part of the South West Metropolitan Region Training Scheme. He was the director of clinical psychology at the University of Surrey between 1971 and 1987 and was actively involved in the creation of the BPS Division of Legal and Criminological Psychology (DLCP) in 1977, which was renamed the Division of Forensic Psychology (DFP) in 1999 after much professional debate.

Haward's work showed great ingenuity and breadth of experience. According to Ronald Blackburn, Lionel Haward 'pioneered the application of psychology to legal questions in this country' (Blackburn, 1996, p.7). In his groundbreaking book Forensic Psychology Haward (1981) described four broad roles for psychologists when answering legal questions: clinical, experimental, actuarial, and advisory. In the clinical role their contribution was to complement and supplement the contribution of their medical colleagues. The focus was on the assessment of psychological functioning, mental health, capacity, or treatability (i.e. it represents an interaction between a clinician and a client). In the experimental role the psychologist performs an original and unique function by conducting laboratory or field research. The actuarial role refers to the psychologist relying on the observation of data in order to establish the probability of the occurrence of a particular phenomenon. In the advisory role the psychologist provides counsel with comments and questions to ask witnesses, including experts from the opposite side. Haward subsequently published *A Dictionary of Forensic Psychology* (Haward, 1990) and a joint publication on forensic psychology in practice (Gudjonsson & Haward, 1998).

Haward (1981) discussed the need for psychologists to produce their findings independently to the court, as the common practice at that time was for psychological findings to be incorporated into a medical report and presented as 'hearsay' evidence: '...they [psychologists] often find that their reports are embodied into those of medical practitioners with whom they work, sometimes without their consent, sometimes against their wishes, and sometimes even without their knowledge' (Haward, 1981, p.58).

Haward first testified in a criminal case in 1958 after a psychiatrist colleague had been unable to answer searching questions in court regarding test findings that he had taken from Haward's assessment and incorporated into his own testimony. The trial judge ruled that this aspect of the psychiatrist's evidence was hearsay and Haward used this ruling to prepare a substantive paper in 1965 for the BPS on the rule of hearsay in relation to psychological reports. In spite of Haward's efforts, it was not until the early 1980s that psychologists truly began to give evidence in their own right in the criminal courts. In 1980 and 1981 Haward testified for the defence, along with Olive Tunstall and Gisli Gudjonsson, in a major fraud case at the Old Bailey. This was Gudjonsson's first evidence in court, and it was Haward's last. Alice Heim appeared in rebuttal for the prosecution. The proposed evidence of the late Hans Eysenck was not admitted, because it was of general nature about intelligence testing, focusing on the review of experimental research. At the time there was scepticism about the real value of forensic clinical psychology in court proceedings, which led to lengthy and hostile cross-examination of the three defence experts and raised a number of professional issues for the BPS (Tunstall et al., 1982). The courts' hostility towards psychological evidence and reluctance to admit their evidence remained for a decade until a landmark victory in the Court of Appeal in 1991 in the case of Engin Raghip – one of the 'Tottenham Three' (Gudjonsson, 2003a). This was a key turning point for forensic clinical psychology. Sadly, Haward never had the opportunity of testifying in the Court of Appeal, but his influence was to build a solid foundation for the new generation of forensic clinical psychologists. His legacy was to establish the independence of forensic clinical psychologists from their medical colleagues in the courtroom.

Surveys of psychologists as 'expert witness'

Table 22.1 provides the key findings from five surveys regarding psychologists providing expert evidence in court or at a tribunal. Four of the surveys (Castell, 1966; Gudjonsson, 1985, 1996, 2008) were commissioned by the BPS and focused on members of different Divisions. The Edmundson (1995) survey focused on a selected group of prison psychologists who were involved in the 'Discretionary Life Panel' process. The main conclusions from the surveys can be summarised as follows:

1. Prior to the early 1980s, psychologists were typically producing reports for medical (psychiatrist) colleagues who often incorporated their findings into their evidence in court, which caused problems with hearsay evidence. The surveys show that since the 1980s, most psychologists receive referrals directly from lawyers and testify about their evidence in court. This improves transparency, accountability, and professionalism.
2. In the 1960s the majority of psychologists involved in court work were educational psychologists, but since the 1980s their involvement declined. This is probably due to the recognition and developing role of clinical and forensic psychologists and the fact that BPS only represented educational psychologists until 1962; thereafter they formed the Association of Educational Psychologists (AEP) which remains their professional body (Martin, 2013).
3. There has been a rapid growth in the involvement of psychologists in civil cases, particularly compensation cases, which does not appear to have increased to the

same extent in other areas of court work. This is now where the largest number of reports is being completed. However, the surveys show that psychologists only testify on about 1 to 2 per cent of the cases where they have produced written reports in contrast to criminal and family/matrimonial proceedings where psychologists commonly have to testify in court.

4. Psychologists typically found giving evidence stressful and did not feel well trained or psychologically prepared for giving evidence.

Table 22.1 The results from surveys on psychologists' court work

Survey	Year	Method	Main findings
Castell (1966)	1965	A questionnaire was sent out to members of the English and Scottish Divisions of the BPS about involvement in court work.	113 responded and of those who had written reports 86% had produced written reports. Of those, 48% had given evidence in court. The respondents were exclusively educational (57%) and clinical (43%) psychologists. Castell concluded that educational psychologists produced more reports than clinical psychologists, but are less likely to be called to give oral evidence. This may reflect the different type of reports provided: clinical psychologists more often addressed questions to do with diagnosis, whereas educational psychologists focused more on intellectual assessment, disposal and prognosis, particularly in juvenile cases. The majority of the referrals came from medical colleagues and the psychologists' findings were mostly incorporated into the psychiatric report, without any payment to the psychologist, and often inappropriately interpreted in court. This was of greatest concern to the psychologists participating in the survey.
Gudjonsson (1985)	1984	A 20-item questionnaire sent to all divisions of the BPS to address questions about frequency of presenting evidence in court and disclosure of confidential test material in open court. Only those who had given oral evidence in court or tribunal during the previous five years were asked to complete the questionnaire. The survey was conducted because of professional issues arising from expert psychological evidence presented at the Old Bailey (Tunstall et al., 1982).	The 185 respondents were mainly clinical (71%) and educational (22%) and 181 had given evidence in court in civil and/or criminal cases. The evidence was mainly based on behavioural assessments/interviews, followed by cognitive tests. 80% had received their instructions from solicitors. The psychologists were commonly asked to disclose details of the psychometric tests in court. Many of the respondents reported being poorly informed, prepared and supported. They found giving evidence to be highly stressful.
Gudjonsson (1996)	1995	A similar questionnaire to that used in the 1984 survey with the addition of more detailed questions. The purpose was to obtain information about court and tribunal work of psychologists during the previous five years. In contrast to the 1984	There were 522 respondents who were mainly clinical (80%) and educational (12%) psychologists. Most reports were produced for civil (55%) and family/juvenile/matrimonial (22%) proceedings, followed by criminal cases (15%) and tribunal cases (4%). In contrast, psychologists were least likely to testify in civil cases (2%) and most commonly in criminal cases (20%) with 10% testifying in

continued

Table 22.1 *continued*

Survey	Year	Method	Main findings
		survey psychologists from all divisions who had written reports (not merely given oral evidence in court or tribunal) were asked to complete the questionnaire.	family/juvenile/matrimonial cases. 80% had received their instructions from solicitors, which is identical to that found in the 1984 survey, but the number of psychologists involved in providing expert testimony appeared to have increased substantially over the previous 10 years. Out of the total sample, 27% of the respondents reported that they had on one or more occasions been asked to modify their report to make it more favourable to the defence. Only three psychologists reported having testified in the Court of Appeal (criminal cases).
Gudjonsson (2008)	2007	A shortened and substantially adapted version of the questionnaire from the 1995 survey was used. Only members of the BPS Directory of Expert Witnesses were asked to complete the questionnaire and 191 completed it.	The majority of respondents were clinical psychologists (62%), followed by forensic (18.5%) and educational (14%) psychologists. Most of the report involvement was in relation to civil cases (60%) and family/matrimonial proceedings (51.6%), followed by criminal cases (50.5%) and tribunal reports (34.5%). So far as oral testimony was concerned, as a proportion of reports produced, the psychologists most commonly testified in tribunal (46%), criminal (31%), and family proceedings (22%), with only 1% of reports resulting in oral testimony in civil cases. Only four psychologists reported having testified in the Court of Appeal (criminal cases).
Edmundson (1995)	1993	104 questionnaires were sent to prison psychologists who had been involved in the 'Discretionary Life Panel' process. 89 (86%) replied and 47% reported that they had written one or more reports on 'lifers' for a Discretionary Life Panel.	The psychologists orally testified on 31% of cases where a report had been produced. They were typically called to give evidence on behalf of prisoners or their representatives. The cross-examination typically involved questioning regarding whether change was associated with the treatment provided in prison, and risk assessment. The psychologist's recommendations were accepted in 77% of the cases. Many of the psychologists reported feeling apprehensive about appearing as a witness. This appeared to be a confidence problem rather than a skills issue.

Forensic hypnosis

Haward (1990) proposed three roles for the application of forensic hypnosis in the UK: (a) preparation of a witness for court (i.e. a form of anxiety management); (b) a psychological investigation of the accused; and (c) improving the memory recall of witnesses. According to Haward the application of forensic hypnosis in the UK increased substantially in the 1970s and in one year his own caseload peaked to 34 cases. The primary role related to memory enhancement, particularly of rape victims. Ordinary witnesses were also hypnotised on occasions. The main concerns about the use of investigative hypnosis for judicial purposes were the absence of scientific validity, possible memory contamination effect, inflated confidence for what is recalled, and problems with the admissibility of evidence produced by witnesses who had been hypnotised.

In the late 1980s the use of hypnosis with witnesses came under close scrutiny and criticism (e.g. the case of *R* v. *Costa* in Maidstone Crown Court in 1987, which resulted in the Home Office producing guidelines about the use of hypnosis for court purposes and discouraging its use). The Division of Clinical Psychology (DCP) and Division of Clinical and Legal Psychology (DCLP) produced comments during the consultation period and recommended that all hypnosis interviews be video-recorded and used only with witnesses who are not required to give evidence in court. In 2001, the British Psychological Society produced a position paper and concluded that 'hypnosis may result in false memories and misplaced confidence in recall. Consequently, if hypnosis is used at all for investigative purposes, any evidence elicited should be treated with the utmost caution' (BPS, 2001, p.8). It has since been used for other purposes. Box 22.1 (overleaf) describes how hypnosis was used in 2001 at the London Central Criminal Court (the 'Old Bailey') to assist a defendant to regain his eyesight after having allegedly lost it during legal arguments at the beginning of his trial.

The use of the polygraph

The polygraph, when used for lie detection purposes, has been used for criminal investigations, personnel selection and security vetting (Gale, 1988). In the aftermath of the Geoffrey Prime spy case in 1982, the British Government announced its intention to undertake pilot studies on the use of the polygraph for security vetting purposes. The Employment Committee was concerned about the government's apparent faith in the use of the polygraph for security and employment screening and set up a public inquiry in order to review the polygraph's evidence base. The BPS submitted evidence to the inquiry and published its objections. The Scientific Affairs Board then set up a working group under the chairmanship of Professor Gale and its findings were published in 1986, concluding that the use of polygraph testing for lie detection purposes was contrary to the spirit of the Society's *Code of Conduct*.

In 2004, the British Psychological Society commissioned a working party to review the scientific status and the application of the polygraph, including its clinical application, as in the UK it had been used for clinical purposes, including:

- to establish the identity of an alleged amnesic patient;
- to diagnose genuine blood injury phobia in an appeal case of suspected drunken driving;
- postconviction sex-offender testing to assist with sex-offender management and treatment (Grubin, 2008). This more recent application of the polygraph will probably replace the use of the penile plethysmograph, which is physically more intrusive and dependent on the availability and ethical acceptability of appropriate stimulus material.

Other methods of lie detection have been used. Alan Smith's (2011) application of the psychological stress evaluator (PSE) in the 1970s is of historical interest. It was developed by three former US Army intelligence officers, who in 1970 marketed a machine that supposedly measured the suppression of microtremor in the voice during stress. Unlike the polygraph, the machine did not require any electrodes being attached to the person, and stress could be measured retrospectively from a taped recorded conversation. Smith experimented with its use over several years and reported that it was better at providing an indication of overall stress level (i.e. anxiety) than as a 'lie detector' test. He concluded:

> There has been no further progress in establishing voice patterns as a measure of anxiety or stress or arousal. Thirty years on, my 1977 study is still being quoted by PSE operators in support of this machine, although of course anyone who reads it will see that it is irrelevant to lie detection. (Smith, 2011, p.77)

Psychological vulnerabilities

The English legal system was shaken in the early 1970s by a miscarriage of justice in the case of the murder of Maxwell Confait, resulting from police-coerced false confessions by three vulnerable teenagers. In the early 1980s, following the report of the Royal Commission on Criminal Procedure in 1981, which resulted in the implementation of the Police and Criminal Evidence Act and its Codes of Practice in 1986, there became greater awareness of psychological vulnerabilities in police interviews and how they might affect reliability and voluntariness. This resulted in an increased demand for psychological assessments relating to confession evidence and the reliability of victims' statements.

In December 1981 Gudjonsson gave evidence for the prosecution in a case that was to strongly influence his thinking and this motivated him to develop the Gudjonsson Suggestibility Scales. The case involved assessing the capacity of an intellectually disabled woman to give evidence in court (Gudjonsson & Gunn, 1982). It became clear that it was important to assess suggestibility, but no suitable instrument was available for this purpose. There existed some research on the topic and, while the experimental work of Elizabeth Loftus in the US was influential, it was not well suited for an individual difference approach to the measurement of suggestibility during police questioning (Gudjonsson & Clark, 1986). As a result Gudjonsson developed the Gudjonsson Suggestibility Scales.

The application of the Gudjonsson Suggestibility Scales in relation to unreliable confession evidence was first heard in the Court of Appeal in November 1991 in the case of Engin Raghip, known as one of the 'Tottenham Three' convicted of the murder of police officer Keith Blakelock (Gudjonsson, 2003a, 2003b). This was a landmark judgement that broadened the criteria for the admissibility of expert psychological evidence to include 'borderline' IQ and personality traits of suggestibility and compliance. This judgement influenced other cases in the Court of Appeal as well as cases in the lower court. In December 2001 the House of Lords quashed the conviction of Donald Pendleton, whose appeal against his conviction for murder had failed in June 2000, on the basis of psychological evidence that was in part based on the appellant's high level of suggestibility and compliance.

Adverse inferences and support in court

The implementation of the Criminal Justice and Public Order Act 1994 meant that adverse inferences may be drawn from failure of suspects to answer questions

Box 22.1 Hypnosis of a defendant with psychogenic blindness

On 26 April 1999, Jill Dando, the presenter of the BBC programme *Crimewatch*, was shot dead outside her home in Fulham, London. On 2 July 2001 Barry George, who lived nearby, was convicted of her murder. Prior to the trial, three defence experts, Gisli Gudjonsson, Susan Young and Michael Kopelman, had reported that Mr George's fitness to stand trial was contingent on his receiving clinical psychological support in court throughout the trial, which lasted between 23 April to 2 July 2001.

Mr George had a complex presentation, including a long history of primary generalised epilepsy (first identified at age two or three), severely abnormal EEG, intellectual deterioration, significant cognitive and executive deficits, rigid and obsessive personality structure, hypochondriacal preoccupations, and an extreme reaction to stress in the form of anxiety and panic attacks, which increased the frequency of absence epileptic seizures. The court appointed Susan Young, a forensic clinical psychologist, who initially sat in the dock with Mr George and provided him with the required assistance. On 26 April 2001, on the fourth day of the legal arguments and prior to swearing in the jury, Mr George turned to Susan Young and declared, 'I can't see'. Prior to this, Mr George had been observed having difficulties concentrating on the legal arguments and he claimed to be experiencing petit mal epileptic seizures in the dock.

The trial before the jury was due to commence on 2 May, but the court determined that the trial could only proceed if Mr George's eyesight could be restored. On the morning of 1 May, all three defence experts were asked to meet Mr George and try to restore his eyesight by 2.00 p.m. (when court commenced that day). Michael Kopelman conducted a medical examination and informed Mr George that there was no physical explanation for his blindness. All attempts to persuade Mr George that it was in his interest to regain his eyesight proved fruitless; he simply kept saying 'I can't see'. At 12.30 p.m. Gisli Gudjonsson, who was trained in hypnosis techniques, suggested that hypnosis might prove successful in bringing back his sight. Mr George agreed to this approach. After an initial induction to the process, Mr George was asked to imagine that he was being taken through a tunnel, accompanied by suggestions that his eyesight would gradually return during that journey and improve further during the one-hour lunch break (i.e. posthypnotic suggestion). After being brought out of the hypnosis, Mr George said he could see but his eyesight was blurred. He was reassured that it would continue to improve and by 2.00 p.m. his eyesight had fully recovered and after the final legal arguments that afternoon, the trial commenced before the jury.

The defence experts construed Mr George's blindness as being psychogenic in origin caused by his inability to cope with the stress generated during the legal arguments (i.e. putting a physical barrier between himself and the court), which was unlocked by the process of hypnosis. This was not the first time Mr George had presented with psychogenic symptoms as he had presented with a functional aphonia (i.e. nonorganic loss of speech) following a stressful environmental event in 1994. Psychogenic blindness and psychogenic aphonia are both a form of a 'conversion disorder' and are often caused by stress that manifests itself as physical symptoms *(*DSM-5*)*.

under caution (when charged) and failure to give evidence at trial. This may influence the outcome of cases as it implies guilt. This created a new role for forensic clinical psychologists in cases when adverse inferences should not be drawn if 'it appears to the court that the physical or mental condition of the accused makes it undesirable for him to give evidence' (Section 35). The leading case with regard to the evaluation of 'undesirability' is *R* v. *Billy-Joe Friend* ([1997] 2 Cr.App.R 231). Mr Friend did not give evidence at his trial in 1996 and a direction by the trial judge to explain the reason was not provided. This was appealed in 1997 when the Court of Appeal decided that 'there is no right test' for assessing undesirability, this being dependent on the individual case. The case again made legal history of relevance to forensic clinical psychology when Mr Friend's conviction was overturned in a subsequent appeal in 2004 on the basis of a report from Susan Young, which demonstrated that at the time of his trial in 1996 he had attention deficit hyperactivity disorder (ADHD) and his symptoms and functional impairments adversely affected his fitness to plead and stand trial (Gudjonsson & Young, 2006). The appeal judgement showed that ADHD, when properly diagnosed, is relevant to issues surrounding adverse inferences and fitness to plead and stand trial.

The establishment of an 'intermediary' was introduced in the Youth Justice and Criminal Evidence Act 1999 in order to further the communication of witnesses in court, but was not incorporated into practice until 2009. Brendan O'Mahony, who is a registered forensic psychologist, persuaded the Court of Appeal in July 2011 (CO/5404/2011) that a young defendant with ADHD required the presence of a 'registered intermediary' to further communication during his trial (i.e. he 'would benefit from having access to a registered intermediary while providing his evidence to the court to enable him to give his best evidence and receive a fair trial'). The role of the registered intermediary is usually reserved for victims and witnesses, but may on occasion be used for defendants as shown by this Court of Appeal judgement. The way was paved in the Barry George trial (see Box 22.1) when, for the first time, support was provided throughout the trial for a defendant by a forensic clinical psychologist (see Box 22.2).

The importance of 'translation' of mental vulnerabilities into the legal question

The essence of expert testimony is that psychological findings have to be properly translated into the legal question. When this translation fails at trial then there may be grounds for an appeal. This happened in the case of *R* v. *Andrew Reeves* and resulted in a landmark decision regarding the failure of a clinical psychologist to translate important psychometric findings into legal issues regarding the 'unreliability' of confession evidence produced voluntarily to close relations while Mr Reeves was on remand in prison (on unrelated charges). The case was heard in the Court of Appeal in London in November 2010. Fresh expert written and oral psychological testimony was provided by Gisli Gudjonsson and Susan Young and their evidence resulted in a successful murder appeal on the unreliability of voluntary confessions due to ADHD symptoms.

The importance of this case is that the clinical psychologist who had been commissioned by the defence to address the issue of the reliability of Mr Reeves's

Box 22.2 Support of a psychologically vulnerable defendant by a forensic clinical psychologist

In 2001 Susan Young was commissioned by the court to sit with Barry George in the dock to monitor him and provide psychological support throughout the trial. Mr George suffered with generalised idiopathic epilepsy, cognitive impairment and mental health problems, including acute anxiety and panic attacks. His fitness to plead and stand trial was borderline depending on his mental state, which fluctuated considerably, increasing the likelihood of absence seizures. At great cost, a previous trial had been aborted in February 2001 when Mr George became unfit to stand trial following a rapid deterioration in his mental state in response to intense media coverage and the publication of his photograph. When the second trial started in April 2001, Susan Young sat with Mr George in the dock during the legal arguments but when the trial commenced before the jury the prosecution insisted she move to the well of the court. At the beginning and end of each court day, during lunch and at each hourly court break, she provided Mr George with interventions to control his feelings of anxiety and panic attacks. Mr George was convicted of murder on 2 July 2001. Susan Young was subsequently commissioned by the Court of Appeal to sit in the dock and provide psychological support and treatment and on 15 November 2007 Mr George's conviction was quashed and a retrial ordered. The retrial lasted between 9 June and 1 August 2008 during which time Susan Young was again commissioned by the court and she sat with Barry George in the dock throughout the retrial. This was a unique role that made legal history. Mr George was acquitted. The Judicial Communications Office of HM Courts Service made the following statement on 6 September 2008:

> The judge in Barry George's original trial ordered that a psychologist should be there to assist the defendant, who was clinically assessed as having psychological difficulties in following proceedings. A similar request for medical attendance was granted by the trial judge before the trial which has just been concluded. Providing professional support to vulnerable people is vital to ensuring defendants receive a fair hearing and enable trials to proceed smoothly and swiftly, making best use of court time and money.

confessions did not explain how psychometric findings were likely to have impacted on the reliability of his confessions. The report was not used at trial in spite of it being potentially helpful to the defence. Psychometric findings need to be appropriately interpreted in relation to relevant vulnerabilities that may undermine the reliability of the confession.

The importance of research

The innovative field work of Barrie Irving and Linden Hilgendorf into police interrogation (Irving & Hilgendorf, 1980) was highly influential both in terms of furthering the understanding of the psychology of interrogation and the importance of psychological vulnerabilities of police detainees. It also appears to have impacted on the development of the Police and Criminal Evidence Act and its Codes of Practice, which came into effect in 1986.

The Royal Commission on Criminal Justice, which was set up following the successful appeal of the Birmingham Six in 1991, commissioned 22 research studies (see Gudjonsson, 2003b for a review of the key studies relevant to police questioning and detention). The studies of Clare and Gudjonsson (1992) and Gudjonsson et al. (1993) provided important information about the identification of psychological vulnerabilities and how vulnerable suspects could be better protected to ensure fairness and justice and this was incorporated into police practice in terms of improved screening (Gudjonsson, 2003b).

The Bradley Report (2009) recommended the employment of healthcare practitioners and improved screening of mental health problems of offenders in custody. These recommendations have been implemented at police stations, although unfortunately research suggests that psychological vulnerabilities (such as intellectual disability and ADHD) are still missed. Even when vulnerabilities are identified through the current screening process, the police often fail to act on the information obtained to ensure that suspects are provided with the required support and protection (Young et al., 2013). This type of research is essential for evaluating legal reforms and for identifying a way forward and demonstrates how research and forensic clinical practice is a reciprocal and integrative endeavour. Legal questions require the need to develop new conceptual models, procedures and assessment tools. Research provides the evidence base that is the foundation for the translation of psychological knowledge to the provision of expert testimony.

Working with offenders

Secure hospitals

Harvey Gordon (2012) refers to four early psychology pioneers at Broadmoor Hospital, one of three maximum security hospitals in England and Wales: Tony Black, Ron Blackburn, David Crawford and Kevin Howells. Tony Black, who in 1959 was the first psychologist appointed to Broadmoor, published a number of papers on his work with mentally disordered offenders, and was head of the Department of Psychology until his retirement in 1986 (Black, 2003). One of Black's first tasks at Broadmoor Hospital was to set up a pre and post admission assessment protocol to assess psychological change in the patients over time.

Since the early 1970s Blackburn has provided an extensive contribution to the assessment, classification and treatment needs of mentally disordered offenders. David Crawford made early attempts at 'social skills' training with sex offenders and Kevin Howells focused on the teaching of prosocial skills to aggressive patients. In the late 1970s and early 1980s interim medium secure units were opened to relieve the pressure on the three maximum security hospitals (Ashworth, Broadmoor and Rampton), followed by purpose-built regional secure units.

Over the past 30 years the assessment and treatment of mentally disordered offenders has become more sophisticated (Gudjonsson & Young, 2007). Today there is demand for evidenced-based treatments designed to reduce antisocial behaviours in mentally disordered offenders; however, offending behaviour programmes were not designed to meet the complex needs of this patient group. The Risk Need Responsivity model suggests that structured and targeted programmes should be delivered which aim to match content and pace of treatment with specific offender characteristics (Andrews & Bonta, 2010). Consistent with this theoretical paradigm, the world-renowned Reasoning & Rehabilitation programme with its strong evidence base for reducing reoffending (Tong & Farrington, 2006) has been adapted to meet the needs of mentally disordered offenders (Cin-Ying Yip et al., 2013; Rees-Jones et al., 2012; Young & Ross, 2007).

Prisons and probation services

Crighton and Towl (2008) provide a brief introduction to the history of psychology in prisons, including young offender institutions and prison headquarters, dating back to the late 1940s. The early 'prison psychologists' focused mainly on staff training and vocational assessment. In the early 1990s a strategy was set up for treating sex offenders in prison, referred to as the Sex Offender Treatment Programme (SOTP), and manualised cognitive behaviour therapy programmes were developed, which aimed at reducing offending.

According to Crighton and Towl (2008) and Towl (2010), there were a number of key factors that shaped the development of forensic psychology services:

- The creation of the DFP and the professional recognition of the specialty 'forensic psychology' in 1999 resulted in an influx of applications for posts in the Prison Service. In fact, the Prison Service became the largest employer in the UK of forensic psychologists, including trainee forensic psychologists, whose main role was to provide risk assessment and implement manual-based group interventions.
- In 2000, a joint post of professional head of psychology was created for the prison and probation services, which widened the remit of psychology services. However, disproportionally fewer psychologists have been employed in the Probation Service.
- In 2003, the first strategic framework document was produced for psychological services within prisons and probation, which included meeting organisational needs for an efficient and effective service delivery, and addressing issues such as a career structure for psychologists. According to Towl (2010), it highlighted the profile of psychology within the prison services, increased the pay of qualified psychologists, and improved supervision arrangements of trainees between 2000 and 2005. Unfortunately, it did not broaden the roles of forensic psychologists, and management has continuously failed to create senior practitioners' positions, which has impacted deleteriously on training, supervision and quality of services provided.

Tensions and controversies

There are tensions between psychology and other professions, particularly law and psychiatry, within the psychology profession itself and between psychology and management.

The long-standing tension between psychologists and lawyers as to what constitutes 'specialist knowledge' versus 'common sense' still remains in relation to experimental eyewitness testimony (Davies & Gudjonsson, 2013), although this is no longer the case for expert psychological evidence in cases of disputed confessions (Gudjonsson, 2003b).

As far as psychiatrists are concerned, some persist in providing the courts with evidence based on their own interpretation of a psychologist's psychometric findings even when this falls outside of their area of training and expertise. In addition, barristers interact more often in court with psychiatrists than psychologists and psychiatrists' medical qualification apparently provides weight to their opinion, while some barristers do not know the difference between psychological and psychiatric evidence (Leslie et al., 2007).

Despite publication of the BPS position paper *Guidelines on Memory and the Law* in 2008, within the psychological profession there remain disagreements regarding the general inferences that can be drawn from memory research and of the role of memory experts in court (see e.g. Conway et al., 2014, in *The Psychologist* and subsequent correspondence in the September and October issues).

Another controversial area within the psychology profession relates to the risk assessment of terrorist offenders. The lack of consensus is well illustrated by the outcome of a working party set up by the BPS in 2008 to develop a position paper on the psychological risk assessment of those convicted for terrorist-related offences for the purpose of assisting psychologists working in this very difficult area. After a draft position paper was sent out for consultation in 2010, it was abandoned due to lack of consensus among those consulted and lack of empirical evidence to produce an informed position paper that could be supported by the BPS (Gudjonsson et al., 2015).

Currently, forensic psychologists mainly work in prisons and forensic clinical psychologists in forensic mental health settings. Forensic psychologists without clinical training have a more limited role as expert witnesses than their clinically trained colleagues, because most civil and criminal cases focus on clinical issues rather than risk assessment. Forensic psychologists may also be disadvantaged when working in mental health settings in terms of role, career progression and pay scale.

With funding restrictions, conflict will continue to exist between management and senior psychologists about the need for a spread of staff calibre employed in forensic settings. Current thinking seems to favour a flat organisational structure over a hierarchy of seniority and expertise. This means that senior staff are often spread too thinly and junior staff (including assistants and trainees) are working in high risk settings without adequate support and supervision.

Acknowledgements

John Hall, Sarah Marks, Derek Perkins, and Graham Towl provided references or material relevant to this chapter. Graham Turpin provided helpful comments regarding a previous draft of this chapter.

References

Andrews, D.A. & Bonta, J. (2010). *The psychology of criminal conduct.* New Providence, NJ: Matthew Bender.

Black, D.A. (2003). *Broadmoor interacts: Criminal insanity revisited.* Chichester: Barry Rose.

Blackburn, R. (1996). What is forensic psychology? *Legal and Criminological Psychology, 1,* 3–16.

Bradley, K. (2009). *The Bradley Report: Lord Bradley's review of people with mental health problems or learning disabilities in the criminal justice system.* London: Department of Health.

British Psychological Society (2001). *The nature of hypnosis.* Leicester: Author.

British Psychological Society (2008). *Guidelines on memory and the law: Recommendations for the scientific study of human memory.* Leicester: Author. Available at www.forcescience.org/articles/Memory&TheLaw.pdf

Castell, J.H.F. (1966). *The court work of educational and clinical psychologists (EDPP).* Leicester: British Psychological Society.

Cin-Ying Yip, V., Gudjonsson, G., Perkins, D. et al. (2013). An evaluation of the R&R2MHP cognitive skills program in high risk male offenders with severe mental illness. *BMC Psychiatry, 13,* 267.

Clare, I. & Gudjonsson, G.H. (1992). *Devising and piloting a new 'Notice to Detained Persons'. Royal Commission on Criminal Justice.* London: HMSO.

Conway, M.A., Justice, L.V. & Morrison, C.M. (2014). Beliefs about autobiographical memory. *The Psychologist, 27,* 502–505.

Crighton, D.A. & Towl, G.J. (2008). *Psychology in prisons.* Oxford: Blackwell.

Davies, G.M. & Gudjonsson, G.H. (2013). Psychologists in the witness box. *The Psychologist, 26,* 496–497.

Edmundson, J. (1995). The psychologist as expert witness. *Forensic Update, 42,* 28–33.

Gale, A. (1988). Introduction. The polygraph test, more scientific investigation. In A. Gale (Ed.), *The polygraph test. Truth, lies and science* (pp.1–9). London: Sage.

Gordon, H. (2012). *Broadmoor.* London: Psychology News Press.

Grubin, D. (2008). The case for polygraph testing of sex offenders. *Legal and Criminological Psychology, 13,* 177–189.

Gudjonsson, G.H. (1985). Psychological evidence in court: Results from the BPS survey. *Bulletin of the British Psychological Society, 38,* 327–330.

Gudjonsson, G.H. (1996). Psychological evidence in court: Results from the 1995 survey. *The Psychologist, 5,* 213–217.

Gudjonsson, G.H. (2003a). Psychology brings justice. The science of forensic psychology. *Criminal Behaviour and Mental Health, 13,* 159–167.

Gudjonsson G.H. (2003b). *The psychology of interrogations and confessions. A handbook.* Chichester: Wiley.

Gudjonsson, G.H. (2008). Psychologists as expert witnesses: The 2007 BPS survey. *Forensic Update, 92,* 23–29.

Gudjonsson, G.H., Clare, I., Rutter, S. & Pearse, J. (1993). *Persons at risk during interviews in police custody: The identification of vulnerabilities. Royal Commission on Criminal Justice.* London: HMSO.

Gudjonsson, G.H. & Clark, N.K. (1986). Suggestibility in police interrogation: A social psychological model. *Social Behaviour, 1,* 83–104.

Gudjonsson, G.H. & Gunn, J. (1982). The competence and reliability of a witness in a criminal court. *British Journal of Psychiatry, 141,* 624–627.

Gudjonsson, G.H. & Haward, L.R.C. (1998). *Forensic psychology: A guide to practice.* London: Routledge.

Gudjonsson, G.H., West, A. & McKee, M. (2015). Risk assessment of terrorist offenders. A challenge too far? In J.J. Pearse (Ed.), *Investigating terrorism: Current political, legal and psychological issues* (pp.123–143). Chichester: Wiley.

Gudjonsson, G.H. & Young, S. (2006). An overlooked vulnerability in a defendant: Attention deficit hyperactivity disorder and a miscarriage of justice. *Legal and Criminological Psychology, 11,* 211–218.

Gudjonsson, G.H. & Young, S. (2007). The role and scope of forensic clinical psychology in secure unit provisions. A proposed service model for psychological therapies. *Journal of Forensic Psychiatry and Psychology, 18,* 534–556.

Haward, L.R.C. (1981). *Forensic psychology.* London. Batsford.

Haward, L.R.C. (1990). *A dictionary of forensic psychology.* Chichester: Barry Rose.

Irving. B. & Hilgendorfe, L. (1980). *Police interrogation: The psychological approach.* Royal Commission on Criminal Procedure. Case Studies No. 1 and No. 2. London. HMSO.

Leslie, O., Young, S., Valentine, T. & Gudjonsson, G. (2007). Criminal barristers' opinions and perceptions of mental health expert. *Journal of Forensic Psychiatry and Psychology, 18,* 394–410.

Martin, H. (2013). From ascertainment to re-construction 1944–1978. In C. Arnold & J. Hardy (Eds.), *British educational psychology: The first hundred years* (pp.49–56). Leicester: British Psychological Society.

Rees-Jones, A., Gudjonsson, G. & Young, S. (2012). A multi-site controlled trial of a cognitive skills programme for mentally disordered offenders. *BMC Psychiatry, 12,* 44.

Smith, G.A. (2011). *From tests to therapy. A personal history of clinical psychology.* Leicester: Matador.

Tong, L.S. & Farrington, D.P. (2006). How effective is the 'reasoning and rehabilitation' program in reducing reoffending? A meta-analysis of evaluations in four countries. *Psychology, Crime and Law*, 12, 3–24.

Towl, G.J. (2010). Psychology in the National Offender Management Service for England and Wales. In J.R. Adler & J.M. Gray (Eds.), *Forensic psychology: Concepts, debates and practice* (pp.305–317). Oxford: Willan.

Tunstall, O., Gudjonsson, G., Eysenck, H. & Haward, L. (1982). Professional issues arising from psychological evidence presented in court. *Bulletin of the British Psychological Society, 35*, 329–331.

Young, S., Goodwin, E.J., Sedwick, O. & Gudjonsson, G.H. (2013). The effectiveness of police custody assessments in identifying suspects with intellectual disabilities and attention deficit hyperactivity disorder. *BMC Medicine, 11*, 248.

Young, S.J. & Ross R.R. (2007). *R&R2 for youths and adults with mental health problems: A prosocial competence training programme.* Ottawa: Cognitive Centre of Canada.

Part 5
National and International Perspectives

Chapter 23 Challenging an anglocentric story

Editors' introduction

It was almost inevitable that the majority of the chapters within this book have been written by English authors describing the development of the profession within different regions of England, despite the fact that the British Psychological Society represents psychologists throughout the British Isles and has had close historical links with the Psychological Society of Ireland. Given that significant differences exist between our nations with respect to legislation, the structures of the health services, religions, cultures and language, such an anglocentric bias will fail to capture the rich diversity of influences on the history of our profession. In an attempt to compensate, we have commissioned a series of short contributions to describe the history of the profession and specific events and challenges within Wales, Scotland, Northern Ireland and the Republic of Ireland. We hope this also reflects the efforts made by the DCP itself over the last decade to establish effective independent chairs and national committees for Wales, Northern Ireland and Scotland.

Although these chapters summarise how the profession has developed distinctly within each of its home nations, readers need also to be reminded of the dramatic and indeed, frequently traumatic events that have surrounded the relationship between these counties and the UK government. We suggest, therefore, that these chapters are read alongside relevant political histories of these times (e.g. Davidson, 2000; Nairn, 1981).

Clinical psychology in Wales: Growth of a profession

Seicoleg glinigol yng Nghymru

David Griffiths & Roger Young

Wales and its National Health Service *(Gwasanaeth Iechyd Gwladol Cymru)* have always had a close and supportive relationship. The Welsh Health Service is a popular, busy, active care system providing about 20 million client contacts each year. At least 80 per cent occur outside hospitals, so clinical psychologists might expect to be busy providing services to the population of over three million people with a national annual growth rate of about 5 per cent. Growth suggests that Wales has its attractions, but it also implies gradually increasing needs for professional groups such as clinical psychology.

Following the establishment of the Welsh Office in 1964, the Secretary of State for Wales assumed responsibility for health and social services in 1969.He was provided with support to ensure the availability of resources to allow appropriate developments. Clinical psychology was one of these. At this time, there were very few clinical psychologist in Wales, but they arrived steadily by various routes from the 1960s. While some clinical psychologists arrived after qualification outside Wales, organised training also developed systematically after 1975, and a regular stream of qualified professionals were produced in both North and South Wales. This has continued to this day and has served to make the country self-sufficient and less dependent on training elsewhere. A fledgling profession which began with a complement of five or less has now grown to a total of about 350 individuals spread over many localities, rural and urban, and providing professional services to a broad range of client groups. The history of clinical psychology in Wales is less than 45 years in total. A great deal has occurred in this time.

As a working context, Wales is distinctive but not unique. It shares a core of legislation with other parts of the UK, but differences have become more apparent since the Welsh Assembly was established after the 1998 Government of Wales Act. Responsibility for the health and social services, and also education and training, underlie the central resourcing of clinical psychology.

Wales is distinctive in that it has two languages and Welsh – spoken fluently and preferentially by up to one in four people, and more in some areas – has a protected legal status which is unique in the UK. It also has a Welsh Language Commissioner. Some clinical psychologists are fluent Welsh speakers and most of these have trained in Wales and more commonly in the North. The North Wales Course has trained at least 30 bilingual trainees, and most have remained to work in the Welsh NHS. All patients have a right to receive a service in Welsh. Wherever possible, trainees have been encouraged to work clinically through the medium of Welsh with a Welsh-speaking supervisor and to submit work in Welsh with translation to support oral presentation.

Wales also has geographical features which influence behaviour and interaction. For example, North and South Wales are separated by considerable distances. It takes four to five hours to travel from the North to the South coast, and at least two to get from West to East. Distance was one factor which eventually gave Wales two separate training courses, and explains the parallel – rather than regularly interactive – existence of professionals at the extremities of the country.

The historical development of clinical psychology: Training and qualification

In 1966 a DCP/BPS publication recorded the presence of six psychologists in the Welsh NHS. They are likely to have qualified as probationers through an apprenticeship model since the BPS Diploma in Clinical Psychology was not available until 1968.

In 1971 a senior lecturer in clinical psychology was appointed in the Department of Psychological Medicine at the Welsh National School of Medicine. The appointee was Dr David Griffiths. His main aim was to teach psychology to medical students as recommended by the 1968 Todd Report on Medical Education. He made a clinical contribution within psychological medicine, and developed support for the five or so local 'probationers' who were already training independently within the BPS framework which had now been operational for three years. This was a precursor to the formal training which followed, and signalled to the local NHS that the profession was developing and committed to progress through training.

In 1975 a new All Wales clinical tutor post was established in the Cardiff Area NHS department. Its remit was to develop a formally organised in-service training course to prepare trainees for the BPS Diploma within the framework of the scientist-practitioner model of applied psychology. Funding for the post and a complement of trainees was made available from 'top sliced' central funds. The tutor appointed was Dr David Griffiths. His teaching of medical students in clinical aspects of psychology continued but was done by other staff and eventually by the Cardiff School of Psychology.

In 1975 the first of regular sequential three-yearly admissions was made to the new Welsh In-service Training Course. The central course was based in Cardiff and clinical placements were available throughout Wales. Over this period, qualified staff were also recruited from within and outside Wales. From the outset, supervisors did most of the central teaching as well as providing a regular supply of high quality clinical placements. They were encouraged to sustain, and indeed assumed, a strong sense of ownership for the course. Without this contribution, for which they received no financial reward, no training course could have come into existence or survived. Trainees were salaried, were attached to local Districts, where they did most of their placements if possible, and were appointed on the understanding (but no legal obligation) that they would seek employment there on qualification. In response to workforce needs, some were funded from sources such as learning disability budgets.

In 1985 the All Wales In-service Course separated into the North and South Wales In-service Courses. Separation was justified by the significant distance between North and South and the problems this caused for organisation, and also the need to stimulate growth in the North. The courses operated in parallel and independently. Laurie Worsley and Dr Peter Higson organised the North Wales Course with regular support from a steering committee which included Professor Tim Miles and Professor Fergus Lowe from the University College of North Wales in Bangor. In the early 1990s, Professor Mark Williams was appointed as director and nine joint academic and clinical appointments were made soon afterwards. Professor Williams's appointment was the first chair of clinical psychology in Wales, and he was succeeded in due course by Professor Isabel Hargreaves who remained as the course head until 2014. In South Wales, Dr Roger Young had become the assistant director of the All Wales Course in 1986, the joint director of the DClinPsy. course in 1994 and the sole director in 2003 at the retirement of Professor David Griffiths. Five senior directors were now responsible for adults, children, learning disability, older adult and research and were soon joined by three specialist tutors to support clinical placements. More recently, the course was among the first in the UK to appoint a service user coordinator to its staff. Professor Reg Morris became the programme director in 2008.

Following negotiations by Professor Mark Williams in North Wales in 1991, and in 1992 by Professor David Griffiths and Dr Roger Young in South Wales, the two courses anticipated national UK trends to develop doctoral level clinical programmes, and affiliated separately to the University of Wales in Bangor and Cardiff. The Welsh courses were the first to establish the qualification at doctoral level in the UK (see chapter 7). From 1991/92 to date, cohorts qualified annually from both courses to meet increasing staffing demands. Central funds have been made available consistently by the Welsh Office through its Welsh Health Common Services Authority and, more recently, the Welsh Government at the Assembly. Pass rates have been about 99 per cent and regular checks on annual cohorts in both courses have revealed that retention rates of qualifiers within NHS Wales have been between 56 and 100 per cent. The investment in training has therefore been worthwhile and internal training has provided an important proportion of the complement of clinicians, managers and researchers providing services in Wales.

People and departments: Growth of the clinical profession

The Welsh Clinical Psychology Advisory Committee, set up in the late 1970s, provided regular opportunities for liaison and decision making in core issues such as staffing and access to psychological help. Membership included representatives of all clinical departments, training courses, academic departments and relevant parts of the civil service such as the Welsh Health Common Services Authority and the National Leadership and Innovation Agency for Health Care. A broad range of issues, including professional matters and service development, were also considered regularly at DCP meetings, such as those organised by the Special Interest Group on the Elderly. Regular contact with the UK was provided by representation and training course officer attendance at the Committee of Organisers of Regional In-Service Courses.

In addition to the regular arrivals of qualified young staff from the internal courses in Wales itself since 1978, qualified staff were also arriving from other courses in the UK. One steady initial source was the Institute of Psychiatry in London beginning with the new senior lecturer in the Welsh School of Medicine and being followed by others (e.g. Dr John Teasdale, Professor David Hawks and Professor Ray Hodgson). Others (e.g. Dr John Hall, David Castell and Dr Charles Twining) came from other clinical and academic centres and a small number arrived from mainland Europe to foster an international atmosphere. The School of Psychology at Cardiff secured its first clinically qualified lecturer, Professor Neil Frude, in 1973 and he eventually became the research director to the South Wales Course. Meanwhile, departments continued to expand.

In North Wales the growth of clinical psychology progressed in both Gwynedd in the West and Clwyd in the East. These counties eventually became part of the largest health organisation in Wales, the Betsi Cadwaladr University Health Board whose current chair, Dr Peter Higson, was instrumental in establishing the North Wales Course in 1985. Another feature of the North Wales scene is that the Psychology Department in Bangor had an early and consistent history of cooperation and integration with the local NHS departments. The attraction of the area has also been maintained by the Centre for Mindfulness Research and Practice at Bangor, and the Institute for Medical and Social Research whose first director in 1997 was Professor Mark Williams. Problems in recruiting to some key posts in the 1990s were resolved successfully by combining clinical and academic resources to allow joint posts which were quickly occupied and allowed developments in teaching, research and clinical work to flourish. Indeed, Robert Jones was appointed in 1992 as Director of Continuing Professional Development and oversaw the first 'top- up doctorate'. The Betsi Cadwaladr Board now has a complement of just under 100 clinical psychologists, the largest in Wales and about 26 per cent of the Welsh total.

In South Wales the South Glamorgan Department (now serving the Cardiff and Vale Board) began its growth in the early 1970s and became one of the more successful area clinical departments in the UK under the initial direction of Professor David Hawks. From 1985 until 2003, it provided a home for the South Wales Training Course, which was the last in the UK to relocate to a university campus in 2012. It has retained its integration and professionalism, and its team in excess of 80 psychologists (about 24 per cent of the Welsh total) have successfully developed a broad range of specialty services.

In other parts of South and Mid Wales, gradually expanding teams of clinical psychologists have provided increasing services from what was initially a low baseline, or indeed no service at all on occasion. Departments have expanded to current approximate numbers of 62 in the Aneurin Bevan Health Board (South East Wales) or 18 per cent of the total for Wales, 50 (about 14 per cent) in Abertawe Bro Morgannwg (Swansea, Neath, Port Talbot and Bridgend area), 27 (8 per cent) in Cwm Taff (Merthyr and Rhondda), 23 (7 per cent) in the Hywel Dda Board (South West Wales) and 12 (3 to 4 per cent) in the Powys (Mid Wales) Teaching Board. Qualifying trainees provided regular recruits and indeed many were attached directly to localities during their training to encourage affiliation to places at some distance from popular spots such as Cardiff.

Wales has also had a significant effect on the development of modern learning disability services in the UK. The Ely Hospital scandal, and the report drafted by Geoffrey Howe in the 1960s, attracted much needed resources to the specialty and led to the Hospital Advisory Service's remit to identify and remedy care failures like Ely (see chapter 17). Within Wales, an innovative framework of care services was developed under firm direction from the All Wales Mental Handicap Strategy. Driven by the Welsh Office and funded appropriately, it provided a model for comprehensive community services in the UK as a whole, and one which also had a clear message for other specialties such as the care of individuals with chronic psychiatric disorder. The model included appropriately sized clinical departments which allowed the recruitment of core professionals such as clinical psychologists in very useful numbers.

In addition to clinical work undertaken routinely by the majority of clinical psychologists, there have also been innovative attempts to explore the applications of psychology in a manner that allows effective and efficient use of scarce resources such as psychological expertise. These have involved a range of service developments such as, for example, Portage parental instruction in the management of developmentally delayed children (Jones, 1983); the development and management of counselling services in primary care (Jenny McBride in Cardiff); training in techniques such as mindfulness meditation (Williams et al., 2007); service-oriented surveys of chronic populations (Ehlert & Griffiths, 1996); the applications of bibliotherapy in client management (Frude, 2004); the evaluation of driving competence in neurologically impaired individuals (McKenna, 2012); the analysis and control of violence associated with alcohol consumption (Smith et al., 2003); and motivational interviewing in patients (Rollnick et al., 2007). Such work applies the reflective scientist-practitioner model which has been a basis for the development of clinical psychology in Wales since its arrival in the 1970s.

Clinical psychology in Scotland

Carole Allan

Introduction

Devolution and the politicisation of health have served to develop a distinct identity for clinical psychology in Scotland. The local focus has been beneficial to clinical psychologists as the smaller scale of the country with five million inhabitants and the establishment of the Scottish Parliament in Edinburgh has enabled engagement with the political agenda, whereas Westminster seems ever more distant.

The political disconnect began in the Thatcher years and has continued to this day when currently Scots voters have returned only one Conservative MP to the UK Parliament out of a possible 45 seats. There has also been a divergence in terms of NHS Scotland: under the direction of the Scottish Nationalist Party, health care has turned its back on the private sector, with the expressed view from the then Cabinet Secretary for Health, Nicola Sturgeon, that public services should be delivered by public servants.

What happens in the rest of the UK will always matter very much in Scotland. The Scottish healthcare workforce including clinical psychologists is highly mobile, not only within the UK but also beyond, and Scots have always travelled abroad in search of opportunities. The link with the UK through the BPS and specifically the DCP has been valued by psychologists so that they are aware of wider developments and can hopefully learn from the successes and mistakes of others across the UK and beyond.

Scottish context

The Scots have a strong national identity fostered by a different legal system based on Roman and Dutch law. It has a different educational system, prints its own banknotes and has a more homogeneous population with little inward immigration from outside the UK. There is less private schooling and less private medicine. It is a poor country compared to England with a history of declining heavy industry, shipbuilding, and mining. Scotland's poor health outcomes compared to Europe have been a consistent finding over a number of years, particularly in the West of Scotland. Despite some improvements, Scottish men and women still die prematurely in comparison to European norms. Causes are multifactorial but more than a million adults in Scotland, over a quarter of the adult population, are now obese or morbidly obese and the high consumption of alcohol has been highlighted as significant contributory factor to mental and physical problems (Whyte & Ajetunmobi, 2012).

The beginning of the NHS in Scotland

Clinical psychology in Scotland is bound up with the NHS, which got off to a flying start in Scotland, as almost half of Scotland was already covered by a state-funded system, the Highlands and Islands Medical Service. This had been set up 35 years earlier, serving the whole of this dispersed rural community and directly run by the Scottish Office in Edinburgh. In addition the Emergency Hospital Service was set up in 1939 to provide extra acute beds for the expected civilian casualties. Scotland was seen as important as a likely source of resistance should Hitler successfully invade the south of England. This service was successfully incorporated into the new Scottish NHS, giving Scotland 15 per cent more beds than the English NHS.

The early development of clinical psychology in Scotland

During the Second World War, a number of Scottish academic psychologists were drafted into various ministries and departments to contribute to the selection and the training of military personnel. Boris Semeonoff, one of the founders of the Edinburgh Course, helped during the war in the selection of special agents (Semeonoff, 1969). A few were seconded to emergency medical services that dealt with the casualties of bombing raids. A number continued to work in hospitals and in due course were absorbed into the new Scottish NHS. At this point, about 10 psychologists were working within the new NHS (Scottish Health Service, 1984).

Clinical psychology training in Scotland

An early and significant contribution to training was made at the Crichton Royal Hospital in Dumfries, where the then physician superintendent, Dr. P. K. McCowan, established departments of clinical and psychological research, with two internationally recognised figures, a psychiatrist, Willi Mayer-Gross, who was recruited in 1939 and a psychologist, John Raven, who was recruited in 1944 (Tait, 1972). The latter worked on a part-time basis for the hospital as he wanted the freedom to pursue his own research.

In 1949 Ralph Hetherington (who went on to found the Liverpool Course) joined John Raven's research department at Crichton Royal, and he noted that in 1951 a 'planned clinical training course' was set up and began to take trainees (Hetherington, 2000), making this one of the earliest in-service training courses in the UK.

At that time there were only two other centres training clinical psychologists and both were in London: the Maudsley Hospital and the Tavistock Clinic. Hetherington noted that both of these institutions had a different approach to the Crichton, which he described as patient-centred and where the clinical interview was central to the process of understanding the patient. Psychometric testing was only undertaken if further investigation was required to clarify the patient's difficulties. Training took two years to complete at the Crichton, rather than three years for training other probationers in Scotland.

The Crichton hospital later linked with the University of Glasgow to form the Glasgow Course, which was formally established in 1960 under the direction of Professor T.F. Rodger (professor of psychiatry) and Bob Mowbray who was now a reader in clinical psychology. According to Reg Herrington, lecturer in psychiatry in the department at the time, it was a period of enthusiasm and optimism in the teaching of psychiatry and psychology, both to medical and psychology undergraduates

The new course took two years to complete and conferred the award of a postgraduate Diploma in Clinical Psychology. The first year was in Glasgow, based at the Southern General Hospital and allowing instruction from other university departments (anatomy, physiology, neuropathology, mental handicap, child psychiatry) and sometimes shared with trainee psychiatrists. Ralph McGuire was the main supervisor for trainees on the Glasgow Course at this point, with contributions from Andrew McGhie, who was a former trainee at the Crichton.

The second year was spent at the Crichton, with an emphasis on clinical practice. There were regular seminars from John Raven and other members of staff. The trainees spent significant periods of time on the wards and there was also a six-month placement in Ladyfield Child Psychiatric Inpatient Unit, one of only two such units in the UK.

Reg Herrington remembers that the important influences were developments in basic sciences, therapeutics and particularly the influence of Hans Eysenck, as a great many people had read his Penguin books and his *Handbook of Abnormal Psychology* that had been published at this time.

In 1964 Gordon Claridge was appointed lecturer in experimental psychology, but Bob Mowbray left the department to go to Australia and so Claridge was obliged to take on the course. He subsequently left to go to Oxford and Neil Brookes was appointed as head of course. Through his work in head injury he established the reputation of the course for excellence in this area, which continues to this day, currently by Tom McMillan (former course director) who was one of the founders of the MSc in Neuropsychology.

Glasgow tended to be the focus of training on behalf of the west of Scotland and Gerry Green was appointed as clinical tutor on a part-time basis, to coordinate placements and supervisors throughout the region, as well as giving input as head of psychology at Gartnavel Royal Hospital. He also undertook a variety of professional roles and was for a number of years BPS Registrar for the Statement of Equivalence, which enabled psychologists from overseas to benchmark their qualifications with those of psychologists in the UK and to be employable within the UK.

When Neil Brookes left his post he was succeeded by Colin Espie, who came to the course with a background in learning disabilities and NHS management but also with research interests in sleep and epilepsy. During his tenure, there was a period of expansion in training numbers as well as training posts. More recent course directors include Liz Campbell, who had a variety of roles within the BPS, most notably as president during the transition to statutory registration; Tom McMillan, who has continued the tradition of neuropsychology; Andrew Gumley, who has undertaken research into psychological interventions in psychosis; and currently Hamish Macleod.

The Edinburgh Course was founded under the direction of Alexander Kennedy (professor of psychiatry) and Boris Semeonoff (lecturer in psychology) and based at the Royal Edinburgh Hospital. The course officially commenced in 1960, but has been considered to have had its start in 1959 when an in-service trainee was appointed to an Edinburgh hospital and was absorbed into the university programme (McGuire, 2000). Most of the clinical teaching and research supervision came from Jim Drewery and Euan McPherson, who were clinicians based in the Royal Edinburgh Hospital.

The course was a joint venture between the NHS, the South Eastern Regional Hospital Board and various hospital boards of management and the University of Edinburgh through the departments of psychology and psychological medicine. Trainees were attached to hospitals in the Lothian area and the Royal Edinburgh Hospitals (REH). Initially, trainees were associated with selected hospitals in the region and were funded and administered by various boards of management. This arrangement proved to be unwieldy and in March 1962 the management of trainees was transferred to the Board of Management for the REH and Associated Hospitals. This change coincided with training being reduced from three to two years, coming into line with the Glasgow and Maudsley courses. Training was primarily focused on assessment. However, Euan McPherson was interested in behaviour therapy and most trainees had exposure to what at this time was considered to be a revolutionary approach.

Graham Foulds, who had an international reputation for research into the relation between personality and mental illness, took over academic responsibilities in 1965. Frank McPherson, who had been an earlier Edinburgh trainee, also took over a major teaching role. After a period of change of personnel and some instability, Ralph McGuire, who had set up the Leeds Course in 1964, was appointed to become course director. Shortly afterwards Dave Peck, who trained in Liverpool, and Ron Lyle, who trained in Birmingham, were appointed as lecturers. An expansion of numbers was planned but lack of funding was an issue. The Edinburgh Course at this time trained graduates from the Republic of Ireland who were under contract to return once training was completed. To support the expansion of training, a supervisors committee was formed, initially led by Euan McPherson and later John Graham-White, who had been director of the Belfast Course, and then Alistair Philip.

The Edinburgh Course had a strong behavioural tradition and Ralph McGuire was an early pioneer of this approach, as was Dave Peck. Ivy Blackburn, who had been at the MRC Brain Metabolism Unit, Edinburgh, advocated and undertook research in cognitive approaches: she became joint course director along with Sue Llewellyn.

The University of Aberdeen had a course which ran for several years (1974–1990) and then folded due to inadequate teaching resources. It was headed by Ron Blackburn and Harry McAllister. Dundee also had an in-service training course which ran for a number of years, and this subsequently was absorbed into the Edinburgh Course.

The Edinburgh Course moved out of the REH and into the Old Medical School buildings in 2005 and became part of the School of Health in Social Science. Recent course directors include Mick Power, Ken Laidlaw and Dave Peck. The current director is Matthias Schwannauer.

Despite the growth in numbers of trainees and frequent discussions about a third course, Glasgow and Edinburgh have continued to be the only two centres which train clinical psychologists in Scotland.

Workforce and service developments

From 1944 until his retirement in 1964, Raven built up the largest clinical department in Scotland, and the Crichton trained clinical psychologists who moved on to have positions of influence in England and abroad. Very few remained in Scotland and it was not until the Glasgow Course got under way in 1960 that clinical psychologists with experience of working at the Crichton went on to find posts in Scotland.

In the early days of clinical psychology there was little planning or thought about the deployment of services as individual psychologists, often on a single-handed basis, worked with medical or nursing colleagues. Generally psychologists were fully committed to fulfilling a range of roles including assessment, teaching and research. There was little in the way of obvious career progression and the only top grades in 1956 were May Davidson, Monte Shapiro, John Raven and Hugh Phillipson (Dabbs, 2000).

Reorganisation of the health service in 1974

A key element was the establishment of a national consultative structure in Scotland which included clinical psychology and which provided a link through the Scottish Health Service Planning Council to the Secretary of State for Scotland and also to the Scottish Home and Health Department (SHHD). This structure enabled clinical psychologists to contribute to the planning of health care and also enabled psychologists to network with a range of other healthcare colleagues.

The Trethowan Report (DHSS, 1977), on the role of psychologists in the health services, did not apply in Scotland but was an important influence in the development of clinical psychology and was finally endorsed by a Scottish circular in 1980 called 'The Organisation of Psychologists in the Health Service'. Like Trethowan, the document affirmed the independent status of clinical psychology as a healthcare profession and provided a model for the organisation of the profession in the NHS.

A further document was published in 1984 called *Clinical Psychology in the Scottish Health Service*, prepared by the clinical psychology subcommittee of the Scottish Health Service Planning Council and authored by Gerry Greene, Alistair Philip and David Clark, who made some important recommendations. The 1970s had seen a rapid expansion in numbers with 158 in post by 1983, but developments were described as erratic and unplanned. The report highlighted the need for a rational workforce planning process and funding for training. At this time Scottish universities, were producing 15 new psychologists per year. The report advocated central funding organised in consultation with the profession, health boards and the SHHD in such a way as to ensure controlled expansion into the areas where there were shortages.

The report also strongly supported establishing a part-time role as an adviser in clinical psychology whose remit would cover equitable distribution of services, provide briefings on psychological issues, liaise with education and social work, and promote better communication between the department and the BPS.

The workforce figures that were available indicated that most psychologists were distributed unevenly across the country and were employed within major conurbations with teaching hospitals and centres with specialist services, namely Lothian, Grampian, Greater Glasgow and Tayside. It noted the development of psychology in primary care as services developed outside mental hospitals, within the community. It also highlighted areas that required expansion, namely physical health and care of the elderly.

The report recognised that there were no formal links between clinical psychologists beyond their own health boards. It highlighted that there are issues that transcend area boundaries which require a more strategic response. This includes training and all aspects of workforce planning, including the equitable distribution of services to individuals regardless of where they live and a research strategy on a national level.

In the years following the report there was little response to the recommendations; however, there were sporadic increases in training numbers, the establishment of service posts and some development of area services, for example in Tayside, so that numbers began to increase.

Devolution and change

The Scotland Act 1998 created a Scottish Parliament and passed to it the powers to make laws on a range of issues. Powers were extended by the Scotland Act in 2012. Issues upon which the Scottish Parliament can make laws are known as devolved matters and cover health and social services (as opposed to reserved matters like defence, which is the province of the UK Parliament). These changes marked the emergence of a national profile and a more coordinated approach for clinical psychology.

In 1999 the Scottish Council for Postgraduate Medical and Dental Education (SCPMDE) assumed responsibility for clinical psychology training across Scotland. This was the first time that there had been a national approach to the funding of training, and to support this development Ann Smyth was appointed as national director of training. SCPMDE published a joint report with Clinical and Applied Psychologists in Scottish Healthcare (CAPISH) chaired by Ray Miller (head of psychology, Royal Edinburgh Hospital), which recommended a national approach to workforce planning and highlighted the significant shortage of psychology workers (SCPMDE/CAPISH, 1999).

In little less than a year after this, the *Clinical Psychology Workforce Planning Report* (2000), sponsored by NHS Education for Scotland (NES) and chaired by John Cameron (clinical director for psychology, Greater Glasgow) was published. The report trod very familiar ground, once again recommending workforce planning processes and highlighting areas of need especially physical health. In contrast to the outcomes from earlier reports, this led to a major development.

The 'Psychology Workforce Planning Project' was initiated in 2001 and was a collaboration between NES (now national commissioners of training for clinical psychology) and the Information Services Division (ISD) of the Scottish Government, responsible for national data collection across health and social care. The project linked individual psychology services, heads of psychology services in Scotland, training providers and statisticians so that data collection could be fine–tuned. It is now publicly available on the ISD website and updated on a quarterly basis ((browse for the latest document via https://isdscotland.scot.nhs.uk/Publications/index.asp).

The NES Psychology Directorate, now headed by Judy Thomson, has developed a national approach to supervision through the provision of CPD modules designed to meet the needs of supervisors. During 2001 to 2003, an education and training needs analysis of all clinical psychology supervisors in NHS Scotland was conducted. One of the key recommendations was to give priority to developing an induction module for new supervisors. This module was developed during 2004/2005, and piloted on two separate cohorts during 2005/2006. New supervisors are expected to complete the required training before taking on their first trainee (Bagnall, 2010).

A further two national documents have been published. The first, *Delivering for Health and Applied Psychology*, was a joint publication between NHS Education Scotland and ISD (2005) utilising the workforce figures to highlight areas for development. As a method of enhancing skill mix, one-year Master's programmes designed to meet the needs of adult primary care services were started in 2005 at the University of Stirling and early interventions for children and young people were started in 2009 at the University of Edinburgh and graduates have found a variety of roles within NHS Scotland as therapists while others have gone on to enter doctoral training.

The second report, entitled *Applied Psychologists and Psychology in NHS Scotland* (or the Wells Report), was commissioned by the Scottish Government and published in March 2011. An expert group was invited to contribute to the report and consisted of senior figures in psychology, nursing and medicine under the chairmanship of Professor Tony Wells (chief executive of NHS Tayside). The report reviewed the availability of psychological services in Scotland and examined how the profession could best contribute to the health and well-being of the people of Scotland. This was prompted by the unprecedented demand for psychological therapies and various targets set by Scottish Government which have focused on improvements in mental health.

The report looked at the range of psychologists who contributed to services within the NHS. In 2009, the majority of these were clinical psychologists (573.7 FTE) with a further 40.5 FTE comprising counselling, forensic, health and neuropsychologists as well as Master's level graduates with a one-year training. Again the recommendations are familiar, including role expansion as trainers and supervisors for a range of staff delivering psychological interventions. The report noted that psychologists are increasingly sought to provide advice at a national level on a variety of matters. However, there is no formal coordination of this input as there is as yet no appointed lead at Scottish Government Health Directorate level.

Improving Access to Psychological Therapies (IAPT)

The aspiration to improve access to psychological therapies has been enacted differently in Scotland. The Scottish Government has given a commitment to increase the availability of evidence-based psychological interventions, but the 'tartan version' has had no additional funding for new services unlike in England. Geraldine Bienkowski (a former chair of DCP Scotland) was appointed as national psychological therapies lead. The approach adopted was to be sustainable and integrative with the overall aim of enhancing service capacity by improving psychological skill levels across a range of health care professionals, to enable a wider range of staff to deliver different levels of psychological intervention across a range of contexts including services in physical health.

The Scottish Government has recently published the Matrix, as a guide to assist Boards in delivering effective psychological therapies that meet national waiting times targets. It provides a summary of the most up-to-date advice on evidence-based interventions, service redesign, strategic planning and robust governance processes to ensure patient safety. Evidence tables were compiled by Kate Davidson (professor of clinical psychology, Glasgow) and Cathy Richards (lead clinician in CAMHs, Lothian) (www.nes.scot.nhs.uk/media/20137/Psychology%20Matrix%202013.pdf).

Despite steady growth in numbers, these initiatives have once again highlighted the shortage of clinical psychologists in Scotland. The current establishment is 808 (674.1 FTE) clinical psychologists and 190 trainees.

Conclusion

Much that has happened in Scotland is mirrored elsewhere within the UK. However, devolution has facilitated a national approach to workforce planning and training as well as postqualification training in supervision. Key figures have been of national relevance throughout our history and more recently in shaping the ability to respond to government targets and initiatives. The future challenges will be a response to the austerity measures that the country faces and the changing political context as health and social care come together.

A Northern Ireland narrative

Chris McCusker

Devolution

Something a little unusual was happening at a DCP-UK executive meeting in 2013. After years of initiatives in England 'coming our way', at this meeting, the then Divisional chairs of Scotland and Northern Ireland were offering a vision to our colleagues on how to make the DCP a more effective and visible professional body in England. Many of the English branches appeared low in morale and confused about role and function. Austerity, job losses, more assertive but reductionistic commissioning and what Glenys Parry has described as the 'industrialisation' of therapies were the threats (see chapter 13). The then chair of DCP-UK (Richard Pemberton) was determined to advance change and looked to our experience and strategy to inform actions. Devolution, more proximal and integrated health and social care structures, key leaders in our profession with political and personal connections, engaging members and nudging a shift in focus from 'What can the DCP do for me?' to 'What can I do through the DCP?' had enabled us to find our own vision and voice in exerting external influence. It was not only in the present day, however, that this devolved nation had shown prescience and innovation.

Prescience in origins

The child guidance movement, primarily at the Royal Belfast Hospital for Sick Children, was the precursor to our profession in Northern Ireland (NI). The establishment of clinical psychology training owed much to the prescience of our psychiatry and educational psychology colleagues involved in child guidance at that time. Professor John Gibson, professor of mental health at Queen's University Belfast (QUB) and Professor George Seth (the first chair of the new discipline of psychology at QUB from 1956), with an educational psychology background, led on convincing the area health authority that Northern Ireland needed clinical psychologists. All were at the vanguard of thinking in the UK in this respect and John Graham-White was appointed in 1959 to develop clinical psychology services in Belfast and to start only the fourth such training programme in the UK.

The founding father of clinical psychology in NI, and indeed one of a small group of such nationally, John Graham-White was ahead of his time. Although the curriculum reflected the standard accreditation criteria of the time (physiological psychology, child psychiatry, behaviour therapy, psychometry and research), Graham-White's writings and presentations all highlight a vision which appears contemporary in outlook and relevance. Much to the consternation of his BPS colleagues on the Committee for Professional Psychologists at the time, he led on the (later to be more widely embraced) belief that by 'giving psychology away' to our more numerous colleagues on the front line of health and social care, we could exert greater good than staying in the clinic and seeing patients ourselves (Graham-White, 1967). Sceptical about the value of 'the psychometric methodology and psychotherapy' (which he called 'two of the weakest boxes of psychological tools', Graham-White, 1972) he believed that we should get out of the clinic and into communities to essentially prevent the escalation of difficulties in 'at-risk populations' through diversion and behavioural shaping. Finally, at a time when our new accreditation standards (BPS, 2014) emphasise the non-therapy skills of leadership and exerting influence, Graham-White had some prophetic words with respect to what was important in training: 'the essential technical skills (psychological assessment, treatment and research) are relatively easy to acquire...other less well defined and perhaps more subtle skills...required in negotiation and management of services are acquired more slowly over a much longer period of time' (Graham-White, 1980). Graham-White was essentially advocating the sorts of secondary prevention, training, consultation and 'exerting influence' activities which are emphasised in contemporary accreditation standards.

Energy and innovation

By 1966 there were seven graduates from the new MSc in Abnormal Psychology which brought the grand total of clinical psychologists in NI to 10. Graham-White had been joined by, among others, Jim Patton, Marjorie Olley, Jeremy Harbison and Donald McKay in supporting the training programme as clinical supervisors and researchers. A prestigious MRC grant was obtained by this early graduate cohort to develop behavioural interventions for sex difficulties (e.g. Quinn et al., 1970). Perhaps this explained why the trainees of the early 1970s recalled teaching on sex therapy as so preponderant in the training curriculum in Belfast. Research-based teaching was alive and well at Queen's.

Branch minutes of the NI BPS meetings throughout the 1960s highlight a vibrant community of applied and academic psychologists coming together to advance the knowledge base and practice of the discipline in NI. The minutes of the 1968 AGM highlight that while branches throughout the UK were losing relevance due to the advent of 'Divisions', those in Northern Ireland and Wales were thriving because, 'we do not get the division between professional and nonprofessional psychologists due to lack of integration of interests'. The integration of the seven Divisions, pursuing common ground with academic colleagues, within the NI BPS branch remains a relatively unique feature of how the DCP in NI continues to operate today. Cross-divisional strategy and activity are not just an aspiration but a reality in NI.

The 'Troubles'

The promise of early beginnings gave way to an altogether more difficult period in the 1970s and early 1980s. The 'Troubles' had erupted and few in the population were untouched by a pouring out of bitter sectarian strife. If these were dark days for the country, so too for clinical psychology.

Graham-White left for Edinburgh in 1974. Funding for the course became less secure and there appeared to be no place for a new, perhaps nonessential, workforce with no critical mass or voice, at a time of growing economic deprivation. Several committed programme leaders from across the university and health care sectors battled valiantly to keep the programme and vision of clinical psychology alive – most notably Don Sykes, Marjorie Olley and Desmond Poole – but it was an uphill battle and morale became low. Training numbers shrank to six every three years for a period of time and accreditation was at risk. Despite the low numbers coming out of training, jobs were scarce, career progression was stagnant and there was a general haemorrhaging of staff to elsewhere due to this situation and indeed the Troubles more generally.

This personally difficult context sheds some light on what has been something of an anomaly to the contemporary profession in NI. Why did clinical psychologists, and indeed the training programme, have so little to say or do about the conflict going on around them? The research that was happening in NI emphasised normalisation and resilience (e.g. Cairns, 1987) and perhaps reinforced what Rooney and Dempsey (2007) describe as a 'culture of silence'. A general survival imperative at this time was to 'keep your head down', but perhaps the profession at that time was simply too small and too much at risk of extinction to think beyond responding to the trauma presenting to clinics and rising to the challenge of the more community-focused perspective that Graham-White had called for.

Fresh starts and reflective practice

Clinical psychology in Northern Ireland was on its knees by the early 1980s. We were undoubtedly aided at this time by developments in England – Trethowan, the MAS report and MPAG – which have been written about elsewhere in this book. However, also instrumental in turning things around was the return to NI of Robin Davidson, a clinical psychologist who trained in Leeds and who used his charm, evidence-based arguments and wily focus to establish a vibrant clinical psychology department at Holywell Hospital in the Northern Board. Davidson embodied the importance of interpersonal skills of leadership and persuasion. He forged alliances with the deputy chief medical officer, among others, and succeeded in establishing and modelling a department of emerging 'specialists' and a career pathway for clinical psychologists. The context was ripe for a relaunch of the training course and Ken Brown (then head of the psychology department at QUB) succeeded in securing new devoted appointments to lead a new three-year MSc in clinical psychology in 1988, with an intake of six every year and with salaried training commissions.

With hindsight, we entered a halcyon period at this time. The other health and social service boards mirrored the Northern Board in appointing 'top grade' psychologists and establishing departments of clinical psychology. This process accelerated with the reorganisation into many more Trusts in 1992 – all of whom had their own 'head of service' who established a widening portfolio of clinical psychology posts as part of their services. Jobs became plentiful, career progression rapid and financial remuneration good.

Perhaps because of this new-found security, the programme at QUB was among the first to focus on what would become known throughout the training community as 'reflective practice'. Although she did not proclaim it at a national level, or it was not heard at a national level, Ann Moriarty, the new programme director, started introducing a culture of critical reflective practice and personal self-awareness into the training of clinical psychologists at the end of the 1980s. This would evolve in later years into something with a more outward-looking, systemic and organisational focus. However, through the 1990s the momentum of progress and expansion seemed unstoppable, we were enjoying the ride and the space to focus on who we were and what we were about.

Research excellence and innovative services

The first part of the first decade of the 21st century continued the expansion and optimism of the 1990s. The first practitioner doctorate at QUB enjoyed a doubling of trainee commissions and a trebling of staff thanks to utilising joint appointments to greater effect. The workforce was growing at a previously unrecognisable rate and, instead of net migration, graduates of other programmes (including the current writer) were coming home to boost numbers and bring greater diversity to the pool of practitioners and supervisors.

Clinical psychologists were extending their reach across an ever-increasing number of specialisms. Of note were developments in clinical health psychology – most notably at the Royal Hospitals (later Belfast) Trust where the new head of service, Nichola Rooney, had established psychological services in a whole spectrum of physical health specialisms (perinatal, multiple paediatric specialisms and across adult health conditions) long before such services had become recommended by NICE and well before contemporary appraisals of such as an important 'future' for our profession. Indeed by the workforce review of 2008 30 per cent of clinical psychologists in NI were working in physical health specialisms.

Advancing the knowledge base in our discipline through a more rigorous research training and engagement with programmatic research became a new hallmark of the QUB course. Clinical psychologists in practice were key collaborators, such as Rooney who had established a landmark 'Clinical Psychology Research Unit', within an NHS setting. A research active culture among clinical psychologists in NI flourished at this time and to the benefit of the training programme. Internationally relevant research, most notably in psychological interventions in physical health conditions, trauma and psychosis (e.g. Hoy et al., 2012; McCusker et al., 2012), flourished.

21st century challenges and directions

Although the 21st century saw an unprecedented recognition of the relevance and effectiveness of psychological interventions, just as with new medical interventions, demand was always going to outstrip what could be delivered through the shrinking public purse and traditional ways of working. Only in Scotland and Northern Ireland, however, was the New Ways of Working (see chapter 5) training vision realised through the establishment of MSc programmes for assistant and associate psychologists to provide a skill mixed economy of psychological care. In England such moves became superseded by IAPT.

It would be premature to judge the impact and success of IAPT, although it is clear from letters in *Clinical Psychology Forum* over the years that this movement has often divided the profession in opinion and response. Most fundamentally, the mushrooming of 'psychological therapists' across multiple professions certainly posed new challenges to the question of what it was clinical psychology had to bring to the table.

This challenge was not going to bypass us in NI and was perhaps the greatest impetus to the transformation in DCP NI from what was effectively a training agency to a professional body. Today the Northern Ireland DCP is a more confident, outward-looking, politically and strategically savvy organisation that our colleagues in England were looking to learn from as outlined at the start of this section. Today our members contribute to and lead on developing statutory guidance across a whole spectrum of health and social care initiatives, advise on workforce development, have a specialty adviser to the Chief Medical Officer, participate in the regulatory body inspections of services, deliver externally facing 'conferences to influence' and engage in effective public discussion through the media and other forums. On the ground, clinical psychologists lead and manage psychological services where psychologists have uniquely defined roles and competencies which complement the psychological therapist colleagues from a range of other backgrounds. This is an uneasy and perhaps fragile success, however, as relentless rationalisation of health care and current austerity drives mean that we can never sit back and rest on our laurels. We look to future leaders in the profession to take this forward.

Review and future scoping

Political devolution has indeed brought into sharper focus the unique identity of clinical psychology in NI. Our key figures, from Graham-White, through Davidson and Rooney, to today's leaders, have been of national relevance in shaping the vision of what we are (and should be) about, of evolving our training curricula, psychological services and professional body activities to ensure we are relevant to, and indeed help shape, a changing health and social care landscape. Research activity across practice, as well as university, settings has contemporary relevance and enhances our professional standing rather than being an anachronistic ideal.

The relentless tides of future challenges will not cease washing over us in NI, however, as elsewhere across the UK. We must train, and at postqualification support, our graduates not to run away from, but to engage with and endeavour to mitigate at least and transform at best, current trends towards reductionistic standardisation, short-sighted regulation and other trends fed by the context of austerity. Initially unsettling, devolution has precipitated a diversity and creativity across our four nations to these common challenges. From this we can all learn, survive and thrive.

The development of clinical psychology in the Republic of Ireland

Alan Carr

The establishment of the academic disciple of psychology in the Republic of Ireland

Although psychology has only recently become an independent field of study in Ireland, scholarship in the subject can be traced back to the early Christian era when philosophical studies flourished in Irish centres of learning (Brady, 1990; Brady & McLoone, 1992; Brock, 2012; McKenna, 1986). In Ireland, as in Britain and elsewhere, psychology was seen as a philosophical discipline for many years. The word 'psychology' first appeared in the title of an Irish academic post in 1909 when a Chair of Logic and Psychology was instituted at University College Dublin (UCD) in the newly founded National University of Ireland. In 1947 Queen's University Belfast launched the first psychology degree programme on the island of Ireland. Eleven years later in 1958 the UCD Diploma in Psychology (known as the UCD Dip Psych) was established by Eamonn Fechín O'Doherty. O'Doherty, a Catholic priest, had completed his PhD in psychology with Frederic Bartlett at Cambridge. The course included academic coursework, research, and a clinical placement. A distinctive feature of the programme was its Catholic ethos. The programme was open to honours graduates from other areas who brought to the course the experience gained in their various professions including teaching, medicine, social science, science and engineering. This ensured that the first psychologists graduating in Ireland, who would be responsible for setting up and developing the clinical psychological services throughout the county, would be mature and experienced people.

In the decade following the founding of the UCD Dip Psych, undergraduate courses in psychology were established at UCD, Trinity College Dublin (TCD), University College Cork and the National University of Ireland, Galway (NUIG). Some of the staff in these departments had completed psychology degrees in the UK and North America. British and North American psychology has had a major impact on the development of academic and clinical psychology in Ireland. In 1999 an undergraduate programme was set up by the newly established psychology department at the National University of Ireland, Maynooth. In 2007 a psychology department was established at the University of Limerick (UL) and an honours undergraduate degree in psychology was first offered in 2009. All six universities offered honours degrees programmes which conferred eligibility for graduate memberships of the Psychological Society of Ireland (PSI) and the British Psychological Society (BPS). Many graduates of these programmes aspired to work as professional clinical psychologists. Until clinical psychology training programmes became established in Ireland in the 1980s, and the profession became better regulated in the 1990s, an apprenticeship model dominated the field. Individuals with a primary degree in psychology took up positions within the Irish public health service, and learned their profession though practice and consultation with peers and senior colleagues.

The development of clinical psychology in the Republic of Ireland

The Irish public health service, from the foundation of the state in 1922, was distinctive insofar as some services were offered by state-run facilities, while others were offered by voluntary organisations established by predominantly Catholic religious orders, and in which professional posts were partly or wholly state-funded. Such organisations, which provided services for children and adults with intellectual disabilities and mental health problems, led the way in establishing clinical psychology services. They had a distinctive Catholic ethos. The first clinical psychological service was established in Dublin in 1955, by Dr Jock McKenna, a Scotsman, at the Saint John of God Child Guidance Clinic in Rathgar (McKenna, 1982, 1986). The impetus for this development came from the Irish Government and the World Health Organization, not from universities, since academic psychology departments had not yet been established. In the late 1950s a link was established between the UCD Psychology Department and the Saint John of God Child Guidance Clinic which provided clinical placements for UCD Dip Psych students.

From the mid-1950s onwards most clinical psychology posts were established first in child guidance clinics (McKenna, 1982, 1986) and intellectual disability services (McLoone, 1982), and later in adult mental health services. This progression from child and disability service to adult mental health services was in part due to resistance or opposition to the development of clinical psychology by elements within the hierarchy of the Catholic Church and the profession of adult psychiatry (Brock, 2012). Beginning in the late 1980s other specialisms such as clinical psychology and child protection, the clinical psychology of older adulthood, clinical neuropsychology, clinical health psychology, paediatric psychology, and clinical psycho-oncology began to develop. In the early years of the profession psychologists were primarily engaged in carrying out psychological assessments. However, the role of clinical psychologists subsequently evolved dramatically (Carr, 2000). In Ireland in the first decades of the 21st century, clinical psychologists work with all age groups, are employed in many different settings and undertake a wide range of functions, including a variety of assessment and intervention procedures, consultancy, and research (Carr, 2012). Since the mid-1950s in the Irish public health service, the career structure for clinical psychologists included trainee, basic, senior, principal and director grades. This career structure was modelled on a system developed in the UK. Assistant psychologist posts were first piloted in the Republic of Ireland in 2013.

From 2002, the growth of the clinical psychology workforce in the Irish public health service has been documented in a series of reports produced by the Heads of Psychology Services in Ireland (Kelly et al., 2012). In 2002 there were 375 FTE clinical psychologists in the Irish public health service. By 2011 this figure had almost doubled, and risen to 710. This growth reflected the strong emphasis on developing psychology services in the Irish government's mental health policy document *A Vision for Change* (O'Connor, 2006) and the establishment of new clinical psychology training programmes at NUIG and UL.

Psychological Society of Ireland (PSI)

PSI was established in 1970 by a group of 96 psychologists at the Mater Hospital in Dublin (McHugh & McLoone, 1980; Swan, 2013). An academic journal, *The Irish Journal of Psychology*, and a newsletter, *The Irish Psychologist*, were first published by PSI in 1971 and 1974 respectively. The PSI Division of Clinical Psychology was established in 1979. This was preceded in 1975 by the PSI policy statement on *Psychology in the Service of Health* which set out parameters for the development of a clinical psychology service within the Irish public health service. The document includes sections on the functions of psychologists, the organisation and staffing of psychological services and on the qualification and training of clinical psychologists. The establishment of formal university-based courses in clinical psychology was strongly advocated. At the time, no such formal courses were available in Ireland. However, some public health service units had begun to sponsor psychologists to complete clinical psychology courses in the UK, notably in Scotland.

PSI published a range of policy documents relevant to clinical psychology, notably *Guidelines for the Employment of Psychologists in the Health Sector* in 1998. A revised version of this document was accepted by the Irish Department of Health in 2000, when PSI became recognised as the body for scrutiny of clinical psychology qualifications from candidates trained outside Ireland. In 2005 the Irish Health and Social Care Professionals Act was introduced. This marked the beginning of an Irish government initiative to introduce statutory registration for clinical psychologists. In 2014, negotiations between PSI and CORU (the government body overseeing statutory registration) about this issue are ongoing.

Training in clinical psychology in the Republic of Ireland

Since the 1950s small numbers of Irish psychologists had obtained their clinical training abroad, mainly in the UK or North America. It was not until the late 1970s that accredited professional training programmes were first established. There have been two diploma courses in clinical psychology in the Republic of Ireland. A BPS Diploma in Clinical Psychology training scheme was set up with clinical placements offered by the public health service in the Dublin area (known then as the Eastern Health Board) and the academic teaching based in the TCD psychology department, under the direction of Sheila Green at TCD and Maureen Gaffney in the Eastern Health Board. This ran from 1978 until the 1990s. The PSI Diploma in Clinical Psychology, which was modelled on the BPS diploma, was established in 1991 and ran until 2007. Placement rotations were developed in the Irish public health service in some regions. Between 1997 and 2007 the University of Ulster offered taught modules to cover the academic elements of the PSI Diploma, through an MSc programme directed by Roger Woodward.

Four university-based accredited professional training programmes were established in the Republic of Ireland between 1977 and 2004 at UCD, TCD, NUIG and

UL. The UCD Master's programme in clinical psychology was established in 1977 under the direction of Therese Brady, and a similar programme was set up at TCD in 1992 under the direction of Maureen Gaffney. Both were accredited by PSI and BPS. In 1997 the UCD and TCD two-year Master's programmes were converted to three-year doctorates in clinical psychology, under the direction of Alan Carr at UCD and Maureen Gaffney at TCD. Similar doctoral programmes were established at NUIG in 2003, under the direction of Brian Maguire, and UL in 2004, under the direction of Patrick Ryan. Both were accredited by PSI. All four of these programmes were based on the UK clinical psychology training model. They involved a research thesis, academic tuition and placements of supervised clinical practice. Tuition and placements spanned a range of populations including child and adult mental health, disability and other specialisms. In the late 1990s Kevin Tierney became academic director of the TCD programme and Sinead Fitzgerald the clinical director.

Publications

Active research programmes in topics relevant to clinical psychology have been conducted at all universities in the Republic of Ireland since the 1970s, although the volume of publications increased markedly in the 1990s, especially following the establishment of the four doctoral programmes in clinical psychology. A variety of clinical psychology text books have been produced in the Republic of Ireland, notably the UCD handbooks covering the child and adult mental health and intellectual disability aspects of the doctoral curriculum (Carr, 1999, 2006; Carr & McNulty, 2006; Carr et al., 2007), a volume on clinical psychology and older adults (Ryan & Coughlan, 2011) and an introductory clinical psychology textbook for undergraduates (Carr, 2012).

The media

In Ireland clinical psychologists have had significant media presence in newspapers, on radio, TV and the internet. Important contributors include Patricia Redlich, Maureen Gaffney (who was director of the TCD clinical psychology programme for much of the 1990s), Tony Bates, Marie Murray, David Coleman and Eddy Murphy, all of whom directed various clinical psychology and mental health services. Gary O'Reilly, joint director of the UCD clinical psychology programme, developed an internet-based cognitive behaviour therapy assisted programme for adolescents called Pesky Gnats which became the most highly accessed eCBT programme for adolescents in the world.

Child abuse

In the Republic of Ireland clinical psychologists played a critical role in addressing the issue of child sexual abuse (CSA). In the late 1980s and early 1990s, clinical psychologists were integral members of the first specialist CSA units in university teaching hospitals (Carr & O'Reilly, 2004). During this same period, the Stay Safe CSA prevention programme, which was rolled out nationally, was developed by a team in which the clinical psychologist Deirdre MacIntyre played a central role (MacIntyre & Carr, 1999). The psychology service within the Irish prison system was established by a clinical psychologist, Des O'Mahony, in the 1980s, and developed the first Irish treatment programme for sex offenders (O'Reilly et al., 2010). The first Irish outpatient programme for clerical sex offenders was established at the Saint John of God's mental health service and led by Patrick Walsh, a clinical psychologist. Psychologists played a central role in the development of the National Counselling Service, established in 2000 to provide psychotherapy to adult survivors of CSA (HSE NCS, 2009). A clinical psychologist, Fred Lowe, sat on the Commission to Inquire into Child Abuse in religiously affiliated institutions which produced the Ryan Report (2009).

Conclusion

In Ireland clinical psychology emerged in the mid-1950s as an integral part of the public health service for people with mental health problems and intellectual disability. The structure of the profession and training system which evolved were based on the UK model. The number of clinical psychologists, the range of specialisms in which they work and roles that clinical psychologist fulfil have developed significantly, especially during the 21st century. PSI, psychologists within the public health service, and the four clinical psychology training programmes have worked together to foster the growth of the profession. Clinical psychology research and textbooks have been published by Irish clinical psychologists, and they have also had significant media presence. Clinical psychologists also had a significant impact on major societal issues such as CSA. Statutory registration is the next major profession development on the horizon for the profession of clinical psychology in the Republic of Ireland.

Editors' concluding reflection

What is striking between the accounts of the devolved nations is that the local focus has provided relatively better political relationships with benefit for the development of clinical psychology in terms of training and workforce. The funding and performance of health care within the devolved administrations has not been without its critics, and a report from the Nuffield Foundation (Bevan et al., 2011) has highlighted that historically Scotland, Wales and Northern Ireland have had higher levels of funding per capita for the NHS than in England. The claim that this has not been matched by greater productivity or better health outcomes means that financial issues will become even more important in the future. Perhaps a reminder that to secure funding from the public purse the profession must continue to demonstrate that psychology can be harnessed for the public good.

References

Bagnall, G. (2010). Preparing for clinical supervision in psychology: What can we learn from the Scottish experience? *Clinical Psychology Forum, 216*, 15–20.

Bevan, G., Mays, N. & Connolly, S. (2011). *Funding and performance of health care systems in the four countries of the UK before and after devolution.* London: The Nuffield Trust.

Brady, T. (1990, November). Clinical psychology in Ireland. *Clinical Psychology Europe* [Special issue of *Clinical Psychology Forum*], 2–7.

Brady, T. & McLoone, J. (1992). Ireland. In V.S. Sexton & J.D. Hogan (Eds.), *International psychology. Views from around the world* (2nd edn, pp.229–340). Lincoln: University of Nebraska Press.

British Psychological Society (2014). *Standards for the accreditation of doctoral programmes in clinical psychology.* Leicester: Author.

Brock, A. (2012). Ireland. In D. Baker (Ed.), *The Oxford handbook of the history of psychology. Global perspectives* (pp.289–306). Oxford. Oxford University Press.

Cairns, E. (1987). *Caught in the crossfire: Children and the Northern Ireland conflict.* Belfast: Appletree.

Carr, A. (1999). *Handbook of clinical child and adolescent psychology: A contextual approach.* London: Routledge.

Carr, A. (2000). *Clinical psychology in Ireland, volume 1: Empirical studies of professional practice.* Lampeter: Edwin Mellen Press.

Carr, A. (2006). *Handbook of clinical child and adolescent psychology: A contextual approach* (2nd edn). London: Routledge.

Carr, A. (2012). *Clinical psychology: An introduction.* London: Routledge.

Carr, A. & McNulty, M. (Eds.) (2006). *Handbook of adult clinical psychology: An evidence-based practice approach.* London: Brunner-Routledge.

Carr, A. & O'Reilly, G. (2004). *Clinical psychology in Ireland, volume 5: Empirical studies of child sexual abuse.* Lampeter: Edwin Mellen Press.

Carr, A. O'Reilly, G., Walsh, P. & McEvoy, J. (Eds.) (2007). *Handbook of clinical psychology and intellectual disability.* London: Brunner-Routledge.

Dabbs, A. (2000). Personal reflections on a career in clinical psychology, or 'We have WAIS and MEAMS to make you talk'. *Clinical Psychology Forum, 145,* 9–13.

Davidson, N. (2000). *The origins of Scottish nationhood.* London: Pluto Press.

Department of Health and Social Security (1977). *The role of psychologists in the health service (Trethowan Report).* London: HMSO.

Ehlert, K. & Griffiths, R.D.P. (1996). Quality of life: A matched group comparison of long stay individuals and day patients manifesting psychiatric disabilities. *Journal of Mental Health, 5*(1), 91–100.

Frude, N. (2004). Bibliotherapy as a means of delivering psychological therapy. *Clinical Psychology, 39,* 8–10.

Graham-White, J. (1967). Clinical psychology in Northern Ireland: The first seven years. *Bulletin of the British Psychological Society, 20*(67), 19–23.

Graham-White, J. (1972). What is wrong with clinical psychology? *Bulletin of the British Psychological Society, 25,* 101–106.

Graham-White, J. (1980). Reflections of training: The making of a twentieth century psychologist. *The Irish Psychologist,* 7(5), 27–30.

Hetherington, R. (2000). Early days in clinical psychology. *Clinical Psychology Forum, 145,* 6–8.

ISD/NES (2005). *Delivering for health and applied psychology: Current workforce and future potential.* www.isdscotland.org/Health-Topics/Workforce/Psychology/Delivering%20for%20Health%20and%20Applied%20Psychology%20.pdf

Hoy, K., Barrett, S., Shannon, C. et al. (2012). Childhood trauma and hippocampal and amygdalar volumes in first episode psychosis. *Schizophrenia Bulletin, 36,* 1162–1169.

HSE NCS (2009). *HSE National Counselling Service strategic framework for service planning and delivery.* Dublin: Author.

Jones, C. (1983). The development of a practicable assessment linked language training curriculum for use with the handicapped child. *British Journal of Learning Disabilities, 11,* 30–32.

Kelly, J., Byrne, M. & Faherty, D. (2012). *Heads of Psychology Services Ireland (HPSI) workforce planning survey report 2011.* Roscommon: HPSI.

MacIntyre, D. & Carr, A. (1999). Evaluation of the effectiveness of the Stay Safe primary prevention programme for child abuse. *Child Abuse and Neglect, 23,* 1307–1325.

McCusker, C., Doherty, N., Molloy, B. et al. (2012). A randomised controlled trial to promote adjustment of children with congenital heart disease entering school and their families. *Journal of Pediatric Psychology, 37,* 1089–1103.

McGuire, R. (2000). Early years of the Edinburgh Course. *Clinical Psychology Forum, 145,* 27–28.

McHugh, M. & McLoone, J. (1980). The roots that clutch: The origins and growth of PSI. *The Irish Psychologist, 6,* 1–8.

McKenna, J. (1982). The development of clinical psychology. *The Irish Psychologist, 6,* 50–51.

McKenna, J. (1986). The development of clinical psychology in Ireland. *Thornfield Journal, 14,* 34–47.

McKenna, P. (2012). When to give up driving. *The Psychologist, 25*, 668–671.
McLoone, J. (1982). Psychologists in mental handicap services. *The Irish Psychologist, 6*, 51.
Nairn, T. (1981). *The break-up of Britain: Crisis and neo-nationalism.* London: Verso.
NHS Education for Scotland (2000). *Clinical psychology workforce planning report.* www.isdscotland.org/wf_psychology/clinicalpsychologywfp.pdf
O'Connor, J. (2006). *A vision for change.* Dublin: Stationery Office.
O'Reilly, G. Carr, A. Murphy, P.M. & Cotter, A. (2010). Evaluation of a prison-based sexual offender intervention programme. *Sexual Abuse, 22*(1), 95–111.
Psychological Society of Ireland (1975). *Psychologists in the service of health.* Dublin: Author.
Psychological Society of Ireland (1998). *Guidelines for the employment of psychologists in the health sector.* Dublin: Author.
Quinn, J.T., Harbison, J.J. & McAllister, H. (1970). An attempt to shape penile responses. *Behaviour Research and Therapy, 8*, 213–216.
Rollnick S., Miller W.R. & Butler C. (2007). *Health care: Helping patients change behaviour.* New York: Guilford Press.
Rooney, N. & Dempsey, A. (2007, October). *'The elephant in the room': How has the clinical psychology profession in Northern Ireland responded to meet the psychological needs of children and families affected by the 'Troubles'?* Paper presented at the Centre for the Study of Youth and Political Violence Working Group Conference, Cape Town, South Africa.
Ryan, P. & Coughlan, B. (2011). *Ageing and older adult mental health: Issues and implications for practice.* London: Routledge.
Ryan, S. (2009). *Report of the Commission to Inquire into Child Abuse.* Dublin: Stationery Office. www.childabusecommission.com/rpt/pdfs/
Scottish Health Service (1984). *Clinical psychology in the Scottish Health Service.* Edinburgh: Author.
SCPMDE/CAPISH (1999). *Psychology services in Scottish health care.* Edinburgh: Author.
Scottish Government (2011). *Applied psychologists and psychology in NHS Scotland (Wells Report).* Edinburgh: Author.
Semeonoff, B. (1969). Changing horizons: An essay in autobiography. *Bulletin of the British Psychological Society, 22*, 169–179.
Smith A.J., Hodgson R.J., Bridgeman, K. & Shepherd, J.P. (2003). A randomised control trial of a brief intervention after alcohol-related facial injury. *Addiction, 98*(1), 43–52.
Swan, D. (2013). The Psychological Society of Ireland – of what is past, and passing and to come. *Irish Journal of Psychology, 34*(3–4), 123–136.
Tait, A.C. (1972). History of Crichton Royal. *Medical History, 16*(2), 178–184.
Whyte, B. & Ajetunmobi, T. (2012). *Still the sick man of Europe? Scottish mortality in a European context 1950–2010.* www.gcph.co.uk/publications/391_still_the_sick_man_of_europe
Williams J.M.G., Teasdale J.M., Segal, Z.V. & Kabat-Zinn, J. (2007). *The mindful way through depression: Freeing yourself from chronic unhappiness.* New York: Guilford Press.

Chapter 24 The international context of British clinical psychology

Steve Melluish, Gary Latchford & Sarah Marks

Introduction

Psychology is international, of course, and a great deal of research and therapeutic innovation originates outside of the UK but influences UK practice – and vice versa. As clinical psychology was beginning to be established in the UK, however, outside influences were more apparent. Models of training in the UK followed pioneering developments in the US, and as the profession grew in the UK it benefited enormously from a number of talented psychologists from different countries who helped to shape the profession. As clinical psychology became established in the UK and elsewhere, the exchange of ideas continued, with changes in the job market leading to many clinical psychologists moving to the UK from different countries, bringing with them a diversity of ideas from which the profession has benefited – and continues to benefit – enormously. As training has become better established in the UK, so ideas and people have been exported to those lower income nations still establishing psychology, but with obvious need. Though there are caveats, these developments hold promise that all involved may be enriched by the experience.

The influence of the US on the clinical psychology profession in the UK

One of the most significant and long-running connections informing the development of clinical psychology in Britain in the 20th century was with theories and practices developed in the US. The importance of US-based publications, such as the *Journal of Abnormal and Clinical Psychology*, cannot be overstated, both in having a wide readership internationally, and in providing a forum for British psychologists to publish research. British psychologists also followed the developments in American behaviourism from the 1950s, not only in terms of key book publications, but also with a number of British figures from the Maudsley conducting study visits to the US, including May Davidson, Grace Rawlings and Hans Eysenck and, later, William Yule (Yule, interview with Sarah Marks, 2 August 2014). Eysenck claimed that 'much of it [American psychology] I admired...during my whole working life psychology has been predominantly North American, and is likely to remain so for the foreseeable future' (Eysenck, 1990, p.ix).

With such significant interest in the US from British psychologists, it is worth tracing the origins of American clinical psychology: some argue that Boulder, Colorado, is the closest thing the profession has to a birthplace internationally. The reason for this is a meeting that took place in Boulder in the summer of 1949 to formally agree on training standards in clinical psychology. The meeting included the most influential psychologists in North America at that time. A contemporary photograph published in an article to commemorate the 50th anniversary (Benjamin & Baker, 2000) shows the attendees smiling for the camera, having presumably finished their business. They are almost all middle-aged, there are no nonwhite faces, and they are nearly all men, but they came up with principles sound enough to maintain their influence over six decades.

The first clinical psychology clinic is usually seen as that established by Lightner Witmer in Pennsylvania in 1896; he also set up a summer course in clinical psychology the year after. Over the next 50 years eight institutions in the US began offering some form of clinical psychology training (Routh, 2000), but in fact most psychologists on both sides of the Atlantic were more likely to be involved in testing than treatment. That was set to change following the Second World War. As the US prepared for war, psychologists were consulted about their contribution to the war effort, seen as being both testing recruits and – in a significant departure from previous thinking – also preparing for the return of these recruits after combat. To achieve the latter meant establishing clear training routes in clinical psychology for the first time.

They were proved right to do so. At the end of the war over 40,000 servicemen in the US were admitted to psychiatric hospitals run by the veterans association (VA). It was clear that psychiatry was unable to recruit anything like the numbers needed to cope with this increase in demand, and the VA looked to clinical psychology (Capshew, 1999). A committee was formed on training in clinical psychology, headed by David Shakow. Their recommendations (APA, 1947) were formally accepted at the Boulder conference which established a consensus on the core components of clinical psychology training (Baker & Benjamin, 2000). Unsurprisingly, this was influenced by established systems for postgraduate study in the US and designed around a PhD (with clinical internships). Most importantly, however, it established the principle of the 'scientist-practitioner', that clinical psychologists are trained as psychological scientists and in the application of this science to clinical practice. The foundation of training was to be the 'holy trinity' of assessment, research and therapy (Raimy, 1950).

The scientist-practitioner model quickly came to be the primary principle underpinning clinical psychology training in the US and elsewhere. All UK clinical psychology programmes are arguably descendants of the principles decided at the Boulder conference, and we suspect that the phrase 'scientist-practitioner' features at least once in every application to clinical psychology training. In the US, however, the dominance of the model has not been so straightforward. Concerns were raised relatively early that the emphasis on a research PhD risked undervaluing training in clinical skills (though it was also noted that graduates from the new training programmes tended not to actually do research or publish once they were trained).

These concerns came to a head in 1973 at a conference in Vail, Colorado, that proposed an alternative training model based on practitioner doctorates. Influenced by professional programmes in medicine and law, the proposal was to address the perceived imbalance in the scientist-practitioner model by shifting content of training more towards the practitioner arm, the argument being that you can be a highly academic consumer and interpreter of research as it applies to practice without having to produce research yourself. In the US there was a tradition of some doctoral degrees (such as the MD) being awarded without the need for a research dissertation or thesis, and the Vail model proposed something similar for clinical psychology – a PsyD award.

Graduates from clinical psychology training in the US based on the Vail model now significantly outnumber those trained on courses based upon the previous model, though most do include clinical research as a component. Different models of training continue to have an impact on the profession in the US. Though this often leads to 'model wars', Bell and Hausman (2014) argue that what overrides training models and unites the profession is a focus on science and competencies.

Clinical psychology training begins in the UK: The crucial role of émigrés

1947, the year of Shakow's report, was also the year that the first clinical psychology training course in the UK was established. Hans Eysenck, who had come to the UK from Germany in the 1930s, had been asked by eminent psychiatrist Professor Sir Aubrey Lewis to establish a department of clinical psychology, and he urged him to visit the US to see how clinical psychology training was becoming established (Gibson, 1981). Eysenck saw much to admire, particularly the way training was to be founded on academic psychology (Rachman, 2003). Eysenck had his own views on how scientific this foundation needed to be, however, rejecting psychodynamic therapy as being unscientific and lacking evidence for clinical usefulness. Eysenck outlined his ideas in an article on the new course in *American Psychologist* in 1949, arguing that clinical psychology training should focus on only two of the three areas set out at Boulder: assessment and research (Eysenck, 1949).

Eysenck was not a clinician and appointed others to lead the clinical section. Monte Shapiro was the first, later succeeded by Jack Rachman. Both, as it happens, originated from Southern Africa, with Rachman having studied with South African psychiatrist Joseph Wolpe (Wolpe, 1958). Shapiro came to the UK from what was then Rhodesia before the Second World War, in which he had flown as a navigator in Bomber Command. He was, above all, an empiricist, 'advocating a scientific approach to the study of individuals with psychopathology as early as 1951' (Barlow & Nock, 2009, p.19). By the 1950s, led by Shapiro, the psychologists at the Maudsley were already doing therapy, though this was disguised as research (see chapters 9 and 14; Buchanan, 2010).

It is notable that many of the key players in the early years during which clinical psychology training became established in the UK were not themselves originally from the UK. As William Yule has argued, it was significant in particular that they were not members of the 'British Establishment', and were perhaps therefore not beholden to local traditions and practices (Yule, interview with Sarah Marks, 2 August 2014). The leap from assessment to intervention was certainly influenced by Shapiro and Rachman, and later Eysenck. It is hard to say how much their upbringing outside of the institutions and divisions of UK society contributed to their willingness to challenge the status quo. Rachman (personal communication, 19 August 2014) thinks that the influence of outsiders might be overstated, acknowledging that most of the psychology department at the Maudsley in the early days were British born, including Reg Beech, Don Kendrick, H. Gwynne Jones and many others. He adds too, that Aubrey Lewis, who became the fiercest critic of psychologists providing treatment and breaking with the established order, was himself an Australian.

Shaping clinical psychology in the UK: People and ideas from Europe and beyond

In addition to acknowledging the anglophone influence of the US, an account of international influences on clinical psychology in the UK needs to reference so many European ideas that a chapter would not be long enough. Of course, the primary source for all developments in behaviour therapy can be traced to physiologist Ivan Pavlov's initial work on conditioning in Russia. This influenced a generation of psychologists in the UK, such as Jeffrey Gray, who translated work from key Russian psychological laboratories himself. Other key Russian figures include Aleksander Luria, who influenced neuropsychology and developmental psychology in the UK, and Luria's teacher, Lev Vygotsky, whose work remained largely unknown in the West until the 1970s, when there was an explosion of interest from cognitive and developmental psychology. Luria, notably, was on the founding editorial board of the BPS *Journal of Social and Clinical Psychology* as a result of his connections with the Maudsley psychologist Neil O'Connor, according to BPS Council minutes from 1960–1961.

Most European countries could similarly cite psychologists and therapists that have influenced practice in the UK, from pioneering therapists such as Freud (Austria) and Erik Erikson and Erich Fromm (both originally from Germany), developmental psychologist Jean Piaget (Switzerland), to the Milan school of family therapy in Italy. Indeed, the emigration of psychologists such as Anna Freud and Melanie Klein to Britain prior to the Second World War also opened up the possibility for these traditions to become institutionalised in British training and practice.

More useful, perhaps, is to continue the earlier theme of recognising individual psychologists from other countries who contributed significantly to the development of the profession. This predates even the first training course. Born in South Africa, May Davidson was an early pioneer in establishing clinical psychology services in Oxford. She had been part of the first committee of professional psychologists in the BPS in 1943, and went on to become the first adviser on clinical psychology to the Department of Health and Social Security in 1973. Similarly, the first chair of the Division of Clinical Psychology was Mahesh Desai, who played a major role in establishing the relatively new profession of clinical psychology within the NHS.

International influences and the mobility of clinical psychologists: The 1980s and beyond

Some of the most important international influences on British clinical psychology over the last 30 years have been from those moving to the UK from the country of their birth (and often of their clinical training). Registration issues are now handled by the Health and Care Professions Council, but for many years the BPS had a subcommittee whose job it was to vet applications for chartership in the UK. The Committee for the Scrutiny of Individual Qualifications in Clinical Psychology (CSIQ, known to all as 'seasick') had a thankless task. Relying on volunteers, they had to interpret the qualifications in clinical psychology submitted by applicants from all over the world, work out how closely they were equivalent to training provided in the UK at the time the candidates trained, and set a list of requirements to be undertaken, examined and passed, based on the difference. This could include clinical placements, research and essays. The applicants came from across Europe, South Africa, India, Australia, Russia, North America and more. It was, of course, also very difficult for these applicants, many of whom already had successful careers in their home country and were in the uncomfortable situation of having their qualifications examined and often 'judged wanting' by people they didn't know. But the system worked well enough. Local psychologists and training courses often supported colleagues going through this process, and as demand for psychology posts in the 1990s outstripped the capacity of UK training programmes to fill them, psychologists trained overseas became a major part of the expansion of services. This group became a major source, not just of new talent, but of new ideas. Many went on to become highly influential in the profession, with a number playing a role in training.

The development of clinical psychology in continental Europe during the 1980s and 1990s also eventually contributed to many psychologists from European countries joining the UK workforce. Official British involvement with associations of psychologists in other European countries did not really begin in earnest until the early 1990s, even though the European Federation of Psychologist's Associations (EFPA) had been founded in Germany in 1981, with a biennial conference, the European Congress of Psychologists, becoming established in Amsterdam in 1989, enabling exchange of research and practices across national boundaries. Ingrid Lunt, a UK-based psychologist, was one of a number of BPS members who were keen to increase the Society's involvement with European colleagues, and she became twice president of the EFPA in the 1990s, a time when a number of associations from the former Eastern Bloc became members of the organisation. She is credited by the EFPA for her active involvement in promoting a set of universal European standards for accreditation and training of psychologists through the EuroPsy project, partly through the EU's Leonardo da Vinci funding scheme to develop a common European psychology qualification (EFPA, 1990; Freeman, 2011). This work in standardisation was crucial for further enabling mobility of psychologists across national borders, allowing the UK to strengthen its workforce in particular.

The situation regarding European qualifications in clinical psychology, and recognition to practice as a clinical psychologist or psychotherapist has varied considerably throughout the European continent. Indeed, this is probably one of the major reasons that EFPA has tried to regulate applied psychology as opposed to the more specialised UK Divisions. However, in parallel with efforts to standardise applied psychology, various attempts have also been made to define clinical psychology within a European context.

There are several reasons for there being such disparate qualifications and definitions of clinical psychology throughout Europe, and these highlight the differences between Europe and the UK. First, there is the question of qualifications in psychology. Prior to attempts to harmonise degrees throughout Europe through the implementation of the Bologna Process (see chapter 7), the duration and level of qualification varied considerably. In many EU countries, the basic undergraduate qualification tended to be four or five years. For example, in Germany three years would be spent studying psychology generically and a further two years with some kind of academic specialisation (e.g. clinical, organisational) leading to the qualification of the Diploma after five years of study. However, the more applied aspects studied later in the degree were usually from an academic perspective and seldom included any clinical practice or supervision. Indeed, it is very common throughout Europe for qualifications in clinical psychology to be solely academically orientated and university-based.

Whether a graduate with an academic qualification is able to practise will depend upon that country's legislation concerning regulation and psychotherapy. Many countries do not have statutory regulation for psychology, and graduates may have to do further training in psychotherapy before they can practise. Indeed, at one time in Italy, you could only practise as a clinical psychologist if you were medically qualified. However, throughout the EU there has been a trend towards unifying the regulation and registration of psychologists and psychotherapists. Similarly, European universities are also offering bachelor's degrees and Master's qualifications usually after four as opposed to five years of study.

There have also been formal attempts to harmonise clinical psychology qualifications and regulation within the EU via the adoption of an EU curriculum for clinical psychology. One such project was the MAPS-C (Masters of Advanced Psychological Studies – Clinical) that was hosted by the University of Vienna and published a report suggesting common training routes and curricula in 2005 (www.univie.ac.at/master_clinicalpsych/InformationsBroschuere.pdf).

Exporting ideas

This influx of clinical psychologists from outside the UK from the 1980s onwards, while shaping practice within the profession, did not seem to lead to the creation of many formal links between UK clinical psychology and other countries. Apart from a few published reports in *Clinical Psychology Forum* on clinical psychology in other countries (Campbell & Phiri, 1996; Collins, 1993) and some personal reflections (Atchison, 2000; Chinn, 1994), the focus of the profession from 1980 to the present was somewhat myopic and culturally and nationally bounded. This can perhaps be seen as a product of the unique way in which clinical psychology developed in the UK with the NHS as the profession's monopoly employer. As a consequence, clinical psychology tended to be defined as a clinical practice rather than an applied branch of an academic discipline. While this allowed the profession to successfully grow within the UK, its development was moulded by the specific demands and structural restraints of the NHS.

Where international links were developed, these tended to be established by those clinical psychologists working in university departments and involved in clinical psychology training. Universities have always been international environments and the exchange of ideas across borders a feature of academic life. From the mid-1990s the internationalisation of higher education accelerated as a result of the enormous advances in global communication technology and also as part of a wider process of globalisation. The higher education context provided scope for interested individuals to develop international links.

An example of such a link is that developed with Japan by a number of British clinical psychologists, including several chapter authors of this book. In Japan the distinctions between clinical psychology, counselling psychology and psychotherapy are harder to make, with training and practice models having been developed through a careful option appraisal of British, European and American models, including the use of indigenous models of psychotherapy, such as Morita therapy. An Association of Clinical Psychology, originally founded in 1964, was refounded in 1982 with a predominantly Jungian orientation. The development of clinical psychology in Japan has been led by Professor Haruhiko Shimoyama from the University of Tokyo, and Sue Llewelyn, Bill Yule, Graham Turpin, and John Hall have all contributed to this programme (Shimoyama, 2011).

Many of the international links created, however, have been with lower- and middle-income countries and have involved collaborative research projects, the development of clinical psychology training courses, involvement in disaster relief and work with war-affected populations.

Lower- and middle-income countries

While for some the attraction of international work is that it is seen as 'exotic' there is also a strong altruism in the profession of clinical psychology and a desire to help improve mental health in other countries, particularly lower- and middle-income countries (LMICs). This 'desire to help' is explored by Rachel Brown (Brown, 2014). She reflects on how Western psychological knowledge is often viewed as superior to the understandings and resources of people in LMICs, and how the import (or export) of Western models of mental health may be viewed as a form of 'psychological colonisation' (Patel et al., 2000).

From a historical perspective, it is important to be mindful of the extent of the influence of the UK's colonial past. In 1922, a fifth of the world's population, 58 countries across the world and a third of Africa, were part of the British Empire. Many of the LMICs where UK clinical psychologists have developed links were former British colonies. This colonial legacy is also part of the history of psychology itself, with the cultural roots of clinical psychology being based on many Western assumptions developed during periods of slavery and colonisation (Patel et al., 2000). Clinical psychologists working in LMICs have struggled with this cultural and historical legacy. Questions about how UK clinical psychologists should practise in LMICs and how to respect and work with local indigenous psychologies have been at the forefront of their work. The concern that Western professionals' involvement in LMICs may do more harm than good and may be at risk of 'trampling local expression of grief, suffering and healing' (Watters, 2010) has been the subject of much deliberation (Brown, 2014; White & Ebert, 2014). Many of those UK psychologists motivated to work in LMICs have also contributed to creating a reflective and critical discourse about these issues (White, 2013; Patel, 2003; Tribe, 2012, 2013).

In the 1990s there were a few published accounts of clinical psychologists visiting LMICs and describing aspects of different services. Two articles in *Clinical Psychology Forum* were published on Zambia (Campbell & Phiri, 1996; Chinn, 1994) and one on Malawi (Collins, 1993). In 1994, with the democratic elections in South Africa marking the end of apartheid, two accounts were also published about the psychological and social transformations in that country (Parker, 1994; Wright, 1994). These published accounts were personal reflections and not reports on any ongoing involvement of UK clinical psychologists in those countries. In the 1990s, however, two UK clinical psychologists did become involved in developing clinical psychology in LMICs: Graham Powell in Bangladesh and Helen Liebling-Kalifani in Uganda.

Graham Powell became involved in Bangladesh in 1994 when he was invited by the Overseas Development Administration of the UK government to advise on how to set up a clinical psychology programme in collaboration with Dr Anisur Rahman, the Head of Psychology at the University of Dhaka. In 1995 a formal proposal was made to establish an MSc followed by a two-year MPhil course linked with University College London, and the programme received approval on 7 October 1996. Graham Powell has continued to work in Dhaka and is now the Professor of Clinical and Neuropsychology at the University of Dhaka, where he has written about the need for long-term sustainable involvement in LMICs (Powell et al., 2014).

A year later Helen Liebling-Kalifani became involved in establishing clinical psychology in Uganda when she was invited by the University of Makerere to support the development of an MSc clinical psychology programme. In collaboration with Liverpool University and Manchester University clinical courses, a three-year British Council academic partnership was set up to fund exchange visits between the UK and Uganda, leading to the creation of a clinical psychology Master's programme in 1998. Between 1998 and 1999, Helen Liebling-Kalifani worked as a senior lecturer at Makerere University, assisting with the clinical psychology course and teaching on the Master's in counselling course. Her work in Uganda also led her to undertake work with women war survivors in Uganda and also in the Democratic Republic of Congo, Liberia and Rwanda as described in the next section.

The new millennium

With the arrival of the new millennium, the plight of many in LMICs became a focus of global concern and raised hopes for a global response to problems such as extreme poverty and hunger, lack of universal primary education, gender inequality, child mortality, maternal health, HIV/AIDS and malaria, environmental sustainability and development (United Nations, 2000). The justification for the choice of UN Millennium Development Goals was criticised at the time (Haines & Casells, 2004), and 14 years on progress has been uneven, with many LMICs having made little or no progress and instead having to use development monies for debt repayments. Explicit reference to mental health was absent from the millennial goals but became part of the global agenda for LMICs in 2004 when the World Health Organization (WHO) published a report called *The Treatment Gap in Mental Health Care* (Kohn et al., 2004). This report highlighted the pressing mental health needs of populations within LMICs and the injustice that LMICs receive less than 20 per cent of the share of the global mental health resource when they make up 80 per cent of the population (Patel and Prince, 2010; WHO, 2007). The WHO argued to scale up mental health services in LMICs (WHO, 2008, 2011) and this created a context for the development of what has become known as the Movement for Global Mental Health (Horton, 2007). The momentum of this movement and the wider acknowledgment of mental health as a global priority have provided a context in which there have been opportunities for the development of clinical psychology in LMICs. Although once again this scaling up and the assumptions of the Global Mental Health Movement have been criticised as pushing a Western agenda and a Western conception of mental health (Summerfield, 2008), Western mental health professionals have been involved in helping to develop mental health plans in LMICs.

During the first decade of the new century, collaborations between UK clinical psychologists and psychologists in LMICs led to the creation of a number of new clinical psychology training programmes. In Tanzania, a formal proposal to develop an MSc in clinical psychology at Muhimbili University was made in 2009 supported by staff from the Oxford clinical psychology programme led by John Hall (Hogan et al., 2010). The first intake was in 2010 and since then the programme has continued to develop (Hall, 2014).

In 2006 Ethiopia adopted its first national mental health policy based on the results of an assessment by the WHO of the country's mental health system, and this set the context for the development of mental health services. A number of psychiatrists from Leicester were involved in establishing a link between Leicester University, the local mental health trust and Gondar University in Ethiopia. Nic Bunker, a clinical psychologist from Leicester, was also active in supporting the link and the development of the clinical psychology course at Gondar with Yemataw Wonde (Wonde, 2014).

In the same period, other clinical psychologists developed exchange programmes. For example, the clinical psychology programme at Lancaster University developed an exchange with Uganda (Kampala) (Davies, 2014) and the University of Leicester with Cuba (Holguin), Ethiopia (Gondar) and India (Chennai). These exchange programmes offered opportunities for trainee placements in LMICs. A number of personal reflections on these experiences have been published in *Clinical Psychology Forum* (Jones, 2014; Sharkey & Tindale, 2010; Swancott et al., 2014). Some of the exchange programmes were reciprocal, offering opportunities for psychologists from LMICs to come to the UK to observe practice and contribute to training (Davies, 2014; Vasquez Monnar & Gutierrez Alvarez, 2010).

For some UK clinical psychologists, working in LMIC settings, where biomedical systems of care were less well established, offered an opportunity to see how a different form of mental health provision could be developed, with alternative explanations for the distress people experience. In 2003, David Winter was involved with the twinning of Sierra Leone psychiatric hospital and Barnet, Enfield and Haringey NHS Trust. He led two delegations of UK mental health professionals to provide training for staff working in the psychiatric hospital, focusing on introducing a more therapeutic ethos in the wards and facilitating links between traditional healers and staff in the hospital. His work led to a 50 per cent reduction in the number of chains used on inpatients (Liebling et al., 2014). His work in Liberia also extended to war-affected populations.

Disaster relief and work in war-affected populations

On 26 December 2004 the Indian Ocean earthquake, the third largest earthquake ever recorded, created one of the deadliest natural disasters in recorded history, affecting people in Indonesia, Sri Lanka, India and Thailand and prompting a worldwide humanitarian response. Many people from the UK and other countries travelled to the area motivated by a desire to help. This influx of volunteers created a problem, as many lacked the right support and clarity of role and also could not really give informed consent to the tasks that confronted them in the wake of the disaster. In response to the large number of British nationals affected by the aftermath of the disaster, either as victims themselves or as helpers who became traumatised by their involvement in the aid effort, the Foreign Office contacted the British Red Cross for help.

Sarah Davidson, a clinical psychologist who had worked as a volunteer for the British Red Cross for 35 years and was then on the board of trustees, was asked to look into providing psychological support. Her role involved working with British nationals on normalising their experiences, offering psychoeducation and facilitating coping strategies. She went on to develop CALMER (Davidson, 2010a, 2010b), an approach to working with trauma. In 2010 she was appointed as head of psychosocial support for the Red Cross and since then has been involved in supporting the development of psychosocial support across other national Red Cross societies.

The strong desire to 'do something' following a natural disaster or 'to help' a population recovering after conflict often leads to a flow of volunteers entering the affected country, creating a difficulty of coordination and in many cases reducing the efficiency of the international response. Angela Simcox and Bridie Gallagher (Simcox & Gallagher, 2014) found this in Cambodia where they developed a clinical psychology service in Phnom Penh. Cambodia was a country that had emerged from a long and bloody civil war in which an estimated third of the population had been killed. They found that the country was 'flooded with (largely untrained) helping professionals offering support to local people who had experienced trauma, sexual abuse, trafficking, rape and stigma' (p.28). After initially working in a bottom-up way they found that it was more effective to support local psychologists through offering supervision and to be involved in the evaluation of the projects run by NGOs.

A number of UK clinical psychologists have been involved in providing psychosocial support to war-affected people. Helen Liebling-Kalifani was involved in looking at the specific needs of women war survivors in Uganda, Sierra Leone and Liberia through her work with Isis-Women's International Cross-Cultural Exchange (Isis-WICCE; www.isis.or.ug) (Liebling-Kalifani et al., 2011).

Ross White and Beate Ebert worked with clinical psychologists from Europe and the US in Sierra Leone to train local workers in psychosocial interventions. Their involvement was part of an organisation, Commit and Act, which provides training in acceptance and commitment therapy (ACT). Their work in Sierra Leone again raises questions about the applicability of Western psychological models (mostly based on intrapsychic phenomena) to people living in collectivist societies. They felt that flexibility within the ACT approach made it adaptable and that working in LMICs offers opportunities for UK clinical psychologists 'to look afresh at the assumptions underlying their practice' (White & Beate, 2014).

The clinical psychology programme at Queen's University, Belfast, also collaborated on interventions with war-affected communities, child soldiers and victims of gender-based violence in Uganda and the Democratic Republic of Congo. Their involvement reinforces the complexities of working with war-affected communities and the challenges it brings around assumptions of victimhood and what an outcome of 'help' might be. As O'Callaghan et al. (2014) state: 'Children are makers of their own meaning who are influential actors, not passive participants in political conflicts' and 'violence may be seen as an acceptable way to replace the existing social order and achieve justice and economic and political opportunities' (p.26).

Human rights and international solidarity

The distinction between the psychological implications of natural disasters giving rise to humanitarian crises and psychological implications of systematic human rights violations committed in the context of war has been a focus for clinical psychologists adopting a human rights-based approach. Nimisha Patel's psychological work is within a human rights framework (e.g. Patel, 2003), which addresses the psychological, economic, political and social consequences of gross human rights violations, including torture and rape, in the context of war, organised violence and state persecution and oppression. Her psychological work internationally is as much an act of solidarity with oppressed and persecuted populations, including with health and social care professionals working in those settings, such as in the Gaza Strip and in the UN refugee camps for Palestinians from Lebanon, Syria and Gaza, as it is about working at different levels of prevention, training health professionals and the judiciary in different countries, engaging in strategic litigation to change domestic and international law to effect structural change, and seeking formal justice for human rights violations (e.g. Patel, 2011). In 2012 she established an interdisciplinary charitable organisation, the International Centre for Health and Human Rights, that works to support the implementation of international human rights standards for health and rehabilitation and justice for survivors of torture and other human rights violations. She has worked in many countries, including Somaliland, Kosovo, Jordan, Libya, Gaza, Lebanon and Romania, including consulting to various ministries of health, UN and other international organisations.

She points out how conflicts give rise to often vast amounts of international aid where many health professionals from different countries clamber to seek 'international contracts', often conducting one-off, short-term projects or trainings in psychological interventions. She emphasises the importance of starting from a critical and questioning position and to ask for whose benefit is this involvement, how culturally and context-appropriate and sustainable is what we are offering, who gets to decide what help is needed, who and how are outcomes defined, and by whom. She also argues for a recognition that there are no quick solutions to working in countries where there is ongoing conflict or in postconflict or transitional societies, and that any involvement of clinical psychologists has to be long-term and part of a broader public health and human rights-based agenda which is context-appropriate, and which seeks sustainable change, led by people who live in those countries.

Conclusion

As historian of science James Secord has argued, knowledge and practices within the sciences are not constrained by national boundaries, with transformations and translations occurring as concepts and practitioners travel across borders (Secord,

2004). With clinical psychology itself being a relatively young profession, and a product of a century in which air travel, communication technology and migration were more developed than ever before, consideration of its international context is particularly important. In this chapter we have tried to provide a historical context to the international influences on clinical psychology, looking at how the profession has been shaped by ideas imported from other countries but also how UK clinical psychologists have increasingly been involved in working in other countries, particularly LMICs. This flow of ideas and people across borders has been enriching and has been an inextricable part of development of UK clinical psychology. While it is difficult to tease out the exact influences of these cultural flows, there have been a few key imports, such as the Boulder and Vail models, that have been central to the profession's identity.

In the last 10 years, the growing interest among UK clinical psychologists in LMICs is a positive development and offers the potential for greater humanity and awareness of others across the globe. At the same time, these developments raise many questions about the role of the clinical psychologist, the extent to which psychological knowledge is culture-bound and the legacy of the UK's colonial past on work abroad.

The increasing international context of clinical psychology seems inevitable with the dramatic pace of global interconnectedness. While technology may be shrinking the world and making it easy to connect, true connections are only formed through genuine curiosity to understand the experiences of others in other countries and an openness to learn about how cultural and social differences play out in a global context. The reflective nature of the profession of clinical psychology places it in a good position to avoid any universalising approach and to advocate for people to be understood in their own terms, using their own language and the concepts of their own societies.

References

Atchison, L. (2000). A clinical psychology training placement in Bangladesh. *Clinical Psychology Forum, 144,* 11–12.

American Psychological Association, Committee on Training in Clinical Psychology (1947). Recommended graduate training programme in clinical psychology. *American Psychologist, 2,* 539–558.

Baker, D.B. & Benjamin, L.T. Jr (2000). The affirmation of the scientist-practitioner: A look back at Boulder. *American Psychologist, 55,* 241–247.

Barlow, D.H. & Nock, M.K. (2009). Why can't we be more idiographic in our research? *Perspectives on Psychological Science, 4,* 19–21.

Bell, D.J. & Hausman, E.M. (2014). Training models in professional psychology doctoral programs. In W.B. Johnson & N.J. Kaslow (Eds.), *The Oxford handbook of education and training in professional psychology* (pp.33–51). New York: Oxford University Press.

Benjamin, L.T. Jr (2005). A history of clinical psychology as a profession in America (and a glimpse at its future). *Annual Review of Clinical Psychology, 1,* 1–30.

Benjamin, L.T. Jr & Baker, D.B. (2000). Boulder at 50. *American Psychologist, 55,* 233–236.

Brown, R. (2014). 'The desire to help' in low economic countries. *Clinical Psychology Forum, 258,* 19–22.

Buchanan, R.D. (2010). *Playing with fire: The controversial career of Hans J. Eysenck.* Oxford: Oxford University Press.

Callaghan, P., McCullen, J. & Shannon, C. (2014). Hamlet or omelette? Debates in the field of interventions of war affected children. *Clinical Psychology Forum, 258,* 23–27.

Campbell, T. & Phiri, M. (1996). Group counselling for safer sex in Zambia. *Clinical Psychology Forum, 93*, 4–8.
Capshew J.H. (1999). *Psychologists on the march: Science, practice, and professional identity in America, 1929–1969.* New York: Cambridge University Press.
Chinn, D. (1994). Confronting two worlds: Psychiatry and bewitchment in Zambia. *Clinical Psychology Forum, 209*, 2–4.
Collins, S. (1993). Clinician heal thyself? A role for clinical psychology in Malawi. *Clinical Psychology Forum, 52*, 25–26.
Davidson, S. (2010a). The development of the British Red Cross Psychosocial framework. 'Calmer'. *Journal of Social Work Practice, 24*(1), 29–42.
Davidson, S. (2010b) . Psychosocial support within a global movement. *The Psychologist, 23*, 2–5.
Davies, J. (2014). Growing international relationships: Some reflections and implications for our training community. *Clinical Psychology Forum, 258*, 37–40.
European Federation of Psychologists' Associations (EFPA) (1990). *Optimal standards for the professional training in psychology.* www.efpa.eu/professional-development/optimal-standards-for-professional-training-in-psychology
Eysenck, H.J. (1949). Training in clinical psychology: An English point of view. *American Psychologist, 4*, 173–176.
Eysenck, H.J. (1990). *Rebel with a cause.* London: W.H. Allen.
Freeman, R. (2011). The history and organization of the European Federation of Psychologists' Associations (EFPA) – reflections on the first 30 years of EFPA. *European Psychologist, 16*(2), 90–99.
Gibson, H. (1981). *Hans Eysenck: The man and his work.* London: Peter Owen.
Haines, A. & Casells, A. (2004). Can the millennium development goals be attained? *British Medical Journal, 329*(7462), 394–397.
Hall, J. (2014). Clinical psychology in Tanzania: Four years on. *Clinical Psychology Forum, 258*, 66–69.
Hogan, M., Mrumbi, K., Ayazi, T. & Hall, J. (2010). Clinical psychology training in Tanzania: Getting started. *Clinical Psychology Forum, 215*, 36–39.
Horton, R. (2007). Launching a new movement for mental health. *The Lancet, 370*(9590), 806.
Jones, T. (2014). A trainee abroad: Reflections on a long term clinical psychology placement in a developing world context. *Clinical Psychology Forum, 258*, 33–36.
Kohn, R., Saxena, S., Levav, I. & Saraceno, B. (2004). The treatment gap in mental health care. *Bulletin of the World Health Organization, 82*, 858–871.
Liebling, H., Winter, D., Ruratotoye, B. et al. (2014). Resilience in the face of adversity: Case studies in Sierra Leone and Eastern Congo. *Clinical Psychology Forum, 258*, 61–65.
Liebling-Kalifani, H., Mwaka, V., Ojiambo-Ochieng, R. et al. (2011) Women war survivors of the 1989-2003 conflict in Liberia: The impact of sexual and gender-based violence. *Journal of International Women's Studies, 12*(1), 1–21.
Parker, I. (1994). Psychology and societal transformation in South Africa. *Clinical Psychology Forum, 68*, 10–12.
Patel, N. (2003). Clinical psychology: Reinforcing inequalities or facilitating empowerment? *International Journal of Human Rights, 7*(1), 16–39.
Patel, N. (2011). Justice and reparation for torture survivors. *Journal of Critical Psychology, Counselling and Psychotherapy, 11*(3), 135–147.
Patel, N., Bennett, E., Dennis, M. et al. (Eds.) (2000). *Clinical psychology, 'race' and culture: A training manual.* Leicester: BPS Books.
Patel, V. & Prince, M. (2010). Global mental health. *Journal of the American Medical Association, 303*(19), 1976–1977.
Powell, G., Chowdhury, K., Uddin, Z. & Rahman, A. (2014). Establishing and sustaining clinical psychology in Bangladesh. *Clinical Psychology Forum, 258*, 50–55.
Rachman, J. (2003). Eysenck and the development of CBT. *The Psychologist, 16*, 588–91.
Raimy, V.C. (Ed.) (1950). *Training in clinical psychology.* Englewood Cliffs, NJ: Prentice Hall.
Secord, J. (2004). Knowledge in transit. *Isis, 95*, 654–72.
Sharkey, S. & Tindale, A. (2010). A placement in Uganda. *Clinical Psychology Forum, 215*, 31–35.
Shimoyama, H. (Ed.) (2011). *An international comparison of clinical psychology: West meets East.* Tokyo: Kazama Shobo.

Simcox, A. & Gallagher, B. (2014). What is the role of a cross-cultural clinical psychologist? Experiences from practice in Cambodia. *Clinical Psychology Forum, 258*, 28–32.
Summerfield, D. (2008). How scientifically valid is the knowledge base of global mental health? *British Medical Journal, 336*, 992–994.
Swancott, R, Uppal, G. & Crossley, J. (2014). Globalisation of psychology: Implications for the development of psychology in Ethiopia. *International Review of Psychiatry, 26*(5), 579–585.
Tribe, R. (2012, July). *Deconstructing global mental health.* Paper presented at the Global mental health: Bridging the perspectives of cultural psychiatry and public health conference, Montreal.
Tribe, R. (2013). Is trauma-focused therapy helpful for victims of war and conflict? In K. Bhui (Ed.), *Critical essays on culture and mental health. A training manual* (pp.1–6). London: Royal College of Psychiatrists.
United Nations (2000). *United Nations Millennium Declaration.* www.un.org/millennium/declaration/ares552e.htm
Vasquez Monnar, O. & Gutierrez Alvarez, A. (2010). Clinical psychology in Cuba. *Clinical Psychology Forum, 215*, 43–46.
Watters, E. (2010). *Crazy like us: The globalisation of the American psyche.* New York: Free Press.
White, R. (2013). The globalisation of mental illness. *The Psychologist, 26*(3), 182–5.
White, R. & Ebert, B. (2014). Working globally, thinking locally: Providing psychosocial intervention training in Sierra Leone. *Clinical Psychology Forum, 258*, 41–45.
Wolpe, J. (1958). *Psychotherapy by reciprocal inhibition.* Stanford, CA: Stanford University Press.
Wonde, Y. (2014). Reflections on the development of psychology in Ethiopia and future directions. *International Review of Psychiatry, 26*(5), 585–589.
World Health Organization (2007). *World health statistics.* Geneva: Author.
World Health Organization (2008). *Mental health gap action programme (mhGAP). Scaling up care for mental, neurological and substance abuse disorders.* Geneva: Author.
World Health Organization (2011). *The mental health atlas.* Geneva: Author.
Wright, J.C. (1994). Time out in South Africa. *Clinical Psychology Forum, 73*, 17–21.

Part 6
Reflections

Chapter 25 Overview: Recurring themes and continuing challenges

David Pilgrim, Graham Turpin & John Hall

Introduction

We have written this overview to reflect on the messages offered by the authors from their differing perspectives and disciplines, and to provide some analysis and explanation for our disparate readership.

When we planned the chapters of this book we were aware of the very different audiences that might read these histories, our primary audience being clinical and other health care psychologists, both qualified and in training. Hopefully, the book will also be of interest to other health professionals with an interest in psychological approaches to health care, and to historians and sociologists. One purpose in writing this text was to stimulate greater academic interest in the history of the psychological disciplines and psychological therapies. In order to draw our audiences together, and to present a critical analysis of some of the issues that both we as editors and our authors have had to confront, we have constructed an overview of what we consider to be the more important themes and ongoing challenges identified within the book.

We also think it important to try to make sense of the twists and turns that the profession's development has taken with respect to major contextual influences that have influenced its values and opportunities for development and expansion. This has required a sociological and political analysis of the context of post–Second World War British society, and particularly of its health and welfare systems up to the present day. Important contextual factors that we have identified include the differentiation of clinical psychology from its host discipline of psychology, and a similar separation from medicine and neuroscience. We examine the critical impact of institutions such as the old asylums and the organisations responsible for their management and upkeep, and in particular the impact of the NHS and government policy. The complex political histories of the constituent parts of our islands and recent changes to relationships within the United Kingdom have also been responsible for different national paths and identities followed by the profession.

In addition to the influence of national identity, we were struck by the recurring theme about the 'true identity' of the profession. We have focused on two important questions: are we scientists or therapists, and do we intervene with individuals, families, organisations, or communities?

Finally, we look forward and attempt to assess what the profession has achieved, and what challenges it is likely to face in the future. We examine the tensions between psychologists, trying to be humane and doing good for their clients and society, and the expectations of the public, and the requirements of a state-controlled healthcare system. However, every profession has its own agenda, areas of self-interest and history of abuse and exploitation. We attempt to create a balance sheet for clinical psychology. By avoiding past practices that were dubious or morally unsound, we can construct a more positive future. So our final section anticipates the 50th anniversary of the profession in 2016 in seeking lessons from the past which are still relevant for today's practising psychologists and those at the start of their careers in training.

Historical perspectives

Introduction: Dilemmas of writing histories

This book has been written by authors from a number of different backgrounds. The majority are themselves trained as clinical psychologists, and many have played a significant role in the intellectual and institutional development of their profession. But two of our authors are historians (Sarah Marks and John Stewart), three are academic psychologists (Alan Collins, Juliet Foster and Katherine Hubbard) and one of the editors (David Pilgrim) has spent half of his career as an academic sociologist, rather than being a practising psychologist.

Consequently it is a particularly nuanced genre of history writing, which has attempted to balance both positive and critical reflections on the past, as well as making use of a broad variety of printed, archival and oral primary source materials, in addition to personal testimony. Our authors have taken different approaches to writing their chapters, and with the relative absence of previous historical writing in this area, it was inevitable that the chapters reflect a wide range of writing styles. We hope this chapter will alert those readers naive to historical analysis to reflect more critically on the accounts of our discipline's and profession's development.

One criticism often made about histories of science and medicine written by professional scientists and doctors, rather than professional historians, is that they are written from an 'internalist' perspective and run the risk of 'Whiggism'. This refers to uncritical and self-congratulatory narratives of progress (Jardine, 2003). Such histories, it is argued, overlook important social and intellectual questions about the development of knowledge and practice within professions, as well as often neglecting to consider the more ethically problematic aspects of practice in the past. Especially when dealing with biographical material relating to founding members or significant contributors, such histories may become 'hagiographies', canonising the secular saints of the field (Terrall, 2006) and there are some examples of this tendency in some of the previous chapters.

Nonetheless, such forms of historical writing play a function in identity formation within professions. Historians of science have written in depth about practices of commemoration, and the role that the recognition of historical figures, events and institutions has had for creating traditions at a disciplinary, professional, or even national level (Abir-Am & Elliot, 1999). This volume contains a number of examples of such practices, establishing a 'collective memory' for clinical psychologists: a legacy to be passed on to the next generation of practitioners through the commemoration of particular key publications, individuals, government reports and training institutions. While these may provide inspirational examples for the profession, it is hoped that they will also encourage critical reflection.

Critical histories of psychology

A key text in the history of psychology is Danziger's *Constructing the Subject* (1990). With other historical texts from British authors, including Smith (1997) and Jones and Elcock (2001), they together advocate a greater reliance on primary sources and a more critical reading of them. The introduction to Michael Billig's book on the roots of critical psychology also points to the association between critical psychology and historical reflexivity (Billig, 2008). The American Benjamin Lovett (2006) discusses the idea of a 'new history of psychology', which can be contrasted with an 'old history of psychology'. He argues that it is the task of critical historians to expose 'origin myths' in psychology – of which the role assigned to Wundt is a prime example.

These general critical reflections about the discipline of psychology are relevant for the fresh task presented in this book of addressing a specific form of applied psychology from a historical perspective that spans over 70 years, from the Second World War to the present. Given that the profession is relatively young, and for many years has been a small one, it has attracted little attention from external professional historians (either critical or Whiggish). Historical interest in the 'psy disciplines' has tended to favour psychiatry or abnormal psychology as an object of study over other areas (e.g. Thomson, 2006). In addition, there is substantially more historical literature on Freud and psychoanalysis than any other area of psychology, as Borch Jacobsen and Shamdasani (2011) point out. This is in part due to 'legend-making' within the psychoanalytic community itself, which has then been replicated by psychoanalytically orientated historians (e.g. Gay, 1988). This has resulted in a 'Freudocentric' narrative of the history of psychology, in which other important traditions and practices have become overshadowed or ignored.

Given an absence of external interest, the impetus to reflect upon the history of British clinical psychology has come from within the ranks of the profession itself, with all of the costs and benefits of historical appraisal that this largely internalist account brings. We have encouraged critical histories but are also aware that the book's chapters are a mixture of old and new forms of historical account, reflecting the inevitably mixed ideologies and particular sensibilities of their authors. Indeed, some of the accounts, or sections of them, have been largely celebratory whereas others were largely critical. Others alternated in style. Thus clinical psychology, like other health and welfare professions, is Janus-faced. It does exist to 'do good' within the assumptions of its parent society (in our case, post-Second World War Britain), and it might be able to demonstrate that it has succeeded. But it has also been self-absorbed, and has created and enacted strategies of self-interest, according to the opportunities created by shifting external circumstances (Pilgrim & Treacher, 1992).

Professional leaders and gender balance

As Richards (2010) notes, until the 1970s most histories of psychology were written, at least in part, to prove its scientific credentials, and typically they told the story of its 'great men' – and most of them were men – and what they had accomplished. There is then a tension between identifying those people who are widely regarded as being pioneers of the profession, and those who have been role models for others, and recognising that they thought and worked collaboratively with others.

In relation to early British clinical psychology, the preceding chapters have referred to a number of individual men, including Don Bannister, Alan Clarke, Mahesh Desai, Hans Eysenck, Graham Foulds, John Graham-White, H. Gwynne

Jones, Lionel Haward, Ralph Hetherington, Miller Mair, Peter Mittler, Bob Payne, Stanley 'Jack' Rachman, John Raven, Joseph Sandler, Monte Shapiro, David Smail, Jack Tizard, Oliver Zangwill… the list goes on (see as well the same trend in the national stories for the British Isles provided in chapter 23). There have been many important women leaders and role models, and with some relatively younger women they include Mary Boyle, Ann Clarke, Liz Campbell, May Davidson, Fay Fransella, Uta Frith, Una Holden, Lucy Johnstone, Freda Newcombe, Glenys Parry, Grace Rawlings, Anne Richardson and Barbara Wilson, to name some key individuals. But the second list is shorter and less well known historically than the first. And most of those in both the male and female lists were white (except for the Indian Mahesh Desai), even if some were wartime or post-war émigrés rejuvenating British empiricism in psychology (see chapter 4).

Throughout the 20th century the profession was male-dominated with the majority of leadership roles occupied by men, despite the growing numbers of women entering training, and filling more junior posts within the NHS. However, with the current dominance of women both as trainees and also as qualified staff, the majority of leadership roles in the 21st century, both in the NHS and the DCP, are now filled and being filled by women. In 2014, 20 out of 30 officers of the DCP (DCP faculty chairs and directors, executive officers, etc.) were women, and 23 out of 28 members of the editorial team of *Clinical Psychology Forum* were female.

This first attempt to prepare an account of the history of the profession has been made by three white male editors, John Hall, David Pilgrim and Graham Turpin. If another version of this book were to be produced in 20 years time, the gendered and racialised composition of any editorial group would probably be very different. But to date it has not been merely a matter of women not being represented respectfully in historical accounts; there has also been a real and actual absence of their leadership role relative to their overall numbers in the profession.

Contextual influences

From public control to user accountability

In arranging the order of chapters for this book we assumed that the discipline and profession should be primarily accountable for its impact upon, and duty towards, the people it serves. We have given primacy to a review of service user involvement with psychological services, even though this is only a recent formal history (chapter 2).

This concern with client-centredness reflects the health policy context of the past 20 years, but it was not the driver of the profession before that period. The intention of the early clinical psychologists, like the bulk of those entering the profession today, was to enhance the psychological functioning of their patients, but this was mediated by medical concerns and priorities. However, the health systems they entered, especially the mental health systems, had other purposes; they served a wider function for the British state.

Winding back in time, it is obvious that there was a preceding historical context that situated, and largely determined, the form and content of the emergent profession of British clinical psychology. The late 19th and early 20th centuries were periods when the social problems of civil society and warfare set public policy agendas (chapters 1 to 4). How was Britain, or any modern industrial economy, to manage perceived threats to order, and the socioeconomic burden of forms of mental deviance or incompetence? Those too old or too young to work, and those who had incomplete powers of reason (or in the case of the insane those who had lost it) had to be managed by the British state (Cohen & Scull, 1983).

Clinical psychologists then, unwittingly perhaps, became part of a state-delegated matrix or 'psy complex' which both participated in the coercive control of psychological deviance and codified that deviance in ways that framed its nature and regulated it, often in a state of welcoming compliance (Rose, 1990; cf. Bean, 1986). The most obvious example of this is where psychologists are working directly with people involved in both the health and criminal justice systems. Subjectivity, according to this post-structuralist view of history, was no longer just crushed coercively, it was also co-constructed by voluntary relationships becoming entangled with a 'psychologised' variant of those relationships. That ambiguity, then and now, raises complex ethical and political questions for the profession about the relationship between care and control.

Academic matters and disciplinary ambiguities

As an applied wing of the academic discipline of psychology, the profession's practical orientation and professional language were provided and constrained by its own academic field of operation (chapters 1, 3 and 4). The disciplinary separation of psychology from sociology and anthropology, and especially philosophy and physiology, in the late 19th century and early 20th century created the risk of disciplinary silos, while historical resonances of older disciplinary connections still remained. Indeed, university clinical psychology training programmes were hosted either in psychology departments within social science or science faculties, or in psychiatry departments within medical schools, and occasionally within schools of nursing or health care. This was reflected in the 2008 Research Assessment Exercise when clinical psychology was assessed with psychiatry and clinical neuroscience, having been split away from its host discipline the psychology panel. That ambiguity was earlier reflected in the Zuckerman Report (1968) about hospital scientific services in Britain and its uncertainty about the disciplinary character of psychology.

In practice settings who exactly were psychologists: were they scientists or clinicians? Should psychologists be answerable to medical committees? Were they part of the 'professions allied to medicine' (PAMS)' or were they 'health scientists'? There has never been a very clear consensus on this by service planners, which has frequently meant that psychology has been overlooked in planning, since it failed to fit any of the traditional or existing structures (chapters 1, 5 and 7).

This ambiguity about disciplinary character and organisational 'fit', and the profession's tendency to define its own tribal identity on its own terms, ensured a later challenge for clinical psychologists of reconnecting with colleagues in other disciplines in the academy and the clinic. The dilemma of an inward-looking tribalism straining against the logic of multidisciplinarity, acting in the interests of service efficiency and client welfare, remains today for the profession. The assumption of separate authority in one field (the academy), was translated in the embodied form of trained practitioners to another field (the clinic), as an academic discipline moved into an applied setting, thereby to become a profession. This connotation of 'field' was developed by the sociologist Pierre Bourdieu, to describe a subsystem of society with its own particular norms, mores, rules, and discursive nuances (Bourdieu, 1993).

We can also note here a peculiarity of clinical psychology, compared to other healthcare professions. As an outcrop of a learned society, clinical psychology has been seen by other healthcare professions as having strong academic links, but in some senses has been subordinated to that larger academic community. The BPS had defined entry criteria, issued ethical guidelines, regulated professional standards, and dealt with problems of malpractice until the transfer of these functions to the HCPC in 2009. But this has at times led to friction, especially as clinical psychologists have now become the largest constituent subsystem within the BPS. Despite this, their presence in central bodies of the BPS has not been reflected in proportional committee representation. These tensions have resulted in continuing calls to form an identity separate from the BPS, from May Davidson's suggestion of a College of Applied Psychology around 1976, to the impetus behind the external review of the DCP instituted in the early 2000s (see chapter 5), and to the present day.

Institutional, organisational and legislative contexts

The early work of applied psychologists was also shaped by their embedding in the institutional settings where they worked in the interwar period, especially the child guidance clinics. Even before the NHS emerged there was psychological activity in clinical settings, especially working with children, and dealing with the demands for assessment and therapy set by a nation at war. The emergence of the Tavistock Clinic is one example of this, but the military background to the development of personality theory by Hans Eysenck is another. We cannot understand the history of the profession without also understanding its particular and diverse institutional settings, which provided their own unique constraints and opportunities. The historical scene of the formation of clinical psychology was wartime Britain, even before the NHS came into being.

Not only were there diverse pre-NHS settings, but the new NHS did not stand still as a structure. It was subjected to one reform after another, which has altered its legal context of operation, its tiers of management, and even its geographical boundaries over time, and clinical psychology has had to adapt to these twists and turns of the NHS in flux. The profession is unusual in being coterminous in its birth and development with the NHS, and until quite recently enjoyed a double form of shelter to nurture its security and confidence. First, as it received medical referrals (in primary, secondary and tertiary health care), an older, mature and dominant profession protected it from direct exposure to scrutiny. Second, it operated in a large publicly funded and popular bureaucracy. It was only when 'marketisation' of the NHS was introduced by Margaret Thatcher, and then reinforced by the same trend in the 'New Labour' years, that the profession was exposed to the risks of supply and demand, as well as encroachment upon the supply side by adjacent occupational groups (see chapter 8). These institutional linkages embedding clinical psychology in the NHS might also explain why some paths have not been taken: one very important example is community psychology, seeing the community rather than presented individuals or their families as the focus of work, which has been a minority pursuit in the profession (see Kagan & Burton, 2003).

British clinical psychology has emerged in a particular geographical and political location in Western Europe. The present-day United Kingdom, the result of Acts of Union with Scotland (1707) and Ireland (1800) and of the creation of the Irish Free State in 1922, was subject to differing forms of social administrative and legislative arrangement in England, Scotland, Wales and Northern Ireland in the relevant period of this history. The colonial and postcolonial setting of the early and mid-20th century contributed to large-scale immigration into Britain from its former colonies in the earlier part of the period, with more recent continuing immigration from the European Union. Isolated by its island status but connected to many parts of the developed anglophone world by its native tongue, Britain has been characterised by the import, and more recently export, of forms of psychological theory and practice (noted in chapters 4, 23 and 24) that have created a possibility of a more nationally differentiated profession of clinical psychology.

One major influence on how the profession has developed in a number of different directions in the last couple of decades has been the influence of distinct national legislatures and administrations within the UK, particularly in relation to health and social care. As the authors of chapter 23 have noted, this has led to a variegated organisational picture across the British Isles. This was characterised by a trend of intranational collaboration and consensus outside of England, and regional variations within England, formerly dominated by metropolitan elites and developments. The near separation of Scotland from the Union in 2014 has brought to the fore arguments about the local character of the English regions, which have been reflected in professional developments and priorities in clinical psychology.

Professionalisation in context

Because clinical psychology is a profession, like others over time it has defended its status, argued for control over its own boundaries, expanded its numbers and campaigned for its financial rewards. At first, possibly reflecting the spirit of scientific rationalism and the 'technological fix' when it began to grow in the 1950s, the profession relied little upon formal boundary definitions. For example, the Division of Clinical Psychology was formed nearly 20 years after the first training course was established, unlike other healthcare professions where the establishment of training courses was closely linked to the formation of a professional body. However, once a professional body emerged, a number of ambivalences were there to be resolved, some of which remain unresolved today.

First, could the scientific background of the profession provide it with an inherent and irrefutable mandate in the eyes of employers – who were in the main the NHS? Given that British empiricism and methodological behaviourism were a basis for scientific credibility this was a likely prospect. However, this was compromised when psychodynamic, humanistic and constructivist camps remained in the profession. This has led to continuing pluralism of theory and practice, not one simple core consensus of professional rhetoric for public broadcast (chapter 15).

Second, what was to be done in relation to the older and dominant profession in healthcare settings? The relationship between clinical psychology and medicine has been a mixture of mutual tolerance, recurrent skirmishing and occasional indifference. Here setting was all important (chapter 8). When clinical psychologists relied mostly on psychiatrists for referrals and the latter were, pre-Trethowan, their de facto managers, then political subordination, raw and personal in the workplace, often provoked resistance. One answer was simply to leave the relationship. For example, from the late 1970s many psychologists working in adult mental health opted to work in primary care, abandoning medically dominated statutory secondary services. While GPs were also medical practitioners, they were not a 'psy profession' and so they did not assume a competing stance. But this tension with psychiatry has not meant that clinical psychology has consistently distanced itself from medical formulations of distress. The continuing acceptance of psychiatric diagnosis in mental health settings, rather than advancing the case for formulation on both scientific and ethical grounds, is one example of this point.

Third, how could professional leaders defend current gains and seek new ones in a constant process of adaptation to historical contingencies? Clinical psychology's early pioneers, few in number at first, succeeded substantially in exploiting opportunities within the healthcare bureaucracy of the early NHS, enabling them to maximise their potential, and expand and reinforce the credibility of a small new profession. A shifting open system of health care created opportunities to define and advance the causes of a new and expansive profession, so we need to appreciate 'contexts of possibility'. All professions are prosocial and self-interested in various ratios over time, and sociologists of the professions have noted this ambiguity and analysed it in a variety of ways (Saks, 1983).

Fourth, was there a case to be made for clinical psychology becoming itself a dominant profession? The argument that its practitioners were an extraordinary talent swimming in a sea of healthcare mediocrity was subtle and implicit, but is there to be found. For example, the notion of 'level three' psychological skills, where psychologists at that level offer 'a thorough understanding of varied and complex psychological theories and their application' suggested by the MAS report (1989) is one indicator. The status of a profession is determined in part by training length, so we have also witnessed a lengthening of the postgraduate training period from 13 months on the first Maudsley course, to three years doctoral training today. The profession has opted to mimic the semantic codes of its dominant medical competitors, becoming 'consultants'. From inside a narrative of historical subordination to medicine, clinical psychologists may be less aware themselves of their own sometimes precious and irritating presentation to others (chapter 8). But the development of a rhetoric of justification of their unique credentials and superiority by any profession, compared to other occupational groups, may coexist with internal dissent and self-doubt: clinical psychology from the 1960s has always had its internal dissenters, such as David Smail (1982).

Identities

A scientific or a therapeutic profession?

Successful professionalisation required the development of a rhetoric of justification on three fronts. First, the profession should have a relevance in the academy through its research reputation (chapter 11), and secondly in the clinic through credible forms of assessment and therapy (chapters 10, 12 and 13). Third, it had to justify its unique credentials to mark it out from pre-existing and adjacent professional groups in the NHS, with medicine being the most important of these (chapters 5 and 8). Unique credentials were to come from the establishment of a unique form of training in the British NHS (chapter 7). Immediately after the Second World War, the tension in clinical psychology between a particular scientific self-belief in 'disinterested' research and assessment, and one driven by psychotherapeutic aspiration, was obvious. This was demonstrated most clearly in the ideological differences between the two metropolitan centres of excellence, the Tavistock Clinic and the Institute of Psychiatry (chapters 9 and 13–15).

The content of training during and after the 1950s was to reflect that tension, as a shifting consensus about its proper nature spread to a national level, with training courses being spawned beyond the metropolis (chapter 7). The tension was resolved eventually by the profession offering its clients and employers some mix of science and humanism or 'scientific humanism' (Richards, 1983). Even within the 'scientific' wing of the profession, epitomised by the Eysenckian ideological emphasis at the Institute of Psychiatry, the urge to actually help people beyond the gaze of the dispassionate researcher or assessor kept pushing through. Hans Eysenck (a researcher, not a clinician) could only hold his antitherapy line of reasoning until 1958 and his volte face. More importantly, others like Gwynne-Jones, Meyer, Shapiro and Rachman swept the profession into an irrevocable therapeutic direction of travel (chapter 14).

This broad movement of the profession advancing its credibility in the NHS, as a new and plausible occupational group, meant that there were inevitable historical accretions to its roles which jostled at times uneasily. The initial testing emphasis perseverated, creating ambivalence for the profession. How should it best assess human functioning? That ambivalence was exemplified by the contrast between projective tests rooted in psychodynamic assumptions, and the type of psychometrics flowing from the genetic/eugenic traditions at University College London, traceable through Cyril Burt back to Karl Pearson and Francis Galton (chapters 4 and 10).

And if the science of assessment was a matter of contention, then the research traditions rooted in British empiricism, and the concern to define the profession's legitimacy by methodological rigour or 'methodologism', were to generate an orthodoxy and a continued credible role (at least for academic clinical psychologists). This trend is reflected in the content of chapter 11, but it also became problematic as doubters, such as feminist critics, argued for qualitative research as a riposte to masculine forms of science (chapters 4 and 11). By the time we reached the 1990s, it was no longer clear what precisely was the research orthodoxy, as the contest between different traditions of academic enquiry seeking bids for legitimacy became evident.

A more recent example of the science versus therapy tension is the impact that neuroscience has had in recent years (e.g. George Bush's announcement of the 1990s being the 'Decade of the Brain', www.loc.gov/loc/brain). The promise of neuroscience has been to provide new interventions and drugs to alleviate mental health problems and brain dysfunctions such as dementia. Recent assessments of the impact of neuroscience have been less flattering (Rose & Abi-Rached, 2013), with no real breakthroughs in the efficacy of medications for psychoses or treatments for dementia, and with drug companies withdrawing from research investment in these areas. Indeed, a recent *Nature* editorial (www.nature.com/news/therapy-deficit-1.11477) highlighted the disproportionate investment into neuroscience and drug research related to mental health, versus the scant money available for developing and evaluating psychological treatments. This is despite the fact that many such interventions now have recognisable and demonstrable efficacy.

The focus of psychological interventions

The ambivalence about which roles to adopt was not limited to assessment and research. One argument came from scarcity. Was it feasible for clinical psychologists to limit their concern only to individual client work, given that demand easily outstripped supply? Alternative options were to teach psychological principles to other health professions, as proposed in Trethowan, or to provide organisational consultancy, as recommended by the MAS report. The contention about the MAS report (chapters 5 and 6) brought to the fore a pragmatic challenge for the profession. Despite its eight-fold increase in numbers between 1980 and the present, not all of the clinical challenges faced by the profession could be addressed through individual case work. At the same time, how does any profession acquire and sustain a mandate to operate as an internal consultancy for its own employing organisation? This question remains an open one today.

As well as diversification in how to approach the client – individually, through building psychological skills in others, or offering psychological consultancy to other staff – there has also been an accompanying broadening in the range of clients that psychologists have worked with in the NHS. While practice in adult mental health settings has often dominated the public image of clinical psychology, historically the picture is more varied. Arguably the roots of the profession at the start of the NHS were more in child than adult work (chapters 3, 6 and 7), and equally arguably some of the earliest most distinctive research and practice contributions of psychologists were in work with people with intellectual disabilities. The range of client groups explored in chapters 16 to 22 reflects the wide scope of practice for the profession, and also the difficulty in offering a simple and unitary description of its character and boundaries, either in the past or the present.

The very idea of categorising people into 'client groups' essentially reflects policies and not practice, and ignores the reality of addressing the needs of people with multiple problems. These include not only mentally disordered offenders, but those who have a physical degenerative condition with an eating problem, or those who are elderly, frail or violent. The area of clinical health psychology (chapter 21) reminds us of the mutual interplay of biological and psychological components of what we mean by 'health', but also that all illness is a form of deviancy (Pilgrim, 1984). This social framing of illness-as-deviance reminds us that clinical psychology had, and has, only one part of the answer to health and illness, whether we consider plausible formulations or credible interventions.

We are aware that this part of the book has not covered work with some significant groups of people, perhaps the most obvious example being people with addictions, where a number of clinical psychologists have contributed to both theoretical and practice developments, such as Ray Hodgson (Hodgson, 1987) and Jim

Orford (Orford, 2013). Omissions within the therapeutic chapters include family therapy, a field where several clinical psychologists have been influential, such as Ian Bennun, Rudi Dallos, Paul O'Reilly, Eddie Street and Andy Treacher (e.g. Dallos & Draper, 2010).

Looking to the future

Scientific humanism: The benefits and risks of 'doing good'

One obvious, but little discussed, question hovers above all this argument. What has been the point of British clinical psychology for its host society?

We have noted the summary description by Barry Richards of the profession being characterised by 1980 as a form of 'scientific humanism' (Richards, 1983). While much of the history of the profession has been about arguments in relation to what is, or is not, a legitimate form of psychological knowledge, from the outset the matter of values was implicit and eventually explicit. Most clinical psychologists, past and present, have started their careers with humane motives, whatever psychological science had taught them as incipient experts. As Don Bannister, a dissident from the Institute of Psychiatry, noted, eventually psychologists indeed did begin to take an interest in people, in the way that sailors for good reasons had to take an interest in ships (chapter 15).

Because people operate in a moral order so do psychologists, for the very reason that they are people too and they share particular normative cultural assumptions about their professional interest: the relationship between experience and behaviour within particular personal biographies. A number of philosophical commentators on psychology have noted that the discipline inevitably is a 'moral science' and operates inside, and so cannot escape from, its own target of curiosity of being-human-in-context (Brinkman, 2011; Harré, 2002). This point was also emphasised by Graham Richards about understanding the history of psychology: 'The psychologist is not outside the things which he or she studies, not an external "objective" observer of the human psyche, but an active participant in the collective psychological life of their community, culture and, ultimately, species' (Richards, 2010, p.7).

If we reflect historically on clinical psychology as an applied 'moral science' then how has it fared? One answer is that its historical commitment to the clientele of the NHS has meant that as a profession it has adhered to progressive social policy norms of equity, by being part of a healthcare system free at the point of need. Another answer is that most individual clinical psychologists have done their best to use their skills and knowledge to meet the needs of others. A third answer is that it has had, within its ranks, notable and honourable 'whistleblowers', such as Patricia Bunn at Whittingham Hospital and Moira Potier at Ashworth Hospital, who were central figures in exposing cruel and degrading practices. These examples confirm a defining central claim from the Durkheimian tradition of sociology: professions are 'moral communities', which serve a positive function for society and offer the greatest good for the greatest number.

That claimed integrative societal function of the professions reminds us that the 'psy professions' do have a normative mandate from the majority of the population. They are not merely agents of top-down and state-funded social control. This is also reflected by the ever growing public interest in psychology as evidenced by numerous self-help publications, popular magazines, frequent appearances of psychologists within the media and 'psychological' fictional television programmes, continuing the lay fascination with psychology evident from the early 20th century (noted in chapter 14).

Today psychology is a very popular subject in schools, with high recruitment rates to undergraduate study, especially for young women, generating far more graduates than can ever become trained applied psychologists. Although early clinical psychology never enjoyed this degree of public interest, it is perhaps worth recognising that Hans Eysenck was a leading populariser of psychology in the 1960s, through his Penguin series on 'Introducing Psychology'. Indeed, the popularity of psychology within UK society was specifically commented on as a strength by an international panel of academics responsible for reviewing the status and accomplishments of the discipline in the UK (ESRC, 2011).

One consequence of this is that, after decades of undersupply, highly able applicants complete well-designed postgraduate clinical psychology courses to enter the profession, although the ethnic and gender balance of those graduates is not well matched to populations at need. For now there is no evidence of a diminution of interest in psychology as an academic subject or profession, but the prospects of employment in its applied wing are determined not only by that supply side, but also by demand. Demand certainly shaped the expansion of clinical psychology, but contraction in the future is also a possibility.

However, if any profession is indeed to be judged as a moral community, when and if its practitioners are proved to act in an immoral or amoral way they are fair game for criticism. In the case of British clinical psychology two evident shortcomings have been identified in the preceding chapters. First, some 'therapeutic' rationales are, with hindsight, now deemed to be morally dubious, such as aversion therapy for homosexuality in the late 1960s and the 'pin down' scandal justified within a framework of behavioural psychology (chapter 14). Second, as most of what clinical psychologists have done to date is to practise some form of psychological therapy, then a proportion of them have been found to be abusive (chapter 13) and quasi-judicial procedures, first conducted by the BPS and since 2009 by the HCPC, continue to be needed.

Lessons from the past about future prospects

Speculations about future prospects for the profession have at times focused on its historical legacies and trends (Hall, 1993; Pilgrim, 1997; Turpin, 2012). Drawing on those accounts and the previous chapters we can finish with some general points about the past, present and future. The book illustrates both the continuing impact of the discipline on society, and the changing nature of that 'psychologisation', away from implicitly post-Freudian accounts of human functioning (which perhaps remain for the literati and in the medical humanities, but in few other places), and towards a reconceptualisation of the nature of human distress and dysfunction to offer positive alternatives to medical models. The work of David Smail in particular has offered us an important legacy when exploring the social determination, maybe overdetermination, of distress (Smail, 1987, 2005).

Since the formation of the Division of Clinical Psychology in 1966, the problems addressed by the profession and the settings in which it practises have changed, towards a far wider range of problems than those presented in the historic mental illness and mental handicap settings. A broader range of research methodologies have contributed to a better understanding of psychological mechanisms underlying many conditions, and how to evaluate the effectiveness of psychological and other interventions. A wider range of therapies is practised by psychologists, working alongside colleagues in a range of community and specialist teams and networks. Their therapeutic goals are more likely to be determined by users' concerns, with a political and philosophical shift in health care away from professional dominance and towards patient-centredness. There is still, however, little engagement with overall population need, an issue even more apparent when looking at the export of Western psychology to low income countries.

In the early days of the profession the NHS was virtually a monopoly employer, but since the purchaser–provider split and the marketisation of the NHS under the political regimes of Thatcher, Blair and Brown, settings of practice are now highly variegated. The demands of demonstrating evidence-based practice and compliance with new public management arrangements in both the NHS and in higher education are shaping what practitioners, researchers and trainers will and will not do. And the profession is facing the market threat of other 'psy professions', especially in the therapeutic role, not least by itself contributing to the development of the skills of those other professions.

Clinical psychology began within a protected world, and was in some senses privileged within that world, but is now in an exposed world. Clinical psychology has gone from a norm of overwhelming commitment to the NHS, to an emerging one of practice in diverse forms of private or subcontracted employment. All of the challenges now evident in that new context of practice were unheard of in 1966, when the early DCP's inchoate concerns about professionalisation, and what exactly constituted psychological science in theory and practice, predominated. Recent and prospective demands from a healthcare system in radical flux are dissolving the boundaries around what has been thought of as clinical psychology. Calls to be applied psychologists in health care may mortally wound the shape of the profession of clinical psychology as it has been. Alternatively it may be a context of creative adaptation for its newly recruited practitioners. Time will tell.

References

Abir-Am, P. & Elliot, C.A. (1999). Commemorative practices in science: Historical perspectives on the politics of collective memory. *Osiris, 14*, special edition.

Bean, P. (1986). *Mental disorder and legal control.* Cambridge: Cambridge University Press.

Billig, M. (2008). *The hidden root of critical psychology.* London: Sage.

Borch Jacobsen, M. & Shamdasani, S. (2011). *The Freud files: An inquiry into the history of psychoanalysis.* Cambridge: Cambridge University Press.

Bourdieu, P. (1993). *The field of cultural production: Essays on art and literature.* New York: Columbia University Press.

Brinkman, S. (2011). *Psychology as a moral science.* New York: Springer.

Cohen, S. & Scull, A. (Eds.) (1983). *Social control and the state: Historical and comparative essays.* Oxford: Oxford University Press.

Dallos, R. & Draper, J. (2010). *An introduction to family therapy: Systemic theory and practice.* Maidenhead: Open University Press.

Danziger, K. (1990). *Constructing the subject: Historical origins of psychological research.* Cambridge: Cambridge University Press.

ESRC (2011). *International benchmarking review of UK psychology.* Available at www.esrc.ac.uk/_images/Int_benchmarking_review_UK_psychology_Jan12_tcm8-15433.pdf

Gay, P. (1988). *Freud: A life for our times.* London: J.M. Dent.

Hall, J. (1993). Clinical psychology in context. *Clinical Psychology Forum, 61,* 3–10.

Harré, R. (2002). *Cognitive science: A philosophical introduction.* London: Sage.

Hodgson, R. (1987). Psychology and addiction. *British Journal of Addiction, 82*(4), 329.

Jardine, N. (2003). Whigs and histories: Herbert Butterfield and the historiography of science. *History of Science, 41,* 125–140.

Jones, D. & Elcock, J. (2001). *History and theories of psychology.* London: Arnold.

Kagan, C.M. & Burton, M. (2003). Community psychology: Why this gap in Britain? *History & Philosophy of Psychology, 4*(2), 10–23.

Lovett, B. (2006). The new history of psychology: A review and a critique. *History of Psychology, 9*(1), 17–37.

Management Advisory Service (1989). *Review of clinical psychology services.* Cheltenham: Author.

Orford, J. (2013). *Power, powerlessness and addiction.* Cambridge: Cambridge University Press.

Pilgrim, D. (1984). Some implications for psychology of formulating all illness as deviance. *British Journal of Medical Psychology, 57*(3), 227–34.

Pilgrim, D. (1997). Clinical psychology observed (reprise and remix). *Clinical Psychology Forum, 107,* 3–6.

Pilgrim, D. & Treacher, A. (1992). *Clinical psychology observed.* London: Routledge.

Richards, B. (1983). *Clinical psychology, the individual and the state.* Unpublished PhD thesis, Polytechnic of North East London.

Richards, G.D. (2010). *Putting psychology in its place: Critical historical perspectives* (3rd edn). London: Routledge.

Rose, N. (1990). *Governing the soul.* London: Routledge.

Rose, N. & Abi-Rached, J. (2013). *Neuro: The new brain sciences and the management of the mind.* Princeton, NJ: Princeton University Press.

Saks, M. (1983). Removing the blinkers? A critique of recent contributions to the sociology of the professions. *Sociological Review, 33,* 1–21.

Smail, D. (1982). Clinical psychology homogenized and sterilised. *Bulletin of the British Psychological Society, 35,* 345–346.

Smail, D. (1987). *Taking care: An alternative to therapy.* London: Dent.

Smail, D. (2005). *Power, interest and psychology: Elements of a social materialist understanding of distress.* Ross-on-Wye: PCCS Books.

Smith, R. (1997). *Fontana history of the human sciences.* London: Fontana.

Terrall, M. (2006). Biography as cultural history of science. *Isis, 97,* 306–313.

Thomson, M. (2006). *Psychological subjects: Identity, culture and health in twentieth-century Britain.* Oxford: Oxford University Press.

Turpin, G. (2012). *The next sixty years: Dilemmas and future milestones.* Division of Clinical Psychology Monte Shapiro Award Lecture. www.youtube.com/watch?v=SbJblXFdhnY

Zuckerman Report (1968). *Hospital scientific and technical services.* London: HMSO.

Appendix 1 Timeline for events related to abnormal and clinical psychology in Britain

Note: The original 'A Chronology of Psychology in Britain' was prepared by Geoff Bunn, and the full version available via the BPS History of Psychology Centre website gives references for each entry, which are omitted here. Most of the dates before 1987 were abstracted from Geoff Bunn's chronology, with additional dates added by the editors of this book.

1853 J.D. Morrell (1816–1891) publishes *Elements of Psychology*, the first book published in England to be called 'psychology'.

1859 Thomas Laycock (1812–1876) publishes Mind and Brain, a systematic treatise on the new physiological psychology. Charles Darwin (1809–1882) publishes *On the Origin of Species*. 'In the distant future I see open fields for far more important researches. Psychology will be based on a new foundation, that of the necessary acquirement of each mental power and capacity by gradation. Light will be thrown on the origin of man and his history.'

1874 G.H. Lewes (1817–1878) publishes the first volume of *Problems of Life and Mind*. He coins the term 'psychodynamic'.

1876 Alexander Bain and George Croom Robertson bring out the first issue of *Mind: A Quarterly Review of Psychology and Philosophy*. 'Psychology, so to speak', writes Robertson, 'faces all the other sciences, because its subject, Mind, does, literally and in every other sense of the word, comprehend the subjects of them all.'

1877 Two years before Wilhelm Wundt establishes the first psychological laboratory in the world, the Cambridge University Senate rejects James Ward and John Venn's proposal to establish a laboratory of psychophysics.

1881 C.H. Lake, headmaster of a Chelsea school, applies psychological tests to his pupils.

1883 Francis Galton (1822–1911) publishes his *Inquiries into Human Faculty*.

1884 Galton sets up an anthropometric laboratory at the International Health Exhibition in London. For a small fee, visitors receive an assessment of their mental faculties and physical abilities. The laboratory is continued at the Science Museum until 1891.

1886 Inspired by Galton, London headmistress Sophie Bryant undertakes mental testing.

1892 James Ward's *The Human Mind* is published. It would later be described as 'the most scholarly, comprehensive and well-balanced factual textbook of psychology ever produced by a British psychologist'. Karl Pearson (1857–1936) introduces the terms 'normal curve ' and 'standard deviation'.

1893 The British Child Study Association is founded.

1895 James Sully publishes *Studies of Childhood*.

1897 W.H.R. Rivers establishes a small psychological laboratory in Cambridge.

1898 Charles Myers, William McDougall and W.H.R. Rivers represent British psychology on the expedition to the Torres Straits. Its goal is to study the islanders' psychology, linguistics, sociology, folklore and ethnomusicology. G.F. Stout (1860–1944) publishes his *Manual of Psychology*. The aim is to make the student 'live himself into psychological problems, so as to acquire a real power of thinking for himself on psychological topics'. The book would become the most widely used psychology text in British universities for the next quarter century.

1900 Karl Pearson introduces the χ^2 (chi-square) test for goodness of fit. He also developed the product–moment formula, the method of multiple correlation, and the formula for the probable error of a correlation coefficient.

1901 Ten people meet at University College London and form the Psychological Society. The founder members are: Robert Armstrong-Jones (1859–1943), William Ralph Boyce Gibson (1869–1935), Sophie Bryant (1850–1922), Frank Hales (1878–1952),William McDougall (1871–1938), Frederick Mott (1853–1926), W.H.R. Rivers (1864–1922), Alexander Shand (1858–1936), W.G. Smith (1866–1918) and James Sully (1842–1923). A Department of Experimental Psychology is established at the London County Council Asylum at Claybury with Dr W.G. Smith as director.

1902 W.H.R. Rivers, Charles Myers and William McDougall are appointed as the psychological subcommittee of the British Association for the Advancement of Science (BAAS) set up to recommend methods of conducting anthropometric surveys of the British population at large. Their 1908 report is the first explicitly to suggest the inclusion in such surveys of measures of higher psychological processes, by means of ratings of character and capacity by trained observers, as well as of sensory and motor capacity.

1903 Charles Myers (1873–1946) is appointed part-time Professor of Psychology at King's College, London. He starts a laboratory there and remains in the position until 1909.

1904 Independently of the Psychological Society, the *British Journal of Psychology* begins publication, edited by James Ward and W.H.R. Rivers. Charles Spearman (1863–1945) publishes 'General Intelligence, Objectively Determined and Measured' in the *American Journal of Psychology*. Spearman articulates the idea of factor analysis and proposes a two-factor theory of intelligence.

1905 William McDougall publishes *Physiological Psychology*. He devises a dotting test apparatus, a modified version of which would be widely used in personnel selection in the Second World War.

1906 The Psychological Society changes its name to the British Psychological Society, to distinguish itself from another 'unacademic group'.

1907 After a visit to Kraepelin's clinic in Munich, Frederick Mott (1853–1926) urges the establishment of a university psychiatric hospital for treatment and research. Henry Maudsley donates £30,000 to the London County Council for the realisation of the plan and the Maudsley Hospital in London is eventually built. Francis Galton is instrumental in establishing the Eugenics Society.

1908 The Royal Commission on the Care and Control of the Feeble-Minded (appointed 1904) issues its report. Mental defectives are classified into four main groups: idiots, imbeciles, the feeble-minded and moral imbeciles. The Commission's recommendations become law with the passing of the Mental Deficiency Act of 1913.

1909 Cyril Burt draws attention to the Binet–Simon tests, suspecting that they may be able to distinguish between training and intelligence.

1910 W.H. Winch, an English school inspector, announces his invention of the treatment group in the *Journal of Educational Psychology*: 'I have, I believe for the first time, employed the method of *equal groups* to the solution of questions of fatigue.' Charles Spearman, Cyril Burt, William Brown and Charles Myers contribute to a symposium on mental testing and factor theories at the Sheffield meeting of the British Association for the Advancement of Science.

1911 William Brown (1881–1952) publishes *Essentials of Mental Measurement* in which he criticises Spearman's two-factor theory of intelligence.

1912 With £3000 of an inheritance, Charles Myers establishes the Cambridge Psychological Laboratory. He becomes its first director. James Drever (1873–1950) succeeds in having a psychological laboratory included into the plans for the Moray House training college building design. It becomes the earliest educational laboratory in the country.

1913 The Cambridge Psychological Laboratory is opened. Cyril Burt is appointed to the half-time post of psychologist by the London County Council. The LCC Chief Education Officer describes him as being 'the first official psychologist in the world'. Burt's tasks are 'the examination of children nominated for admission to schools for the mentally defective'. He continues to work for the LCC until 1932.

1914 Charles Myers proceeds on his own initiative to France 'to do what he could to help the war effort'. The Maghull Military Hospital for the treatment of war neuroses is established. The 'Maghull Academy' consists of R.G. Rows, W.H.R. Rivers, William McDougall, Tom Pear and William Brown.

1915 Charles Myers popularises the term 'shell shock' in *The Lancet.* He reports that he has successfully used hypnosis on a number of cases.

1918 By the end of the First World War, the army had dealt with over 80,000 cases of shell shock.

1919 A meeting of the Industrial Psychology Provisional Institute Committee is held in London. Charles Myers outlines his vision for a new Industrial Psychology Section. He remarks that 'it is hoped in the near future to form further Sections for Social Psychology, the Psychology of Aesthetics, Animal Psychology, etc'. The Medical Section of the BPS is established, to act as a forum for debate in psychopathology and psychotherapy.

1920 Hugh Crichton Miller establishes an Institute of Medical Psychology in a private house in Tavistock Square. The Tavistock Clinic is one of the first clinics in the country to provide outpatient psychological treatment for adults and children unable to afford private fees.

1921 With Henry Welch, an industrialist, Charles Myers founds the National Institute of Industrial Psychology (NIIP) 'on an entirely voluntary basis'. It would become the most important avenue of employment for psychologists in Britain prior to the Second World War. Cyril Burt publishes his widely used *Mental and Scholastic Tests.*

1922 Henry Maudsley and Frederick Mott's campaign to establish a clinic for the treatment and study of insanity finally comes to fruition with the opening of the Maudsley Hospital.

1923 Based partly on his experiences treating shell shock cases at Netley and Littlemore hospitals during the First World War, William McDougall publishes his *Outlines of Abnormal Psychology.*

1924 The Board of Education's Consultative Committee publishes *Psychological Tests of Educable Capacity*, 'a turning point in the history of educational psychology, reinforcing public interest in psychological techniques'.

1925 Cyril Burt publishes the plans for a child guidance clinic as an appendix to his 'classic' *The Young Delinquent.* Analysis of variance is first described by R.A. Fisher (1890–1960) in his *Statistical Methods for Research Workers.* At the instigation of the Howard League for Penal Reform, James Drever begins clinical psychological work with children and juveniles at Edinburgh University.

1926 The *Report of the Royal Commission on Lunacy and Mental Disorder* argues that the problem of insanity is essentially a public health problem to be dealt with accordingly.

1927 Under the auspices of the Jewish Health Organization, Noel Burke and Emanuel Miller open the East London Child Guidance Clinic at the Jewish Hospital. Beatrice Edgell is appointed the first woman professor of psychology in Britain.

1928 The London Child Guidance Centre Demonstration Clinic is established in Islington. It deals with 'backward children, delinquents, and "nervous" and "unmanageable" children'. Dr William Moodie is the director. Margaret Lowenfeld founds a Children's Clinic for the Treatment and Study of Nervous and Difficult Children.

1930 With the passing of the Mental Treatment Act 1930, voluntary admission to institutions becomes general.

1931 Margaret Lowenfeld's clinic becomes the Institute of Child Psychology.

1935 W.P. Alexander devises the 'Passalong Test' as a component of the 'Alexander Performance Test, a measure of concrete and abstract intelligence'.

1936 While working at the London Child Guidance Clinic, John Bowlby begins a series of studies into the familial experiences of juvenile thieves.

1938 J.C. Raven publishes his 'Progressive Matrices' intelligence test. It would be adopted on a large scale by the British Armed Services during the Second World War. Thanks to the efforts of Ernest Jones and others, Sigmund Freud escapes Vienna and comes to live in England.

1939 The Feversham Report is published. After the war it would amalgamate numerous bodies to form the National Association for Mental Health, crystallising the division of labour between educational and clinical psychologists and psychiatrists. J.R. Rees of the Tavistock Clinic and Alec Rodger of the NIIP submit a memo to the medical authorities at the War Office calling for a preliminary experiment to assess the contribution to the quality of training of conscripts that might be made by psychological and psychiatric assessments.

1941 The official documents of incorporation are received by the British Psychological Society from the Registrar of Companies. By June, a Directorate of Selection of Personnel has been set up under the Adjutant-General, and psychologists are being extensively used to screen personnel in the Army.

1942 Aubrey Lewis, Clinical Director of the Mill Hill Emergency Hospital, appoints Hans Eysenck to undertake psychological research. Beveridge Report published. John Raven appointed as Director of Psychological Research at Crichton Royal, Dumfries. First meeting of 'Fildes Committee' of psychologists at Child Guidance Council Conference.

1943 Psychology has made major inroads into the military establishment by 1943. A senior psychologist is a member of the staff of the Chief of Naval Personnel and 10 psychologists (aided by around 300 assistants) are working in other parts of the Admiralty. Nineteen psychologists are employed at the War Office where over 30 officers have received psychological training. Four psychologists advise on training methods at the Air Ministry. Group psychotherapy is pioneered at the Mill Hill Hospitals Neurosis Unit. Committee of Professional Psychologists (Mental Health) is formally created within BPS as successor to the Fildes Committee.

1944 There are more than 70 child guidance clinics in Great Britain. The Applied Psychology Unit is established in Cambridge with Kenneth Craik as its first director. The Education Act requires that all children receive secondary education suited to their abilities. It proposes that children should be allocated to grammar, technical or modern schools at 11-plus.

1945 The National Foundation for Educational Research is established with a donation from the Leverhulme Trust.

1946 The NHS Act for England is passed. First intake of students to the Maudsley training course.

1947 A subcommittee of the BPS is appointed to consider the professional status of non-medical people who are already working with children. Hans Eysenck publishes *Dimensions of Personality*. Privy Council Office publishes *Report of an Advisory Committee on the Work of Psychologists and Psychiatrists in the Services.*

1948 The NHS is inaugurated. A deputation of the BPS meets representatives from the Treasury to discuss the official incorporation of psychologists within the Scientific Civil Service. The *Quarterly Bulletin of the British Psychological Society* is launched with Frederick Laws as editor.

1949 Hans Eysenck publishes his views on 'Training in Clinical Psychology' in the *American Psychologist.* He argues that 'the psychologist has sufficient scope in the fields of diagnostic testing and clinical research to make it undesirable for him to become a "Jack-of-all-trades" by also providing therapy'.

1950 BPS Council recommends co-option of psychologists working in the adult field to the CPP(MH). The first meeting of the Sub-Committee of Professional Problems of Psychologists discusses a 'Code of Professional Ethics Governing the Disclosure by Qualified Psychologists of Psychological Information about Individuals', compiled by members of the Society's Australian Branch.

1951 Sponsored by the World Health Organization, John Bowlby publishes *Maternal Care and Mental Health.*

1952 The first Whitley Council Circular relating to clinical psychologists is issued. A working party of the Committee of Professional Psychologists (Mental Health), English Division is set up to consider problems of training psychologists for work in the education and health services in England and Wales.

1954 The British Psychological Society submits a Memorandum to the Royal Commission on the Law Relating to Mental Illness and Mental Deficiency, and A.D.B. Clarke presents oral evidence.

1955 The Underwood Report (Report of the Committee on Maladjusted Children) – 'an important milestone in educational psychology' – draws attention to the ways in which educational psychologists work.

1956 The Association of Child Psychotherapists has three recognised training centres: the Hampstead Child Therapy Course (Anna Freud), the Institute of Child Psychology (Margaret Lowenfeld) and the Tavistock Clinic (John Bowlby). Working for a few years as the first psychologist in the Gold Coast, Gustav Jahoda discovers that so-called tests of abstract ability were no more culture free than intelligence tests. H. Gwynne Jones publishes the first behaviour therapy paper in Britain.

1958 H.J. Eysenck introduces behaviour therapy to British psychiatry in a lecture before the Royal Medico-Psychological Association, and creates a furore. Aubrey Yates publishes his account of 'The Application of Learning Theory to the Treatment of Tics' in the *Journal of Abnormal and Social Psychology*. A.M. and A.D.B. Clarke publish *Mental Deficiency: The Changing Outlook.* Donald Broadbent becomes Director of the Applied Psychology Unit of the Medical Research Council.

1959 Mental Health Act 1959. H.J. Eysenck publishes the *Maudsley Personality Inventory.*

1960 Over half the chairs of psychology in Britain are now held by Bartlett's former students. John Graham-White begins his campaign to introduce clinical psychology into the health services of the six counties of Northern Ireland.

1962 The *British Journal of Social and Clinical Psychology* is launched with Michael Argyle and Jack Tizard as editors. Hospital Plan recommends creation of district general hospitals.

1964 Jack Tizard is appointed the first Professor of Child Development at the University of London Institute of Education.

1965 The Queen grants the British Psychological Society a Royal Charter.

1966 The BPS Division of Clinical Psychology holds its inaugural meeting, and Mahesh Desai is elected to the Chair. Don Bannister argues that psychologists 'have not yet faced up to the issue of reflexivity and the need for reflexivity in psychological thinking'.

1967 The Bene–Anthony Family Relations Test is developed by Eva Bene 'to facilitate the recollection of childhood family feelings [and] obtain these recollections in a form which is systematic and in which they can be quantified'.

A number of papers on aversion therapy are delivered at the BPS Annual Conference in Belfast. Among the conditions deemed suitable for treatment are alcoholism, homosexuality, transvestism and fetishism.

1968 The Summerfield Report *(Psychologists in the Education Services)* is published.

1970 John Shotter calls for the teaching of philosophical psychology, arguing that the belief in a self-corrective experimental methodology warrants replacing with an approach that merges empirical and philosophical inquiries.

1971 Don Bannister and Fay Fransella publish Inquiring Man. The Foster Report on Scientology is published, recommending legislation to control the practice of psychotherapy.

1972 In an article in the *Bulletin of the British Psychological Society*, M.P. Bender describes the role of a community psychologist as being the instigation of change at a field level. A-level Psychology is launched by the Associated Examining Board.

1974 NHS reorganisation unifies the pre-existing tripartite system to create area and regional health authorities, to improve coordination of health and local authority services by coterminosity and improve management.

1975 The Scientific Affairs Board of the BPS investigates the possibility of establishing a permanent display of psychological methods and findings in one or more of the national museums.

1976 Oliver Gillie publishes an article entitled 'Crucial Data Was Faked by Eminent Psychologist' in *The Sunday Times*, and the Cyril Burt scandal erupts.

1977 The Trethowan Report on clinical psychology is published. The BPS Division of Criminological and Legal Psychology holds its inaugural meeting, and D.A. Black is elected to the Chair.

1979 The University of Liverpool Department of Psychology, in collaboration with the British Psychological Society, holds a meeting to mark the centenary of the founding of the first laboratory of experimental psychology in Leipzig. L.S. Hearnshaw argues that Wundt deserves two cheers 'for consciously seizing the opportunity which confronted him' and 'for being an exceptionally hard-working and competent organizer. But we must withhold the third cheer, which we will keep for psychology's man of genius, its Newton, when he turns up'.

1980 Children Act 1980. Fraser Watts, discussing the implementation of the legal registration of psychologists, comments: 'The fact that unqualified practitioners could not use the title of psychologist means that the public would gradually acquire a clearer and better image of a psychologist and his roles.'

1982 Fay Fransella founds the Centre for Personal Construct Psychology in London.

1983 Stephen Newstead discovers that heads of psychology departments in the UK regard B.F. Skinner as the most important living psychologist in the world, with H.J. Eysenck and D.E. Broadbent in second and third places respectively. Freud, Piaget, Pavlov, Skinner and James are considered the five most important psychologists of all time.

1985 D. Middleton and D. Edwards argue 'that psychology as a discipline is best conceptualised not in "pure-applied" terms, but rather as theory and need driven'. Scrivens and Charlton Report on clinical psychology staffing commissioned by the Department of Health.

1986 Kevin Connolly's article 'Can There Be a Psychology for the Third World?' elicits a fierce response from Fathali Moghaddam and Donald Taylor who accuse the author of having a 'colonial attitude'. Peter Furnell argues that 'little research exists on the experience and life-styles of self-identified gay men and lesbian women', the literature on homosexuality having been hitherto dominated by 'issues of treatment and aetiology'.

1987 The BPS History and Philosophy of Psychology Section holds its first annual meeting in Ilkley. On 18 December, the Queen grants amendments to the Charter of the British Psychological Society, which allows the BPS to maintain a Register of Chartered Psychologists.

1989 Hawton et al.'s influential *Cognitive Behaviour Therapy for Psychiatric Conditions: A Practical Guide* is published, still in print in 2015,

1992 Health of the Nation 1992/3 creates 27 national targets in five key areas: coronary heart disease and stroke, cancers, mental illness, accidents, HIV/AIDS and sexual health.

1995 Royal College of Psychiatrists and the British Psychological Society jointly publish *Psychological Therapies for Adults in the NHS.*

1999 National Service Framework for Adult Mental Health.

2001 Centenary of BPS. The BPS and the Science Museum jointly publish G.C. Bunn, A.D. Lovie, and G.D. Richards (Eds.) *Psychology in Britain: Historical Essays and Personal Reflections.*

2004 Department of Health publishes *Organising and Delivering Psychological Therapies.*

2010 R.D. Buchanan's biography of Hans Eysenck *Playing with Fire* is published.

Appendix 2 Chairs of the Division of Clinical Psychology

1966–1967	Mahesh Desai
1967–1968	Mahesh Desai
1968–1969	Mahesh Desai
1969–1970	May Davidson
1970–1971	May Davidson
1971–1972	Jim Drewery
1972–1973	Jim Drewery
1973–1974	Jim Drewery
1974–1975	David Castell
1975–1976	David Castell
1976–1977	David Castell
1977–1978	Frank McPherson
1978–1979	Frank McPherson
1979–1980	Frank McPherson
1980–1981	Bernard Kat
1981–1982	Bernard Kat
1982–1983	Bernard Kat
1983–1984	Fraser Watts
1984–1985	David F. Clark
1985–1986	Chris Cullen
1986–1987	Chris Cullen
1987–1988	Ann Pattie
1988–1989	Jamie Furnell
1989–1990	Ian McPherson
1990–1991	Peter Wilcock
1991–1992	Malcolm Adams
1992–1993	Glenys Parry
1993–1994	Marc Binns
1994–1995	Pat Frankish
1995–1996	Sue Gardner
1996–1997	Adrian Skinner
1997–1998	Pat Guinan
1998–1999	Lesley Cohen
1999/2000	Peter Harvey
2000–2001	Ray Miller
2001–2002	Ray Miller/Ian Gray
2002–2003	Michael Wang
2003–2004	Dorothy Fielding
2004–2005	Peter Kinderman
2005–2006	Graham Turpin
2006–2007	Tim Cate
2007–2008	Tim Cate
2008–2009	Jenny Taylor
2009–2010	Jenny Taylor
2010–2011	Peter Kinderman
2011–2012	Richard Pemberton
2012–2013	Richard Pemberton
2013–2014	Richard Pemberton
2014–2015	Richard Pemberton

Appendix 3 Presidents of the British Psychological Society who were clinical psychologists, or closely involved with clinical or abnormal psychology

1941–1943	Professor Sir Cyril Lodowic Burt
1954–1955	Professor Philip E. Vernon
1957–1958	Professor Alec Rodger
1966–1967	Grace Rawlings OBE
1968–1969	Boris Semeonoff
1970–1971	Professor Harry Gwynne Jones
1972–1973	Professor Max Hamilton
1974–1975	Professor Oliver Louis Zangwill CBE
1975–1976	Professor Jack Tizard CBE
1976–1977	May Alison Davidson CBE
1977–1978	Professor Alan Douglas Benson Clarke CBE
1979–1980	Professor Peter H. Venables
1982–1983	Dr Ralph R. Hetherington
1991–1992	Revd Dr Fraser Norman Watts
1992–1993	Professor Edgar Miller
1997–1998	Professor Christopher Noel Cullen
1999–2000	Dr Patricia Frankish
2002–2003	Professor Graham Davey
2005–2006	Dr Graham Powell
2006–2007	Professor Ray Miller
2008–2009	Dr Liz Campbell
2009–2010	Susan Gardner
2011–2012	Dr Carole Allan
2015–2016	Professor Jamie Hacker Hughes

Appendix 4 Selected workforce data

Graph 1: Clinical Psychology – Headcount in the NHS (1950–2013)

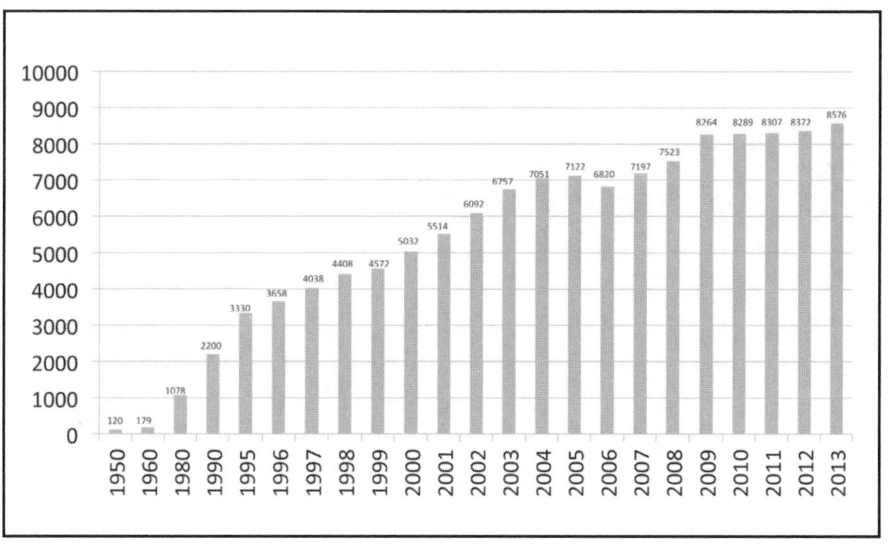

Graph 2: Clinical Psychology – FTE in the NHS (1995–2013)

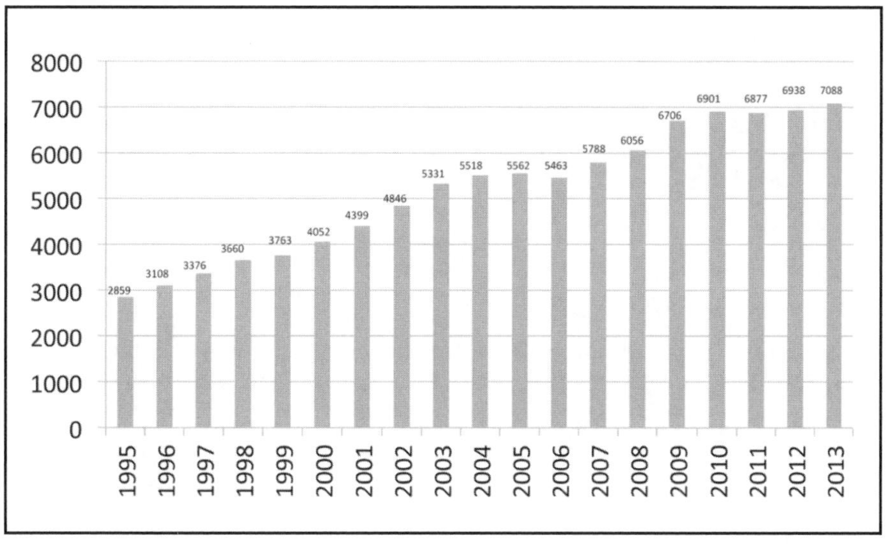

Graph 3: Number of training places in the UK from 1980 to 2014

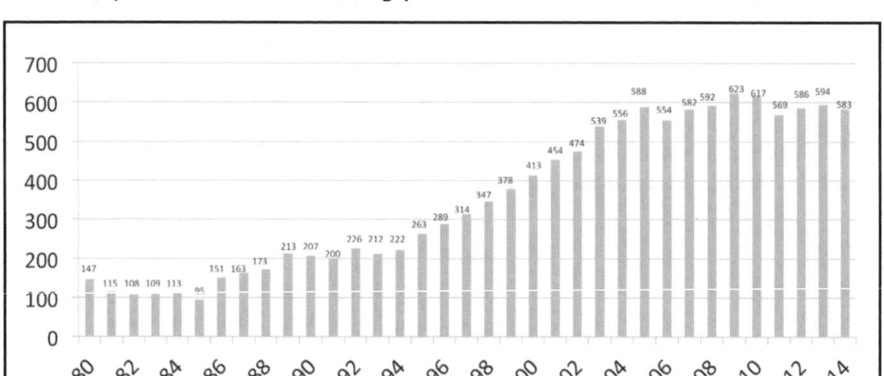

Index

Note: All index entries refer to clinical psychology, unless otherwise mentioned. For this reason, entries are limited under 'clinical psychology' and users are advised to seek more specific index entries. All NHS-related entries refer to England, unless otherwise mentioned.